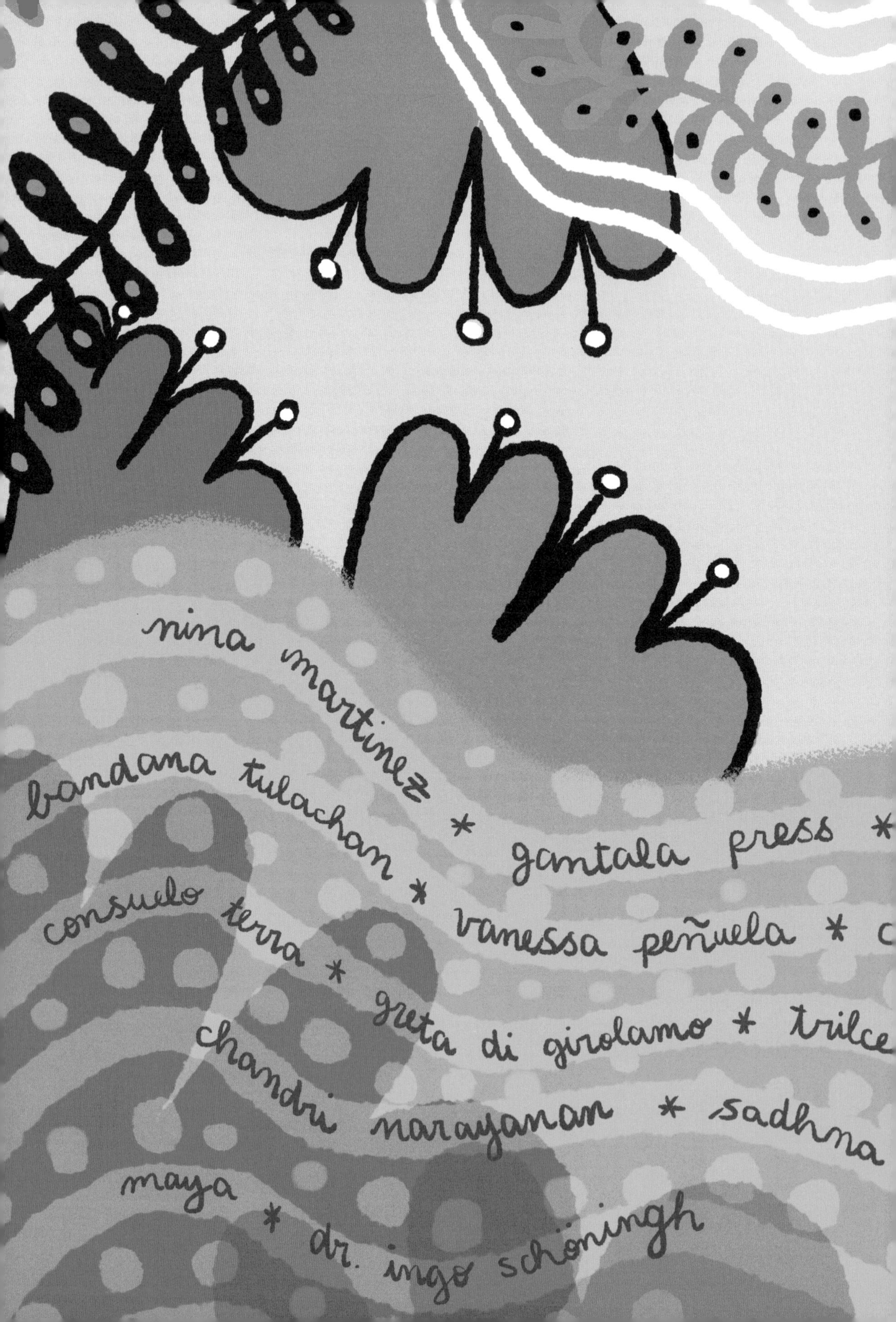
nina martinez * gantala press *
bandana tulachan * vanessa peñuela * c
consuelo terra * greta di girolamo * trilce
chandri narayanan * sadhna
maya * dr. ingo schöningh

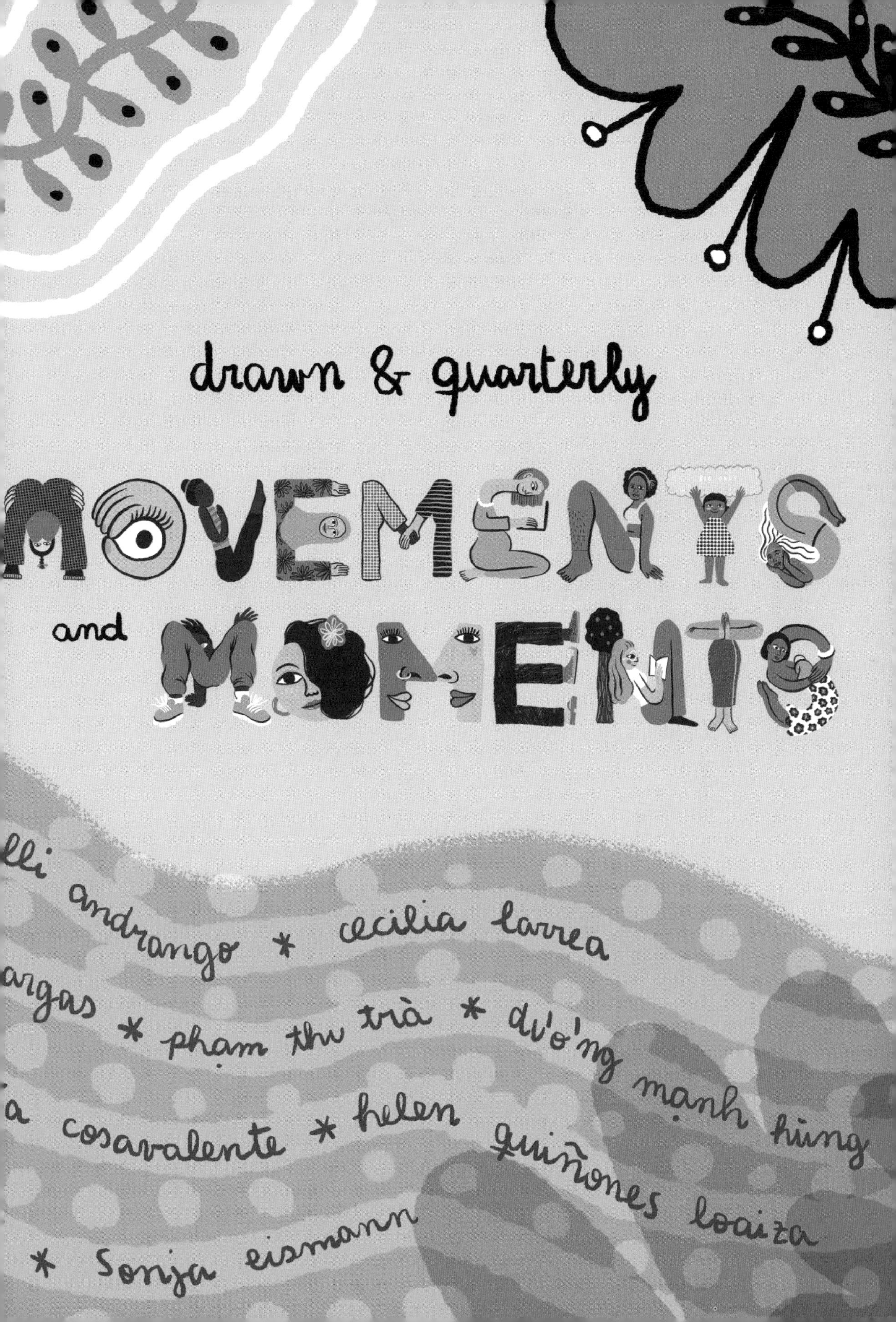
drawn & quarterly
MOVEMENTS
and MOMENTS
lli andrango * cecilia larrea
argas * phạm thu trà * dương mạnh hùng
a cosavalente * helen quiñones loaiza
* sonja eismann

drawnandquarterly.com | goethe.de

978-1-77046-561-9 | First edition: November 2022
Printed in Thailand | 10 9 8 7 6 5 4 3 2 1

Cataloguing data available from Library and Archives Canada

Published in the USA by Drawn & Quarterly, a client publisher of Farrar, Straus and Giroux. Published in Canada by Drawn & Quarterly, a client publisher of Raincoast Books. Published in the United Kingdom by Drawn & Quarterly, a client publisher of Publishers Group UK.

The translation of this work was supported by a grant from the Goethe-Institut.

GOETHE INSTITUT

FSC www.fsc.org MIX Paper | Supporting responsible forestry FSC™ C005748

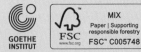

contents

introduction

In the summer of 2018, the Goethe-Institut Indonesien launched an open call for a feminism and pop culture conference in Berlin. Hundreds of applications started pouring in from highly motivated activists, artists, and journalists based in Australia, Aotearoa (New Zealand), and Southeast Asia. Sixteen participants were eventually selected and hosted by *Missy Magazine*.

In February 2019, a follow-up meeting was organized in Jakarta by Anna Maria Strauss, regional Head of Cultural Programs at the time. At these sessions, the absence of an archive for feminist endeavors consistently kept coming up. Such achievements and contributions seldom make it into history books or pop culture canons. To combat the erasure of these herstories, an idea emerged to record them as comics. The medium's tremendous pop-cultural appeal makes these stories accessible to a wide variety of potential readers. In 2020, a Goethe-Institut Excellence Grant made an open call for this project possible.

While an impressive number of graphic novels by women have been published and translated in recent years, feminisms of the Global South have not garnered nearly as much attention. Indigenous feminist activists receive even less credit than their mainstream counterparts. From their perspective, not even feminism is free of Western colonial baggage, and many of them hesitate to claim the label as a result. This makes it all the more important for the rest of us to pay attention, listen, and learn. In light of increasingly frequent natural disasters linked to constant land exploitation, it is becoming clear that the fight for gender-based justice must always be linked to the fight for our planet's preservation.

Movements and Moments saw 218 applications pour in from 325 applicants across forty-two countries. We were overwhelmed but nonetheless exceedingly pleased to discover so many individuals and collectives involved in gender justice and ecology at the grassroots level. With the help of our jury members Urvashi Butalia (India), Auá Mendes (Brazil), and Johann Ulrich (Germany), we selected sixteen of the best stories by creative teams in the Global South. Eight of them appear in this volume, while the rest are available to read online.

We sincerely thank all the Indigenous feminist activists who have generously shared their stories, past and present. We are deeply humbled by your courage and strength as you continue to take up the fight. We must also thank Amruta Patil (India) and Nacha Vollenweider (Argentina) who mentored our finalists. And of course, we would also like to thank the artists, writers, researchers, and translators whose passion and enthusiasm made this project possible. We hope you, as readers, enjoy these inspiring stories as much as we do.

Sonja, Maya, and Ingo

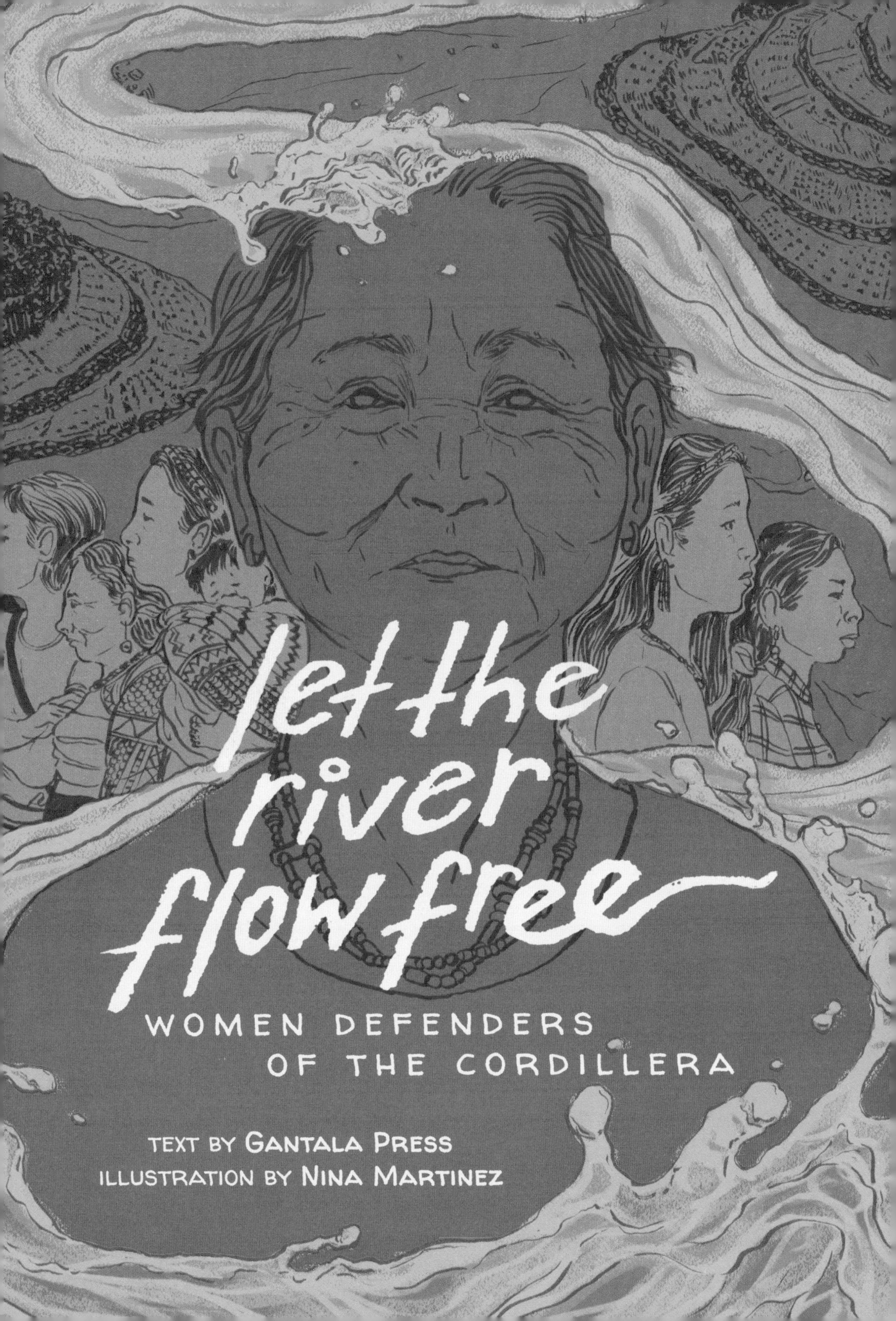
let the river flow free
WOMEN DEFENDERS OF THE CORDILLERA
TEXT BY GANTALA PRESS
ILLUSTRATION BY NINA MARTINEZ

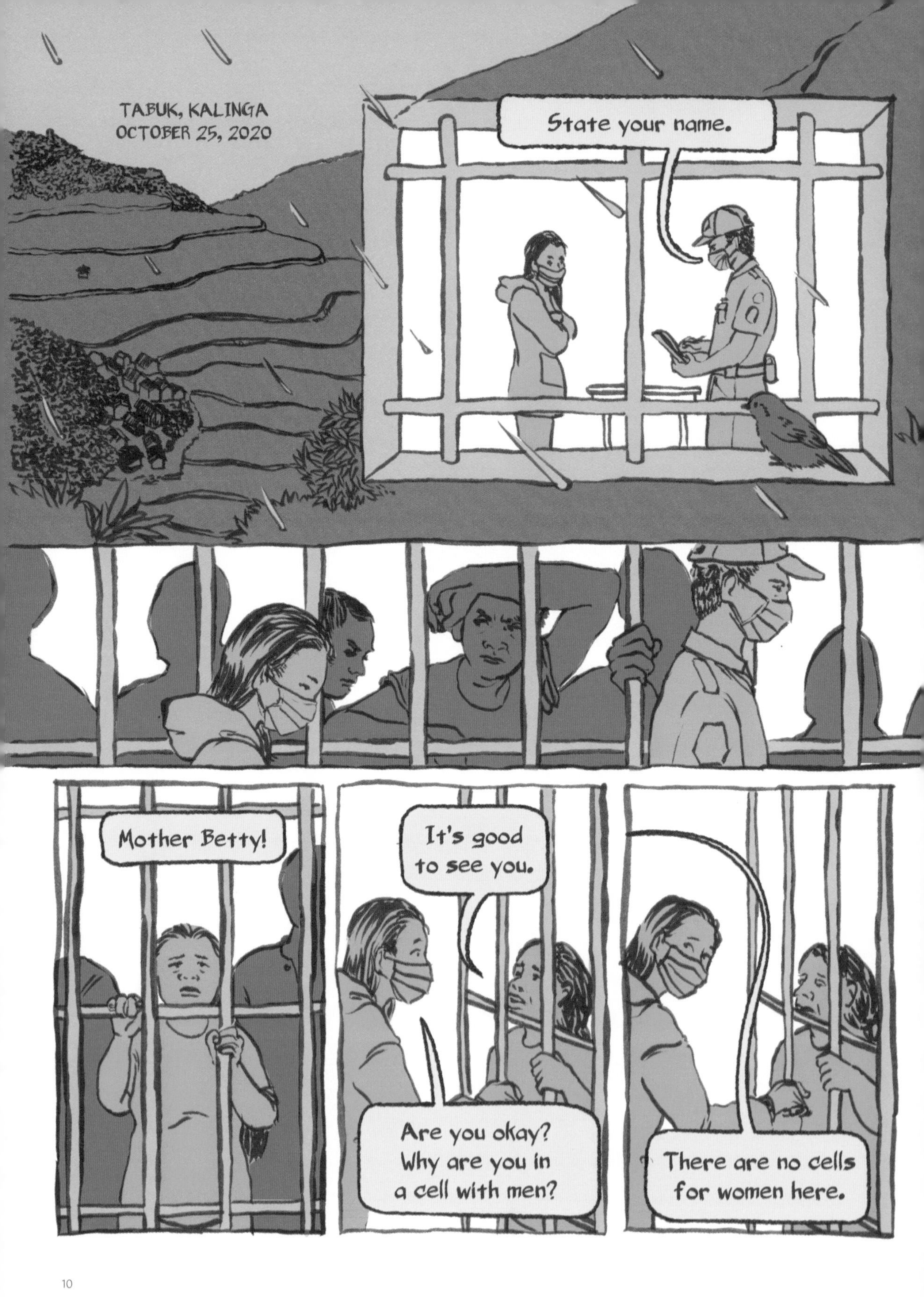
TABUK, KALINGA
OCTOBER 25, 2020
State your name.
Mother Betty!
It's good to see you.
Are you okay? Why are you in a cell with men?
There are no cells for women here.

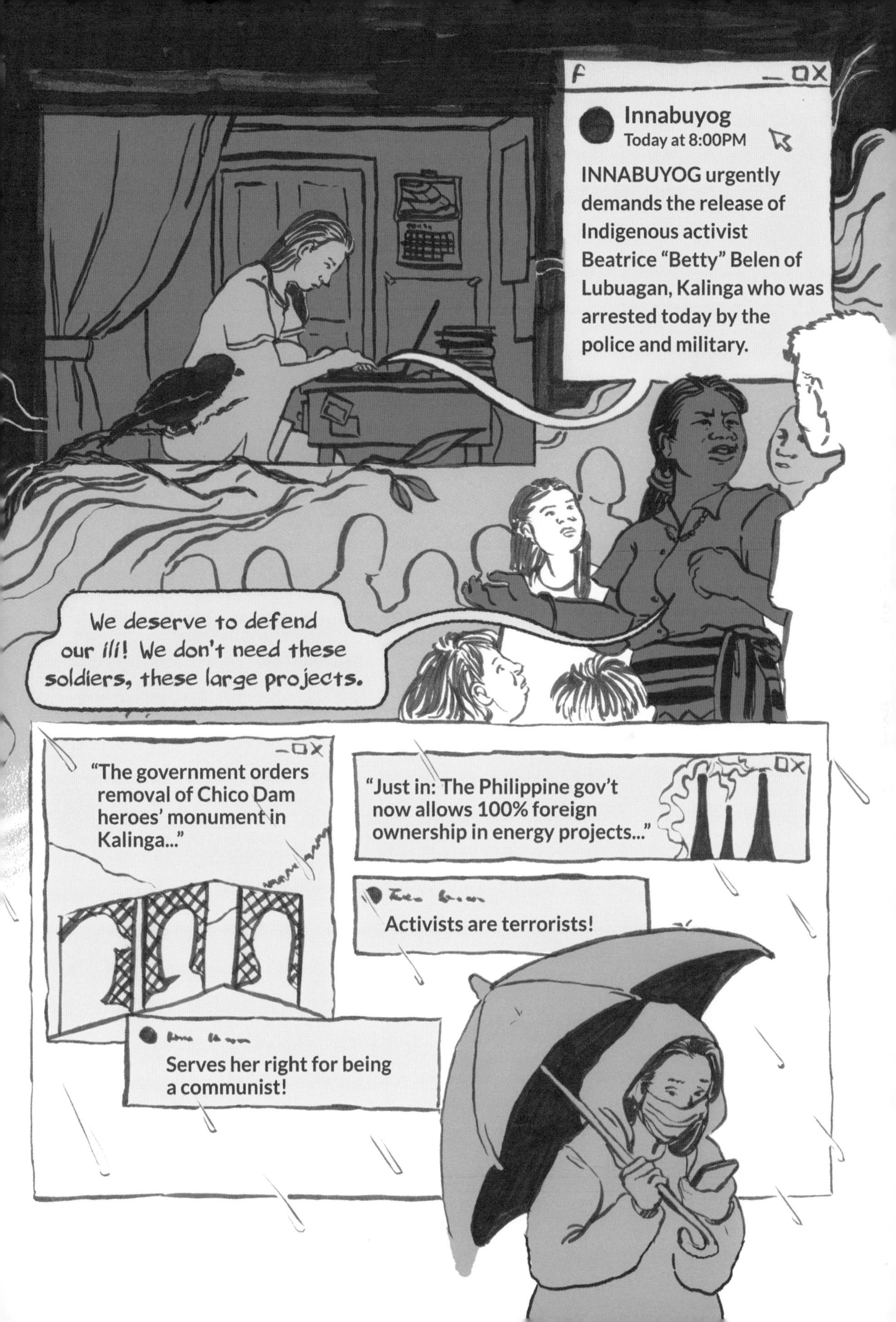

Innabuyog
Today at 8:00PM
INNABUYOG urgently demands the release of Indigenous activist Beatrice "Betty" Belen of Lubuagan, Kalinga who was arrested today by the police and military.
We deserve to defend our *ili*! We don't need these soldiers, these large projects.
"The government orders removal of Chico Dam heroes' monument in Kalinga..."
"Just in: The Philippine gov't now allows 100% foreign ownership in energy projects..."
Activists are terrorists!
Serves her right for being a communist!

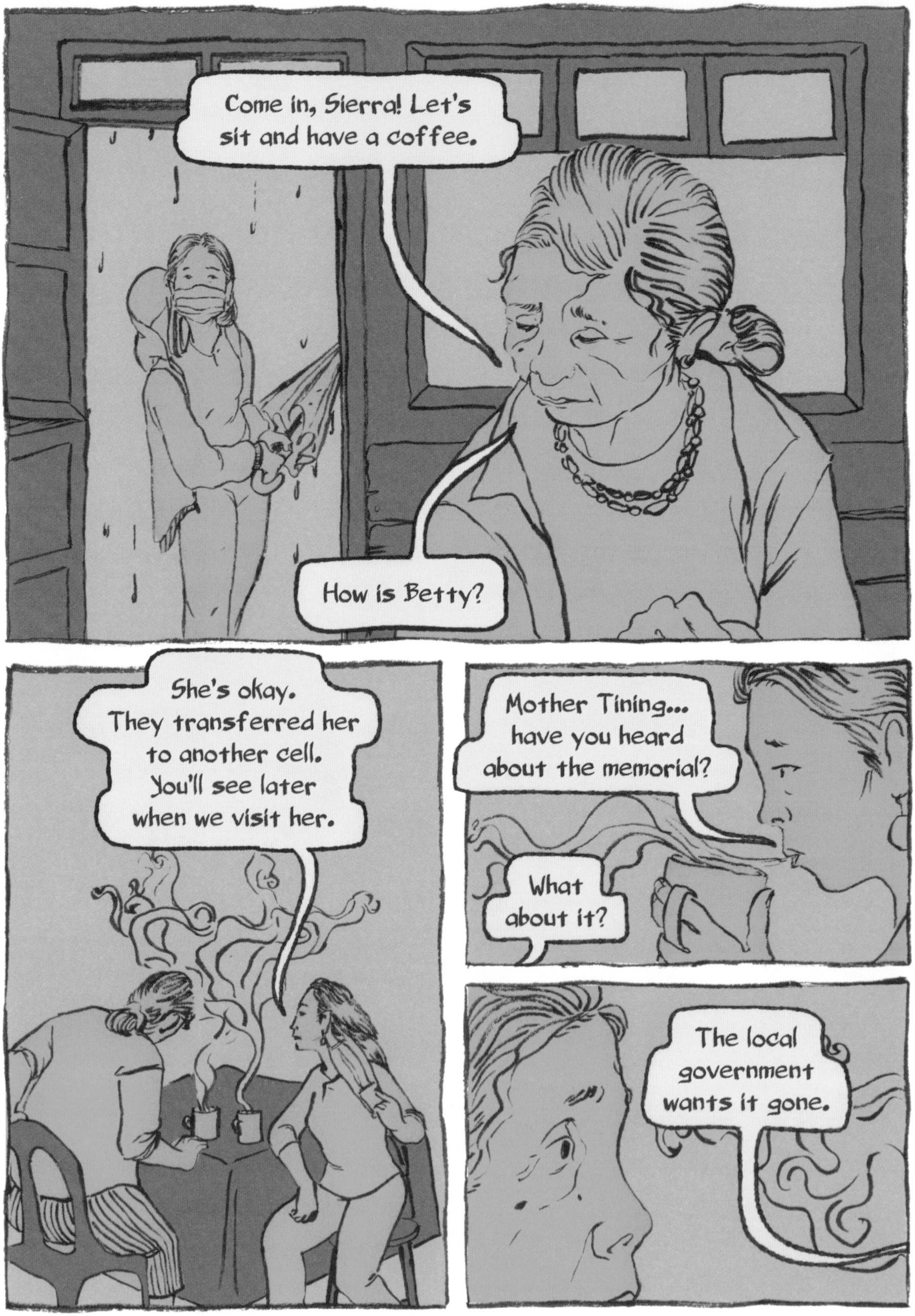
Come in, Sierra! Let's sit and have a coffee.
How is Betty?
She's okay. They transferred her to another cell. You'll see later when we visit her.
Mother Tining... have you heard about the memorial?
What about it?
The local government wants it gone.

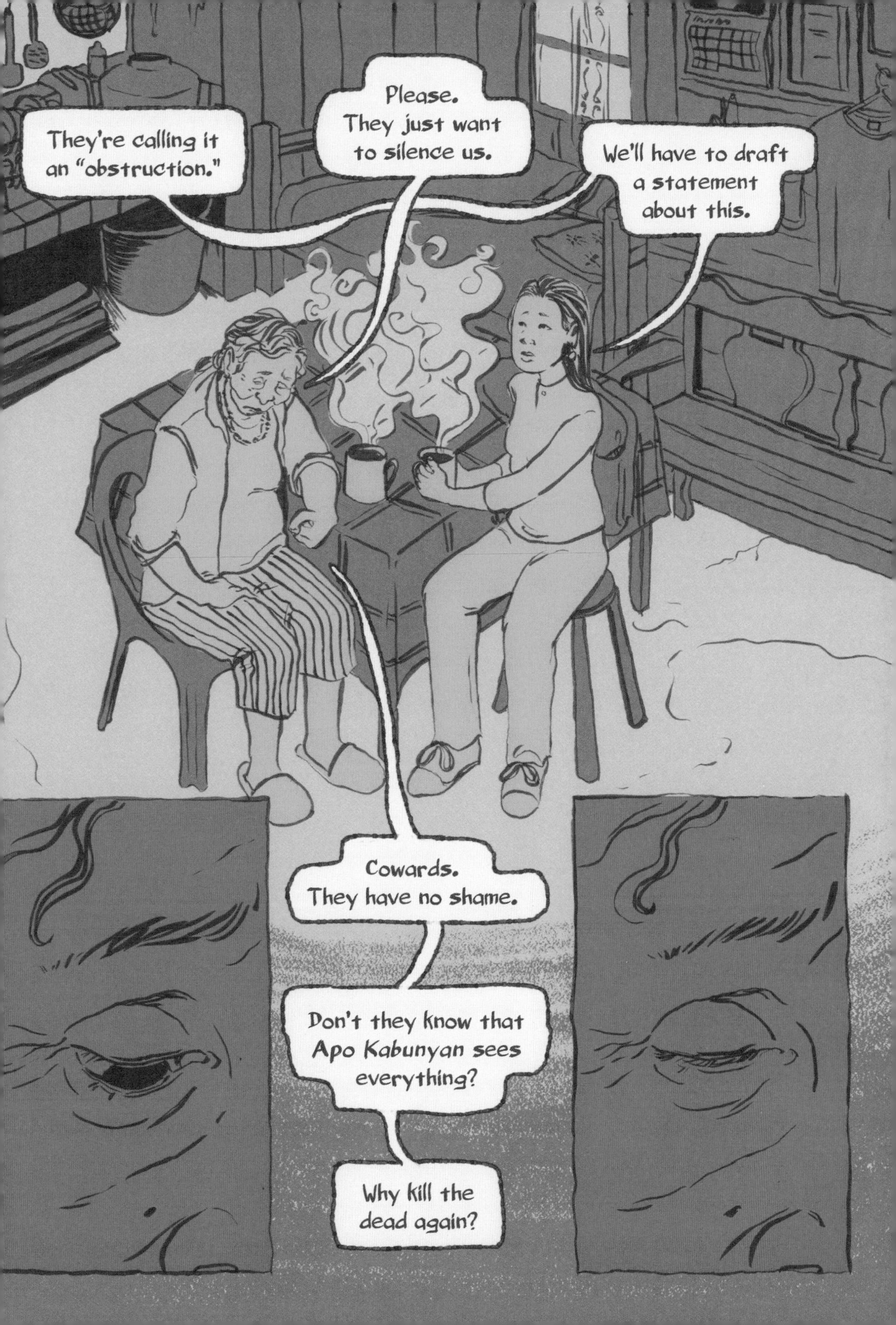
They're calling it an "obstruction."
Please. They just want to silence us.
We'll have to draft a statement about this.
Cowards. They have no shame.
Don't they know that Apo Kabunyan sees everything?
Why kill the dead again?

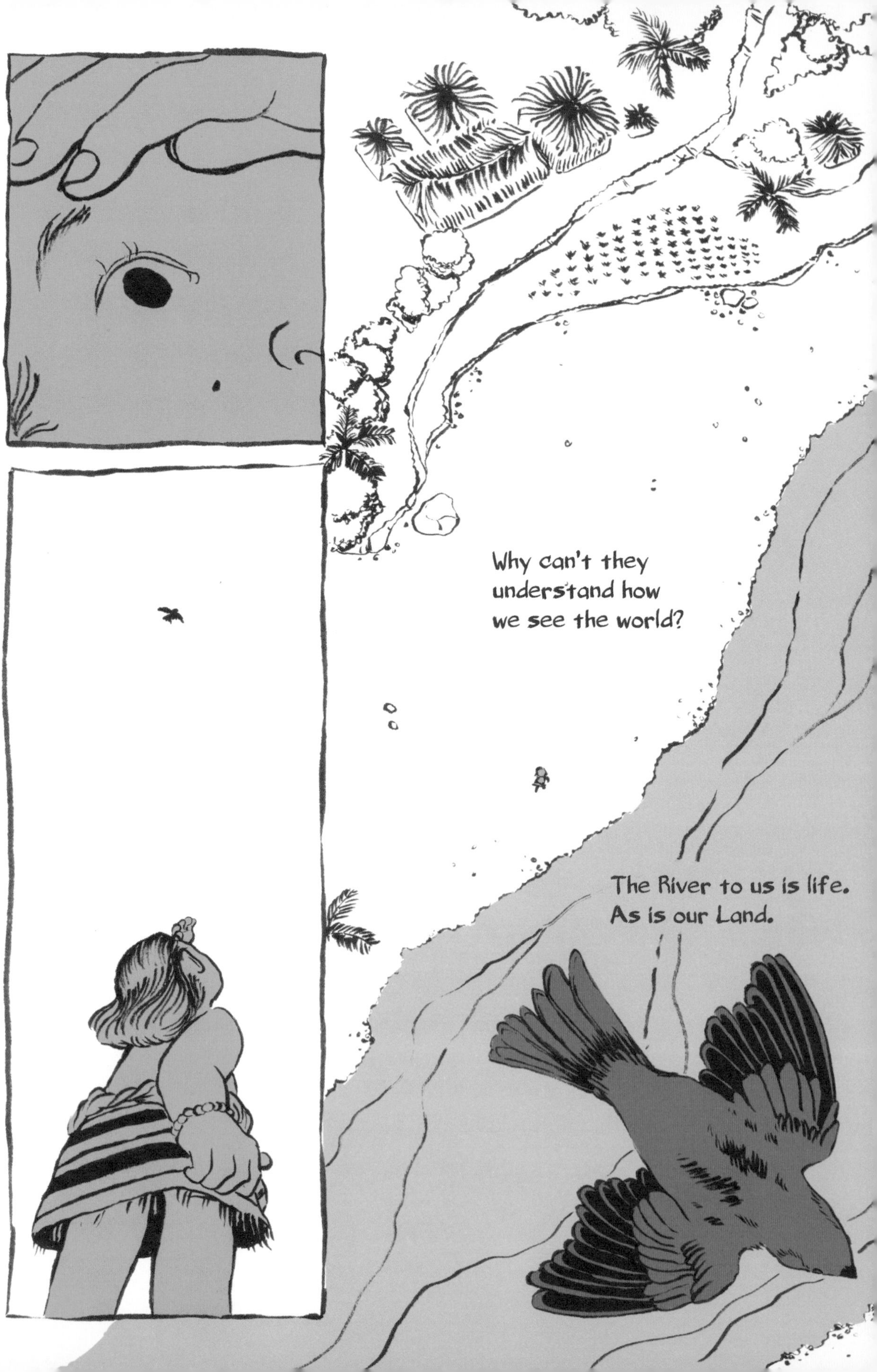
Why can't they understand how we see the world?
The River to us is life. As is our Land.

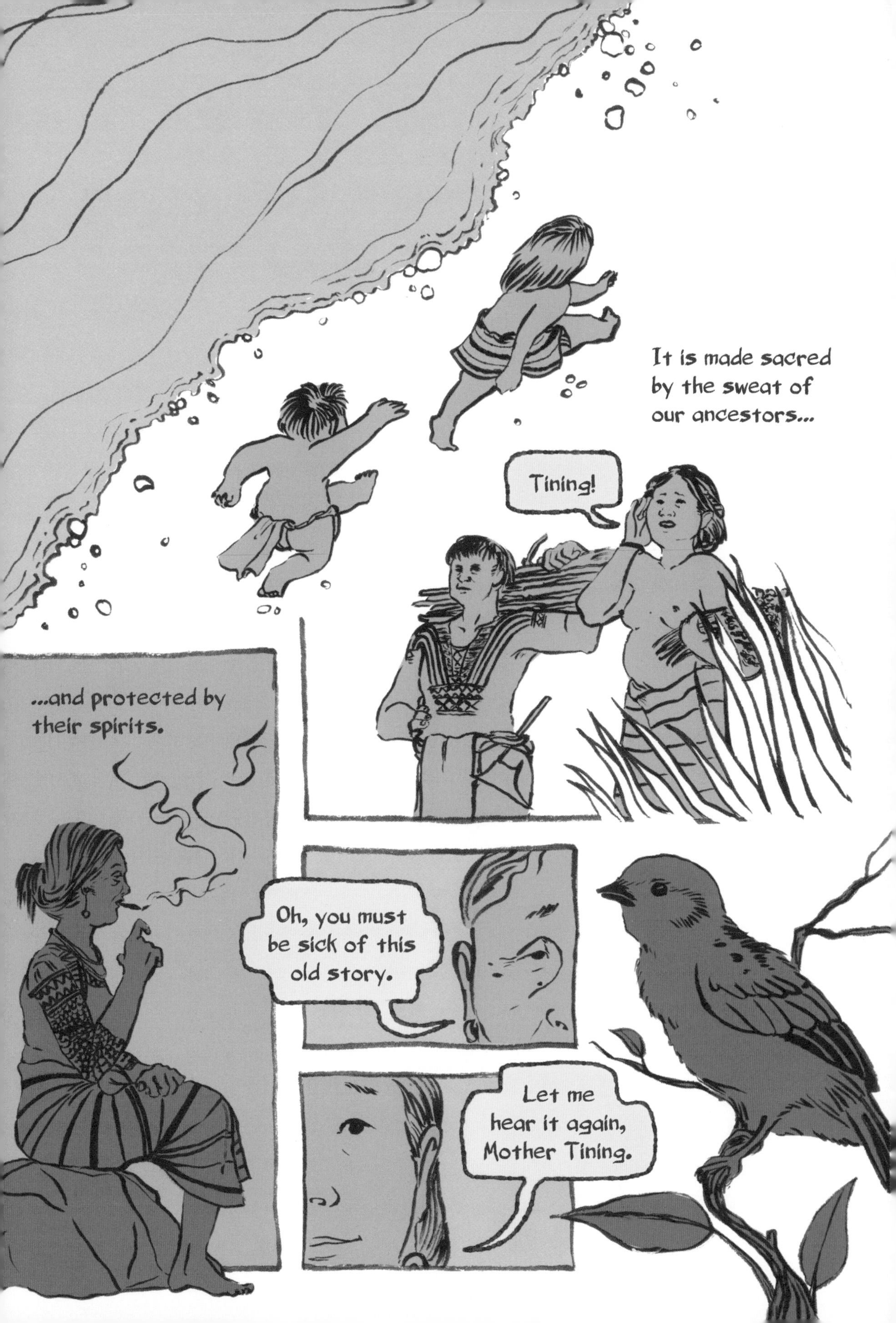
It is made sacred by the sweat of our ancestors...
Tining!
...and protected by their spirits.
Oh, you must be sick of this old story.
Let me hear it again, Mother Tining.

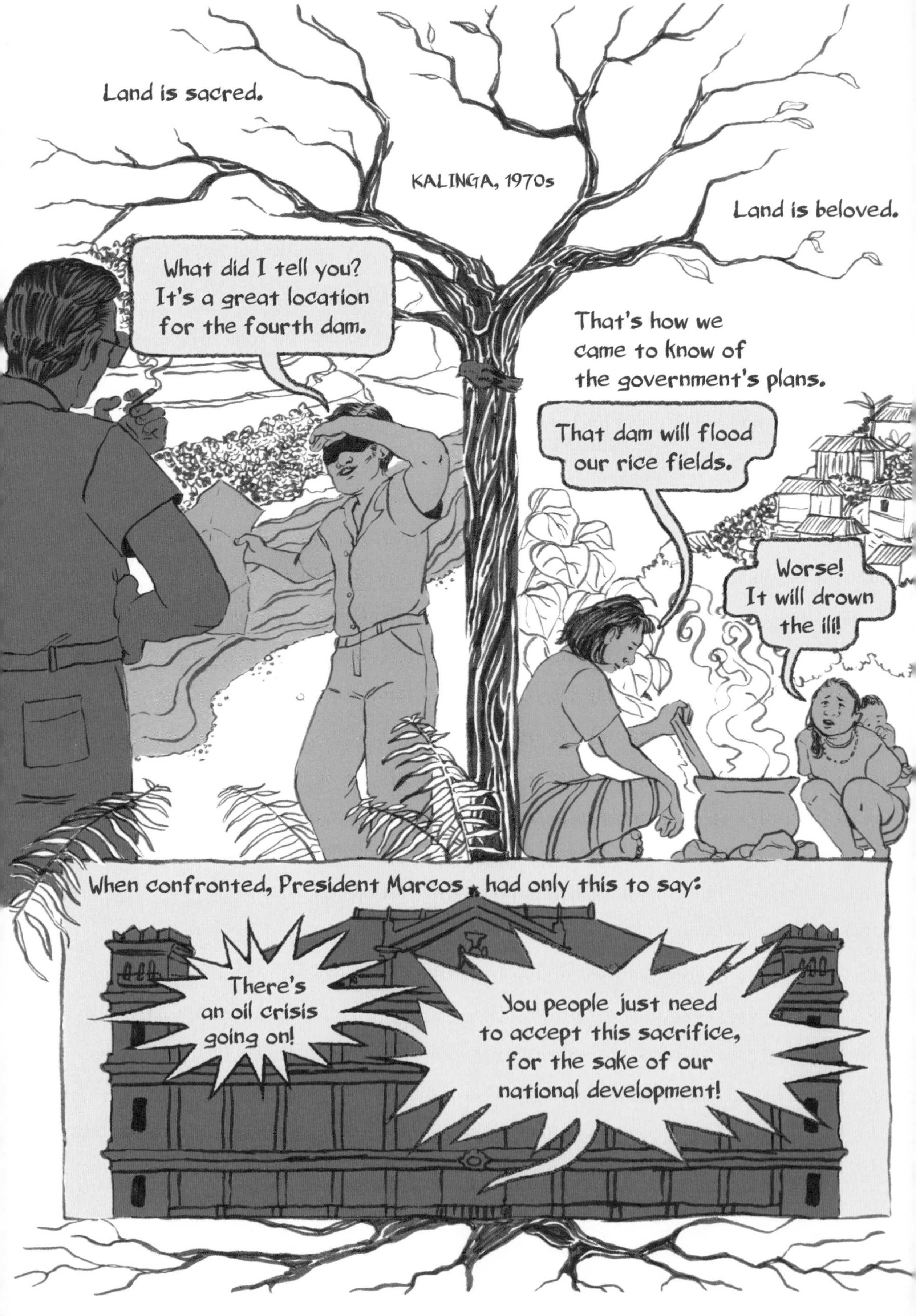
Land is sacred.
KALINGA, 1970s
Land is beloved.
What did I tell you? It's a great location for the fourth dam.
That's how we came to know of the government's plans.
That dam will flood our rice fields.
Worse! It will drown the ili!
When confronted, President Marcos had only this to say:
There's an oil crisis going on!
You people just need to accept this sacrifice, for the sake of our national development!

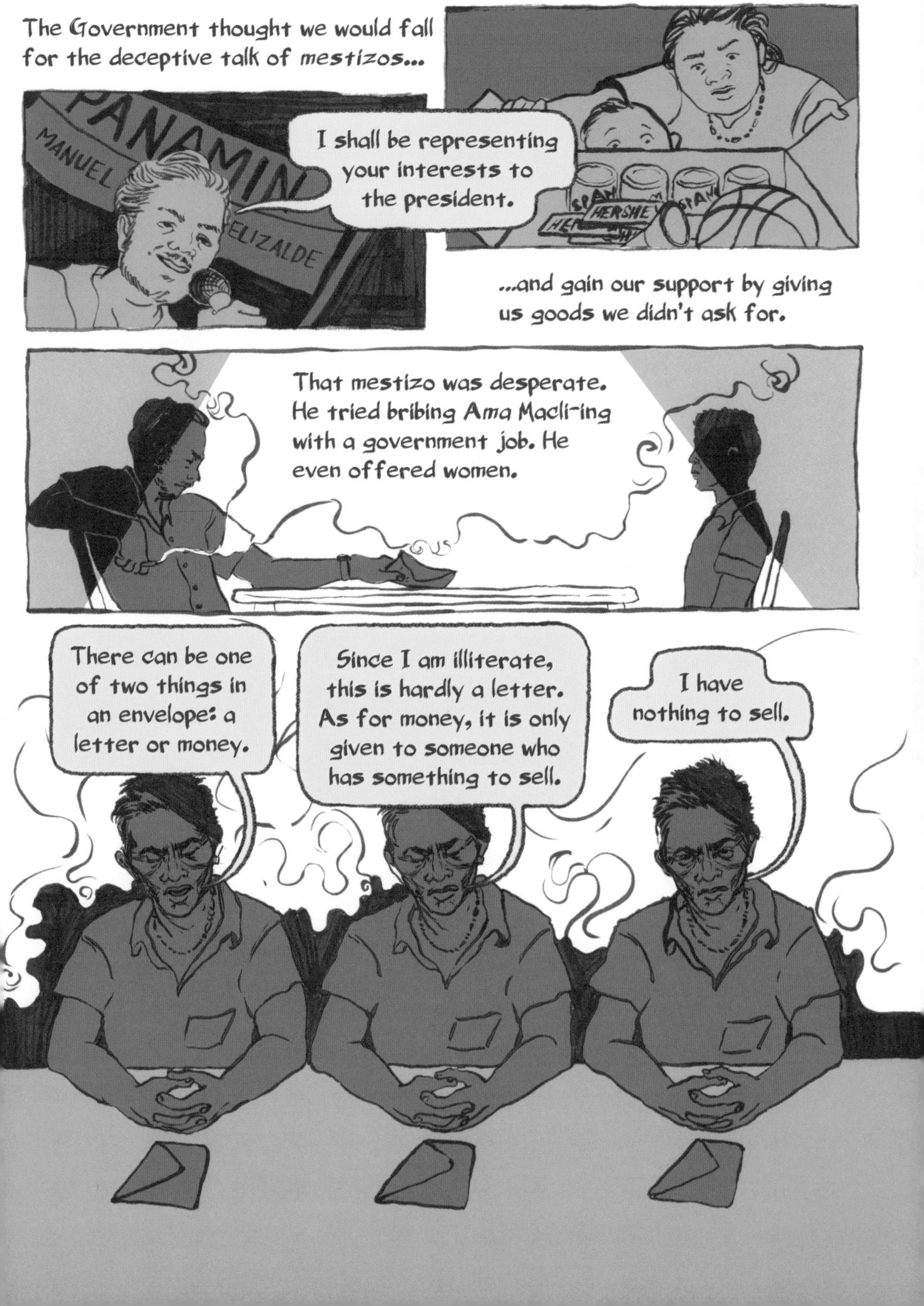

The Government thought we would fall for the deceptive talk of *mestizos*...
PANAMIN
MANUEL
ELIZALDE
I shall be representing your interests to the president.
HERSHEY
...and gain our support by giving us goods we didn't ask for.
That mestizo was desperate. He tried bribing Ama Macli-ing with a government job. He even offered women.
There can be one of two things in an envelope: a letter or money.
Since I am illiterate, this is hardly a letter. As for money, it is only given to someone who has something to sell.
I have nothing to sell.

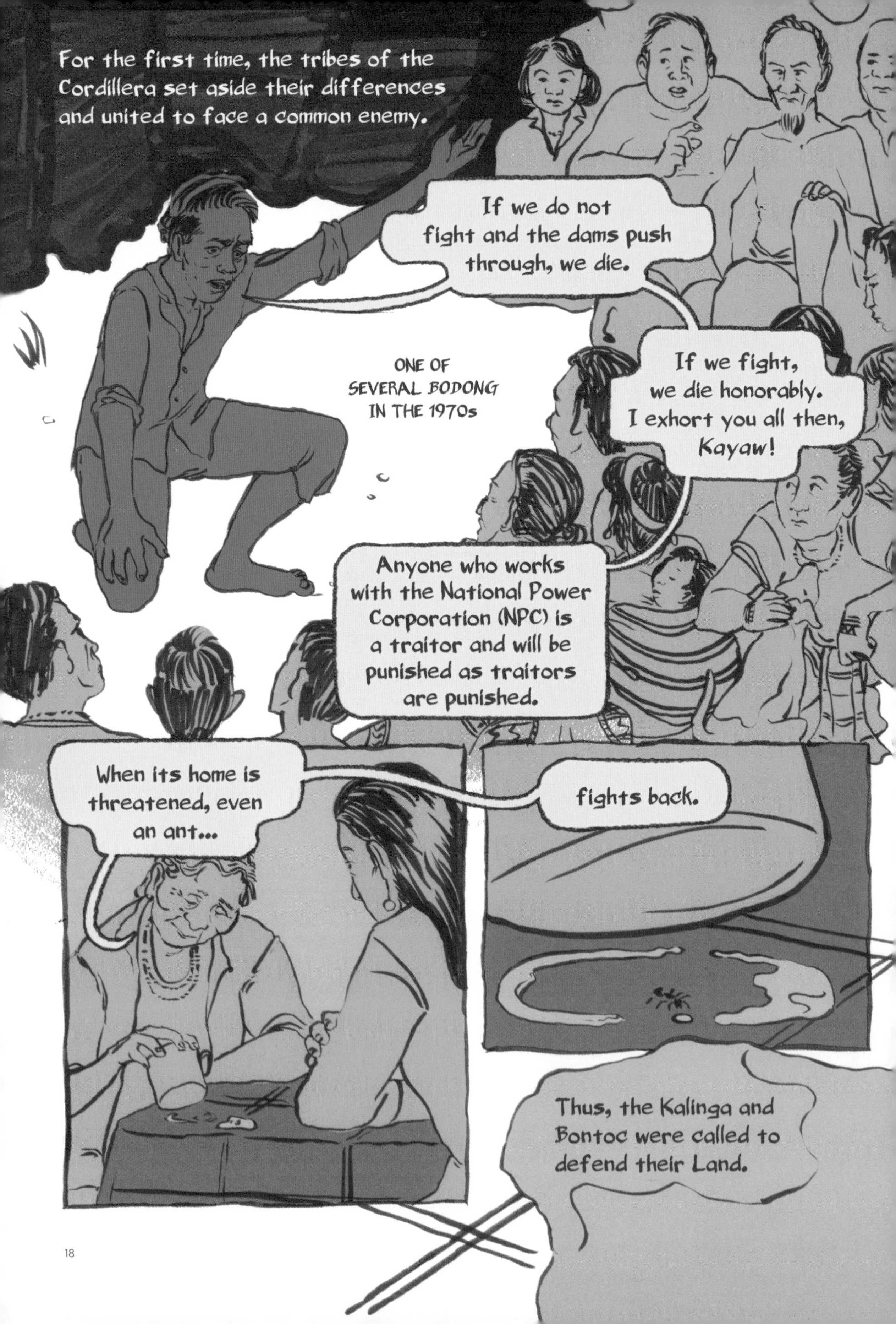
For the first time, the tribes of the Cordillera set aside their differences and united to face a common enemy.
If we do not fight and the dams push through, we die.
ONE OF SEVERAL BODONG IN THE 1970s
If we fight, we die honorably. I exhort you all then, Kayaw!
Anyone who works with the National Power Corporation (NPC) is a traitor and will be punished as traitors are punished.
When its home is threatened, even an ant...
fights back.
Thus, the Kalinga and Bontoc were called to defend their Land.

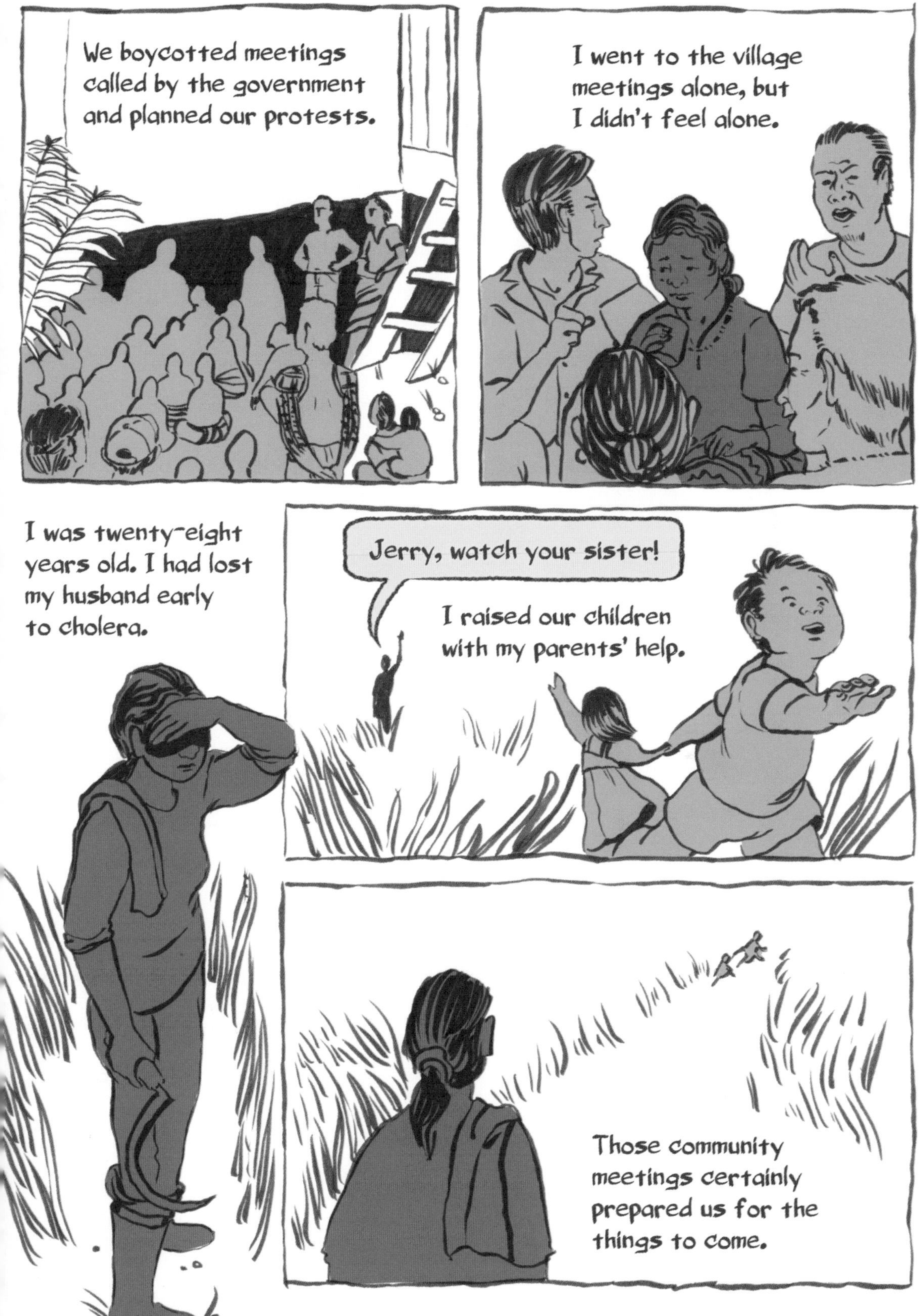
We boycotted meetings called by the government and planned our protests.
I went to the village meetings alone, but I didn't feel alone.
I was twenty-eight years old. I had lost my husband early to cholera.
Jerry, watch your sister!
I raised our children with my parents' help.
Those community meetings certainly prepared us for the things to come.

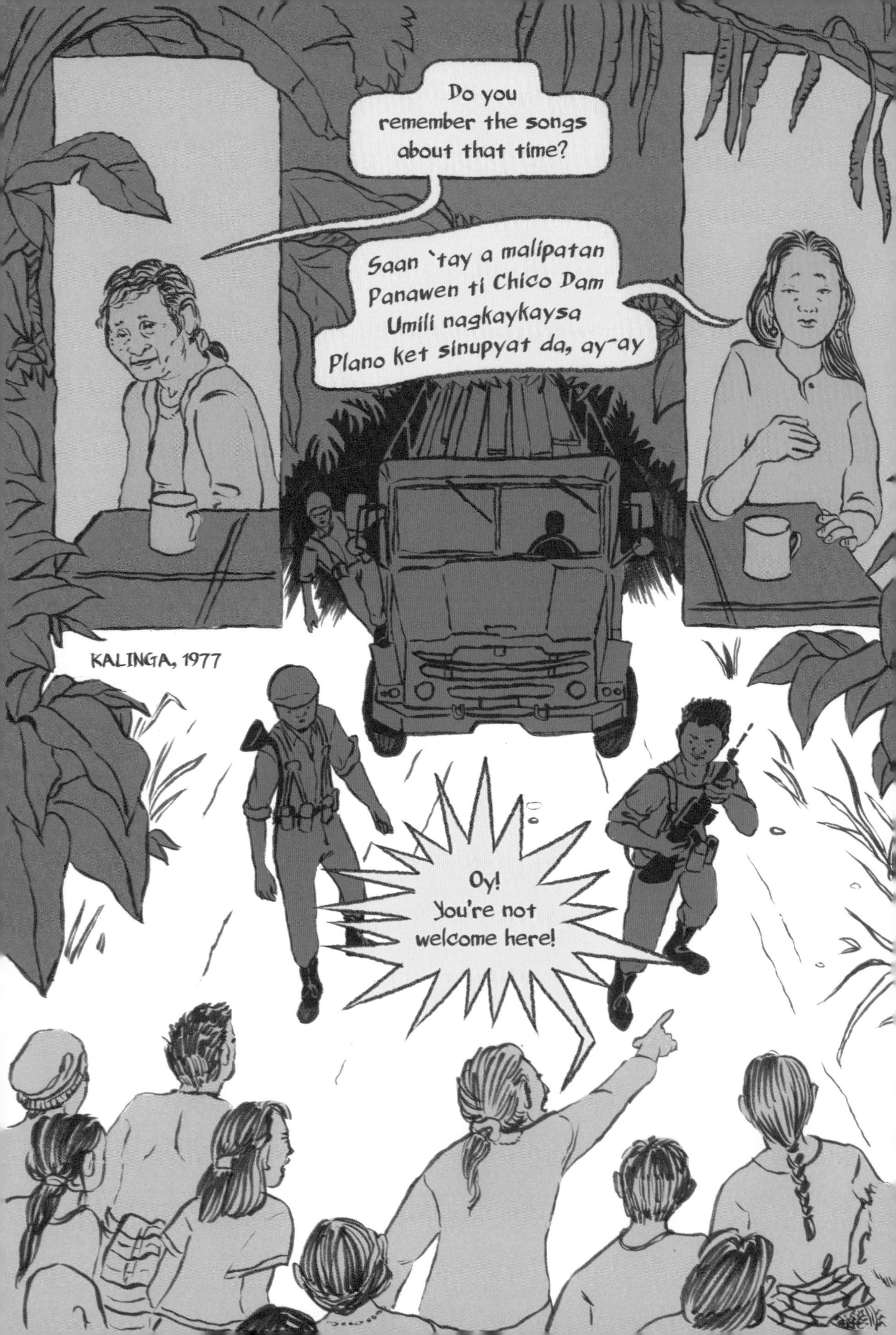
Do you remember the songs about that time?
Saan `tay a malipatan
Panawen ti Chico Dam
Umili nagkaykaysa
Plano ket sinupyat da, ay-ay
KALINGA, 1977
Oy! You're not welcome here!

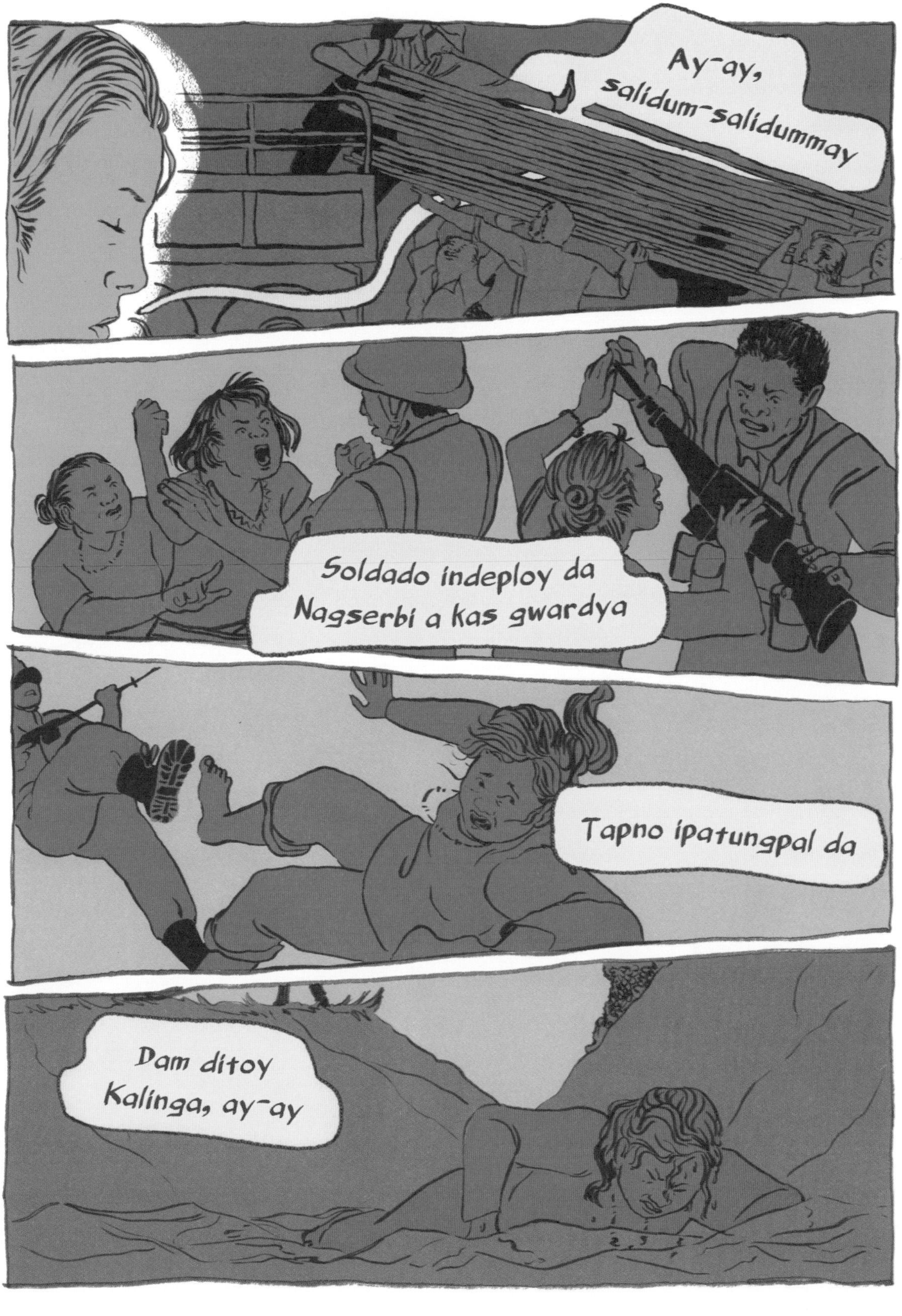

Ay-ay, salidum-salidummay
Soldado indeploy da Nagserbi a kas gwardya
Tapno ipatungpal da
Dam ditoy Kalinga, ay-ay

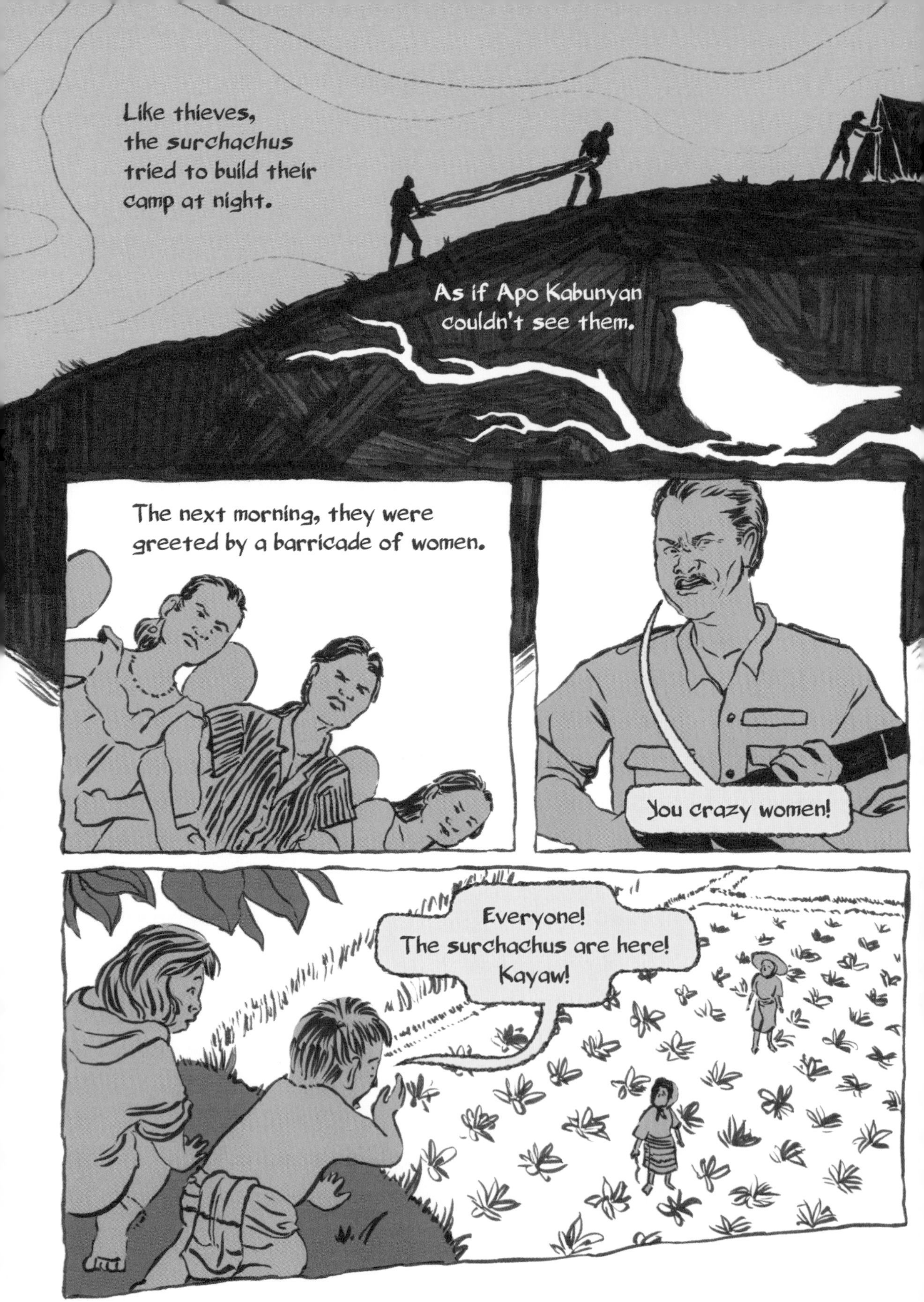
Like thieves, the surchachus tried to build their camp at night.
As if Apo Kabunyan couldn't see them.
The next morning, they were greeted by a barricade of women.
You crazy women!
Everyone! The surchachus are here! Kayaw!

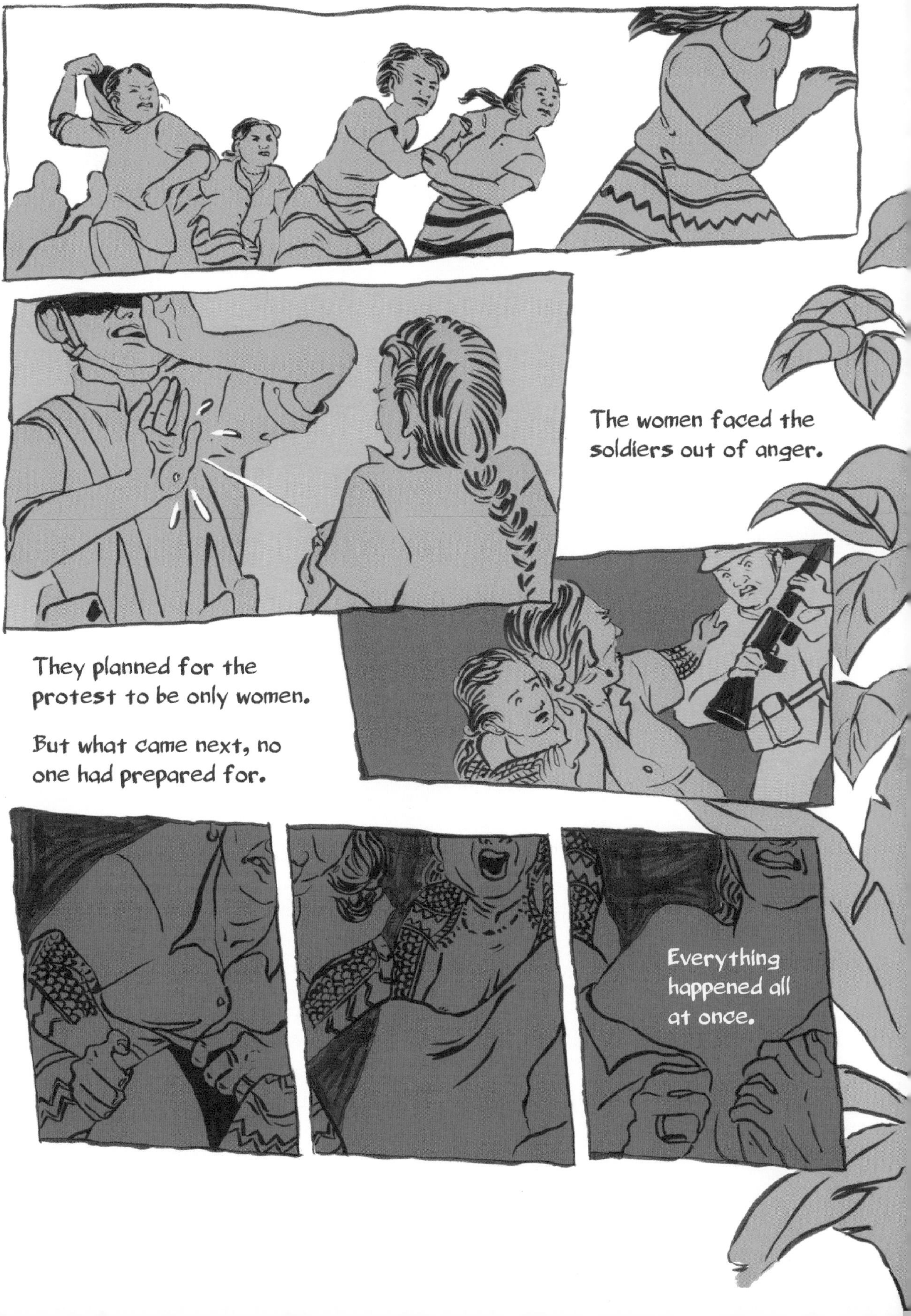
The women faced the soldiers out of anger.
They planned for the protest to be only women.
But what came next, no one had prepared for.
Everything happened all at once.

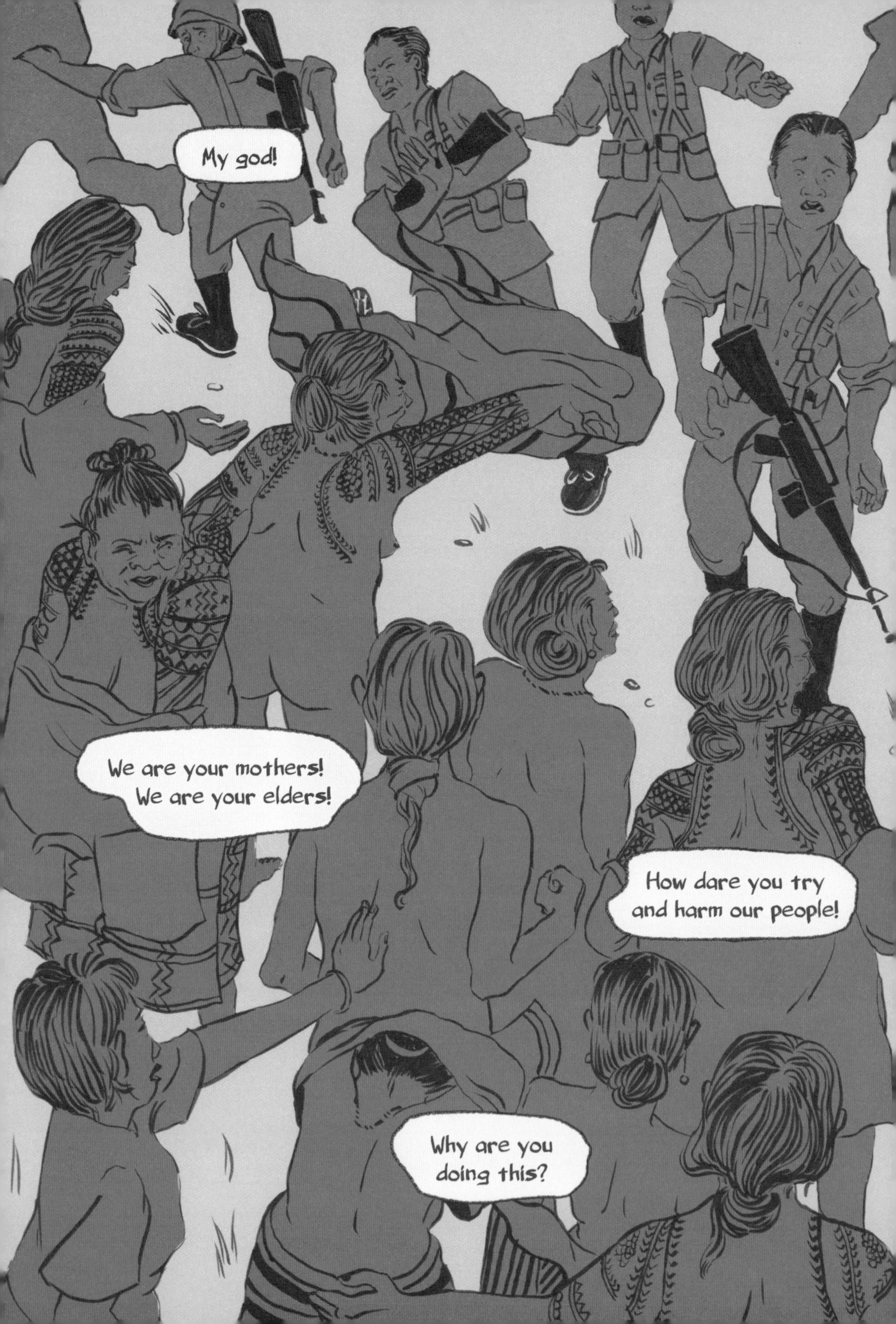
My god!
We are your mothers! We are your elders!
How dare you try and harm our people!
Why are you doing this?

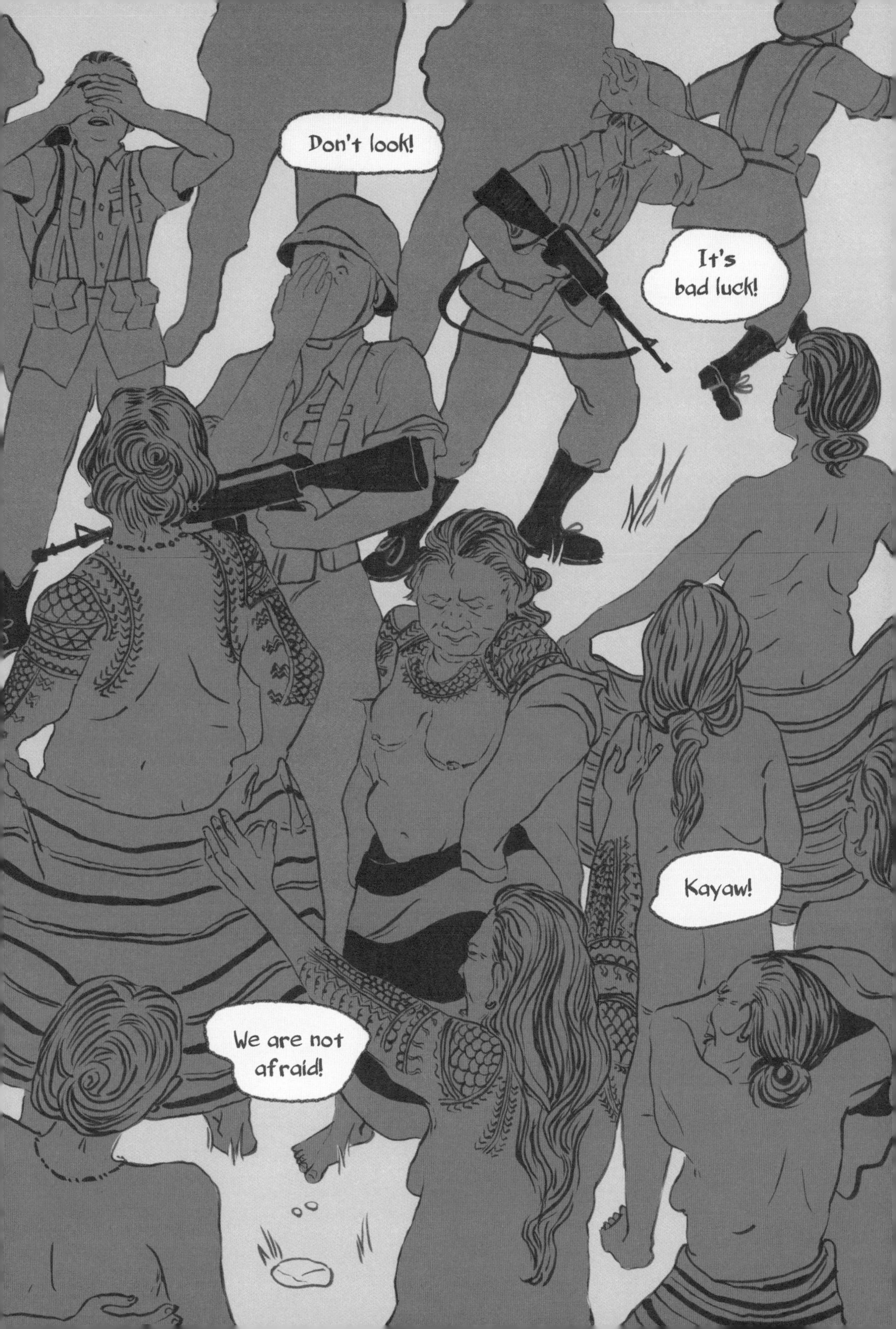
Don't look!
It's bad luck!
Kayaw!
We are not afraid!

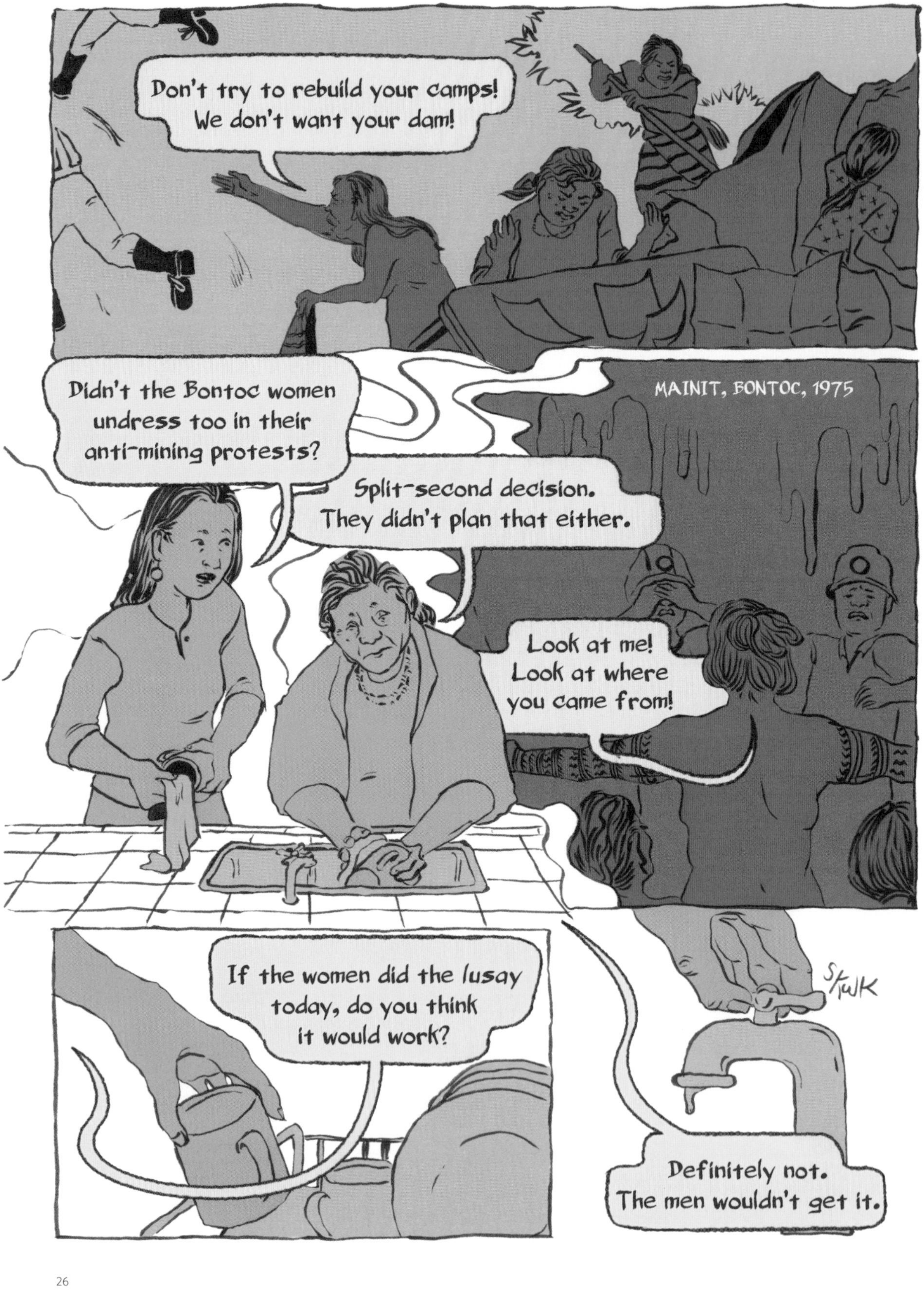
Don't try to rebuild your camps! We don't want your dam!
Didn't the Bontoc women undress too in their anti-mining protests?
MAINIT, BONTOC, 1975
Split-second decision. They didn't plan that either.
Look at me! Look at where you came from!
If the women did the lusay today, do you think it would work?
SKWIK
Definitely not. The men wouldn't get it.

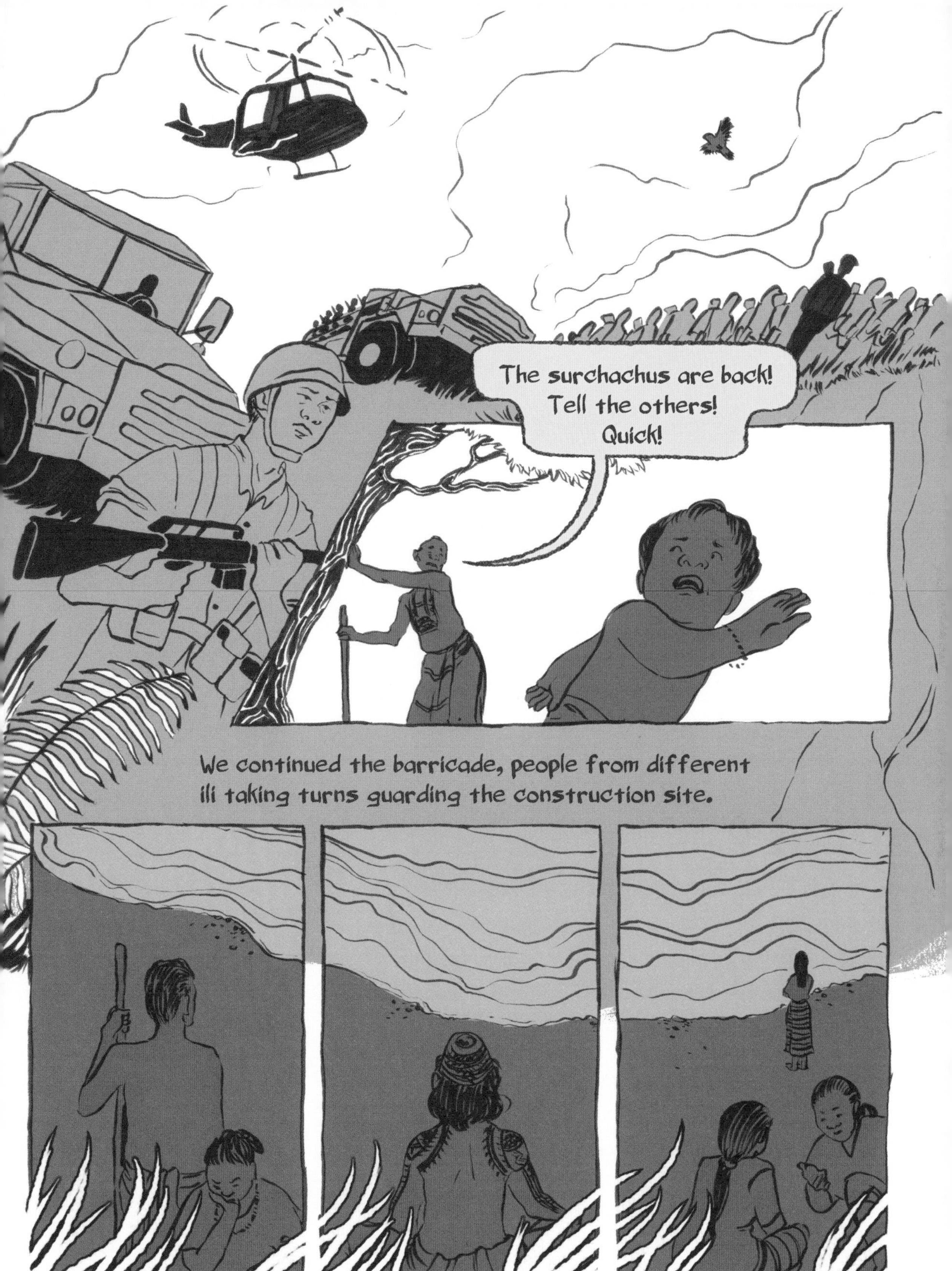
The surchachus are back! Tell the others! Quick!
We continued the barricade, people from different ili taking turns guarding the construction site.

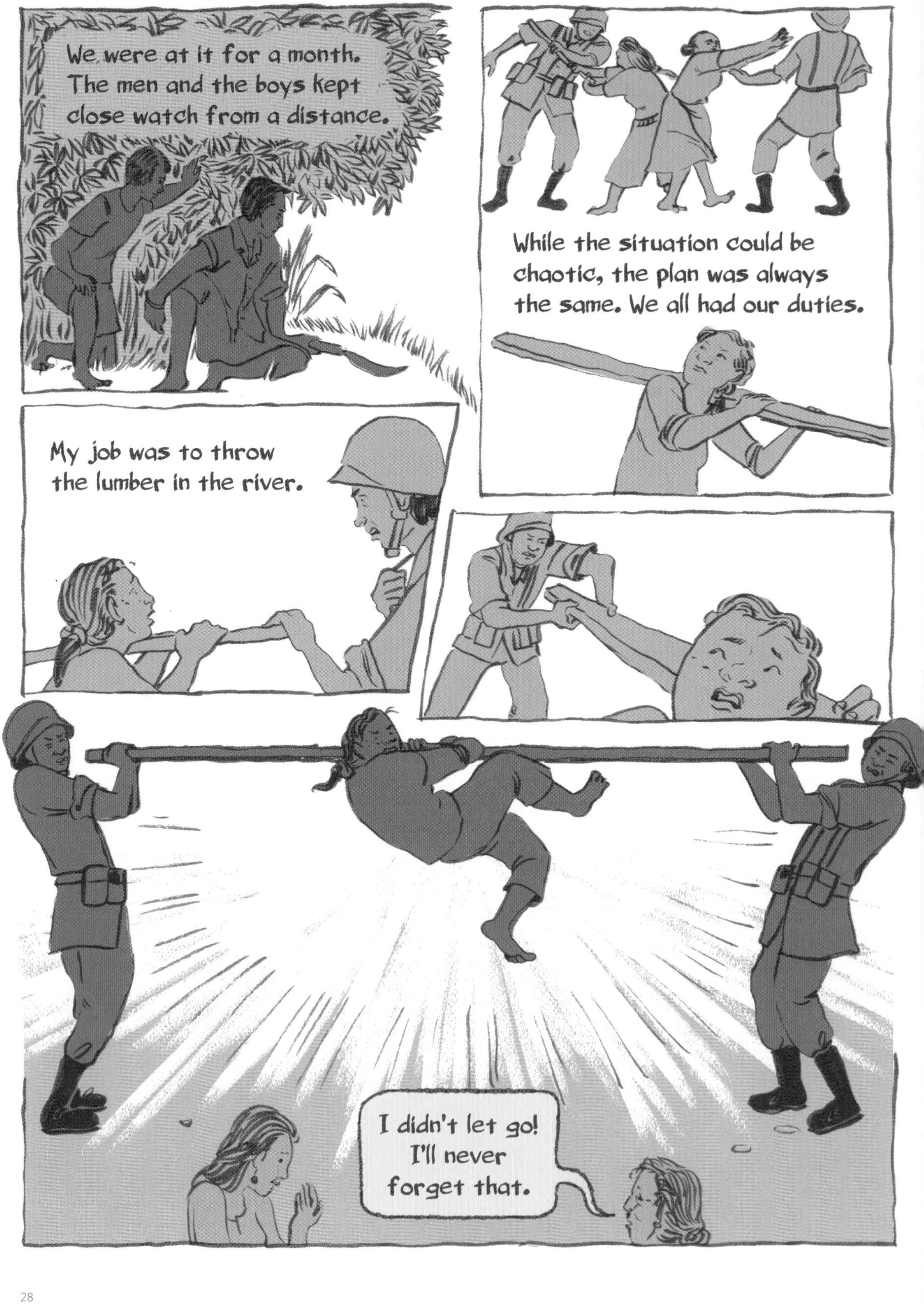
We were at it for a month. The men and the boys kept close watch from a distance.
While the situation could be chaotic, the plan was always the same. We all had our duties.
My job was to throw the lumber in the river.
I didn't let go! I'll never forget that.

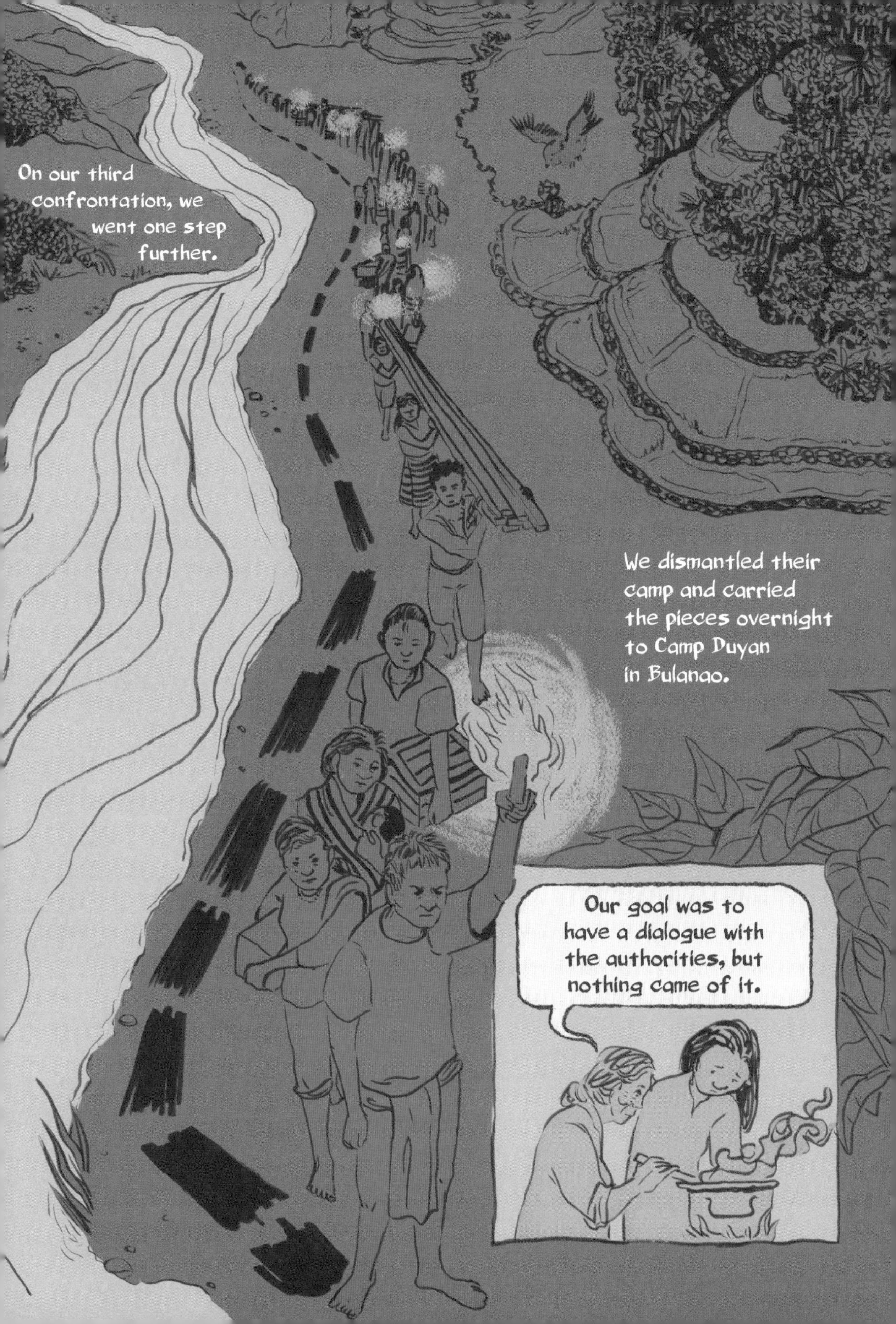
On our third confrontation, we went one step further.
We dismantled their camp and carried the pieces overnight to Camp Duyan in Bulanao.
Our goal was to have a dialogue with the authorities, but nothing came of it.

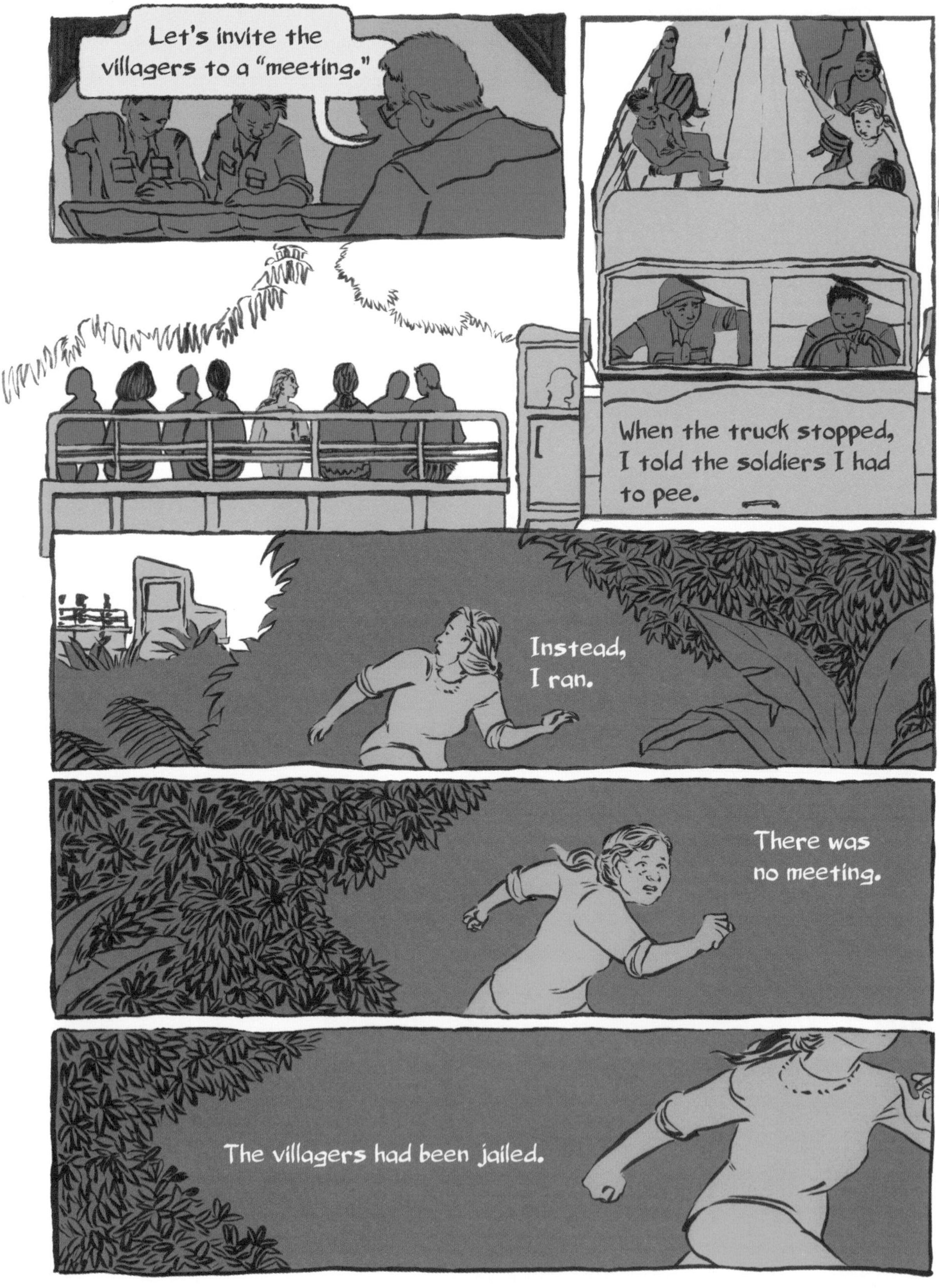

Let's invite the villagers to a "meeting."
When the truck stopped, I told the soldiers I had to pee.
Instead, I ran.
There was no meeting.
The villagers had been jailed.

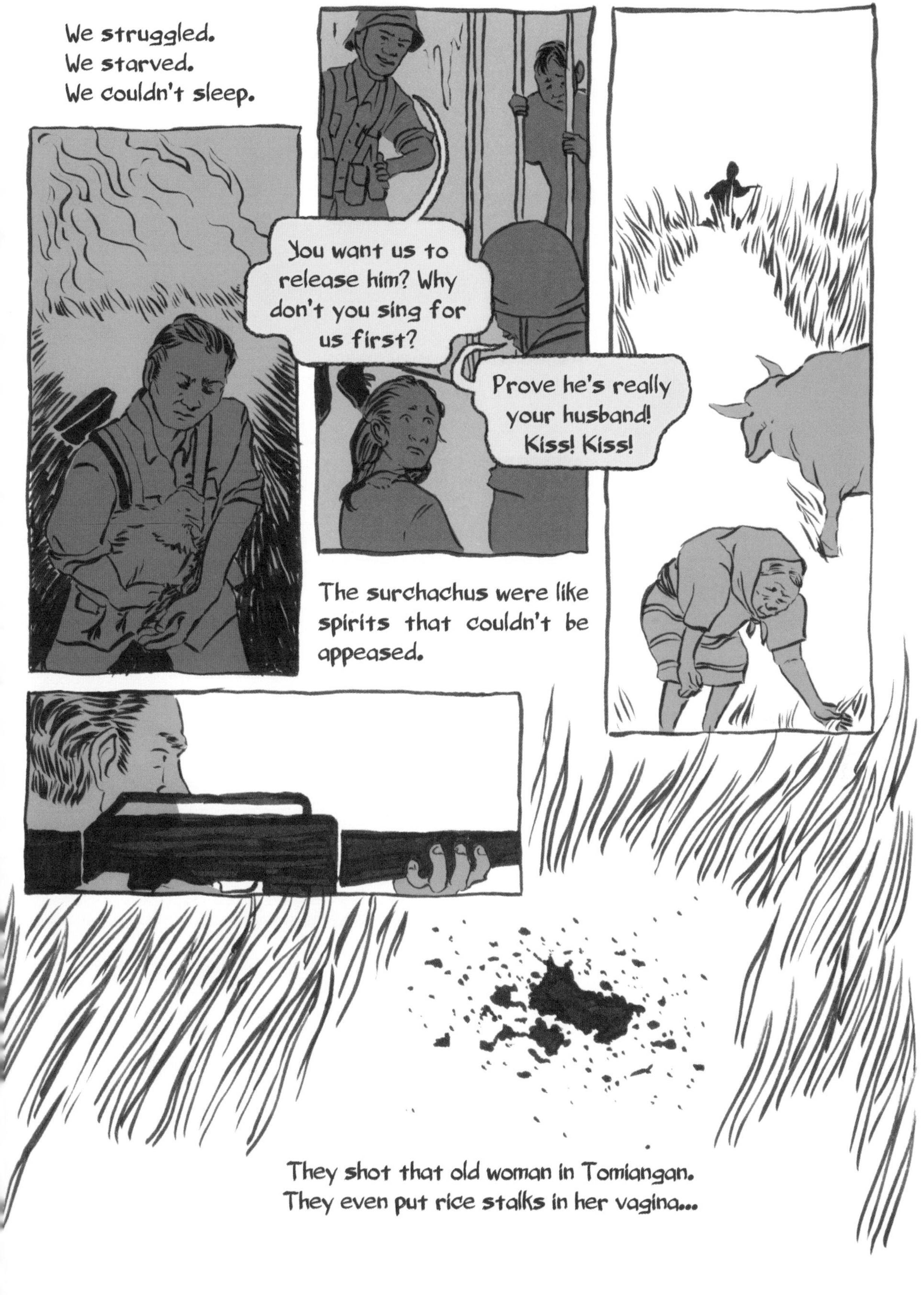
We struggled.
We starved.
We couldn't sleep.
You want us to release him? Why don't you sing for us first?
Prove he's really your husband! Kiss! Kiss!
The surchachus were like spirits that couldn't be appeased.
They shot that old woman in Tomiangan.
They even put rice stalks in her vagina...

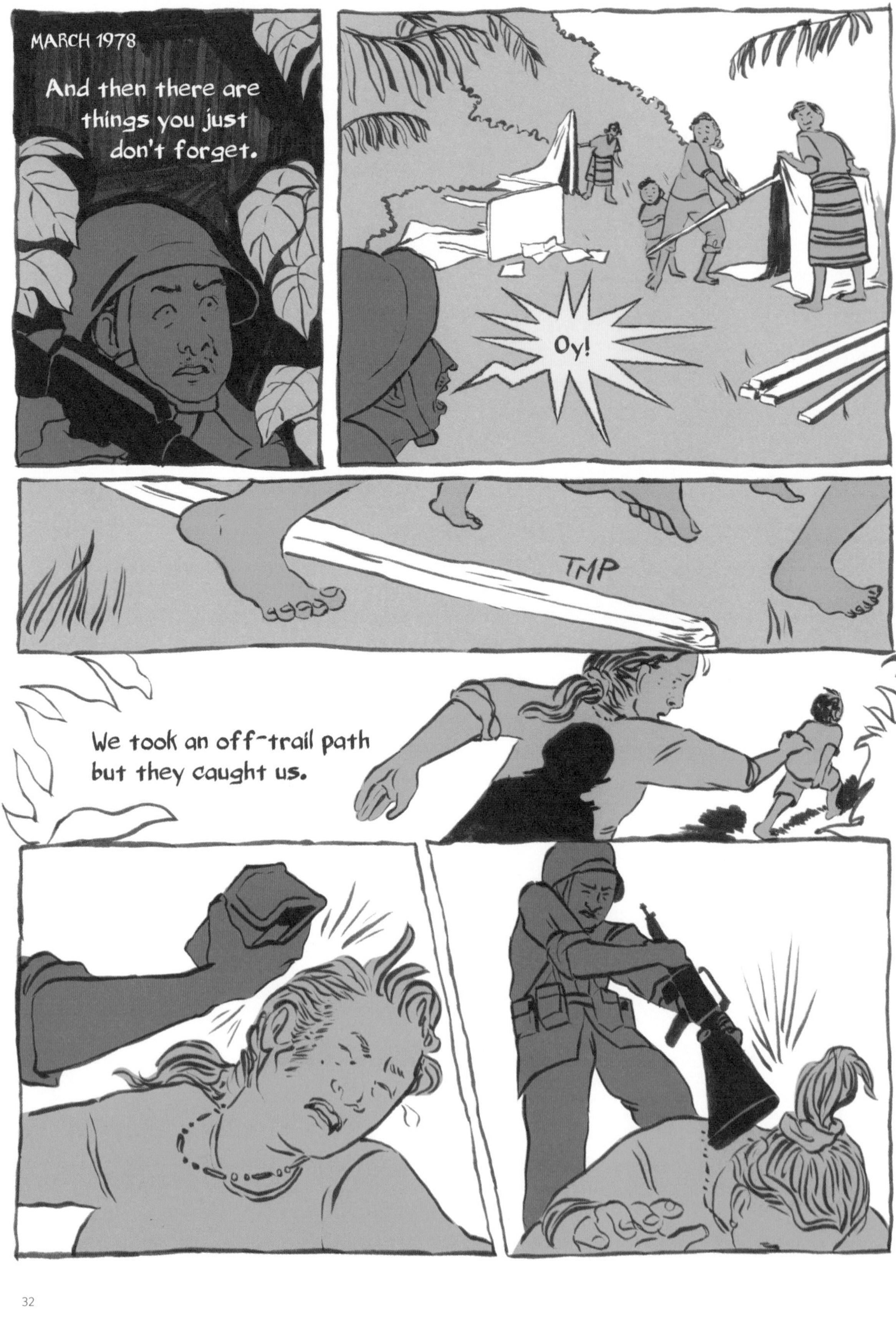
MARCH 1978
And then there are things you just don't forget.
Oy!
TMP
We took an off-trail path but they caught us.

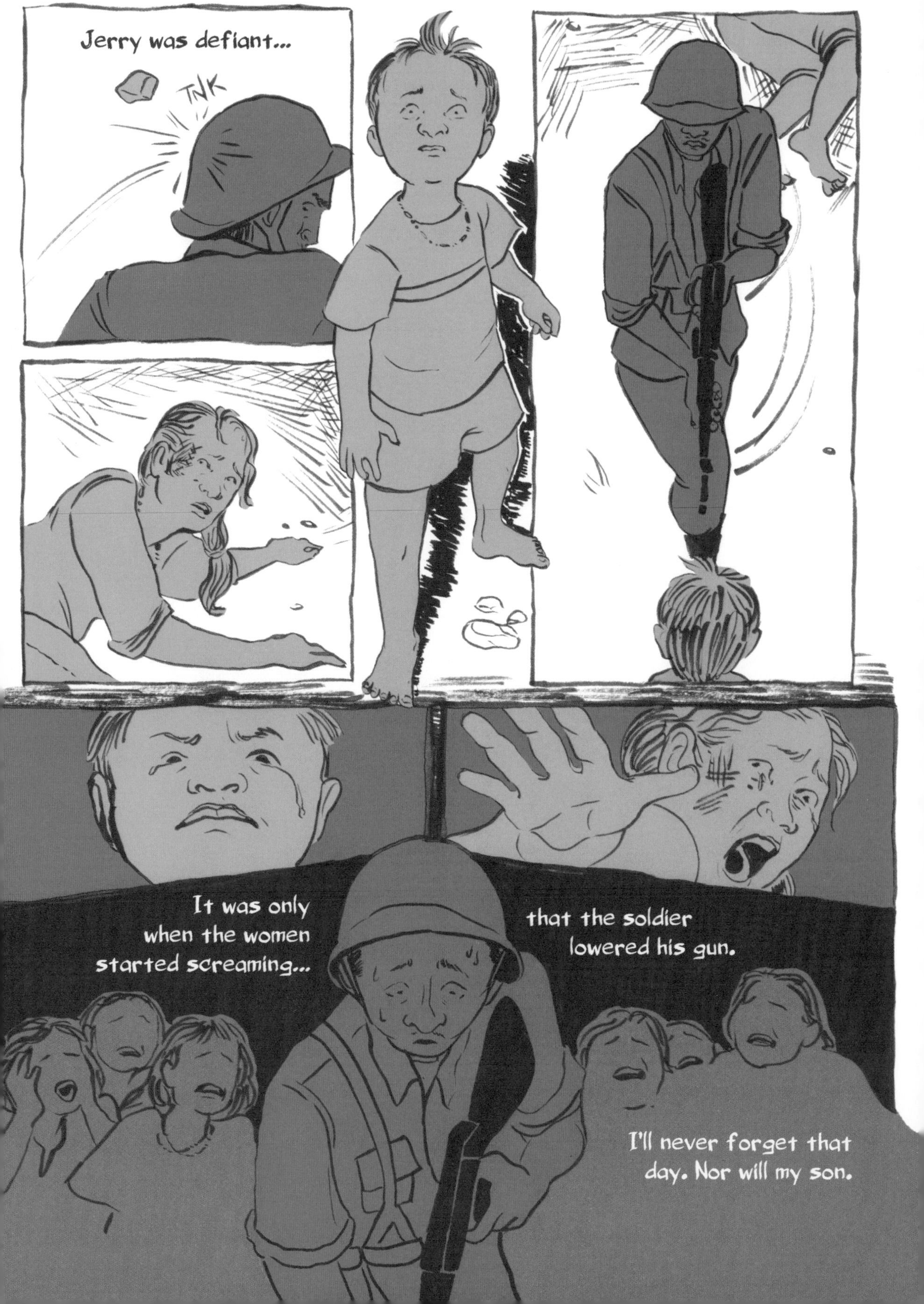
Jerry was defiant...
TNK
It was only when the women started screaming...
that the soldier lowered his gun.
I'll never forget that day. Nor will my son.

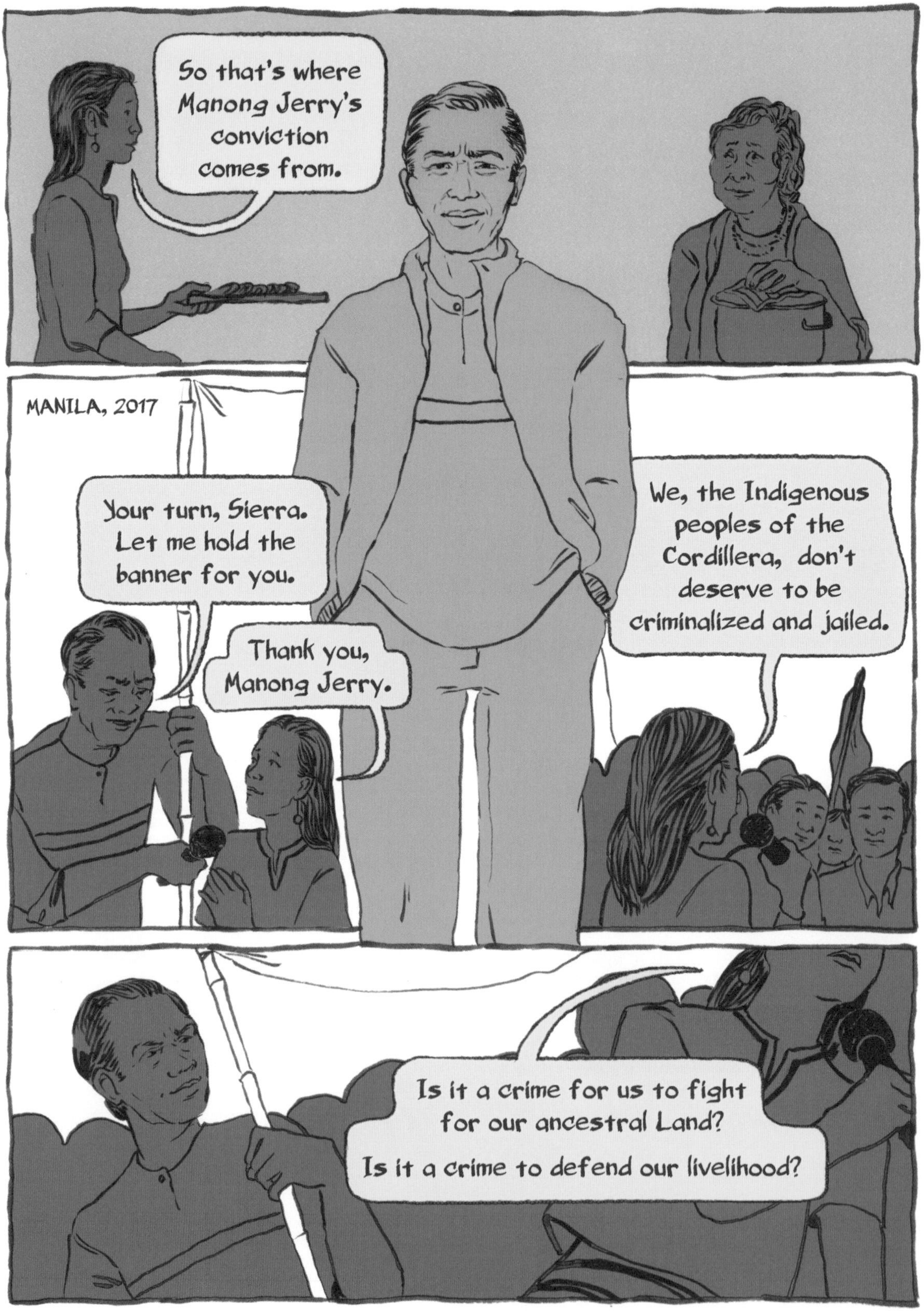
So that's where Manong Jerry's conviction comes from.
MANILA, 2017
Your turn, Sierra. Let me hold the banner for you.
Thank you, Manong Jerry.
We, the Indigenous peoples of the Cordillera, don't deserve to be criminalized and jailed.
Is it a crime for us to fight for our ancestral Land?
Is it a crime to defend our livelihood?

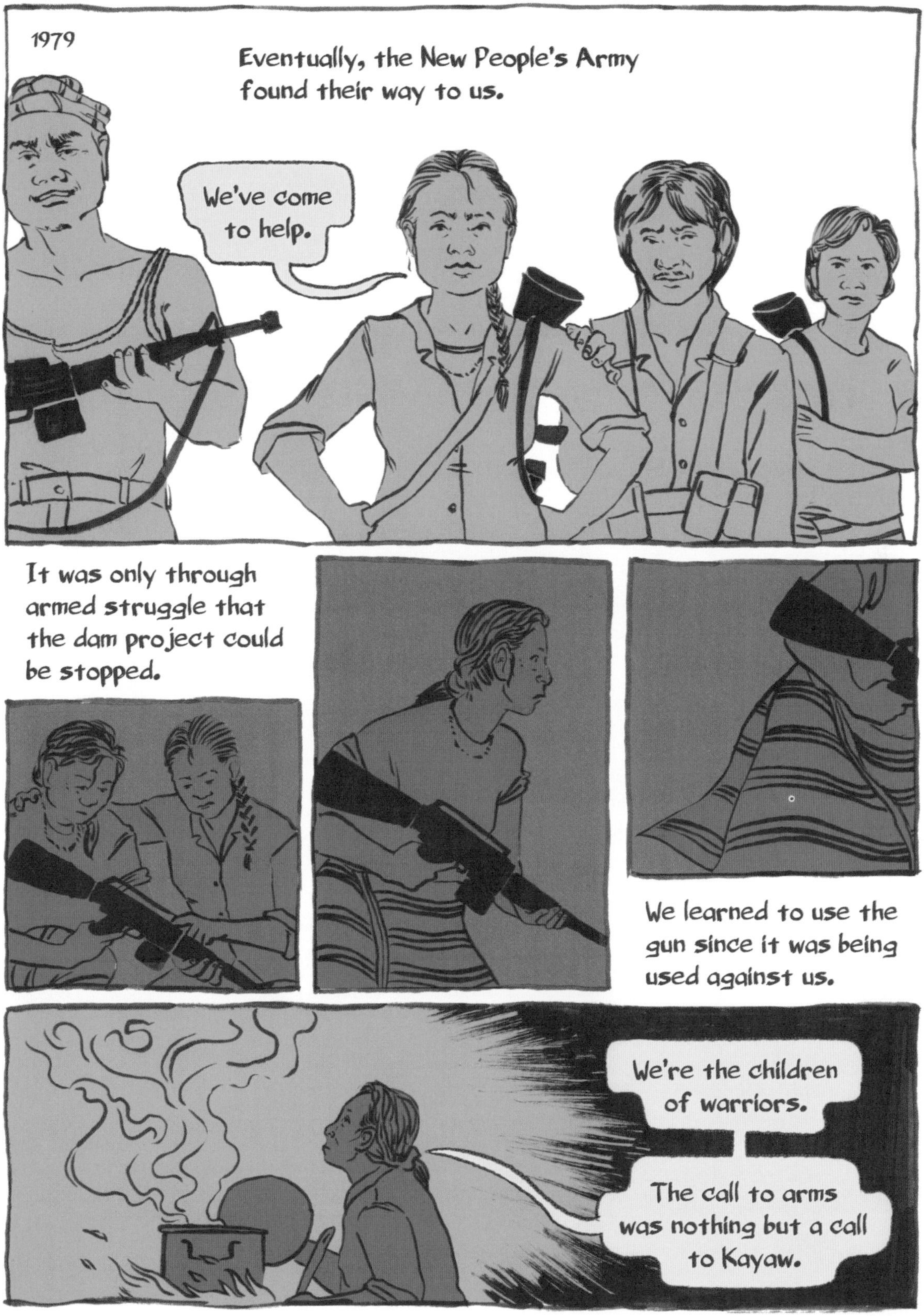
1979
Eventually, the New People's Army found their way to us.
We've come to help.
It was only through armed struggle that the dam project could be stopped.
We learned to use the gun since it was being used against us.
We're the children of warriors.
The call to arms was nothing but a call to Kayaw.

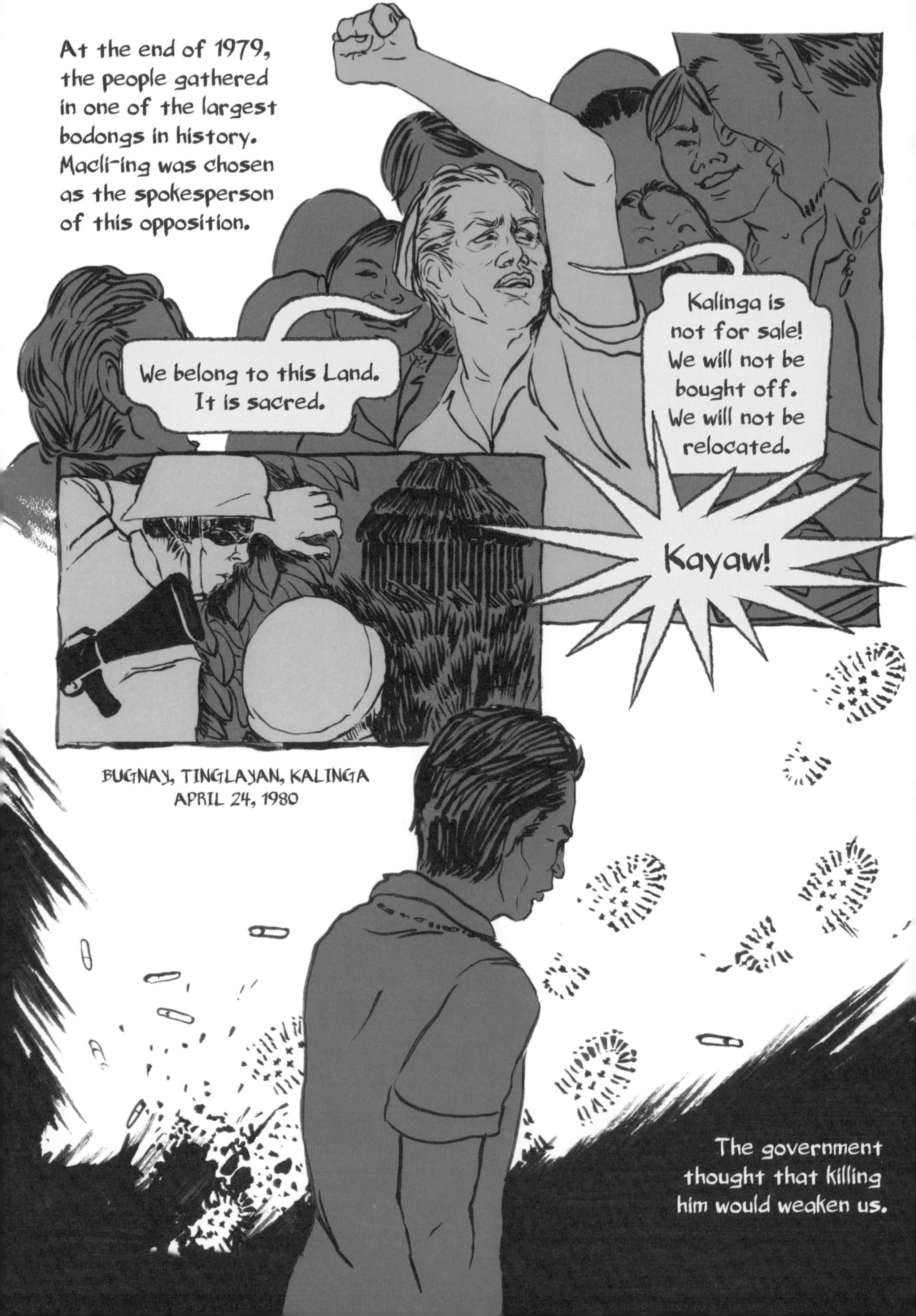
At the end of 1979, the people gathered in one of the largest bodongs in history. Macli-ing was chosen as the spokesperson of this opposition.
We belong to this Land. It is sacred.
Kalinga is not for sale! We will not be bought off. We will not be relocated.
Kayaw!
BUGNAY, TINGLAYAN, KALINGA APRIL 24, 1980
The government thought that killing him would weaken us.

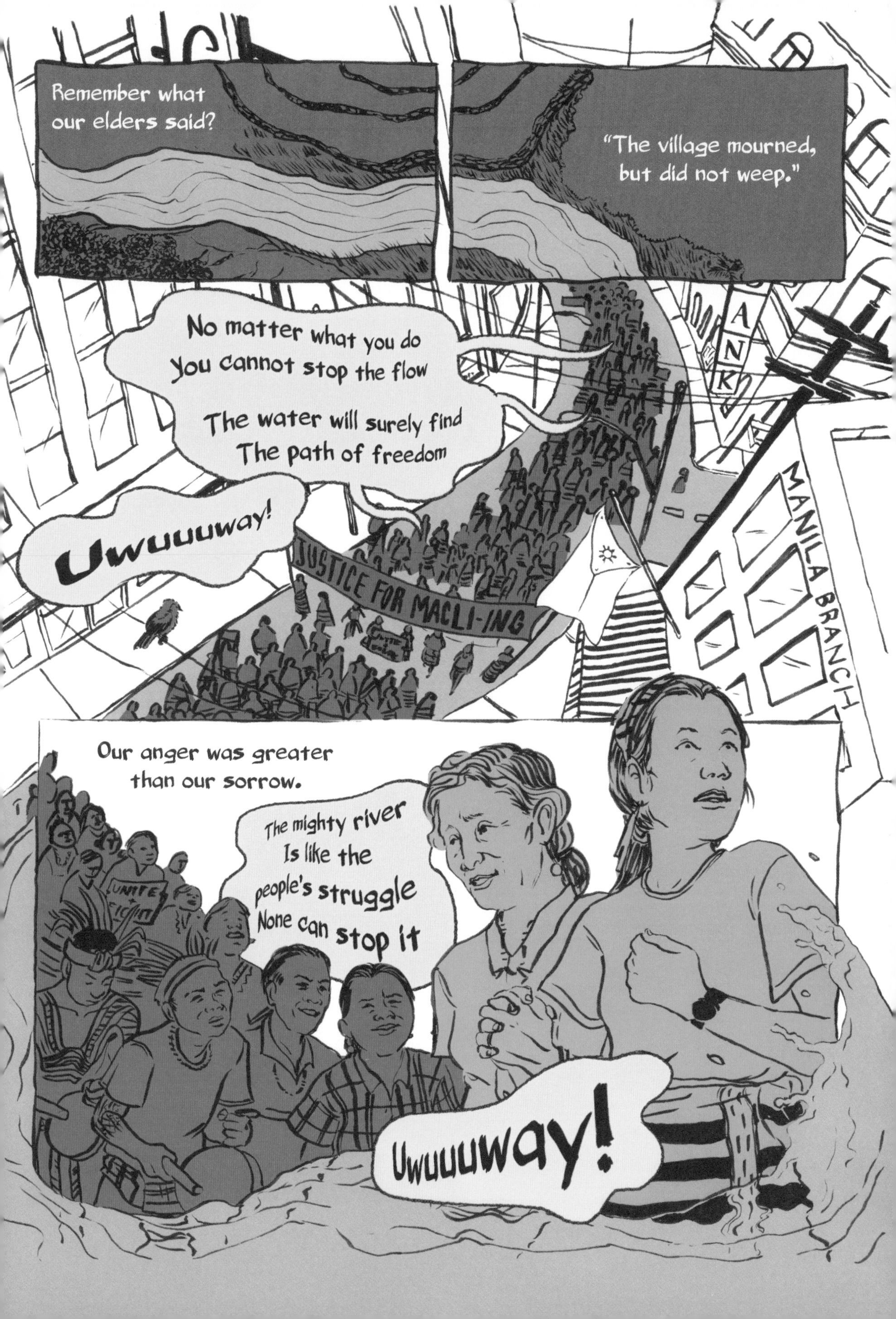

Remember what our elders said?
"The village mourned, but did not weep."
No matter what you do
You cannot stop the flow
The water will surely find
The path of freedom
Uwuuuway!
JUSTICE FOR MACLI-ING
ANK
MANILA BRANCH
Our anger was greater than our sorrow.
The mighty river
Is like the
people's struggle
None can stop it
Uwuuuway!

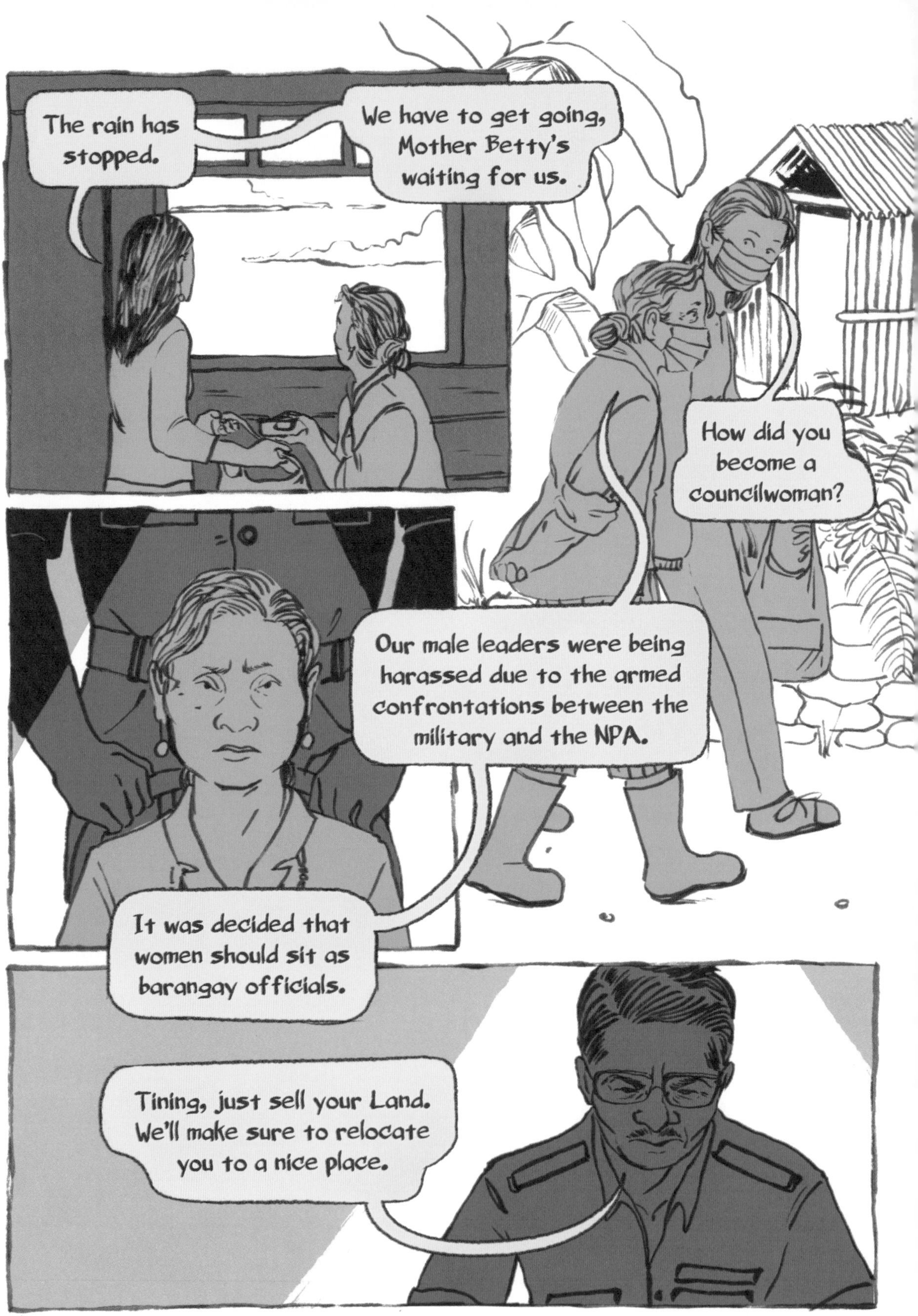

The rain has stopped.
We have to get going, Mother Betty's waiting for us.
How did you become a councilwoman?
Our male leaders were being harassed due to the armed confrontations between the military and the NPA.
It was decided that women should sit as barangay officials.
Tining, just sell your Land. We'll make sure to relocate you to a nice place.

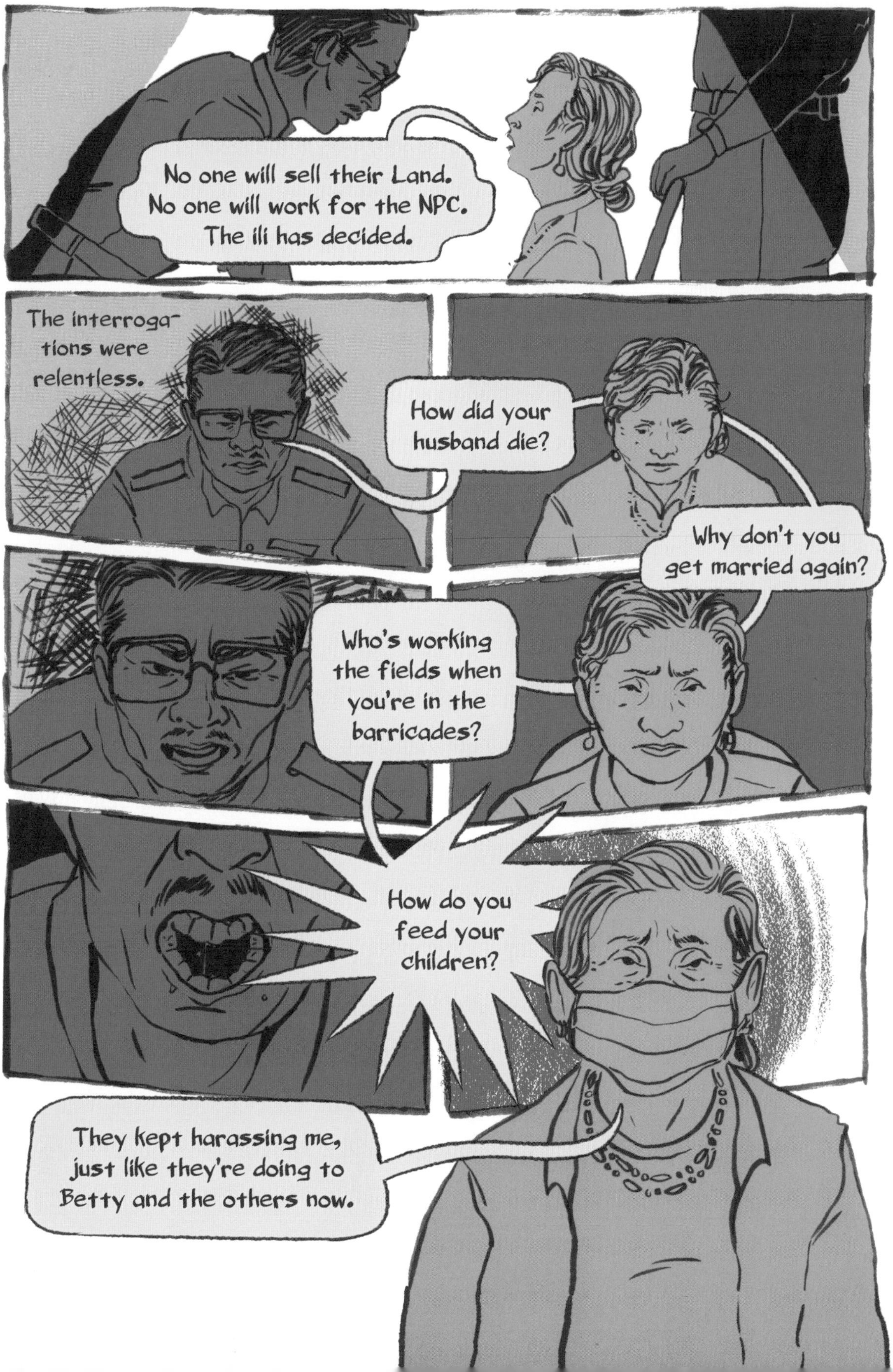
No one will sell their Land. No one will work for the NPC. The ili has decided.
The interrogations were relentless.
How did your husband die?
Why don't you get married again?
Who's working the fields when you're in the barricades?
How do you feed your children?
They kept harassing me, just like they're doing to Betty and the others now.

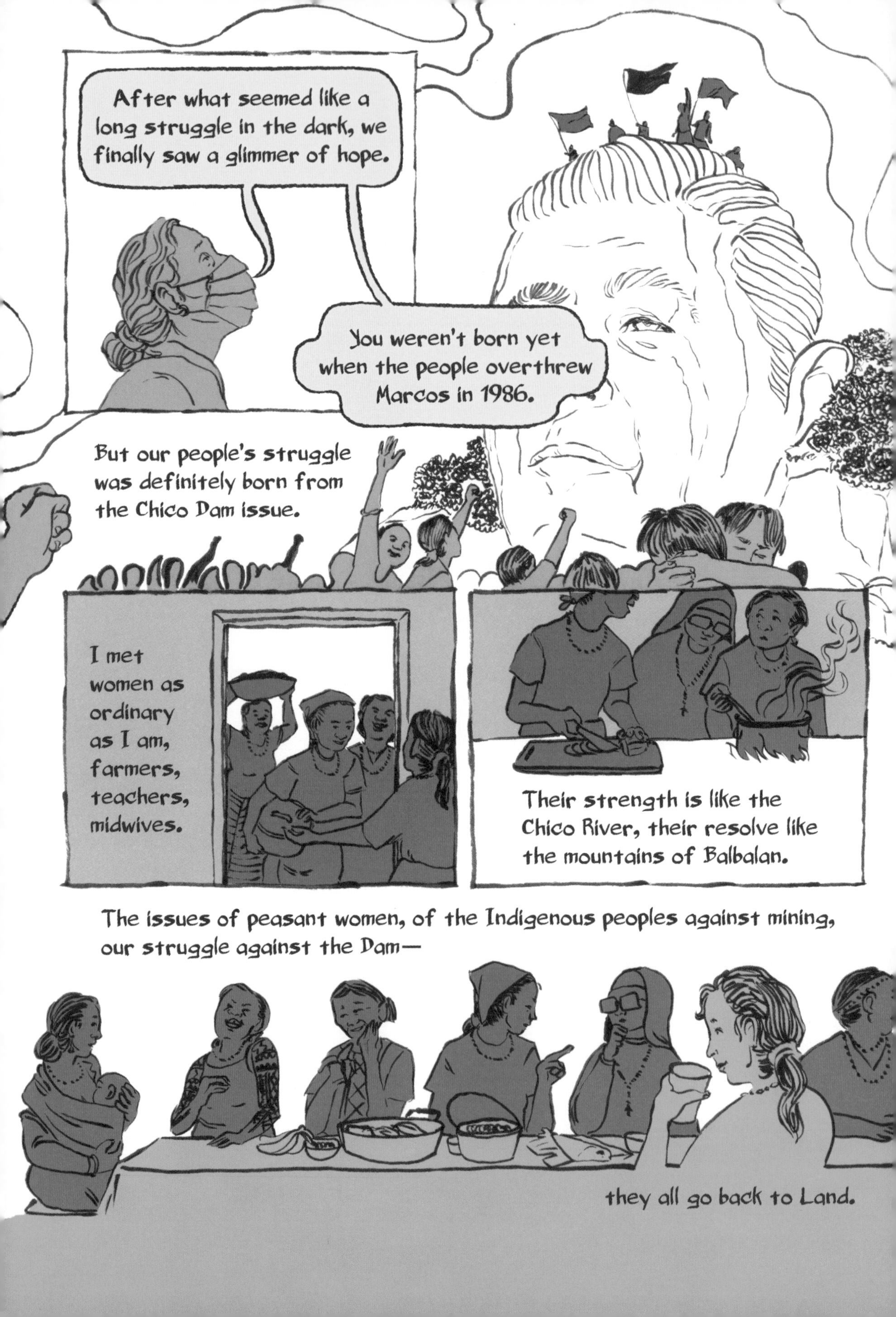
After what seemed like a long struggle in the dark, we finally saw a glimmer of hope.
You weren't born yet when the people overthrew Marcos in 1986.
But our people's struggle was definitely born from the Chico Dam issue.
I met women as ordinary as I am, farmers, teachers, midwives.
Their strength is like the Chico River, their resolve like the mountains of Balbalan.
The issues of peasant women, of the Indigenous peoples against mining, our struggle against the Dam—
they all go back to Land.

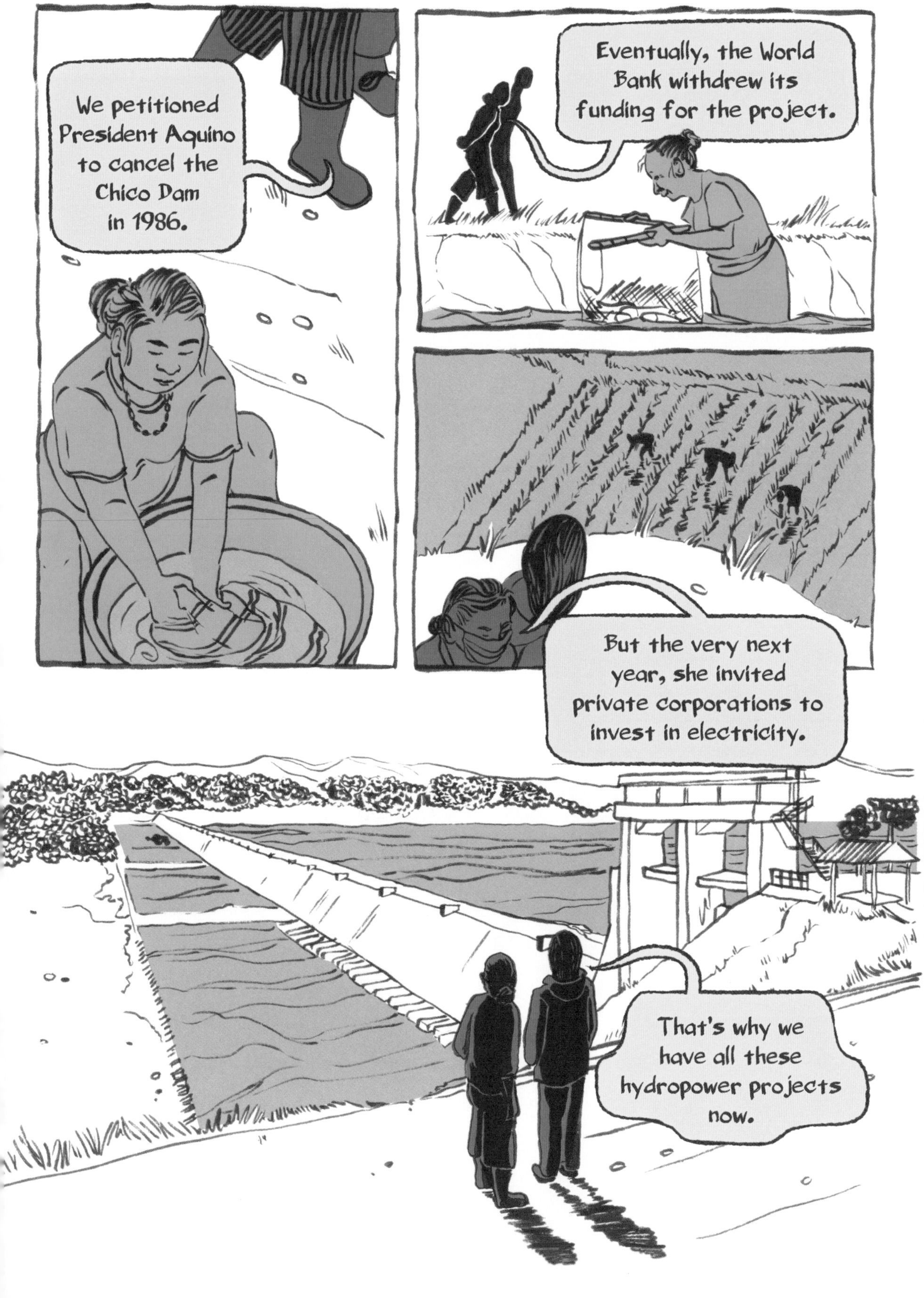
We petitioned President Aquino to cancel the Chico Dam in 1986.
Eventually, the World Bank withdrew its funding for the project.
But the very next year, she invited private corporations to invest in electricity.
That's why we have all these hydropower projects now.

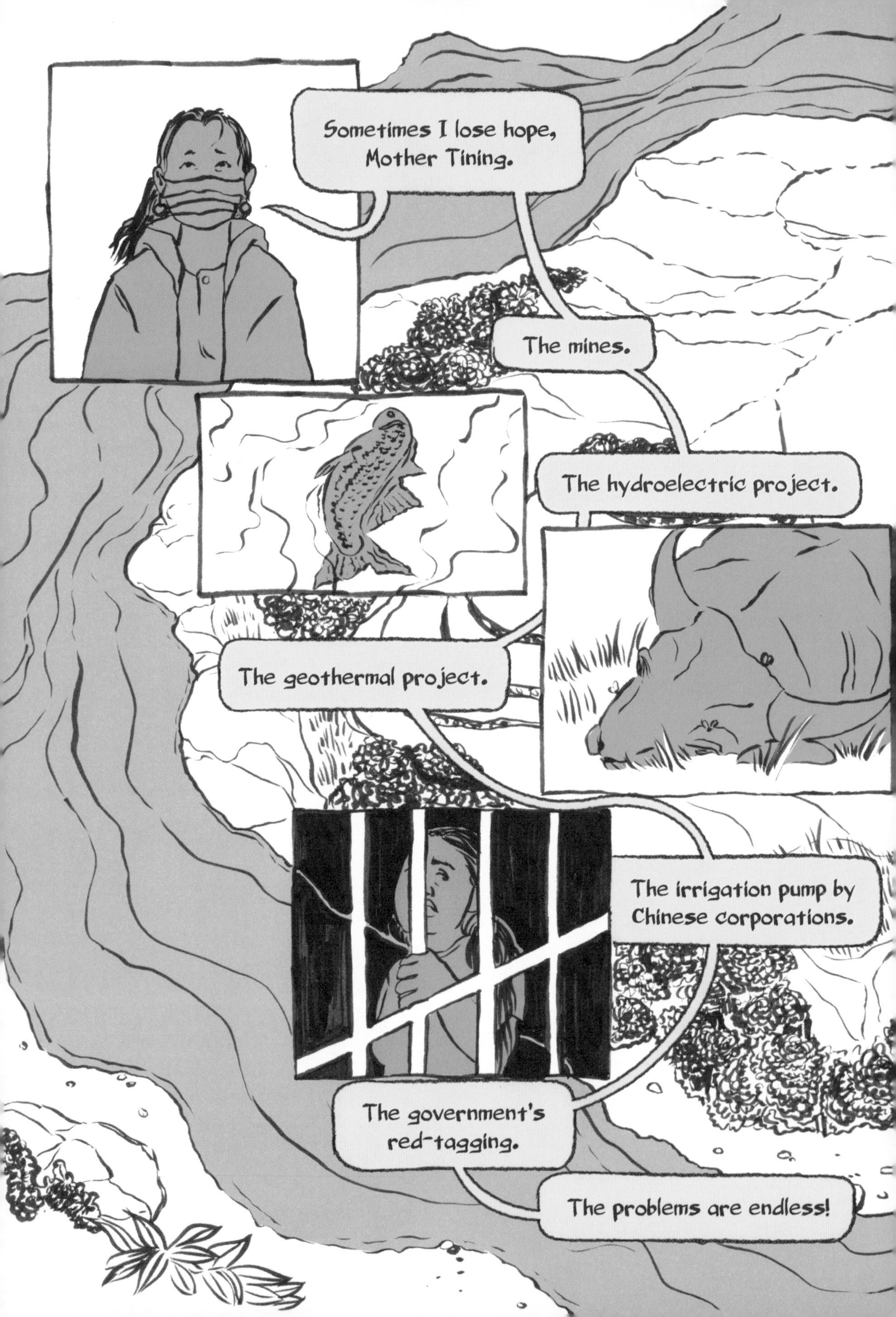

Sometimes I lose hope, Mother Tining.
The mines.
The hydroelectric project.
The geothermal project.
The irrigation pump by Chinese corporations.
The government's red-tagging.
The problems are endless!

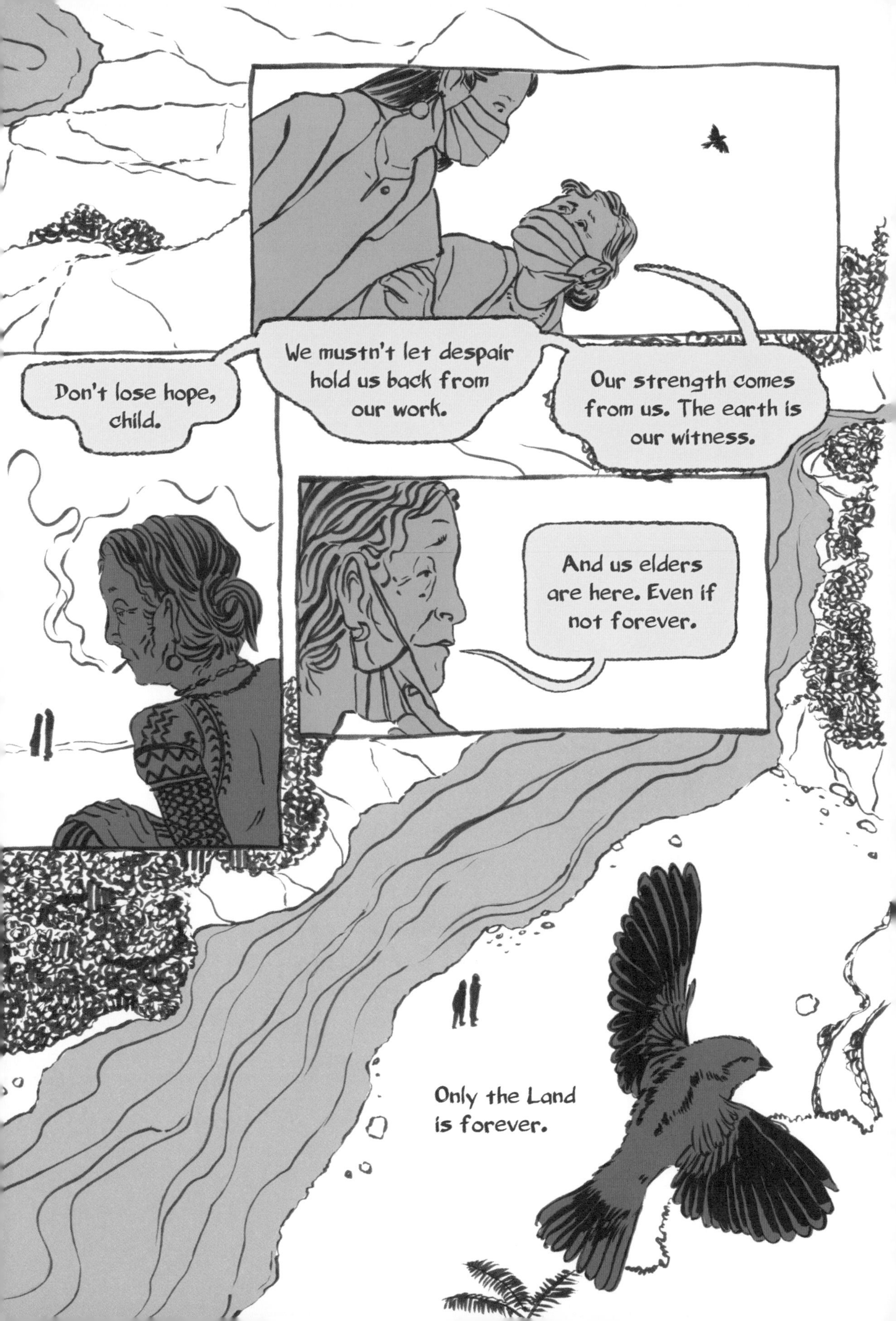
Don't lose hope, child.
We mustn't let despair hold us back from our work.
Our strength comes from us. The earth is our witness.
And us elders are here. Even if not forever.
Only the Land is forever.

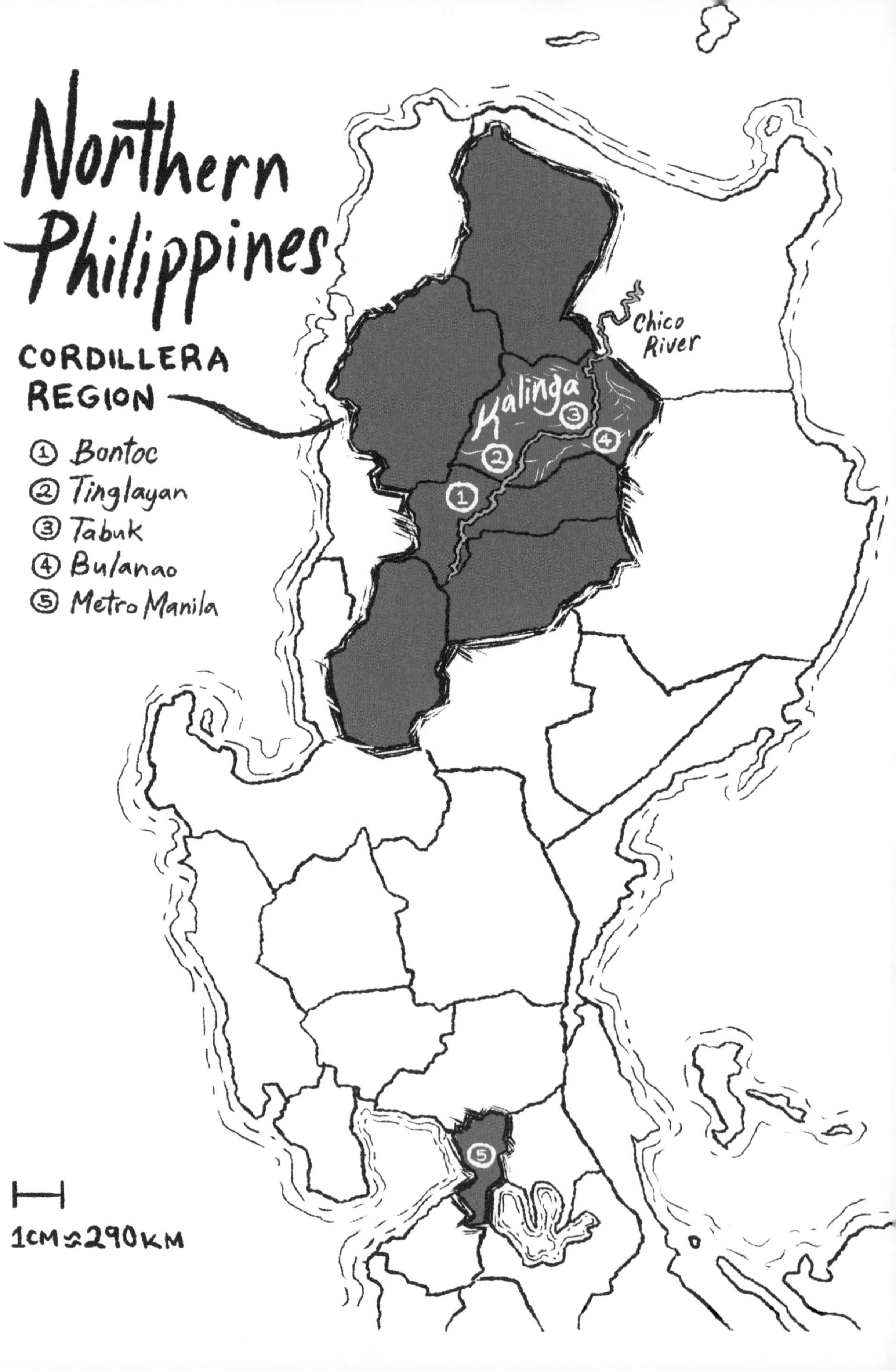
Northern Philippines
CORDILLERA REGION
① Bontoc
② Tinglayan
③ Tabuk
④ Bulanao
⑤ Metro Manila
Chico River
Kalinga
1CM≈290KM

Glossary

Ama Macli-ing — Macli-ing Dulag, chief of the Butbut tribe and leader of the Kalinga in the Chico Dam struggle.

Apo Kabunyan — Supreme Deity in many parts of the Cordillera region, northern Philippines.

bodong — peace pact.

Bontoc — a municipality and capital of Mountain Province, in the Cordillera region of northern Philippines.

Cordillera Heroes' Memorial — a memorial in Tinglayan, Kalinga dedicated to Macli-ing Dulag, Pedro Dungoc Sr., and Ama Lumbaya Gayudan, heroes of the Chico Dam struggle.

Kalinga — a province in the Cordillera region, Northern Philippines; the name comes from the Ibanag and Gaddang term kalinga, which means "headhunter."

ili — village.

Innabuyog-GABRIELA — alliance of women's organizations in the Cordillera region, northern Philippines.

kayaw — Cordillera term for struggle, also refers to a Kalinga headhunting expedition.

lusay — an act in which elderly women disrobe and show their tattooed bodies, thought to bring bad luck to men.

mestizo — Filipinos of foreign, usually European, ancestry; referring here to Manuel Elizalde.

PANAMIN — Presidential Assistant on National Minorities, headed by Manuel Elizalde.

NPC — National Power Corporation.

NPA — New People's Army, armed unit of the Communist Party of the Philippines-National Democratic Front.

"President Marcos" (p. 16) — Ferdinand Marcos, Philippine president (1965-1986).

red-tagging (p. 34) — a strategy historically employed against perceived enemies of the state that labels or accuses such individuals and/or organizations of leftist, communist, or terrorist activites.

"President Aquino" (p. 41) — Corazon Aquino, Philippine president (1986-1992).

surchachus — government army soldiers.

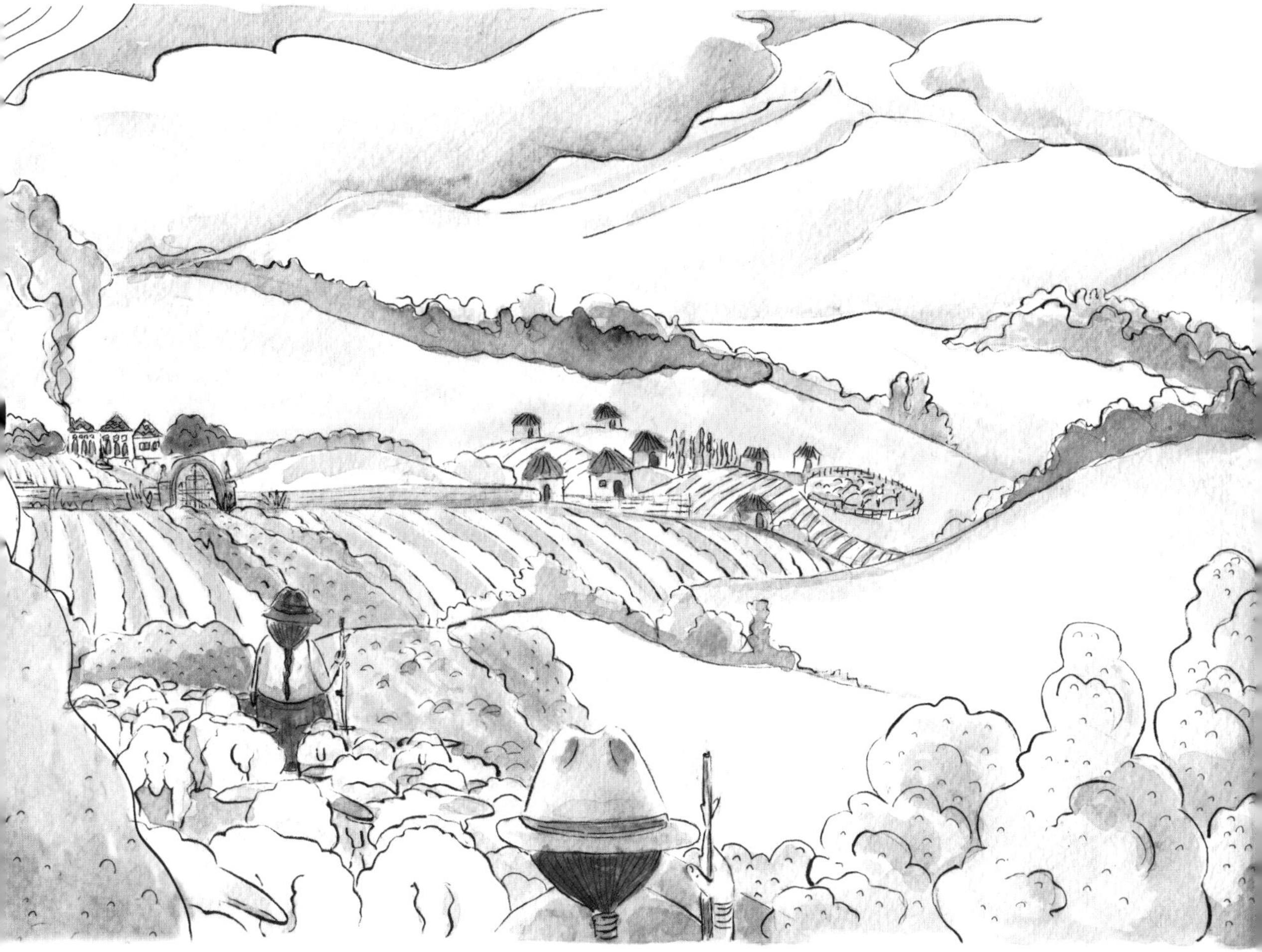

Mama Dulu

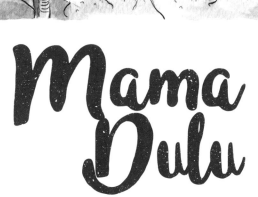

STORY AND ART BY
CITLALLI ANDRANGO
& CECILIA LARREA

TRANSLATED BY
RENATA DUQUE

RUNA MEANS 'HUMAN' IN KICHWA. THIS IS HOW THE ECUADORIAN KICHWA COMMMUNITY IDENTIFIES ITSELF. IN THE NINETEENTH CENTURY, THE RUNAS LIVED UNDER EXTREME CONDITIONS OF EXPLOITATION, POVERTY, AND ABANDONMENT. THEIR ANCESTRAL TERRITORIES HAD BEEN HANDED OVER TO THE CATHOLIC CHURCH AND CONVERTED INTO FARMS AND PLANTATIONS. THE CHURCH, IN TURN, OVERSAW THESE OPERATIONS IN A VIOLENT AND REPRESSIVE MANNER.

PLANTATION OWNERS WOULD HAND OVER SMALL PLOTS OF LAND, CALLED *HUASIPUNGO*, FOR THE RUNAS TO LIVE ON. IN EXCHANGE, THEY WERE EXPECTED TO WORK THE LAND WITHOUT PAY. THEY WERE CHARGED A TITHING TAX. THIS FORCED THEM TO SURRENDER THE FIRST RIGHT OF HARVEST TO THEIR LANDLORDS ALONG WITH TEN PERCENT OF THEIR CROPS. SUCH COLLECTIONS WERE NOT REGULATED, AND PLANTATION OWNERS WOULD OFTEN ABUSE THEIR POWER, TAKING MORE THAN WHAT WAS OWED. ALL OF THIS TOOK PLACE UNDER THE GOVERNMENT'S WATCH.

ECUADOR, LATE NINETEENTH CENTURY

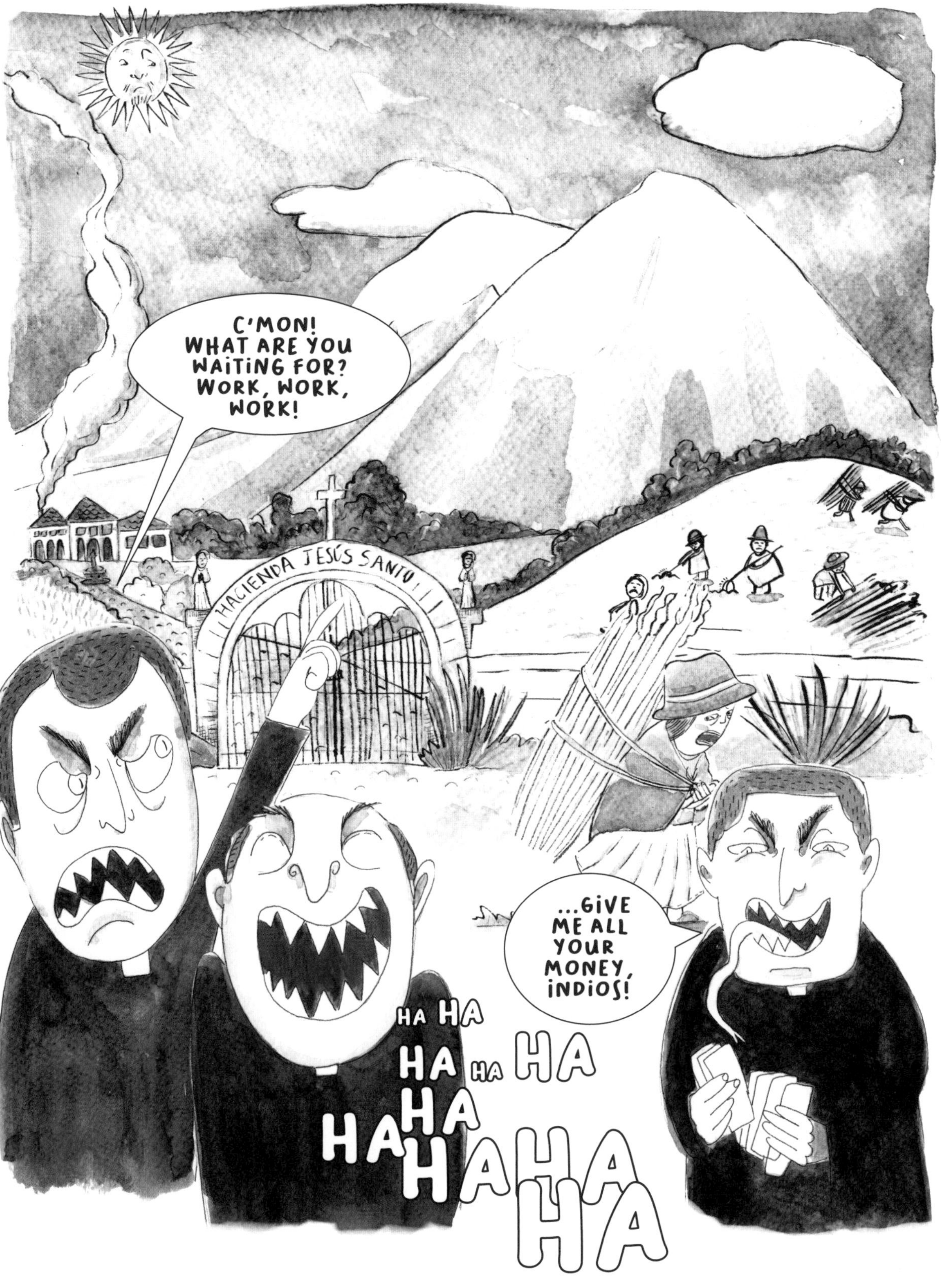
C'MON! WHAT ARE YOU WAITING FOR? WORK, WORK, WORK!
HACIENDA JESÚS SANTO
...GIVE ME ALL YOUR MONEY, INDIOS!
HA HA HA HA HA HA HA HA HA HA HA

WOMEN WERE CONSIDERED A FORM OF PROPERTY.

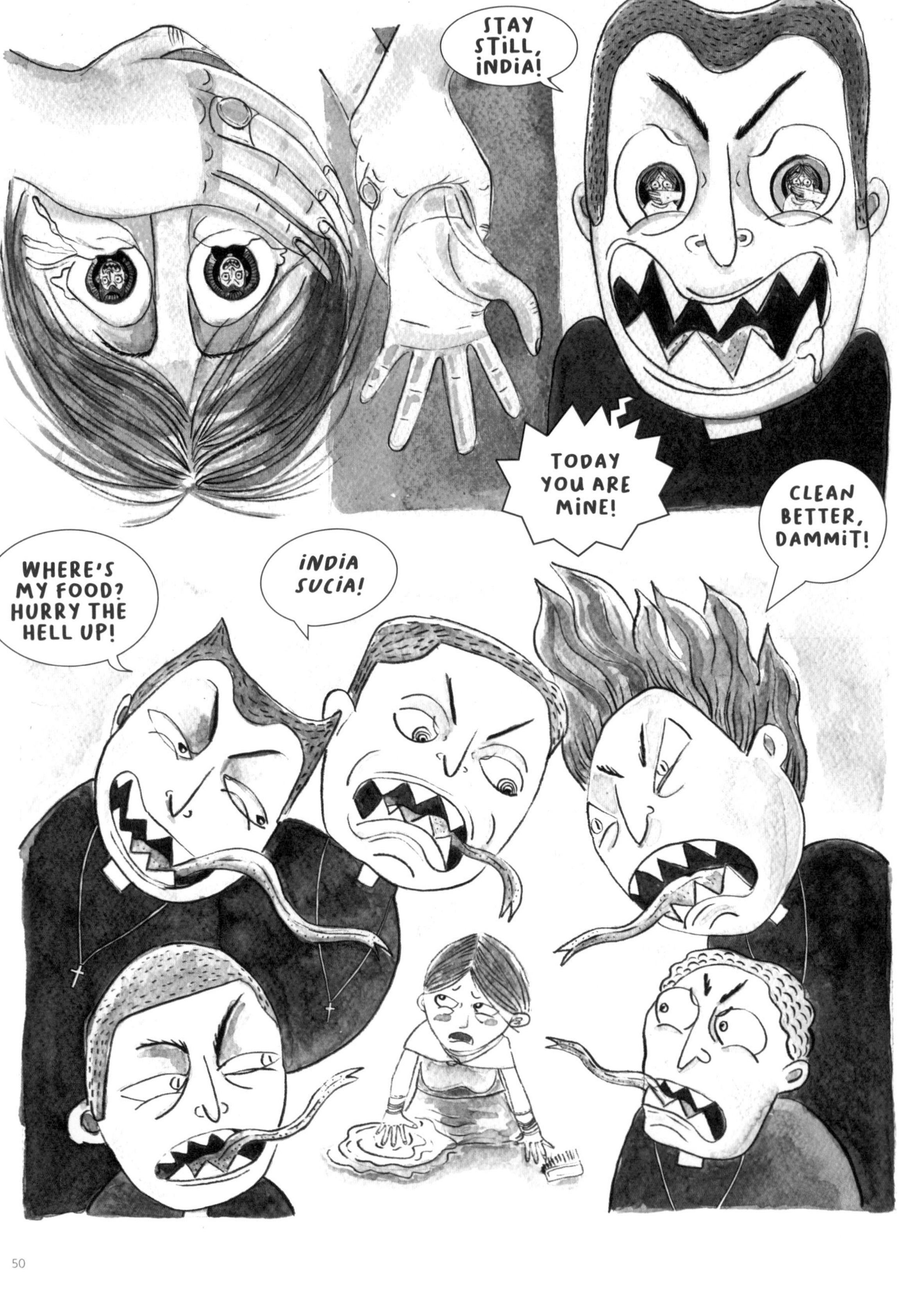
STAY STILL, INDIA!
TODAY YOU ARE MINE!
WHERE'S MY FOOD? HURRY THE HELL UP!
INDIA SUCIA!
CLEAN BETTER, DAMMIT!

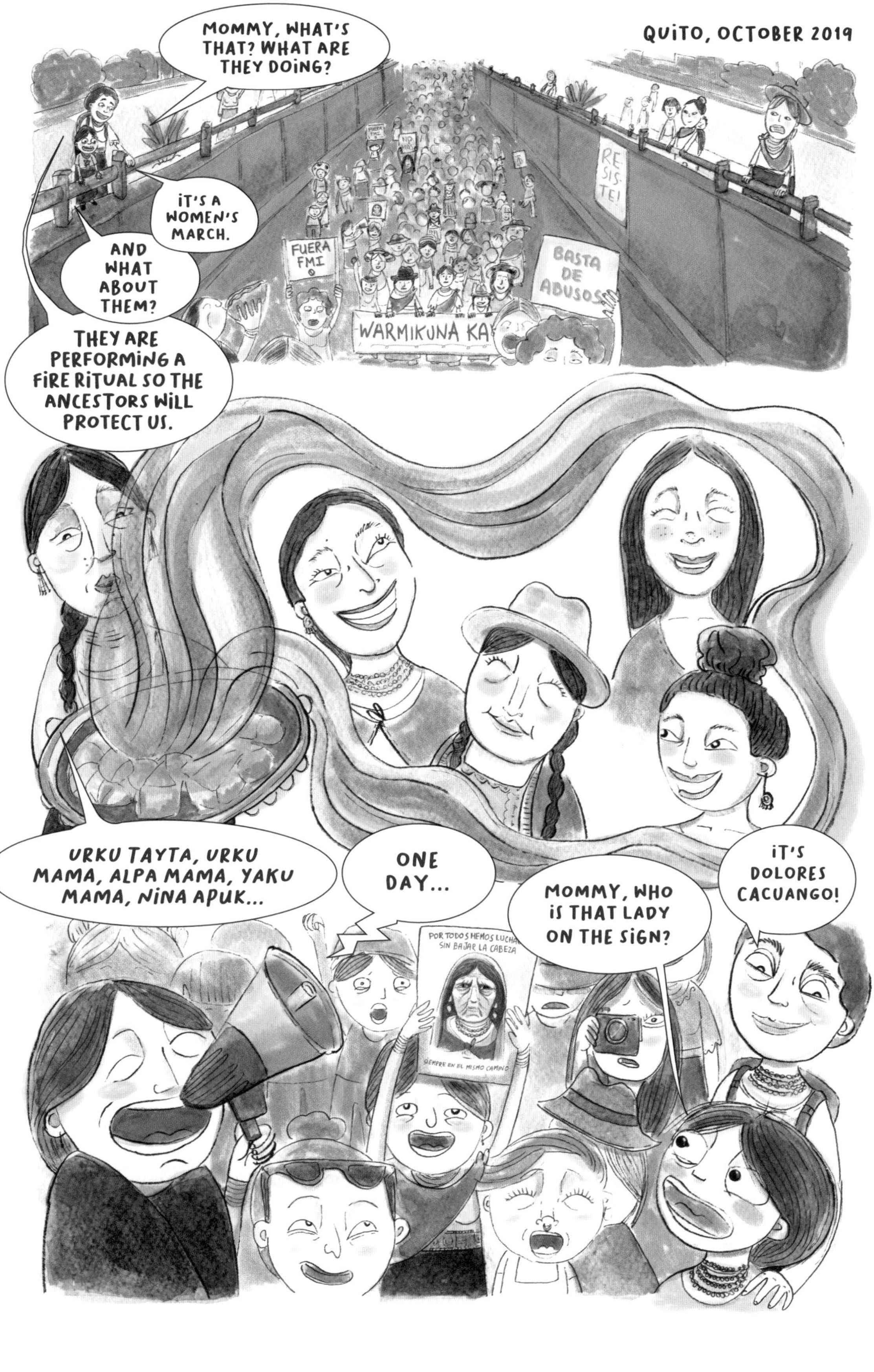
QUITO, OCTOBER 2019
MOMMY, WHAT'S THAT? WHAT ARE THEY DOING?
IT'S A WOMEN'S MARCH.
AND WHAT ABOUT THEM?
THEY ARE PERFORMING A FIRE RITUAL SO THE ANCESTORS WILL PROTECT US.
FUERA FMI
BASTA DE ABUSOS
RE SIS TE!
WARMIKUNA KA
URKU TAYTA, URKU MAMA, ALPA MAMA, YAKU MAMA, NINA APUK...
ONE DAY...
MOMMY, WHO IS THAT LADY ON THE SIGN?
IT'S DOLORES CACUANGO!
POR TODOS HEMOS LUCHA SIN BAJAR LA CABEZA
SIEMPRE EN EL MISMO CAMINO

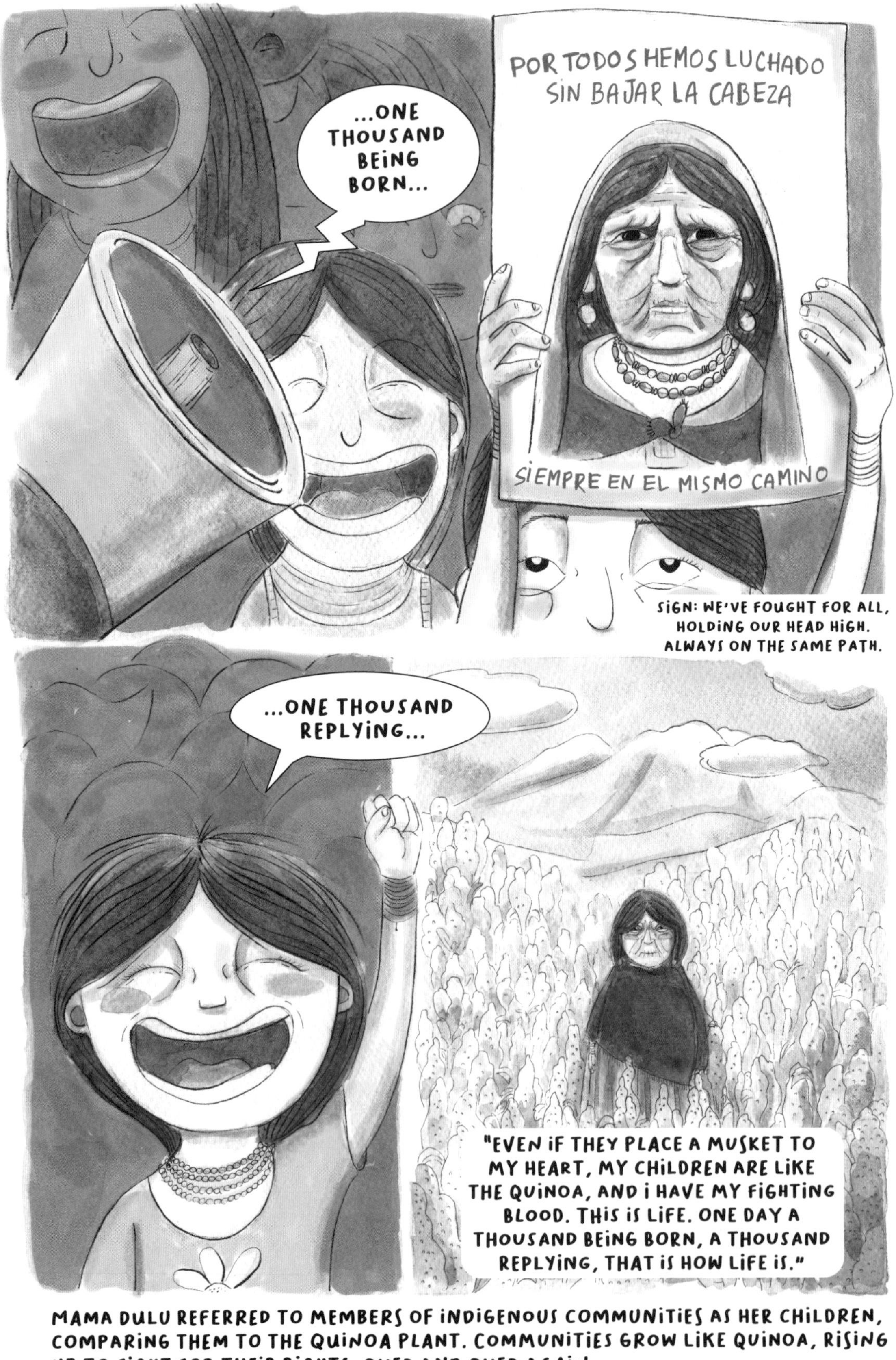
...ONE THOUSAND BEING BORN...
POR TODOS HEMOS LUCHADO SIN BAJAR LA CABEZA
SIEMPRE EN EL MISMO CAMINO
SIGN: WE'VE FOUGHT FOR ALL, HOLDING OUR HEAD HIGH. ALWAYS ON THE SAME PATH.
...ONE THOUSAND REPLYING...
"EVEN IF THEY PLACE A MUSKET TO MY HEART, MY CHILDREN ARE LIKE THE QUINOA, AND I HAVE MY FIGHTING BLOOD. THIS IS LIFE. ONE DAY A THOUSAND BEING BORN, A THOUSAND REPLYING, THAT IS HOW LIFE IS."

MAMA DULU REFERRED TO MEMBERS OF INDIGENOUS COMMUNITIES AS HER CHILDREN, COMPARING THEM TO THE QUINOA PLANT. COMMUNITIES GROW LIKE QUINOA, RISING UP TO FIGHT FOR THEIR RIGHTS, OVER AND OVER AGAIN.

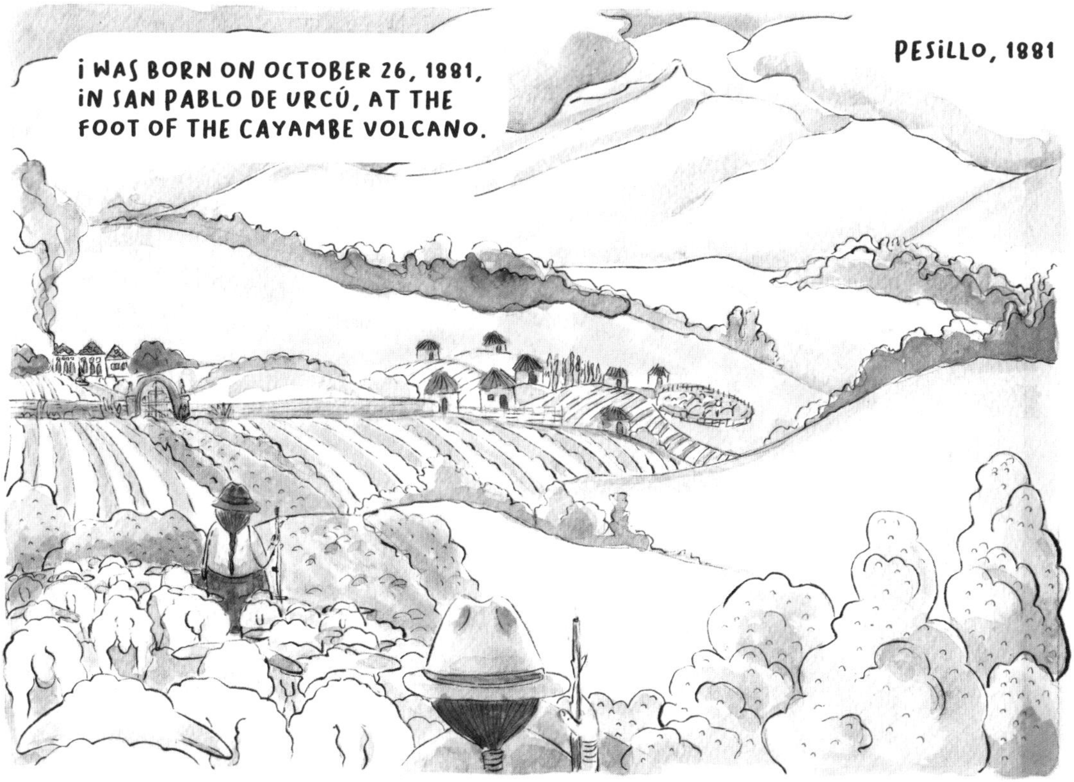
PESILLO, 1881
I WAS BORN ON OCTOBER 26, 1881, IN SAN PABLO DE URCÚ, AT THE FOOT OF THE CAYAMBE VOLCANO.

WHEN I WAS A YOUNG GIRL, I WOULD SEE MAMIKU ANDREA AND HER COMPAÑERAS* FIGHTING FOR US.

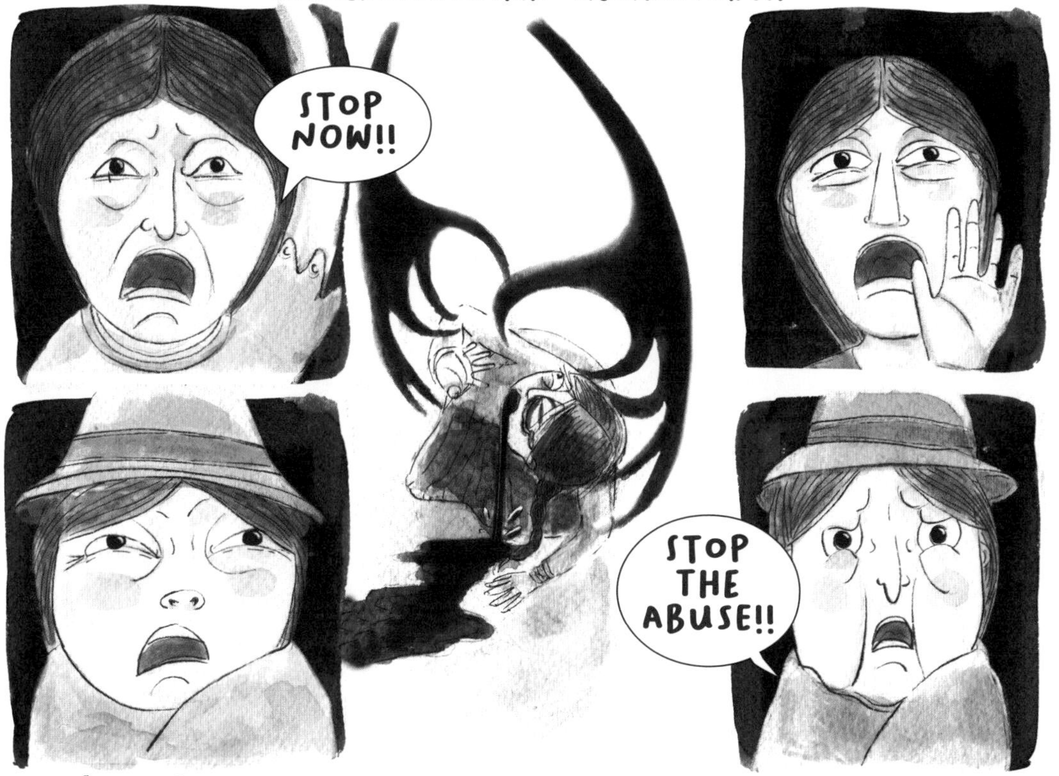
STOP NOW!!
STOP THE ABUSE!!

* COMPAÑERAS: FRIENDS, COMRADES, SISTERS IN ARMS, AND FIGHTING COMPANIONS.

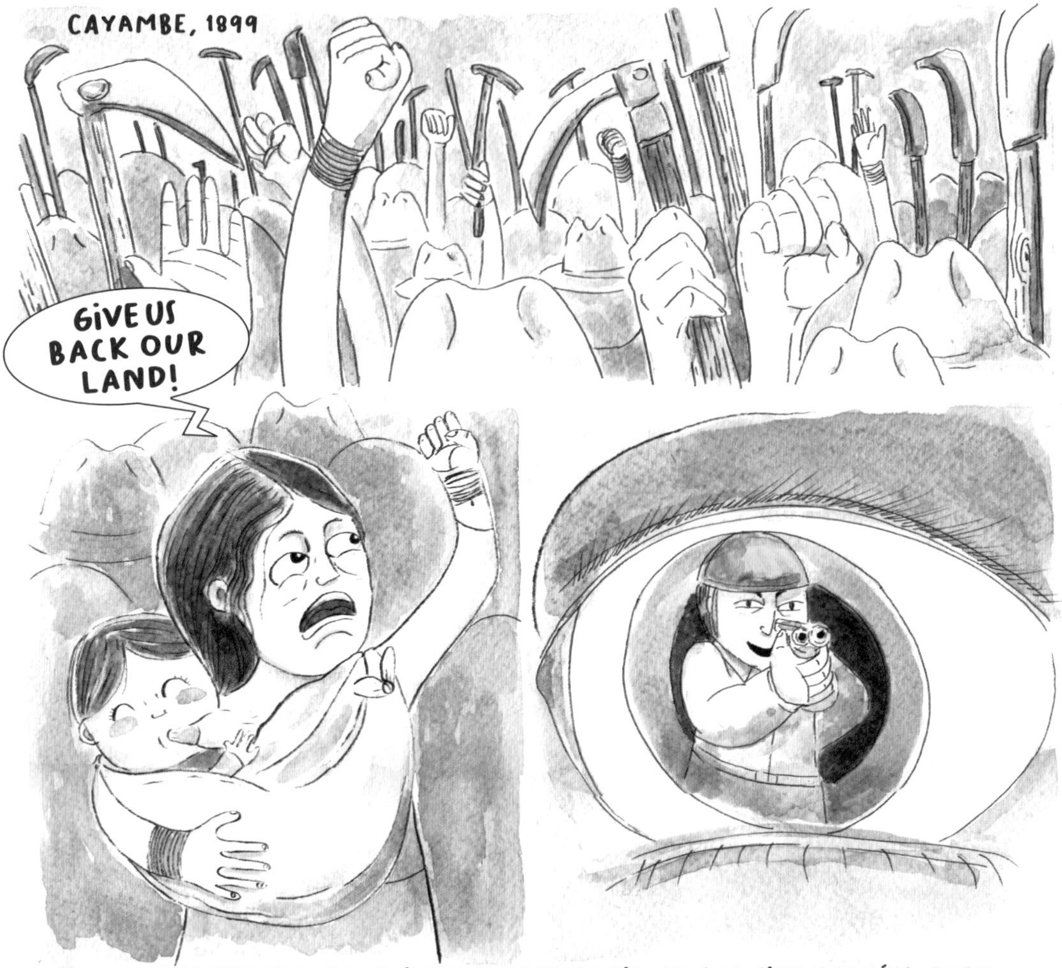
CAYAMBE, 1899
GIVE US BACK OUR LAND!

DURING THE STRUGGLE, I SAW HOW THEY KILLED JUANITA CALCÁN, EVEN WHILE SHE HELD A *WAWA** AT HER BREAST, JUST FOR RAISING HER VOICE.

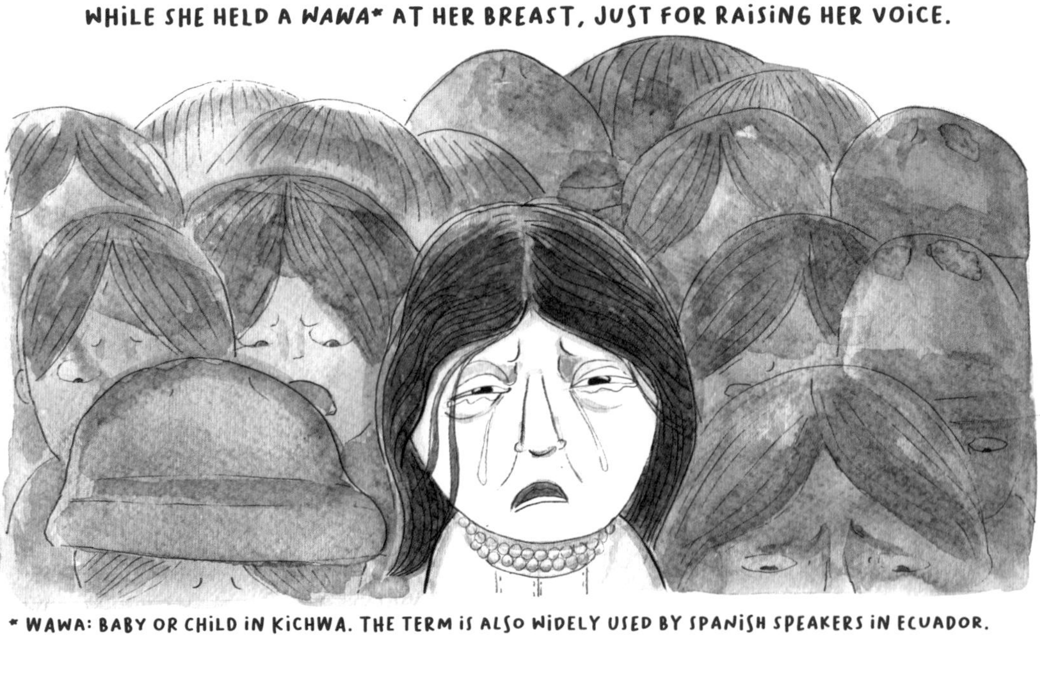

* WAWA: BABY OR CHILD IN KICHWA. THE TERM IS ALSO WIDELY USED BY SPANISH SPEAKERS IN ECUADOR.

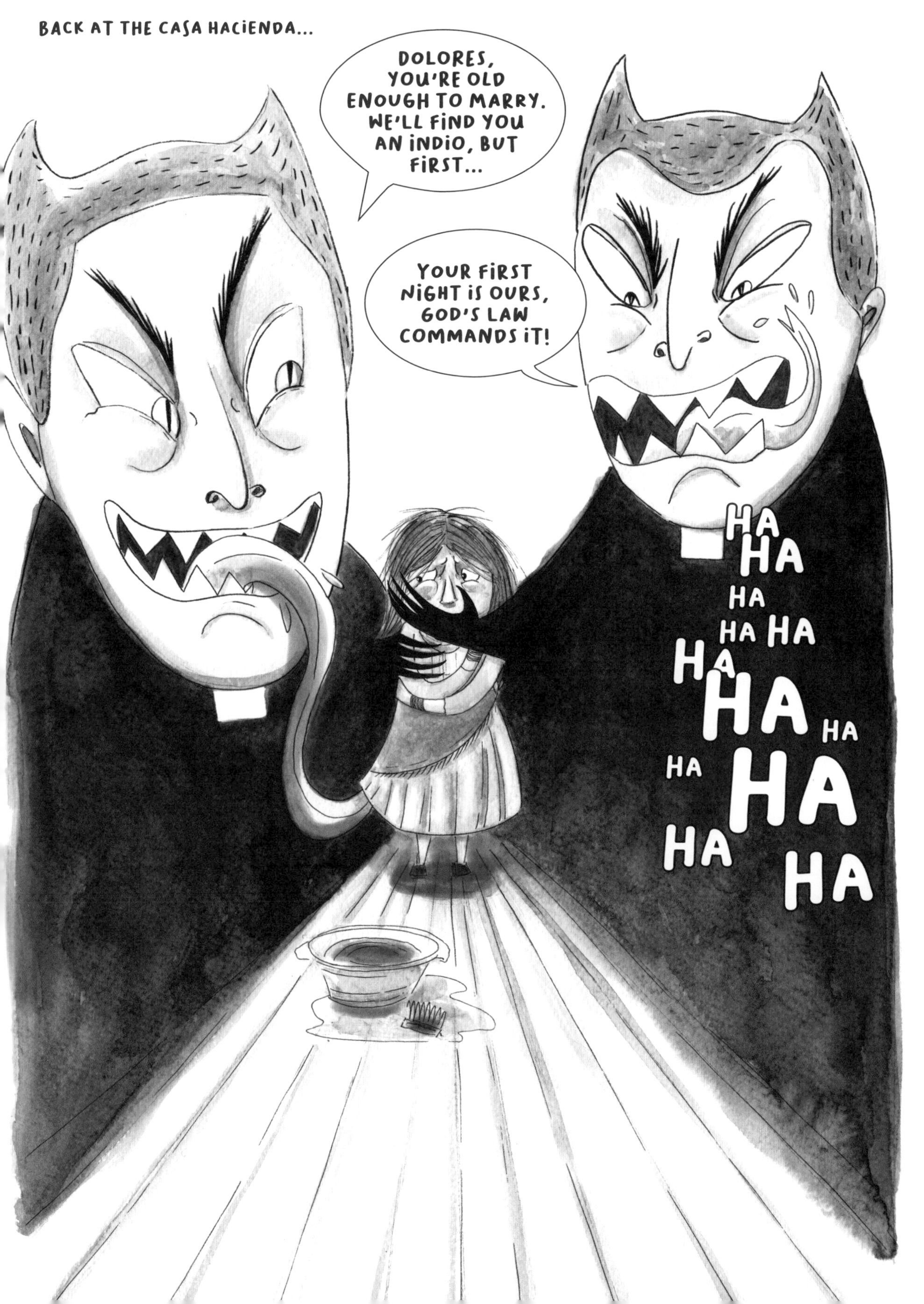
BACK AT THE CASA HACIENDA...
DOLORES, YOU'RE OLD ENOUGH TO MARRY. WE'LL FIND YOU AN INDIO, BUT FIRST...
YOUR FIRST NIGHT IS OURS, GOD'S LAW COMMANDS IT!
HA HA HA HA HA HA HA HA HA HA HA HA

AFTER THAT, I DECIDED TO LEAVE. I'D NEVER BEEN AWAY FROM THE PLANTATION.

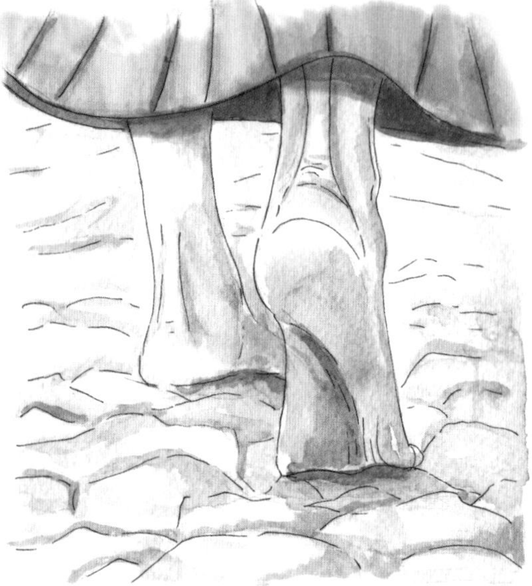

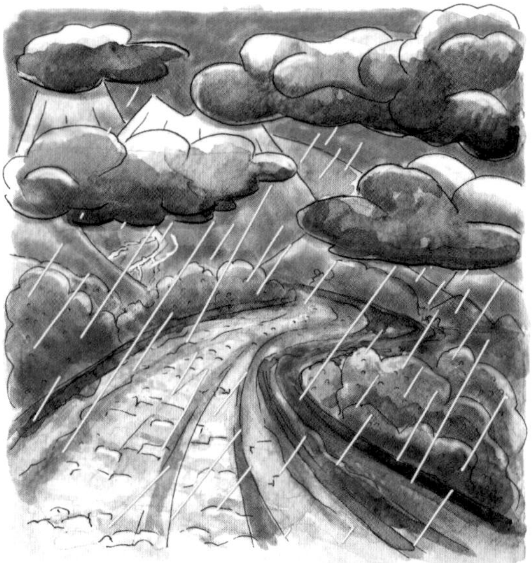

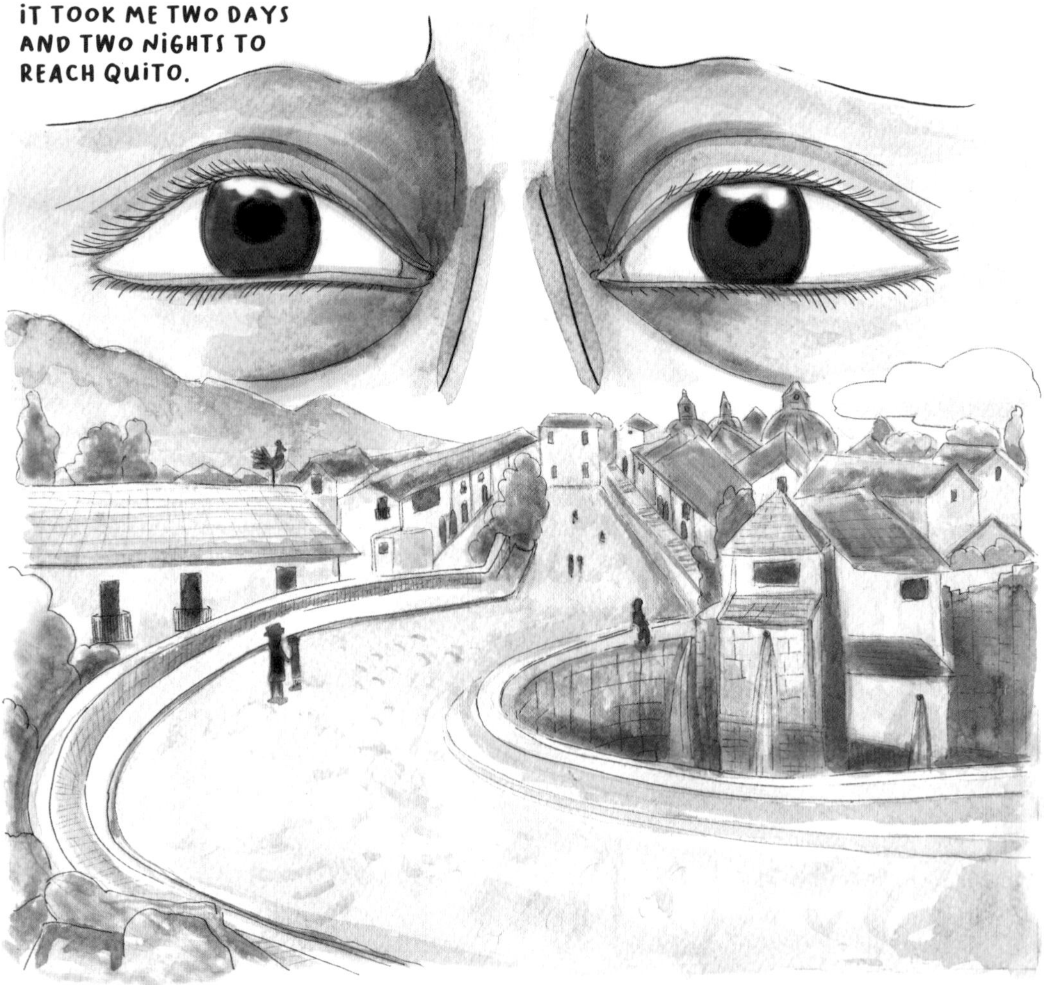
IT TOOK ME TWO DAYS AND TWO NIGHTS TO REACH QUITO.

I STARTED WORKING AT A SERGEANT'S HOUSE AS A HOUSE SERVANT: I CLEANED, I WASHED, I COOKED, I WORKED WELL PAST MIDNIGHT WHILE EVERYONE ELSE RESTED.

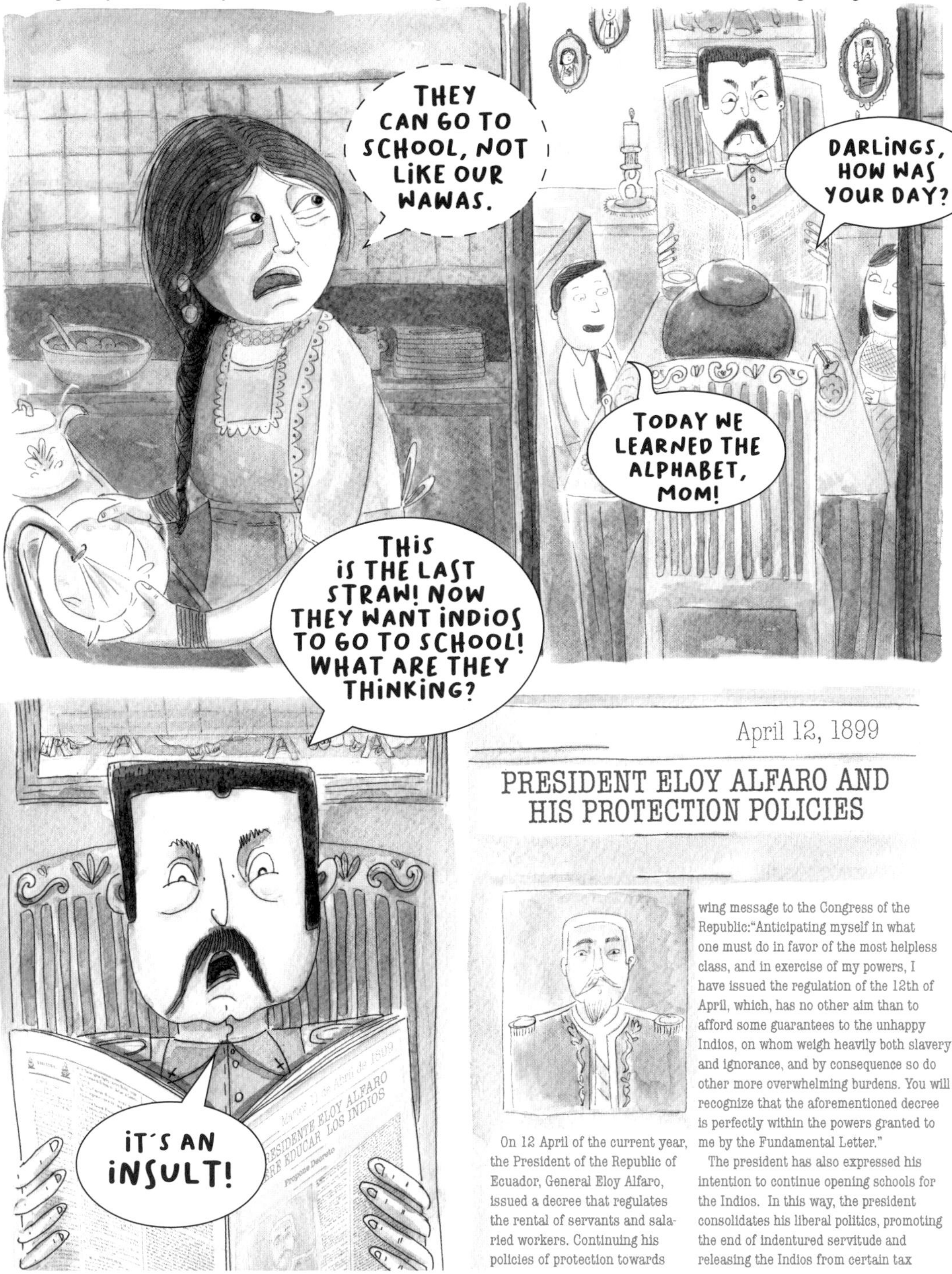
THEY CAN GO TO SCHOOL, NOT LIKE OUR WAWAS.
DARLINGS, HOW WAS YOUR DAY?
TODAY WE LEARNED THE ALPHABET, MOM!
THIS IS THE LAST STRAW! NOW THEY WANT INDIOS TO GO TO SCHOOL! WHAT ARE THEY THINKING?
IT'S AN INSULT!
April 12, 1899
PRESIDENT ELOY ALFARO AND HIS PROTECTION POLICIES
On 12 April of the current year, the President of the Republic of Ecuador, General Eloy Alfaro, issued a decree that regulates the rental of servants and salaried workers. Continuing his policies of protection towards wing message to the Congress of the Republic:"Anticipating myself in what one must do in favor of the most helpless class, and in exercise of my powers, I have issued the regulation of the 12th of April, which, has no other aim than to afford some guarantees to the unhappy Indios, on whom weigh heavily both slavery and ignorance, and by consequence so do other more overwhelming burdens. You will recognize that the aforementioned decree is perfectly within the powers granted to me by the Fundamental Letter."
The president has also expressed his intention to continue opening schools for the Indios. In this way, the president consolidates his liberal politics, promoting the end of indentured servitude and releasing the Indios from certain tax

ALFARO WAS OVERTHROWN BY A MILITARY COUP ON AUGUST 12, 1911, AND BRUTALLY ASSASSINATED ONLY A FEW MONTHS LATER. HIS POLICIES AIMED AT GRANTING RIGHTS TO THE INDIO POPULATION WERE NEVER ACCEPTED BY THE CONSERVATIVE PARTY. A CRISIS FOLLOWED, THAT SAW VARIOUS MEN ASSUME THE PRESIDENCY FOR SHORT PERIODS OF TIME. FINALLY, IN 1916, ALFREDO BAQUERIZO WAS ELECTED PRESIDENT.

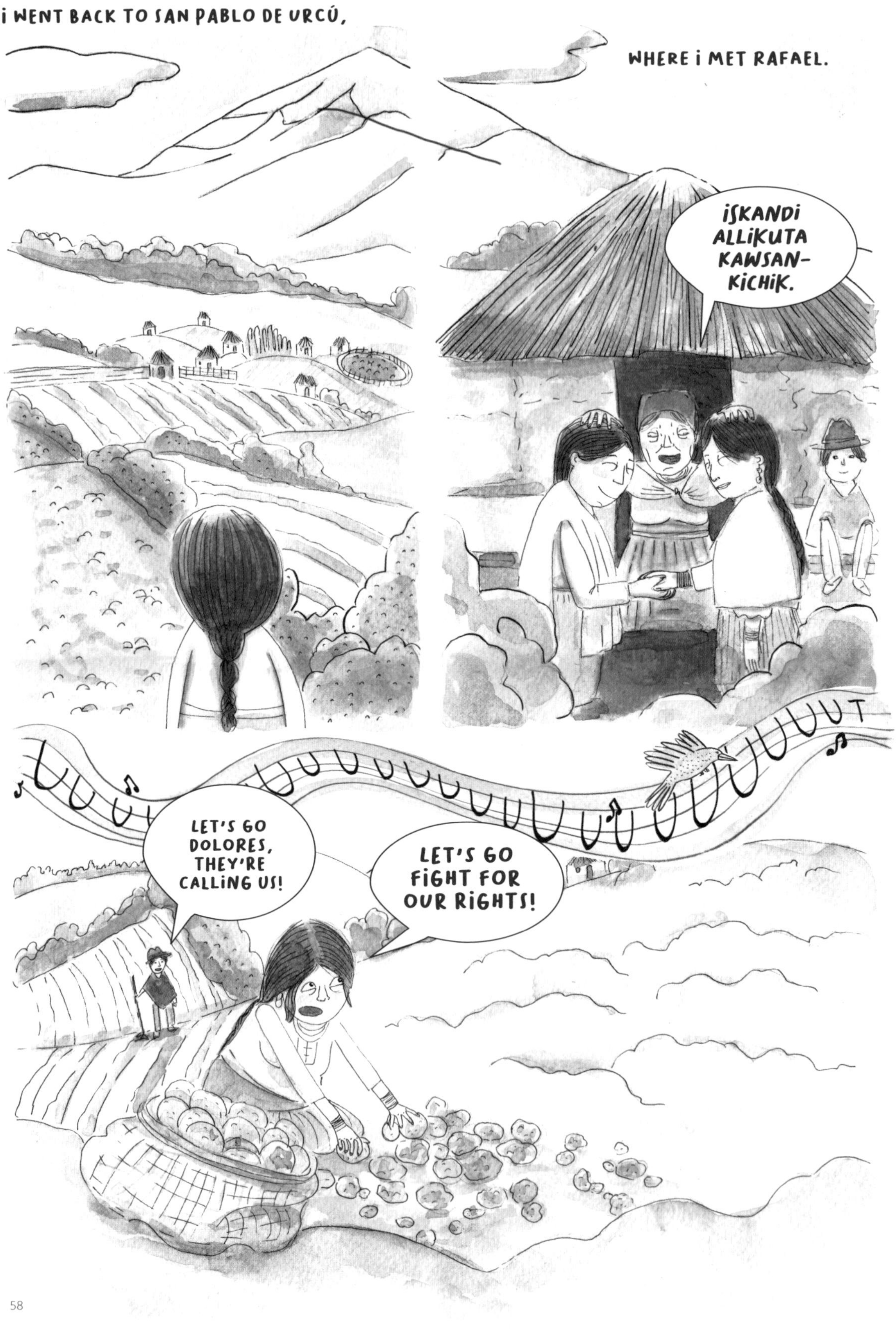
I WENT BACK TO SAN PABLO DE URCÚ,
WHERE I MET RAFAEL.
ISKANDI ALLIKUTA KAWSAN-KICHIK.
UUUUUUUUUUUUUUUUUUUUUUUUUUUT
LET'S GO DOLORES, THEY'RE CALLING US!
LET'S GO FIGHT FOR OUR RIGHTS!

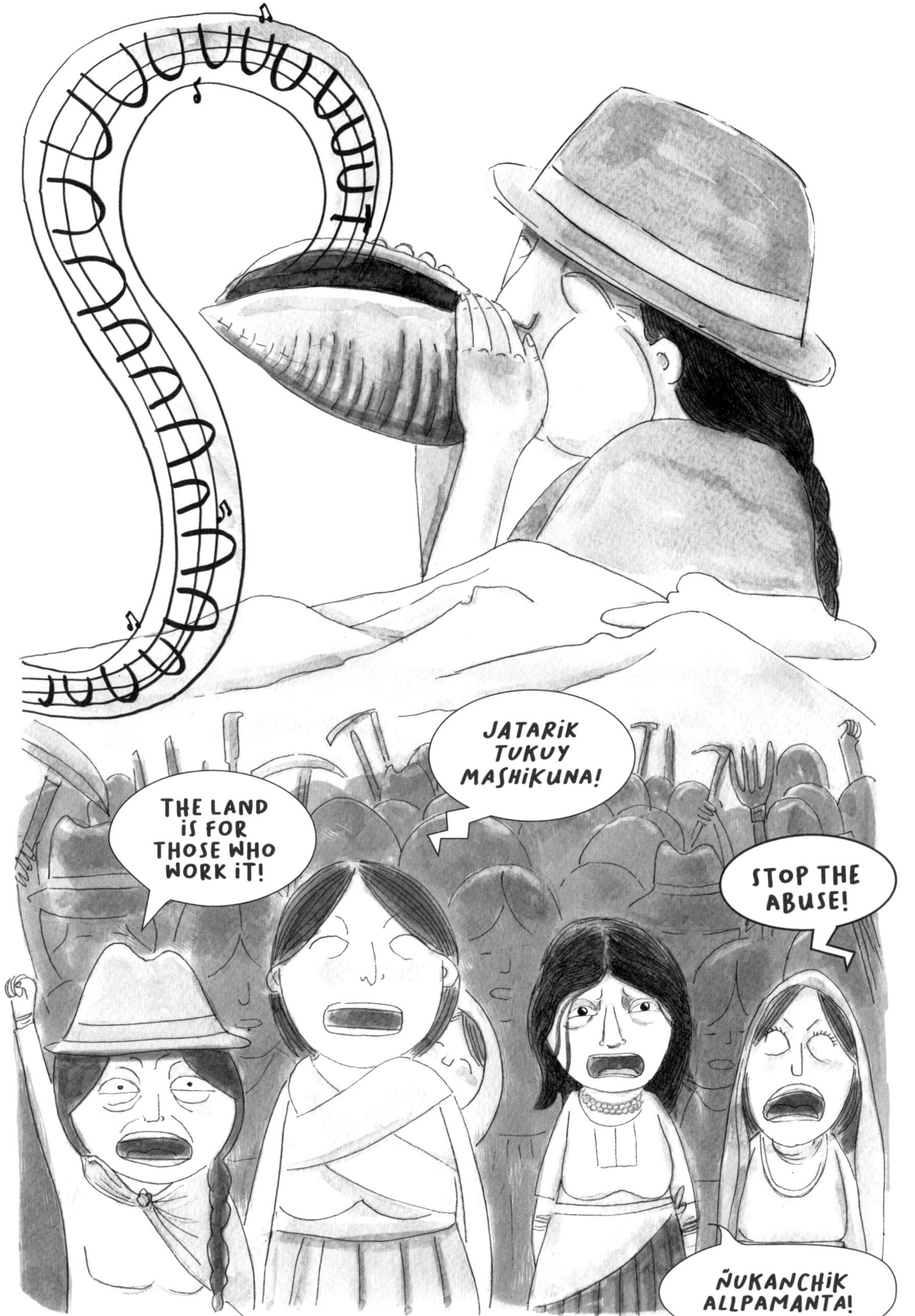
JATARIK TUKUY MASHIKUNA!
THE LAND IS FOR THOSE WHO WORK IT!
STOP THE ABUSE!
ÑUKANCHIK ALLPAMANTA!

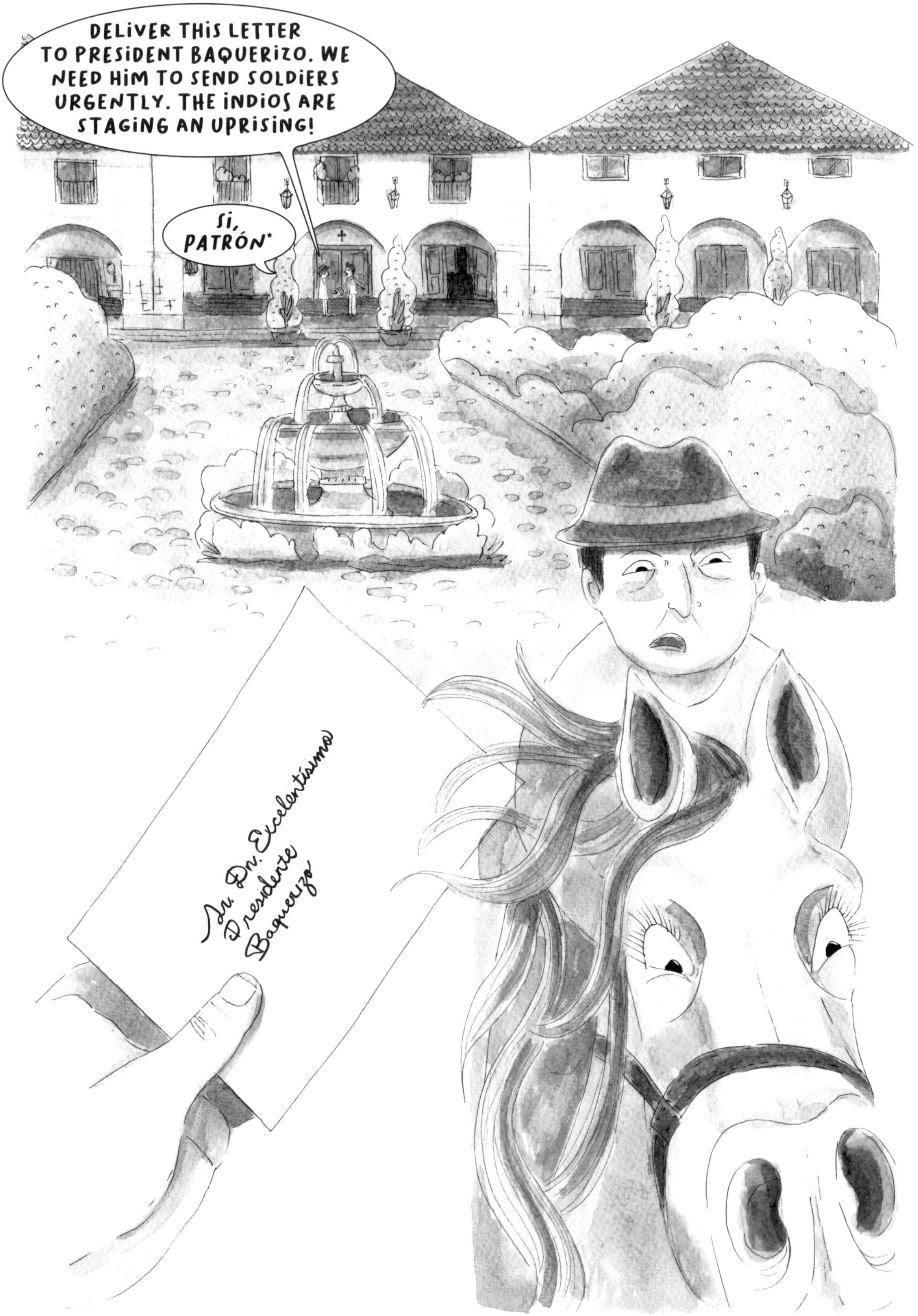
DELIVER THIS LETTER TO PRESIDENT BAQUERIZO. WE NEED HIM TO SEND SOLDIERS URGENTLY. THE INDIOS ARE STAGING AN UPRISING!
SI, PATRÓN*
Sr. Dr. Excelentísimo Presidente Baquerizo

*PATRÓN: MASTER OR BOSS. USUALLY USED TO DENOTE A FARM OR PLANTATION OWNER.

IN 1919, WE ROSE UP IN PESILLO. MANY OF MY FELLOW COMPAÑEROS AND COMPAÑERAS DIED, BUT WE OBTAINED PAYMENT: TWENTY CENTS FOR MEN AND TEN CENTS FOR WOMEN.

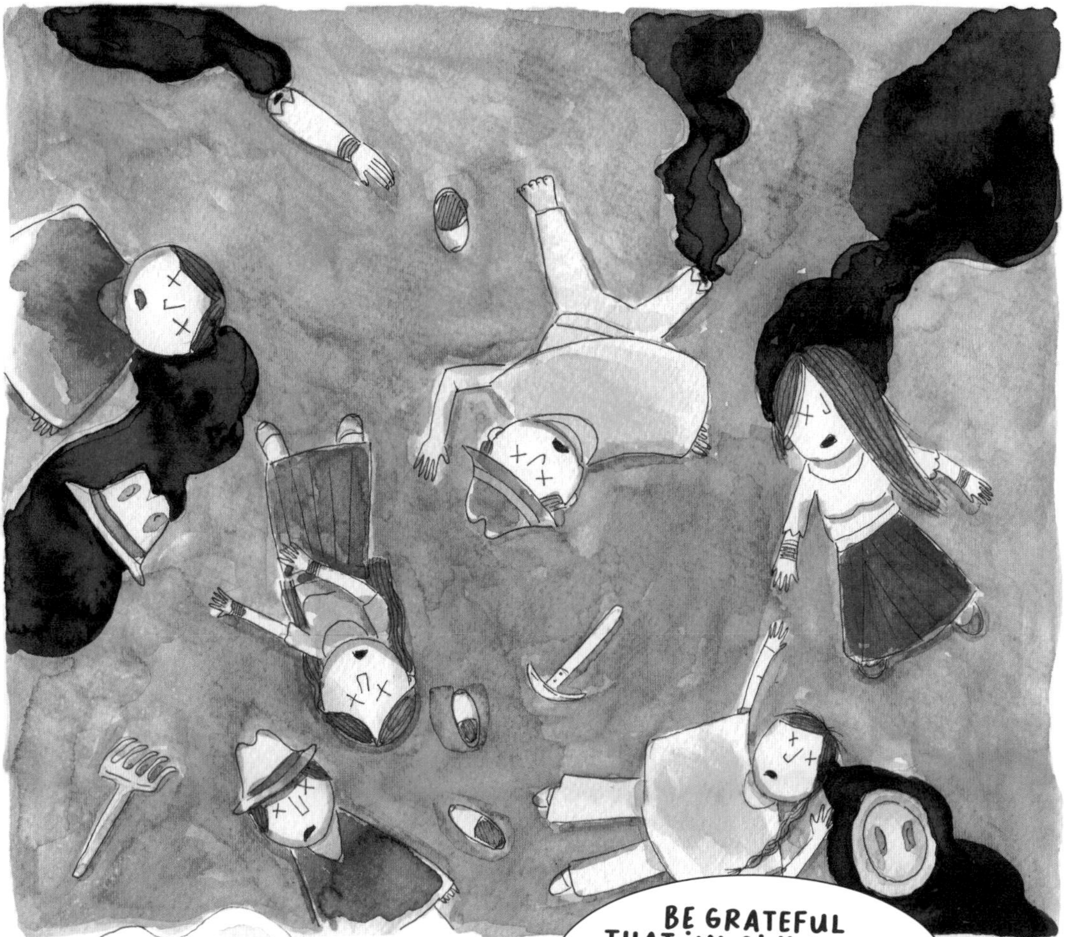

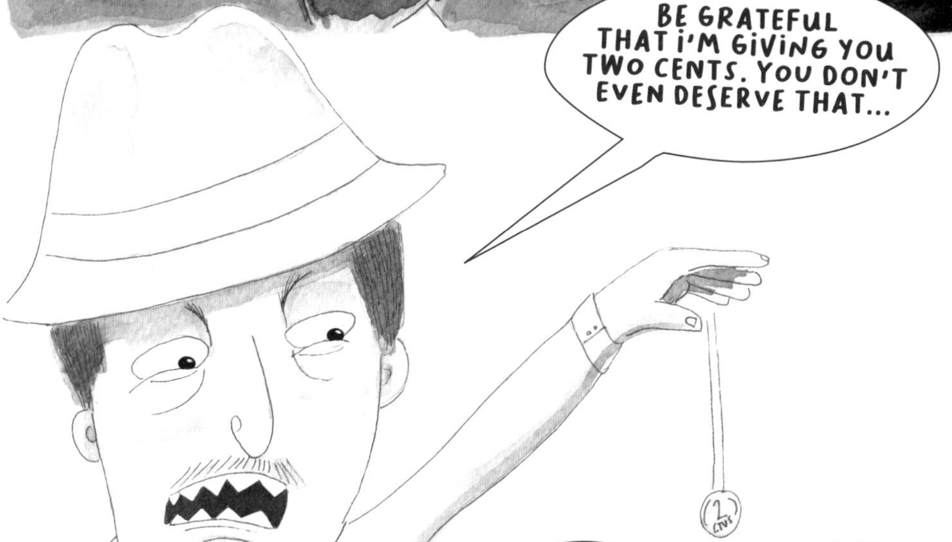
BE GRATEFUL THAT I'M GIVING YOU TWO CENTS. YOU DON'T EVEN DESERVE THAT...
NOW GET OUT!

DESPITE OUR GAINS, THE PATRONES KEPT ABUSING US, PAYING US WHAT THEY WANTED.

CAYAMBE, 1919

AFTER THE PESILLO MASSACRE, WE DECIDED TO JOIN OUR COMPAÑEROS JESÚS GUALAVISÍ, JUAN ALBAMOCHO, AND RICARDO PAREDES. PAREDES WAS ALREADY A MEMBER OF THE COMMUNIST PARTY. WE WANTED TO FORM A UNION.

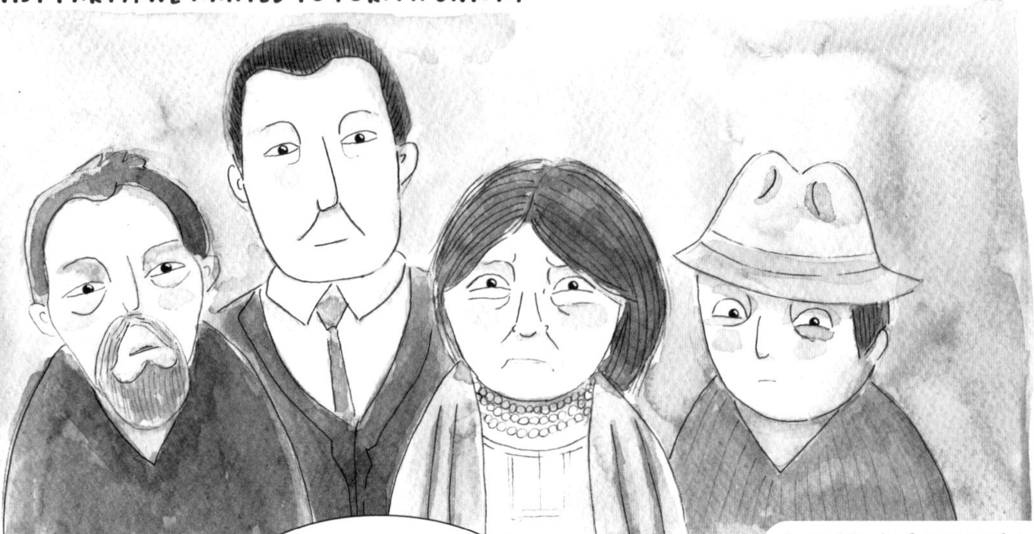

BUT IT WASN'T EASY.

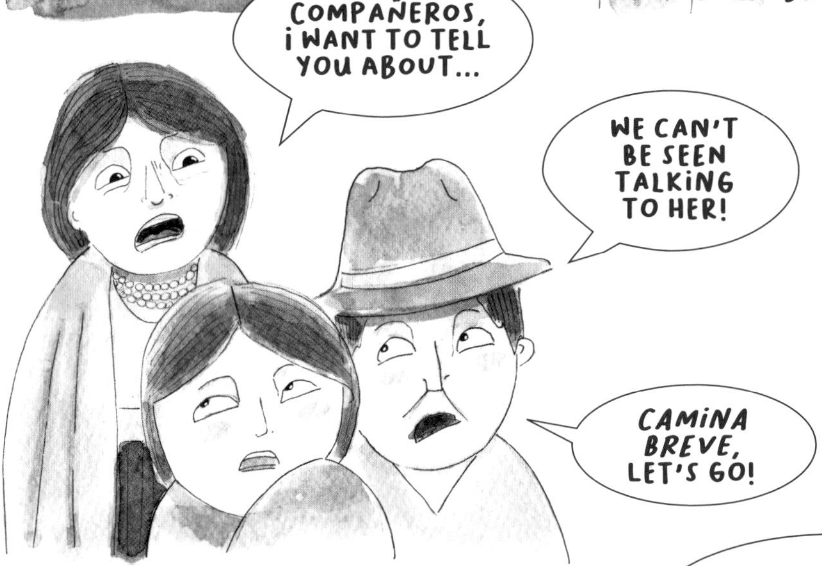
COMPAÑEROS, I WANT TO TELL YOU ABOUT...
WE CAN'T BE SEEN TALKING TO HER!
CAMINA BREVE, LET'S GO!

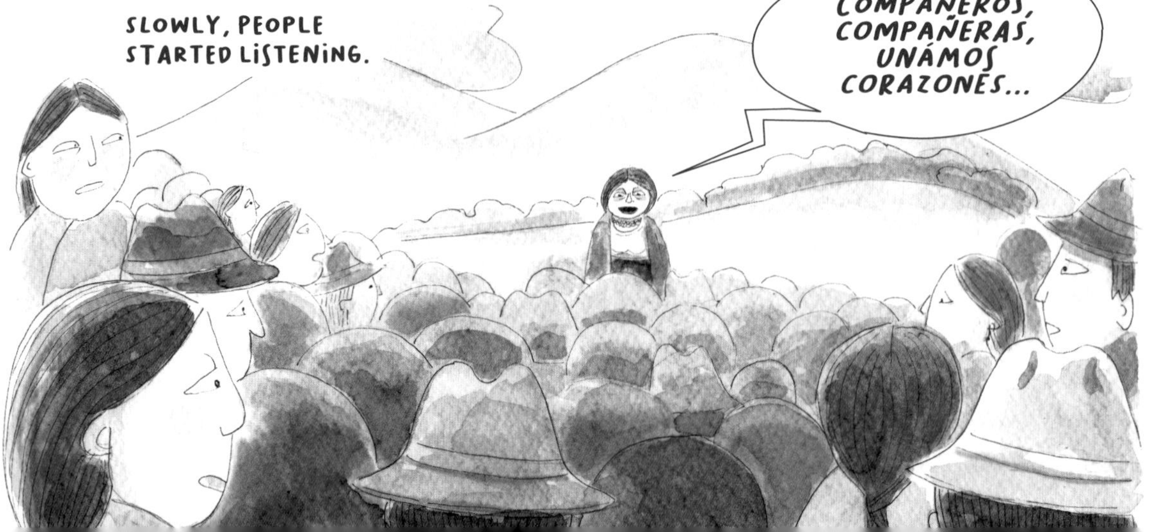
SLOWLY, PEOPLE STARTED LISTENING.
COMPAÑEROS, COMPAÑERAS, UNÁMOS CORAZONES...

IT'S AT ONE OF THOSE MEETINGS WHERE I MET TRÁNSITO.
WE BECAME COMPAÑERAS, SISTERS IN ARMS.

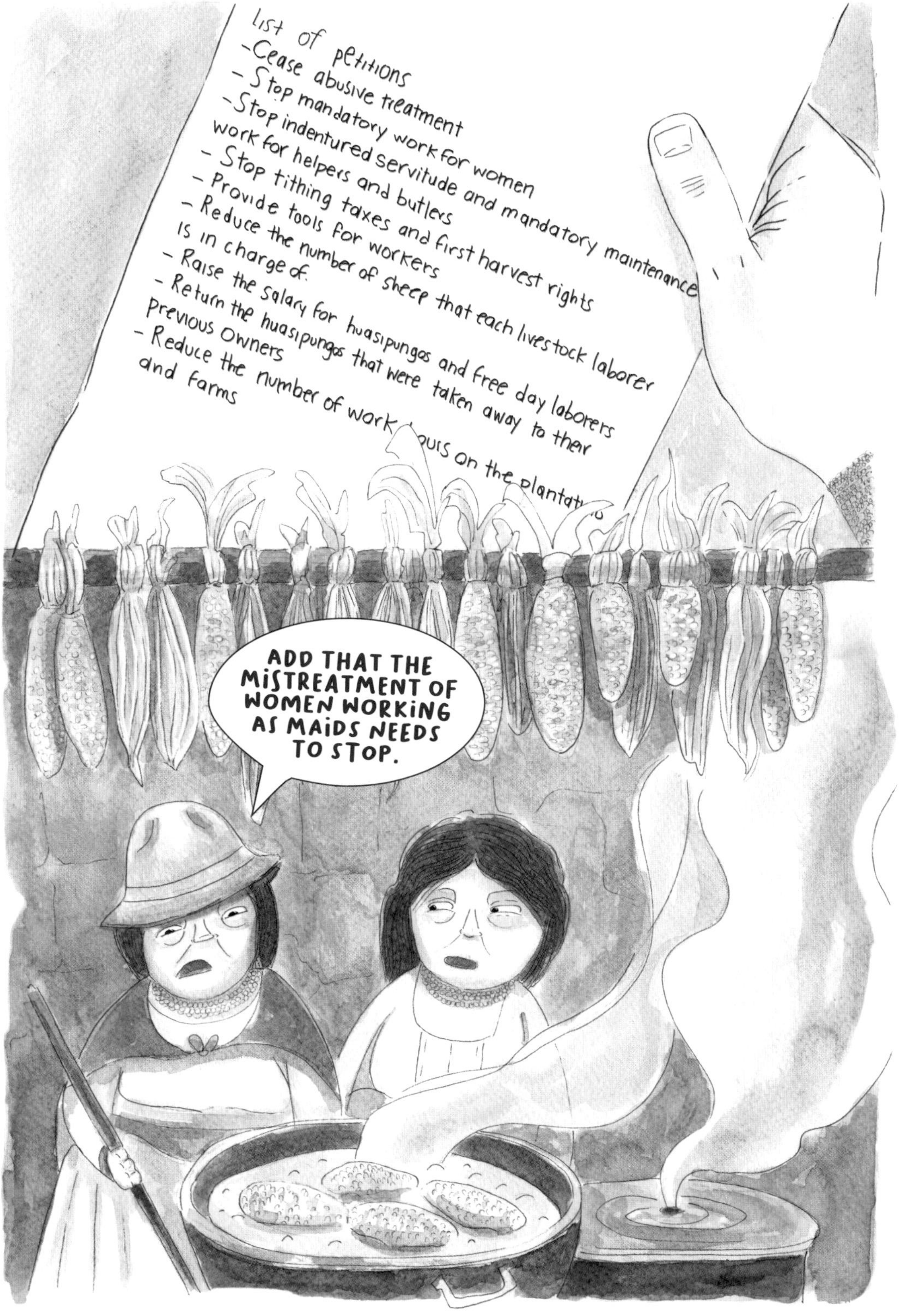
List of petitions
-Cease abusive treatment
- Stop mandatory work for women
-Stop indentured servitude and mandatory maintenance work for helpers and butlers
- Stop tithing taxes and first harvest rights
- Provide tools for workers
- Reduce the number of sheep that each livestock laborer is in charge of.
- Raise the salary for huasipungos and free day laborers
- Return the huasipungos that were taken away to their previous owners
- Reduce the number of work ours on the plantatio and farms
ADD THAT THE MISTREATMENT OF WOMEN WORKING AS MAIDS NEEDS TO STOP.

OUR LIST OF DEMANDS REACHED PATRÓN LUIS DELGADO.

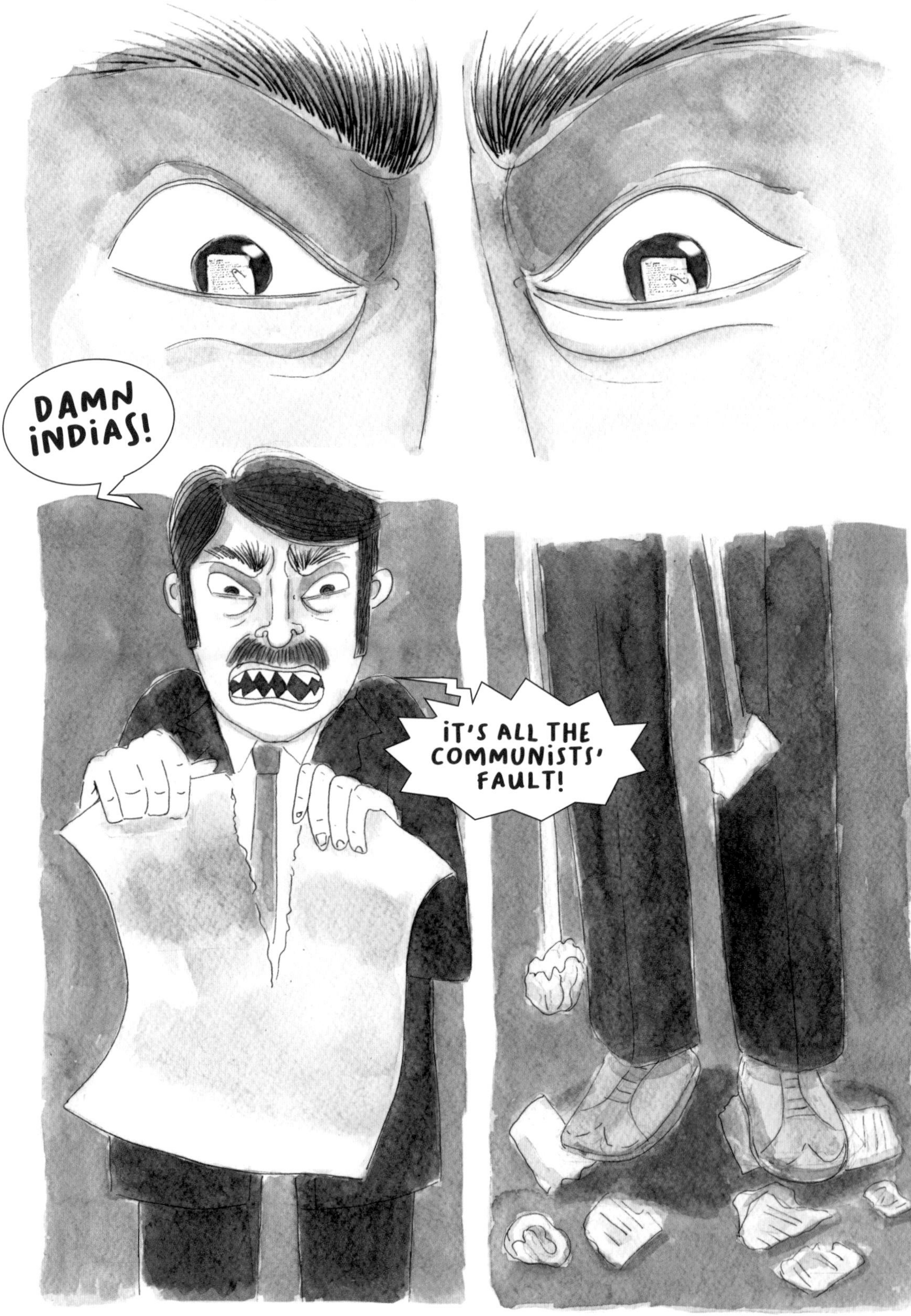
DAMN INDIAS!
IT'S ALL THE COMMUNISTS' FAULT!

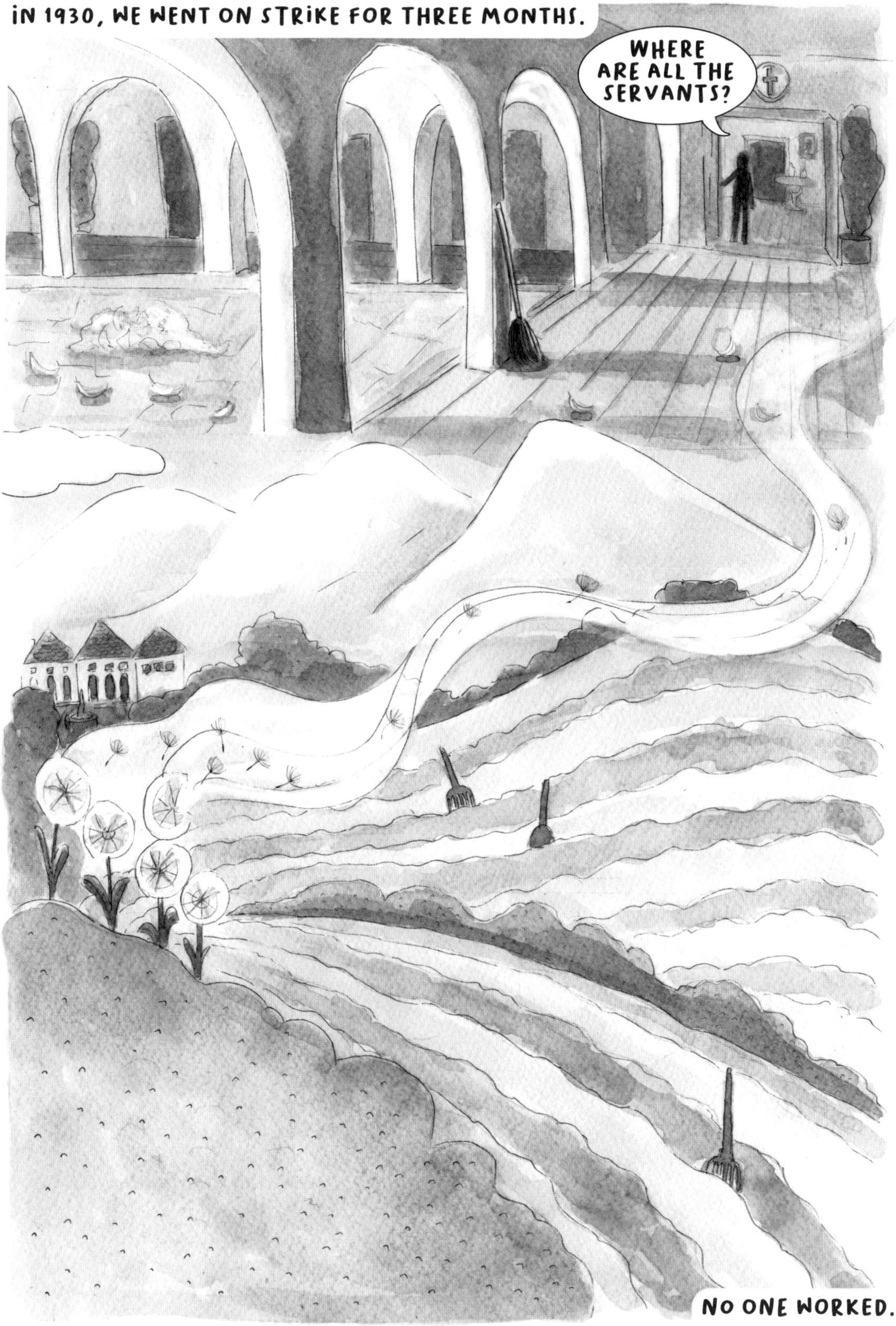
IN 1930, WE WENT ON STRIKE FOR THREE MONTHS.
WHERE ARE ALL THE SERVANTS?
NO ONE WORKED.

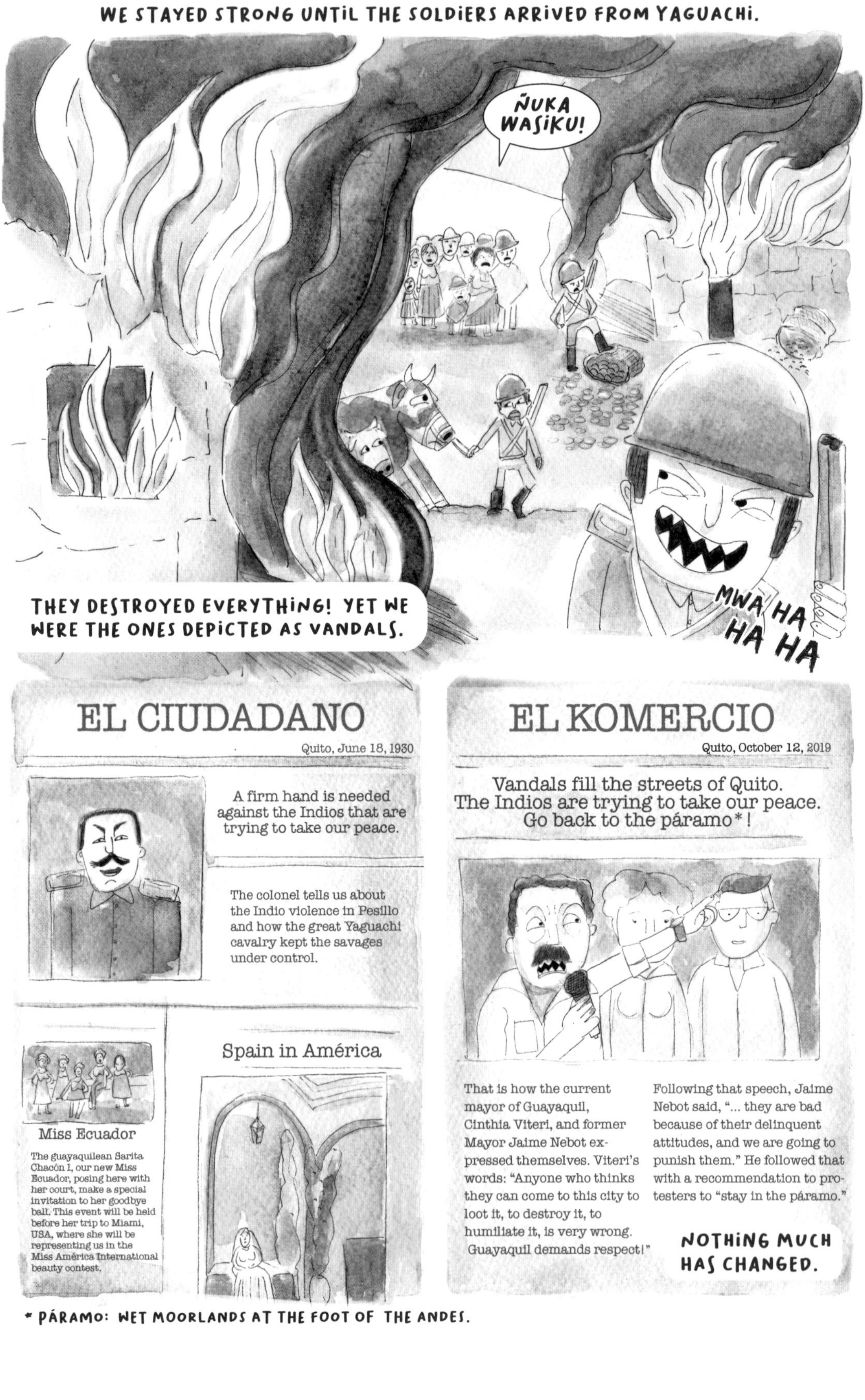

WE STAYED STRONG UNTIL THE SOLDIERS ARRIVED FROM YAGUACHI.
ÑUKA WASIKU!
THEY DESTROYED EVERYTHING! YET WE WERE THE ONES DEPICTED AS VANDALS.
MWA HA HA HA
EL CIUDADANO
Quito, June 18, 1930
A firm hand is needed against the Indios that are trying to take our peace.
The colonel tells us about the Indio violence in Pesillo and how the great Yaguachi cavalry kept the savages under control.
Miss Ecuador
The guayaquilean Sarita Chacón I, our new Miss Ecuador, posing here with her court, make a special invitation to her goodbye ball. This event will be held before her trip to Miami, USA, where she will be representing us in the Miss América International beauty contest.
Spain in América
EL KOMERCIO
Quito, October 12, 2019
Vandals fill the streets of Quito. The Indios are trying to take our peace. Go back to the páramo*!
That is how the current mayor of Guayaquil, Cinthia Viteri, and former Mayor Jaime Nebot expressed themselves. Viteri's words: "Anyone who thinks they can come to this city to loot it, to destroy it, to humiliate it, is very wrong. Guayaquil demands respect!" Following that speech, Jaime Nebot said, "... they are bad because of their delinquent attitudes, and we are going to punish them." He followed that with a recommendation to protesters to "stay in the páramo."
NOTHING MUCH HAS CHANGED.
* PÁRAMO: WET MOORLANDS AT THE FOOT OF THE ANDES.

AFTER THE UPRISING, THEY STARTED LOOKING FOR ME...

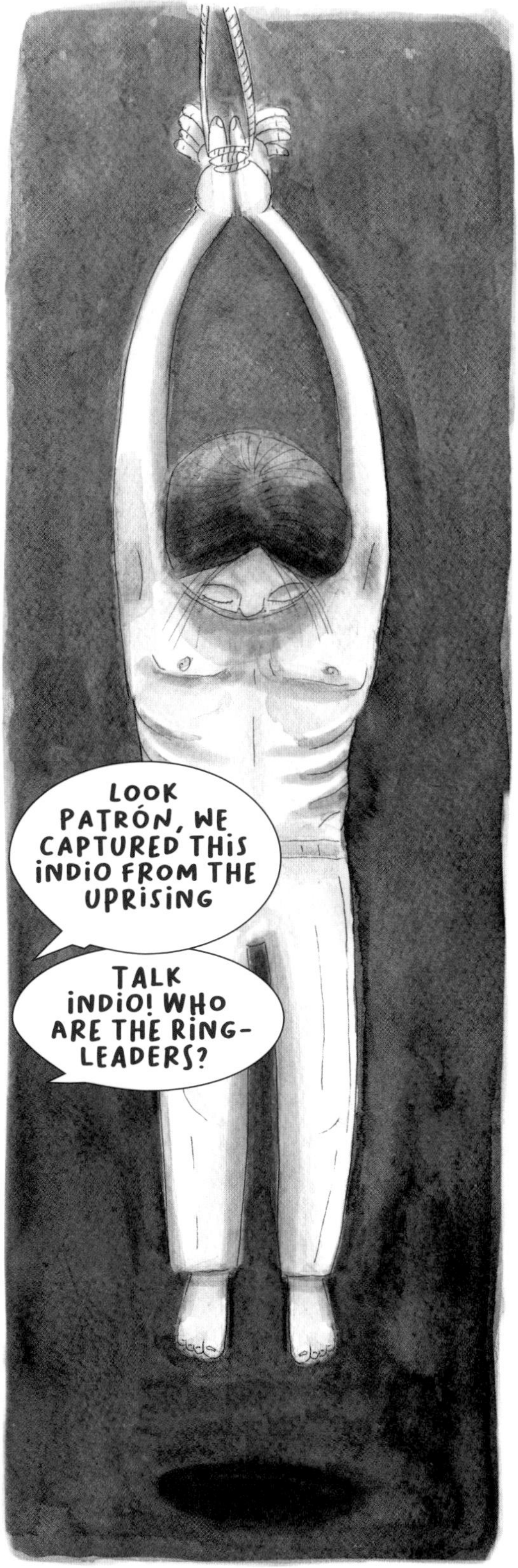
LOOK PATRÓN, WE CAPTURED THIS INDIO FROM THE UPRISING
TALK INDIO! WHO ARE THE RING-LEADERS?

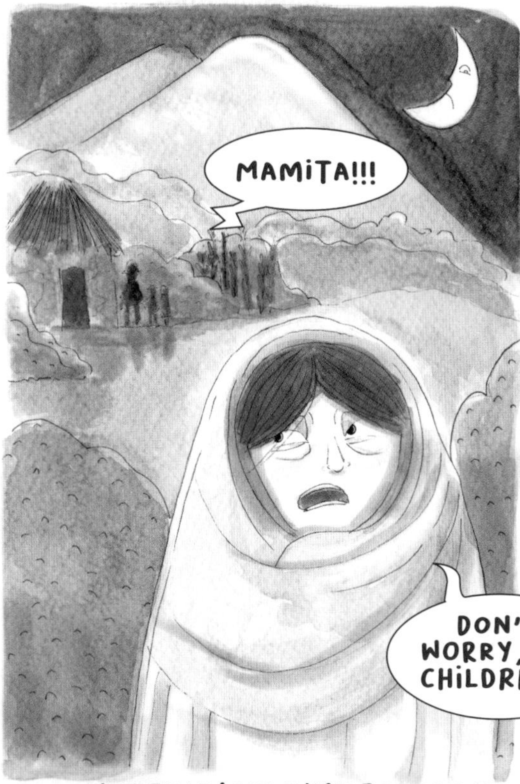
MAMITA!!!
DON'T WORRY, MY CHILDREN...

...NOT THAT I LET MYSELF BE FOUND.

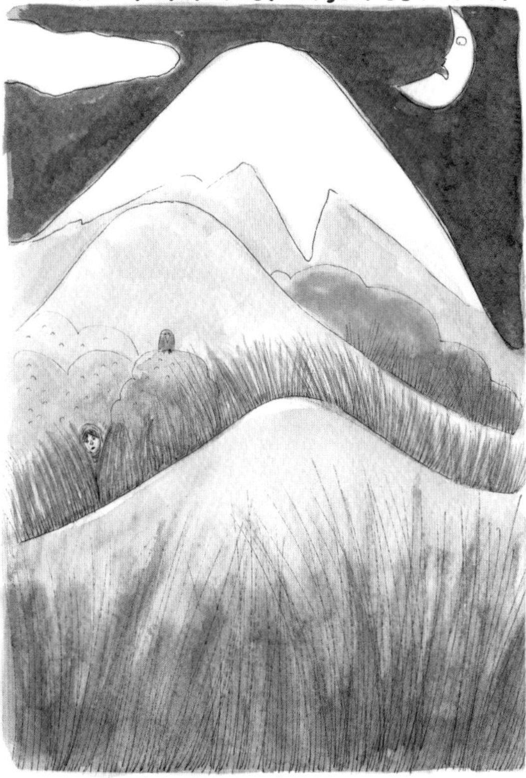

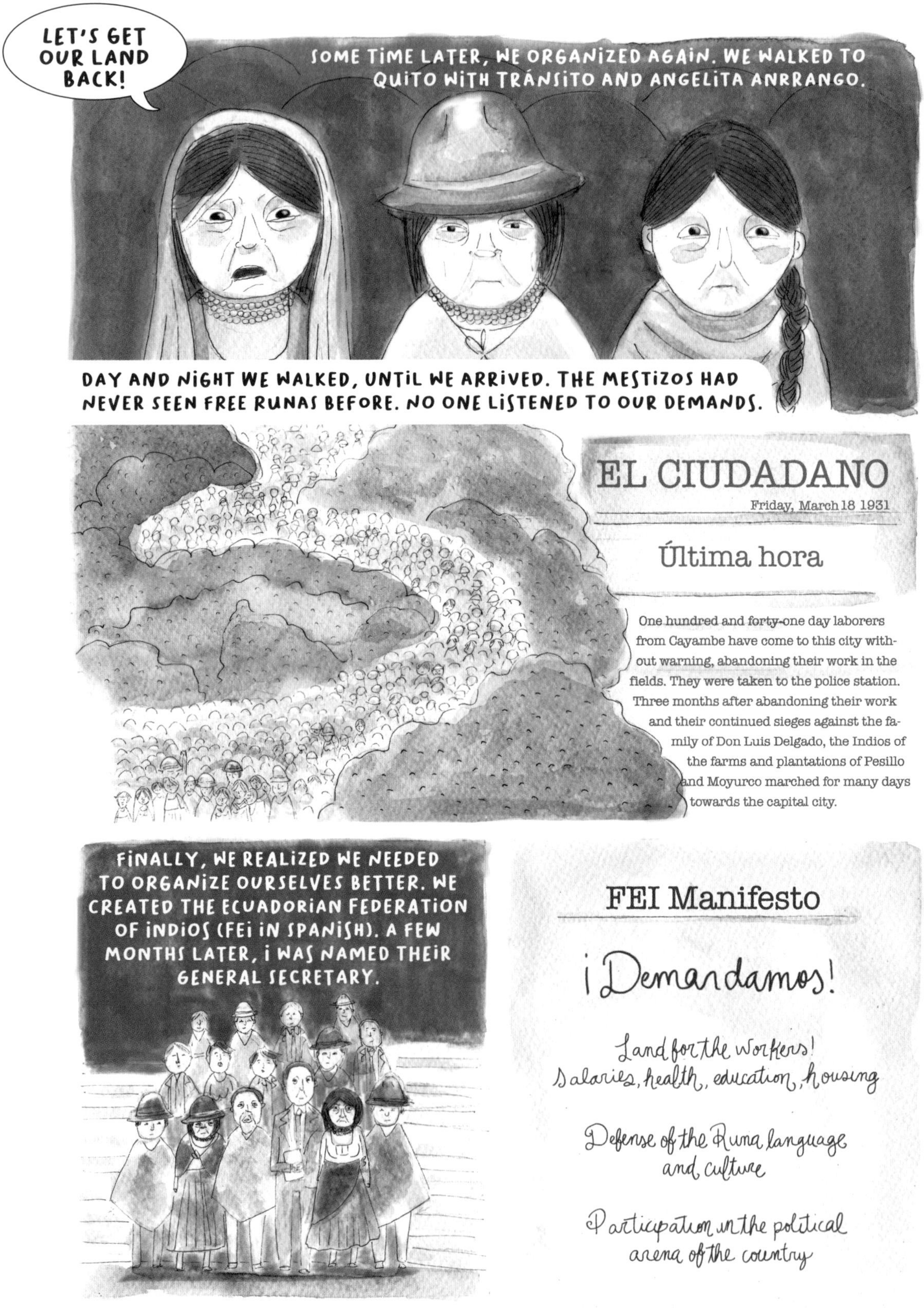
LET'S GET OUR LAND BACK!
SOME TIME LATER, WE ORGANIZED AGAIN. WE WALKED TO QUITO WITH TRÁNSITO AND ANGELITA ANRRANGO.
DAY AND NIGHT WE WALKED, UNTIL WE ARRIVED. THE MESTIZOS HAD NEVER SEEN FREE RUNAS BEFORE. NO ONE LISTENED TO OUR DEMANDS.
EL CIUDADANO
Friday, March 18 1931
Última hora
One hundred and forty-one day laborers from Cayambe have come to this city without warning, abandoning their work in the fields. They were taken to the police station. Three months after abandoning their work and their continued sieges against the family of Don Luis Delgado, the Indios of the farms and plantations of Pesillo and Moyurco marched for many days towards the capital city.
FINALLY, WE REALIZED WE NEEDED TO ORGANIZE OURSELVES BETTER. WE CREATED THE ECUADORIAN FEDERATION OF INDIOS (FEI IN SPANISH). A FEW MONTHS LATER, I WAS NAMED THEIR GENERAL SECRETARY.
FEI Manifesto
¡Demandamos!
Land for the workers!
salaries, health, education, housing
Defense of the Runa language and culture
Participation in the political arena of the country

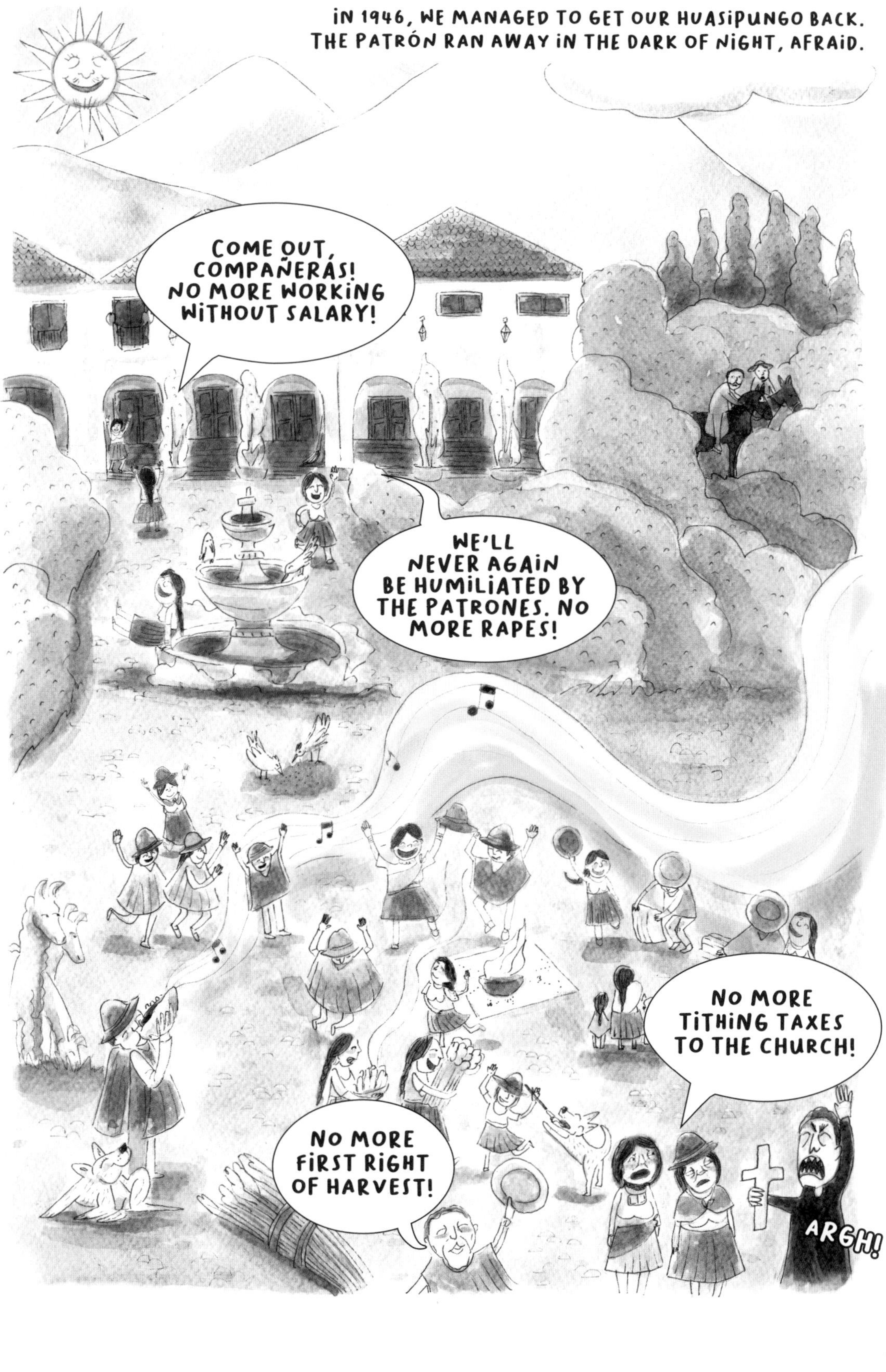
IN 1946, WE MANAGED TO GET OUR HUASIPUNGO BACK. THE PATRÓN RAN AWAY IN THE DARK OF NIGHT, AFRAID.
COME OUT, COMPAÑERAS! NO MORE WORKING WITHOUT SALARY!
WE'LL NEVER AGAIN BE HUMILIATED BY THE PATRONES. NO MORE RAPES!
NO MORE TITHING TAXES TO THE CHURCH!
NO MORE FIRST RIGHT OF HARVEST!
ARGH!

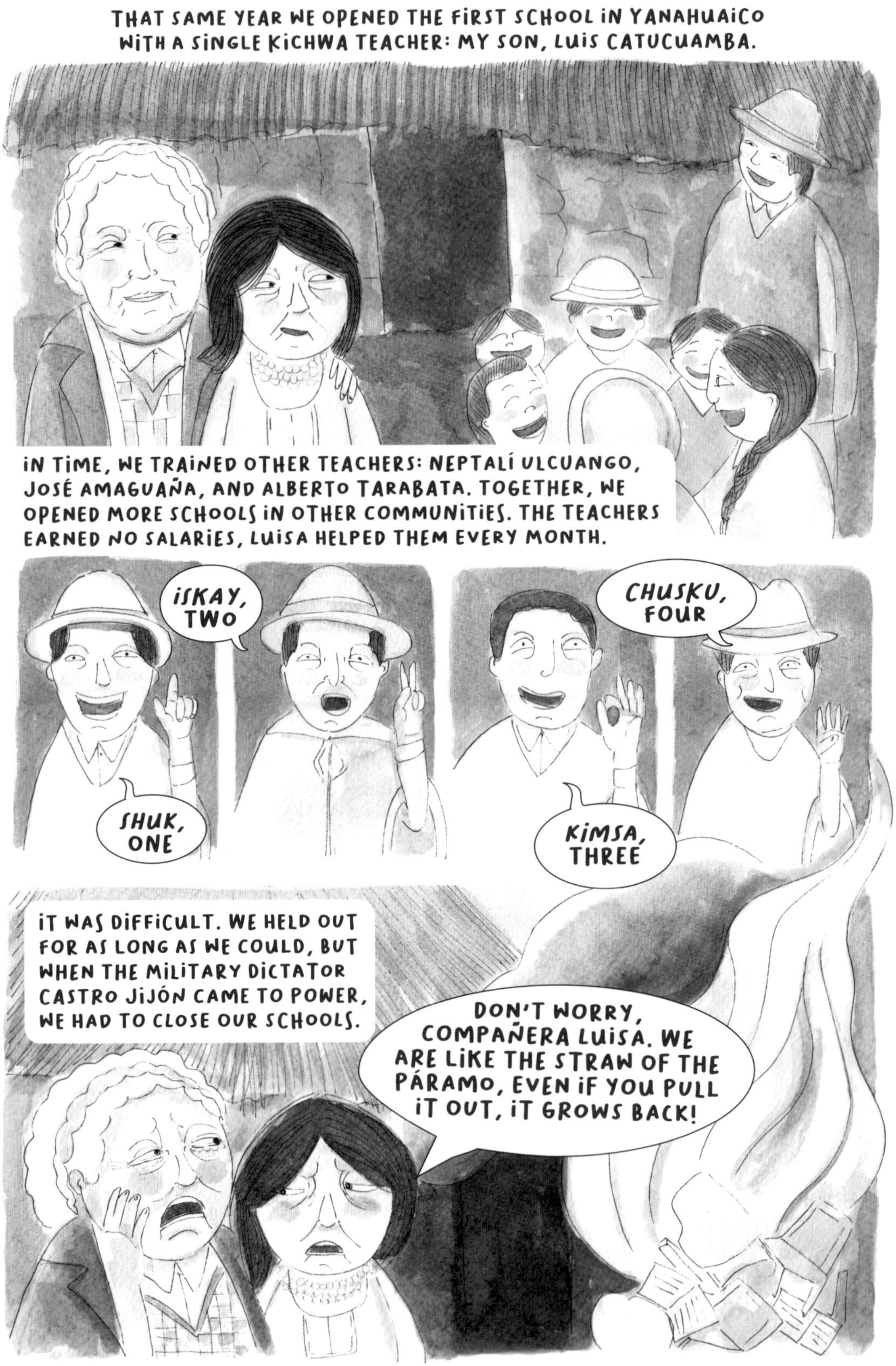
THAT SAME YEAR WE OPENED THE FIRST SCHOOL IN YANAHUAICO WITH A SINGLE KICHWA TEACHER: MY SON, LUIS CATUCUAMBA.
IN TIME, WE TRAINED OTHER TEACHERS: NEPTALÍ ULCUANGO, JOSÉ AMAGUAÑA, AND ALBERTO TARABATA. TOGETHER, WE OPENED MORE SCHOOLS IN OTHER COMMUNITIES. THE TEACHERS EARNED NO SALARIES, LUISA HELPED THEM EVERY MONTH.
SHUK, ONE
ISKAY, TWO
KIMSA, THREE
CHUSKU, FOUR
IT WAS DIFFICULT. WE HELD OUT FOR AS LONG AS WE COULD, BUT WHEN THE MILITARY DICTATOR CASTRO JIJÓN CAME TO POWER, WE HAD TO CLOSE OUR SCHOOLS.
DON'T WORRY, COMPAÑERA LUISA. WE ARE LIKE THE STRAW OF THE PÁRAMO, EVEN IF YOU PULL IT OUT, IT GROWS BACK!

EVENTUALLY, ALL THE EFFORTS WE POURED INTO THE SCHOOLS BORE FRUIT.

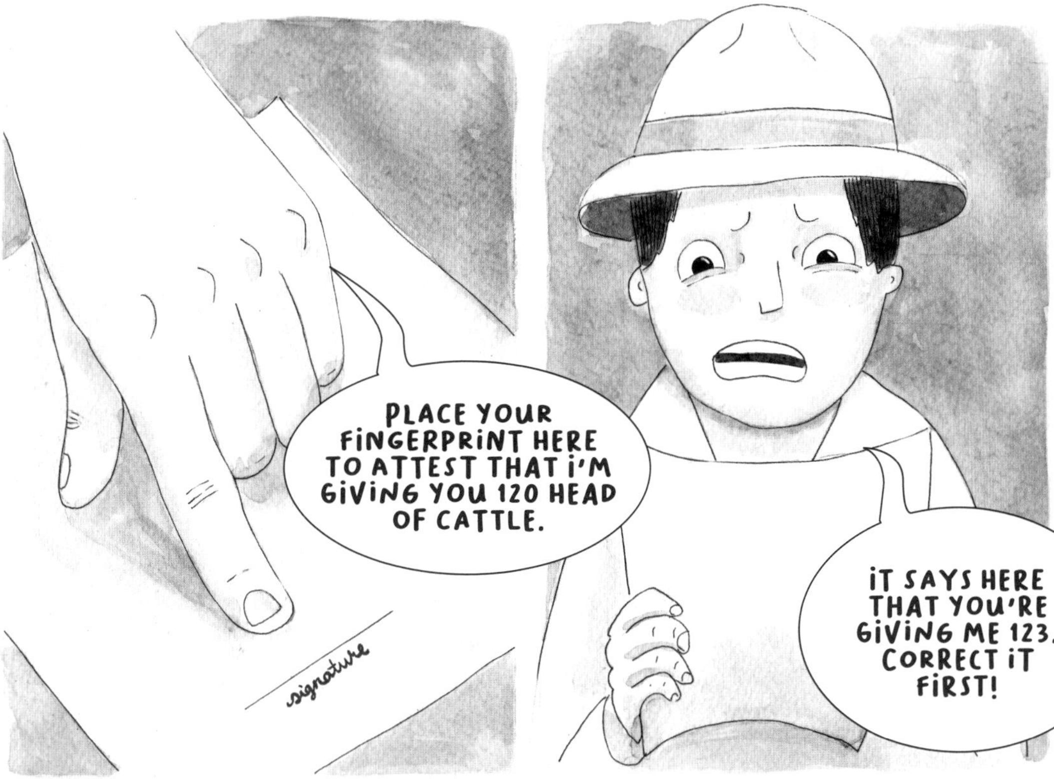

signature
PLACE YOUR FINGERPRINT HERE TO ATTEST THAT I'M GIVING YOU 120 HEAD OF CATTLE.
IT SAYS HERE THAT YOU'RE GIVING ME 123. CORRECT IT FIRST!

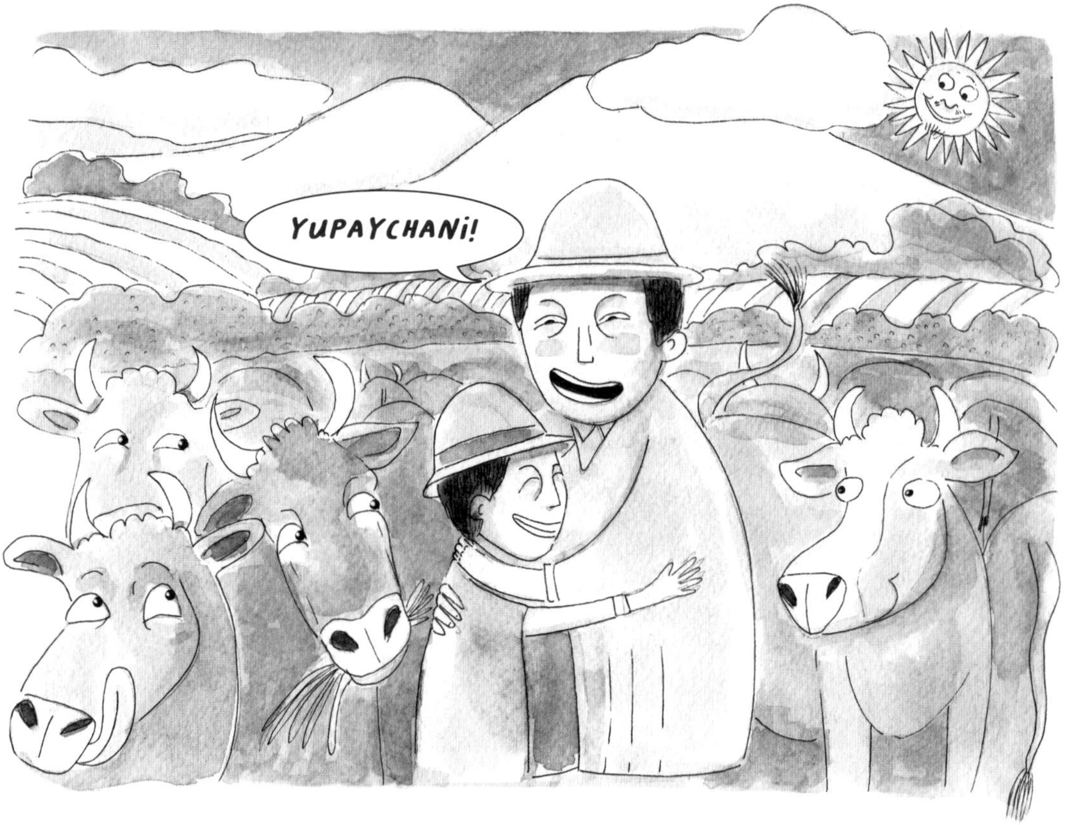

YUPAYCHANI!

ON APRIL 23, 1971, I LEFT MY TIRED BODY WITH THE HOPE THAT THOSE WHO REMAIN WILL CONTINUE THE FIGHT.

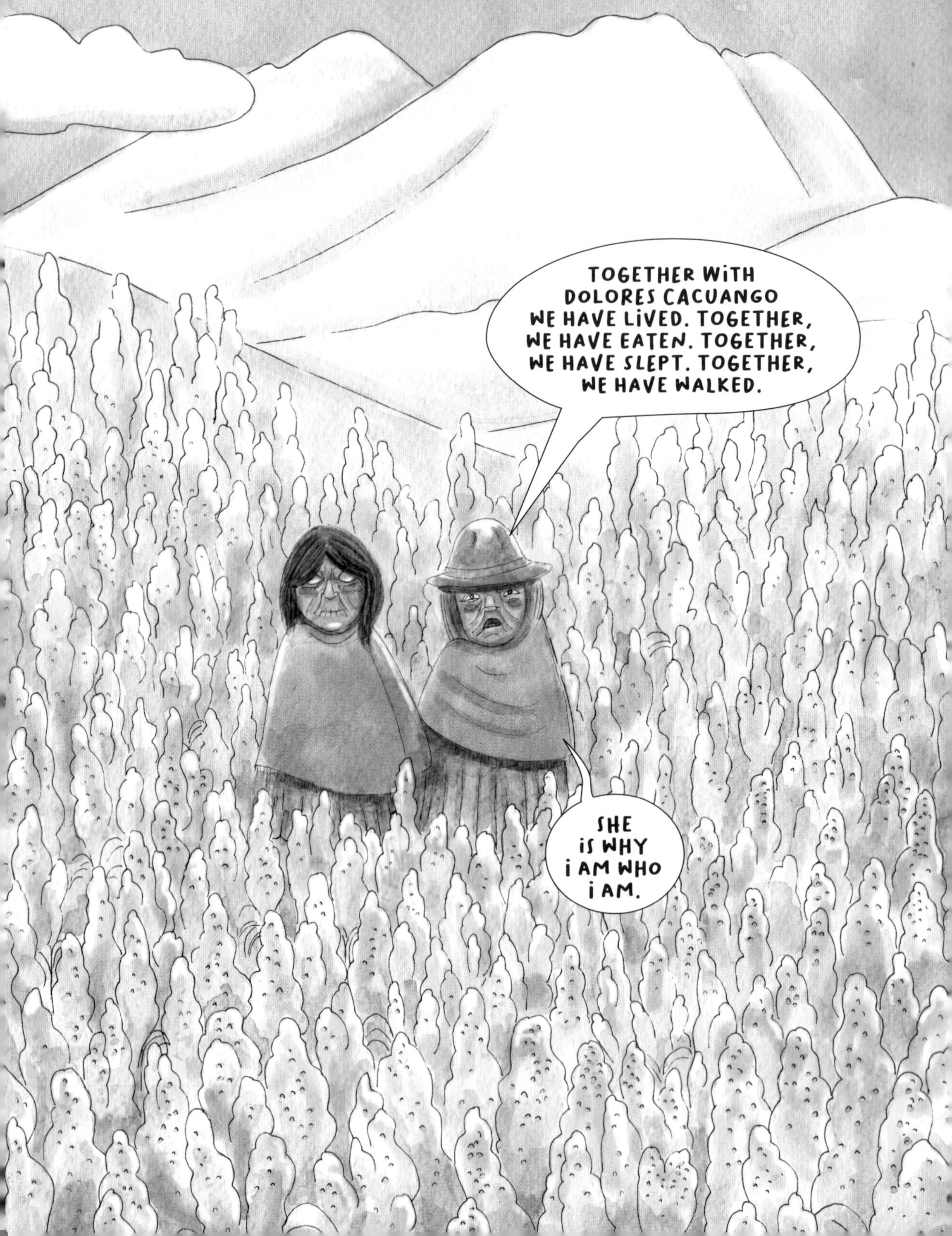
TOGETHER WITH DOLORES CACUANGO WE HAVE LIVED. TOGETHER, WE HAVE EATEN. TOGETHER, WE HAVE SLEPT. TOGETHER, WE HAVE WALKED.
SHE IS WHY I AM WHO I AM.

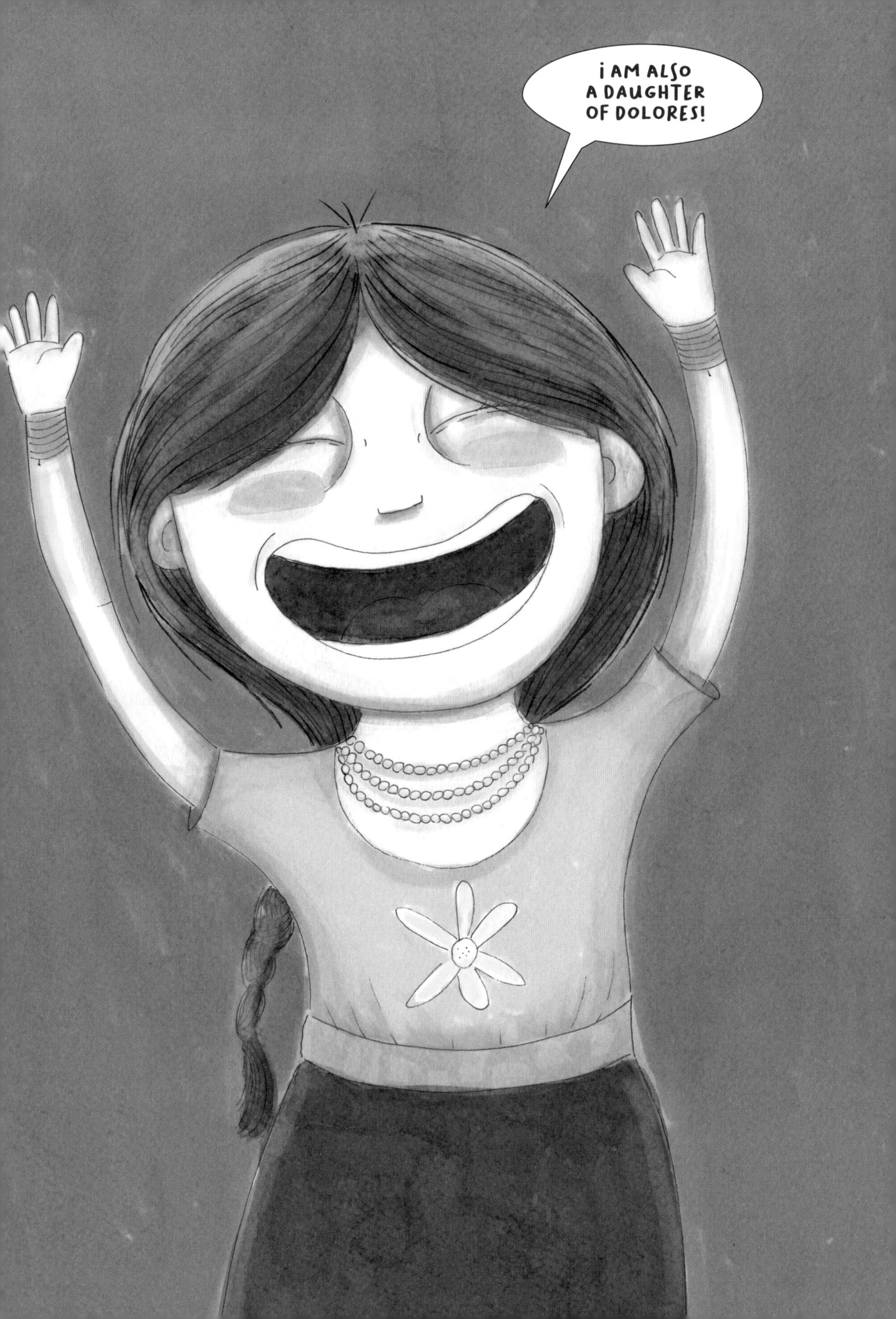
¡AM ALSO A DAUGHTER OF DOLORES!

DOLORES CACUANGO'S STORY IS SYNONYMOUS WITH THE RESISTANCE AND HISTORY OF ECUADOR'S FIRST PEOPLES AND NATIONS. SHE FOUGHT FOR EVERYONE'S RIGHTS, REGARDLESS OF GENDER AND ORIGIN. WHILE SHE IDENTIFIED AS A COMMUNIST, WE ALSO CHOOSE TO REMEMBER AND CELEBRATE HER AS A FEMINIST.

HER LIFE AND STORY CONTINUE TO INSTILL GENERATIONS OF WOMEN WITH THE SPIRIT OF RESISTANCE. THESE ARE SOME OF THE ACTIVISTS FOLLOWING IN HER FOOTSTEPS, CONTINUING THE FIGHT FOR THEIR COMMUNITIES' RIGHTS.

TO READ AN EARLIER VERSION OF THIS STORY, PLEASE VISIT GOETHE.DE/INS/ID/EN/KUL/KUE/MMO/BDL.HTML

THERE'S A DOLORES CACUANGO IN EVERY WOMAN!

PATRICIA YALLICO IS A KICHWA FILMMAKER FROM THE WARANKA PEOPLE. SHE IS WORKING ON A FEATURE-LENGTH FILM HOMAGE TO CACUANGO ENTITLED *DOLORES*, WITH HER COLLEAGUES AT THE AUDIOVISUAL COLLECTIVE ACAPANA. SHE AIMS TO USE FILM AS A TOOL TO AWAKEN POLITICAL CONSIOUSNESS AND EMPOWER COMMUNITIES TO TELL THEIR OWN STORIES.

IT IS WOMEN WHO DEFEND THEIR TERRITORIES. IT'S THE FIRST ACT OF RESISTANCE.

MISHELLE CALLE IS A LAWYER AND CIVIL RIGHTS ACTIVIST FROM CUENCA. SHE IS INVOLVED WITH LOCAL COLLECTIVES WHO PROVIDE LEGAL AID FOR PEOPLE AFFECTED BY MINING IN THE CITY'S RIO BLANCO AREA. THESE COLLECTIVES ALSO PROMOTE FAIR TRADE PRACTICES AND LOCAL TOURISM. THESE SUPPORT SYSTEMS HELP WOMEN BECOME FINANCIALLY INDEPENDENT AND BETTER EQUIPPED TO PROTECT THEIR LAND WITHOUT HAVING TO WORK FOR MINING COMPANIES.

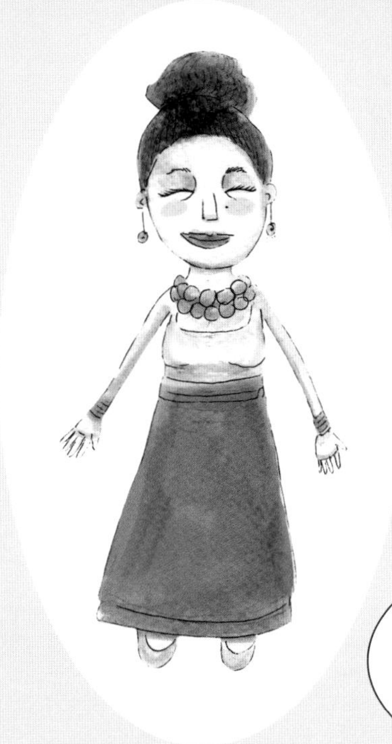
TODAY, WE AS YOUNG PEOPLE CAN QUESTION WHAT WE'VE BEEN TOLD ABOUT WHAT IT MEANS TO BE INDIGENOUS. WE CAN DECONSTRUCT THE WAYS OF THINKING THAT HAVE BEEN IMPOSED.

MARIELA CONDO IS A KICHWA SINGER, AUTHOR, COMPOSER, AND MEMBER OF THE PURUHÁ PEOPLE. BORN INTO THE CACHA COMMUNITY, HER CHILDHOOD MEMORIES ARE MUSICAL. HER PATH WAS INSPIRED BY HER MOTHER AND THOSE AROUND HER, WHO SANG DAILY. THROUGH HER SINGING, SHE EMBRACES AND CELEBRATES A WOMAN'S RIGHT TO FREEDOM, FREEDOMS HER MOTHER AND GRANDMOTHER WERE UNABLE TO ENJOY.

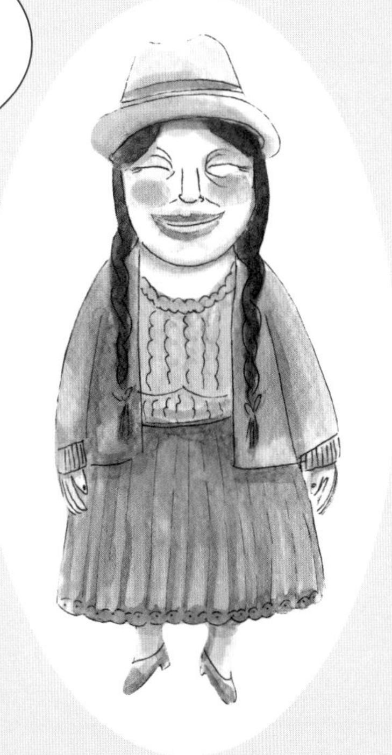
IF WE EAT WELL, TAKE CARE OF OUR SEEDS, AND LIVE IN HARMONY, WE WON'T NEED PESTICIDES FOR OUR PLANTS OR PHARMACIES FOR OUR BODIES.

BÉLGICA JIMÉNEZ IS AN ACTIVIST FOR WOMEN FIELD-WORKER'S RIGHTS. SHE IS ALSO A COORDINATOR FOR RED AGROECOLÓGICA DEL AUSTRO, AN AGROECOLOGICAL NETWORK. SHE FEARLESSLY DEFENDS HER PEOPLE'S TERRITORIES AND MANY COMMUNITIES' RIGHTS TO FOOD SOVEREIGNTY, AND SHE FIGHTS TO ENSURE THE ACCESIBILITY OF HEALTHY ORGANIC PRODUCE.

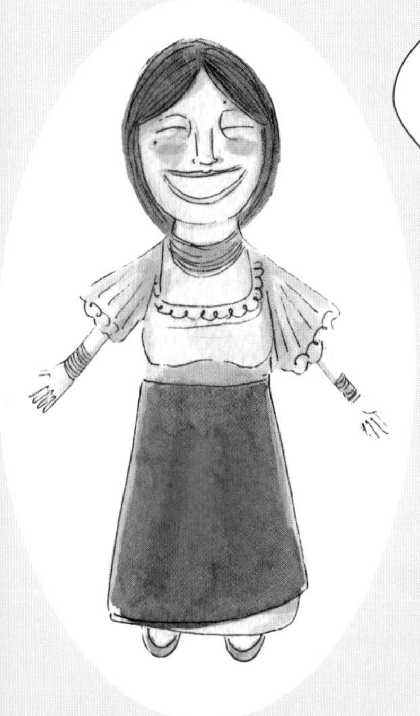
AS MIDWIVES, WE ALSO FIGHT THE SYSTEM THROUGH OUR WORK. OUR DREAM IS TO KEEP TRAINING MORE WOMEN.

MARTHA AROTINGO, OF THE COTACACHI PEOPLE, IS A TRADITIONAL KICHWA MIDWIFE AND REPRESENTATIVE OF THE COUNCIL FOR ANCESTRAL HEALTH, *HAMPIK WARMIKUNA*. SHE USES ANCESTRAL TECHNIQUES AND NATURAL MEDICINE TO PROVIDE PRE-NATAL, LABOR, AND POSTPARTUM CARE. HER MOTHER, WHO WAS ALSO A MIDWIFE, TAUGHT HER EVERYTHING SHE KNOWS. SHE AND HER FELLOW MIDWIVES FIGHT FOR HUMANIZED LABOR POLICIES AND FOR THE RIGHT TO MAINTAIN THEIR ANCIENT PRACTICES BY TRAINING OTHERS, WITHOUT CRIMINALIZATION.

WE ARE LIKE THE STRAW OF THE PÁRAMO,
EVEN IF YOU PULL IT OUT IT GROWS BACK.
WITH THE STRAW OF THE PÁRAMO
WE WILL CULTIVATE THE WORLD.

—DOLORES CACUANGO

*INTI, THE SUN, IS WHISTLING THE SONG "TAMIAJUN" BY THE HUMAZAPAS

SHANTI:
BEYOND THE VEIL

Bandana Tulachan

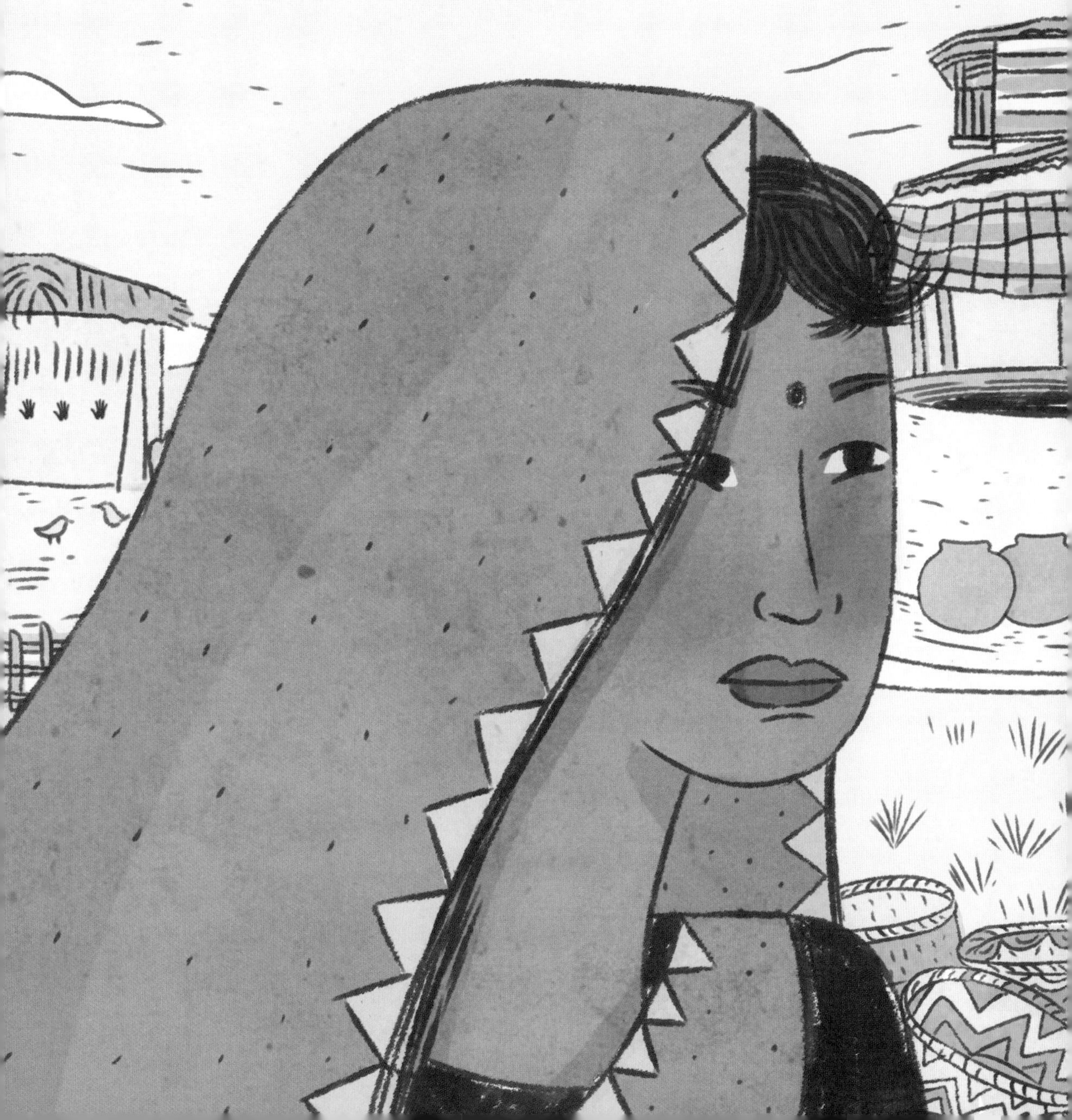

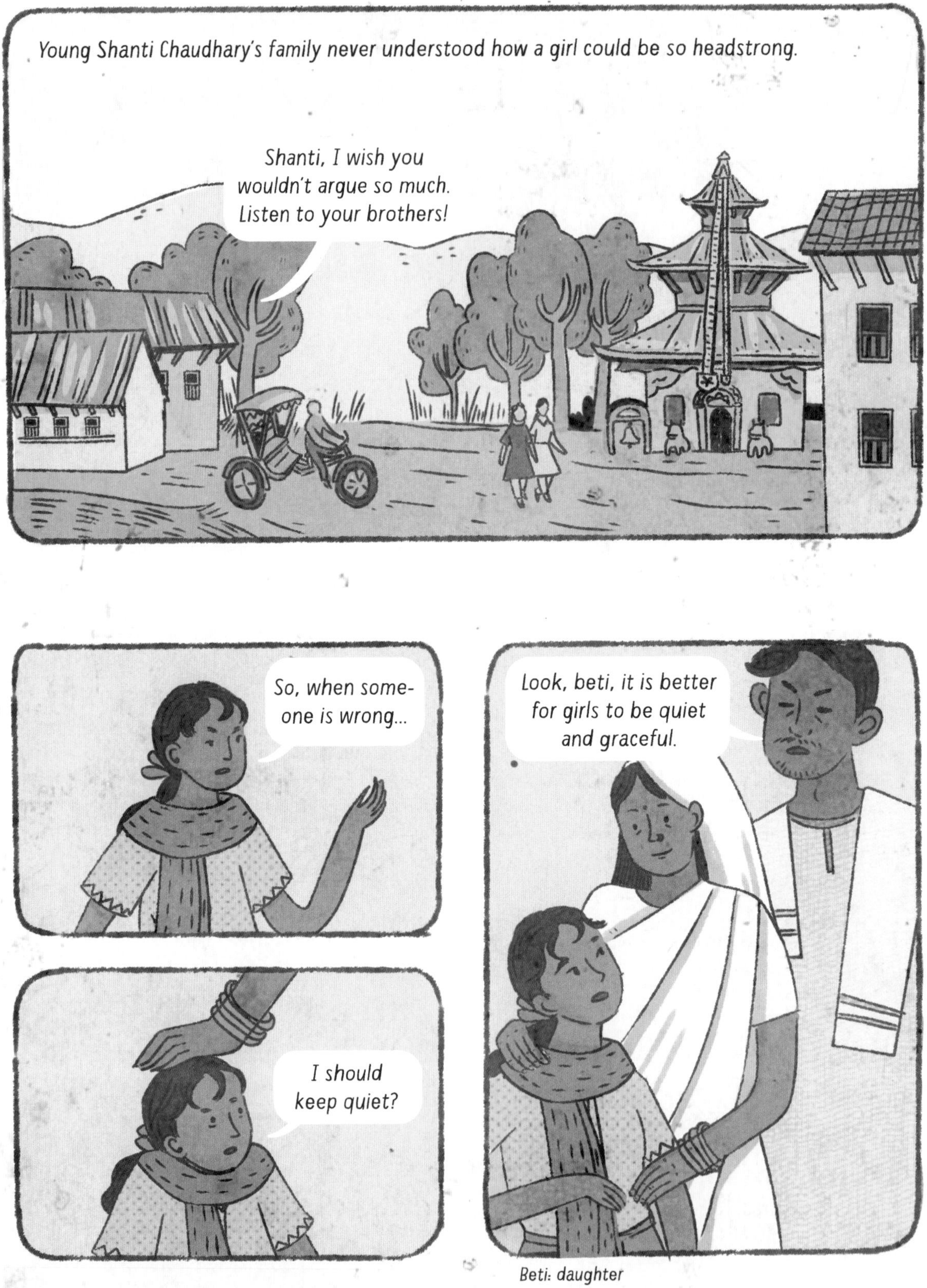
Young Shanti Chaudhary's family never understood how a girl could be so headstrong.
Shanti, I wish you wouldn't argue so much. Listen to your brothers!
So, when some-one is wrong...
I should keep quiet?
Look, beti, it is better for girls to be quiet and graceful.

Beti: daughter

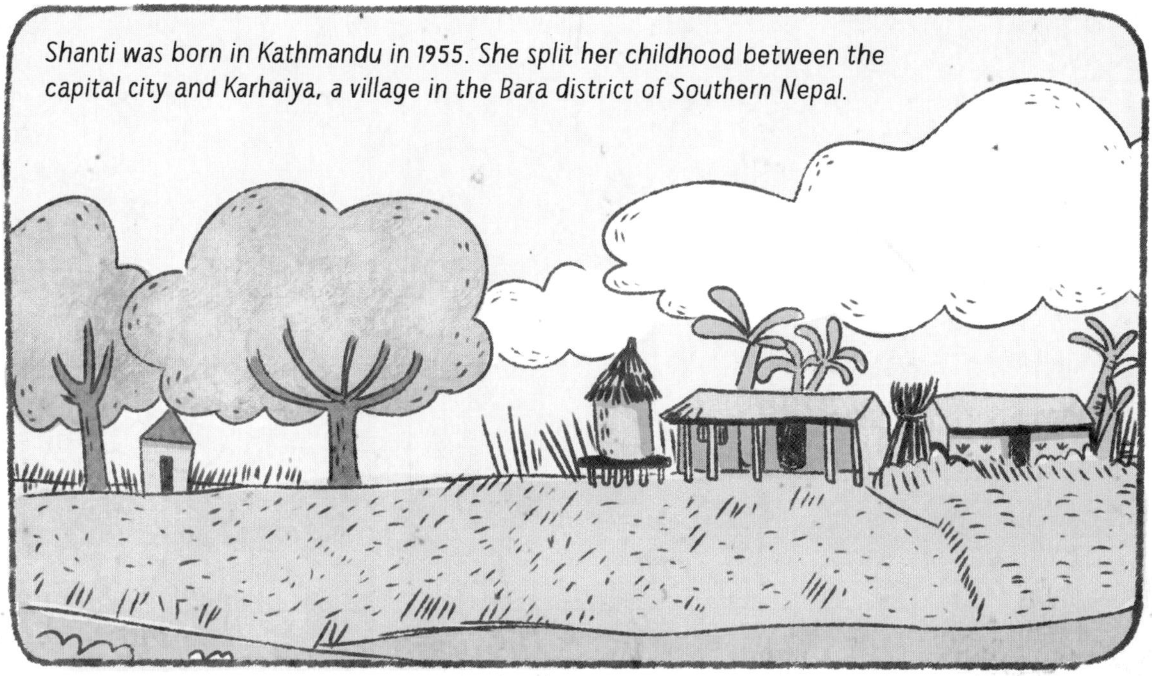
Shanti was born in Kathmandu in 1955. She split her childhood between the capital city and Karhaiya, a village in the Bara district of Southern Nepal.

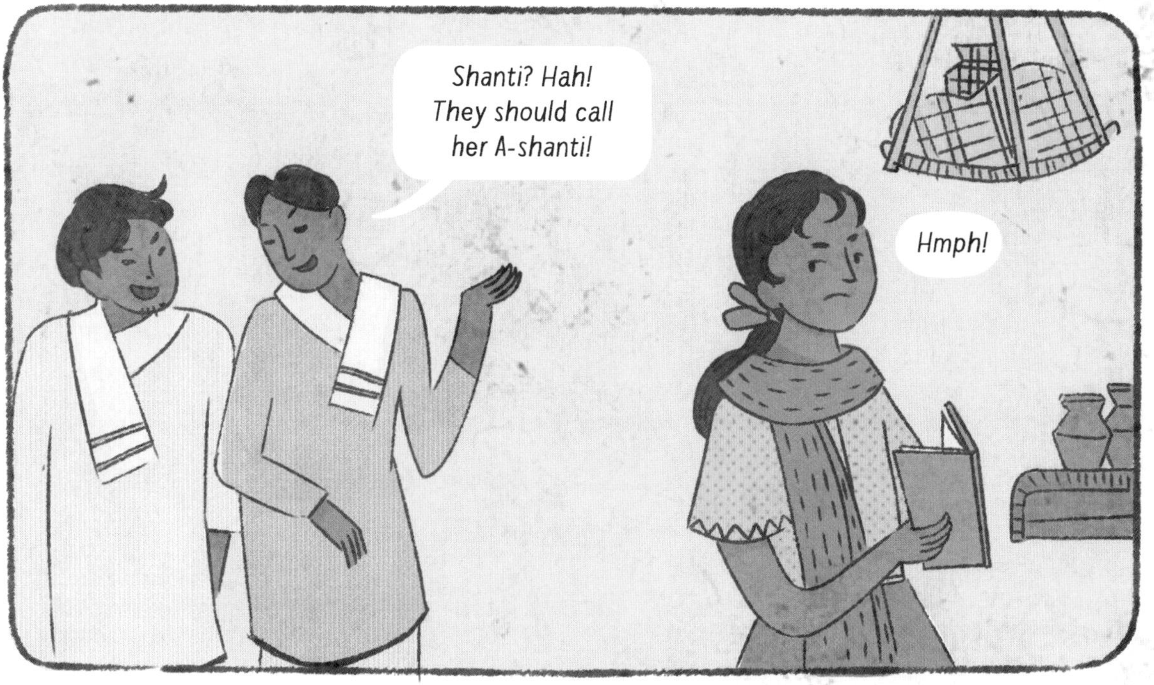
Shanti? Hah! They should call her A-shanti!
Hmph!

Though the name Shanti meant 'peaceful,' she would often be called Ashanti, 'unpeaceful,' until much later in life.

As a child, she watched women toil away behind the veils of their saris, each day filled with menial chores.

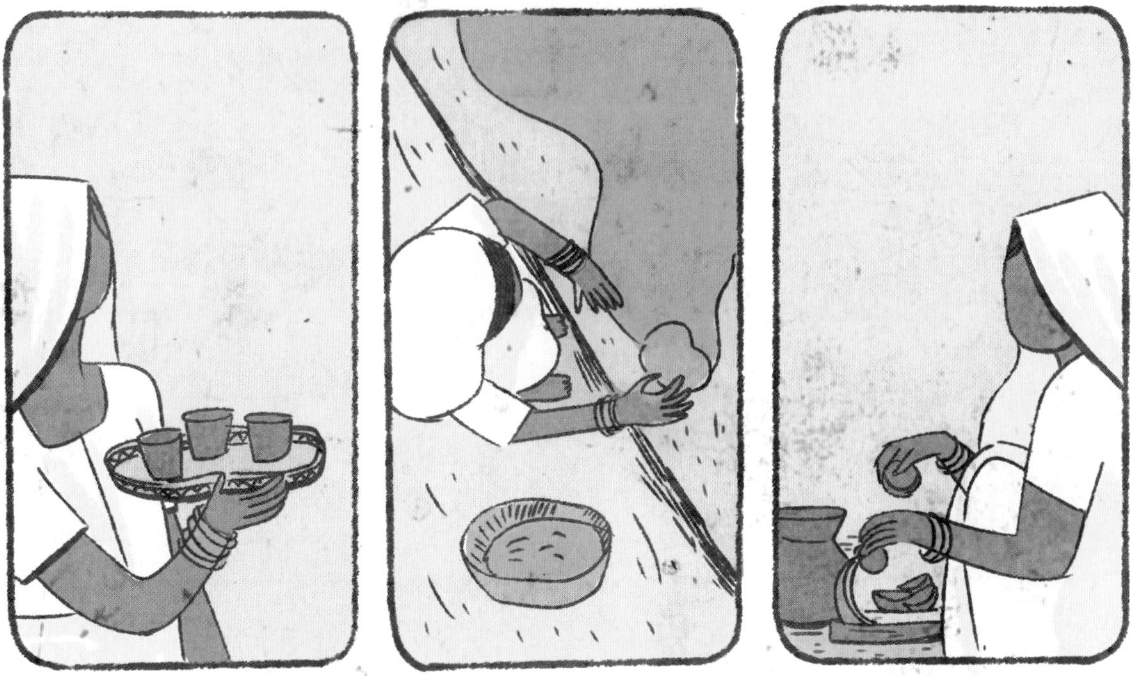

Shanti felt there was hardly any room for thoughts, wishes, or feelings among Tharu women.

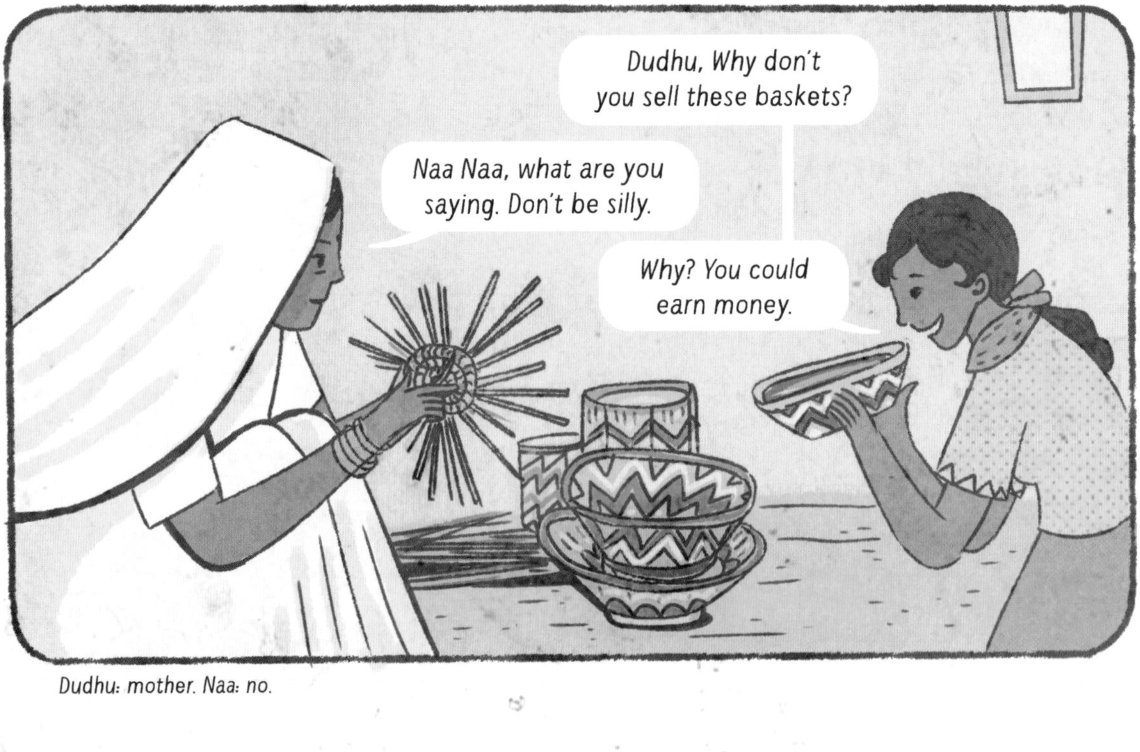
Dudhu, Why don't you sell these baskets?
Naa Naa, what are you saying. Don't be silly.
Why? You could earn money.

Dudhu: mother. Naa: no.

To Shanti, womanhood was the memory of her Dudhu's calloused hands,

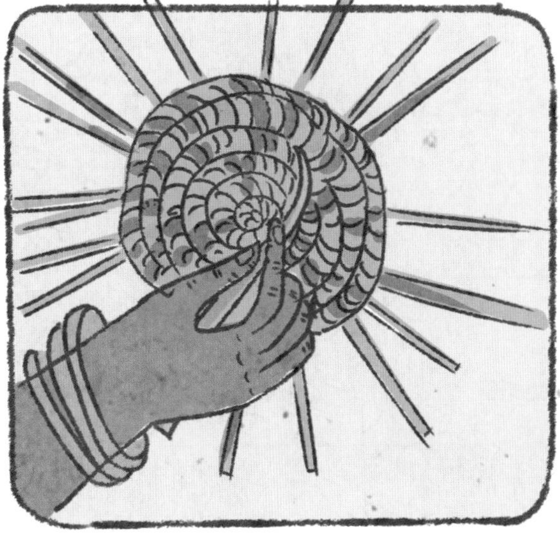

and Dudhu's broken bangles when Baba hit her.

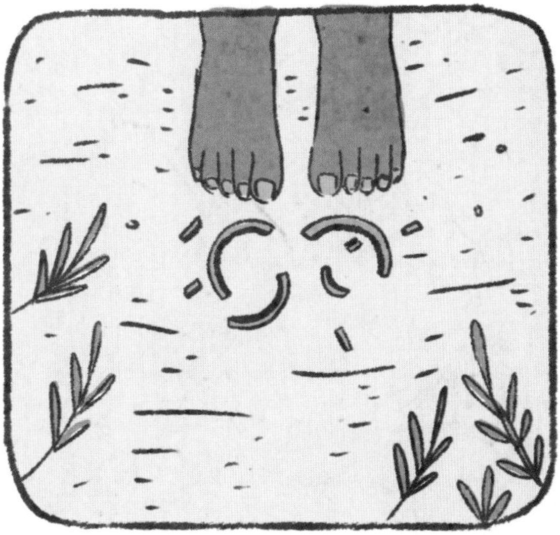

Womanhood was a lesson in endurance, in continuing to live, no matter what.

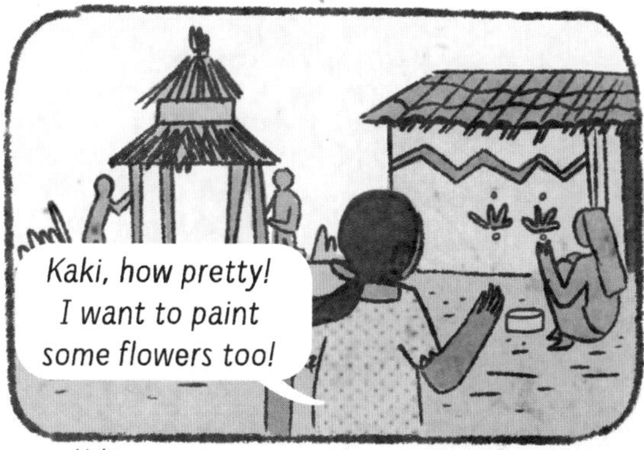
Kaki, how pretty! I want to paint some flowers too!

Kaki: aunt.

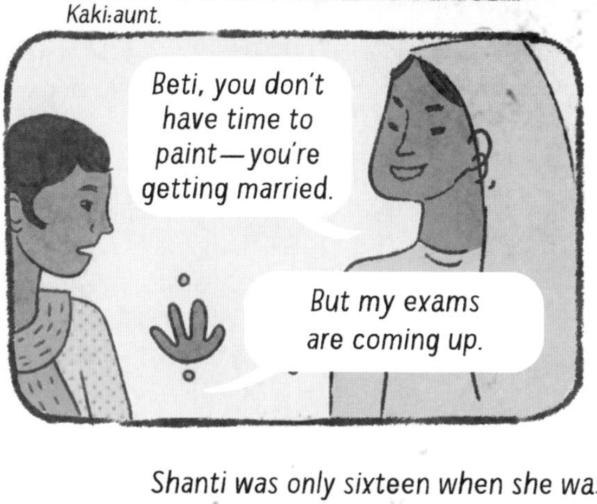
Beti, you don't have time to paint—you're getting married.
But my exams are coming up.

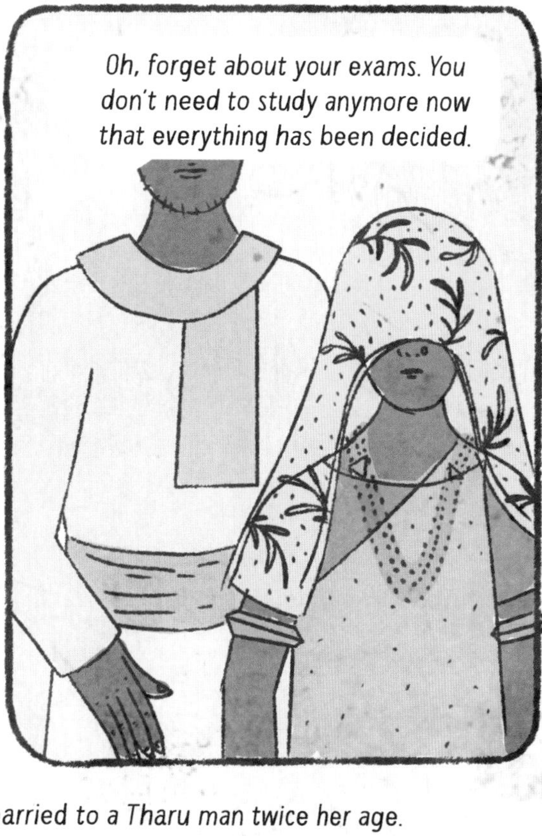
Oh, forget about your exams. You don't need to study anymore now that everything has been decided.

Shanti was only sixteen when she was married to a Tharu man twice her age.

He worked at a cigarette factory in Janakpur, a bustling city 150 km east of Bara, where he lived with his married brother.

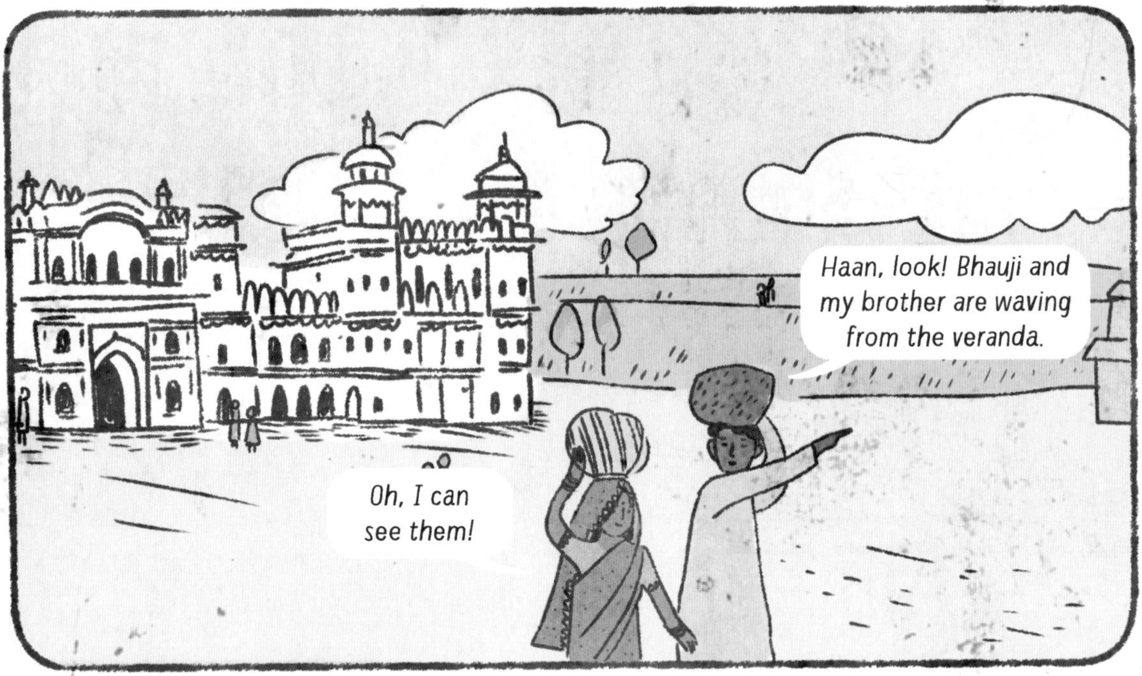
Haan, look! Bhauji and my brother are waving from the veranda.
Oh, I can see them!

Shanti struggled to make sense of her life in a strange new place, with a strange new family.

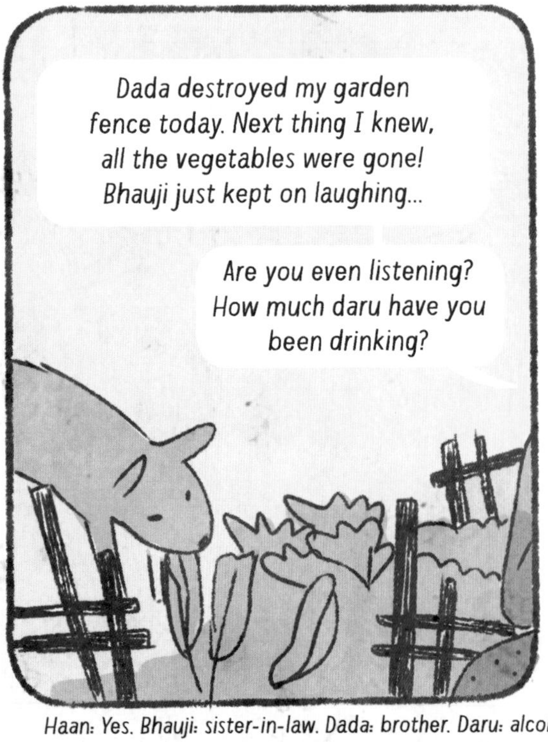
Dada destroyed my garden fence today. Next thing I knew, all the vegetables were gone! Bhauji just kept on laughing...
Are you even listening? How much daru have you been drinking?

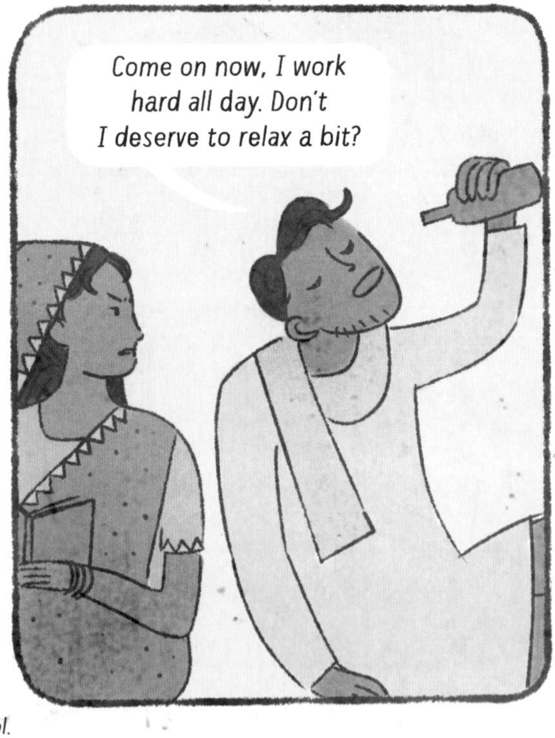
Come on now, I work hard all day. Don't I deserve to relax a bit?

Haan: Yes. Bhauji: sister-in-law. Dada: brother. Daru: alcohol.

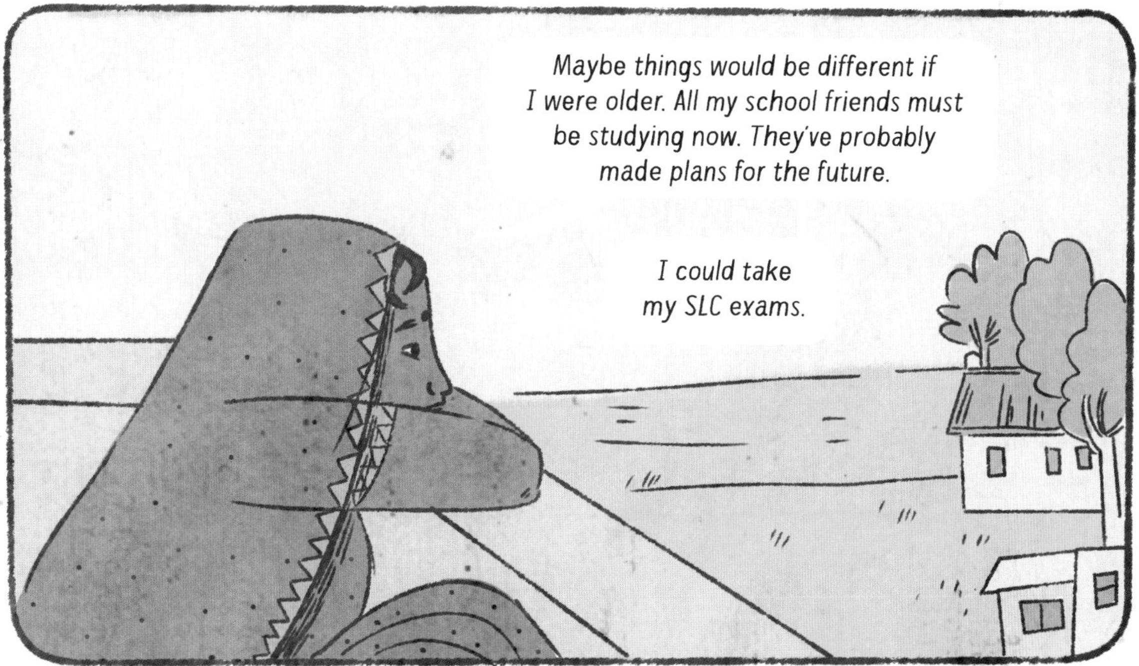
Maybe things would be different if I were older. All my school friends must be studying now. They've probably made plans for the future.
I could take my SLC exams.

SLC: School Leaving Certificate, equivalent to secondary school.

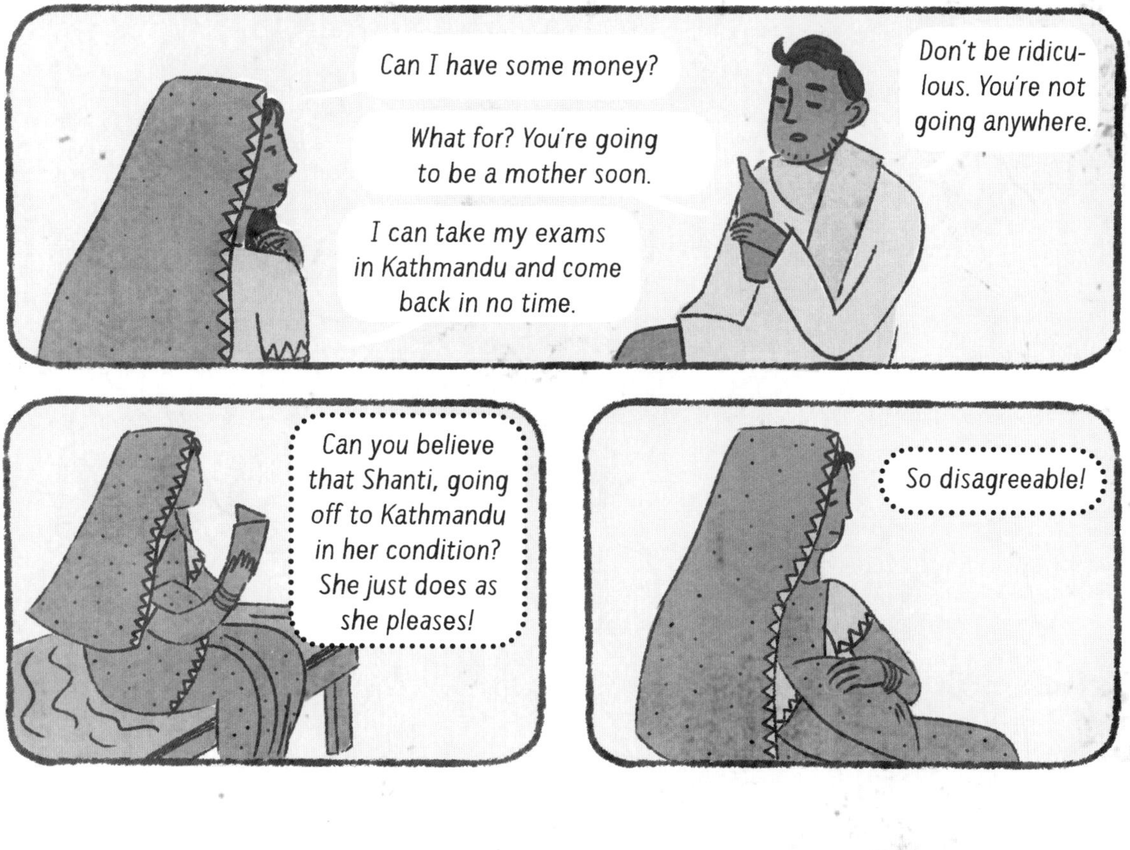
Can I have some money?
What for? You're going to be a mother soon.
I can take my exams in Kathmandu and come back in no time.
Don't be ridicu-lous. You're not going anywhere.
Can you believe that Shanti, going off to Kathmandu in her condition? She just does as she pleases!
So disagreeable!

Shanti was trapped

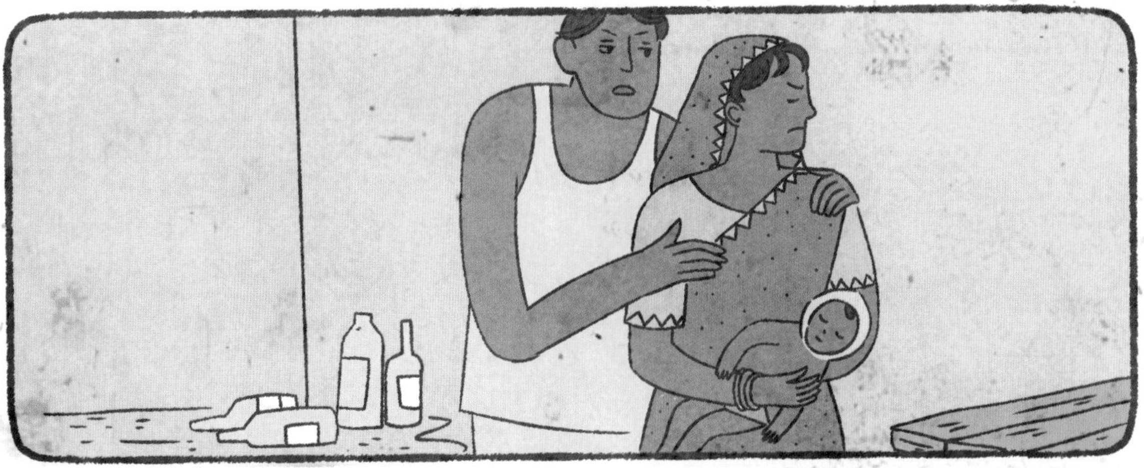

within the walls of her own home

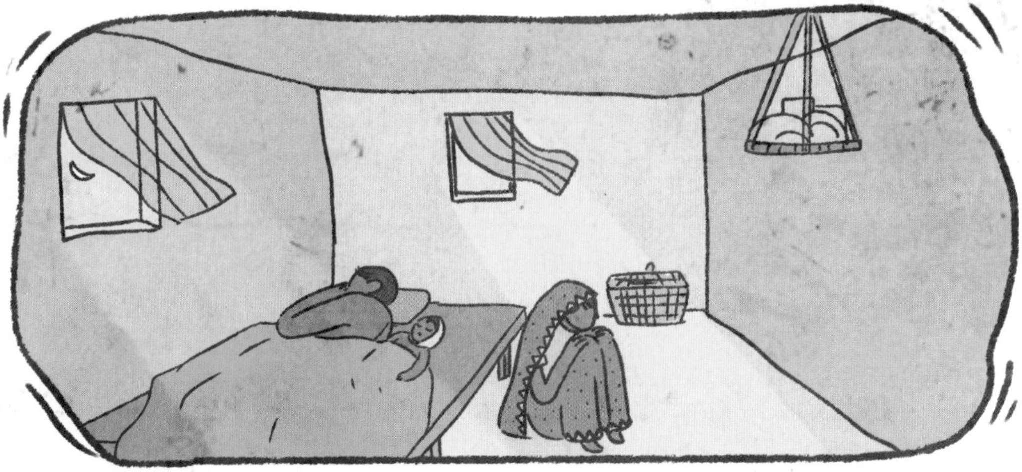

completely alone.

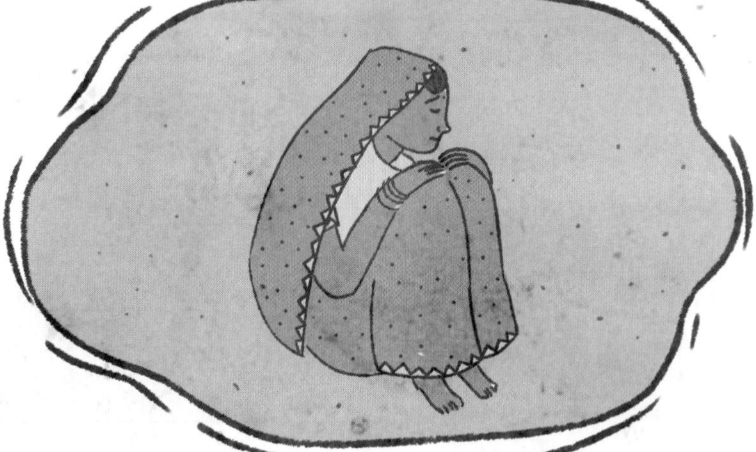

But under the heat of the midday sun and during cool quiet nights while everyone slept, Shanti would stay up and write. She poured all of her feelings—woe, anger, frustration—out onto the page.

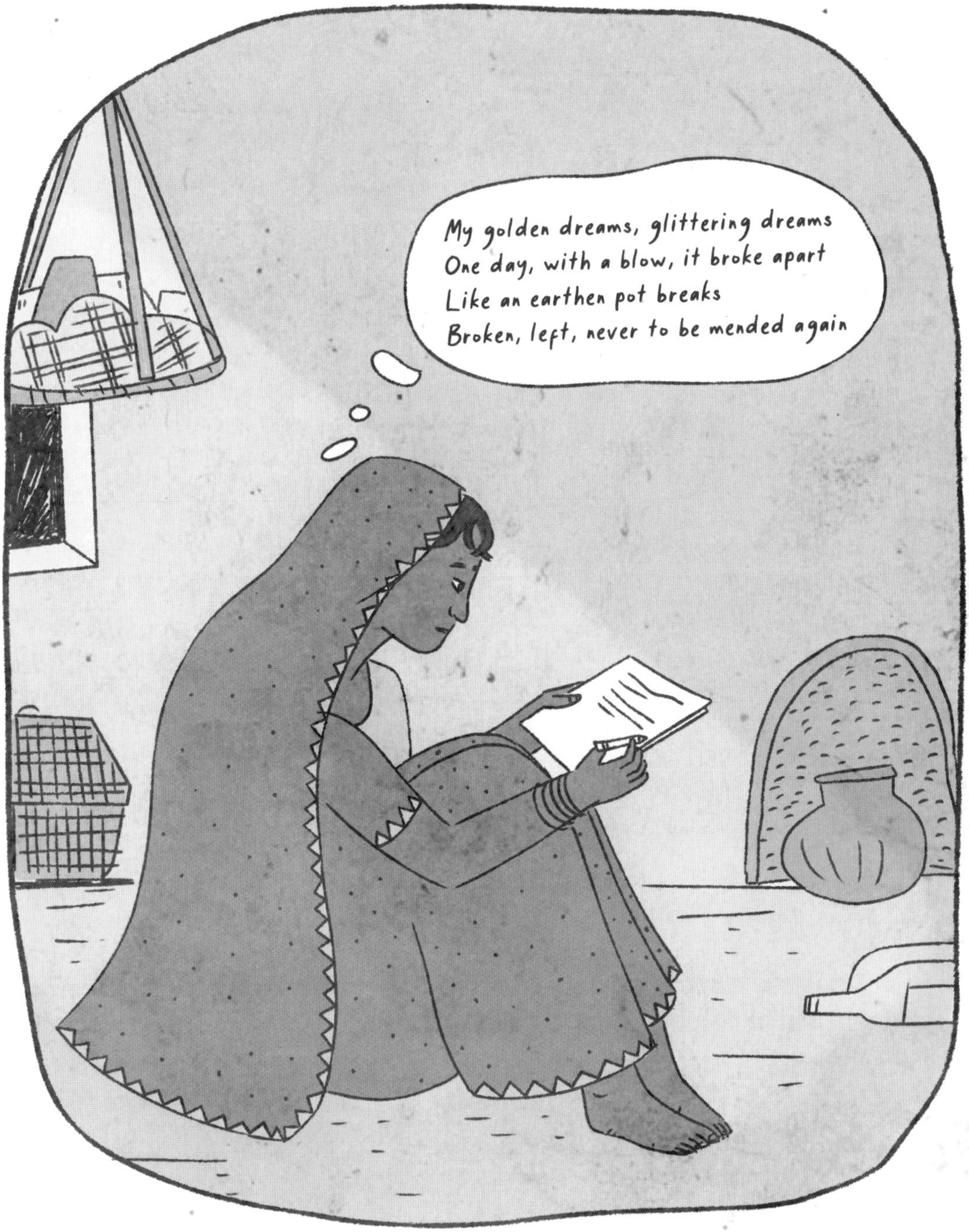
My golden dreams, glittering dreams
One day, with a blow, it broke apart
Like an earthen pot breaks
Broken, left, never to be mended again

These words were her only means of escape.

Once, Shanti almost gave up.

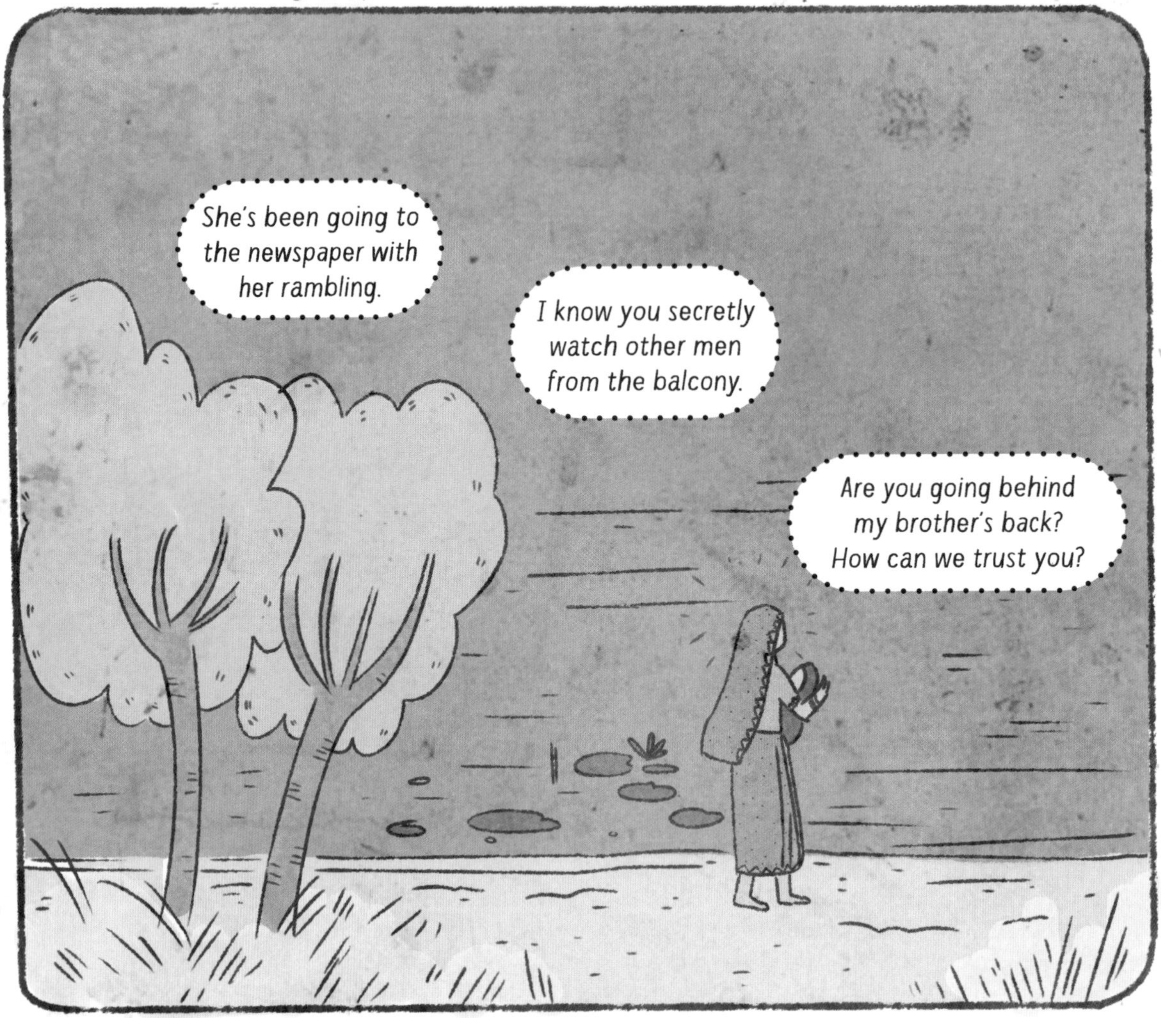
She's been going to the newspaper with her rambling.
I know you secretly watch other men from the balcony.
Are you going behind my brother's back? How can we trust you?

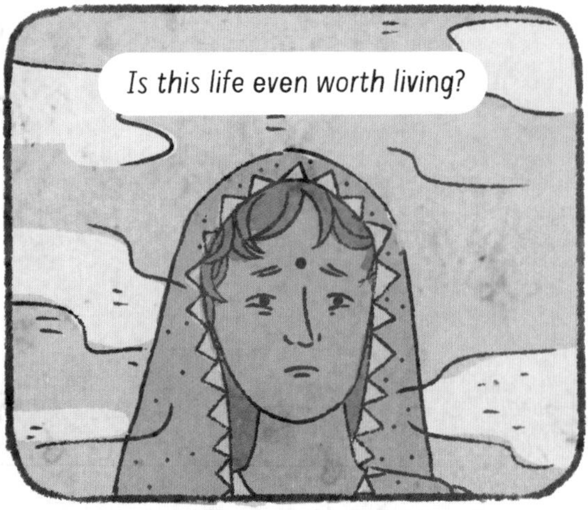
Is this life even worth living?

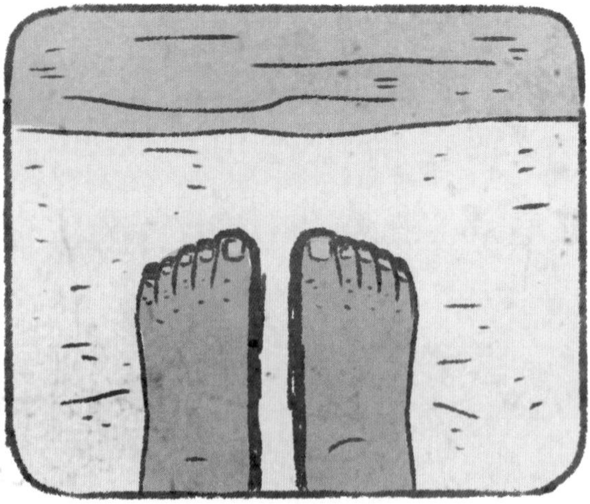

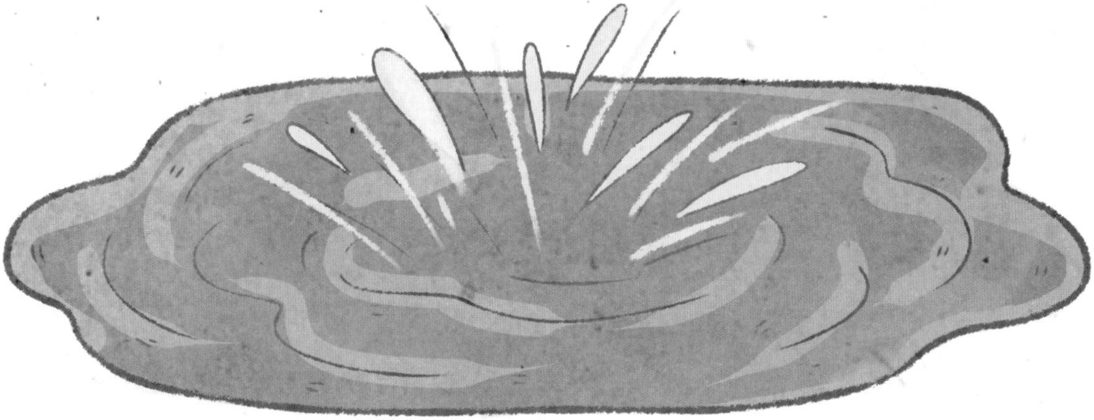

If I died today, would anyone pity me? Would they feel sad for me?

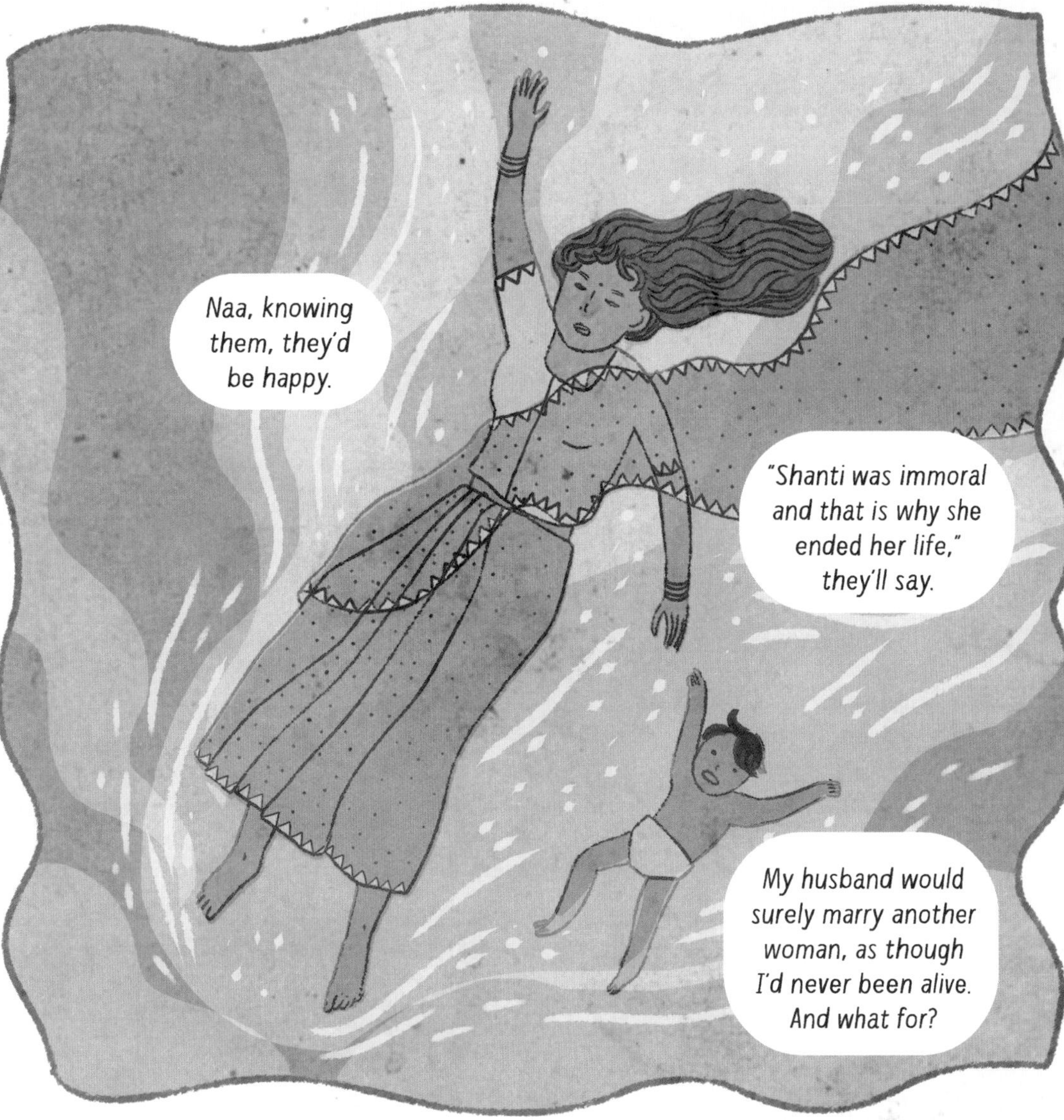
Naa, knowing them, they'd be happy.
"Shanti was immoral and that is why she ended her life," they'll say.
My husband would surely marry another woman, as though I'd never been alive. And what for?

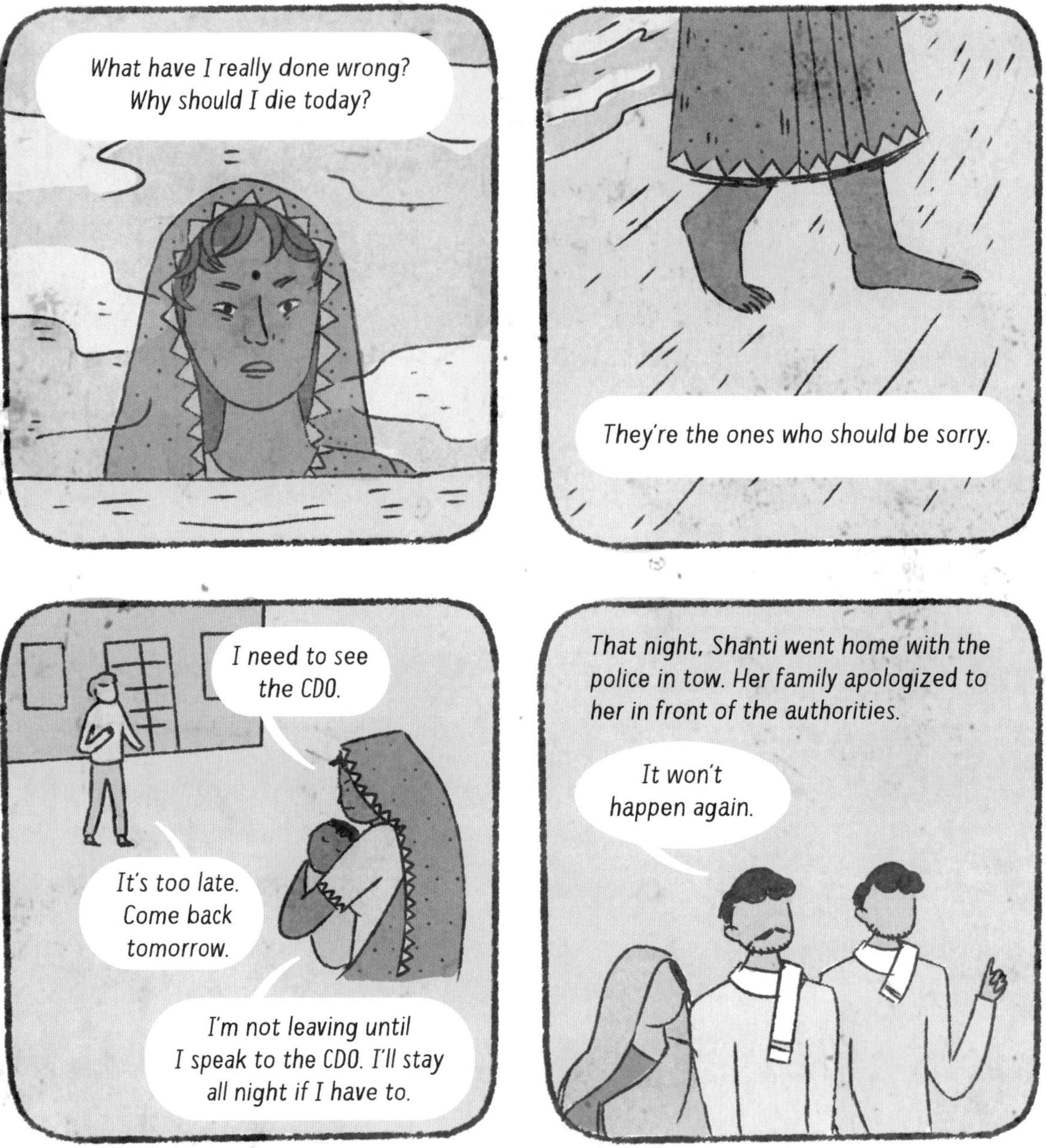
What have I really done wrong? Why should I die today?
They're the ones who should be sorry.
I need to see the CDO.
It's too late. Come back tomorrow.
I'm not leaving until I speak to the CDO. I'll stay all night if I have to.
That night, Shanti went home with the police in tow. Her family apologized to her in front of the authorities.
It won't happen again.

CDO: Chief District Officer.

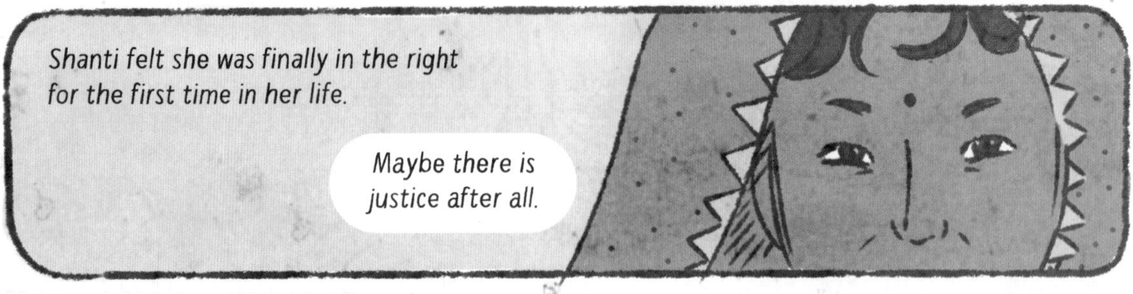
Shanti felt she was finally in the right for the first time in her life.
Maybe there is justice after all.

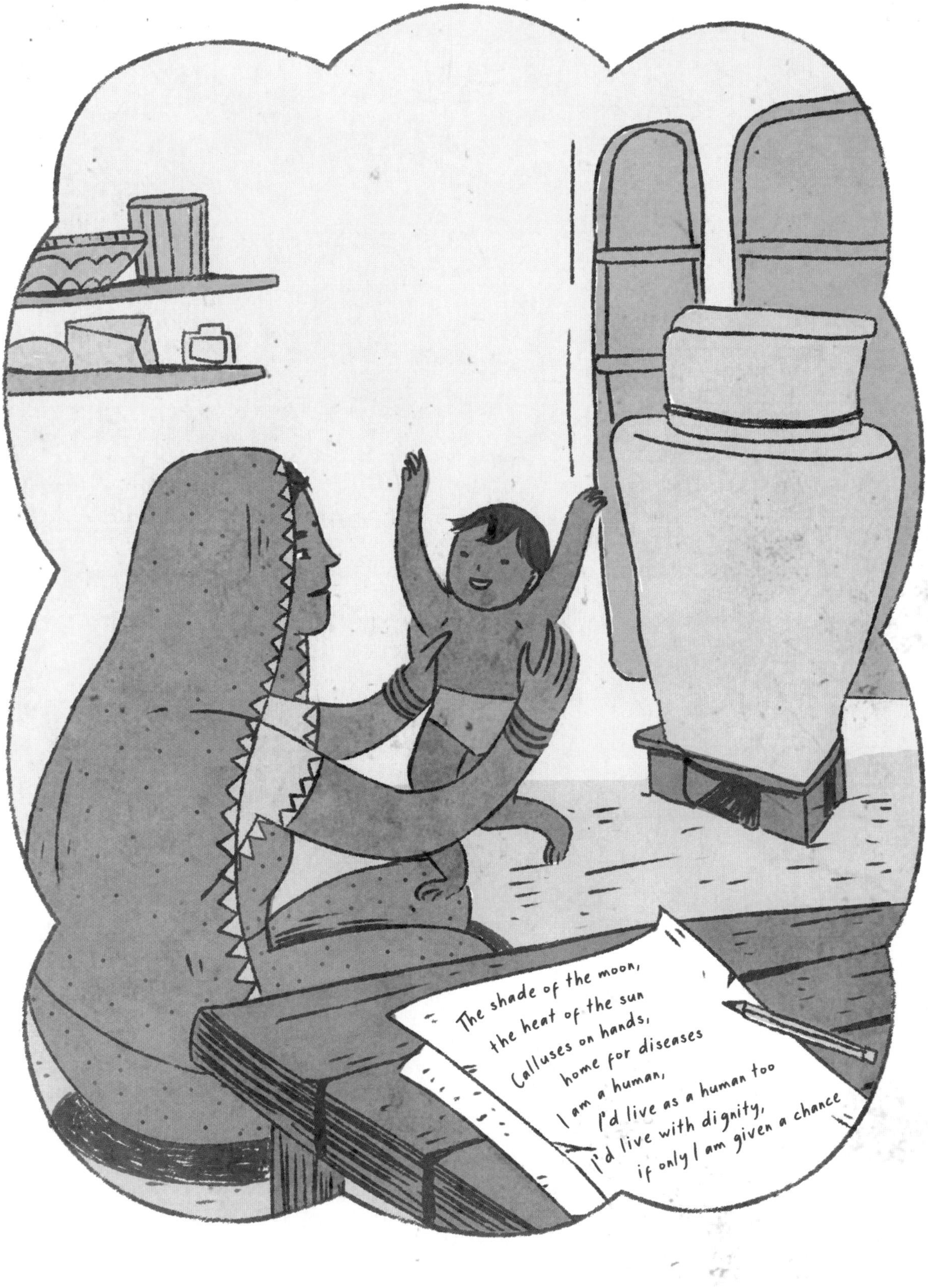

The shade of the moon,
the heat of the sun
Calluses on hands,
home for diseases
I am a human,
I'd live as a human too
I'd live with dignity,
if only I am given a chance

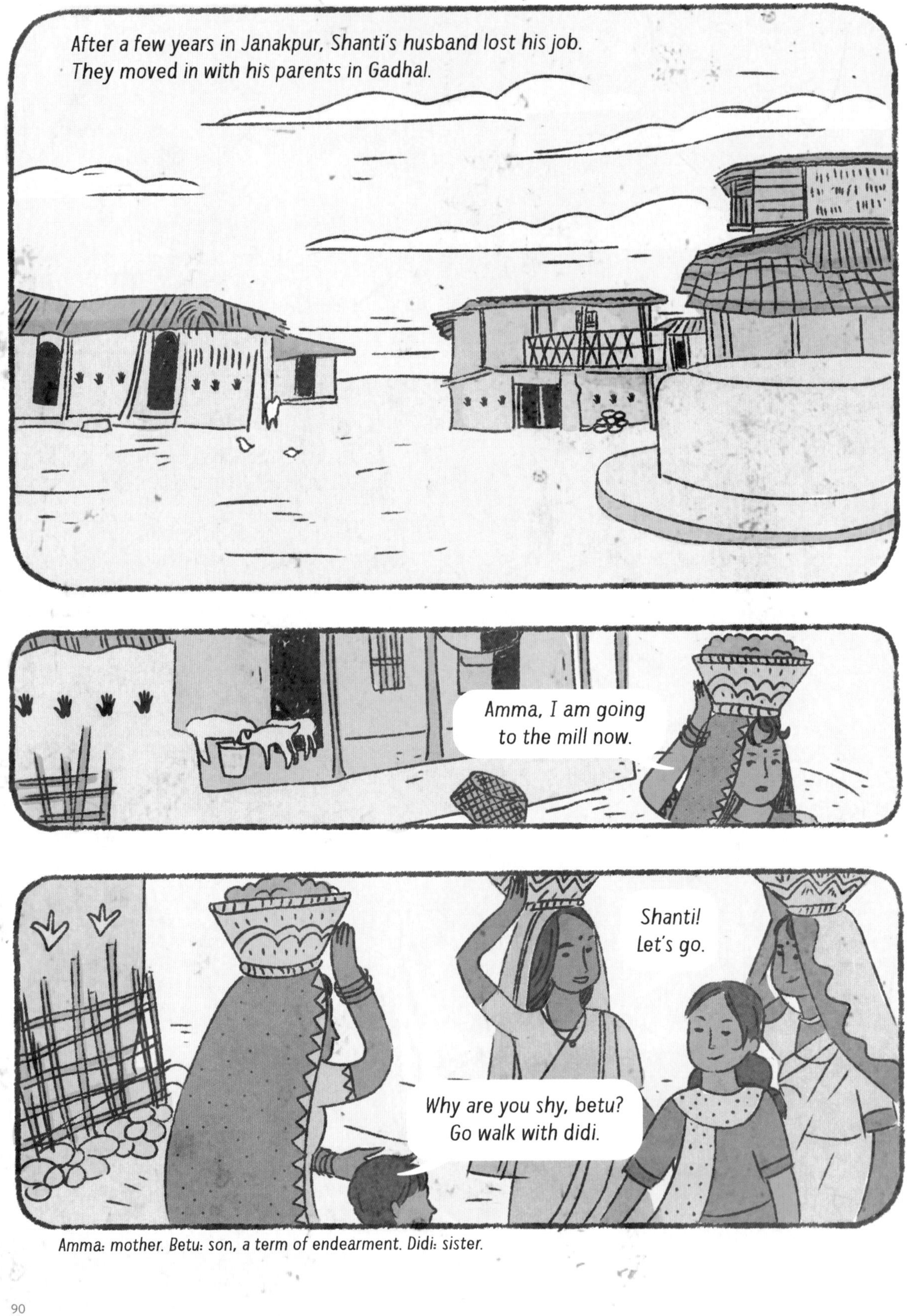
After a few years in Janakpur, Shanti's husband lost his job. They moved in with his parents in Gadhal.
Amma, I am going to the mill now.
Shanti! Let's go.
Why are you shy, betu? Go walk with didi.

Amma: mother. Betu: son, a term of endearment. Didi: sister.

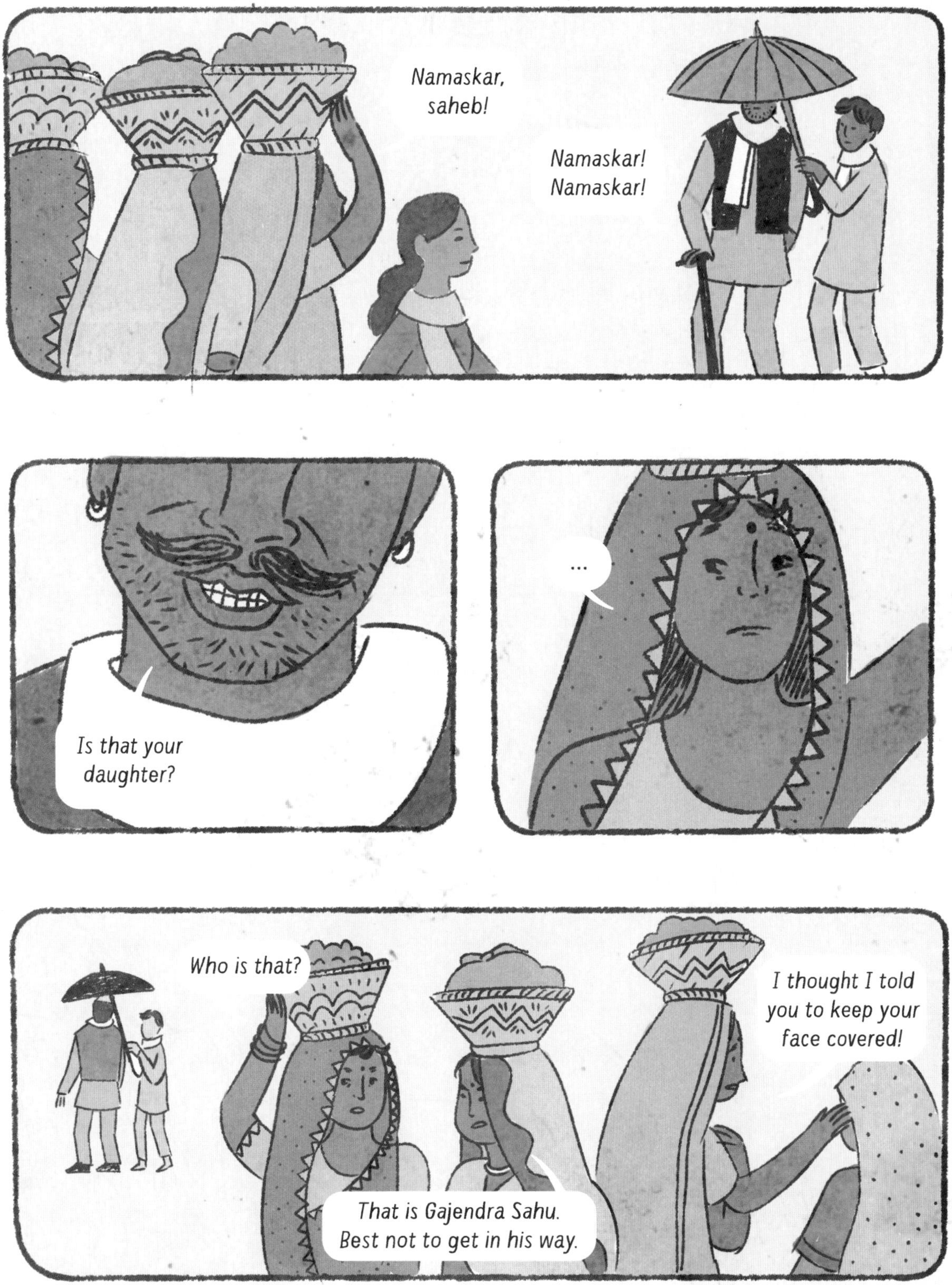
Namaskar, saheb!
Namaskar! Namaskar!
Is that your daughter?
...
Who is that?
That is Gajendra Sahu. Best not to get in his way.
I thought I told you to keep your face covered!

Sahu: landowner, usually a wealthy person of influence.

Gadhal, Shanti found, was nothing like Karhaiya. This village, not so far from her own, was ruled by one of the cruellest Sahus in the area.

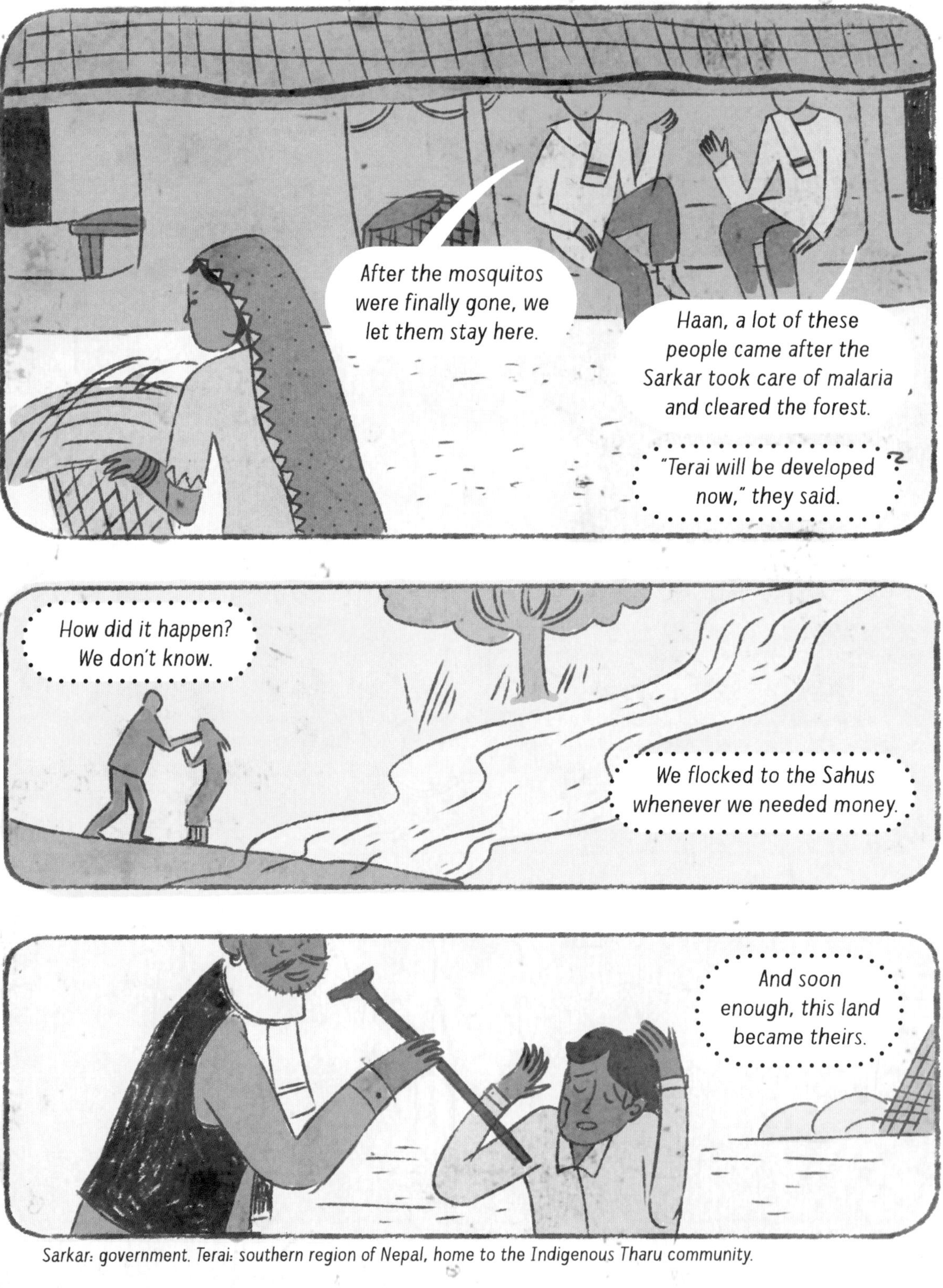

After the mosquitos were finally gone, we let them stay here.
Haan, a lot of these people came after the Sarkar took care of malaria and cleared the forest.
"Terai will be developed now," they said.
How did it happen? We don't know.
We flocked to the Sahus whenever we needed money.
And soon enough, this land became theirs.

Sarkar: government. Terai: southern region of Nepal, home to the Indigenous Tharu community.

But even within the Tharu community, things were far from perfect.

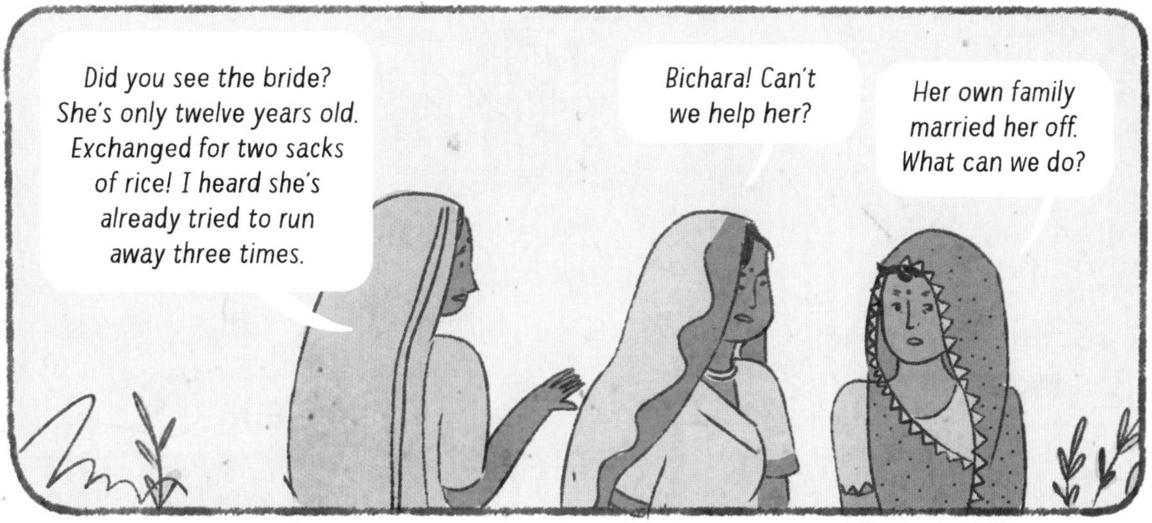
Did you see the bride? She's only twelve years old. Exchanged for two sacks of rice! I heard she's already tried to run away three times.
Bichara! Can't we help her?
Her own family married her off. What can we do?

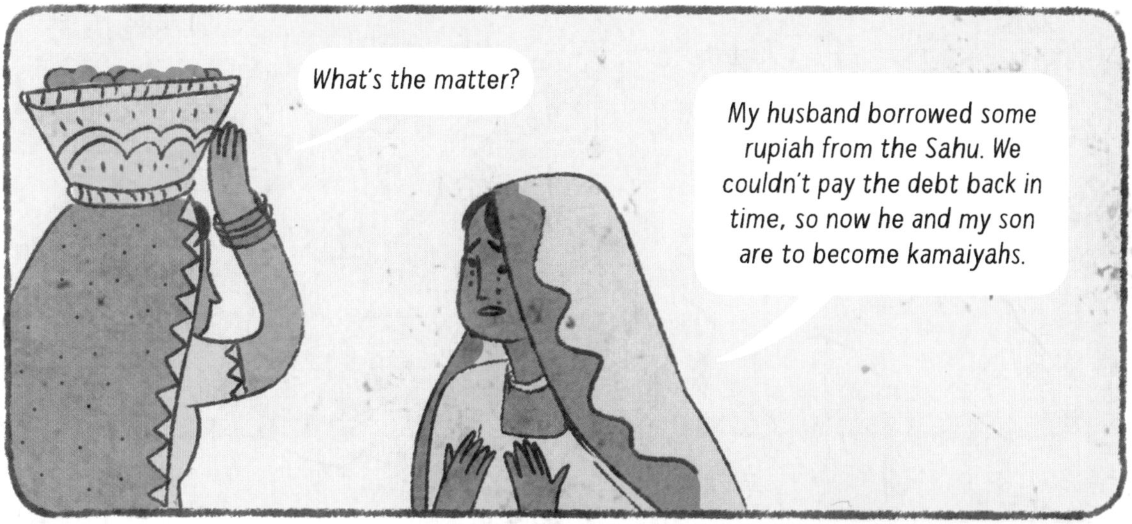
What's the matter?
My husband borrowed some rupiah from the Sahu. We couldn't pay the debt back in time, so now he and my son are to become kamaiyahs.

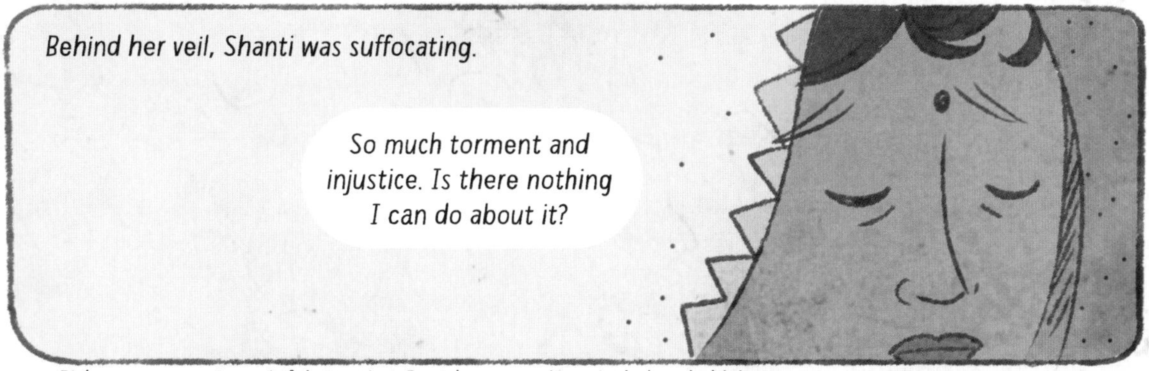
Behind her veil, Shanti was suffocating.
So much torment and injustice. Is there nothing I can do about it?

Bichara: a person in a pitiful situation. Rupiah: money. Kamaiyah: bonded laborer.

Writing, her only source of reprieve, grew elusive as she struggled each day for survival.

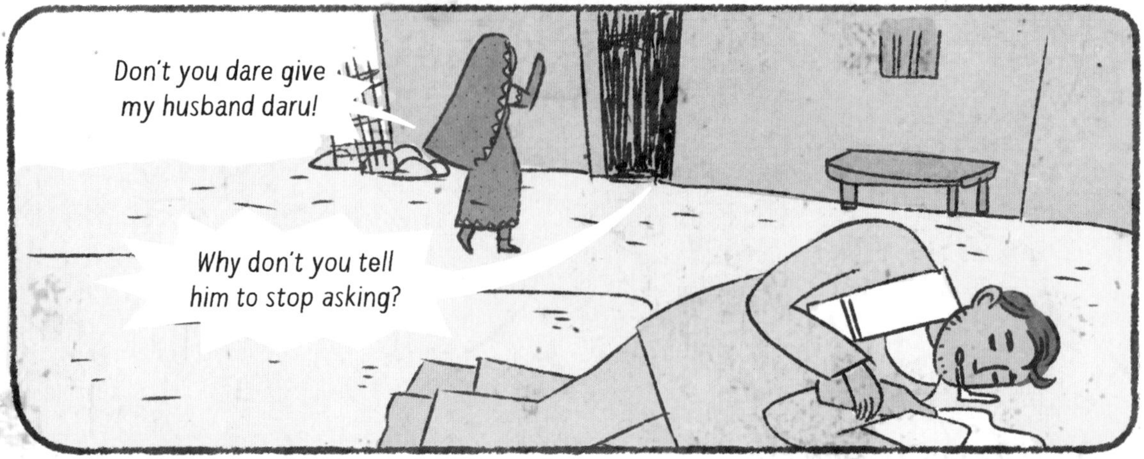
Don't you dare give my husband daru!
Why don't you tell him to stop asking?

The empty pantry, *the daily hustle,*

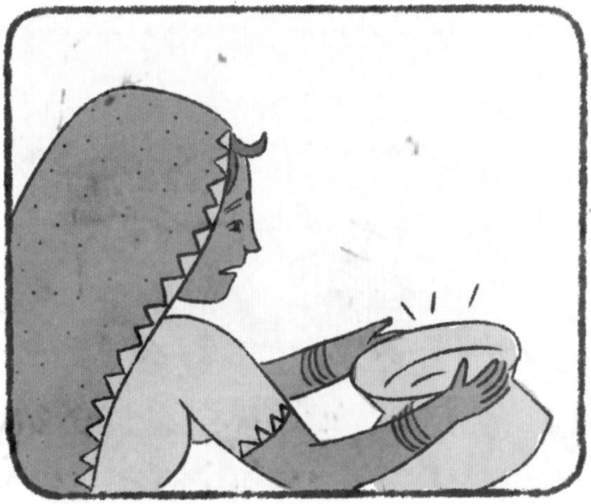

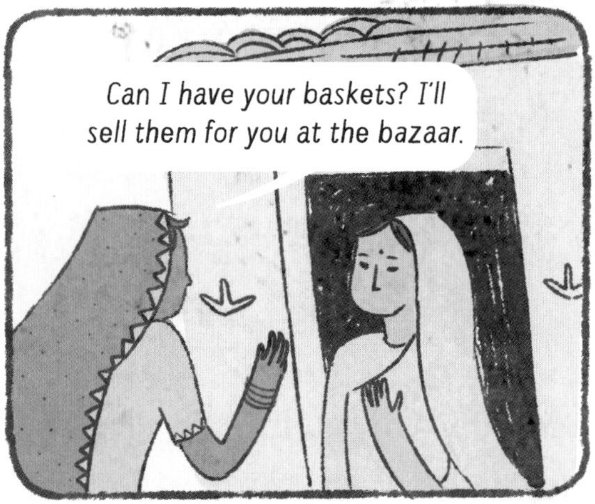
Can I have your baskets? I'll sell them for you at the bazaar.

It took a lot of grit to keep Shanti going.

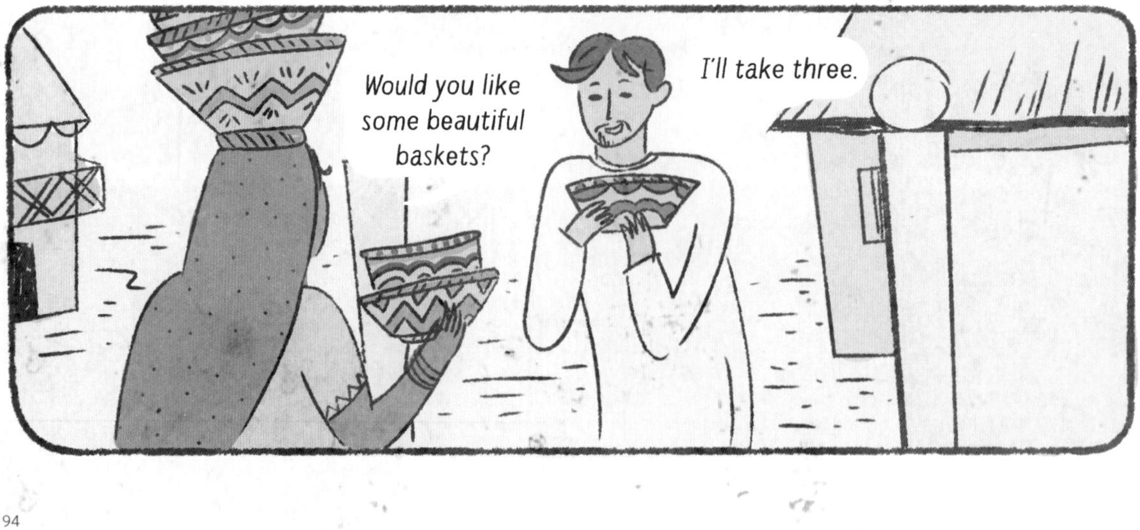
Would you like some beautiful baskets?
I'll take three.

Selling local handicrafts worked out well. Soon, Shanti was taking bundles of Tharu baskets to the city for selling.

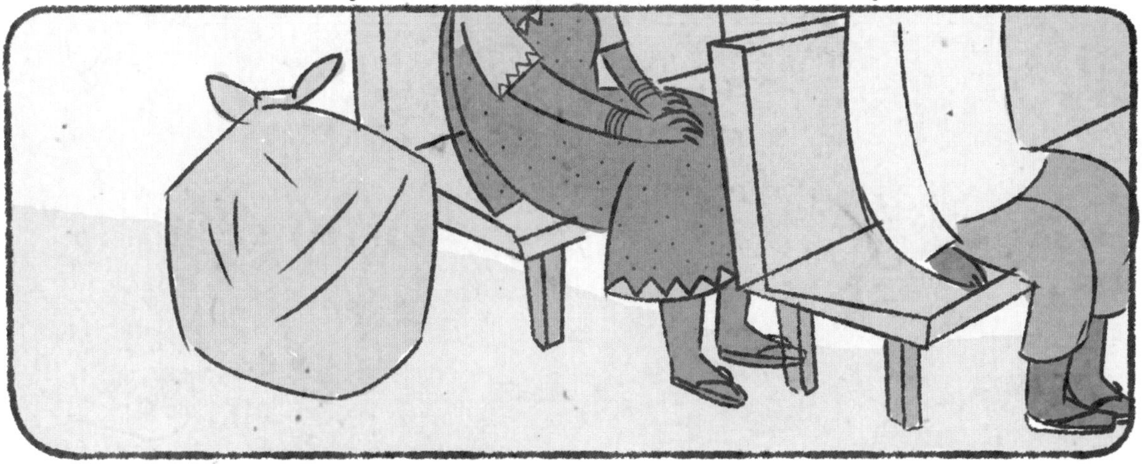

The Kathmandu crafts market was thriving at the time.

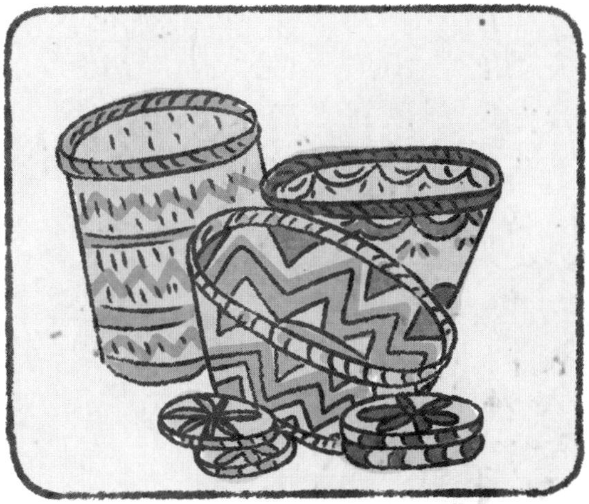

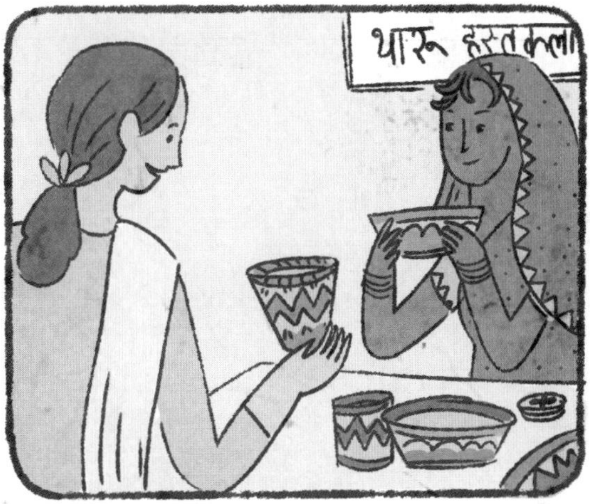

Shanti became the bridge that connected Gadhal to the capital.

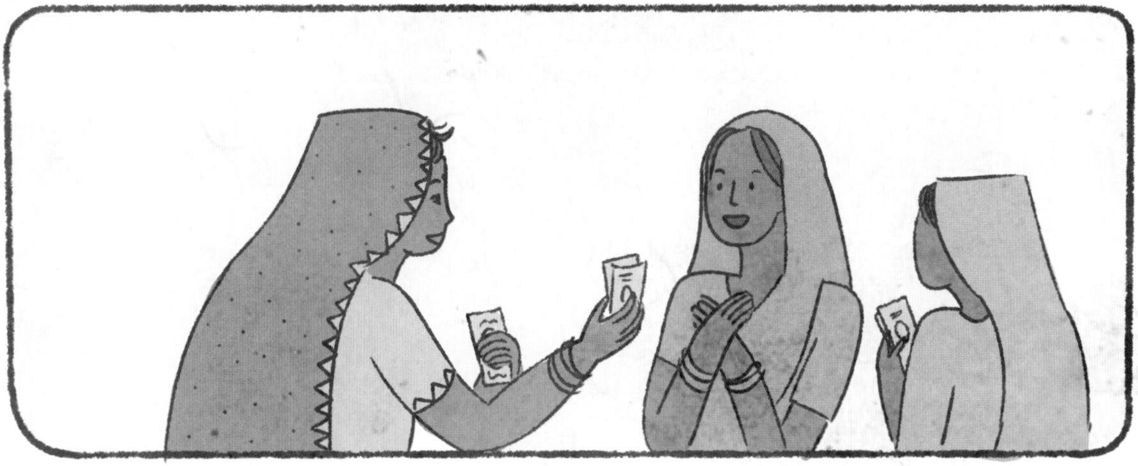

Little by little, change came to Gadhal.

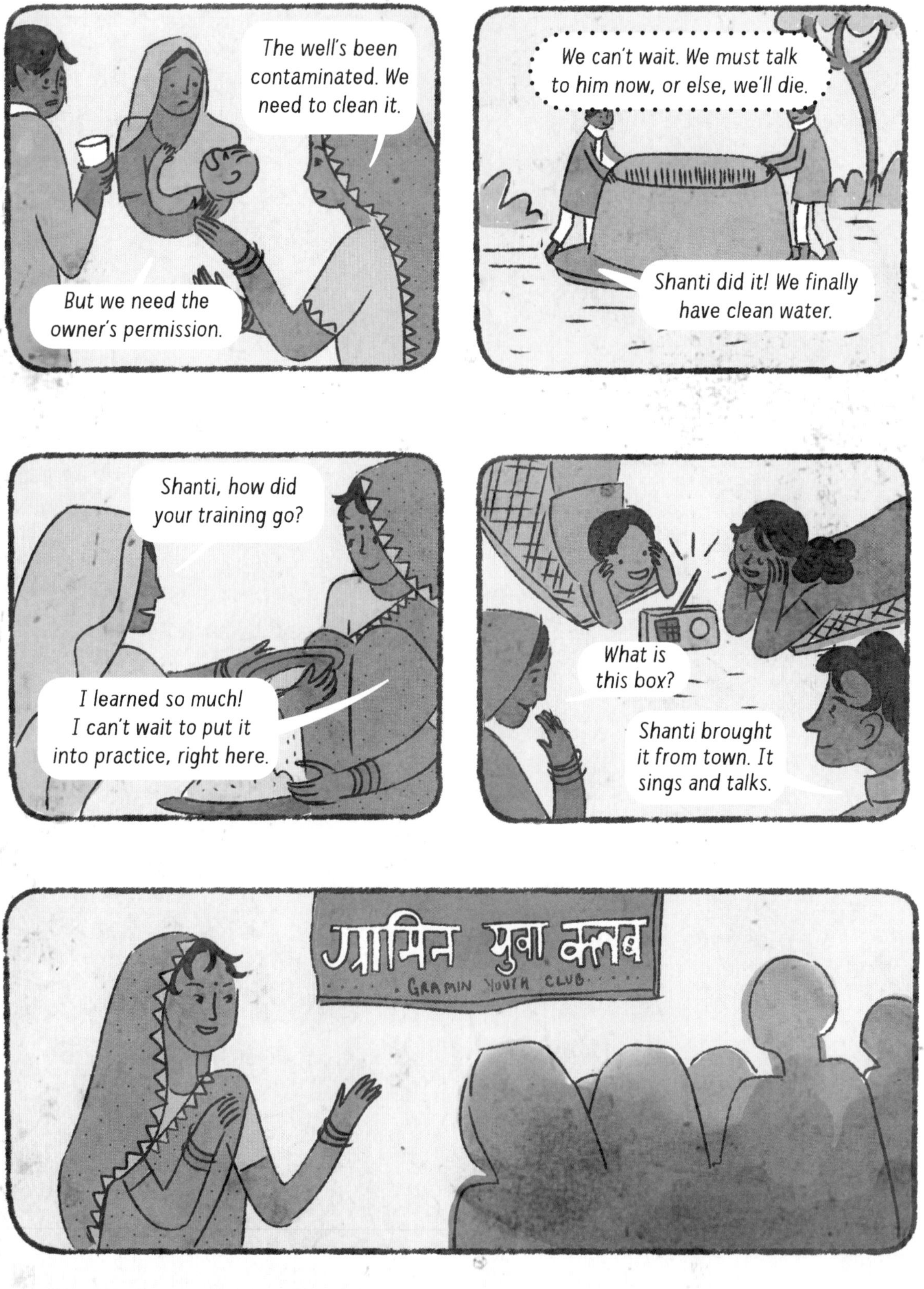
The well's been contaminated. We need to clean it.
But we need the owner's permission.
We can't wait. We must talk to him now, or else, we'll die.
Shanti did it! We finally have clean water.
Shanti, how did your training go?
I learned so much! I can't wait to put it into practice, right here.
What is this box?
Shanti brought it from town. It sings and talks.
ग्रामिन युवा क्लब
GRAMIN YOUTH CLUB

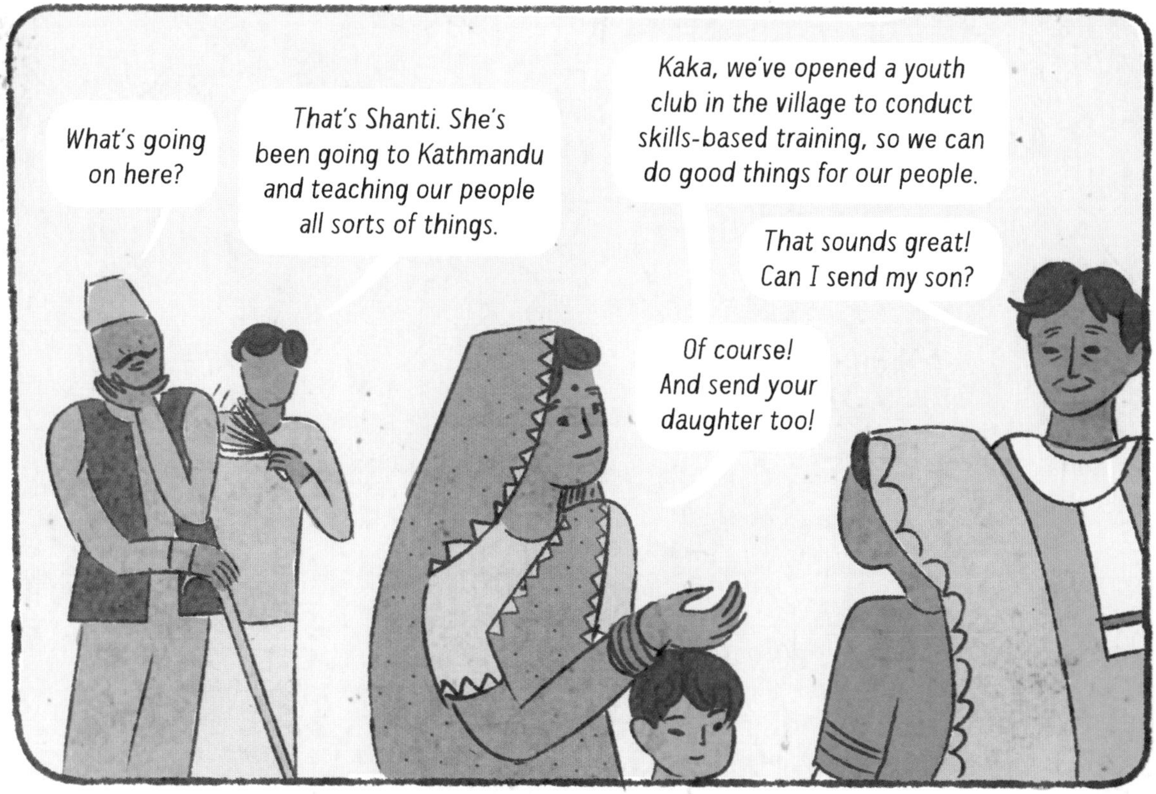
What's going on here?
That's Shanti. She's been going to Kathmandu and teaching our people all sorts of things.
Kaka, we've opened a youth club in the village to conduct skills-based training, so we can do good things for our people.
That sounds great! Can I send my son?
Of course! And send your daughter too!

Things were starting to look up.

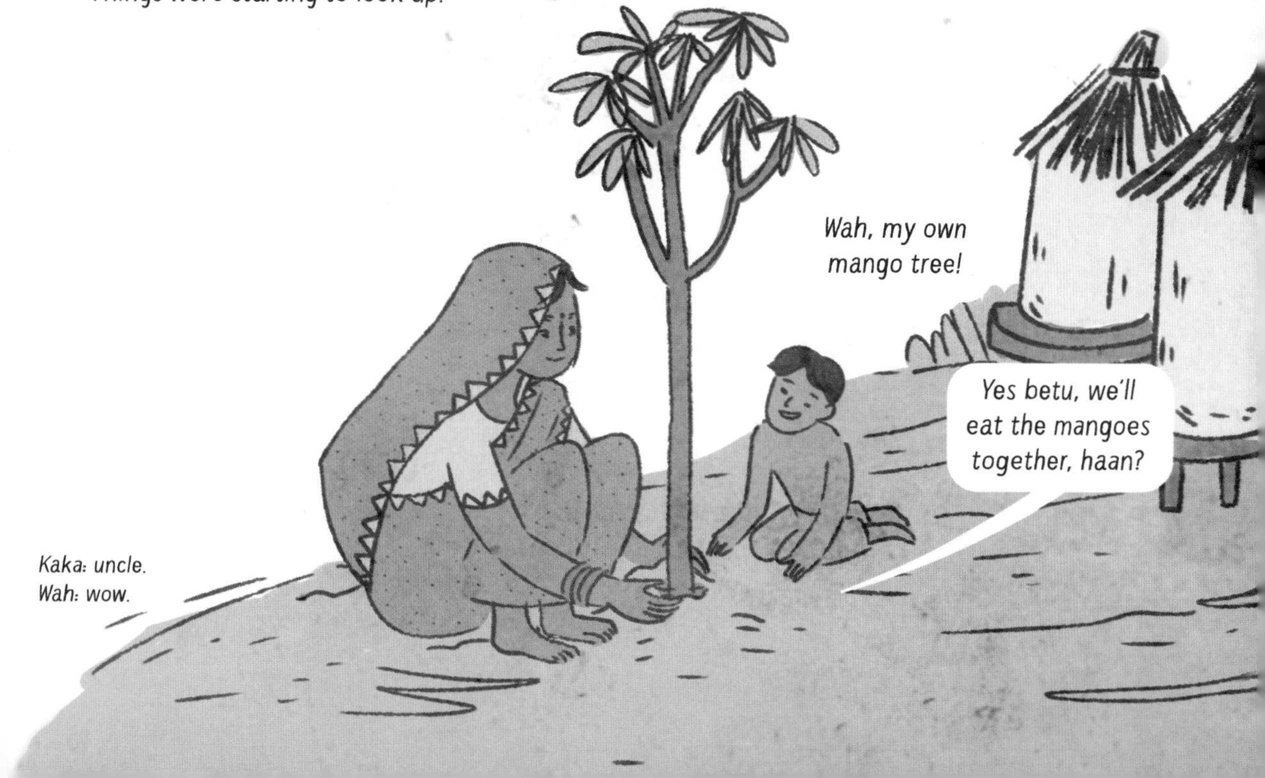
Wah, my own mango tree!
Yes betu, we'll eat the mangoes together, haan?

Kaka: uncle.
Wah: wow.

But the Sahus didn't like seeing progress in the village. They didn't want things to change. One day, Shanti got a notice from the CDO.

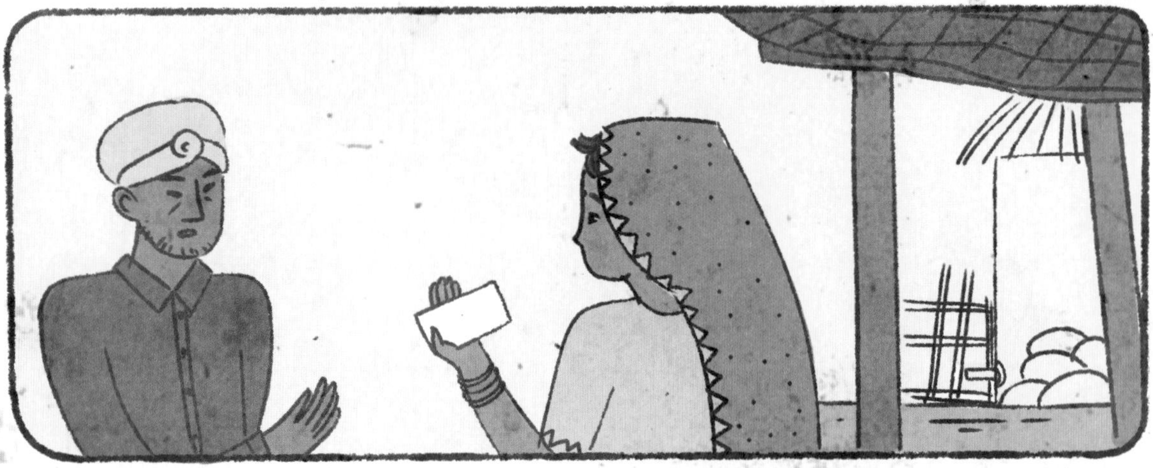

Somebody had filed a complaint against her.

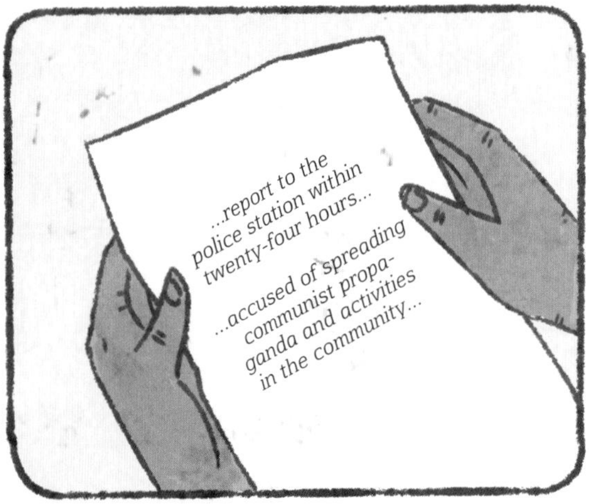
...report to the police station within twenty-four hours...
...accused of spreading communist propaganda and activities in the community...

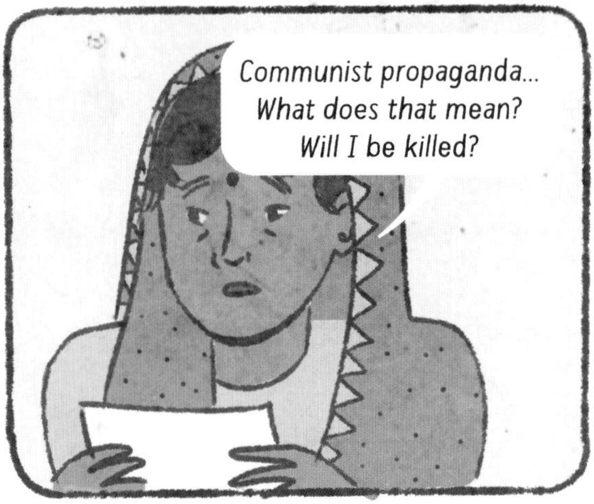
Communist propaganda... What does that mean? Will I be killed?

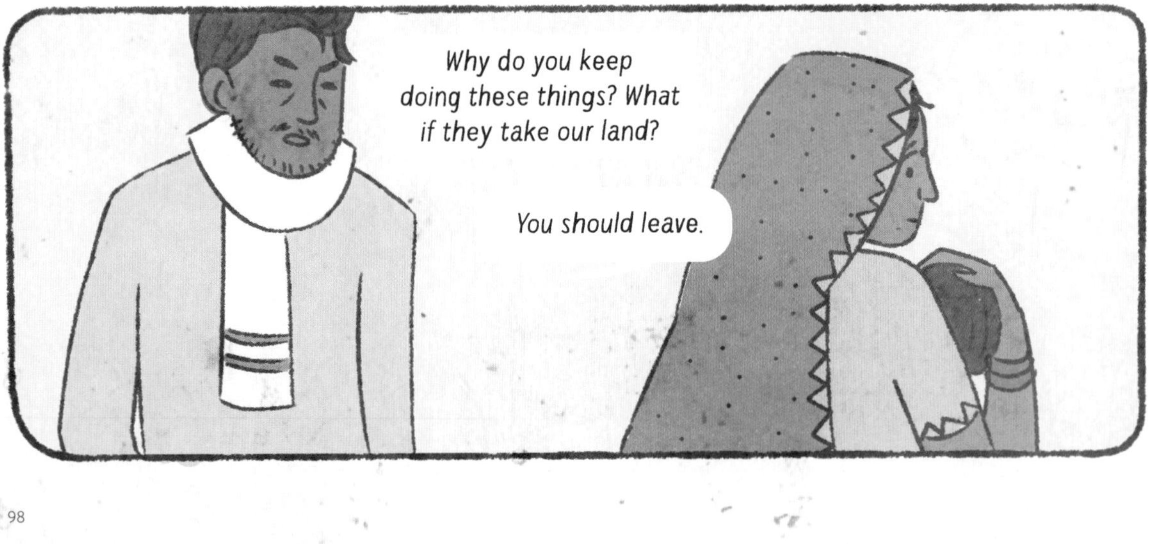
Why do you keep doing these things? What if they take our land?
You should leave.

Shanti fled to Kathmandu with her son to avoid being detained.
She didn't trust the authorities and she couldn't take any chances.

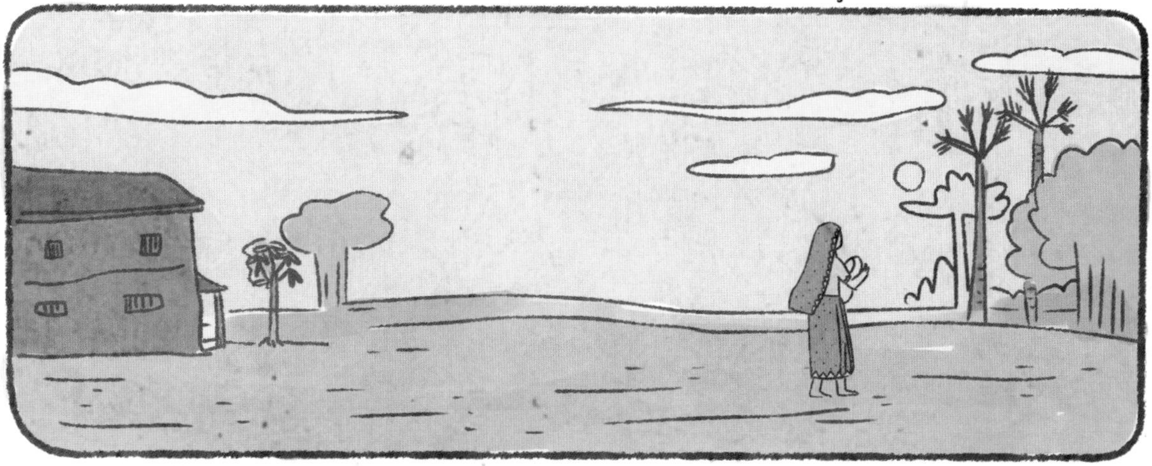

Back in the city, her family pleaded with her to return to her husband.

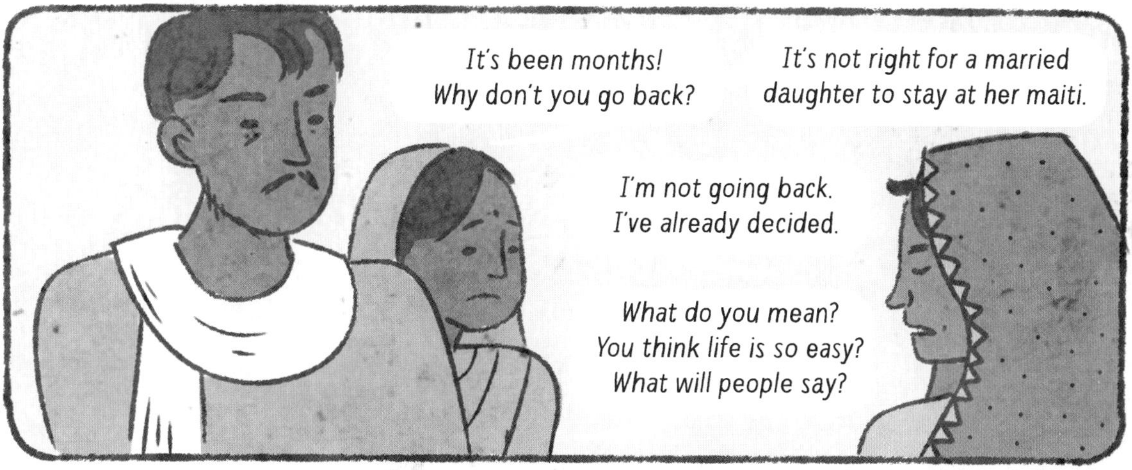
It's been months! Why don't you go back?
It's not right for a married daughter to stay at her maiti.
I'm not going back. I've already decided.
What do you mean? You think life is so easy? What will people say?

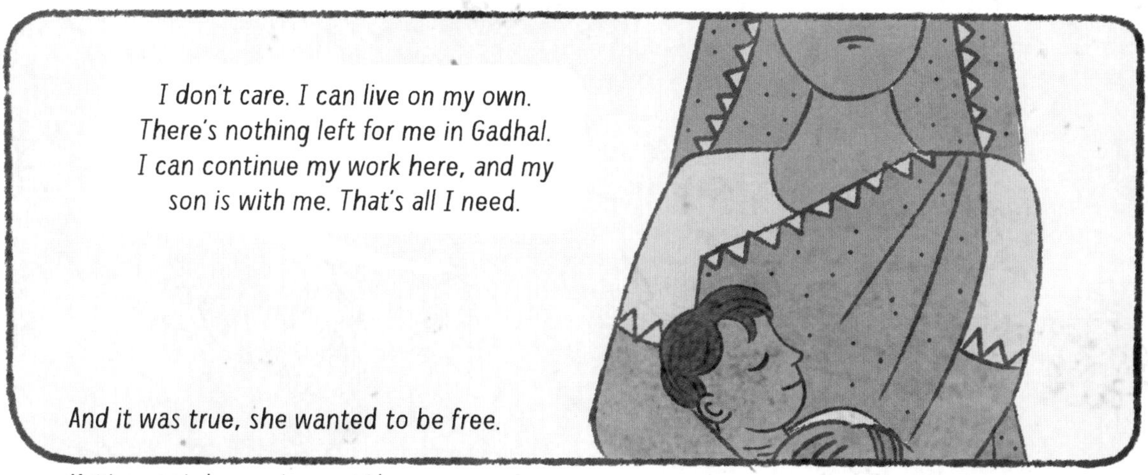
I don't care. I can live on my own. There's nothing left for me in Gadhal. I can continue my work here, and my son is with me. That's all I need.
And it was true, she wanted to be free.

Maiti: a married woman's parents' home.

But life rarely goes as planned. Soon, her husband's family in Janakpur took her son away.

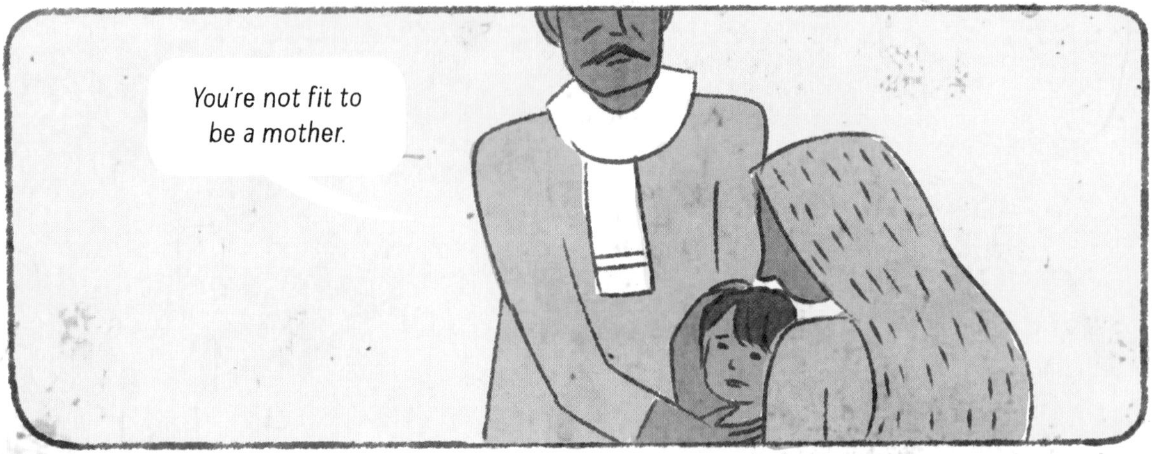
You're not fit to be a mother.

And as much as she tried, they wouldn't let her see him again.

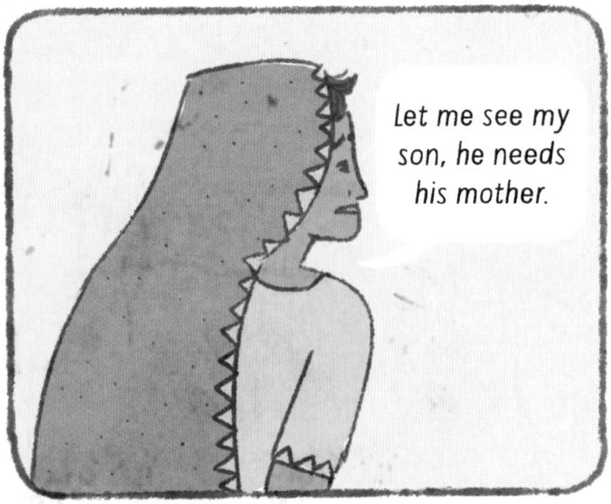
Let me see my son, he needs his mother.

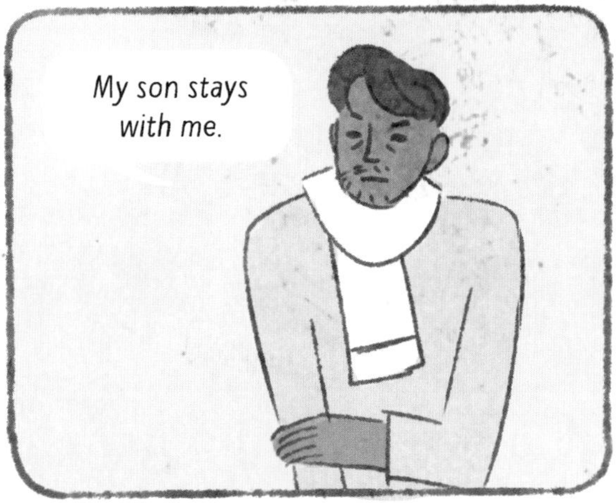
My son stays with me.

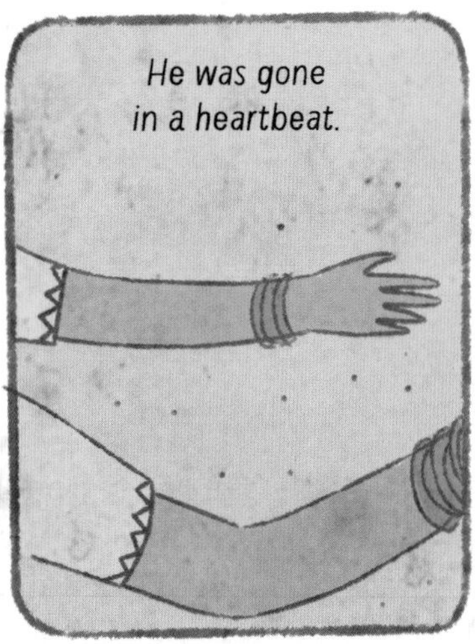
He was gone in a heartbeat.

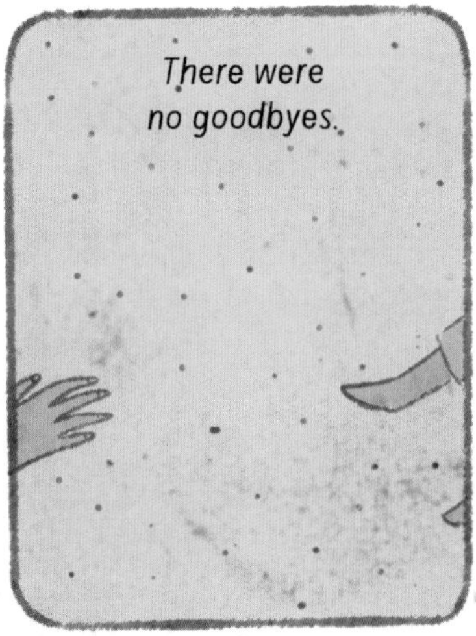
There were no goodbyes.

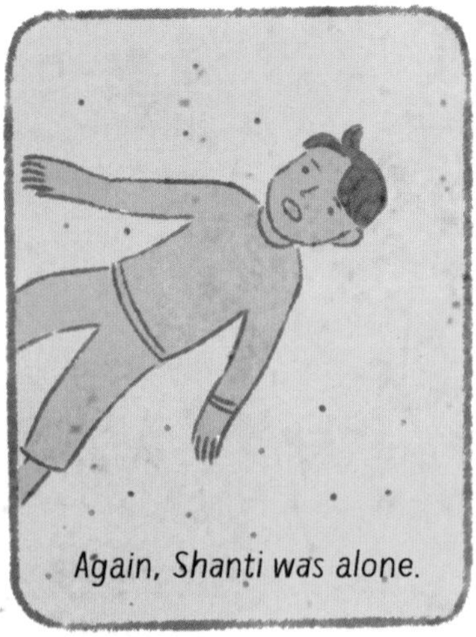
Again, Shanti was alone.

Seasons changed and life moved on.

Shanti had to find the strength to pick herself back up.

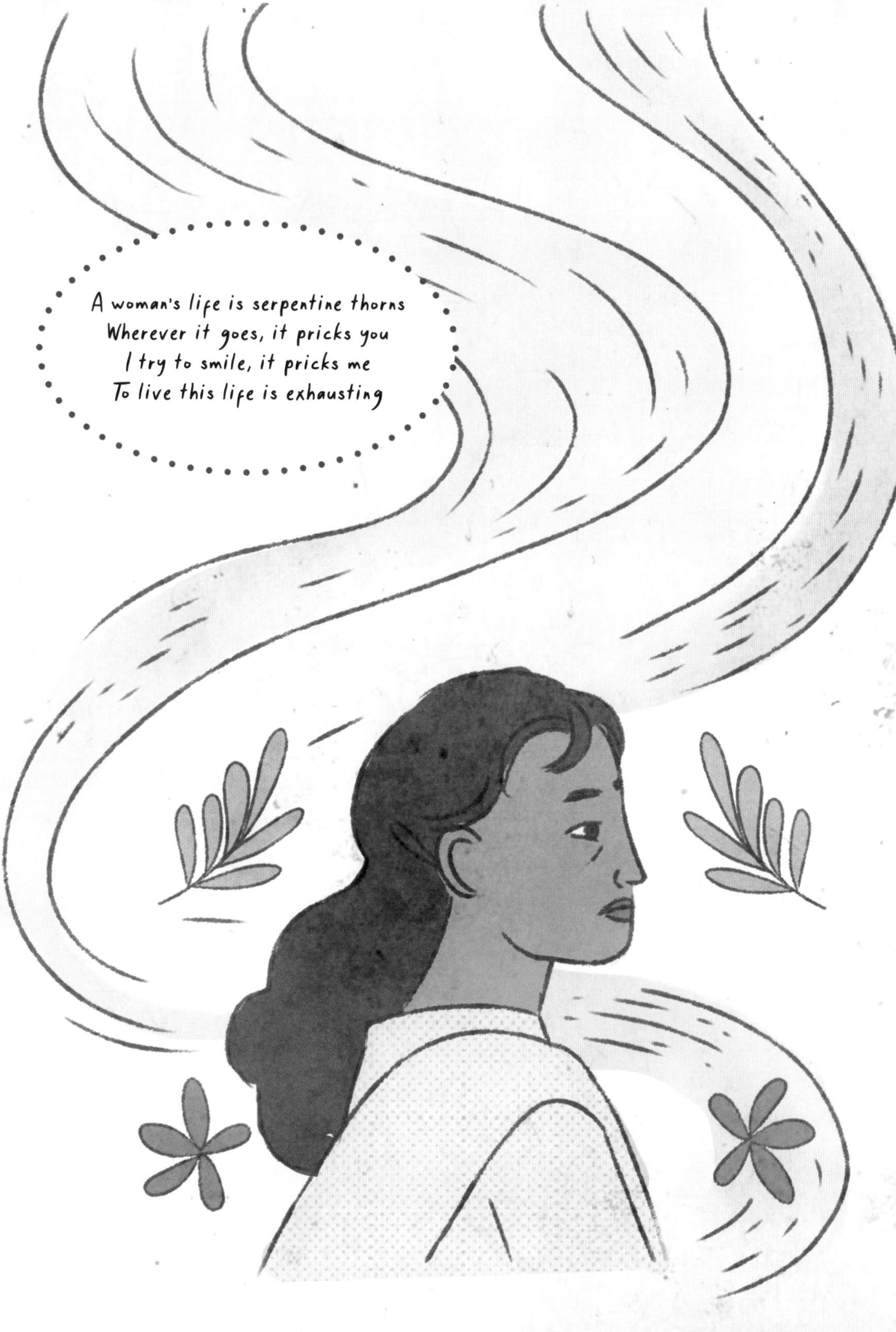
A woman's life is serpentine thorns
Wherever it goes, it pricks you
I try to smile, it pricks me
To live this life is exhausting

In Kathmandu, Shanti worked at a law firm for a while. There, she met many women who'd been exploited because they didn't know their rights.

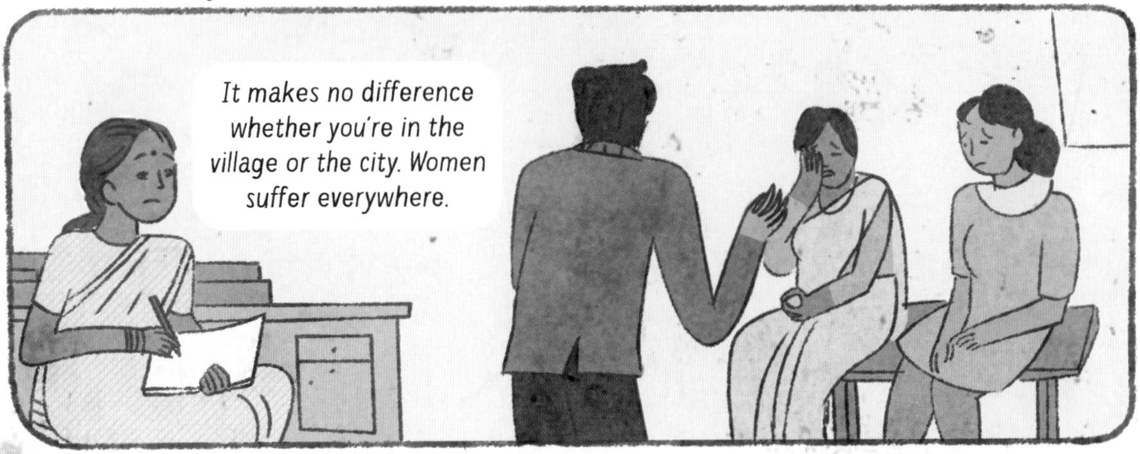
It makes no difference whether you're in the village or the city. Women suffer everywhere.

This is how she found her life's mission. In 1988, she opened the Srijana Bikash Kendra to empower rural women and youth.

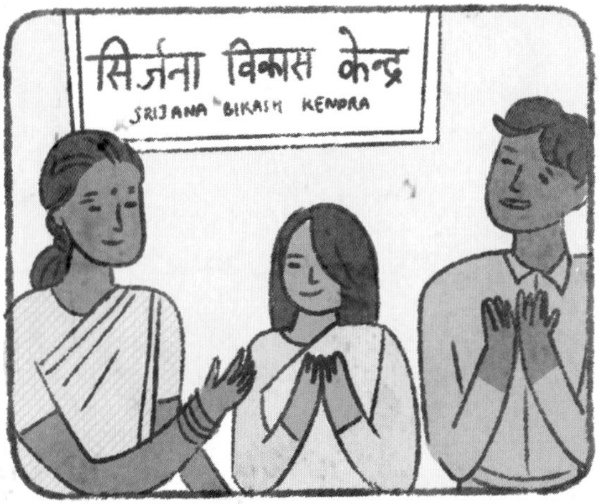
सिर्जना विकास केन्द्र
SRIJANA BIKASH KENDRA

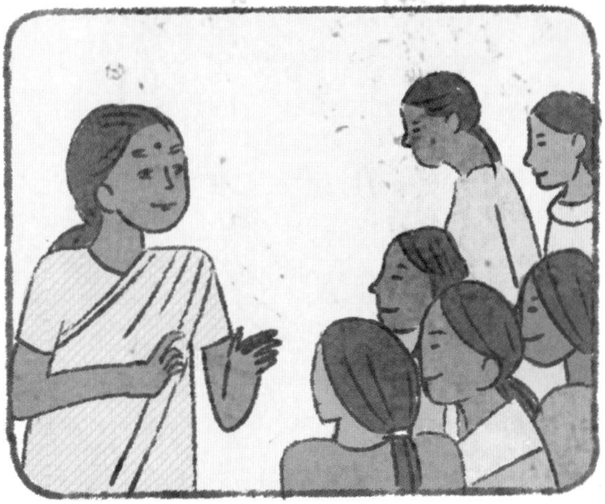

She even started writing again.

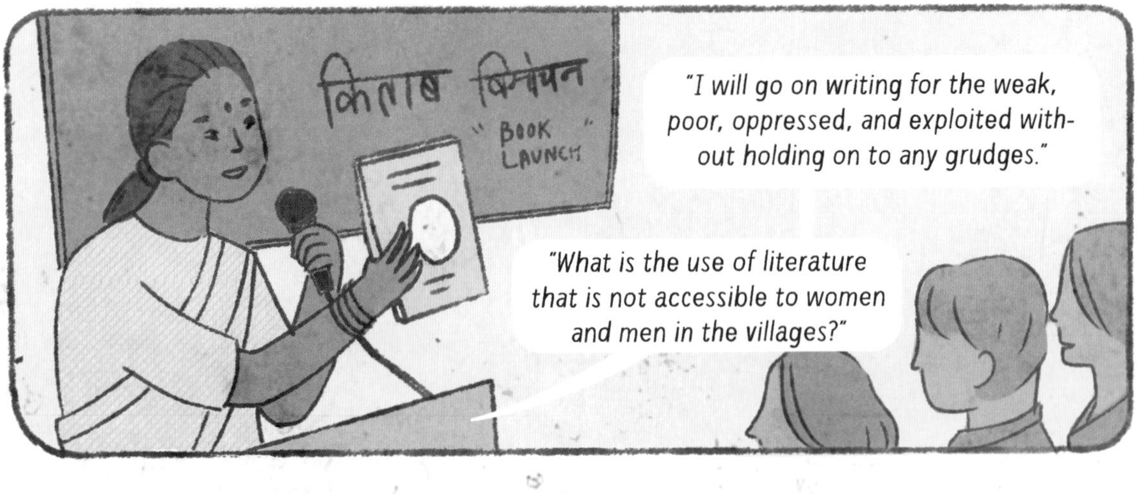
"BOOK LAUNCH"
"I will go on writing for the weak, poor, oppressed, and exploited without holding on to any grudges."
"What is the use of literature that is not accessible to women and men in the villages?"

She didn't need to write in secret anymore. Her work would be published through the Srijana Bikash Kendra and used in grassroots training programs with women and youth.

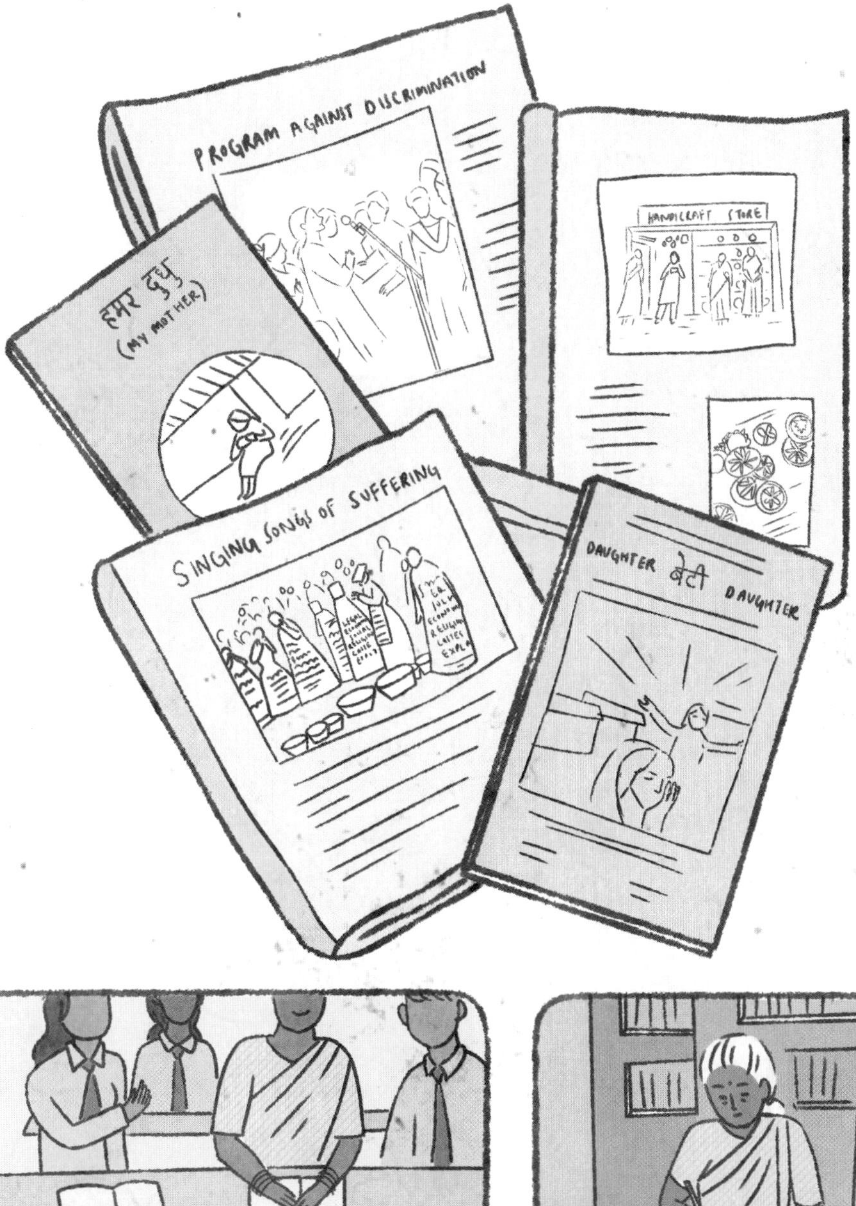
PROGRAM AGAINST DISCRIMINATION
HANDICRAFT STORE
(MY MOTHER)
SINGING SONGS OF SUFFERING
DAUGHTER बेटी DAUGHTER

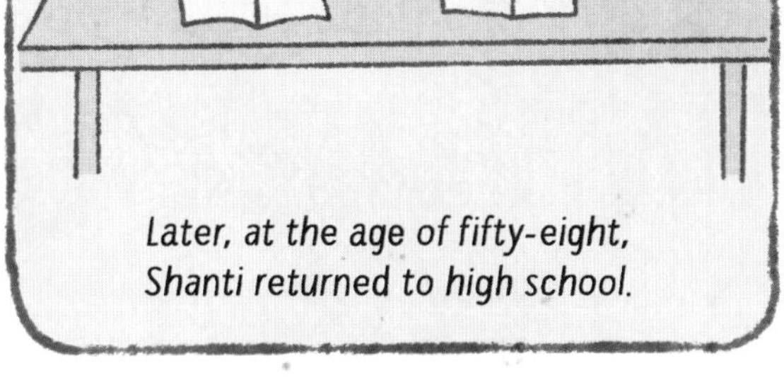
Later, at the age of fifty-eight, Shanti returned to high school.

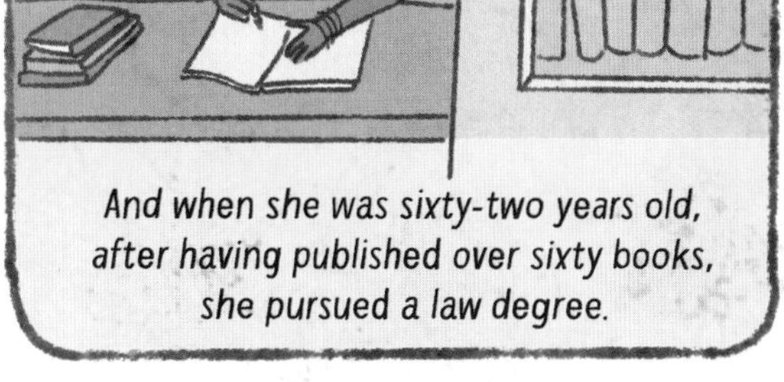
And when she was sixty-two years old, after having published over sixty books, she pursued a law degree.

The girl who was once deemed unpeaceful for speaking her mind ended up finding a strong, loud voice uniquely her own.

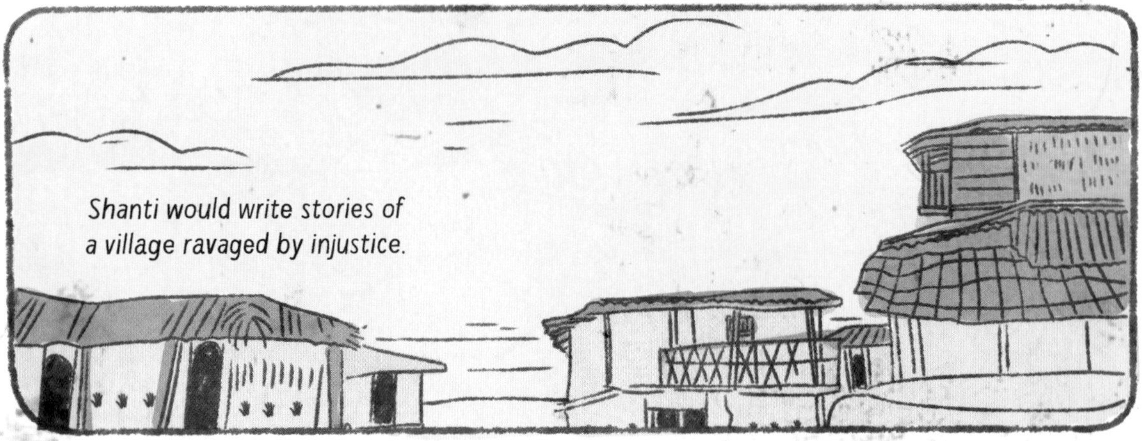
Shanti would write stories of a village ravaged by injustice.

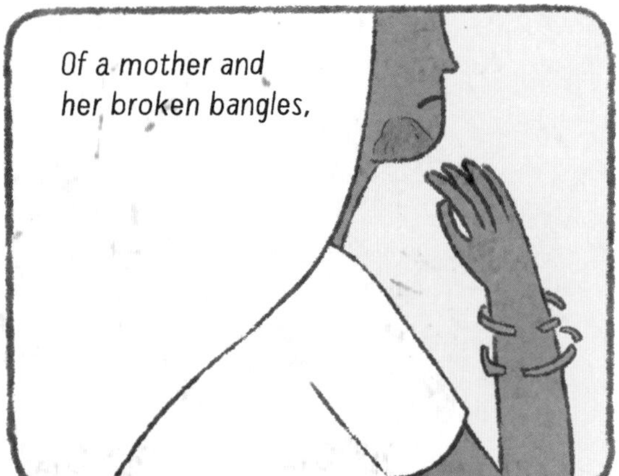
Of a mother and her broken bangles,

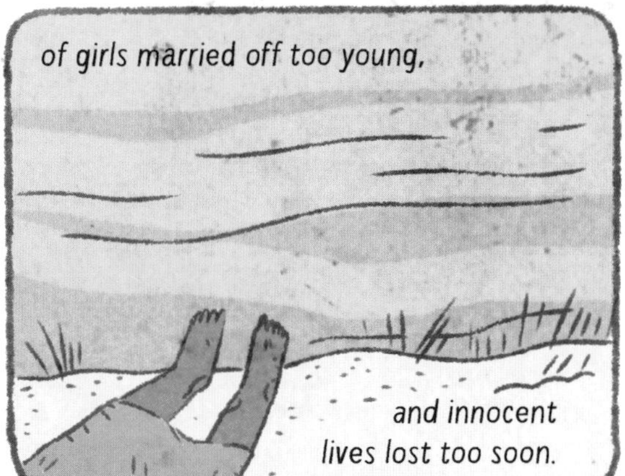
of girls married off too young,
and innocent lives lost too soon.

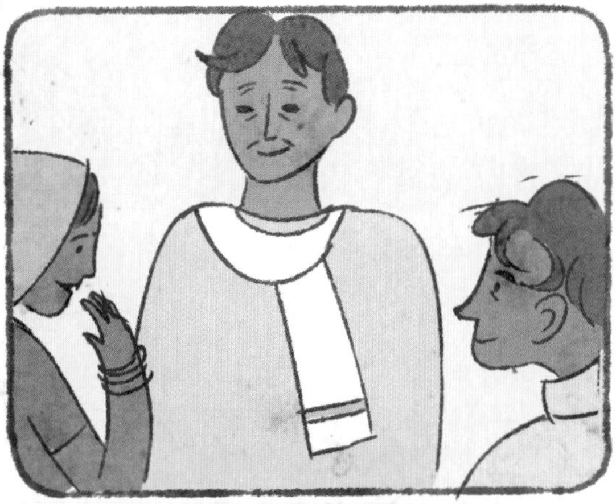

Shanti's stories are about people

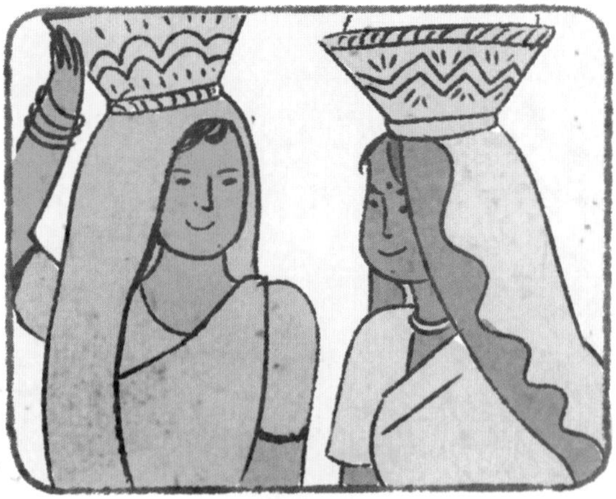

and about women.

Shanti's stories are about her.

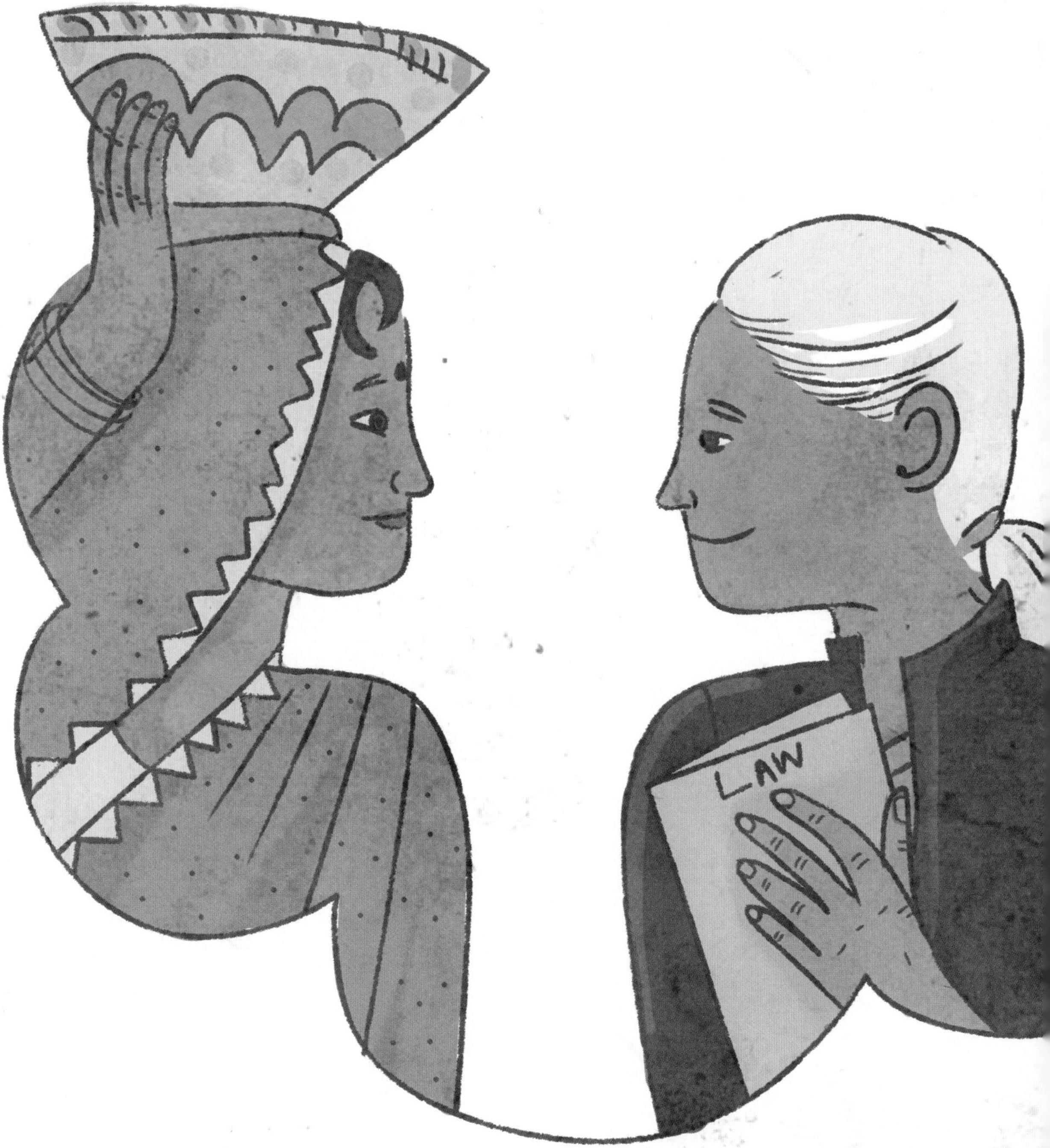
LAW

Acknowledgments

Shanti Chaudhary
Geeta Chaudhary and family
Rajendra Chaudhary
Amruta Patil
Muna Gurung
Nhooja Tuladhar
Madan Puraskar Pustakalaya
and my family

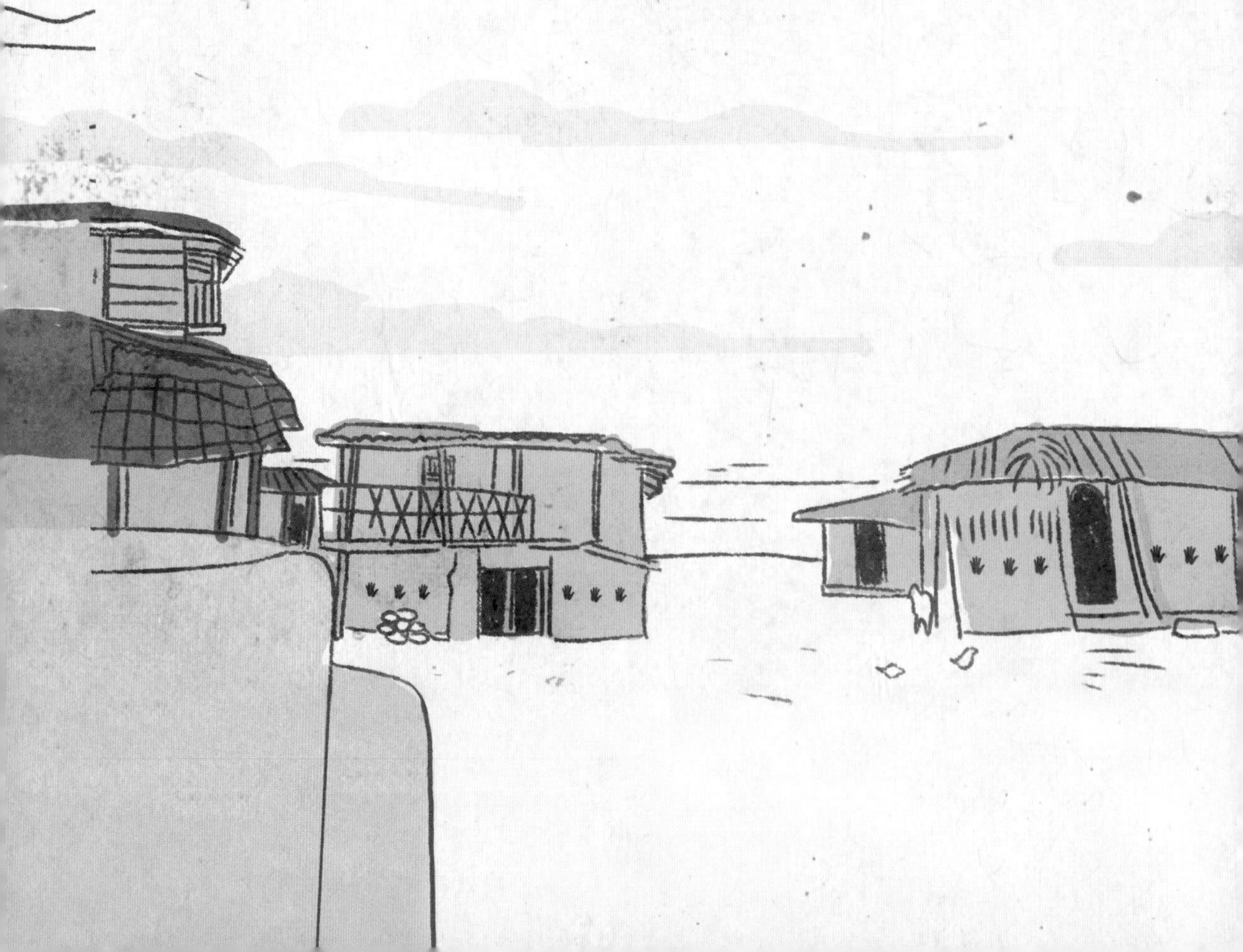

THE ANARCHIST CHOLAS

A SHORT STORY ABOUT A BOLIVIAN FEMALE LIBERTARIAN TRADE UNION

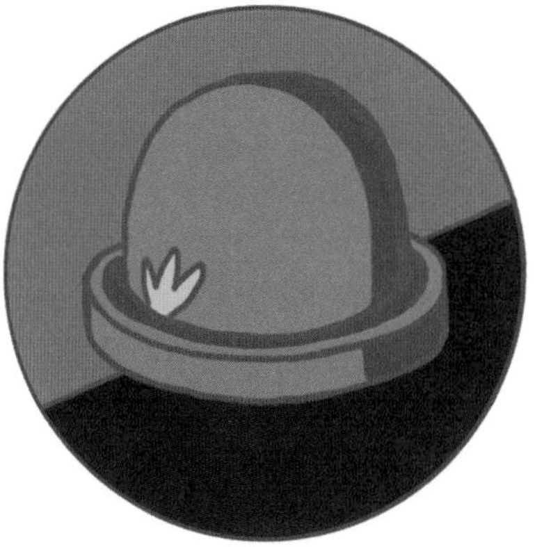

Story and Art: Vanessa Peñuela and César Vargas
Drawing Assistant: Jeisson Cortés
Translation: Felipe Pachón

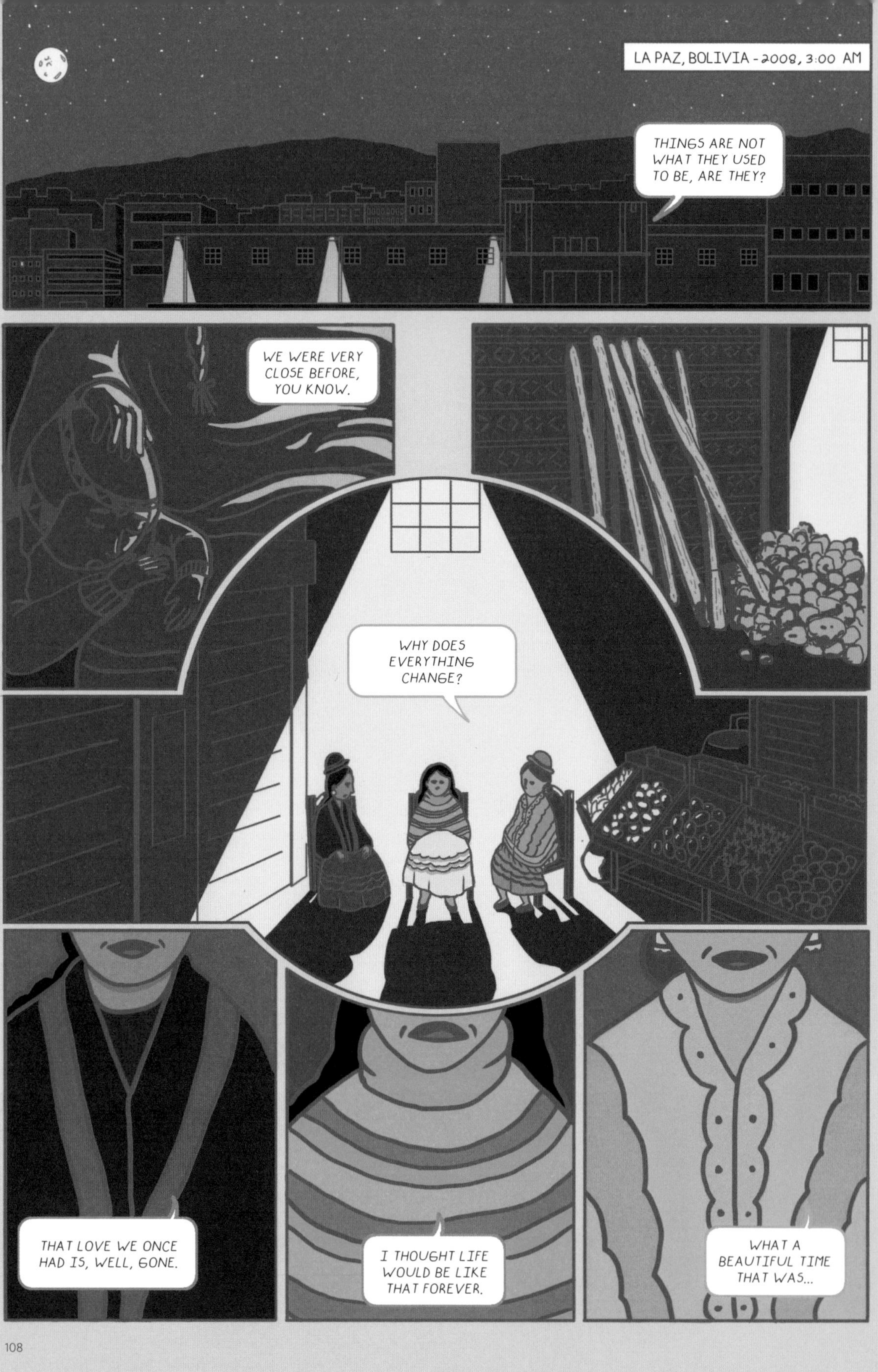

LA PAZ, BOLIVIA - 2008, 3:00 AM
THINGS ARE NOT WHAT THEY USED TO BE, ARE THEY?
WE WERE VERY CLOSE BEFORE, YOU KNOW.
WHY DOES EVERYTHING CHANGE?
THAT LOVE WE ONCE HAD IS, WELL, GONE.
I THOUGHT LIFE WOULD BE LIKE THAT FOREVER.
WHAT A BEAUTIFUL TIME THAT WAS...

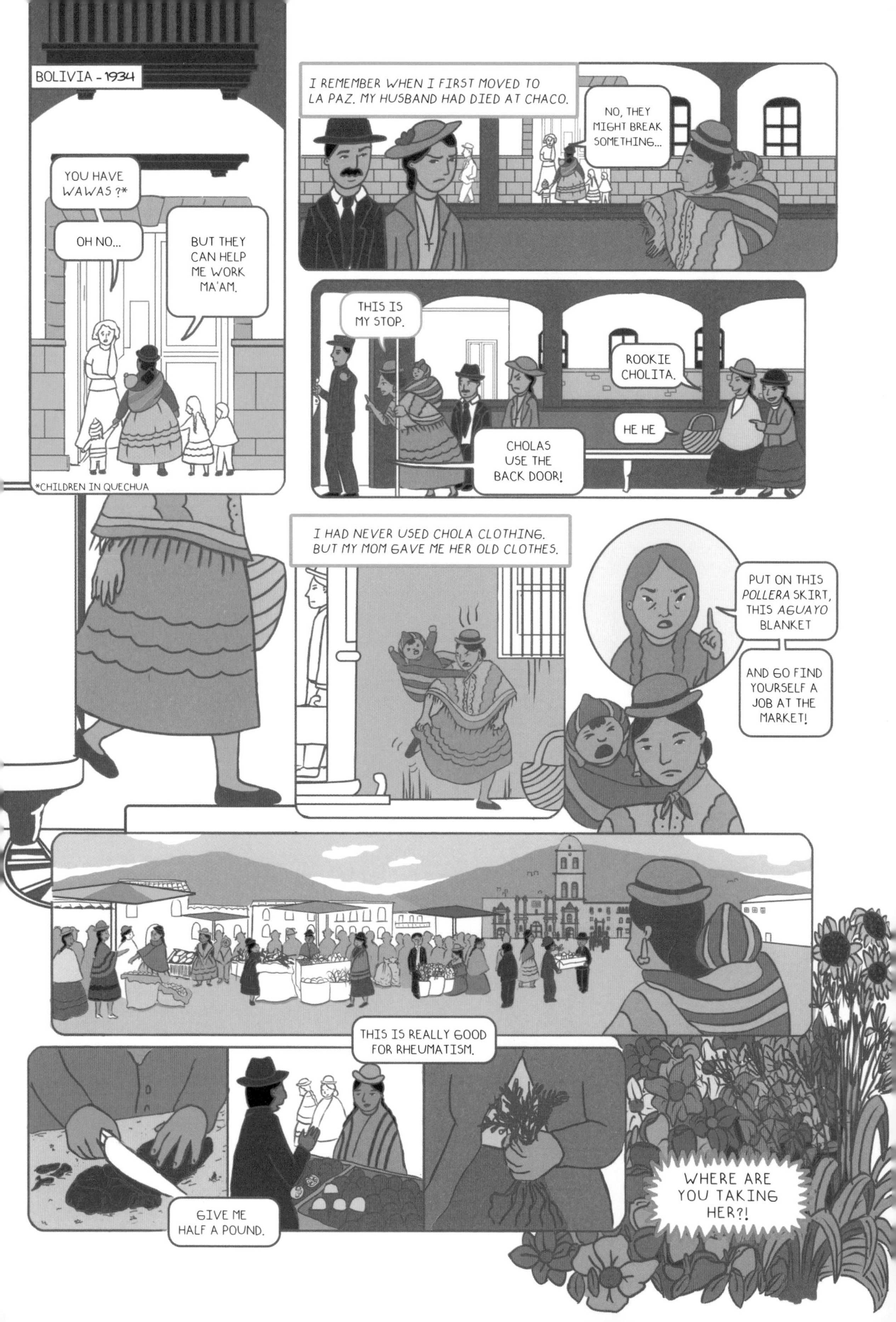
BOLIVIA - 1934
YOU HAVE WAWAS ?*
OH NO...
BUT THEY CAN HELP ME WORK MA'AM.
*CHILDREN IN QUECHUA
I REMEMBER WHEN I FIRST MOVED TO LA PAZ. MY HUSBAND HAD DIED AT CHACO.
NO, THEY MIGHT BREAK SOMETHING...
THIS IS MY STOP.
ROOKIE CHOLITA.
HE HE
CHOLAS USE THE BACK DOOR!
I HAD NEVER USED CHOLA CLOTHING. BUT MY MOM GAVE ME HER OLD CLOTHES.
PUT ON THIS POLLERA SKIRT, THIS AGUAYO BLANKET
AND GO FIND YOURSELF A JOB AT THE MARKET!
THIS IS REALLY GOOD FOR RHEUMATISM.
GIVE ME HALF A POUND.
WHERE ARE YOU TAKING HER?!

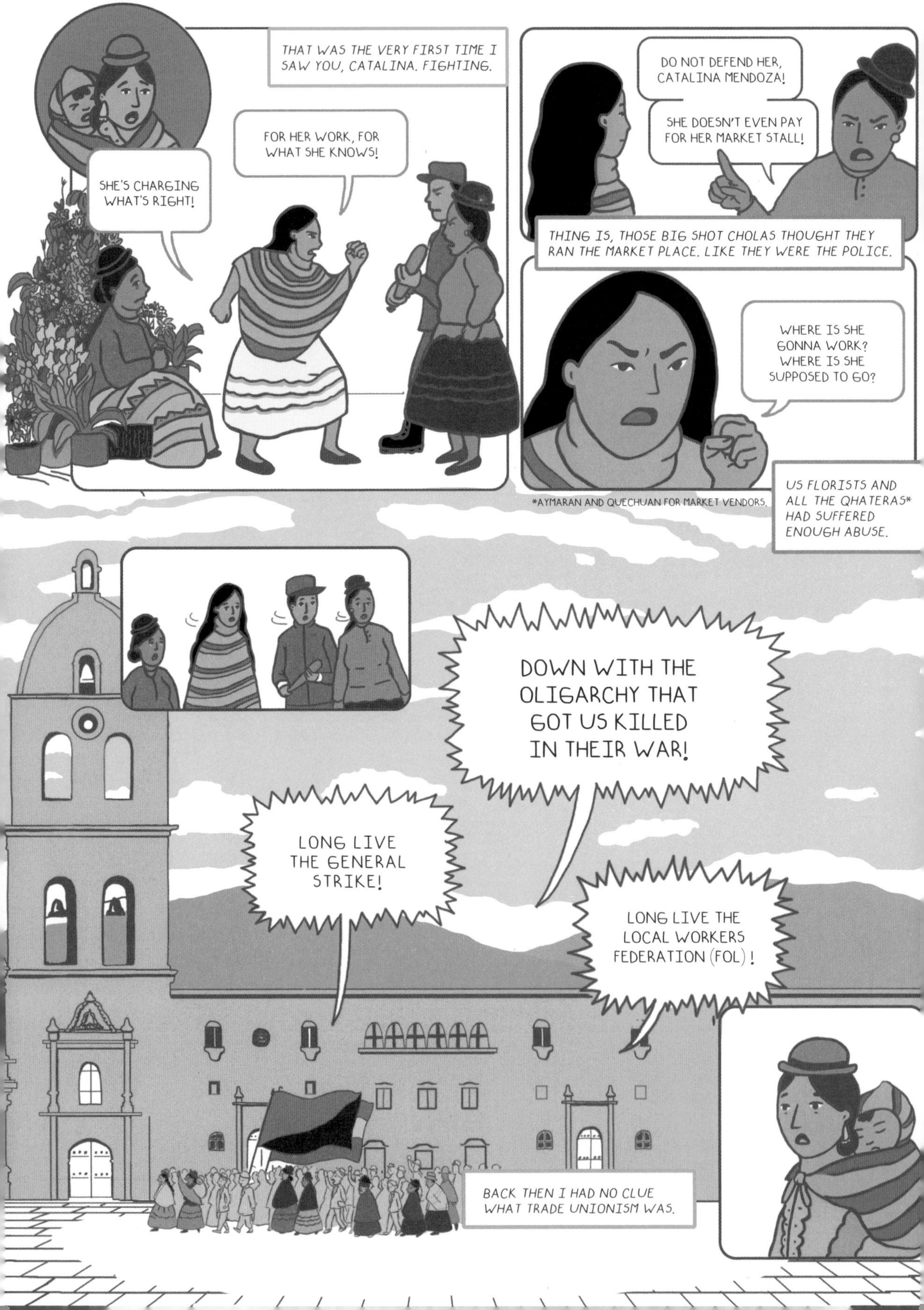
THAT WAS THE VERY FIRST TIME I SAW YOU, CATALINA. FIGHTING.
SHE'S CHARGING WHAT'S RIGHT!
FOR HER WORK, FOR WHAT SHE KNOWS!
DO NOT DEFEND HER, CATALINA MENDOZA!
SHE DOESN'T EVEN PAY FOR HER MARKET STALL!
THING IS, THOSE BIG SHOT CHOLAS THOUGHT THEY RAN THE MARKET PLACE. LIKE THEY WERE THE POLICE.
WHERE IS SHE GONNA WORK? WHERE IS SHE SUPPOSED TO GO?
US FLORISTS AND ALL THE QHATERAS* HAD SUFFERED ENOUGH ABUSE.
*AYMARAN AND QUECHUAN FOR MARKET VENDORS.
DOWN WITH THE OLIGARCHY THAT GOT US KILLED IN THEIR WAR!
LONG LIVE THE GENERAL STRIKE!
LONG LIVE THE LOCAL WORKERS FEDERATION (FOL)!
BACK THEN I HAD NO CLUE WHAT TRADE UNIONISM WAS.

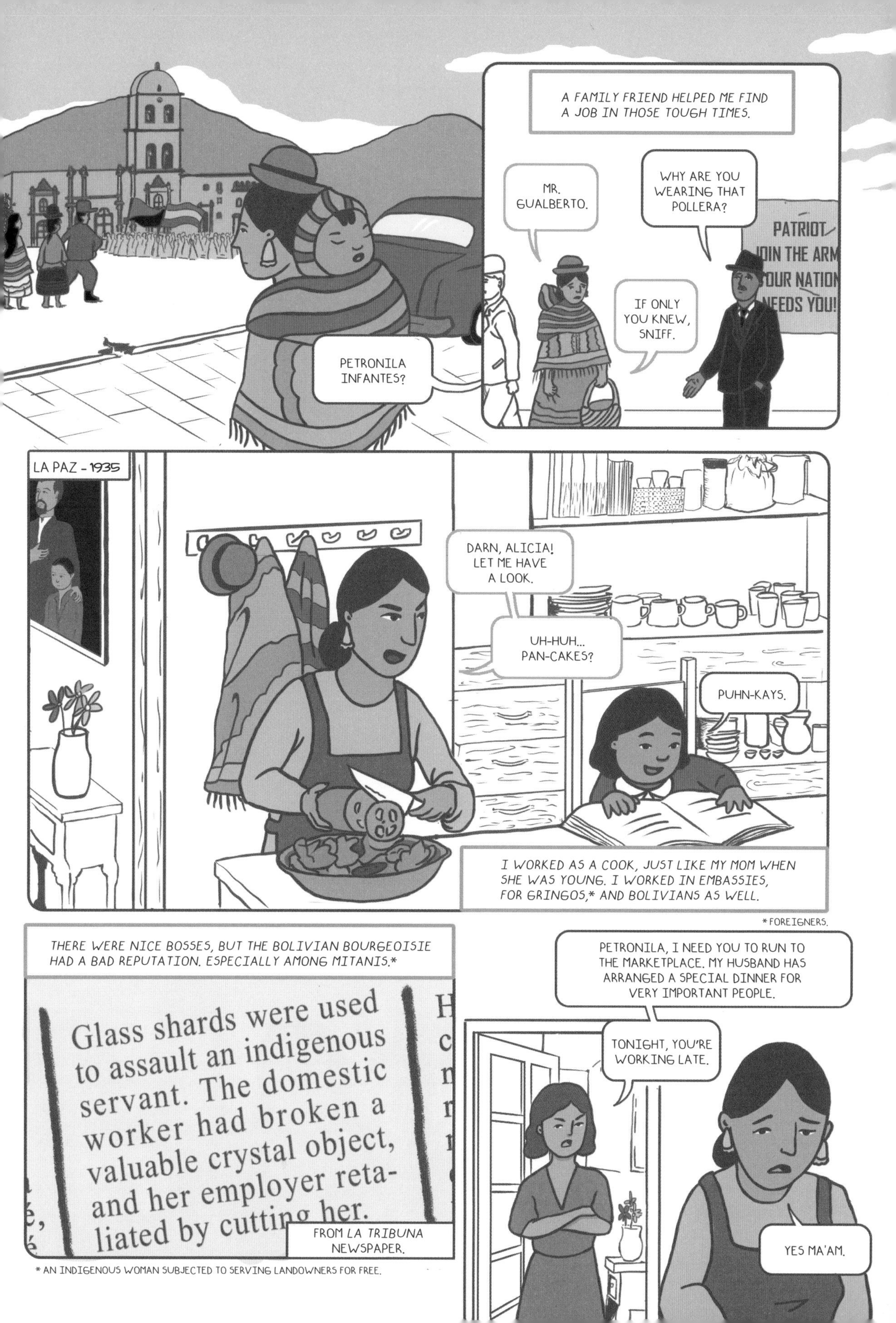
A FAMILY FRIEND HELPED ME FIND A JOB IN THOSE TOUGH TIMES.
PETRONILA INFANTES?
MR. GUALBERTO.
WHY ARE YOU WEARING THAT POLLERA?
IF ONLY YOU KNEW, SNIFF.
PATRIOT
JOIN THE ARM
OUR NATION
NEEDS YOU!
LA PAZ - 1935
DARN, ALICIA! LET ME HAVE A LOOK.
UH-HUH... PAN-CAKES?
PUHN-KAYS.
I WORKED AS A COOK, JUST LIKE MY MOM WHEN SHE WAS YOUNG. I WORKED IN EMBASSIES, FOR GRINGOS,* AND BOLIVIANS AS WELL.
* FOREIGNERS.
THERE WERE NICE BOSSES, BUT THE BOLIVIAN BOURGEOISIE HAD A BAD REPUTATION. ESPECIALLY AMONG MITANIS.*
Glass shards were used to assault an indigenous servant. The domestic worker had broken a valuable crystal object, and her employer reta-liated by cutting her.
FROM LA TRIBUNA NEWSPAPER.
* AN INDIGENOUS WOMAN SUBJECTED TO SERVING LANDOWNERS FOR FREE.
PETRONILA, I NEED YOU TO RUN TO THE MARKETPLACE. MY HUSBAND HAS ARRANGED A SPECIAL DINNER FOR VERY IMPORTANT PEOPLE.
TONIGHT, YOU'RE WORKING LATE.
YES MA'AM.

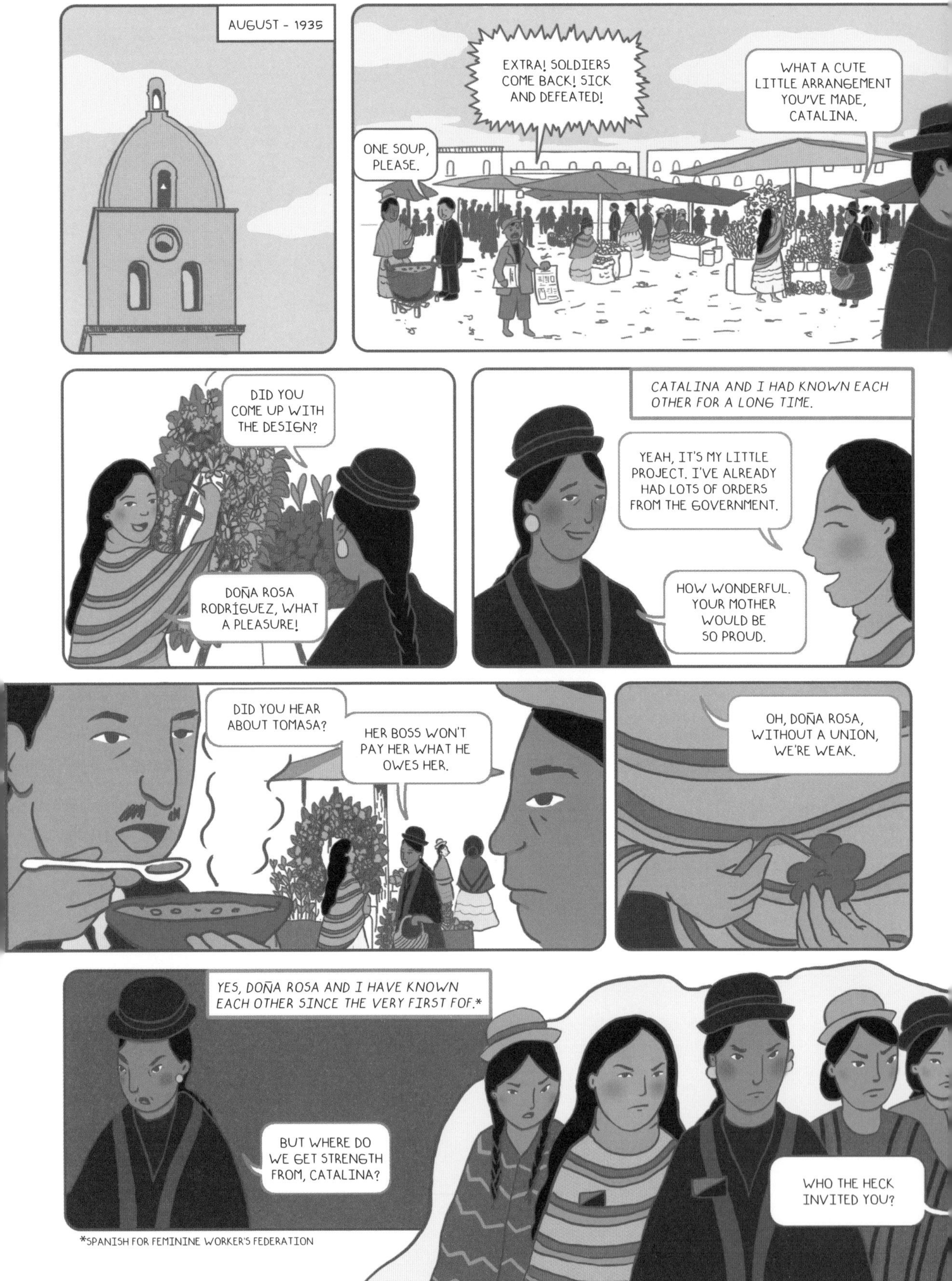
AUGUST - 1935
EXTRA! SOLDIERS COME BACK! SICK AND DEFEATED!
ONE SOUP, PLEASE.
WHAT A CUTE LITTLE ARRANGEMENT YOU'VE MADE, CATALINA.
DID YOU COME UP WITH THE DESIGN?
DOÑA ROSA RODRÍGUEZ, WHAT A PLEASURE!
CATALINA AND I HAD KNOWN EACH OTHER FOR A LONG TIME.
YEAH, IT'S MY LITTLE PROJECT. I'VE ALREADY HAD LOTS OF ORDERS FROM THE GOVERNMENT.
HOW WONDERFUL. YOUR MOTHER WOULD BE SO PROUD.
DID YOU HEAR ABOUT TOMASA?
HER BOSS WON'T PAY HER WHAT HE OWES HER.
OH, DOÑA ROSA, WITHOUT A UNION, WE'RE WEAK.
YES, DOÑA ROSA AND I HAVE KNOWN EACH OTHER SINCE THE VERY FIRST FOF.*
BUT WHERE DO WE GET STRENGTH FROM, CATALINA?
WHO THE HECK INVITED YOU?
*SPANISH FOR FEMININE WORKER'S FEDERATION

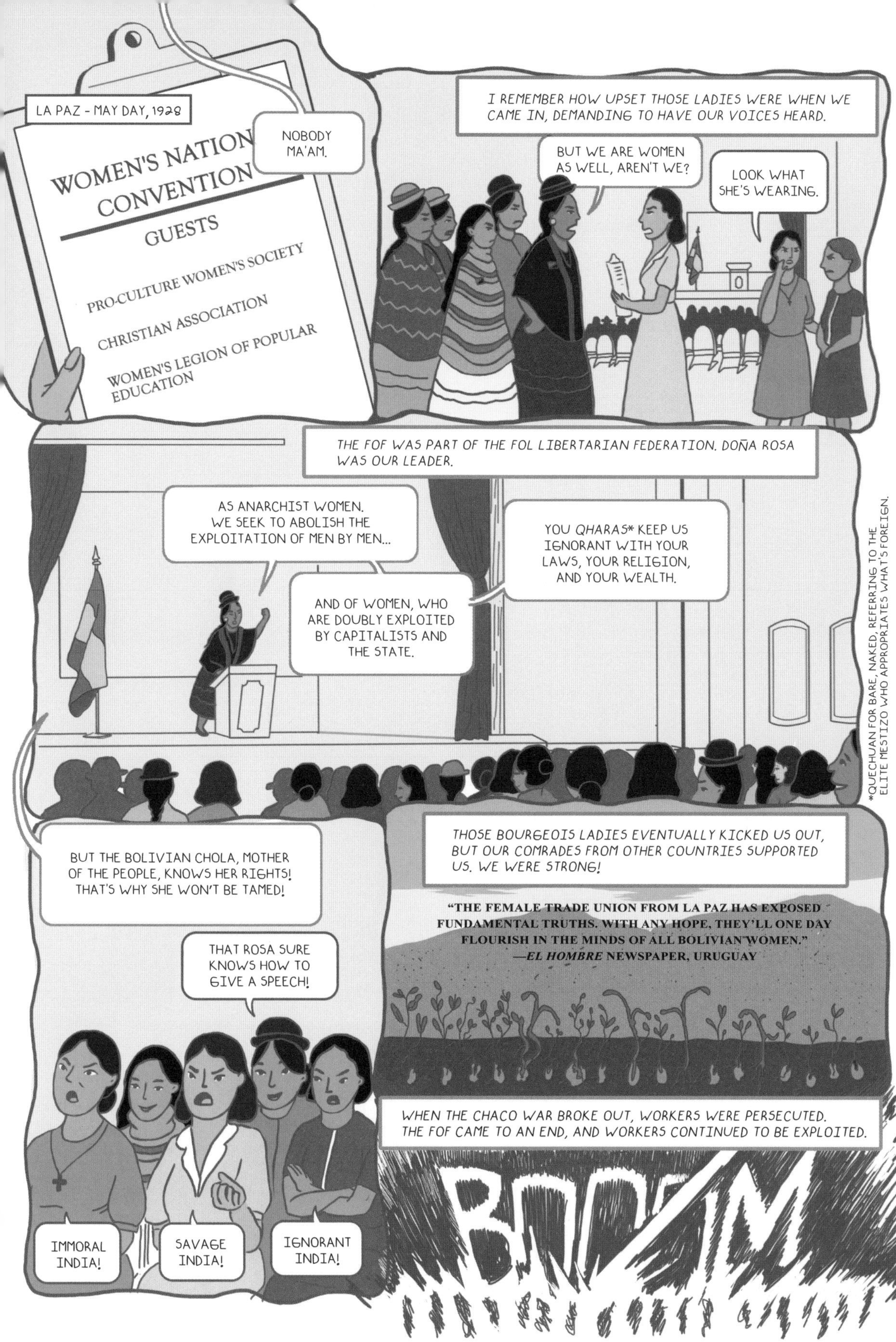
LA PAZ - MAY DAY, 1928
WOMEN'S NATION
CONVENTION
GUESTS
PRO-CULTURE WOMEN'S SOCIETY
CHRISTIAN ASSOCIATION
WOMEN'S LEGION OF POPULAR EDUCATION
NOBODY MA'AM.
I REMEMBER HOW UPSET THOSE LADIES WERE WHEN WE CAME IN, DEMANDING TO HAVE OUR VOICES HEARD.
BUT WE ARE WOMEN AS WELL, AREN'T WE?
LOOK WHAT SHE'S WEARING.
THE FOF WAS PART OF THE FOL LIBERTARIAN FEDERATION. DOÑA ROSA WAS OUR LEADER.
AS ANARCHIST WOMEN. WE SEEK TO ABOLISH THE EXPLOITATION OF MEN BY MEN...
AND OF WOMEN, WHO ARE DOUBLY EXPLOITED BY CAPITALISTS AND THE STATE.
YOU QHARAS* KEEP US IGNORANT WITH YOUR LAWS, YOUR RELIGION, AND YOUR WEALTH.
*QUECHUAN FOR BARE, NAKED, REFERRING TO THE ELITE MESTIZO WHO APPROPRIATES WHAT'S FOREIGN.
BUT THE BOLIVIAN CHOLA, MOTHER OF THE PEOPLE, KNOWS HER RIGHTS! THAT'S WHY SHE WON'T BE TAMED!
THAT ROSA SURE KNOWS HOW TO GIVE A SPEECH!
IMMORAL INDIA!
SAVAGE INDIA!
IGNORANT INDIA!
THOSE BOURGEOIS LADIES EVENTUALLY KICKED US OUT, BUT OUR COMRADES FROM OTHER COUNTRIES SUPPORTED US. WE WERE STRONG!
"THE FEMALE TRADE UNION FROM LA PAZ HAS EXPOSED FUNDAMENTAL TRUTHS. WITH ANY HOPE, THEY'LL ONE DAY FLOURISH IN THE MINDS OF ALL BOLIVIAN WOMEN."
—EL HOMBRE NEWSPAPER, URUGUAY
WHEN THE CHACO WAR BROKE OUT, WORKERS WERE PERSECUTED. THE FOF CAME TO AN END, AND WORKERS CONTINUED TO BE EXPLOITED.
BOOM

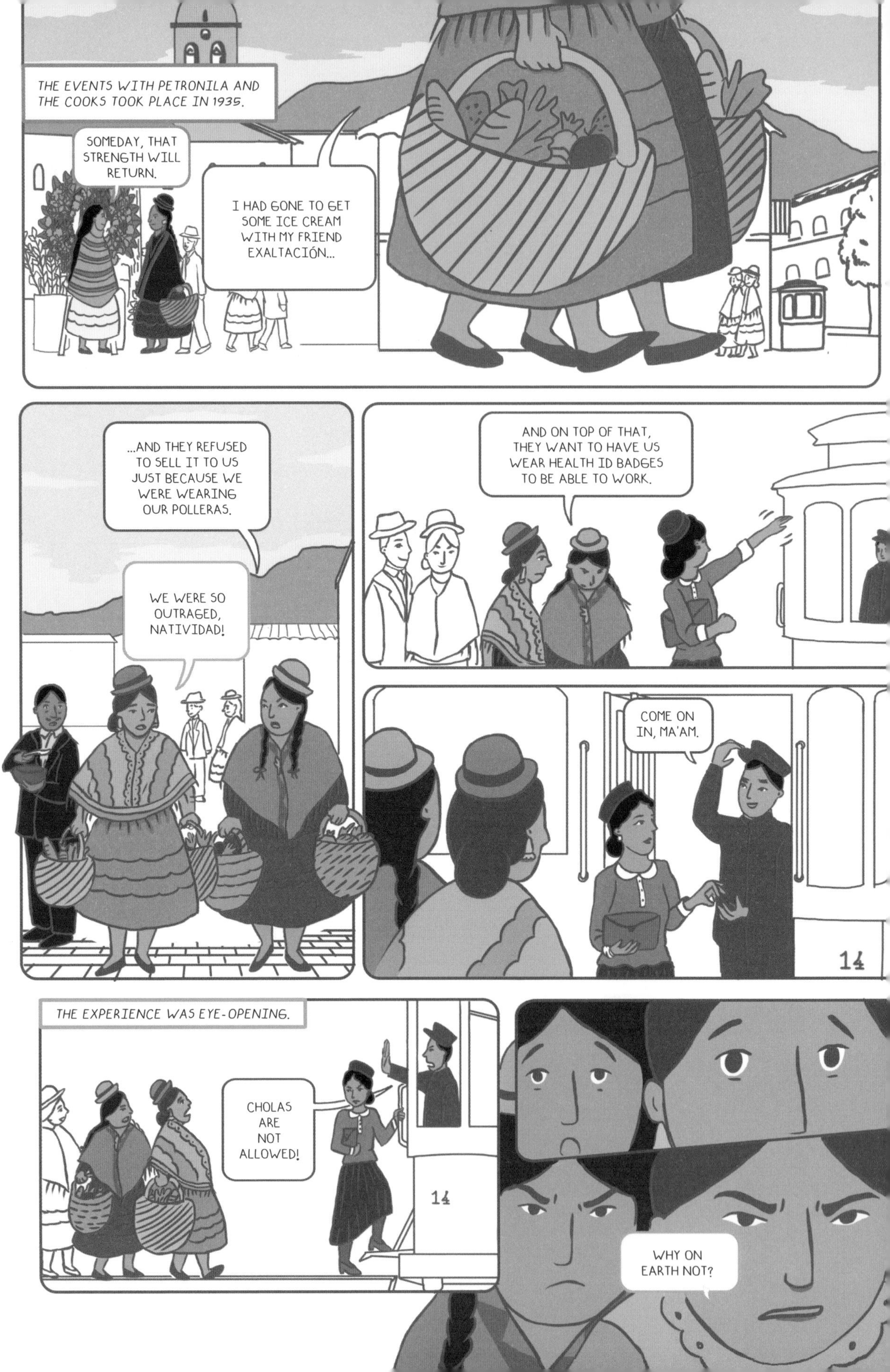
THE EVENTS WITH PETRONILA AND THE COOKS TOOK PLACE IN 1935.
SOMEDAY, THAT STRENGTH WILL RETURN.
I HAD GONE TO GET SOME ICE CREAM WITH MY FRIEND EXALTACIÓN...
...AND THEY REFUSED TO SELL IT TO US JUST BECAUSE WE WERE WEARING OUR POLLERAS.
WE WERE SO OUTRAGED, NATIVIDAD!
AND ON TOP OF THAT, THEY WANT TO HAVE US WEAR HEALTH ID BADGES TO BE ABLE TO WORK.
COME ON IN, MA'AM.
14
THE EXPERIENCE WAS EYE-OPENING.
CHOLAS ARE NOT ALLOWED!
14
WHY ON EARTH NOT?

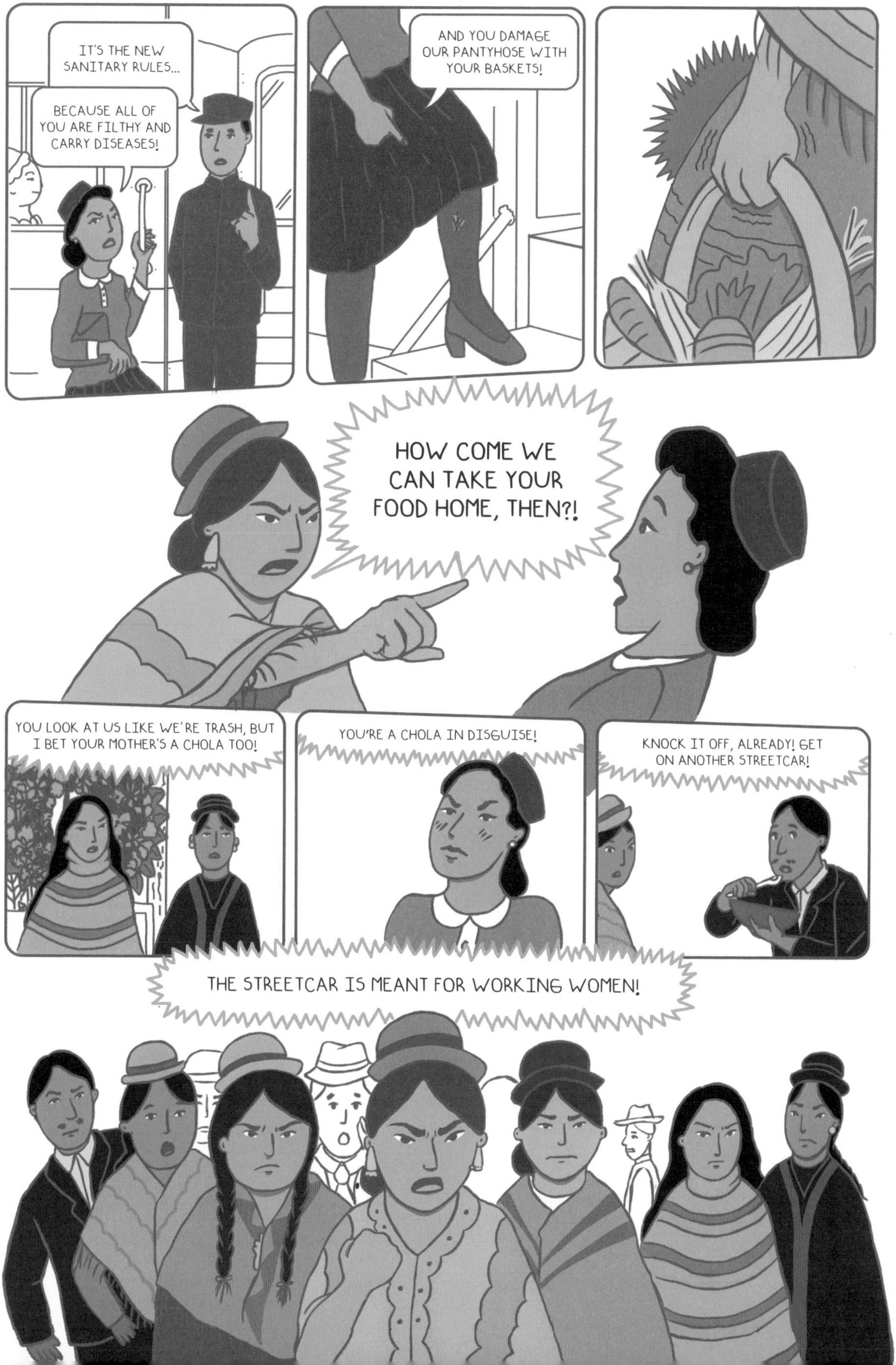

IT'S THE NEW SANITARY RULES...
BECAUSE ALL OF YOU ARE FILTHY AND CARRY DISEASES!
AND YOU DAMAGE OUR PANTYHOSE WITH YOUR BASKETS!
HOW COME WE CAN TAKE YOUR FOOD HOME, THEN?!
YOU LOOK AT US LIKE WE'RE TRASH, BUT I BET YOUR MOTHER'S A CHOLA TOO!
YOU'RE A CHOLA IN DISGUISE!
KNOCK IT OFF, ALREADY! GET ON ANOTHER STREETCAR!
THE STREETCAR IS MEANT FOR WORKING WOMEN!

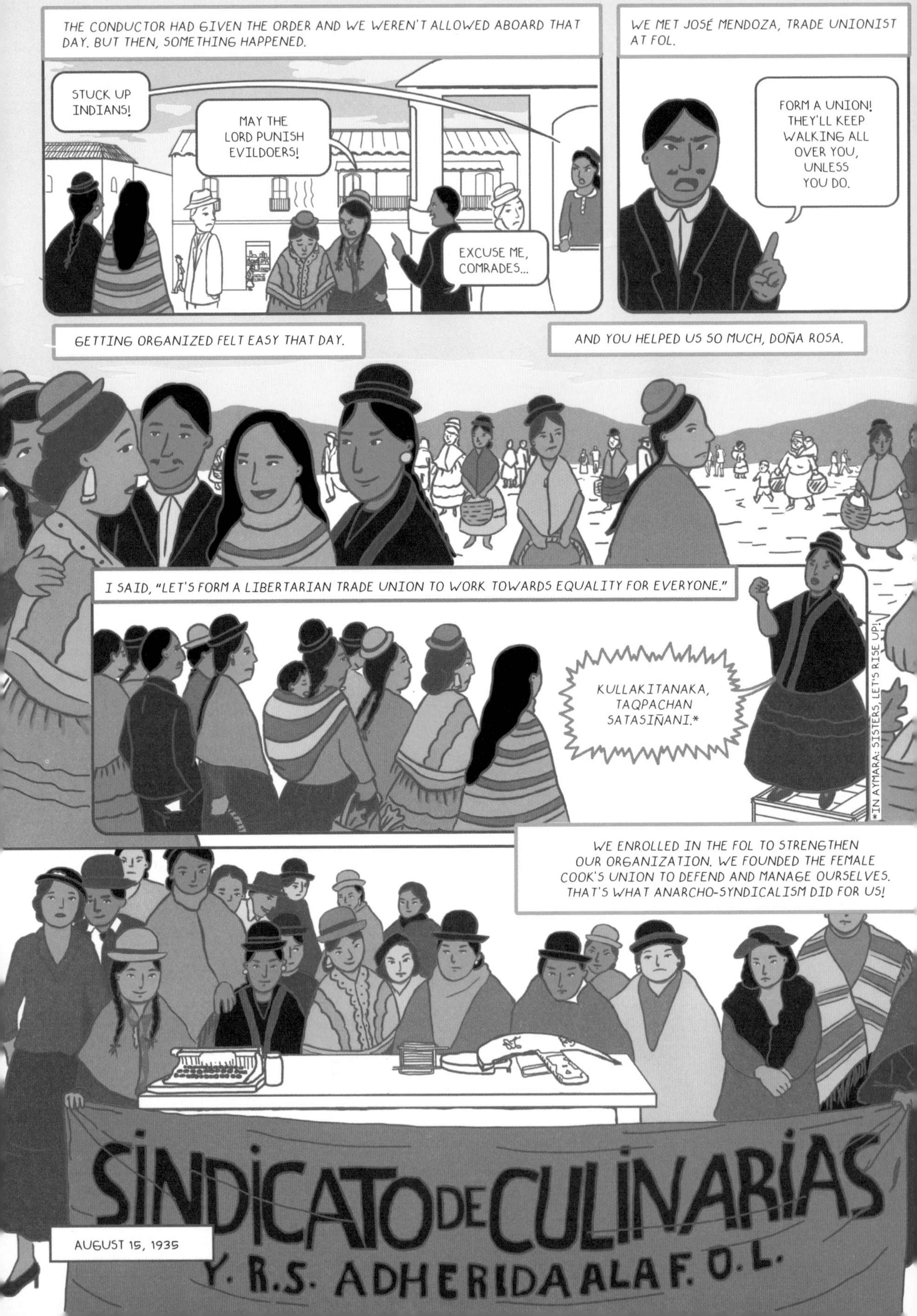

THE CONDUCTOR HAD GIVEN THE ORDER AND WE WEREN'T ALLOWED ABOARD THAT DAY. BUT THEN, SOMETHING HAPPENED.
STUCK UP INDIANS!
MAY THE LORD PUNISH EVILDOERS!
EXCUSE ME, COMRADES...
WE MET JOSÉ MENDOZA, TRADE UNIONIST AT FOL.
FORM A UNION! THEY'LL KEEP WALKING ALL OVER YOU, UNLESS YOU DO.
GETTING ORGANIZED FELT EASY THAT DAY.
AND YOU HELPED US SO MUCH, DOÑA ROSA.
I SAID, "LET'S FORM A LIBERTARIAN TRADE UNION TO WORK TOWARDS EQUALITY FOR EVERYONE."
KULLAKITANAKA, TAQPACHAN SATASIÑANI.*
*IN AYMARA: SISTERS, LET'S RISE UP!
WE ENROLLED IN THE FOL TO STRENGTHEN OUR ORGANIZATION. WE FOUNDED THE FEMALE COOK'S UNION TO DEFEND AND MANAGE OURSELVES. THAT'S WHAT ANARCHO-SYNDICALISM DID FOR US!
SINDICATO DE CULINARIAS
Y. R.S. ADHERIDA A LA F.O.L.
AUGUST 15, 1935

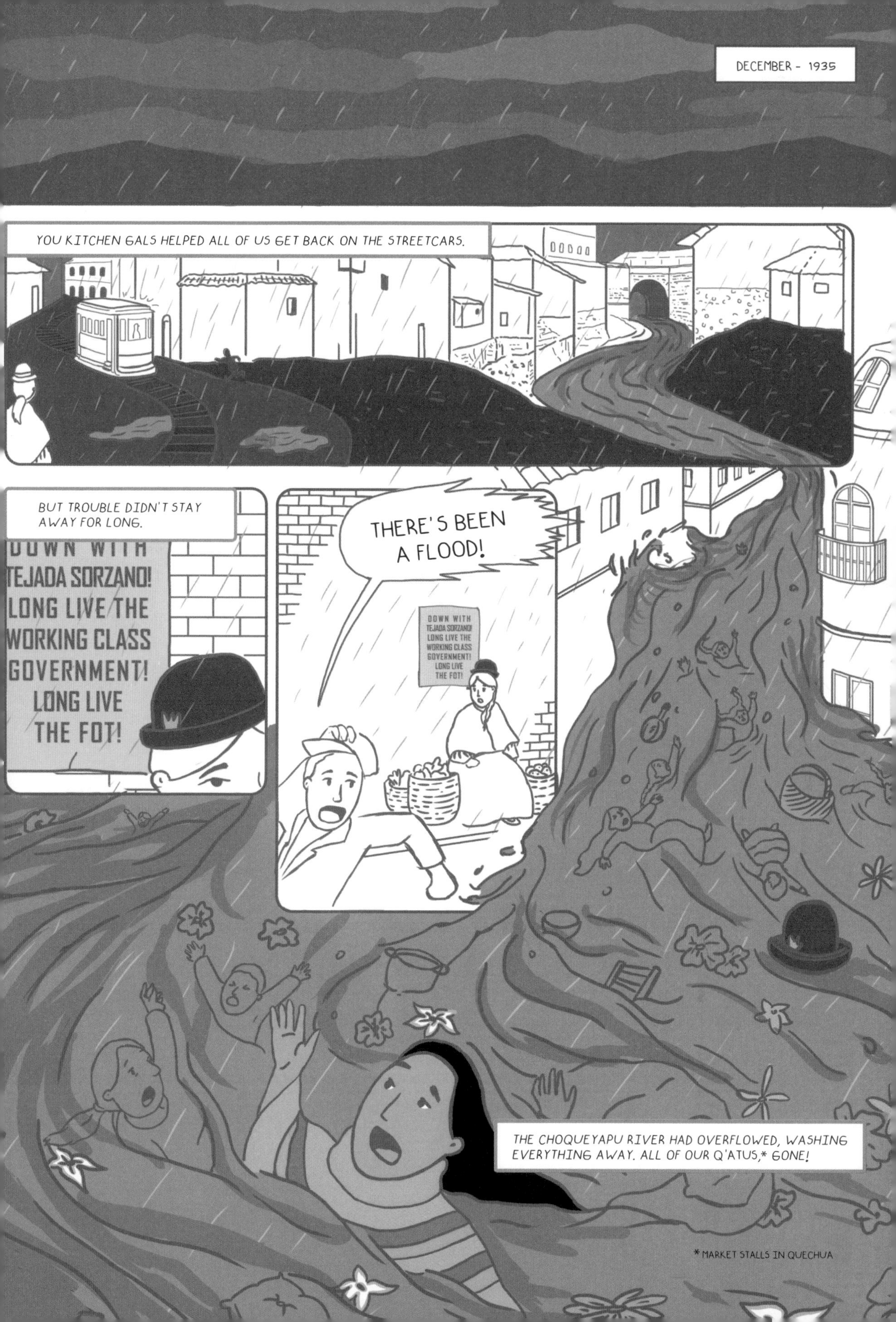
DECEMBER - 1935
YOU KITCHEN GALS HELPED ALL OF US GET BACK ON THE STREETCARS.
BUT TROUBLE DIDN'T STAY AWAY FOR LONG.
DOWN WITH TEJADA SORZANO! LONG LIVE THE WORKING CLASS GOVERNMENT! LONG LIVE THE FOT!
THERE'S BEEN A FLOOD!
DOWN WITH TEJADA SORZANO! LONG LIVE THE WORKING CLASS GOVERNMENT! LONG LIVE THE FOT!
THE CHOQUEYAPU RIVER HAD OVERFLOWED, WASHING EVERYTHING AWAY. ALL OF OUR Q'ATUS,* GONE!
* MARKET STALLS IN QUECHUA

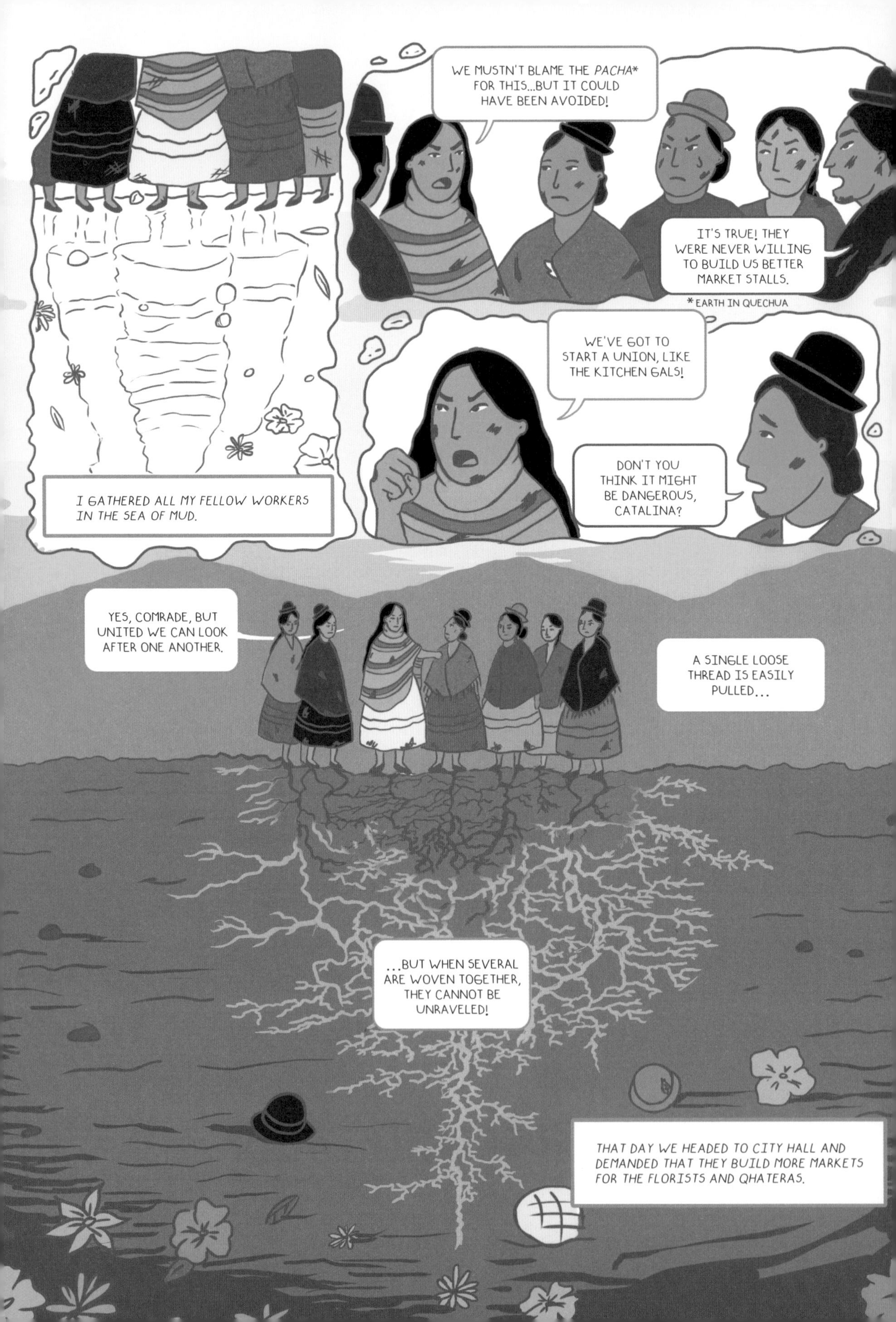
WE MUSTN'T BLAME THE *PACHA** FOR THIS...BUT IT COULD HAVE BEEN AVOIDED!
IT'S TRUE! THEY WERE NEVER WILLING TO BUILD US BETTER MARKET STALLS.
*EARTH IN QUECHUA
I GATHERED ALL MY FELLOW WORKERS IN THE SEA OF MUD.
WE'VE GOT TO START A UNION, LIKE THE KITCHEN GALS!
DON'T YOU THINK IT MIGHT BE DANGEROUS, CATALINA?
YES, COMRADE, BUT UNITED WE CAN LOOK AFTER ONE ANOTHER.
A SINGLE LOOSE THREAD IS EASILY PULLED...
...BUT WHEN SEVERAL ARE WOVEN TOGETHER, THEY CANNOT BE UNRAVELED!
THAT DAY WE HEADED TO CITY HALL AND DEMANDED THAT THEY BUILD MORE MARKETS FOR THE FLORISTS AND QHATERAS.

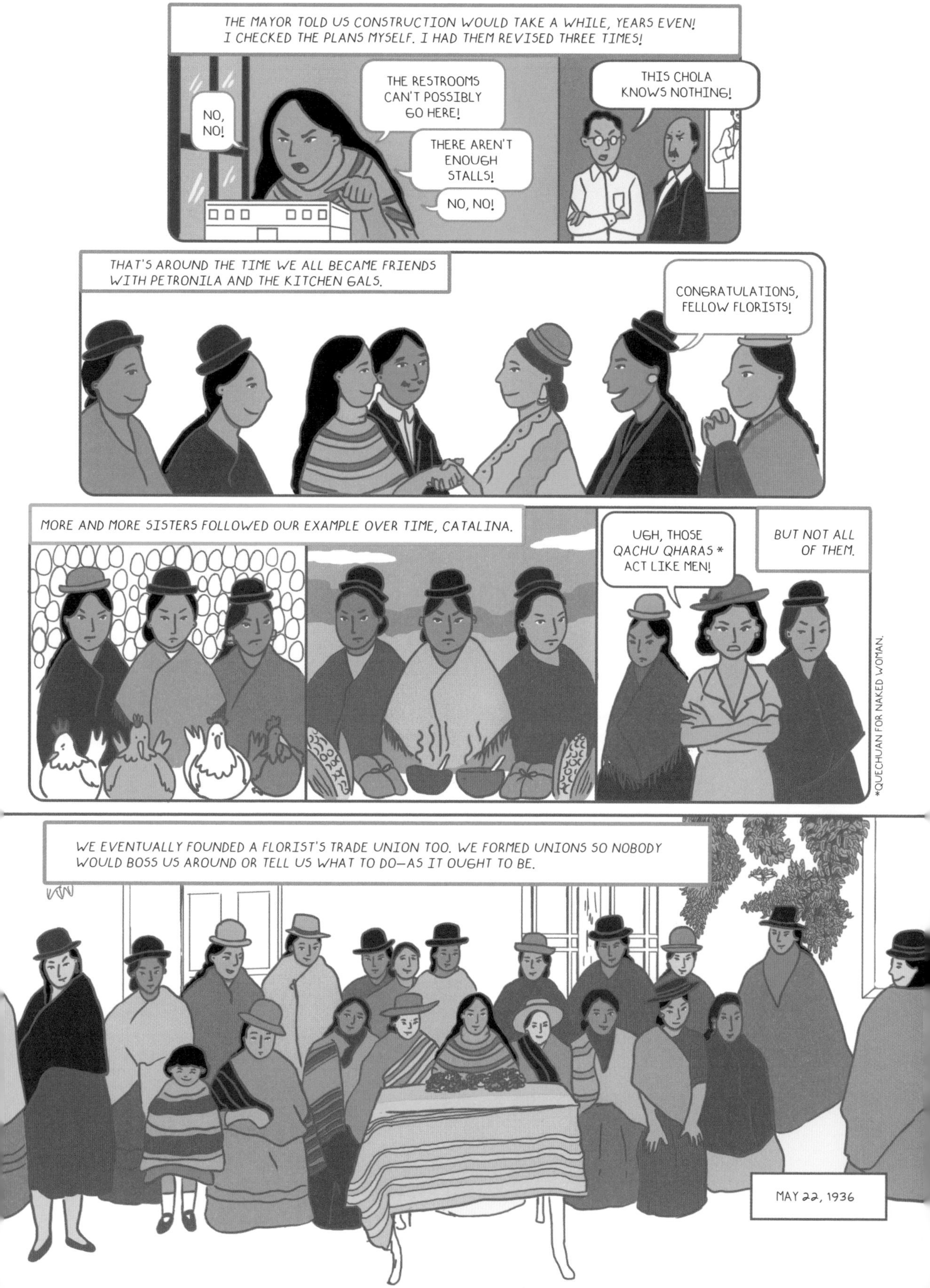
THE MAYOR TOLD US CONSTRUCTION WOULD TAKE A WHILE, YEARS EVEN! I CHECKED THE PLANS MYSELF. I HAD THEM REVISED THREE TIMES!
NO, NO!
THE RESTROOMS CAN'T POSSIBLY GO HERE!
THERE AREN'T ENOUGH STALLS!
NO, NO!
THIS CHOLA KNOWS NOTHING!
THAT'S AROUND THE TIME WE ALL BECAME FRIENDS WITH PETRONILA AND THE KITCHEN GALS.
CONGRATULATIONS, FELLOW FLORISTS!
MORE AND MORE SISTERS FOLLOWED OUR EXAMPLE OVER TIME, CATALINA.
UGH, THOSE QACHU QHARAS * ACT LIKE MEN!
BUT NOT ALL OF THEM.
*QUECHUAN FOR NAKED WOMAN.
WE EVENTUALLY FOUNDED A FLORIST'S TRADE UNION TOO. WE FORMED UNIONS SO NOBODY WOULD BOSS US AROUND OR TELL US WHAT TO DO—AS IT OUGHT TO BE.
MAY 22, 1936

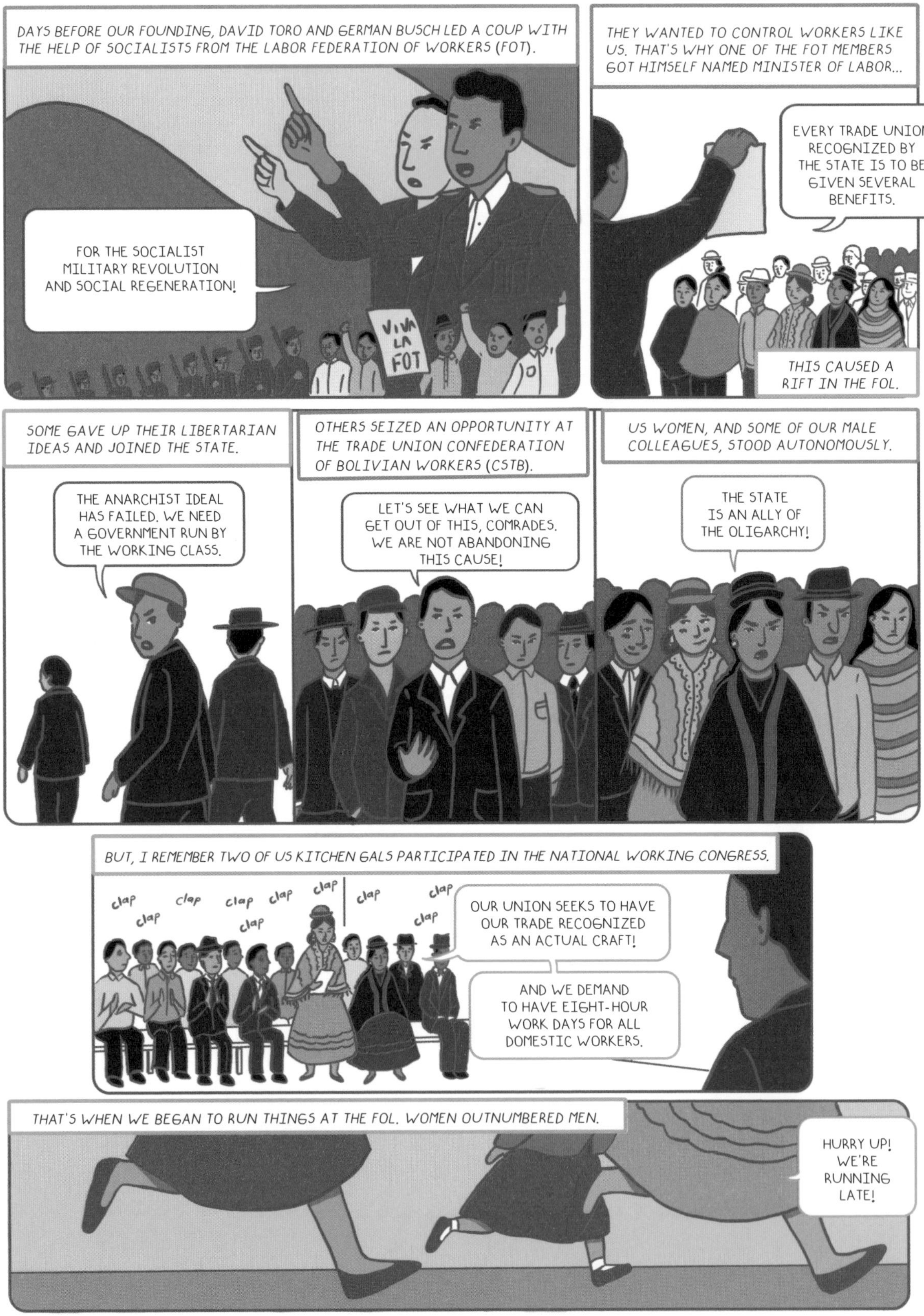
DAYS BEFORE OUR FOUNDING, DAVID TORO AND GERMAN BUSCH LED A COUP WITH THE HELP OF SOCIALISTS FROM THE LABOR FEDERATION OF WORKERS (FOT).
FOR THE SOCIALIST MILITARY REVOLUTION AND SOCIAL REGENERATION!
VIVA LA FOT
THEY WANTED TO CONTROL WORKERS LIKE US. THAT'S WHY ONE OF THE FOT MEMBERS GOT HIMSELF NAMED MINISTER OF LABOR...
EVERY TRADE UNION RECOGNIZED BY THE STATE IS TO BE GIVEN SEVERAL BENEFITS.
THIS CAUSED A RIFT IN THE FOL.
SOME GAVE UP THEIR LIBERTARIAN IDEAS AND JOINED THE STATE.
THE ANARCHIST IDEAL HAS FAILED. WE NEED A GOVERNMENT RUN BY THE WORKING CLASS.
OTHERS SEIZED AN OPPORTUNITY AT THE TRADE UNION CONFEDERATION OF BOLIVIAN WORKERS (CSTB).
LET'S SEE WHAT WE CAN GET OUT OF THIS, COMRADES. WE ARE NOT ABANDONING THIS CAUSE!
US WOMEN, AND SOME OF OUR MALE COLLEAGUES, STOOD AUTONOMOUSLY.
THE STATE IS AN ALLY OF THE OLIGARCHY!
BUT, I REMEMBER TWO OF US KITCHEN GALS PARTICIPATED IN THE NATIONAL WORKING CONGRESS.
clap clap clap clap clap clap clap clap clap clap
OUR UNION SEEKS TO HAVE OUR TRADE RECOGNIZED AS AN ACTUAL CRAFT!
AND WE DEMAND TO HAVE EIGHT-HOUR WORK DAYS FOR ALL DOMESTIC WORKERS.
THAT'S WHEN WE BEGAN TO RUN THINGS AT THE FOL. WOMEN OUTNUMBERED MEN.
HURRY UP! WE'RE RUNNING LATE!

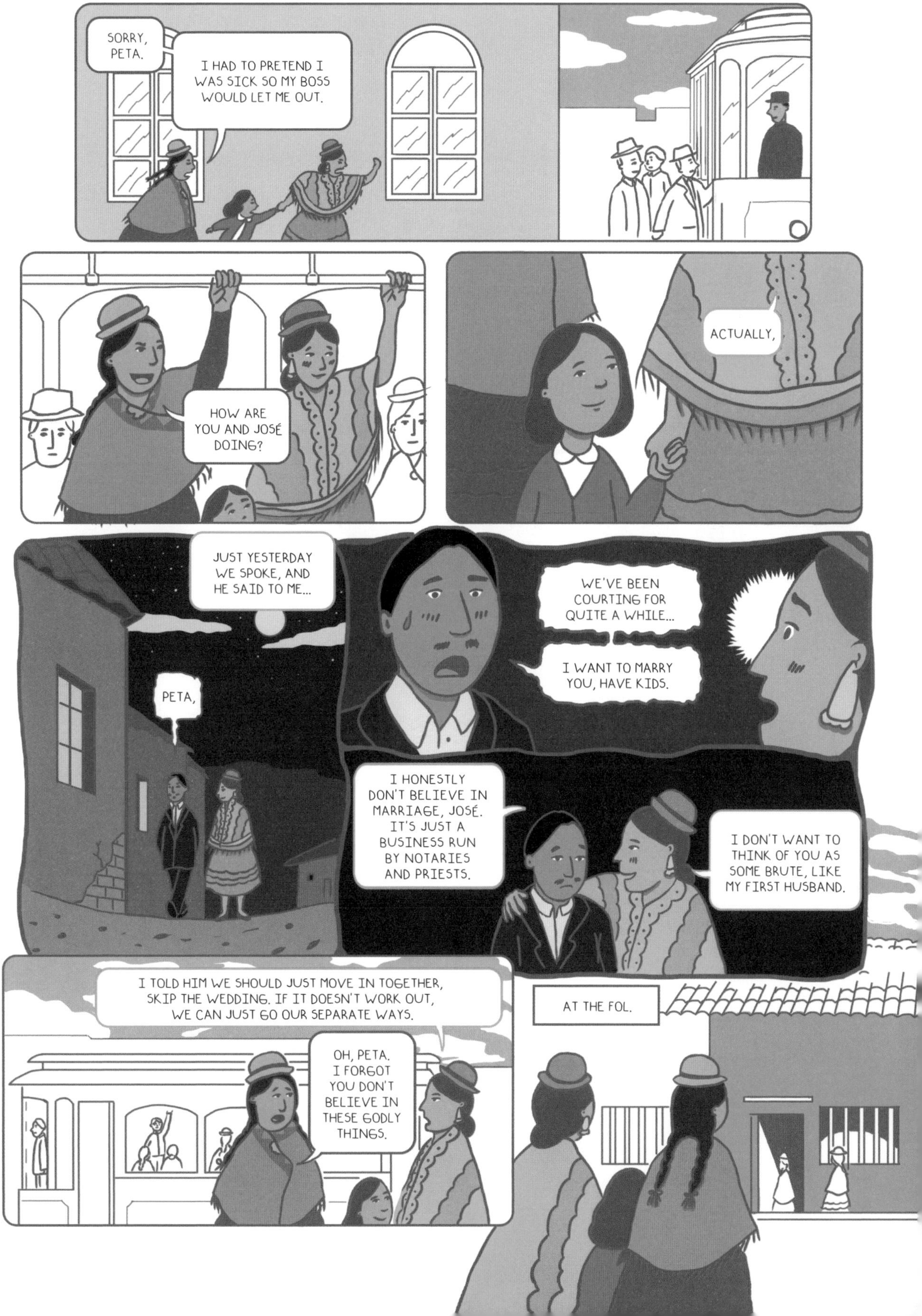
SORRY, PETA.
I HAD TO PRETEND I WAS SICK SO MY BOSS WOULD LET ME OUT.
HOW ARE YOU AND JOSÉ DOING?
ACTUALLY,
JUST YESTERDAY WE SPOKE, AND HE SAID TO ME...
PETA,
WE'VE BEEN COURTING FOR QUITE A WHILE...
I WANT TO MARRY YOU, HAVE KIDS.
I HONESTLY DON'T BELIEVE IN MARRIAGE, JOSÉ. IT'S JUST A BUSINESS RUN BY NOTARIES AND PRIESTS.
I DON'T WANT TO THINK OF YOU AS SOME BRUTE, LIKE MY FIRST HUSBAND.
I TOLD HIM WE SHOULD JUST MOVE IN TOGETHER, SKIP THE WEDDING. IF IT DOESN'T WORK OUT, WE CAN JUST GO OUR SEPARATE WAYS.
OH, PETA. I FORGOT YOU DON'T BELIEVE IN THESE GODLY THINGS.
AT THE FOL.

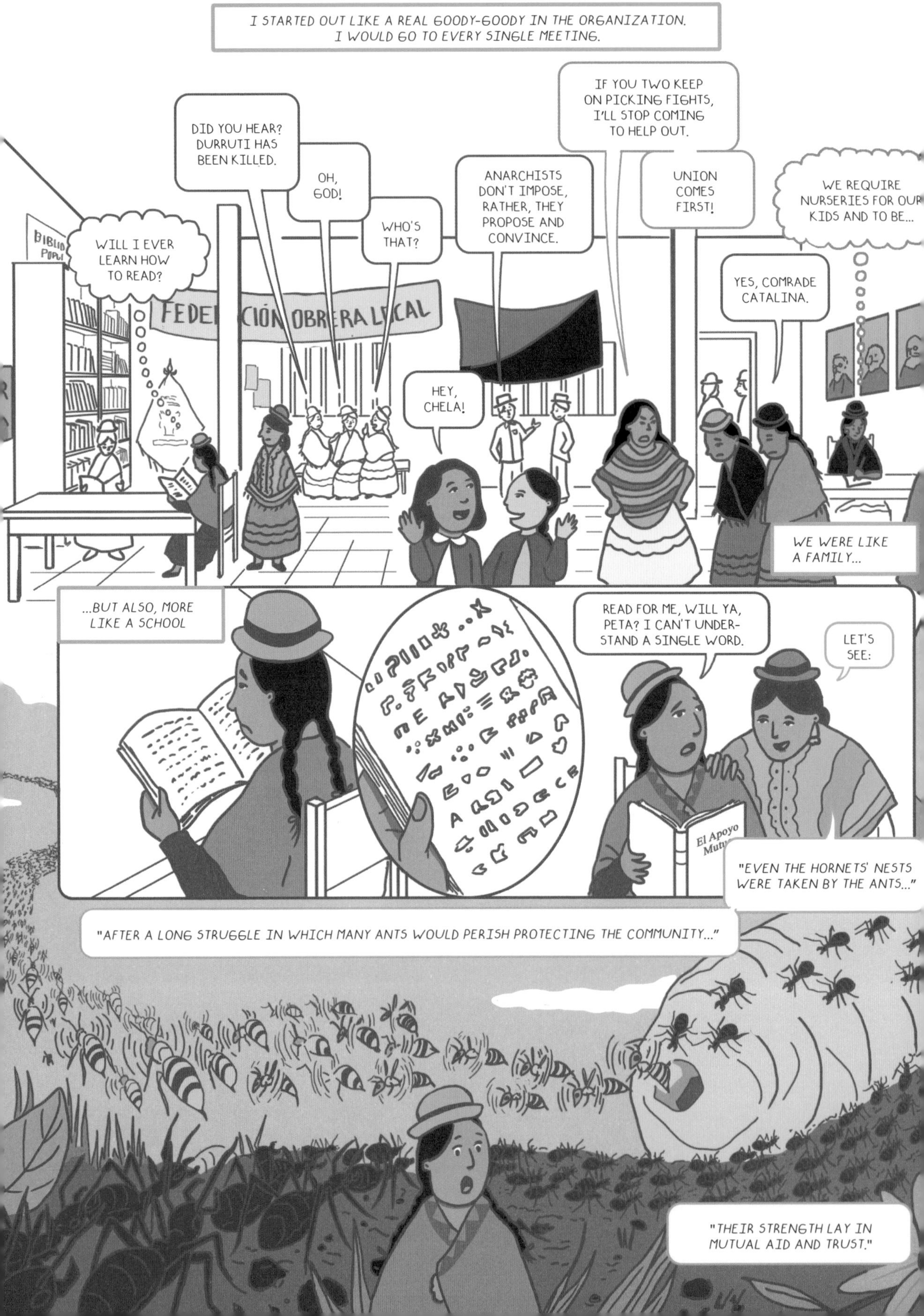

I STARTED OUT LIKE A REAL GOODY-GOODY IN THE ORGANIZATION. I WOULD GO TO EVERY SINGLE MEETING.
WILL I EVER LEARN HOW TO READ?
DID YOU HEAR? DURRUTI HAS BEEN KILLED.
OH, GOD!
WHO'S THAT?
ANARCHISTS DON'T IMPOSE, RATHER, THEY PROPOSE AND CONVINCE.
IF YOU TWO KEEP ON PICKING FIGHTS, I'LL STOP COMING TO HELP OUT.
UNION COMES FIRST!
WE REQUIRE NURSERIES FOR OUR KIDS AND TO BE...
YES, COMRADE CATALINA.
HEY, CHELA!
FEDE CIÓN OBRERA LOCAL
WE WERE LIKE A FAMILY...
...BUT ALSO, MORE LIKE A SCHOOL
READ FOR ME, WILL YA, PETA? I CAN'T UNDERSTAND A SINGLE WORD.
LET'S SEE:
El Apoyo Mutu
"EVEN THE HORNETS' NESTS WERE TAKEN BY THE ANTS..."
"AFTER A LONG STRUGGLE IN WHICH MANY ANTS WOULD PERISH PROTECTING THE COMMUNITY..."
"THEIR STRENGTH LAY IN MUTUAL AID AND TRUST."

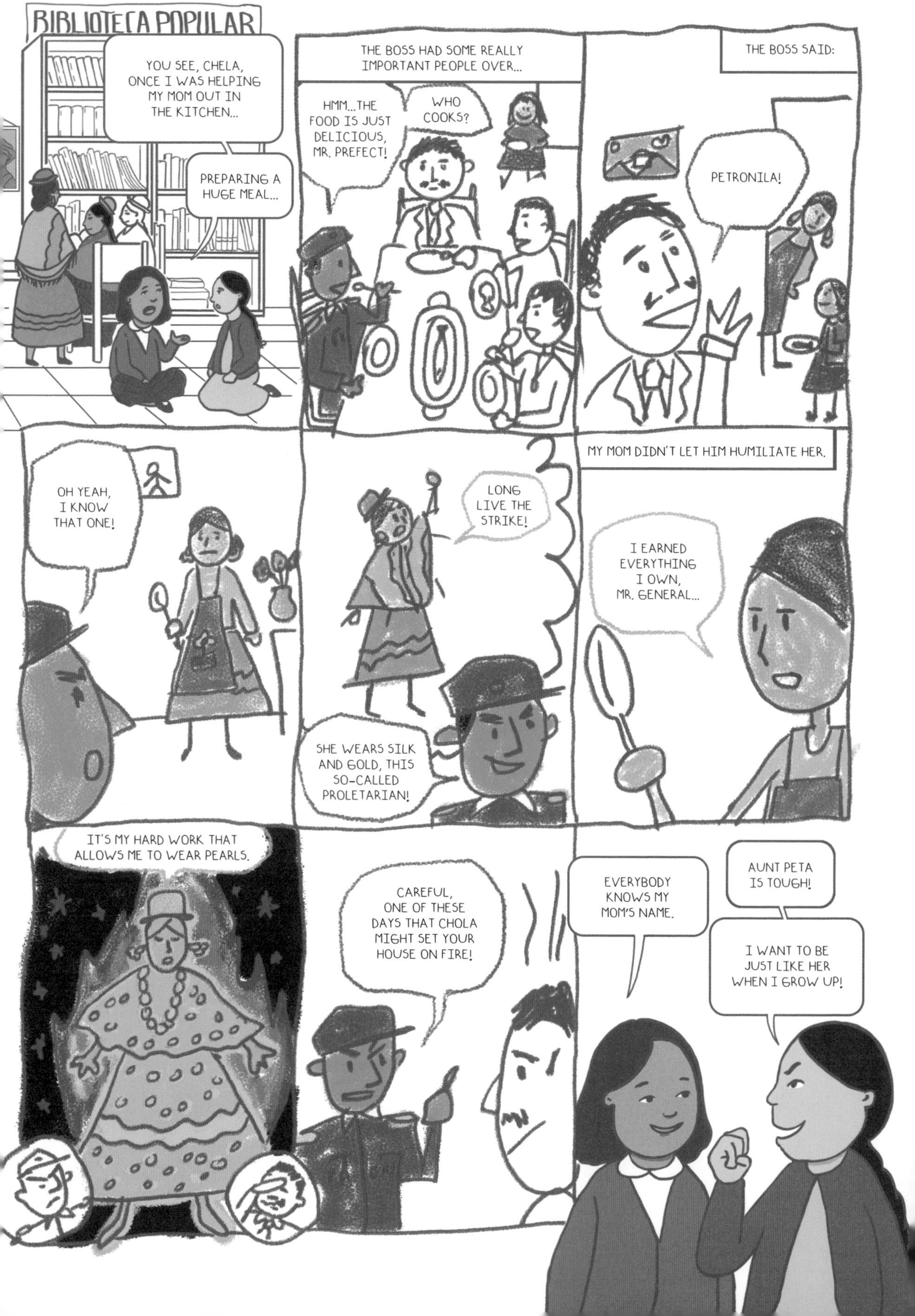
BIBLIOTECA POPULAR
YOU SEE, CHELA, ONCE I WAS HELPING MY MOM OUT IN THE KITCHEN...
PREPARING A HUGE MEAL...
THE BOSS HAD SOME REALLY IMPORTANT PEOPLE OVER...
HMM...THE FOOD IS JUST DELICIOUS, MR. PREFECT!
WHO COOKS?
THE BOSS SAID:
PETRONILA!
OH YEAH, I KNOW THAT ONE!
LONG LIVE THE STRIKE!
SHE WEARS SILK AND GOLD, THIS SO-CALLED PROLETARIAN!
MY MOM DIDN'T LET HIM HUMILIATE HER.
I EARNED EVERYTHING I OWN, MR. GENERAL...
IT'S MY HARD WORK THAT ALLOWS ME TO WEAR PEARLS.
CAREFUL, ONE OF THESE DAYS THAT CHOLA MIGHT SET YOUR HOUSE ON FIRE!
EVERYBODY KNOWS MY MOM'S NAME.
AUNT PETA IS TOUGH!
I WANT TO BE JUST LIKE HER WHEN I GROW UP!

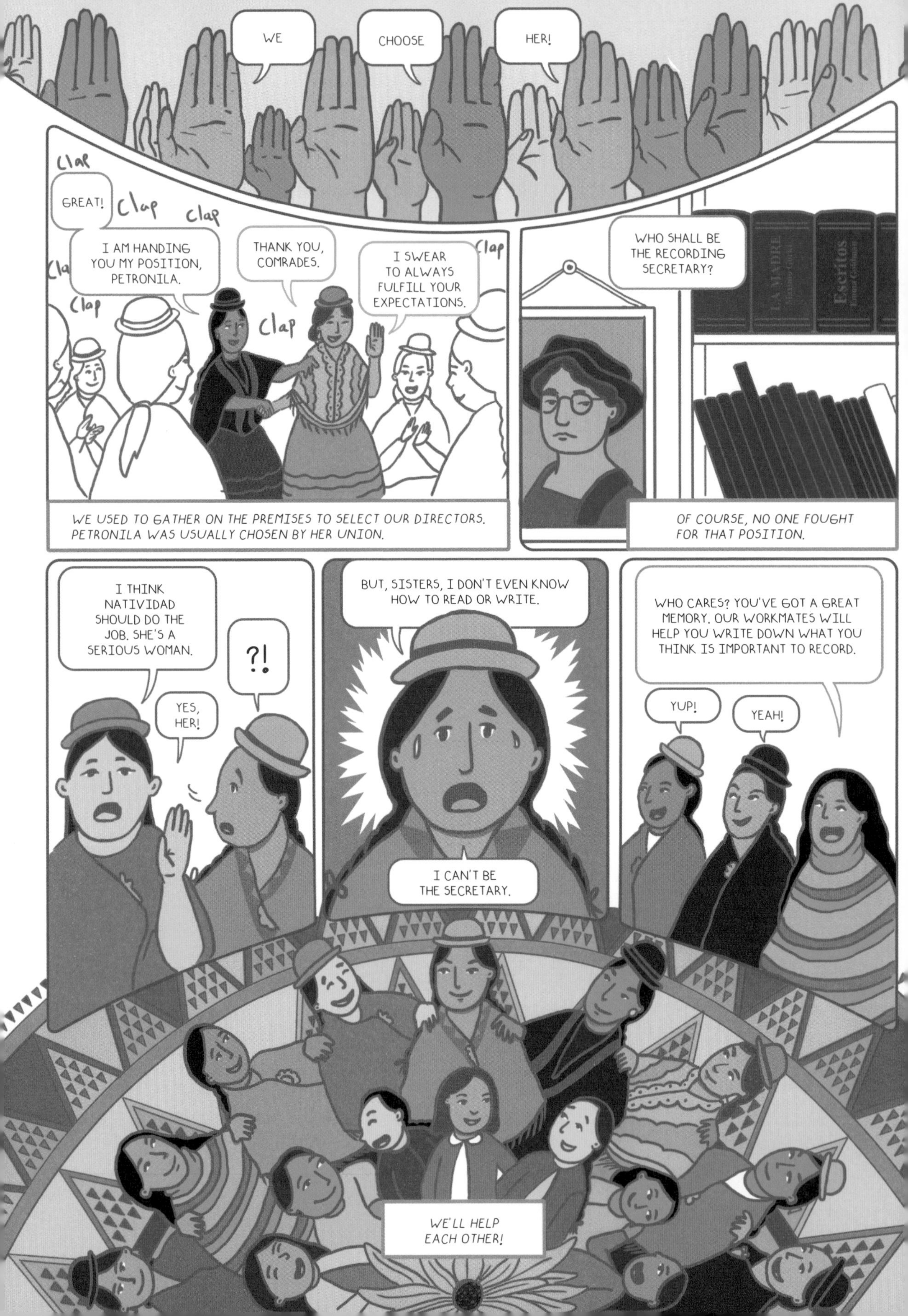

WE
CHOOSE
HER!
Clap
GREAT!
Clap
Clap
I AM HANDING YOU MY POSITION, PETRONILA.
THANK YOU, COMRADES.
Clap
I SWEAR TO ALWAYS FULFILL YOUR EXPECTATIONS.
Clap
Clap
WE USED TO GATHER ON THE PREMISES TO SELECT OUR DIRECTORS. PETRONILA WAS USUALLY CHOSEN BY HER UNION.
WHO SHALL BE THE RECORDING SECRETARY?
LA MADRE
Escritos
OF COURSE, NO ONE FOUGHT FOR THAT POSITION.
I THINK NATIVIDAD SHOULD DO THE JOB. SHE'S A SERIOUS WOMAN.
?!
YES, HER!
BUT, SISTERS, I DON'T EVEN KNOW HOW TO READ OR WRITE.
I CAN'T BE THE SECRETARY.
WHO CARES? YOU'VE GOT A GREAT MEMORY. OUR WORKMATES WILL HELP YOU WRITE DOWN WHAT YOU THINK IS IMPORTANT TO RECORD.
YUP!
YEAH!
WE'LL HELP EACH OTHER!

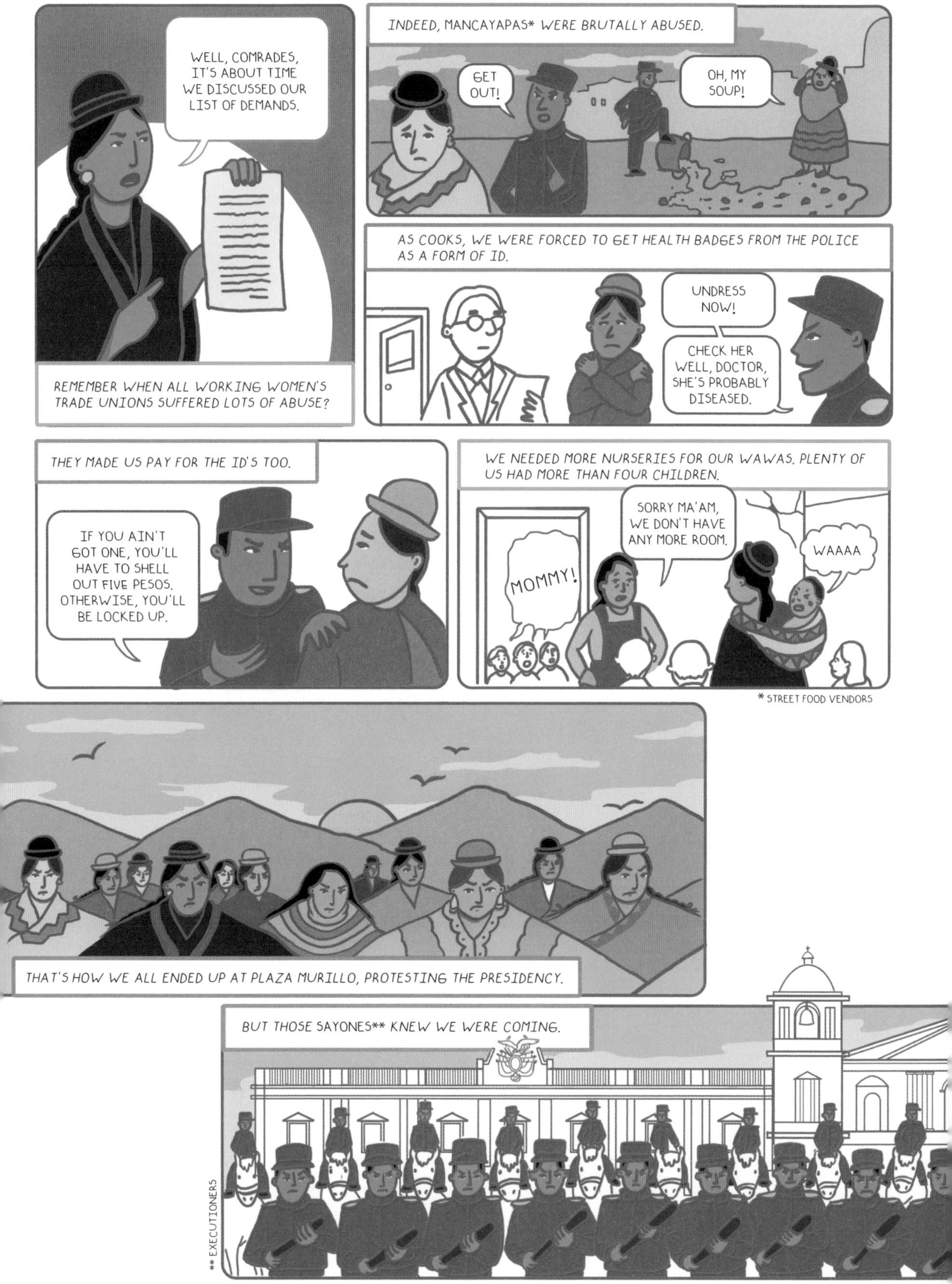
WELL, COMRADES, IT'S ABOUT TIME WE DISCUSSED OUR LIST OF DEMANDS.
REMEMBER WHEN ALL WORKING WOMEN'S TRADE UNIONS SUFFERED LOTS OF ABUSE?
INDEED, MANCAYAPAS* WERE BRUTALLY ABUSED.
GET OUT!
OH, MY SOUP!
AS COOKS, WE WERE FORCED TO GET HEALTH BADGES FROM THE POLICE AS A FORM OF ID.
UNDRESS NOW!
CHECK HER WELL, DOCTOR, SHE'S PROBABLY DISEASED.
THEY MADE US PAY FOR THE ID'S TOO.
IF YOU AIN'T GOT ONE, YOU'LL HAVE TO SHELL OUT FIVE PESOS. OTHERWISE, YOU'LL BE LOCKED UP.
WE NEEDED MORE NURSERIES FOR OUR WAWAS. PLENTY OF US HAD MORE THAN FOUR CHILDREN.
MOMMY!
SORRY MA'AM, WE DON'T HAVE ANY MORE ROOM.
WAAAA
THAT'S HOW WE ALL ENDED UP AT PLAZA MURILLO, PROTESTING THE PRESIDENCY.
BUT THOSE SAYONES** KNEW WE WERE COMING.

* STREET FOOD VENDORS

** EXECUTIONERS

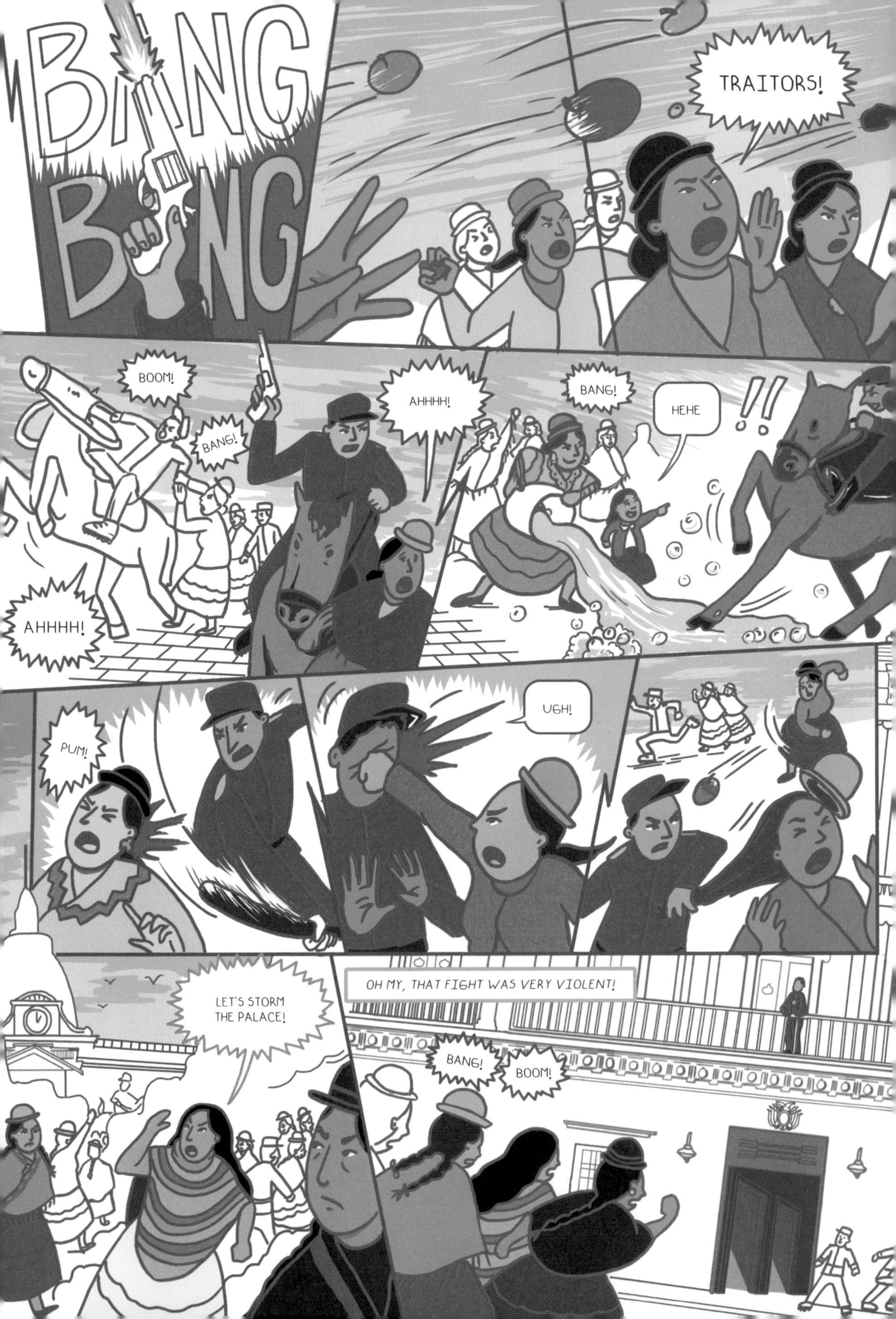
BANG
BANG
TRAITORS!
BOOM!
BANG!
AHHHH!
AHHHH!
BANG!
HEHE
!!
PUM!
UGH!
LET'S STORM THE PALACE!
OH MY, THAT FIGHT WAS VERY VIOLENT!
BANG!
BOOM!

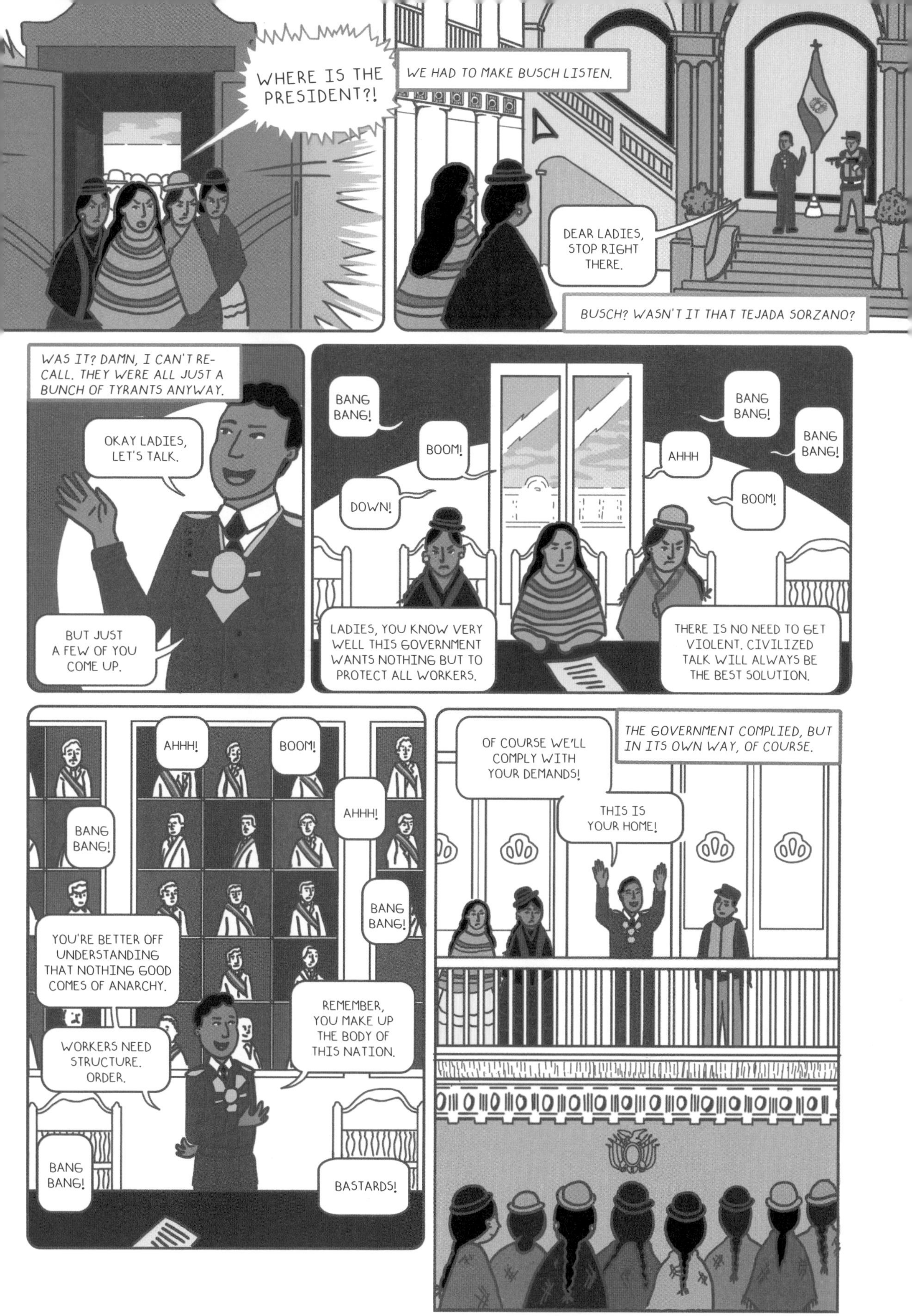
WHERE IS THE PRESIDENT?!
WE HAD TO MAKE BUSCH LISTEN.
DEAR LADIES, STOP RIGHT THERE.
BUSCH? WASN'T IT THAT TEJADA SORZANO?
WAS IT? DAMN, I CAN'T RE-CALL. THEY WERE ALL JUST A BUNCH OF TYRANTS ANYWAY.
OKAY LADIES, LET'S TALK.
BUT JUST A FEW OF YOU COME UP.
BANG BANG!
BOOM!
DOWN!
BANG BANG!
AHHH
BANG BANG!
BOOM!
LADIES, YOU KNOW VERY WELL THIS GOVERNMENT WANTS NOTHING BUT TO PROTECT ALL WORKERS.
THERE IS NO NEED TO GET VIOLENT. CIVILIZED TALK WILL ALWAYS BE THE BEST SOLUTION.
AHHH!
BOOM!
AHHH!
BANG BANG!
BANG BANG!
YOU'RE BETTER OFF UNDERSTANDING THAT NOTHING GOOD COMES OF ANARCHY.
WORKERS NEED STRUCTURE. ORDER.
REMEMBER, YOU MAKE UP THE BODY OF THIS NATION.
BANG BANG!
BASTARDS!
THE GOVERNMENT COMPLIED, BUT IN ITS OWN WAY, OF COURSE.
OF COURSE WE'LL COMPLY WITH YOUR DEMANDS!
THIS IS YOUR HOME!

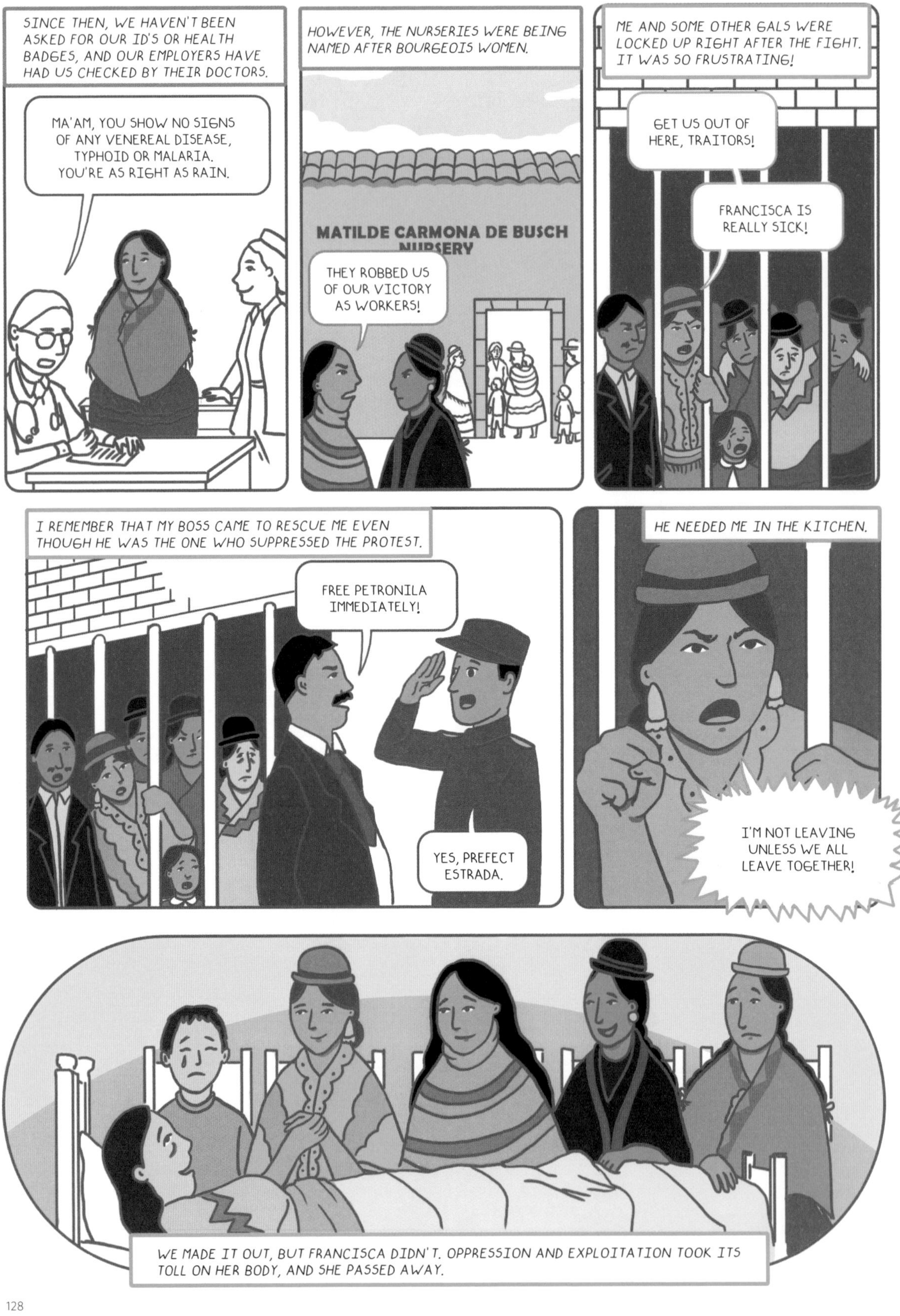

SINCE THEN, WE HAVEN'T BEEN ASKED FOR OUR ID'S OR HEALTH BADGES, AND OUR EMPLOYERS HAVE HAD US CHECKED BY THEIR DOCTORS.
MA'AM, YOU SHOW NO SIGNS OF ANY VENEREAL DISEASE, TYPHOID OR MALARIA. YOU'RE AS RIGHT AS RAIN.
HOWEVER, THE NURSERIES WERE BEING NAMED AFTER BOURGEOIS WOMEN.
MATILDE CARMONA DE BUSCH NURSERY
THEY ROBBED US OF OUR VICTORY AS WORKERS!
ME AND SOME OTHER GALS WERE LOCKED UP RIGHT AFTER THE FIGHT. IT WAS SO FRUSTRATING!
GET US OUT OF HERE, TRAITORS!
FRANCISCA IS REALLY SICK!
I REMEMBER THAT MY BOSS CAME TO RESCUE ME EVEN THOUGH HE WAS THE ONE WHO SUPPRESSED THE PROTEST.
FREE PETRONILA IMMEDIATELY!
YES, PREFECT ESTRADA.
HE NEEDED ME IN THE KITCHEN.
I'M NOT LEAVING UNLESS WE ALL LEAVE TOGETHER!
WE MADE IT OUT, BUT FRANCISCA DIDN'T. OPPRESSION AND EXPLOITATION TOOK ITS TOLL ON HER BODY, AND SHE PASSED AWAY.

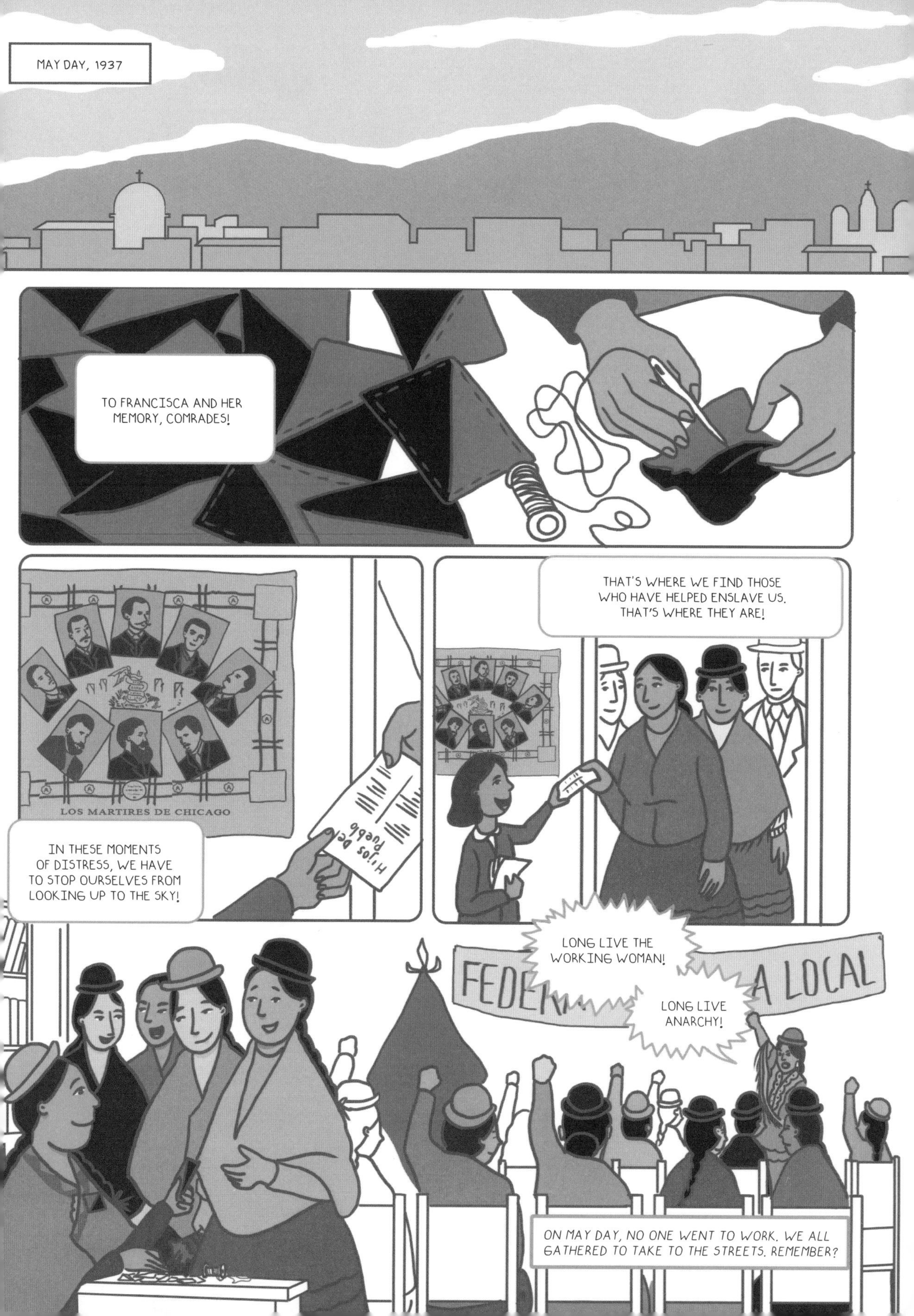
MAY DAY, 1937
TO FRANCISCA AND HER MEMORY, COMRADES!
LOS MARTIRES DE CHICAGO
Hijos del Puebl
IN THESE MOMENTS OF DISTRESS, WE HAVE TO STOP OURSELVES FROM LOOKING UP TO THE SKY!
THAT'S WHERE WE FIND THOSE WHO HAVE HELPED ENSLAVE US. THAT'S WHERE THEY ARE!
LONG LIVE THE WORKING WOMAN!
FEDE
A LOCAL
LONG LIVE ANARCHY!
ON MAY DAY, NO ONE WENT TO WORK. WE ALL GATHERED TO TAKE TO THE STREETS. REMEMBER?

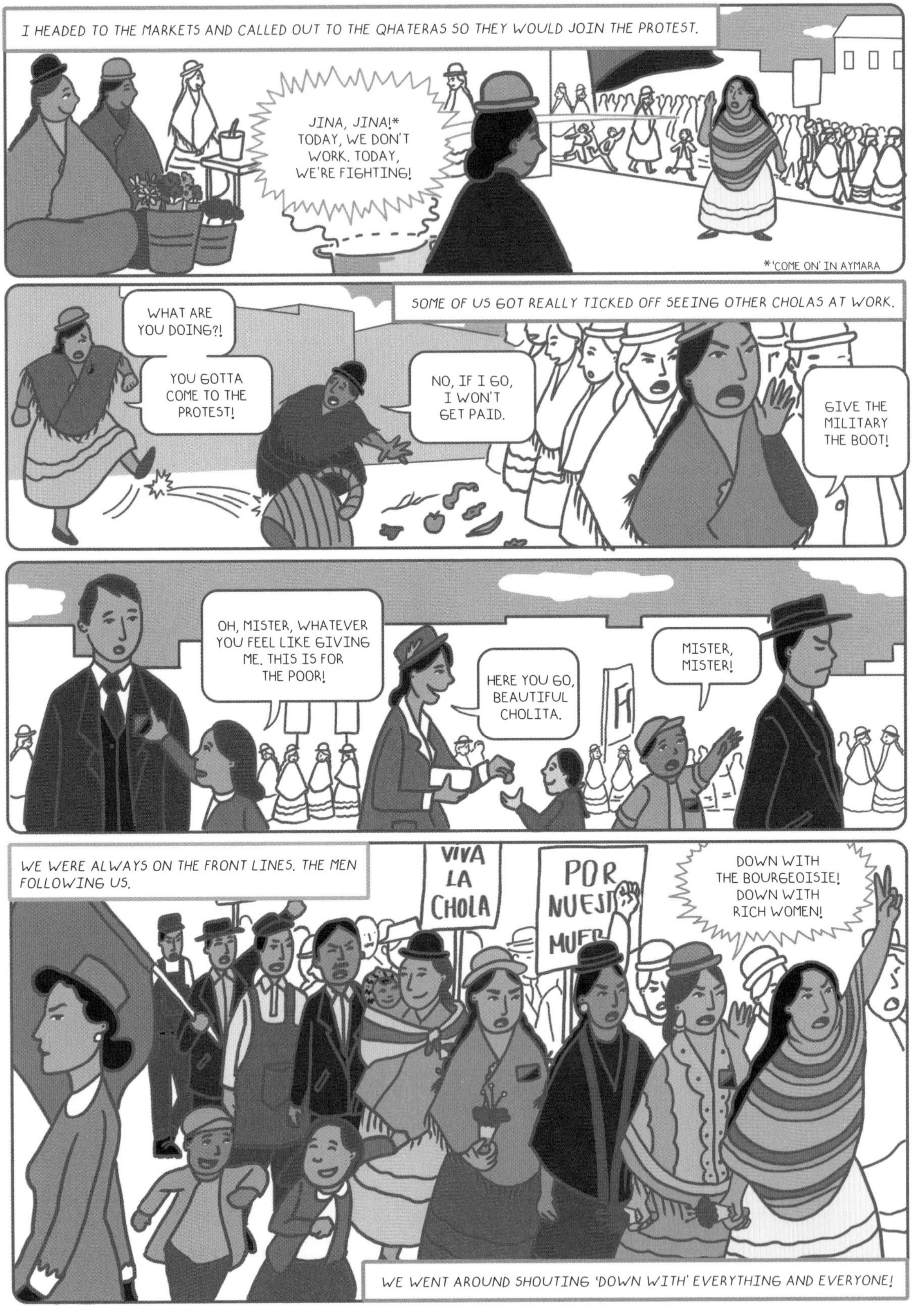

I HEADED TO THE MARKETS AND CALLED OUT TO THE QHATERAS SO THEY WOULD JOIN THE PROTEST.
JINA, JINA!* TODAY, WE DON'T WORK. TODAY, WE'RE FIGHTING!
*'COME ON' IN AYMARA
SOME OF US GOT REALLY TICKED OFF SEEING OTHER CHOLAS AT WORK.
WHAT ARE YOU DOING?!
YOU GOTTA COME TO THE PROTEST!
NO, IF I GO, I WON'T GET PAID.
GIVE THE MILITARY THE BOOT!
OH, MISTER, WHATEVER YOU FEEL LIKE GIVING ME. THIS IS FOR THE POOR!
HERE YOU GO, BEAUTIFUL CHOLITA.
MISTER, MISTER!
WE WERE ALWAYS ON THE FRONT LINES. THE MEN FOLLOWING US.
VIVA LA CHOLA
DOWN WITH THE BOURGEOISIE! DOWN WITH RICH WOMEN!
WE WENT AROUND SHOUTING 'DOWN WITH' EVERYTHING AND EVERYONE!

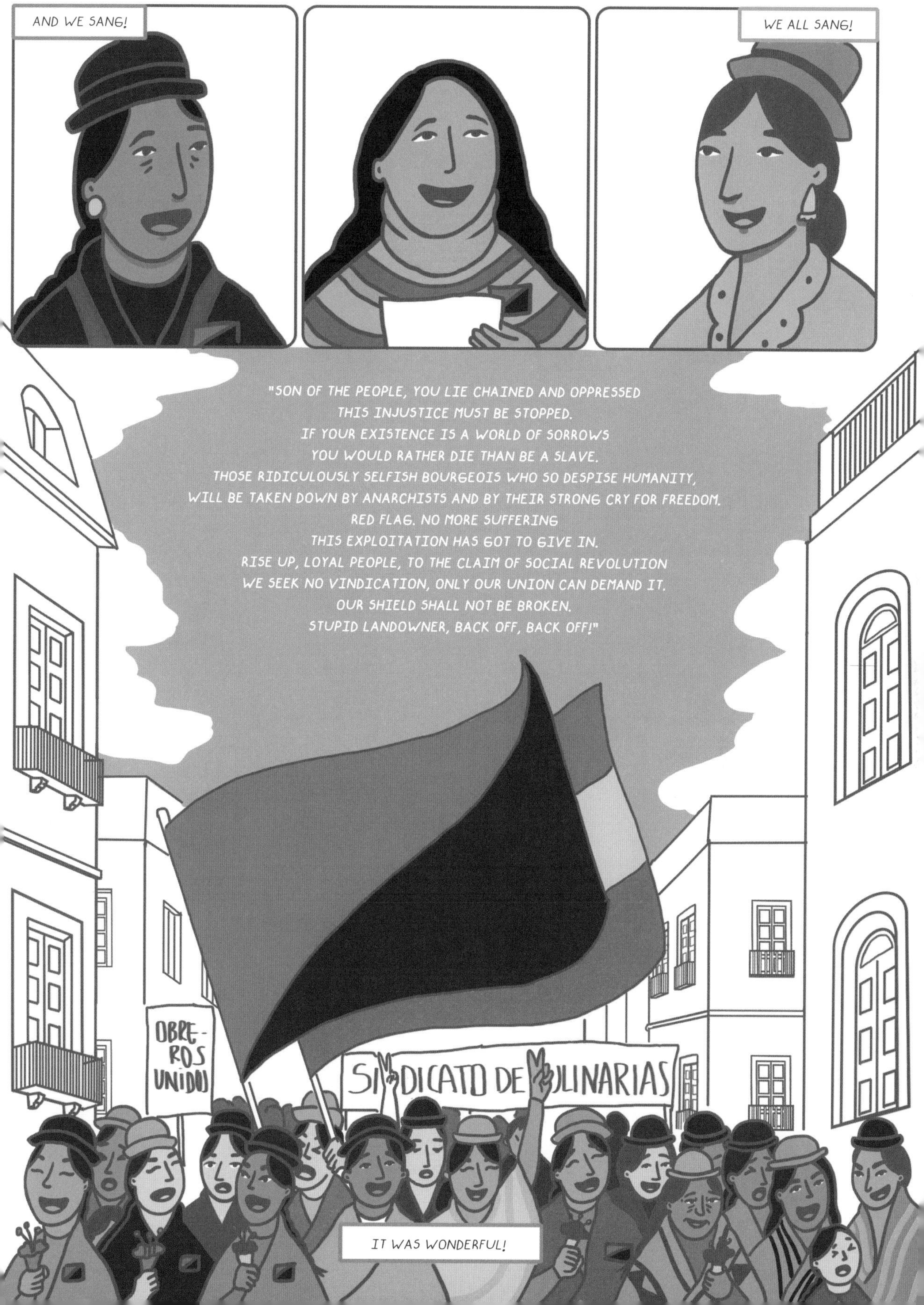
AND WE SANG!
WE ALL SANG!
"SON OF THE PEOPLE, YOU LIE CHAINED AND OPPRESSED
THIS INJUSTICE MUST BE STOPPED.
IF YOUR EXISTENCE IS A WORLD OF SORROWS
YOU WOULD RATHER DIE THAN BE A SLAVE.
THOSE RIDICULOUSLY SELFISH BOURGEOIS WHO SO DESPISE HUMANITY,
WILL BE TAKEN DOWN BY ANARCHISTS AND BY THEIR STRONG CRY FOR FREEDOM.
RED FLAG. NO MORE SUFFERING
THIS EXPLOITATION HAS GOT TO GIVE IN.
RISE UP, LOYAL PEOPLE, TO THE CLAIM OF SOCIAL REVOLUTION
WE SEEK NO VINDICATION, ONLY OUR UNION CAN DEMAND IT.
OUR SHIELD SHALL NOT BE BROKEN.
STUPID LANDOWNER, BACK OFF, BACK OFF!"
OBRE-ROS UNIDOS
SI DICATO DE ULINARIAS
IT WAS WONDERFUL!

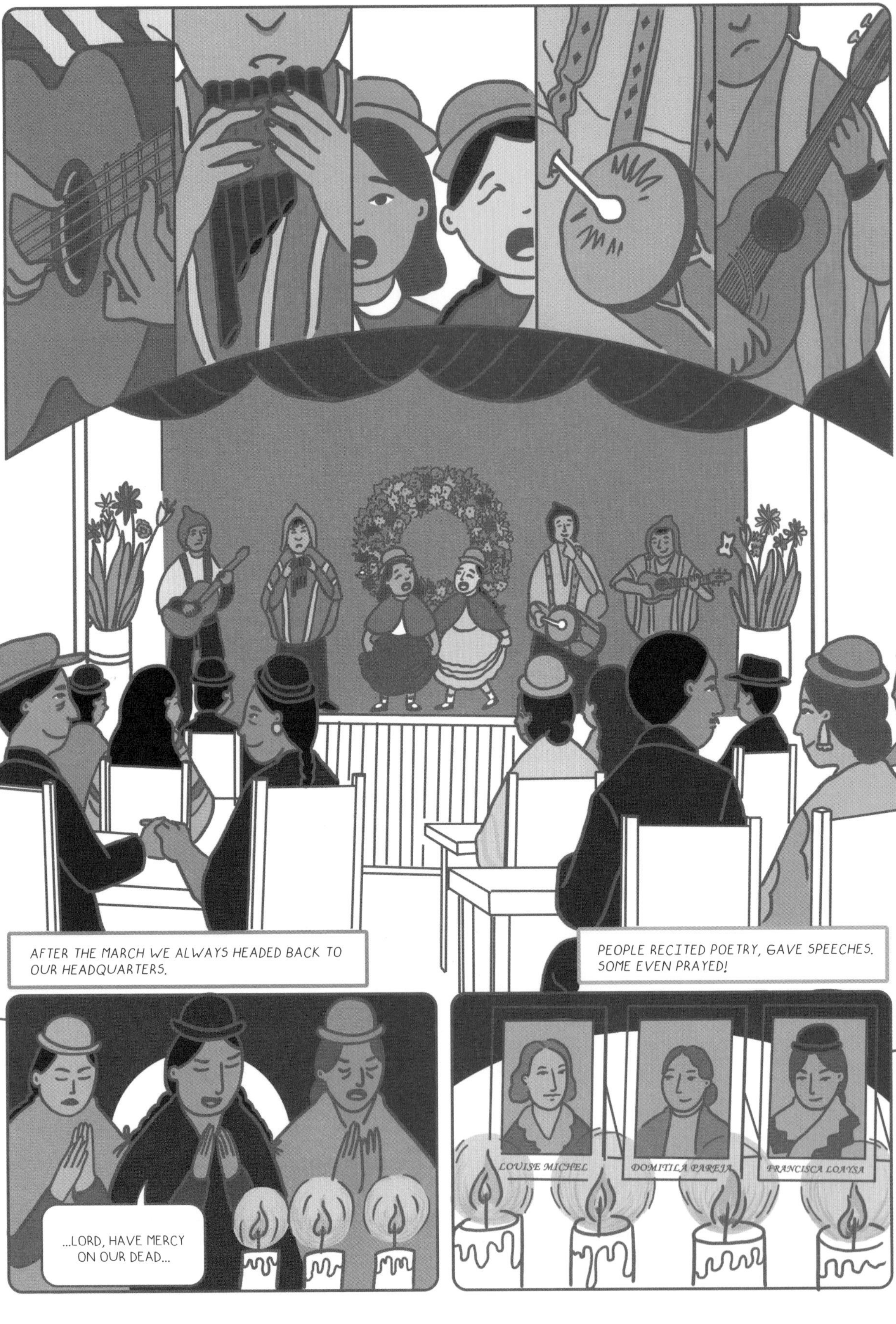
AFTER THE MARCH WE ALWAYS HEADED BACK TO OUR HEADQUARTERS.
PEOPLE RECITED POETRY, GAVE SPEECHES. SOME EVEN PRAYED!
...LORD, HAVE MERCY ON OUR DEAD...
LOUISE MICHEL
DOMITILA PAREJA
FRANCISCA LOAYSA

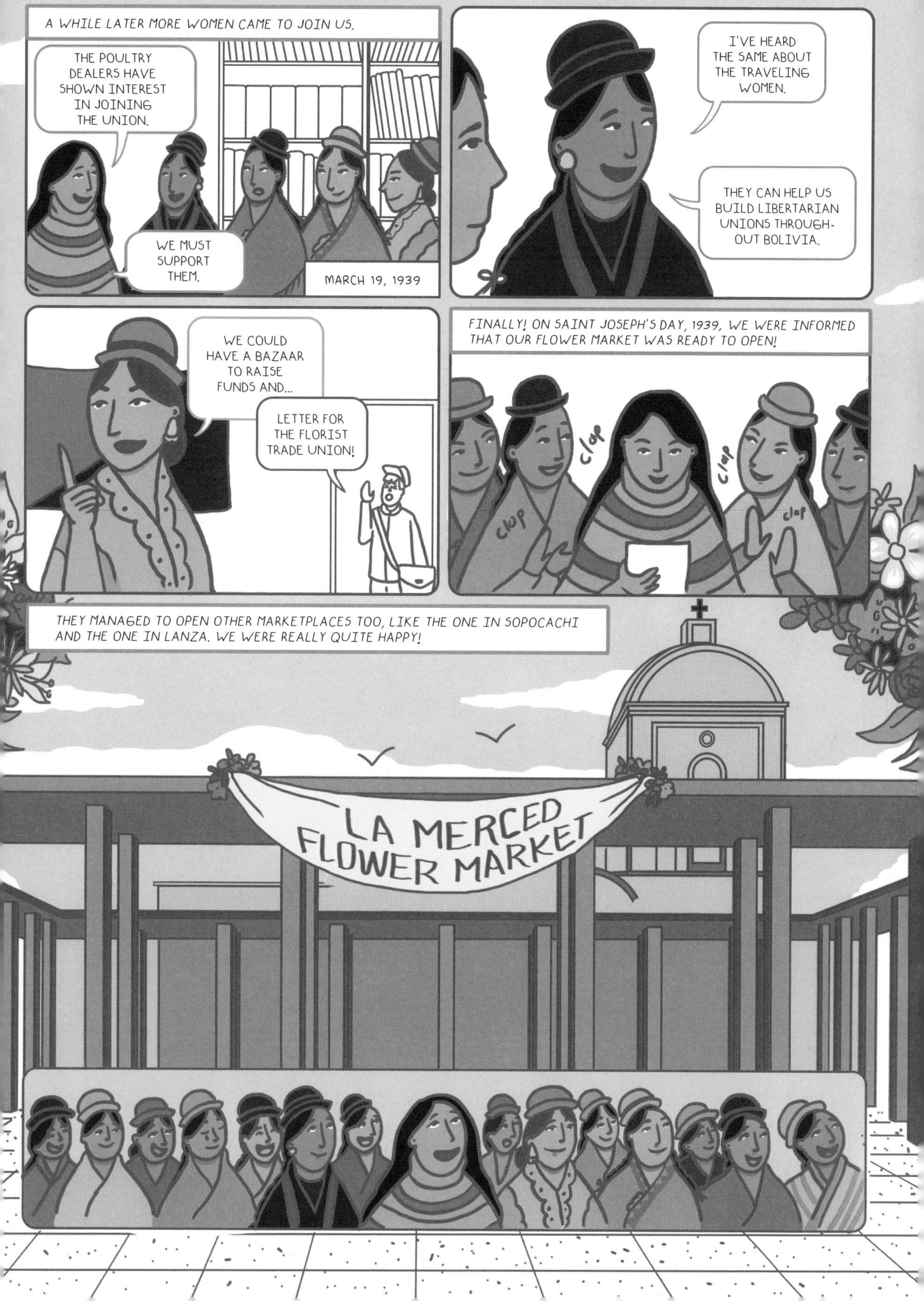
A WHILE LATER MORE WOMEN CAME TO JOIN US.
THE POULTRY DEALERS HAVE SHOWN INTEREST IN JOINING THE UNION.
WE MUST SUPPORT THEM.
MARCH 19, 1939
I'VE HEARD THE SAME ABOUT THE TRAVELING WOMEN.
THEY CAN HELP US BUILD LIBERTARIAN UNIONS THROUGH-OUT BOLIVIA.
WE COULD HAVE A BAZAAR TO RAISE FUNDS AND...
LETTER FOR THE FLORIST TRADE UNION!
FINALLY! ON SAINT JOSEPH'S DAY, 1939, WE WERE INFORMED THAT OUR FLOWER MARKET WAS READY TO OPEN!
clap
clap
clap
clap
THEY MANAGED TO OPEN OTHER MARKETPLACES TOO, LIKE THE ONE IN SOPOCACHI AND THE ONE IN LANZA. WE WERE REALLY QUITE HAPPY!
LA MERCED FLOWER MARKET

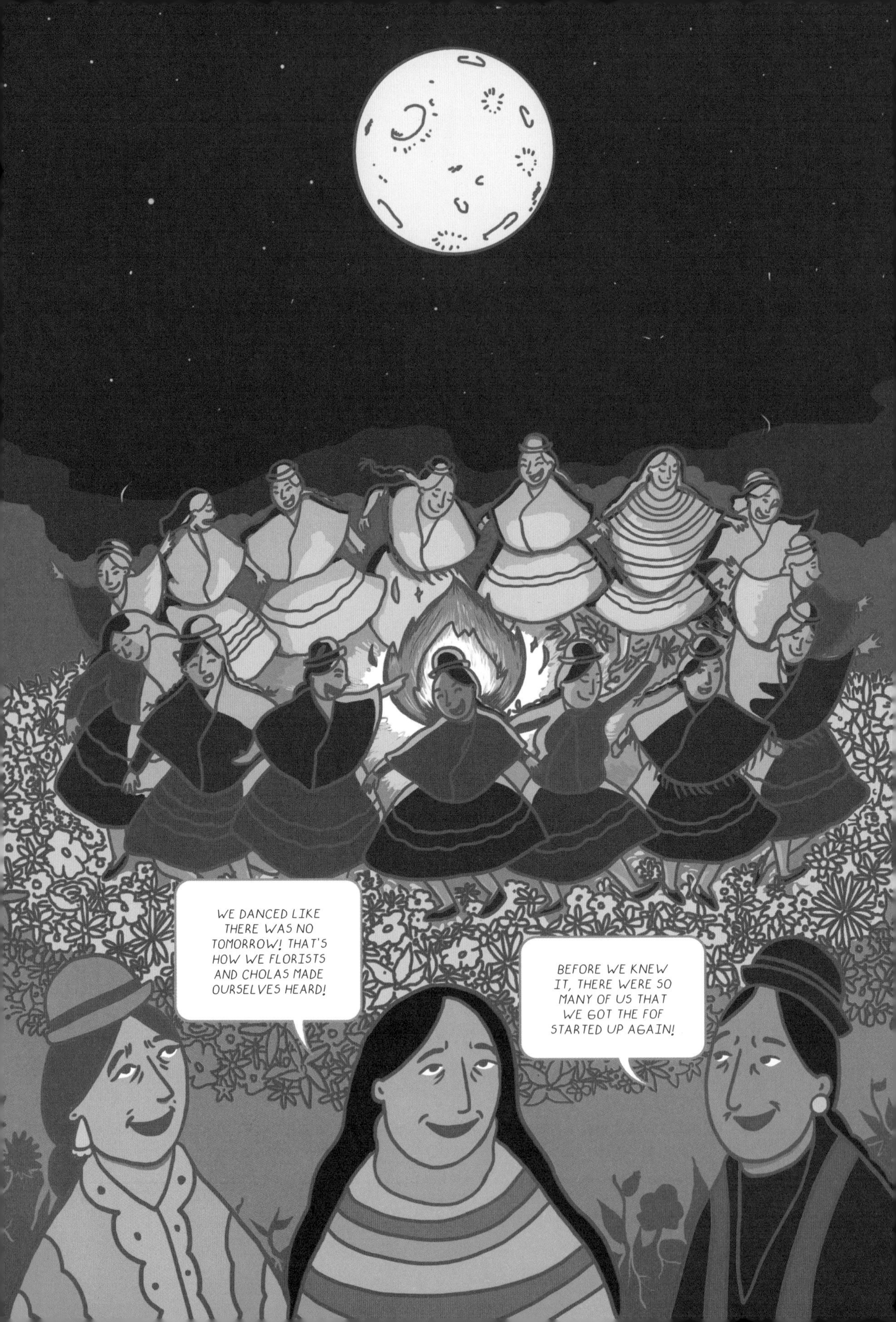
WE DANCED LIKE THERE WAS NO TOMORROW! THAT'S HOW WE FLORISTS AND CHOLAS MADE OURSELVES HEARD!
BEFORE WE KNEW IT, THERE WERE SO MANY OF US THAT WE GOT THE FOF STARTED UP AGAIN!

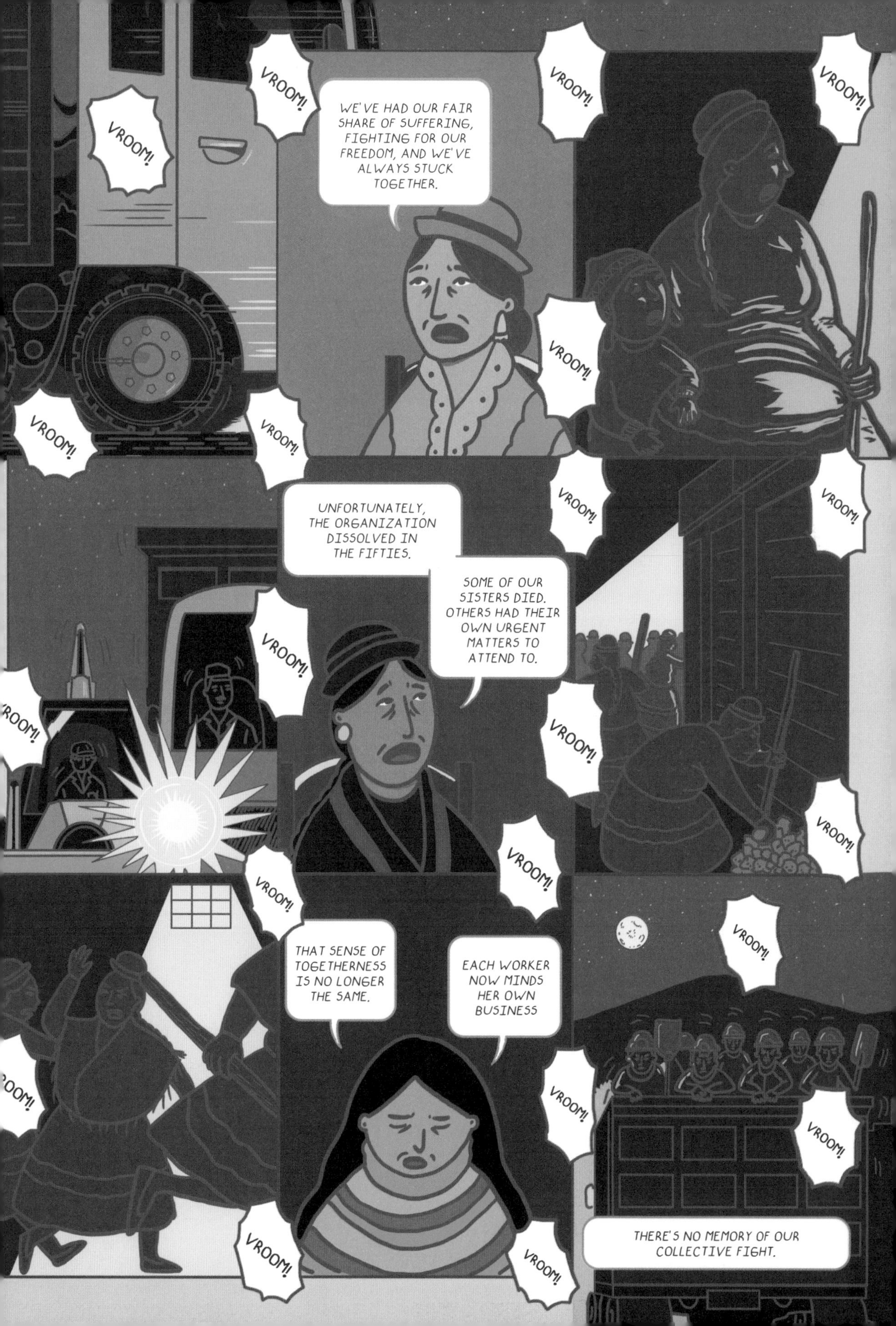
VROOM!
VROOM!
VROOM!
WE'VE HAD OUR FAIR SHARE OF SUFFERING, FIGHTING FOR OUR FREEDOM, AND WE'VE ALWAYS STUCK TOGETHER.
VROOM!
VROOM!
VROOM!
VROOM!
UNFORTUNATELY, THE ORGANIZATION DISSOLVED IN THE FIFTIES.
SOME OF OUR SISTERS DIED. OTHERS HAD THEIR OWN URGENT MATTERS TO ATTEND TO.
VROOM!
VROOM!
VROOM!
VROOM!
VROOM!
VROOM!
VROOM!
THAT SENSE OF TOGETHERNESS IS NO LONGER THE SAME.
EACH WORKER NOW MINDS HER OWN BUSINESS
VROOM!
VROOM!
VROOM!
VROOM!
THERE'S NO MEMORY OF OUR COLLECTIVE FIGHT.

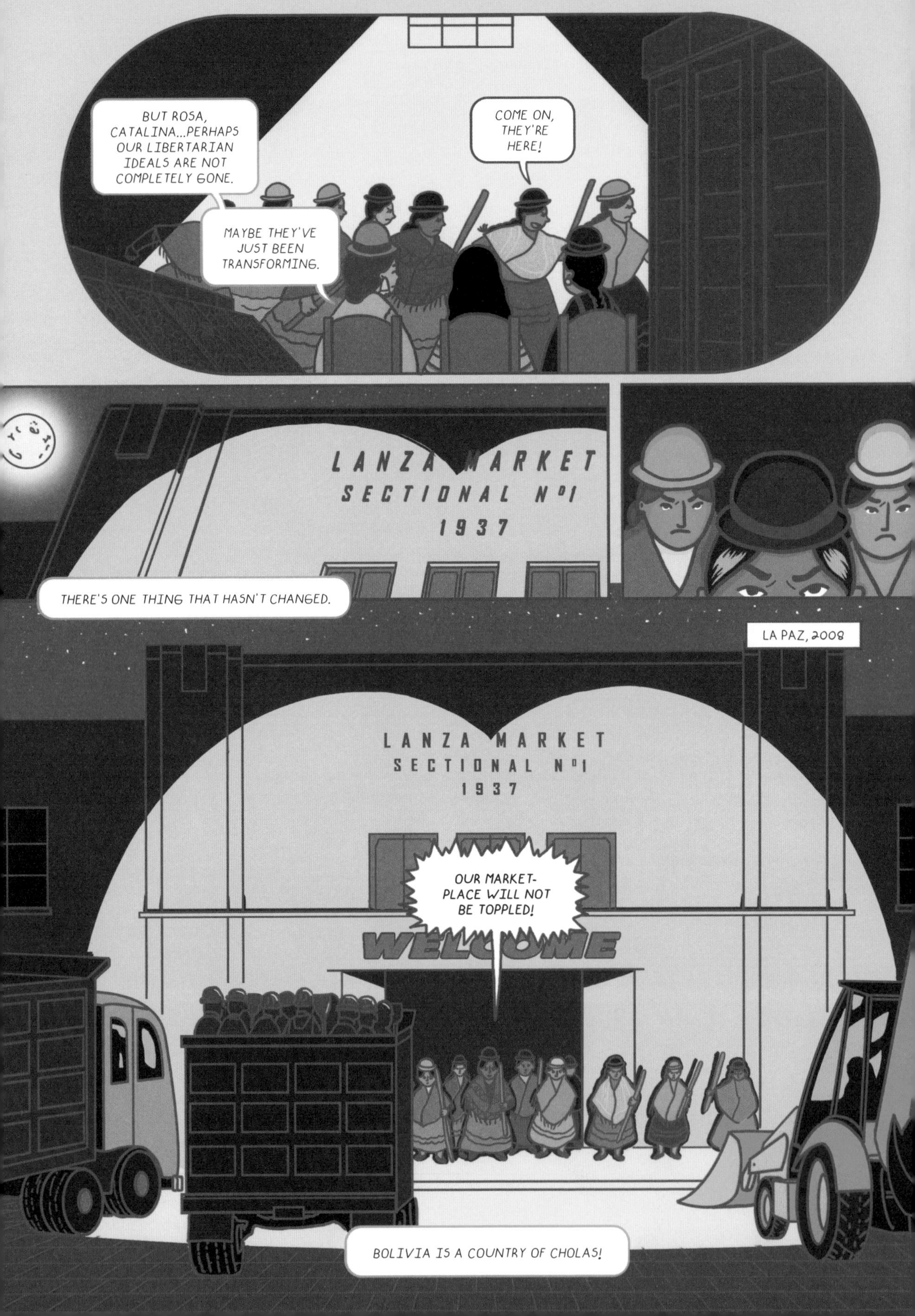
BUT ROSA, CATALINA...PERHAPS OUR LIBERTARIAN IDEALS ARE NOT COMPLETELY GONE.
MAYBE THEY'VE JUST BEEN TRANSFORMING.
COME ON, THEY'RE HERE!
LANZA MARKET
SECTIONAL Nº1
1937
THERE'S ONE THING THAT HASN'T CHANGED.
LA PAZ, 2008
LANZA MARKET
SECTIONAL Nº1
1937
OUR MARKET-PLACE WILL NOT BE TOPPLED!
WELCOME
BOLIVIA IS A COUNTRY OF CHOLAS!

BIBLIOGRAPHY

DIBBITS, INEKE, ELIZABETH PEREDO, RUTH VOLGGER AND CECILIA WADSWORTH (1989). POLLERAS LIBERTARIAS. FEDERA-CIÓN OBRERA FEMENINA (1927-1965). LA PAZ: TAHIPAMU/HISBOL.

LEHM, Z., RIVERA CUSICANQUI, S. (1986) LOS ARTESANOS LIBERTARIOS Y LA ÉTICA DEL TRABAJO. THOA: LA PAZ.

MANSILLA CORTEZ, N. (2016) "DE HERENCIAS LIBERTARIAS A SOBRE VIGENCIAS CONTESTATARIAS" IN ANARQUISMO EN BOLIVIA AYER Y HOY. USS-CESU: COCHABAMBA.

MARGARUCCI, I. (2015) "COCINANDO LA REVOLUCIÓN EN LA CIUDAD DE LA PAZ, 1927-1946" IN REVISTA ARCHIVOS DE HISTORIA DEL MOVIMIENTO OBRERO Y LA IZQUIERDA. AÑO IV, NO 7. UBA: BUENOS AIRES

MARGARUCCI, I. (2022) ANARQUISMOS Y ANARQUISTAS EN LA REGIÓN ANDINA. UNA HISTORIA DEL MOVI-MIENTO LIBERTARIO EN BOLIVIA, 1905-1952. DOCTORAL THESIS IN HISTORY, PHILOSOPHY AND LITERATURE FACULTY, UNIVERSITY OF BUENOS AIRES.

RIVERA CUSICANQUI, S. (2016) "COMUNALIDADES ANARQUISTAS. UNA APROXIMACIÓN TESTIMONIAL" IN ANARQUISMO EN BOLIVIA AYER Y HOY. USS-CESU: COCHABAMBA.

RODRÍGUEZ GARCÍA, H. (2010) LA CHOLEDAD ANTIESTATAL. EL ANARCOSINDICALISMO EN EL MOVIMIENTO OBRERO BOLIVIANO (1912-1965). LIBROS DE LOS ANARRES: BUENOS AIRES.

WADSWORTH, A.C., DIBBITS, I. (1986) AGITADORAS DEL BUEN GUSTO. HISTORIA DEL SINDICATO DE CULINARIAS (1935-1950). TAHIPAMU: LA PAZ.

NOTES

THIS COMIC INTENDS TO SHOW CERTAIN ASPECTS OF THE HISTORY OF A TRADE UNION MOVEMENT THROUGH FICTION. WE CHOSE OUR PROTAGONISTS ROSA RODRÍGUEZ DE CALDERÓN, CATALINA MENDOZA, AND PETRONILA INFANTES, WELL-KNOWN LEADERS OF THE FEDERATION, BECAUSE THEY APPEAR IN THE TESTIMONIALS OF CHOLAS RECORDED IN BOOKS EDITED BY THE THOA, THE TAHIMPAU, AND OTHER AVAILABLE LITERATURE ON THE FOF. NEVERTHELESS, MANY OTHER WORKING WOMEN PARTICIPATED AND LED THE ORGANIZATION. PLEASE REFER TO THE BIBLIOGRAPHY TO FIND OUT THEIR NAMES, STORIES, AND LIBERTARIAN STRUGGLES.

PAGE 109: PETRONILA INFANTES REPORTED THAT HER EX-HUSBAND DIDN'T ACTUALLY DIE IN THE CHACO WAR, BUT THEY SEPARATED DUE TO HIS BEING ABUSIVE. (RODRÍGUEZ GARCÍA, 2010). PETRONILA WAS PORTRAYED AS A MOTHER OF ONLY ONE DAUGHTER, WHEN IN REALITY SHE HAD TWO CHILDREN DURING HER FIRST MARRIAGE.

PAGE 113: BASED ON IVANNA MARGARUCCI'S RESEARCH (2022), FOF CHOLAS IN 1929 DID NOT USE SUCH STRONG ANARCHIST SPEECH IN PUBLIC, BUT RATHER PRIVATELY WITHIN THE ORGANIZATION. WE SPECIFICALLY WANTED TO COMMUNICATE THEIR ANARCHIST POSITION.

PAGE 120: TORO AND BUSCH'S COUP HAPPENED ON MAY 17, 1936, DURING A MASSIVE ANTI-GOVERNMENT STRIKE LED BY TEJADA SORZANO. IT IS WORTH NOTING THAT DESPITE THE FOT'S SUPPORT FOR THE COUP, FOL TRADE UNIONISTS ALSO PARTICIPATED.

PAGE 120 AND 122: WHILE IT IS TRUE THAT THE FOL WELCOMED BOTH COOKS AND FLORISTS, EACH UNION GATHERED INDEPENDENTLY AND CHOSE THEIR LEADERS SEPARATELY. ONCE THE NEW FOF WAS CONSOLIDATED IN 1940, A COLLECTIVE ELECTION FOR FEDERATION REPRESENTATIVES WAS HELD.

PAGE 123: THESE EVENTS TOOK PLACE BETWEEN 1947 AND 1949. ACCORDING TO PETRONILA AND ALICIA'S TESTIMONIES (WADSWORTH AND DIBBITS, 1989), THIS DINNER WAS HELD IN THE PRESENCE OF PRESIDENT HERTZOG. PETRONILA DID, HOWEVER, SERVE BUSCH AS WELL.

PAGE 125-26: WE COMBINED DEMANDS THAT WEREN'T NECESSARILY MADE DURING THE TORO/BUSCH GOVERNMENT IN ORDER TO PORTRAY THE BREADTH OF THIS COLLECTIVE DEMONSTRATION. THE FIGHT FOR HEALTH BADGES AND CHILD CARE CENTERS TOOK PLACE BETWEEN 1934 AND 1936, UNDER TEJADA SORZANO'S GOVERNMENT. EVERY OTHER ISSUE WAS ADDRESSED OVER EXTENDED PERIODS OF TIME.

PAGE 127: THE COOKS STORMED THE PALACE DURING TEJADA SORIANO'S TENURE, NOT BUSCH'S. WE CHOSE TO DEPICT THE ANARCHIST CHOLAS' PERSPECIVES ON STATE AUTHORITIES IN BROAD STROKES.

PAGE 128: FEMALE TRADE UNION LEADERS WERE JAILED FOR DIFFERENT REASONS. THIS FICTIONAL SCENE WAS BASED ON PETRONILA'S EXPERIENCE IN PRISON. SHE WAS NOT, HOWEVER, JAILED FOR PARTICIPATING IN THIS PARTICULAR DEMONSTRATION. FRANCISCA LOAYZA, ON THE OTHER HAD, DID IN FACT DIE FOLLOWING HER INCARCERATION IN 1937.

PAGE 133: THE LA MERCED MARKET, NAMED AFTER A TEMPLE OF THE SAME NAME LOCATED JUST ACROSS THE WAY, WAS BUILT SPECIFICALLY FOR FLORISTS IN 1939. CONSTRUCTION ON THE LANZA AND OTHER MARKETS BEGAN IN 1937. IN OUR VERSION, CATALINA MENDOZA FONDLY RECALLS THE DAY SHE WAS GIVEN HER STALL AT LA MERCED (LEHM AND RIVERA CUSICANQUI, 1986).

PAGE 136: IN 2008, DEMOLITION BEGAN IN PREPARATION FOR THE RECONSTRUCTION OF THE OLD LANZA MARKET. THIS WAS A UNILATERAL DECISION MADE BY THE LA PAZ GOVERNMENT WITHOUT ANY INPUT FROM ITS EXISTING VENDORS. ALTHOUGH THE TRADE UNION WASN'T AS STRONG AS IT ONCE WAS, CHOLAS STILL PLAYED A KEY ROLE IN PROTESTING DEMOLITION. (MANSILLA CORTEZ, 2016).

ACKNOWLEDGEMENTS

WE WOULD LKE TO THANK THE ANARCHIST CHOLAS FOR THEIR INSPIRING PURSUIT OF A DECENT, AUTONOMOUS LIFE WORTH LIVING. SPECIAL THANKS ALSO GOES TO RESEARCHER IVANNA MARGARUCCI FOR HER KINDNESS, AND FOR PROVIDING DOCUMENTS ESSENTIAL TO THE CREATION OF THIS COMIC, AS WELL AS FOR TAKING THE TIME TO REVIEW OUR DRAFTS AND SUBSEQUENT INPUT. WE WOULD SIMIILARLY LIKE TO THANK THE CARTOONIST NACHA VOLLENWEIDER FOR HER ASSISTANCE AND HER SUGGESTIONS THROUGHOUT OUR CREATIVE PROCESS, AND TO JEISSON CORTÉS FOR ACCOMPANYING US ON THIS JOURNEY. THANKS TO JORGE ALEMÁN AND ANDRÉS BELTRÁN FOR READING OUR WORK AND SHARING THEIR VALUABLE INSIGHTS. WE WOULD ALSO LIKE TO THANK SILVIA RIVERA C. AND ZULEMAN LEHM FOR SHARING THESE WOMEN'S COLLECTED TESTIMONIALS. WITH THESE DOCUMENTS, WE WERE ABLE TO PORTRAY THEM AS THE PEOPLE-CENTERED ACTIVISTS AND FIGHTERS THAT THEY WERE.

BASED ON THE RESEARCH STUDY BY SILVIA RIVERA C. AND ZULEMAN LEHM (THOA),*
TAHIMPAMU GROUP,** IVANNA MARGARUCCI, AND HUASCAR RODRÍGUEZ G.
ADDITIONAL DRAWING ASSISTANCE PROVIDED BY JEISSON CORTÉS @JEISSON5252.

*SPANISH FOR ORAL HISTORY WORKSHOP.
**HISTORY AND WOMEN'S PARTICIPATION WORKSHOP.

Tracing between colors of the highlands

Dương Mạnh Hùng

Phạm Thu Trà

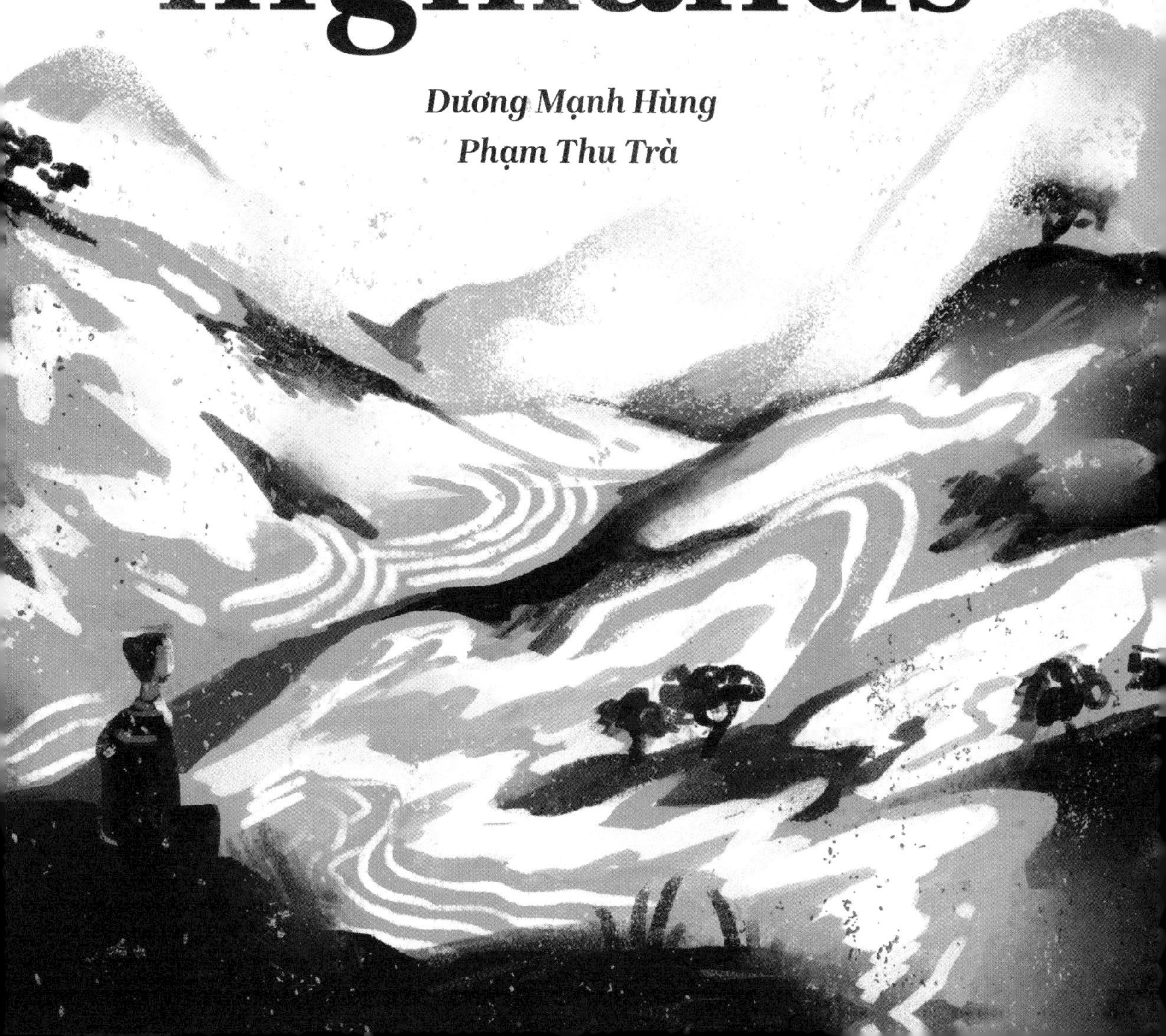

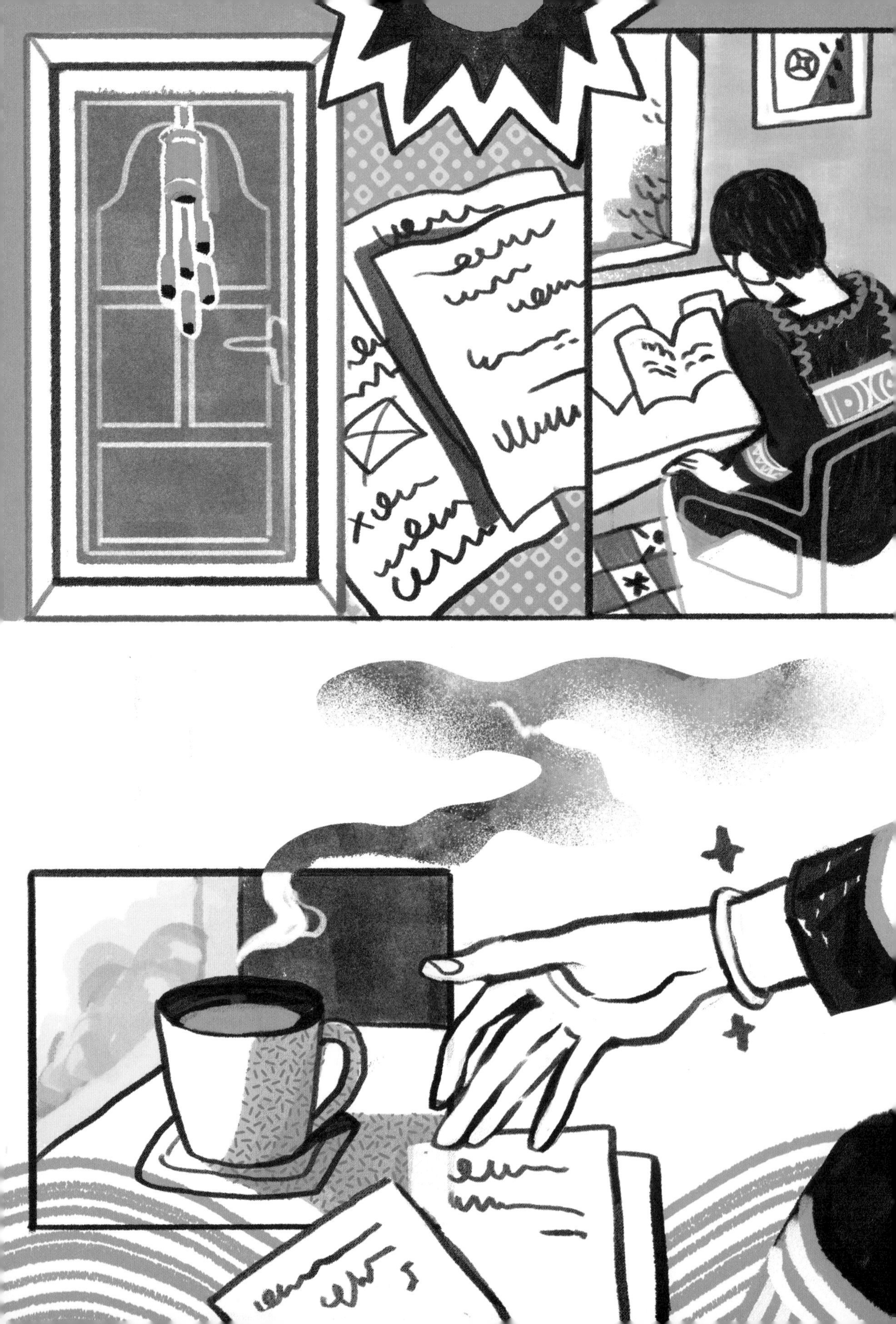

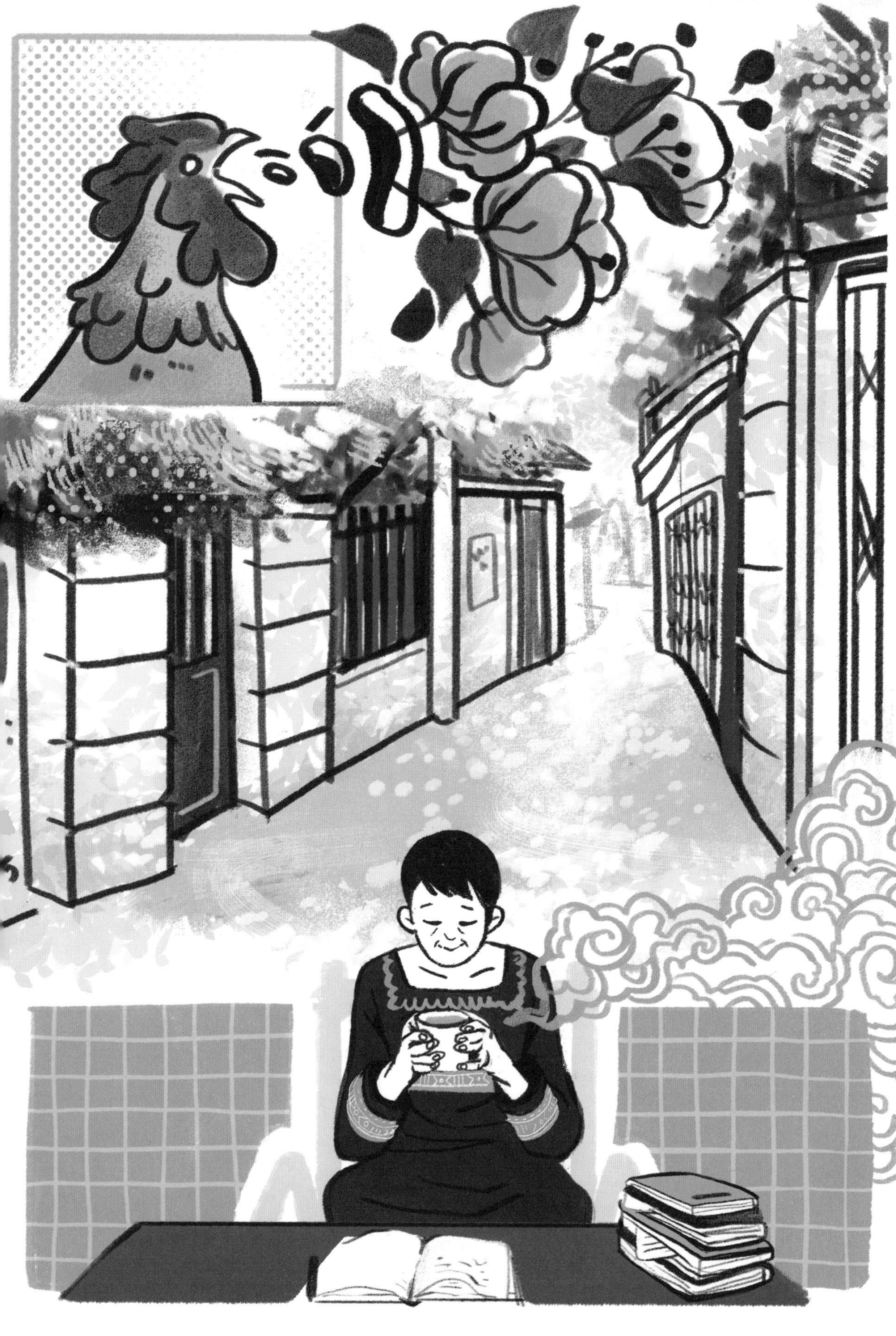

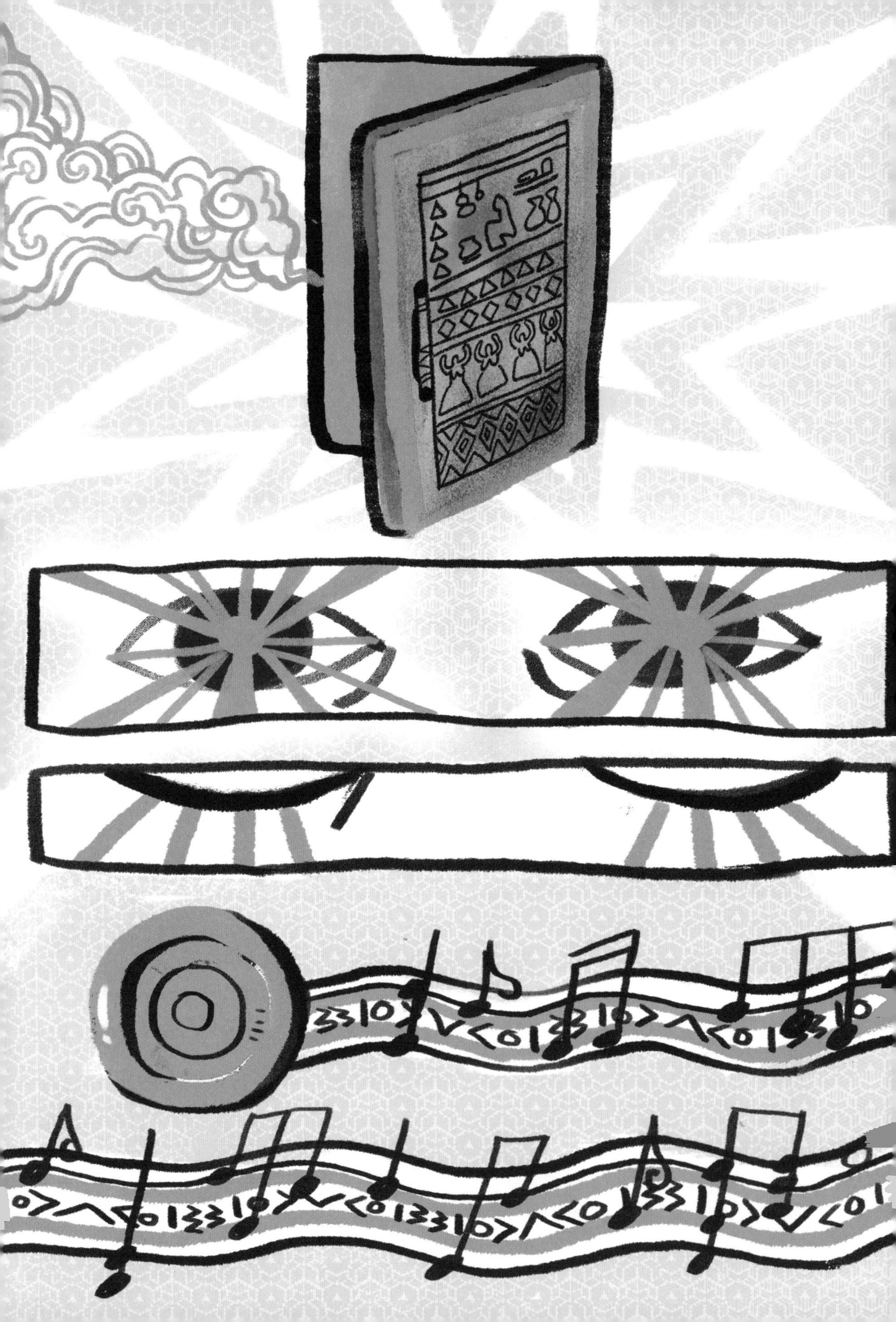

Chapter 1: The Culture Cradle

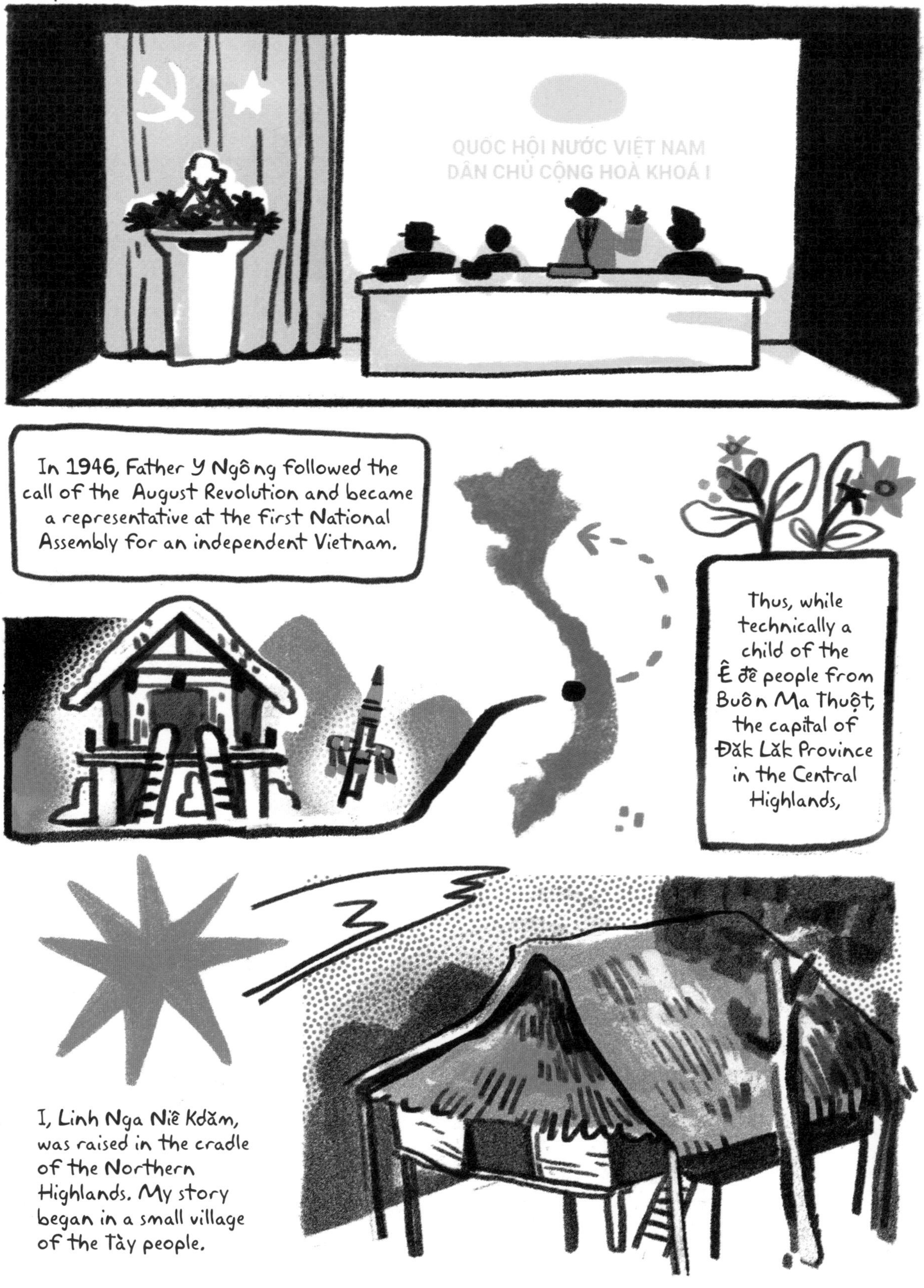
QUỐC HỘI NƯỚC VIỆT NAM
DÂN CHỦ CỘNG HOÀ KHOÁ I
In 1946, Father Y Ngông followed the call of the August Revolution and became a representative at the first National Assembly for an independent Vietnam.
Thus, while technically a child of the Ê đê people from Buôn Ma Thuột, the capital of Đăk Lăk Province in the Central Highlands,
I, Linh Nga Niê Kdăm, was raised in the cradle of the Northern Highlands. My story began in a small village of the Tày people.

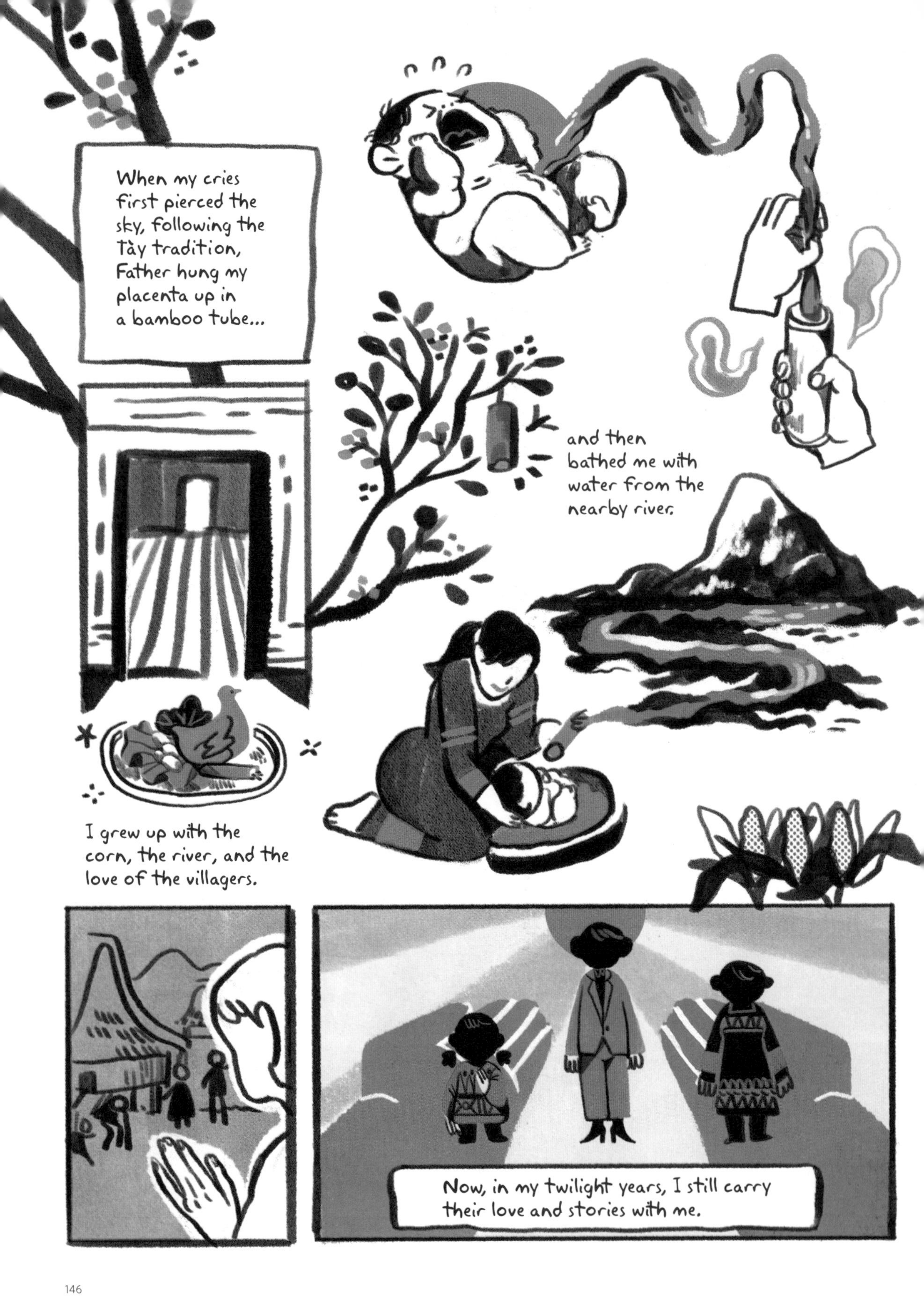
When my cries first pierced the sky, following the Tày tradition, Father hung my placenta up in a bamboo tube...
and then bathed me with water from the nearby river.
I grew up with the corn, the river, and the love of the villagers.
Now, in my twilight years, I still carry their love and stories with me.

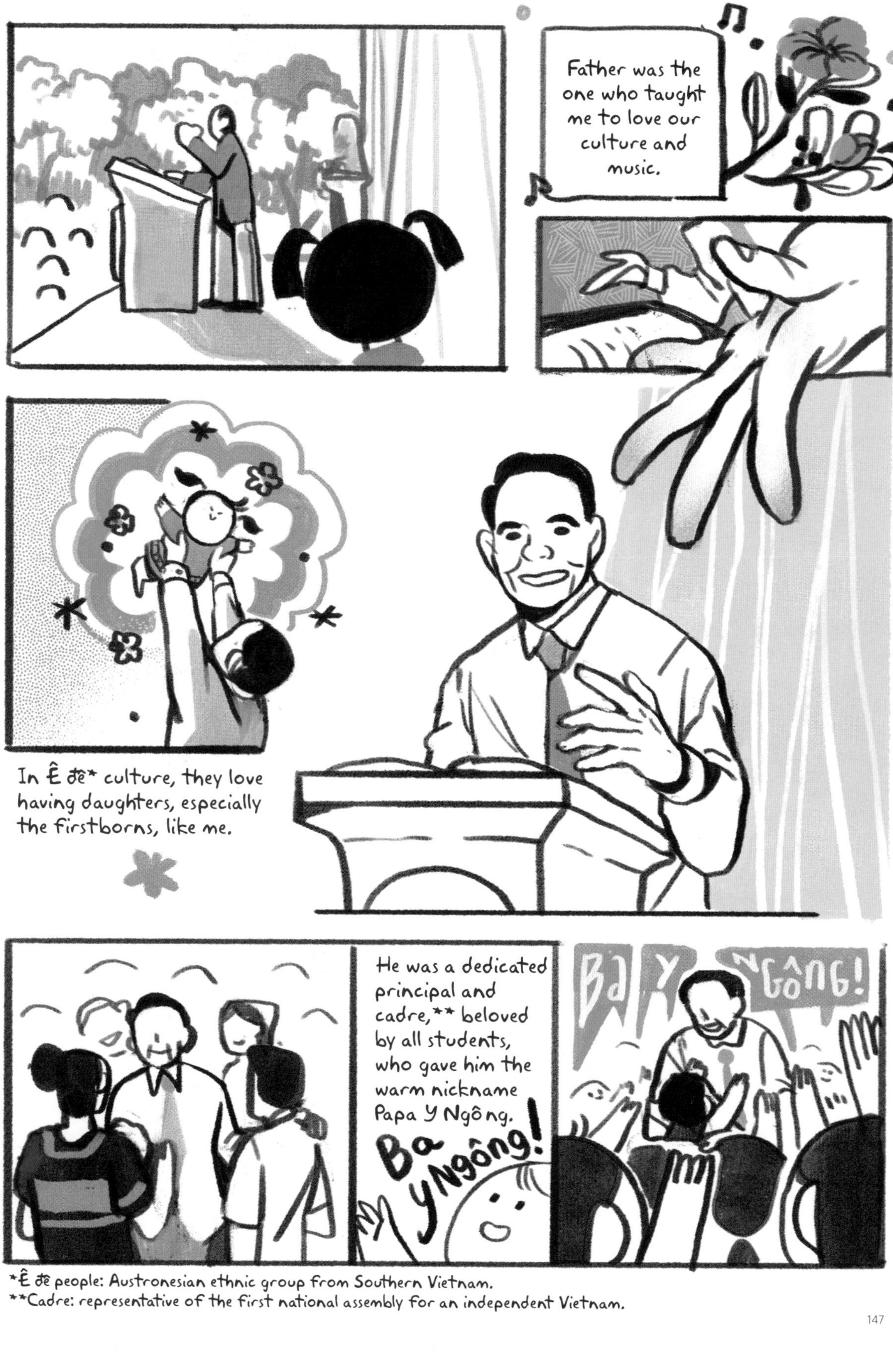
Father was the one who taught me to love our culture and music.
In Ê đê* culture, they love having daughters, especially the firstborns, like me.
He was a dedicated principal and cadre,** beloved by all students, who gave him the warm nickname Papa Y Ngông.
Ba Y Ngông!
Ba Y Ngông!

*Ê đê people: Austronesian ethnic group from Southern Vietnam.
**Cadre: representative of the first national assembly for an independent Vietnam.

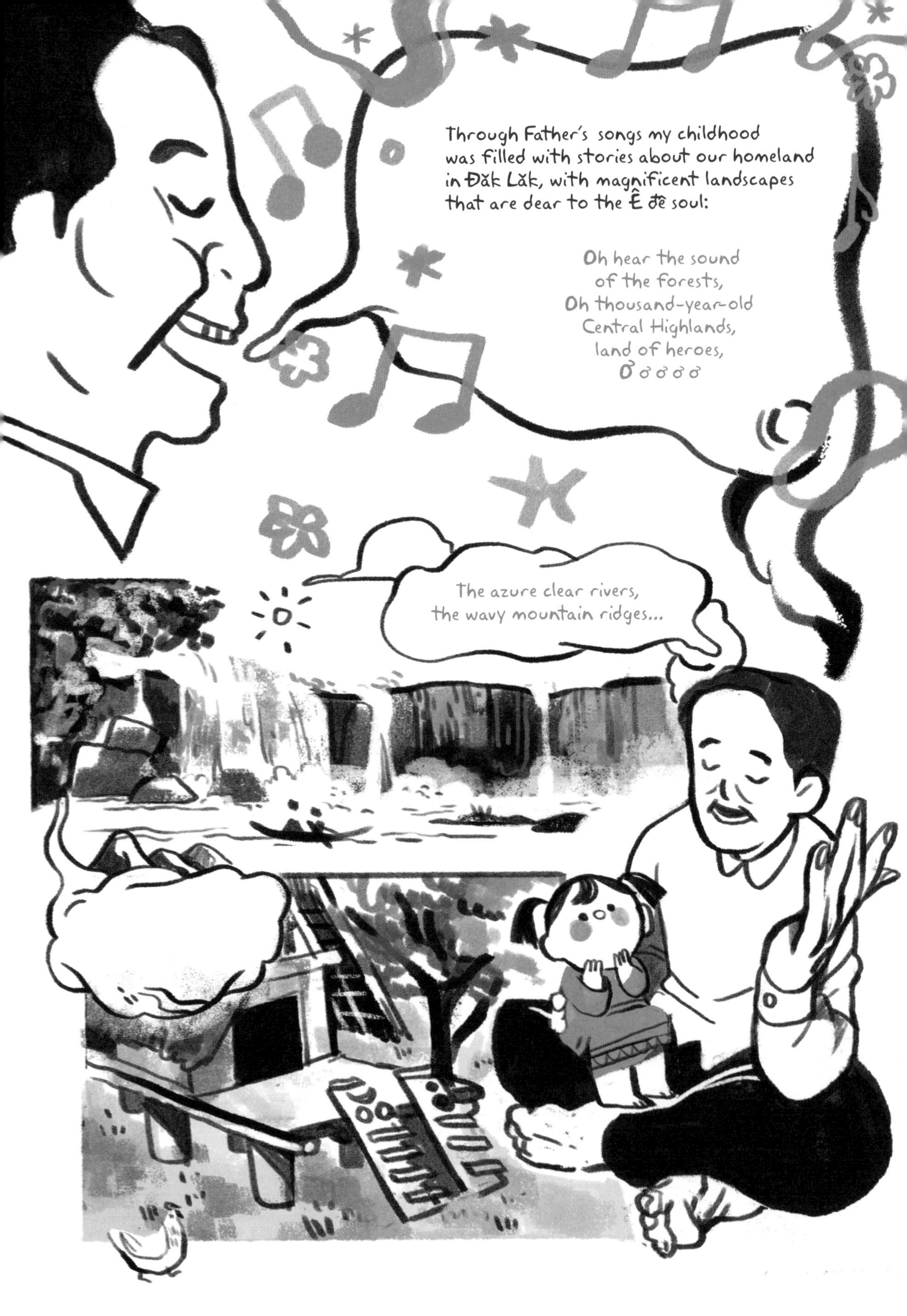
Through Father's songs my childhood was filled with stories about our homeland in Đăk Lăk, with magnificent landscapes that are dear to the Ê đê soul:
Oh hear the sound of the forests, Oh thousand-year-old Central Highlands, land of heroes, Ơ ơ ơ ơ ơ
The azure clear rivers, the wavy mountain ridges...

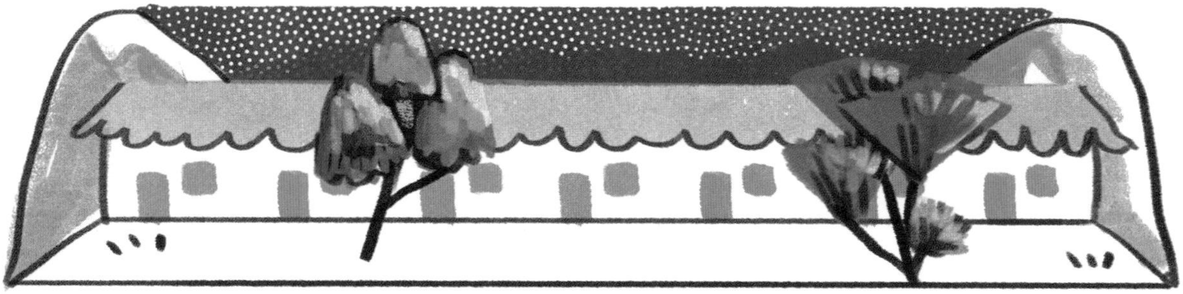

The school for Southern students, where Father was the headmaster, was also home to hundreds of cadres from the Central Highlands.

They decorated their houses according to their customs, even bringing everyday objects from home: from livestock to musical instruments.

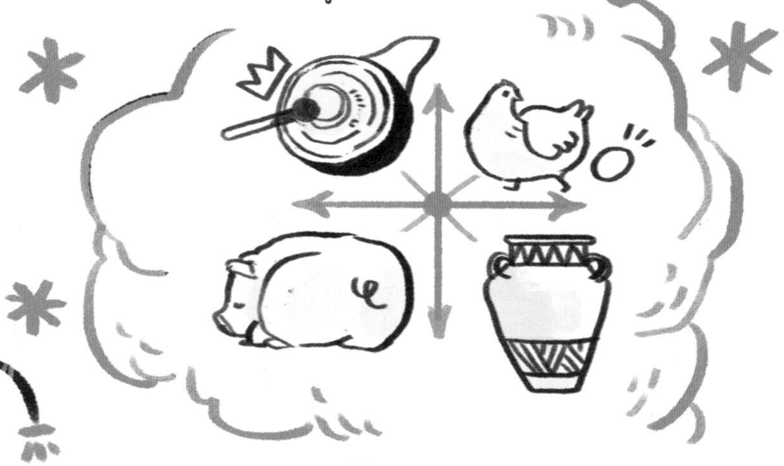

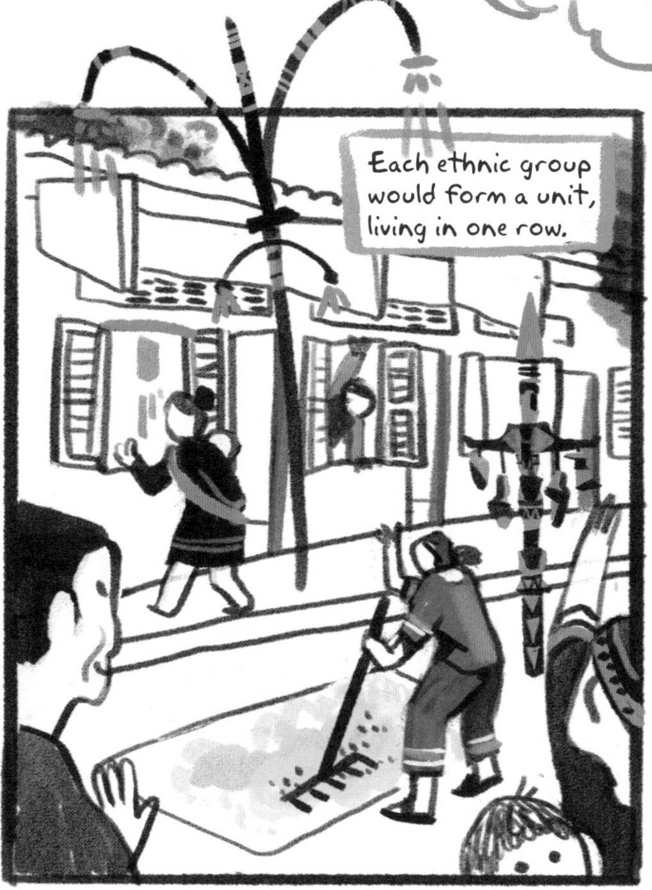

Each ethnic group would form a unit, living in one row.

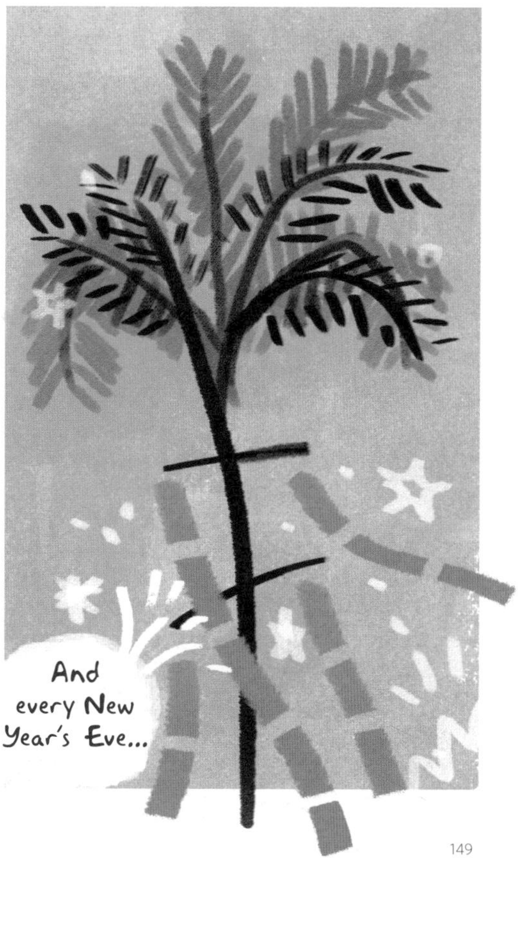

And every New Year's Eve...

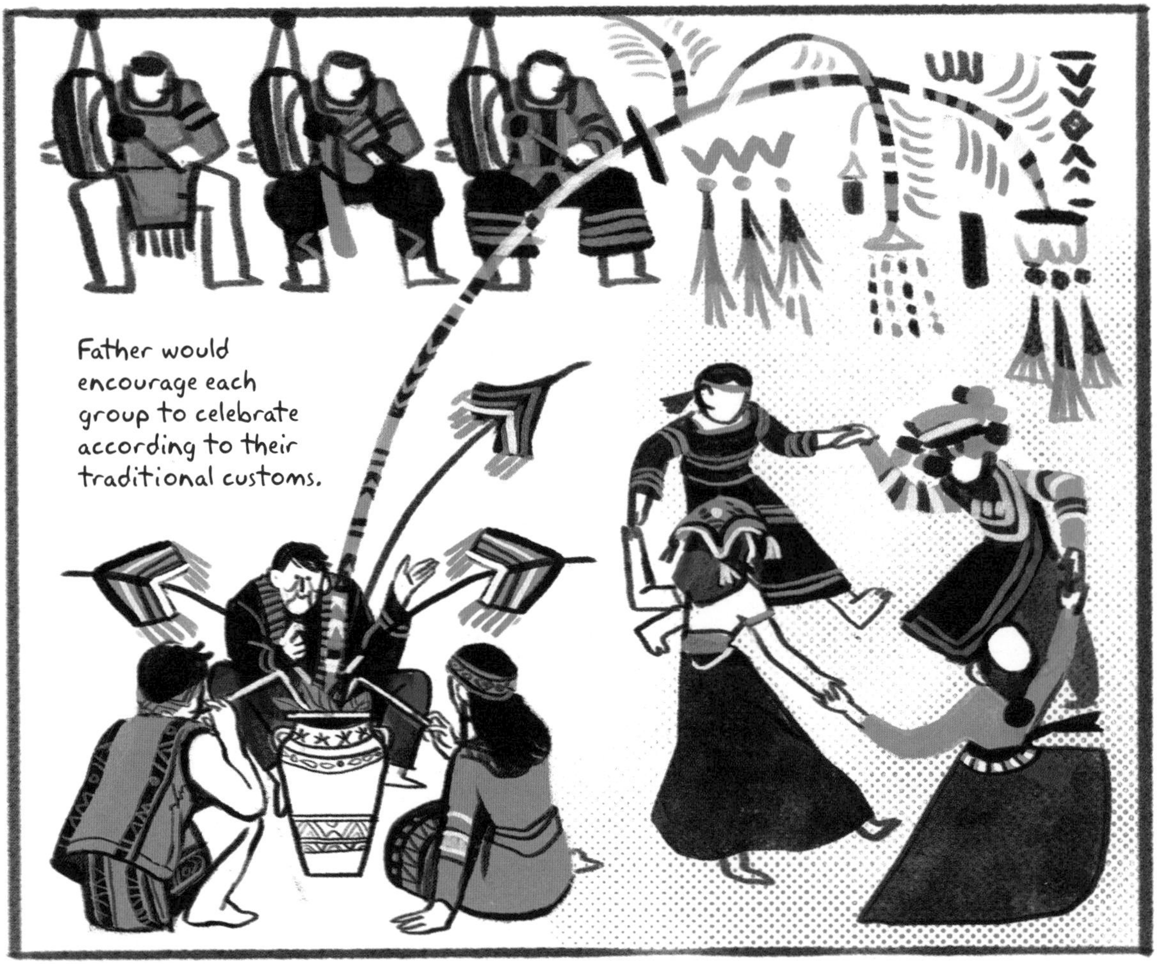
Father would encourage each group to celebrate according to their traditional customs.

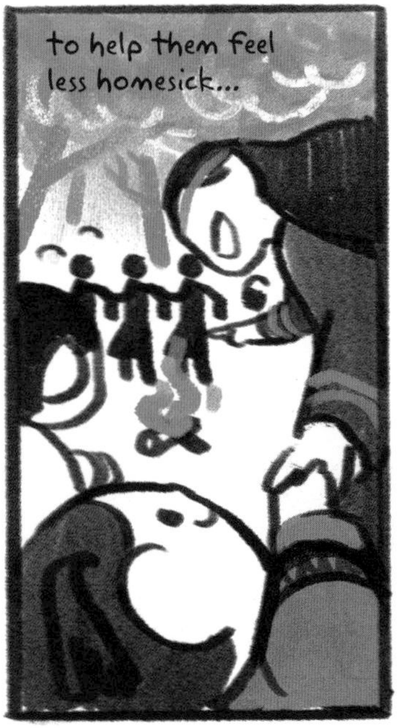
to help them feel less homesick...

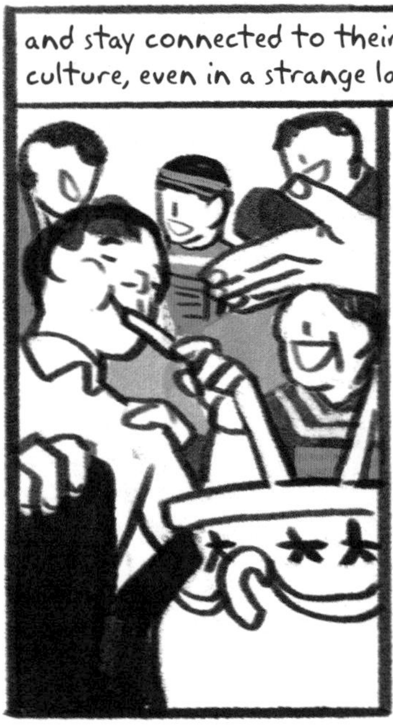
and stay connected to their culture, even in a strange land.

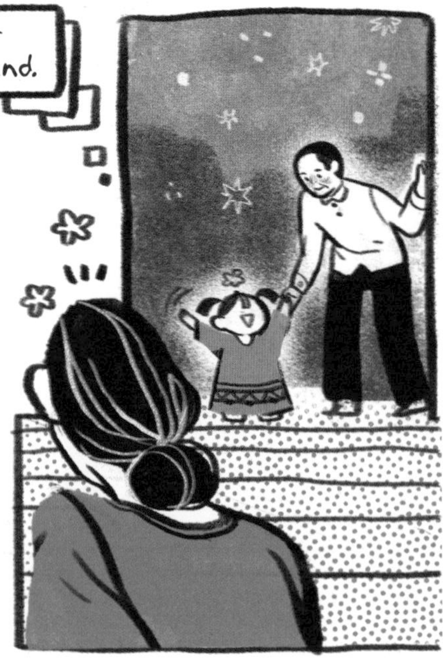

In line with Highland tradition, Father and I were gifted a small string of meat to bring home with us when we visited their homes during the celebrations.

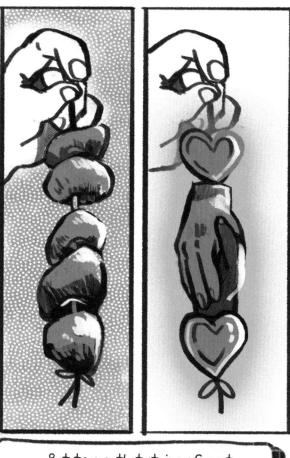

Mother would always complain that the fat stained father's suit.

But to me, that string of meat was the core of collective life: communities sharing food and love.

In that small gift lies a whole culture of how to treat others.

Chapter 2: Guidance from the Folk Performers

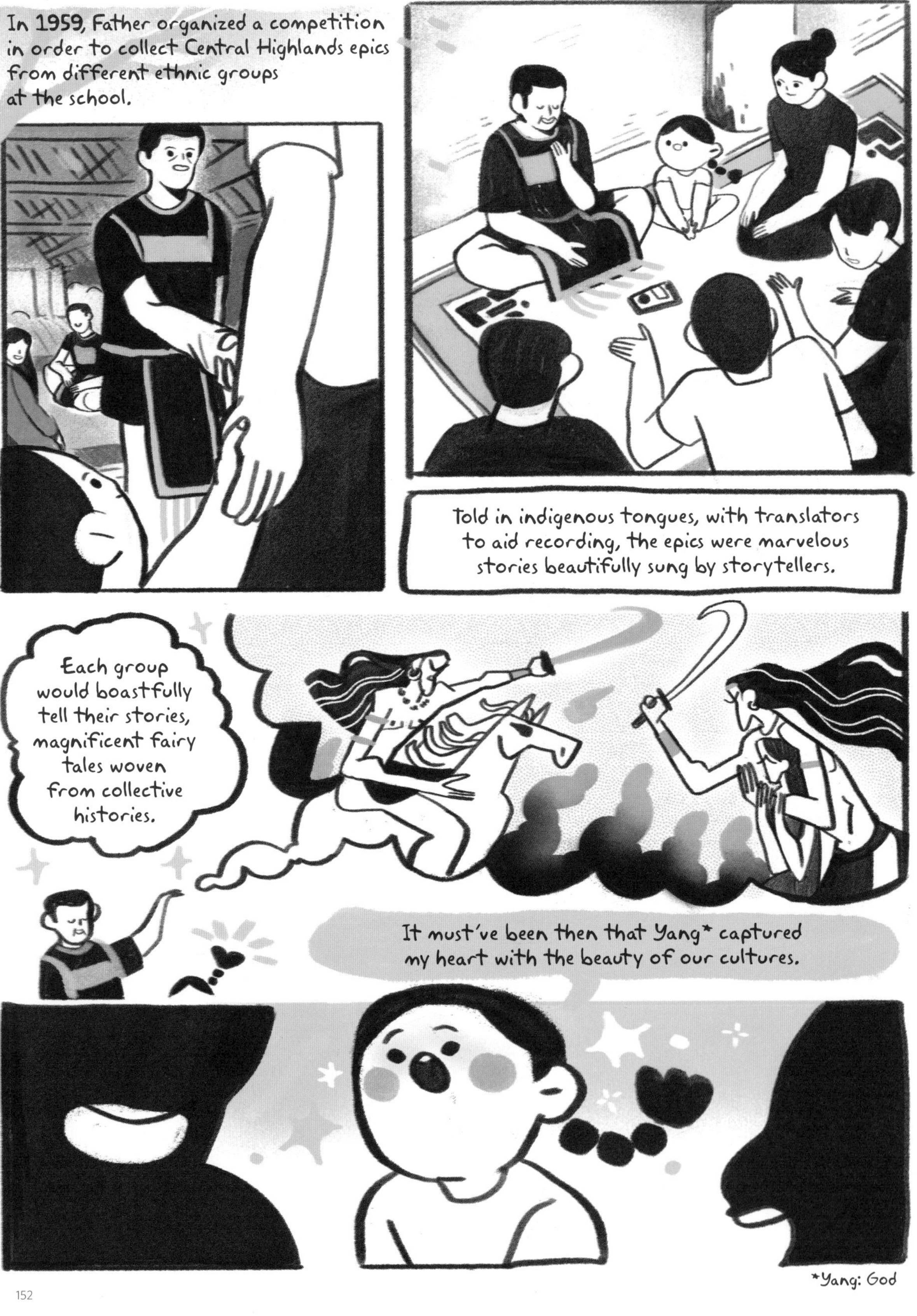
In 1959, Father organized a competition in order to collect Central Highlands epics from different ethnic groups at the school.
Told in indigenous tongues, with translators to aid recording, the epics were marvelous stories beautifully sung by storytellers.
Each group would boastfully tell their stories, magnificent fairy tales woven from collective histories.
It must've been then that Yang* captured my heart with the beauty of our cultures.

*Yang: God

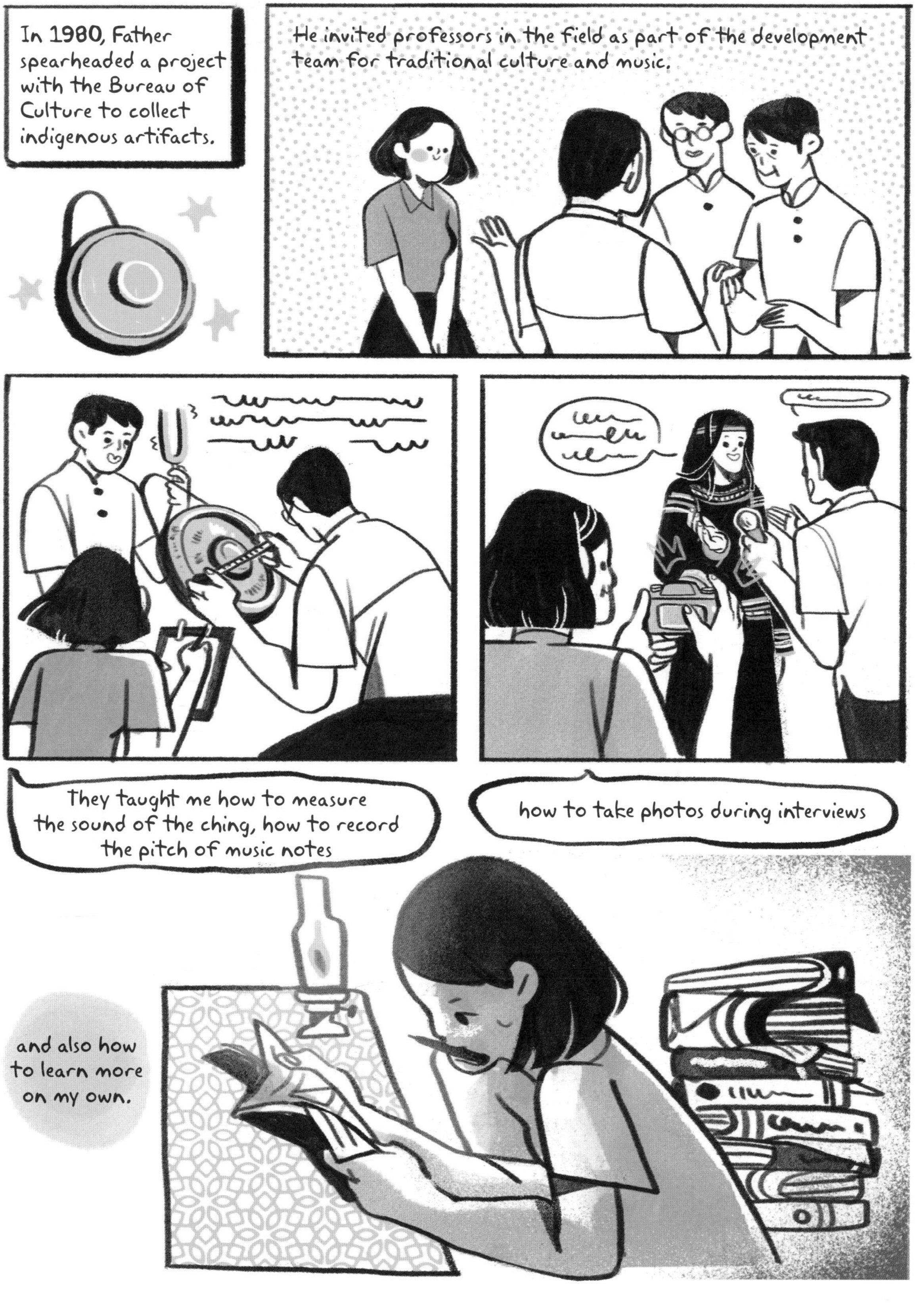
In 1980, Father spearheaded a project with the Bureau of Culture to collect indigenous artifacts.
He invited professors in the field as part of the development team for traditional culture and music.
They taught me how to measure the sound of the ching, how to record the pitch of music notes
how to take photos during interviews
and also how to learn more on my own.

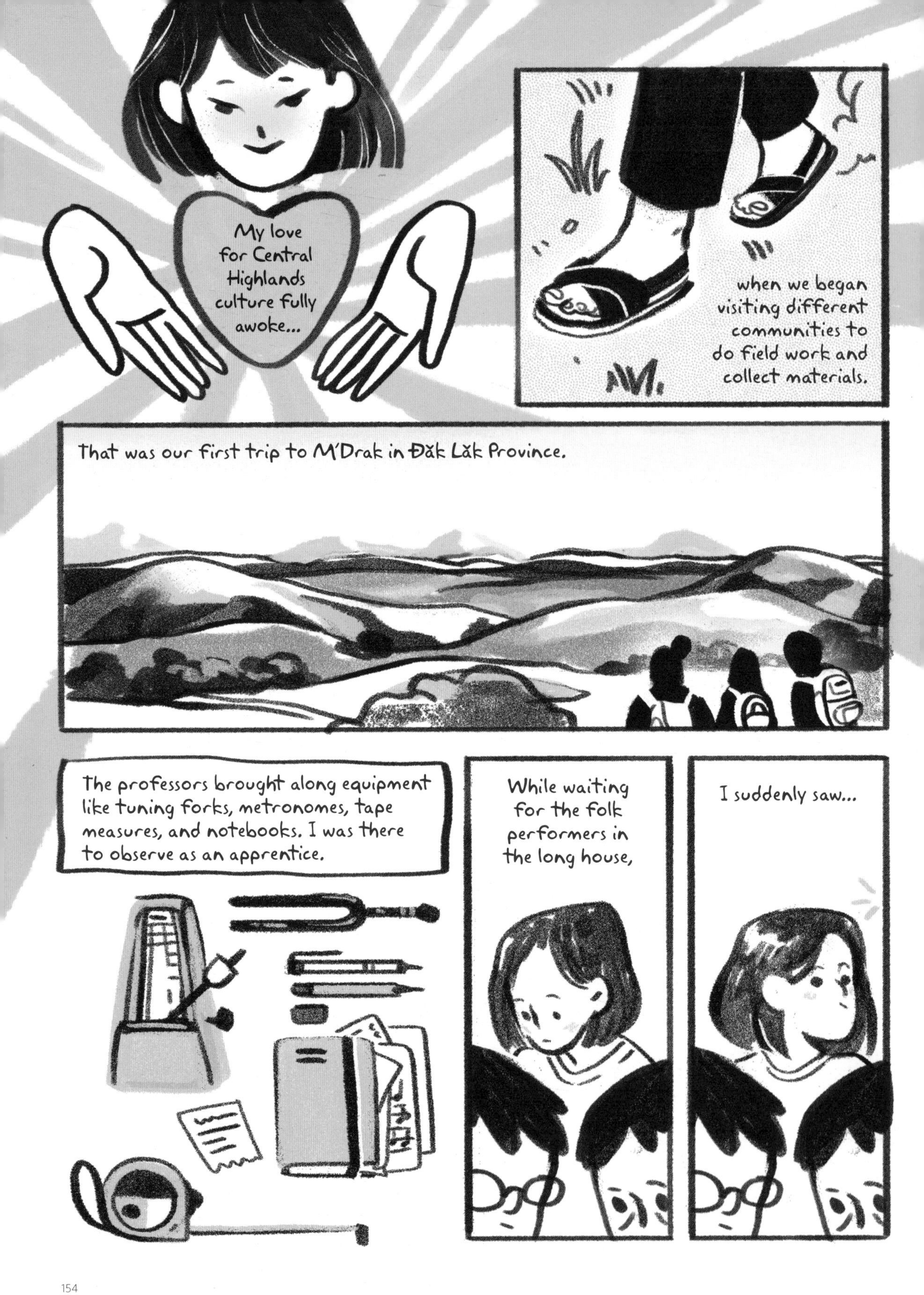
My love for Central Highlands culture fully awoke...
when we began visiting different communities to do field work and collect materials.
That was our first trip to M'Drak in Đăk Lăk Province.
The professors brought along equipment like tuning forks, metronomes, tape measures, and notebooks. I was there to observe as an apprentice.
While waiting for the folk performers in the long house,
I suddenly saw...

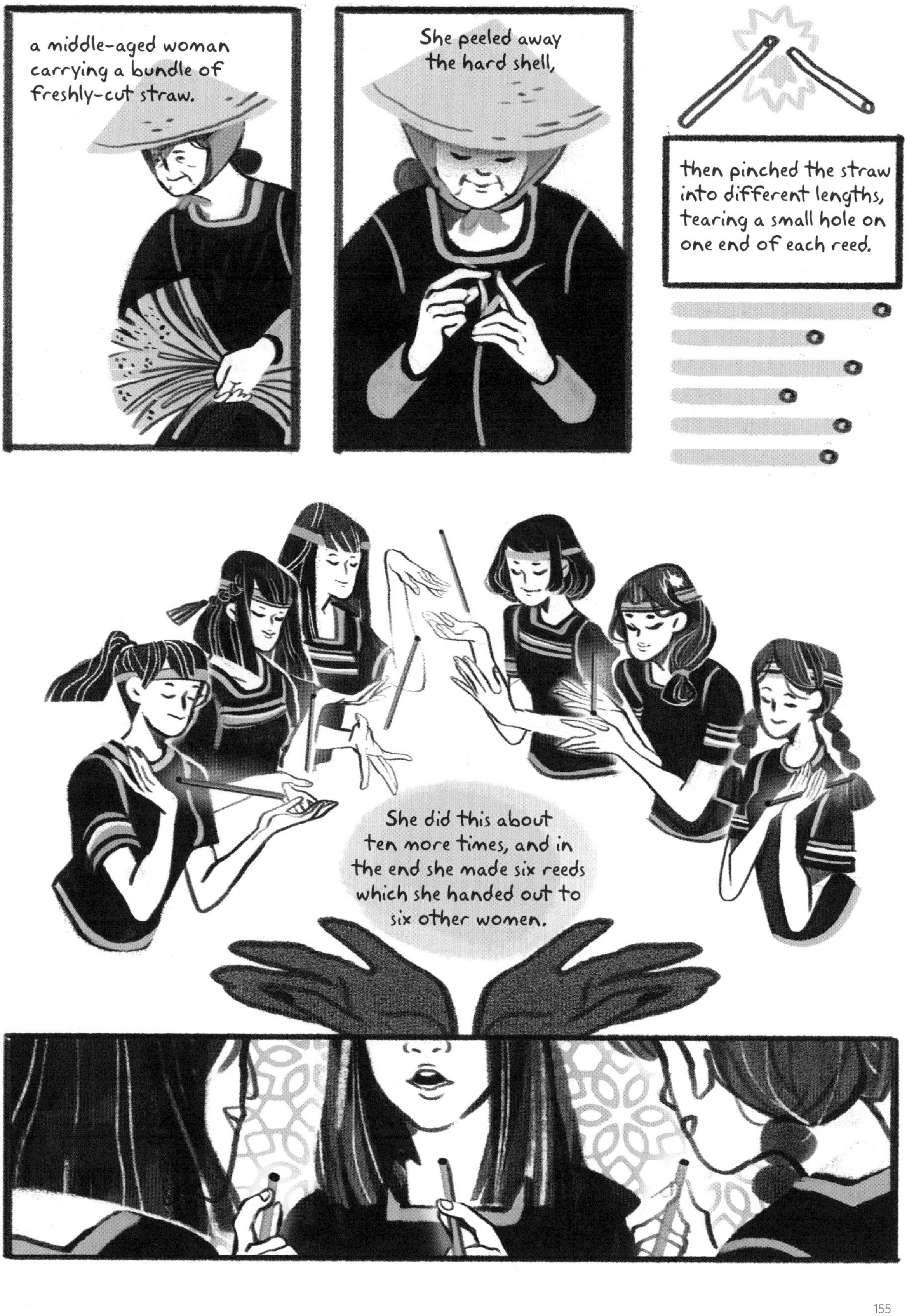
a middle-aged woman carrying a bundle of freshly-cut straw.
She peeled away the hard shell,
then pinched the straw into different lengths, tearing a small hole on one end of each reed.
She did this about ten more times, and in the end she made six reeds which she handed out to six other women.

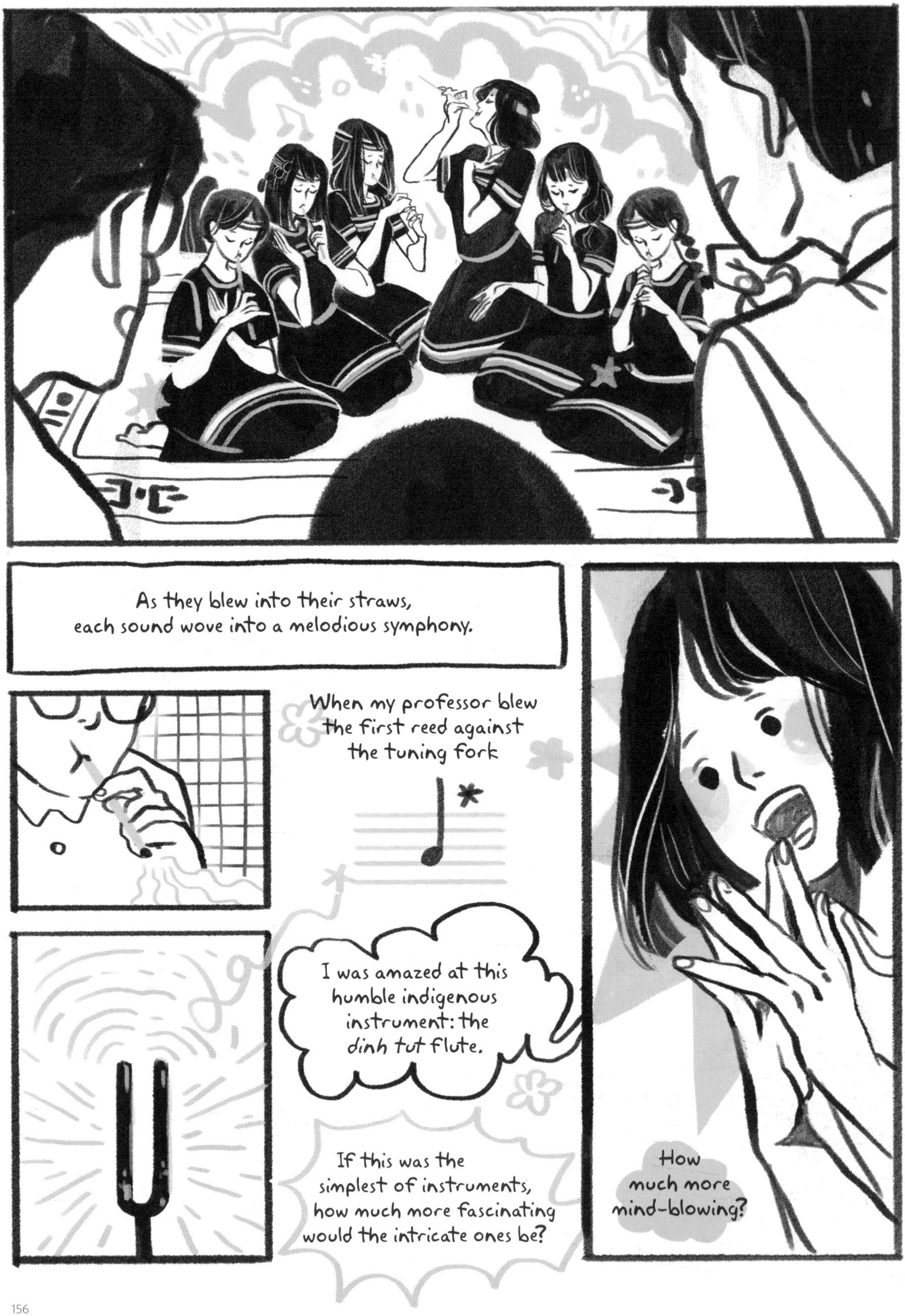
As they blew into their straws,
each sound wove into a melodious symphony.
When my professor blew the first reed against the tuning fork
I was amazed at this humble indigenous instrument: the *dinh tut* flute.
If this was the simplest of instruments, how much more fascinating would the intricate ones be?
How much more mind-blowing?

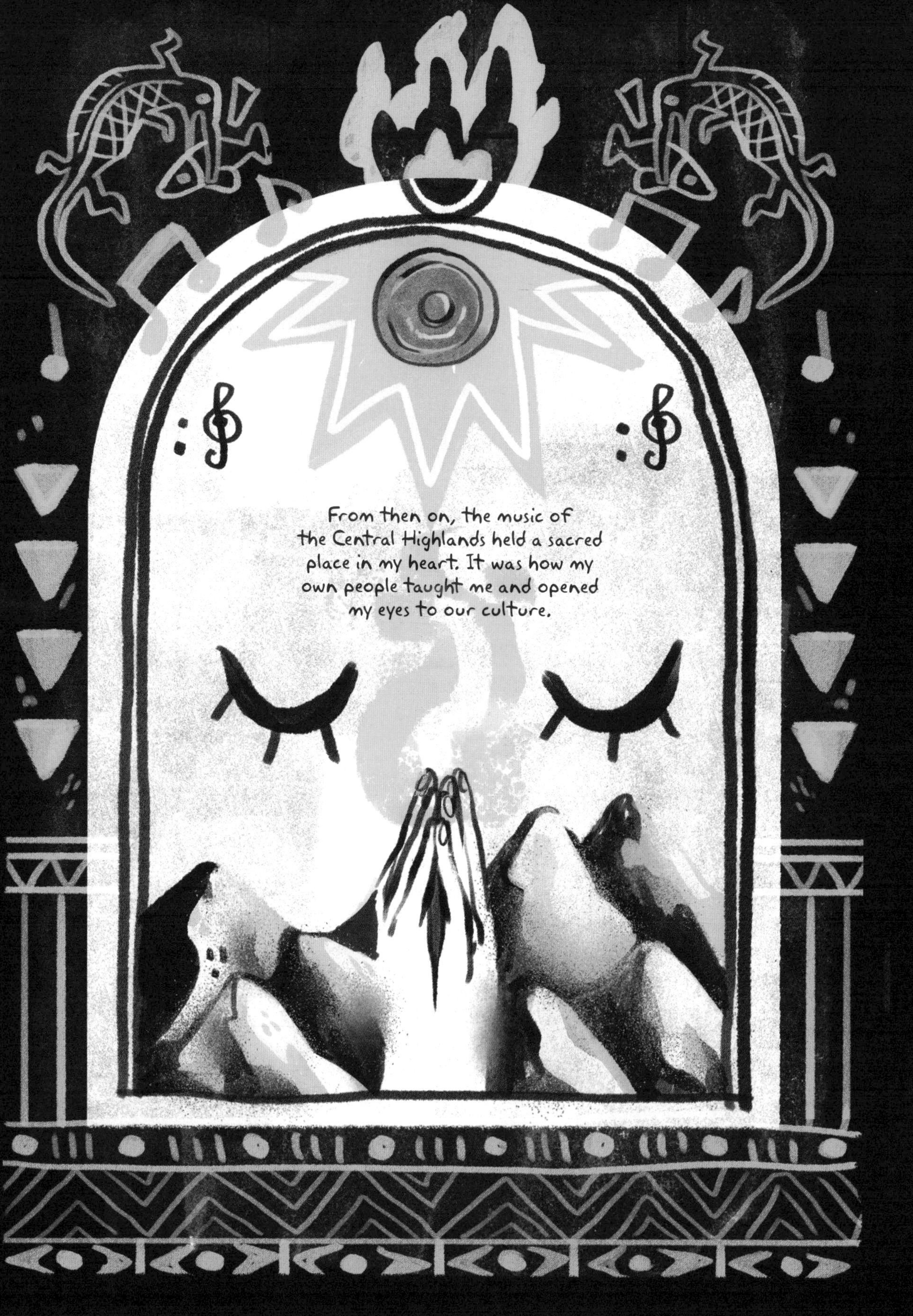
From then on, the music of the Central Highlands held a sacred place in my heart. It was how my own people taught me and opened my eyes to our culture.

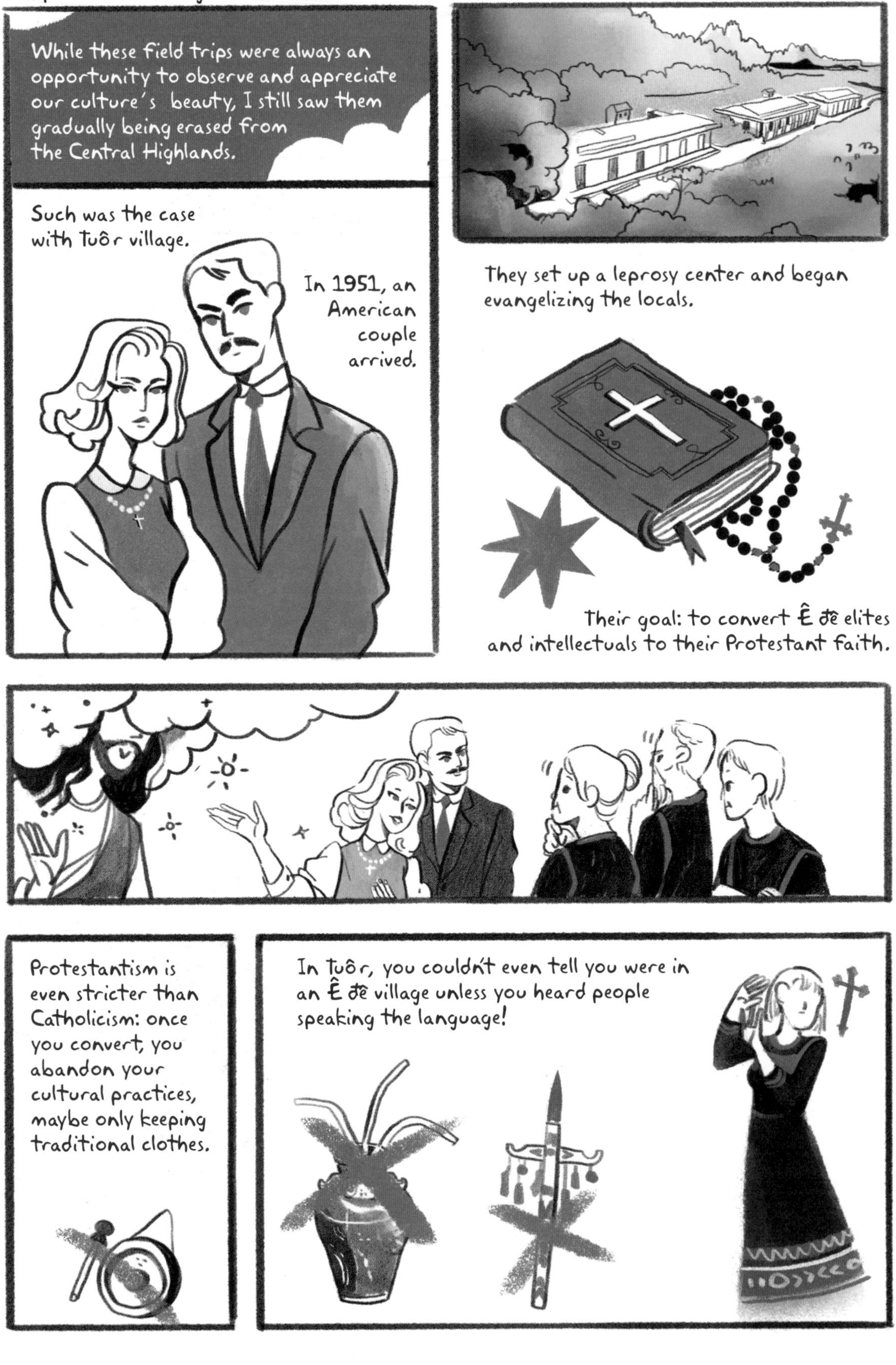
While these field trips were always an opportunity to observe and appreciate our culture's beauty, I still saw them gradually being erased from the Central Highlands.
Such was the case with Tuôr village.
In 1951, an American couple arrived.
They set up a leprosy center and began evangelizing the locals.
Their goal: to convert Ê đê elites and intellectuals to their Protestant faith.
Protestantism is even stricter than Catholicism: once you convert, you abandon your cultural practices, maybe only keeping traditional clothes.
In Tuôr, you couldn't even tell you were in an Ê đê village unless you heard people speaking the language!

Upon our first encounter,
the villagers were very suspicious.

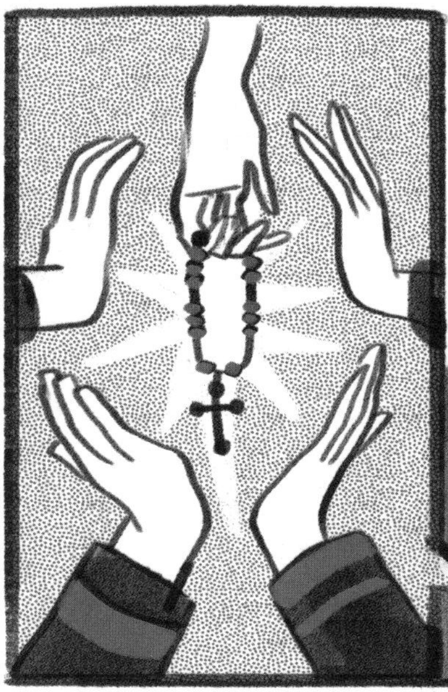

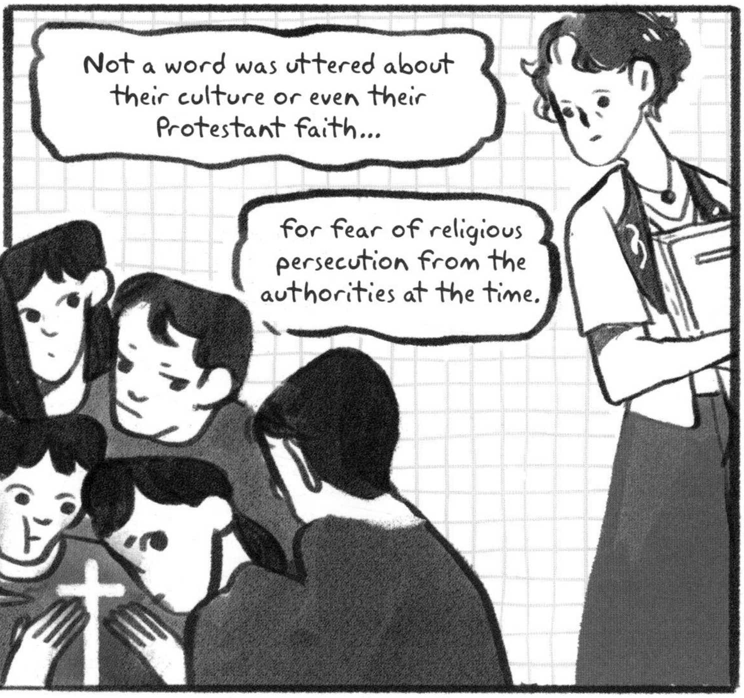
Not a word was uttered about their culture or even their Protestant faith...
for fear of religious persecution from the authorities at the time.

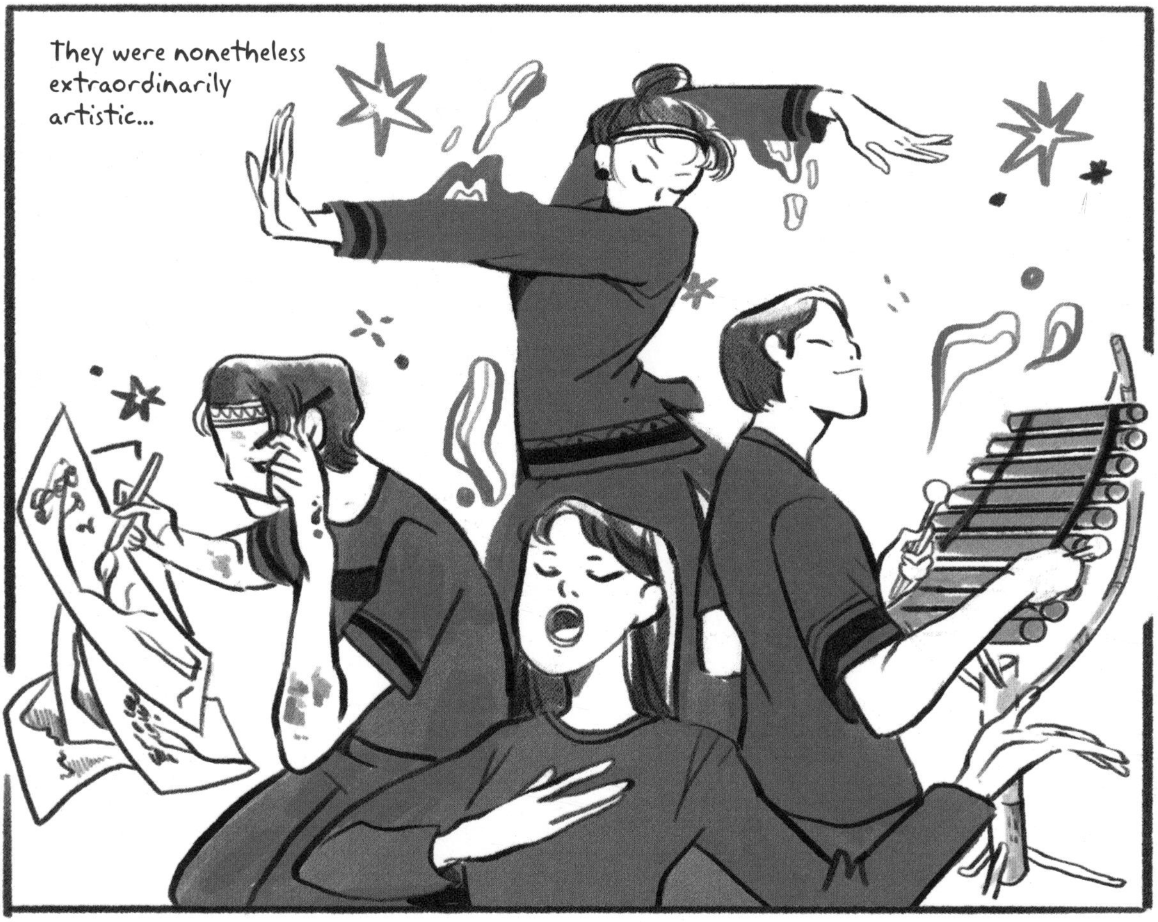
They were nonetheless extraordinarily artistic...

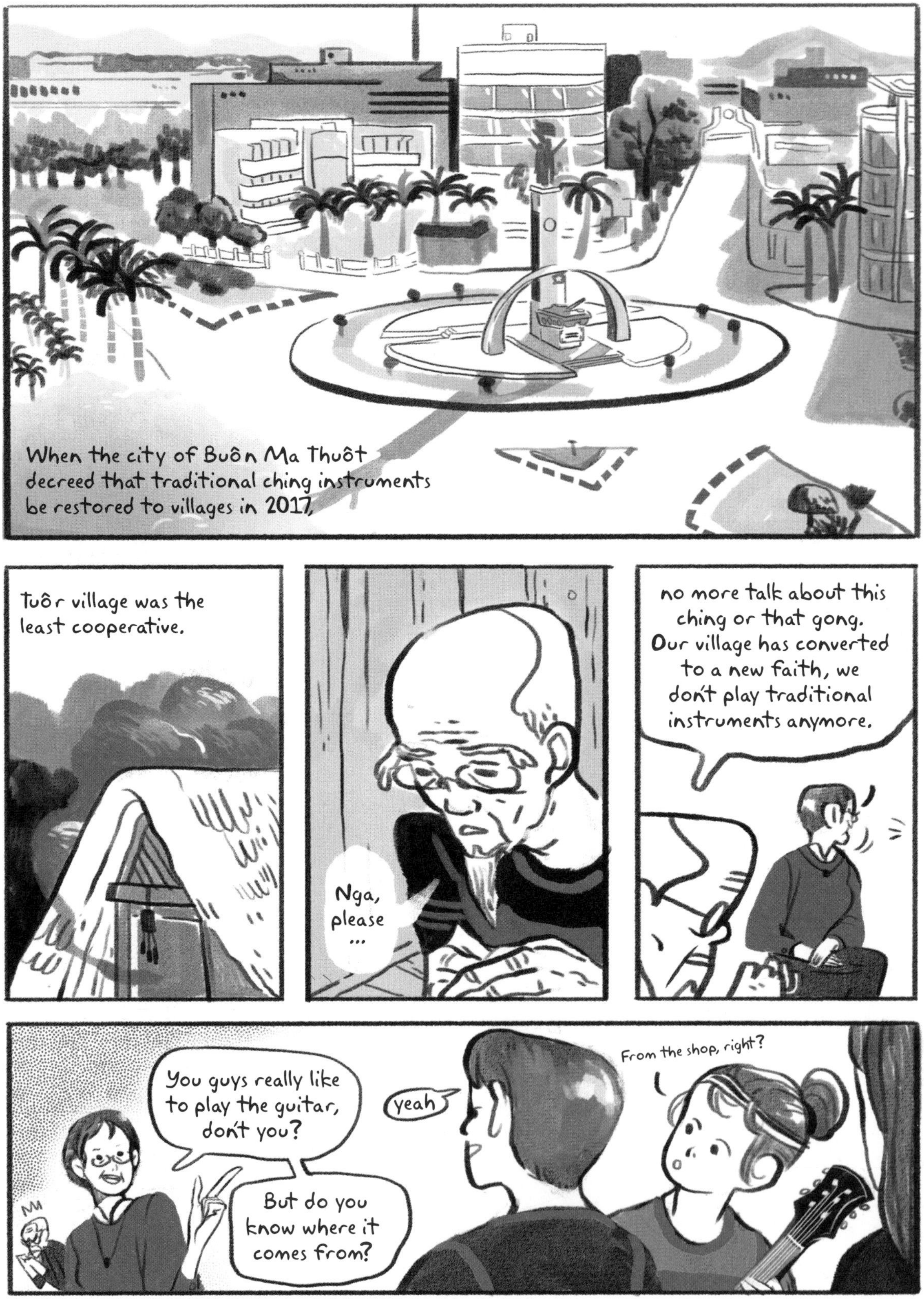

When the city of Buôn Ma Thuột decreed that traditional ching instruments be restored to villages in 2017,
Tuôr village was the least cooperative.
Nga, please ...
no more talk about this ching or that gong. Our village has converted to a new faith, we don't play traditional instruments anymore.
You guys really like to play the guitar, don't you?
But do you know where it comes from?
yeah
From the shop, right?

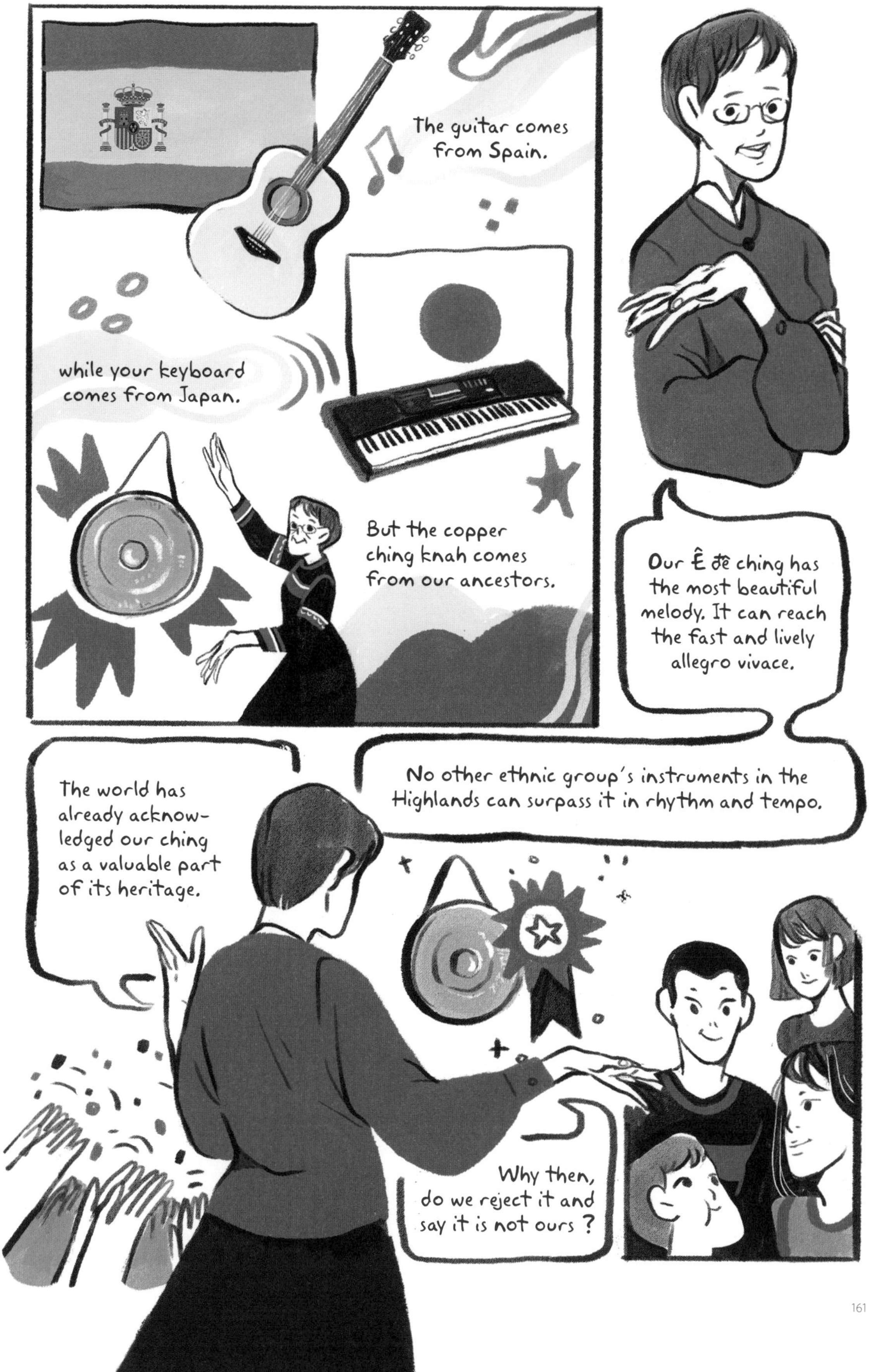

The guitar comes from Spain.
while your keyboard comes from Japan.
But the copper ching knah comes from our ancestors.
Our Ê đê ching has the most beautiful melody. It can reach the fast and lively allegro vivace.
No other ethnic group's instruments in the Highlands can surpass it in rhythm and tempo.
The world has already acknow-ledged our ching as a valuable part of its heritage.
Why then, do we reject it and say it is not ours ?

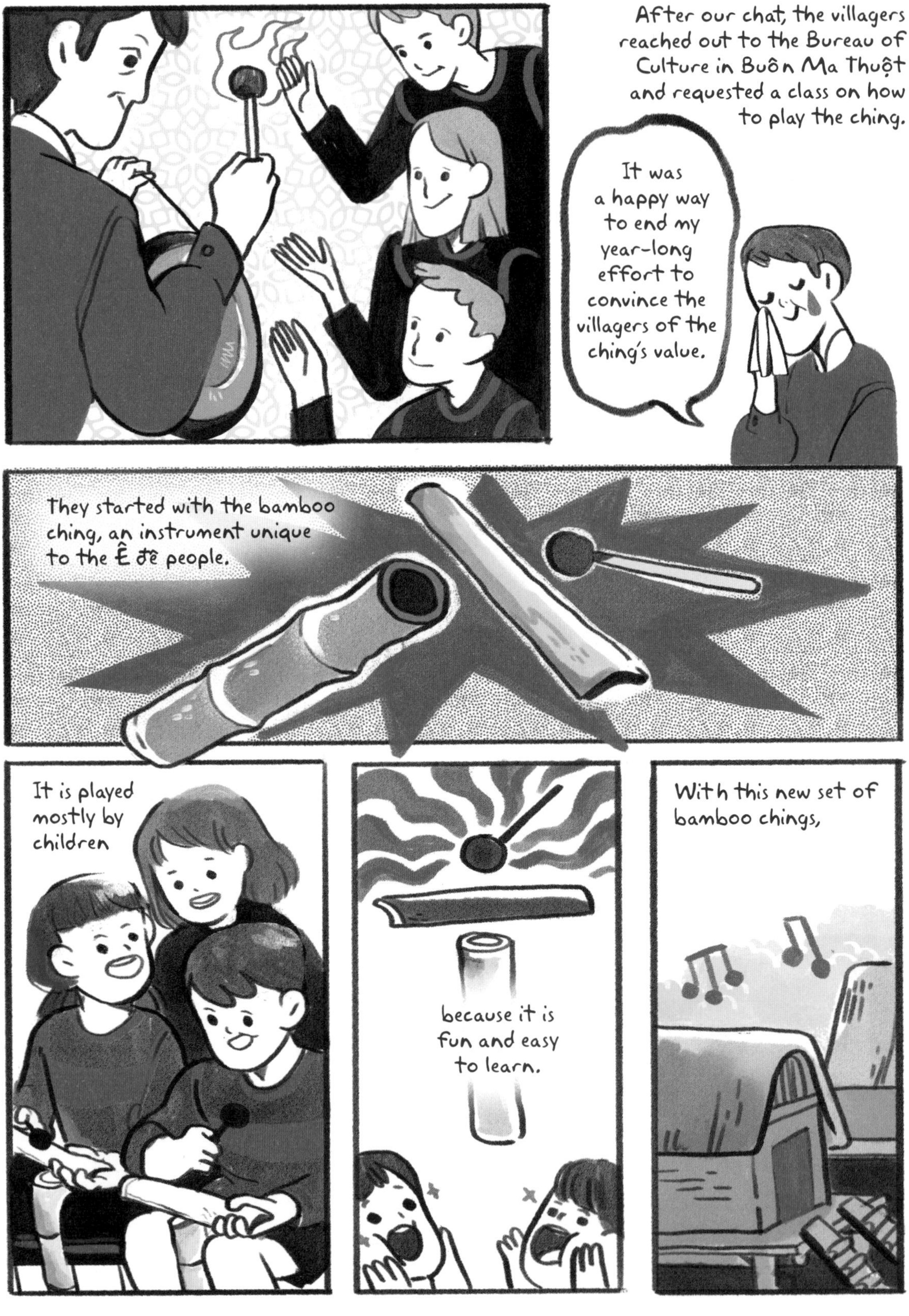
After our chat, the villagers reached out to the Bureau of Culture in Buôn Ma Thuột and requested a class on how to play the ching.
It was a happy way to end my year-long effort to convince the villagers of the ching's value.
They started with the bamboo ching, an instrument unique to the Ê đê people.
It is played mostly by children
because it is fun and easy to learn.
With this new set of bamboo chings,

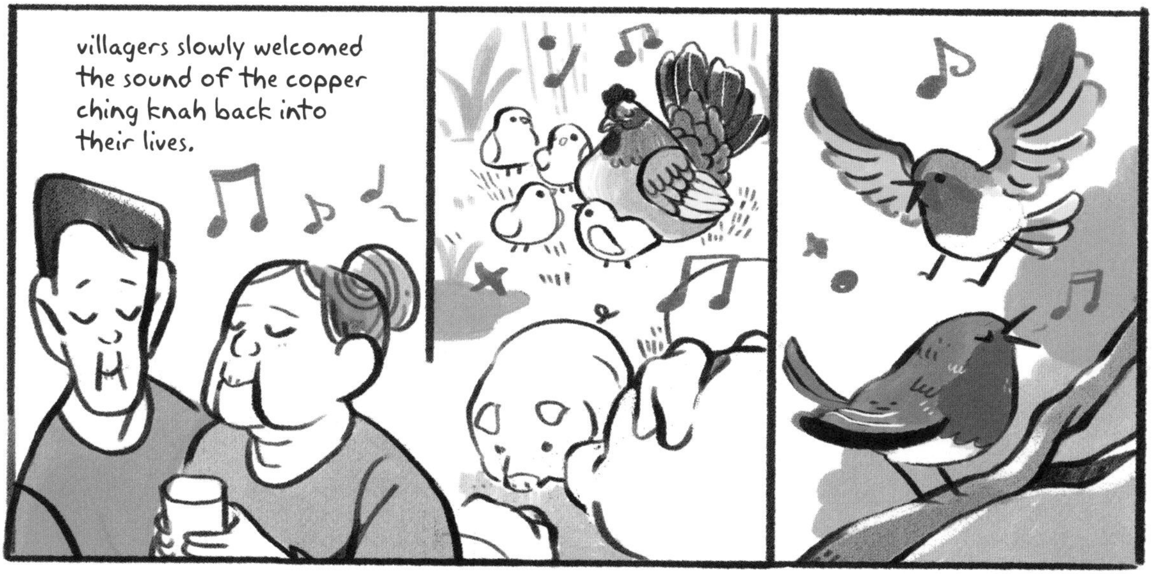
villagers slowly welcomed the sound of the copper ching knah back into their lives.

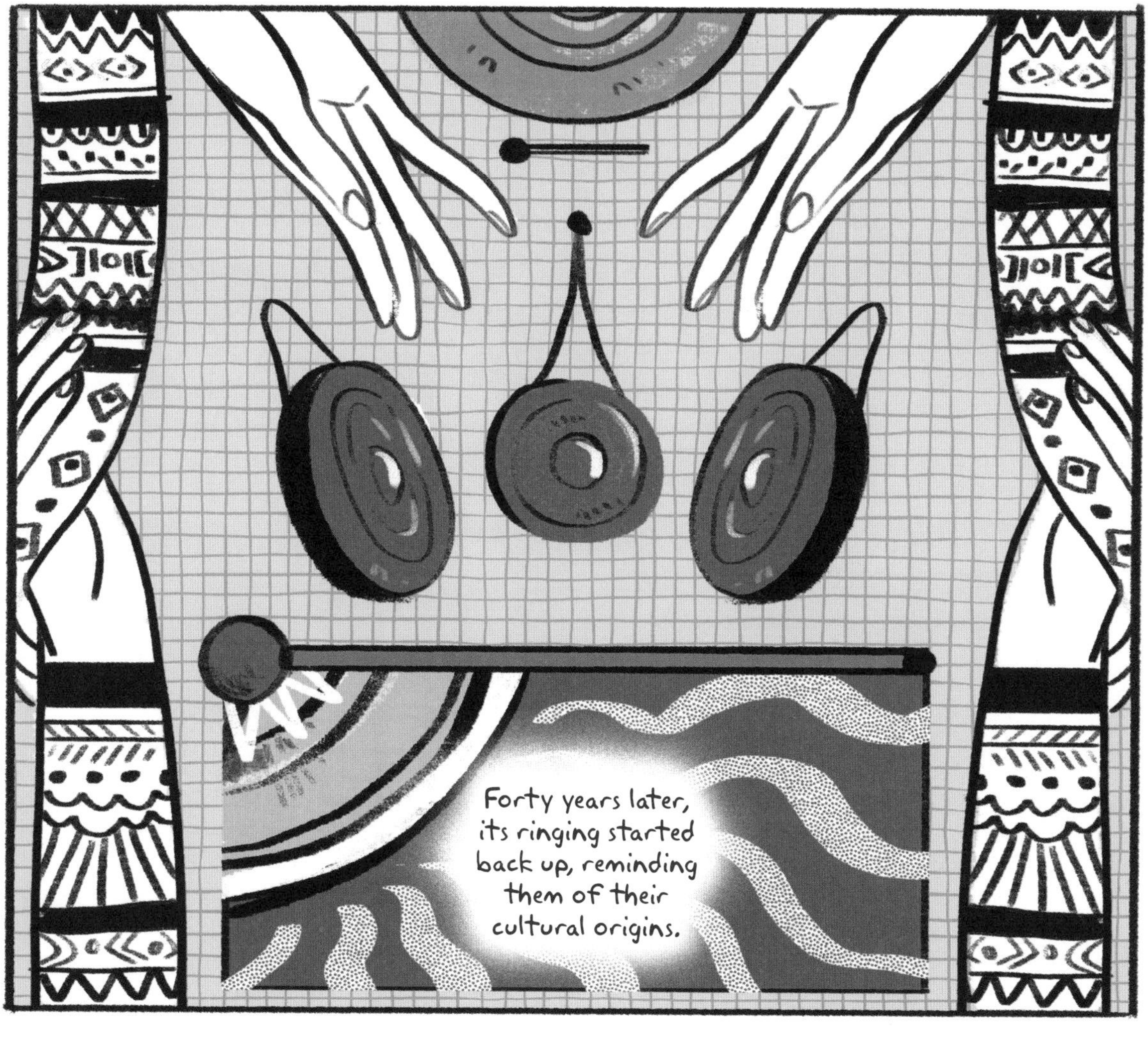
Forty years later, its ringing started back up, reminding them of their cultural origins.

Chapter 4: The Central Highland-ist

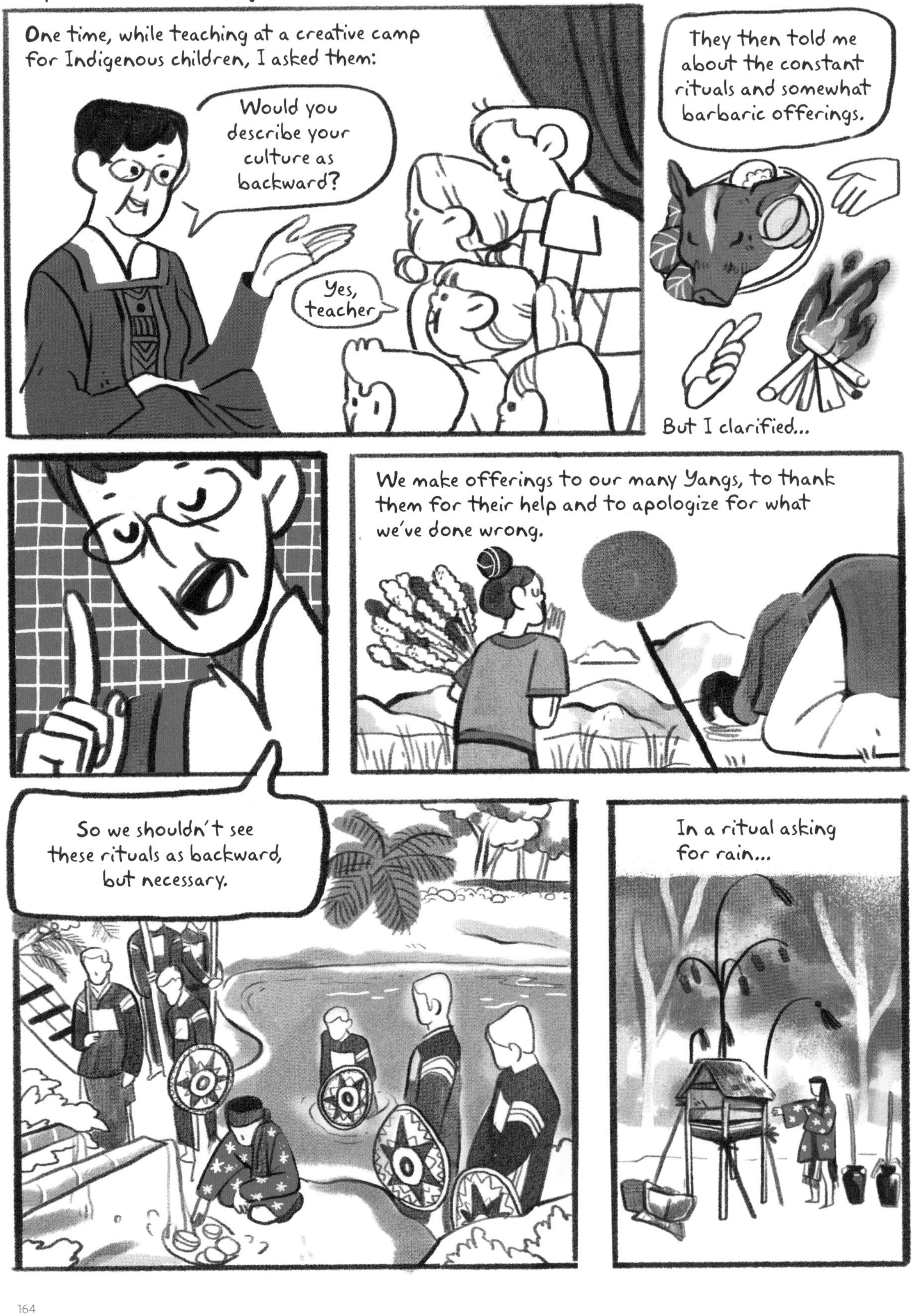
One time, while teaching at a creative camp for Indigenous children, I asked them:
Would you describe your culture as backward?
Yes, teacher
They then told me about the constant rituals and somewhat barbaric offerings.
But I clarified...
We make offerings to our many Yangs, to thank them for their help and to apologize for what we've done wrong.
So we shouldn't see these rituals as backward, but necessary.
In a ritual asking for rain...

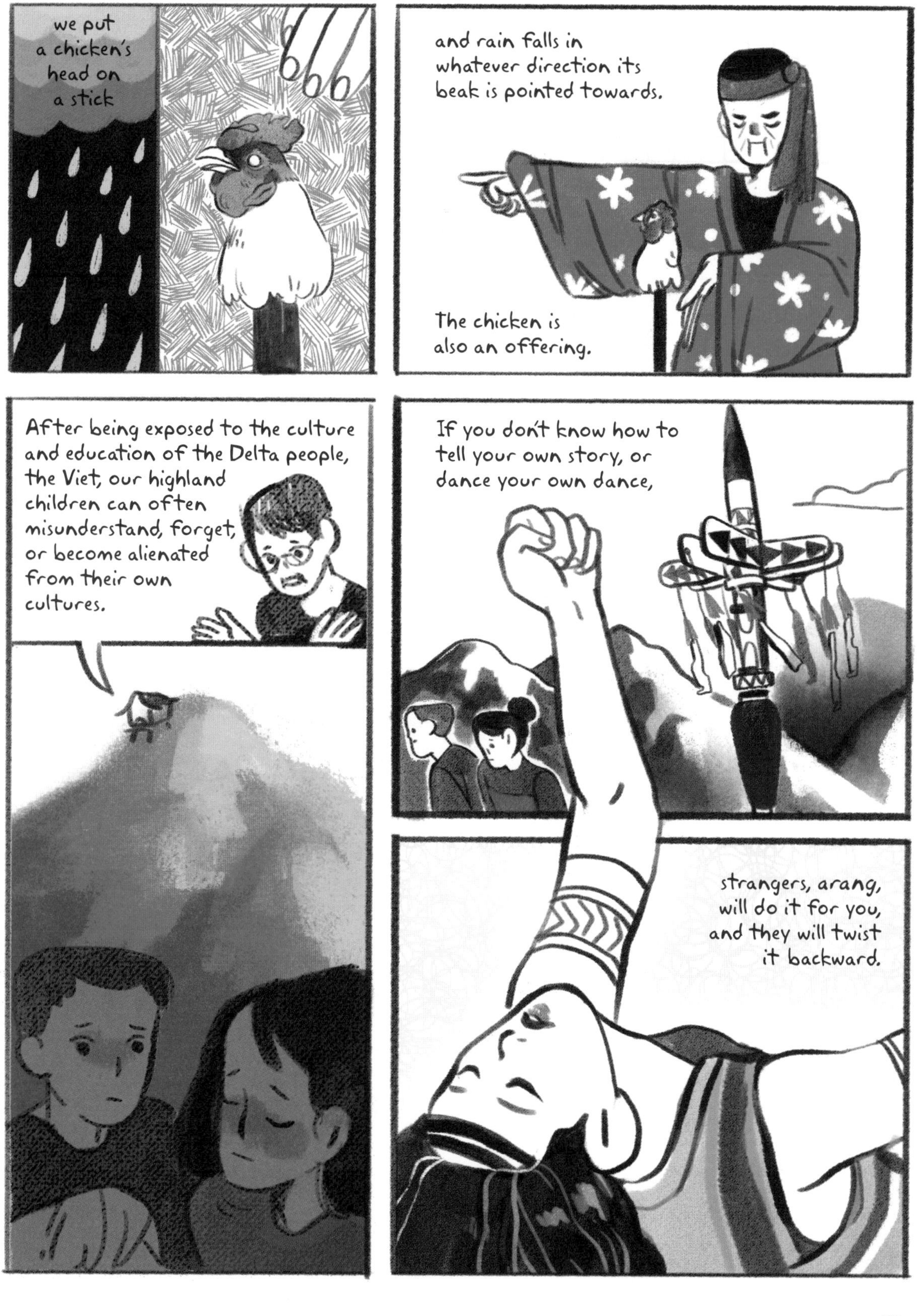
we put a chicken's head on a stick
and rain falls in whatever direction its beak is pointed towards.
The chicken is also an offering.
After being exposed to the culture and education of the Delta people, the Viet, our highland children can often misunderstand, forget, or become alienated from their own cultures.
If you don't know how to tell your own story, or dance your own dance,
strangers, arang, will do it for you, and they will twist it backward.

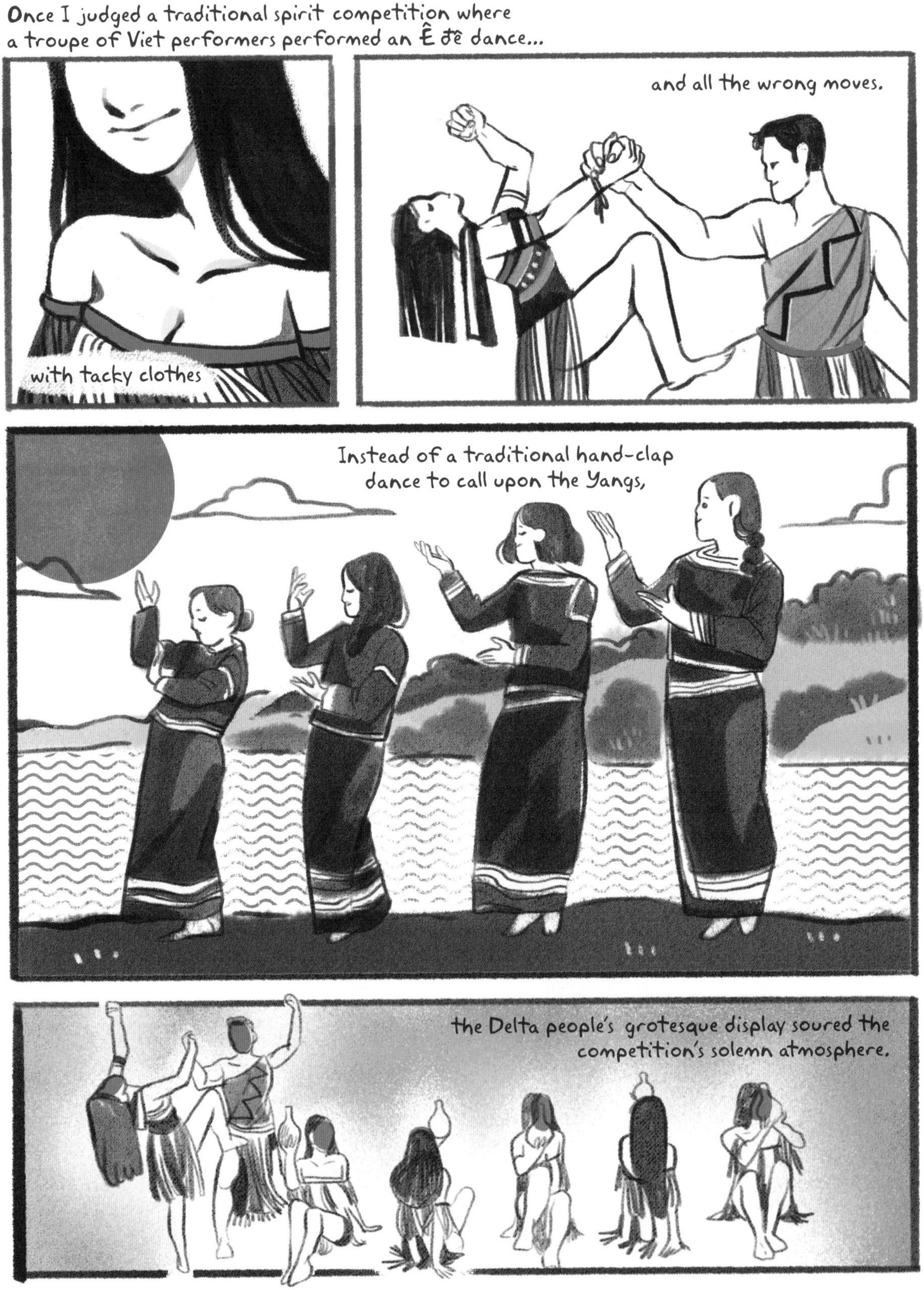
Once I judged a traditional spirit competition where a troupe of Viet performers performed an Ê đê dance...
with tacky clothes
and all the wrong moves.
Instead of a traditional hand-clap dance to call upon the Yangs,
the Delta people's grotesque display soured the competition's solemn atmosphere.

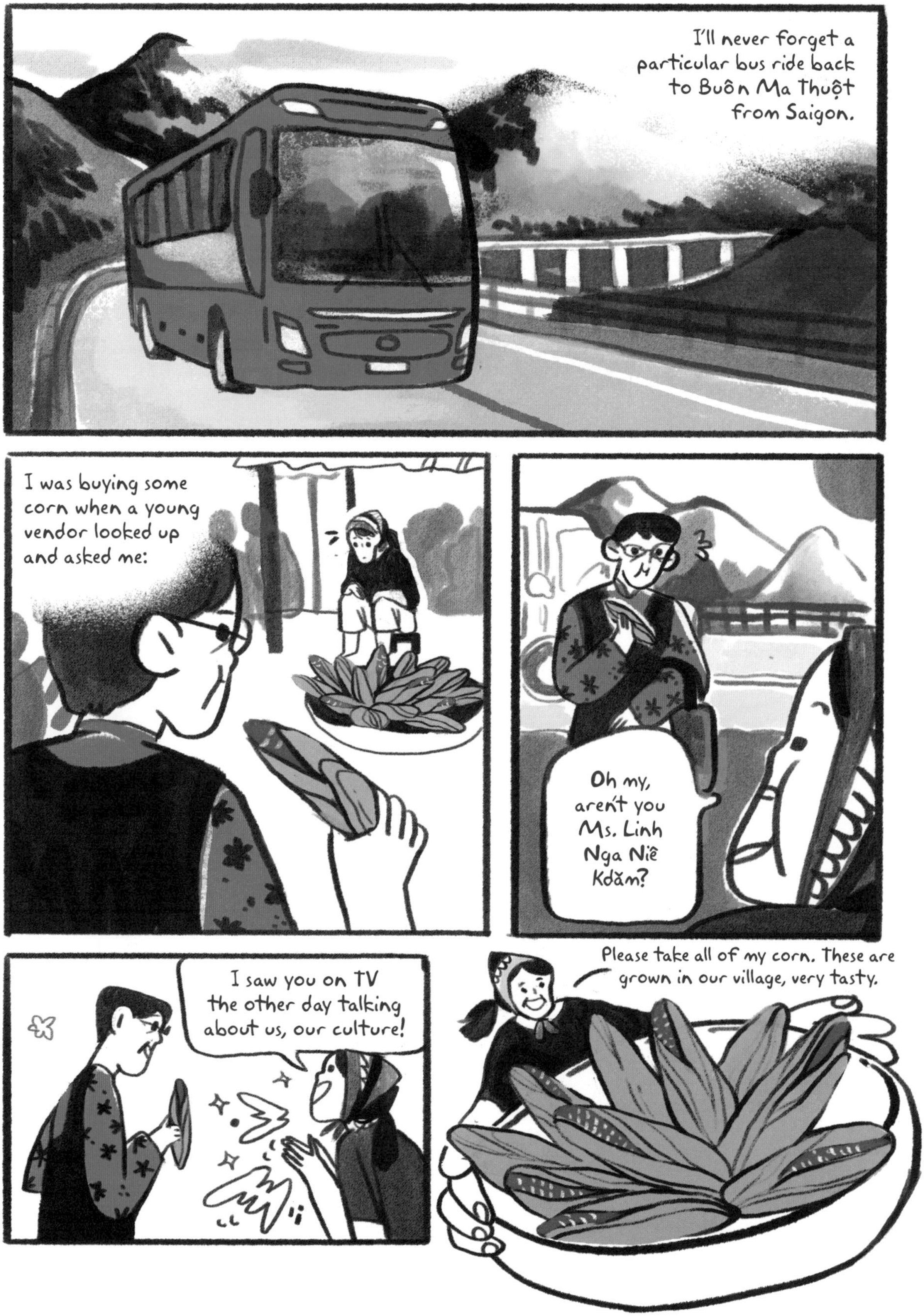
I'll never forget a particular bus ride back to Buôn Ma Thuột from Saigon.
I was buying some corn when a young vendor looked up and asked me:
Oh my, aren't you Ms. Linh Nga Niê Kdăm?
I saw you on TV the other day talking about us, our culture!
Please take all of my corn. These are grown in our village, very tasty.

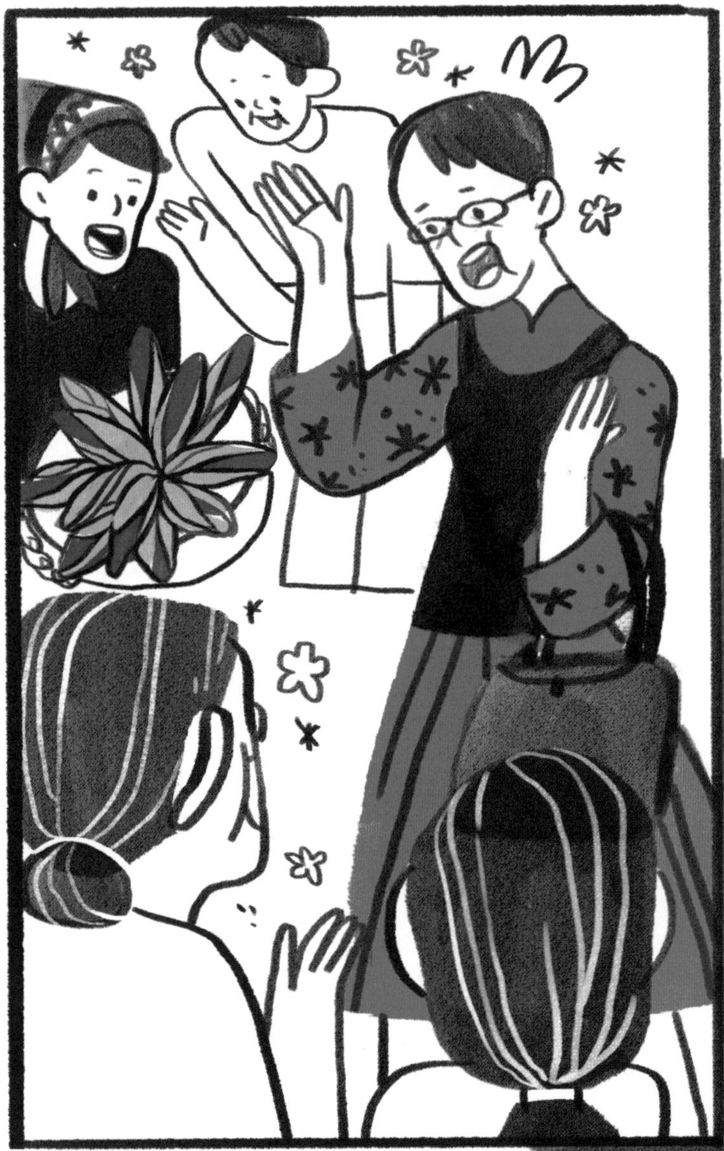

Other vendors began crowding in, chatting in Ê đê; everyone wanted to gift me their corn.

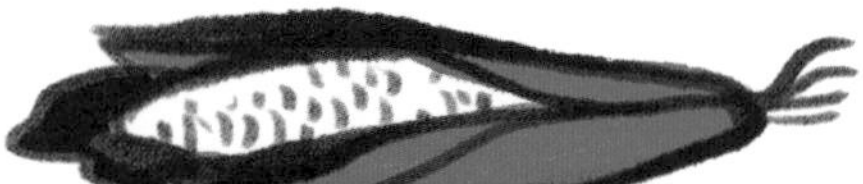

In the end, I took one from each of them to show my gratitude and appreciation.

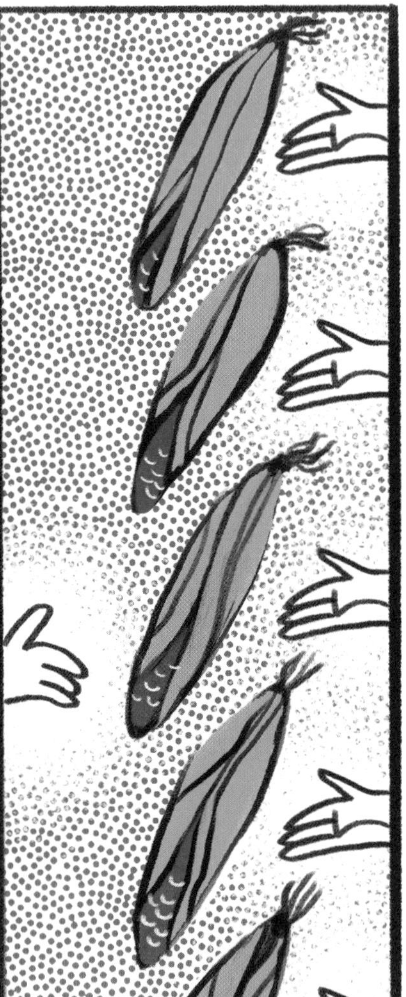

I was Elated. My people saw what I was doing for our community. They understood that I was dedicated to protecting our culture with love.

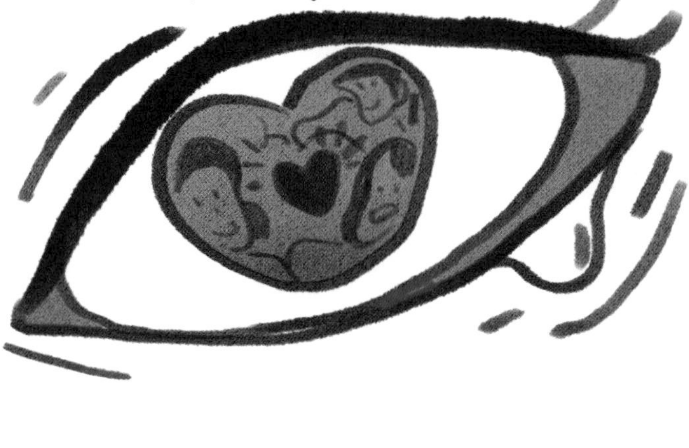

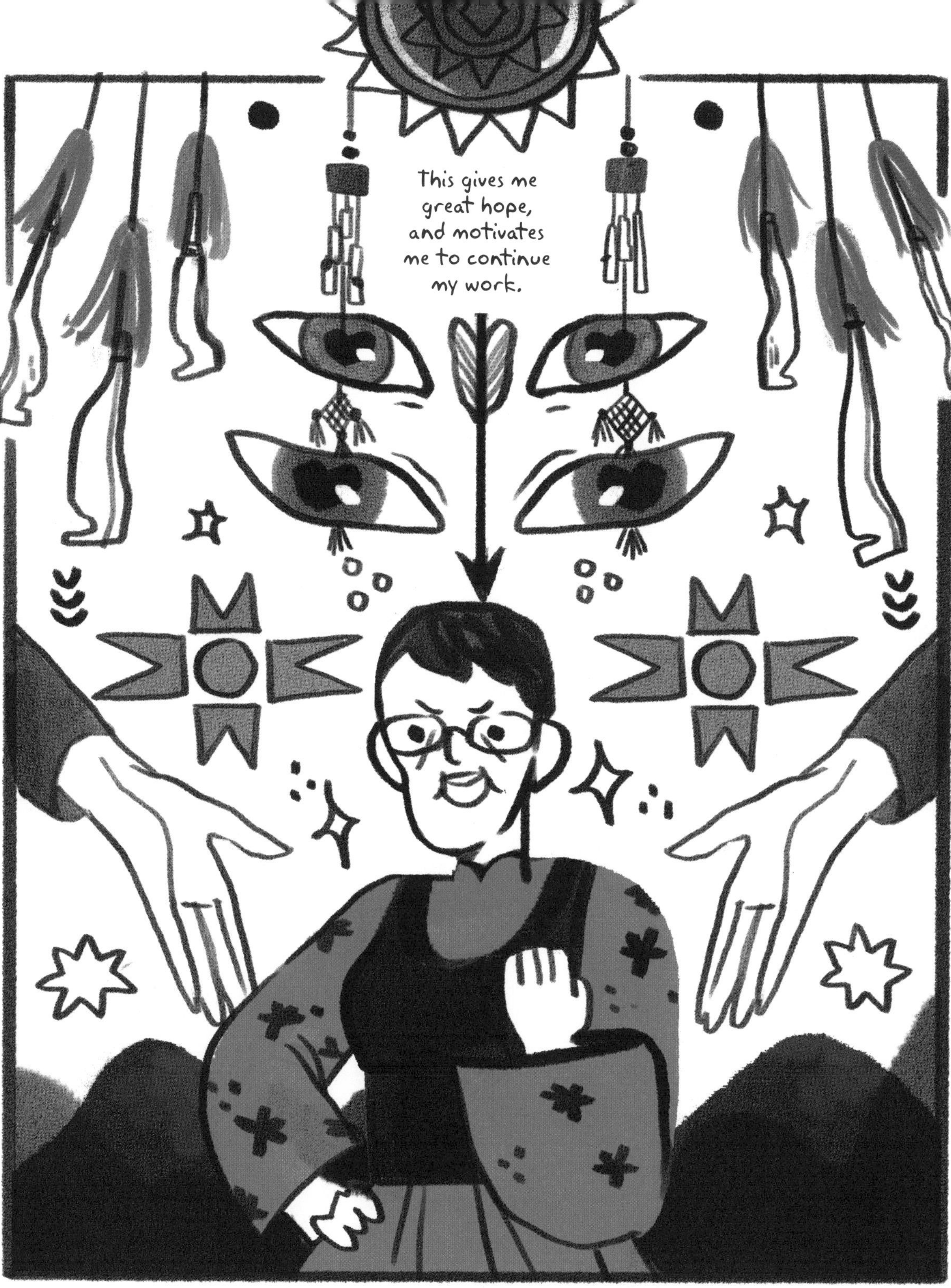
This gives me great hope, and motivates me to continue my work.

The Yangs still watch over me, and have granted me the good health to continue pursuing what I most treasure. That to me, is more than enough. There is truly nothing for me to regret.

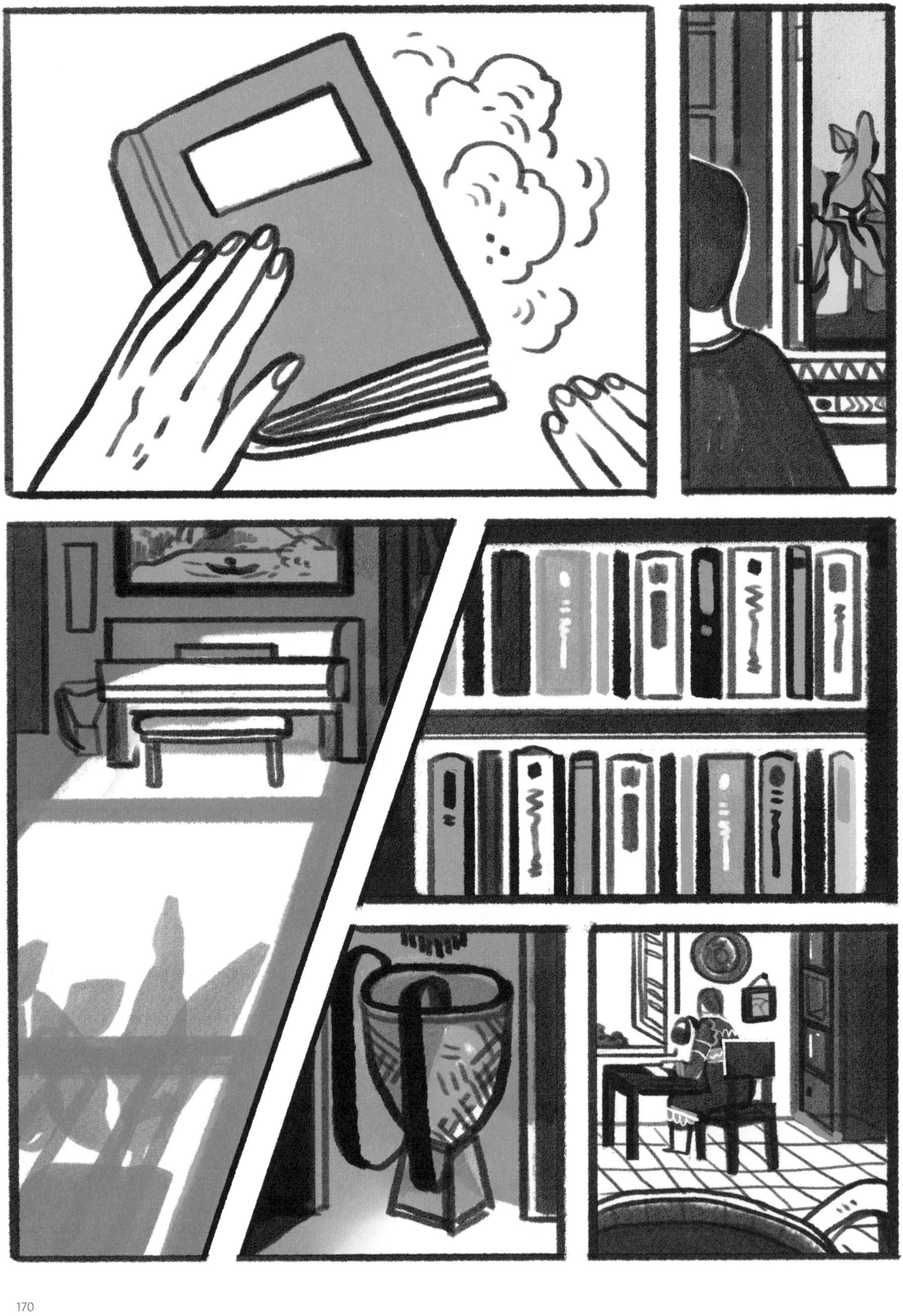

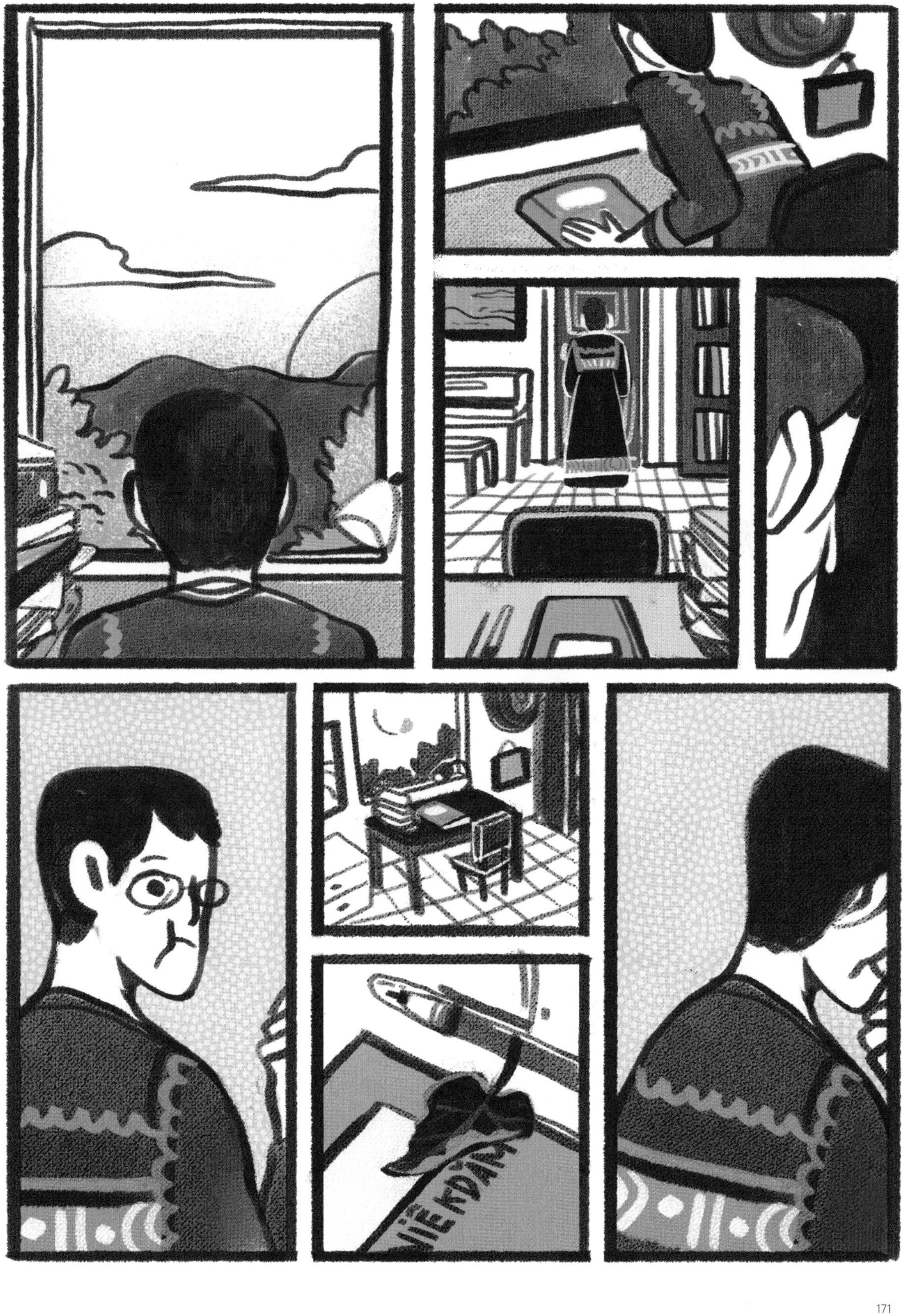

To Ms. Linh Nga Niê Kdam
and the Ê đê communities
in Buôn Ma Thuột,

Our undying gratitude.

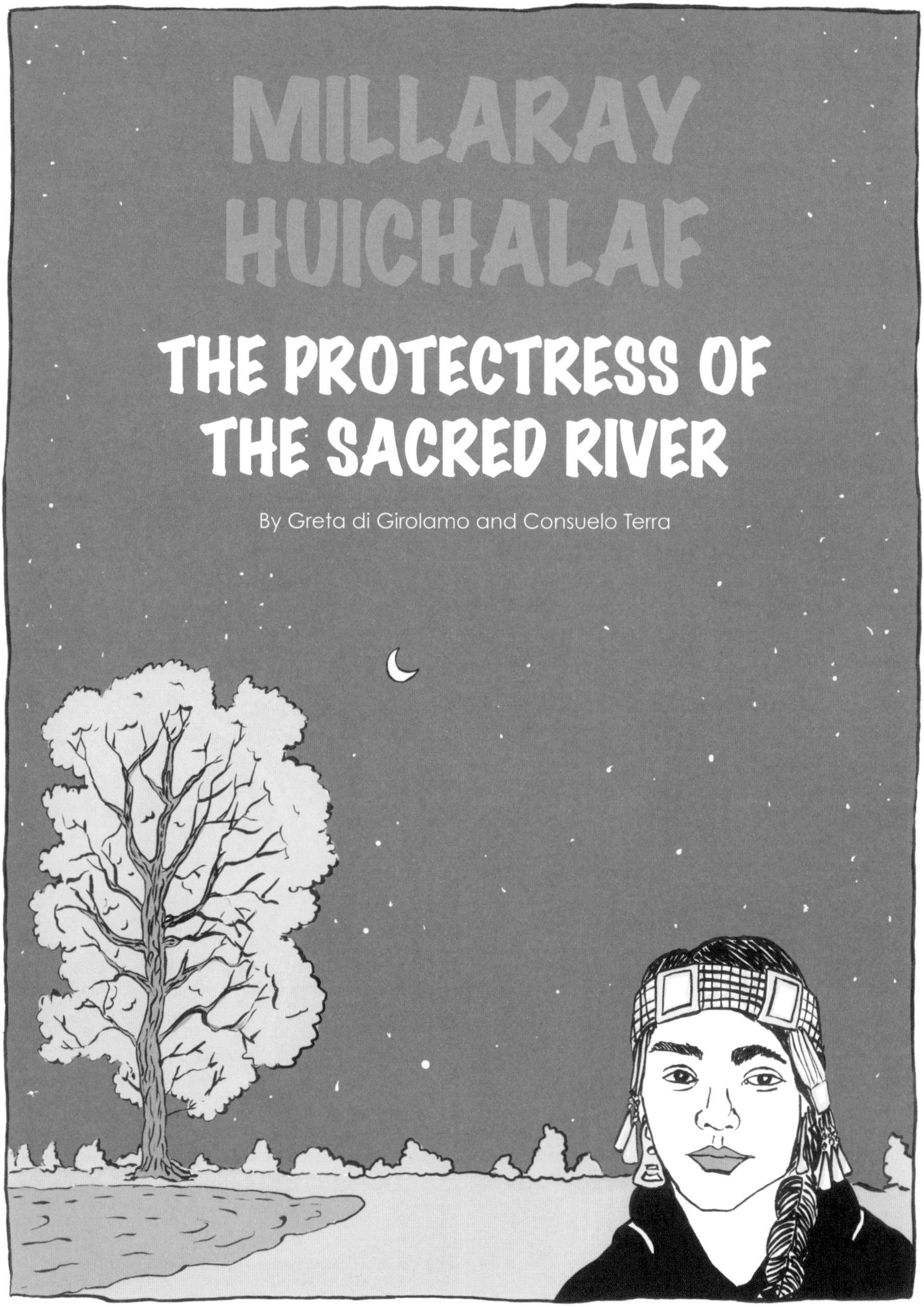
MILLARAY HUICHALAF
THE PROTECTRESS OF THE SACRED RIVER
By Greta di Girolamo and Consuelo Terra

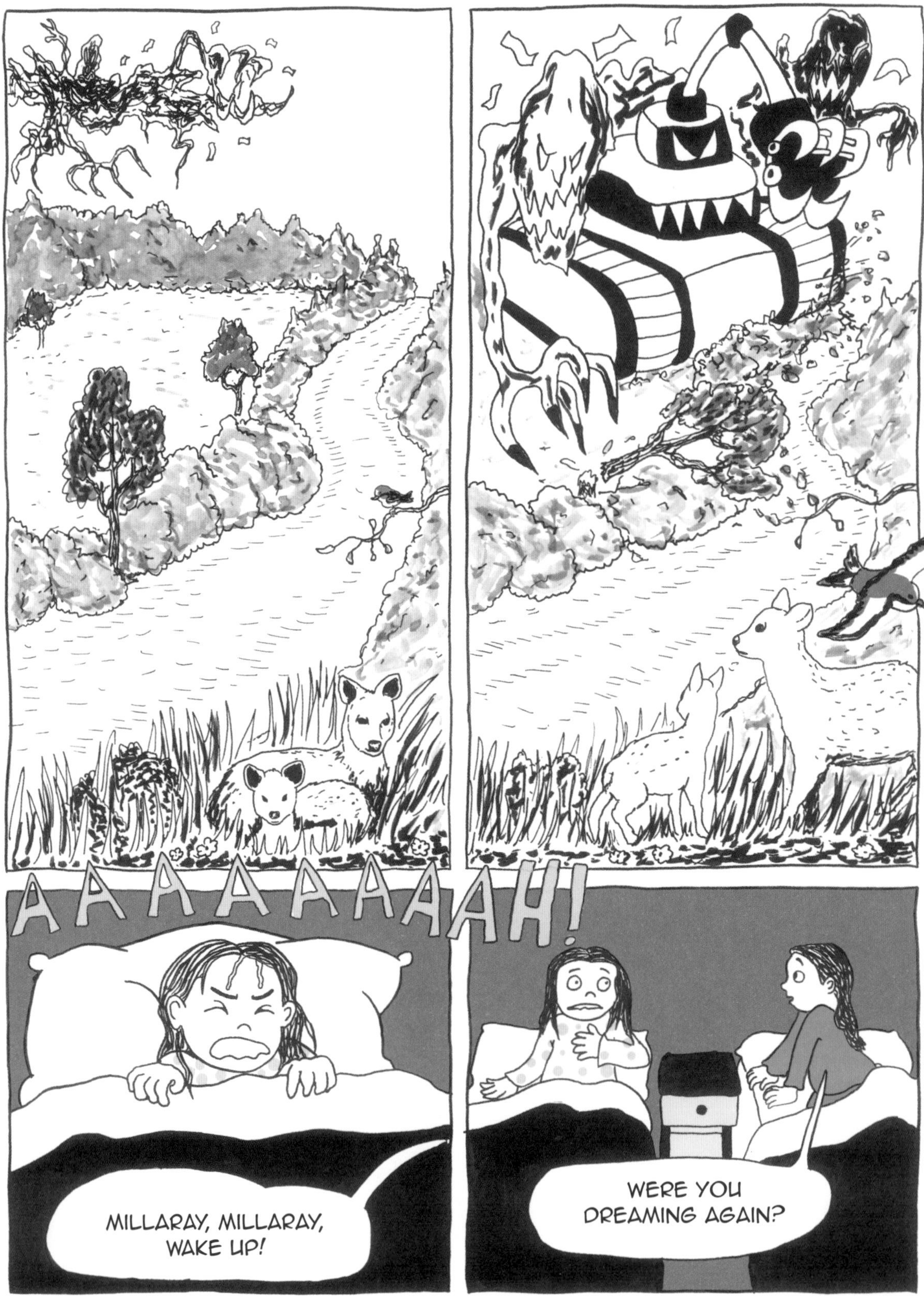
AAAAAAAAH!
MILLARAY, MILLARAY, WAKE UP!
WERE YOU DREAMING AGAIN?

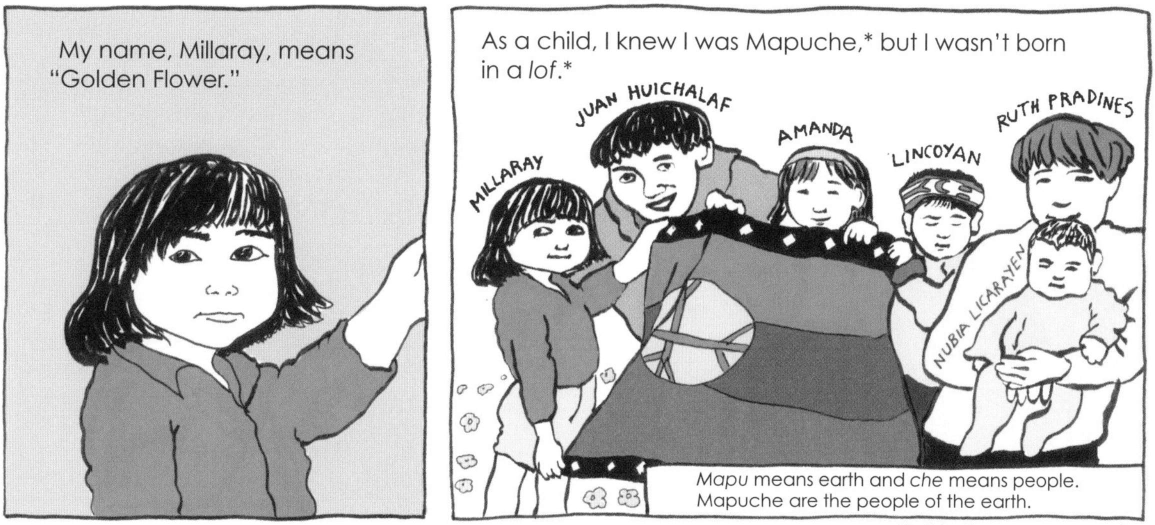
My name, Millaray, means "Golden Flower."
As a child, I knew I was Mapuche,* but I wasn't born in a *lof*.*
MILLARAY
JUAN HUICHALAF
AMANDA
LINCOYAN
RUTH PRADINES
NUBIA LICARAYEN
Mapu means earth and *che* means people. Mapuche are the people of the earth.

*Lof: Indigenous community

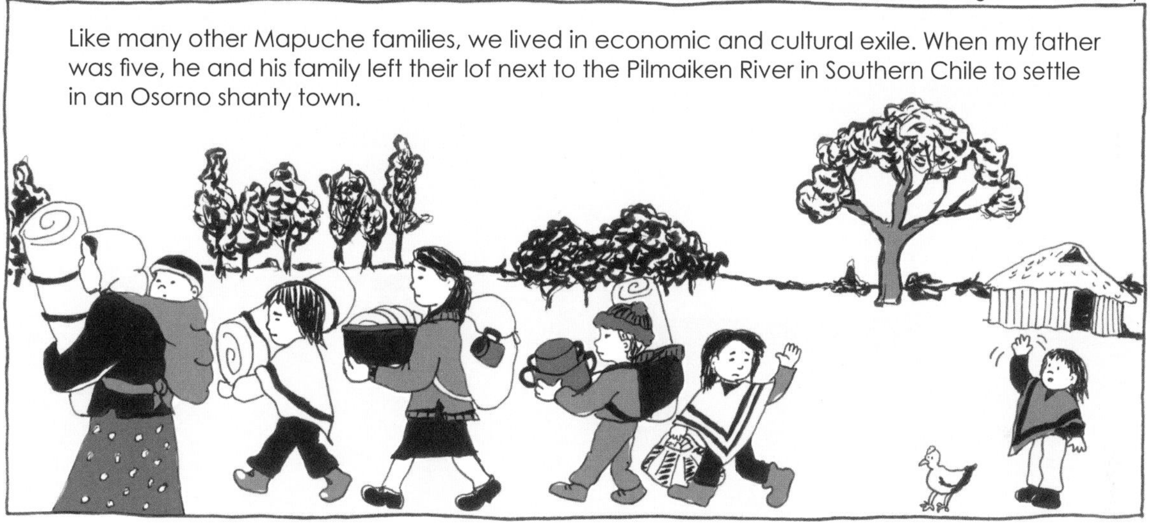
Like many other Mapuche families, we lived in economic and cultural exile. When my father was five, he and his family left their lof next to the Pilmaiken River in Southern Chile to settle in an Osorno shanty town.

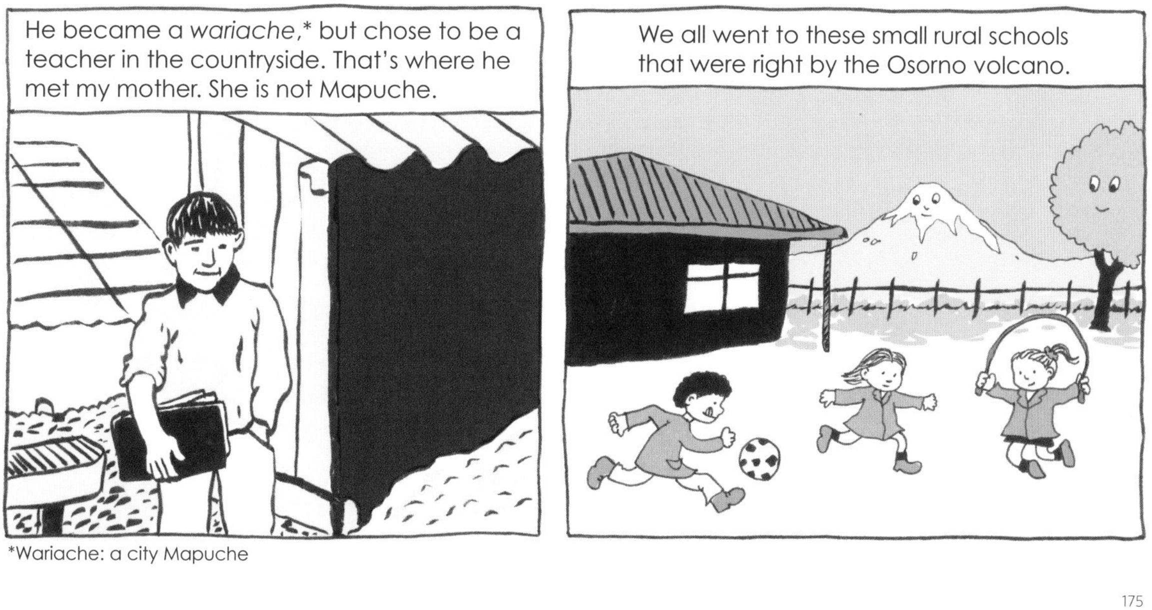
He became a *wariache*,* but chose to be a teacher in the countryside. That's where he met my mother. She is not Mapuche.
We all went to these small rural schools that were right by the Osorno volcano.

*Wariache: a city Mapuche

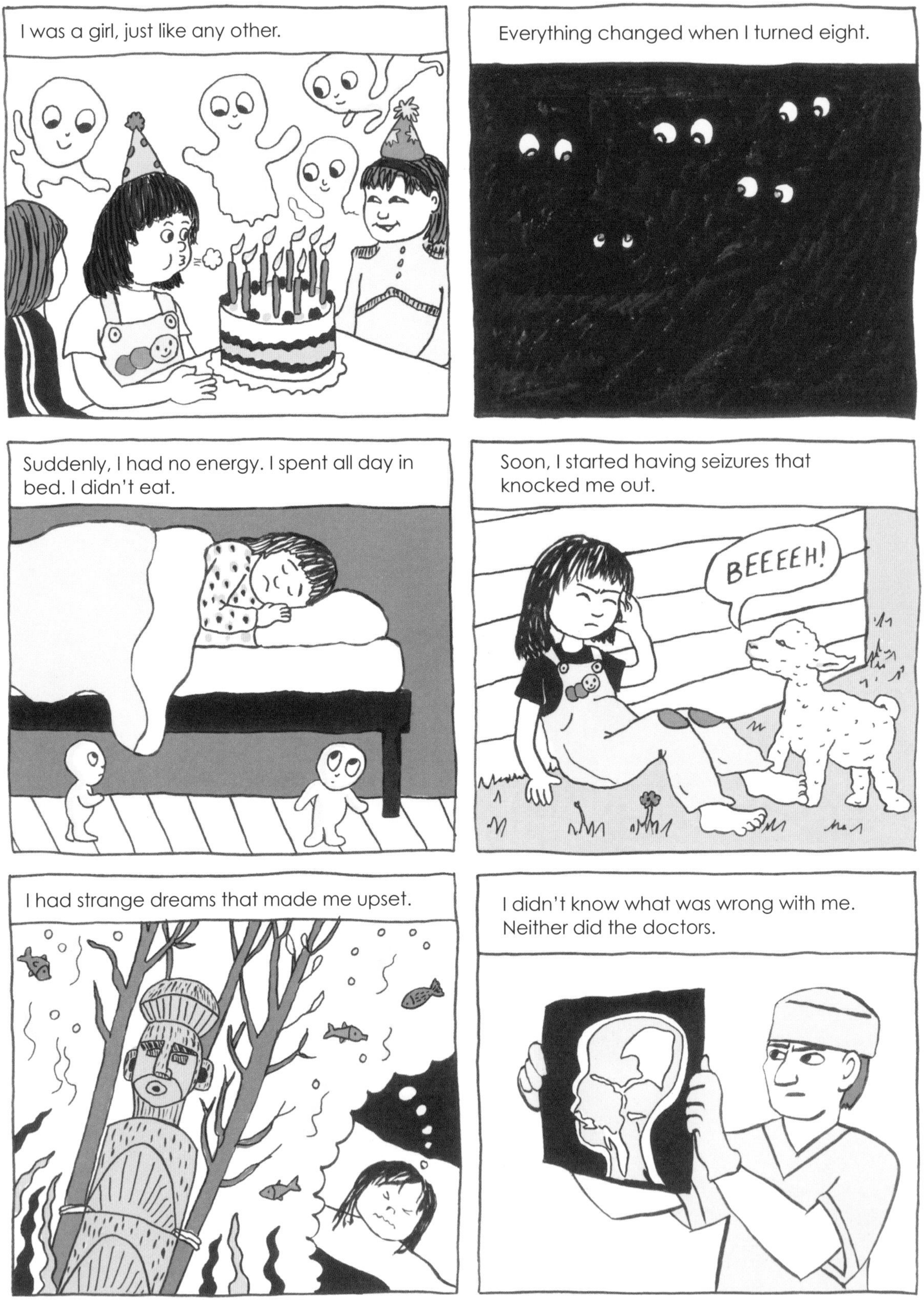
I was a girl, just like any other.
Everything changed when I turned eight.
Suddenly, I had no energy. I spent all day in bed. I didn't eat.
Soon, I started having seizures that knocked me out.
BEEEEH!
I had strange dreams that made me upset.
I didn't know what was wrong with me. Neither did the doctors.

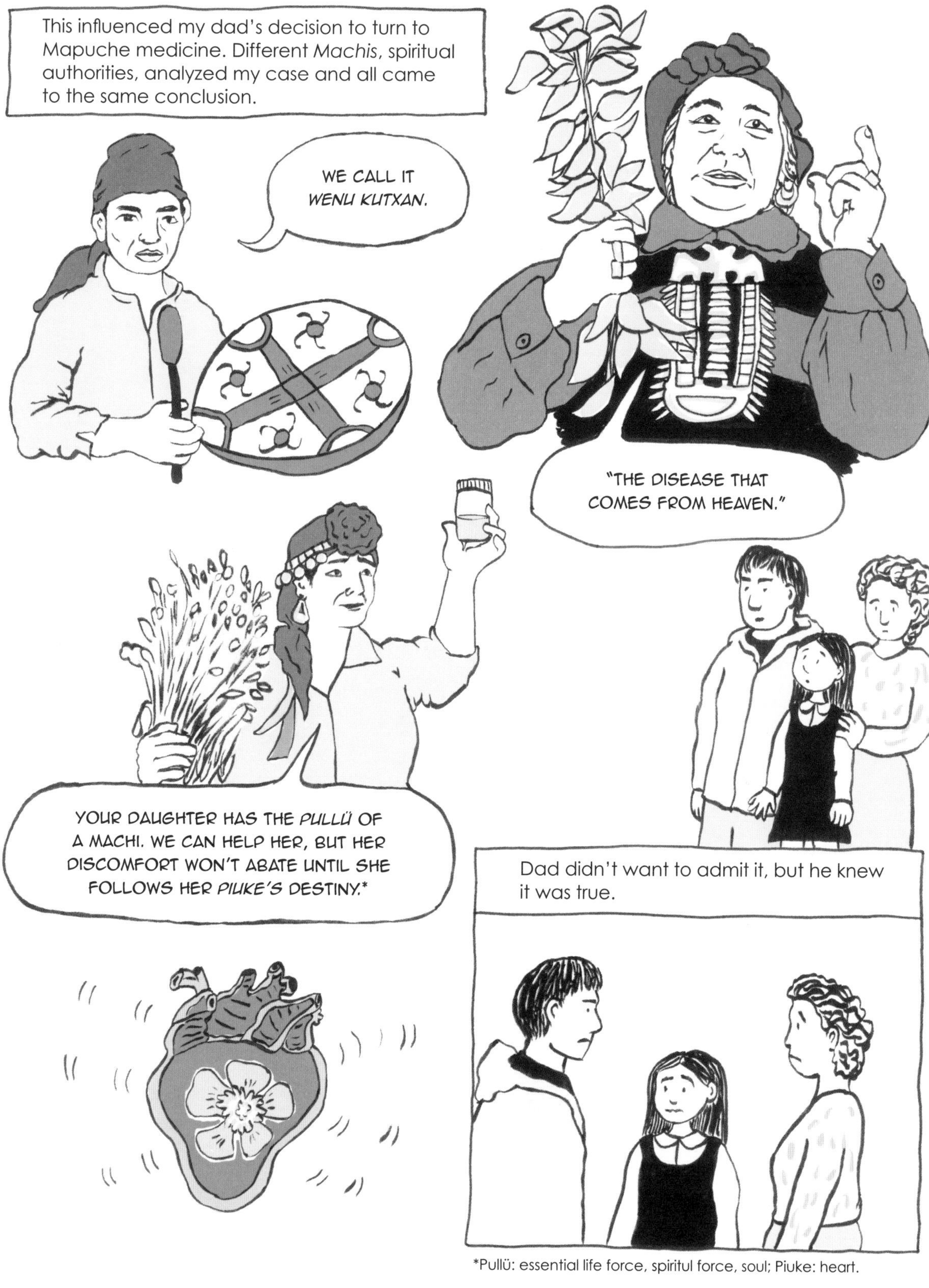
This influenced my dad's decision to turn to Mapuche medicine. Different *Machis*, spiritual authorities, analyzed my case and all came to the same conclusion.
WE CALL IT *WENU KUTXAN*.
"THE DISEASE THAT COMES FROM HEAVEN."
YOUR DAUGHTER HAS THE *PULLÜ* OF A MACHI. WE CAN HELP HER, BUT HER DISCOMFORT WON'T ABATE UNTIL SHE FOLLOWS HER *PIUKE'S* DESTINY.*
Dad didn't want to admit it, but he knew it was true.

*Pullü: essential life force, spiritul force, soul; Piuke: heart.

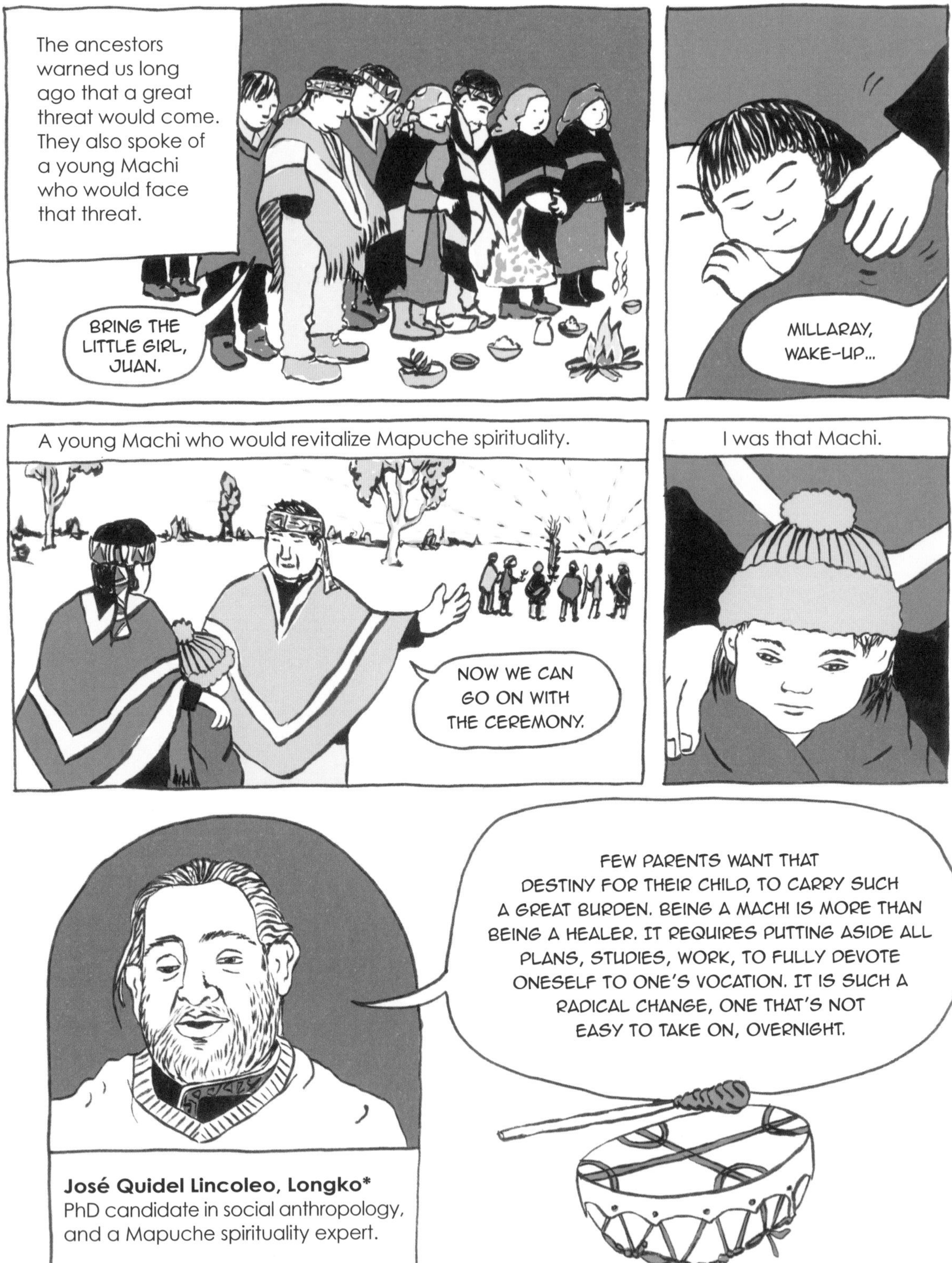
The ancestors warned us long ago that a great threat would come. They also spoke of a young Machi who would face that threat.
BRING THE LITTLE GIRL, JUAN.
MILLARAY, WAKE-UP...
A young Machi who would revitalize Mapuche spirituality.
NOW WE CAN GO ON WITH THE CEREMONY.
I was that Machi.
FEW PARENTS WANT THAT DESTINY FOR THEIR CHILD, TO CARRY SUCH A GREAT BURDEN. BEING A MACHI IS MORE THAN BEING A HEALER. IT REQUIRES PUTTING ASIDE ALL PLANS, STUDIES, WORK, TO FULLY DEVOTE ONESELF TO ONE'S VOCATION. IT IS SUCH A RADICAL CHANGE, ONE THAT'S NOT EASY TO TAKE ON, OVERNIGHT.
José Quidel Lincoleo, Longko*
PhD candidate in social anthropology, and a Mapuche spirituality expert.

*Longko: leader

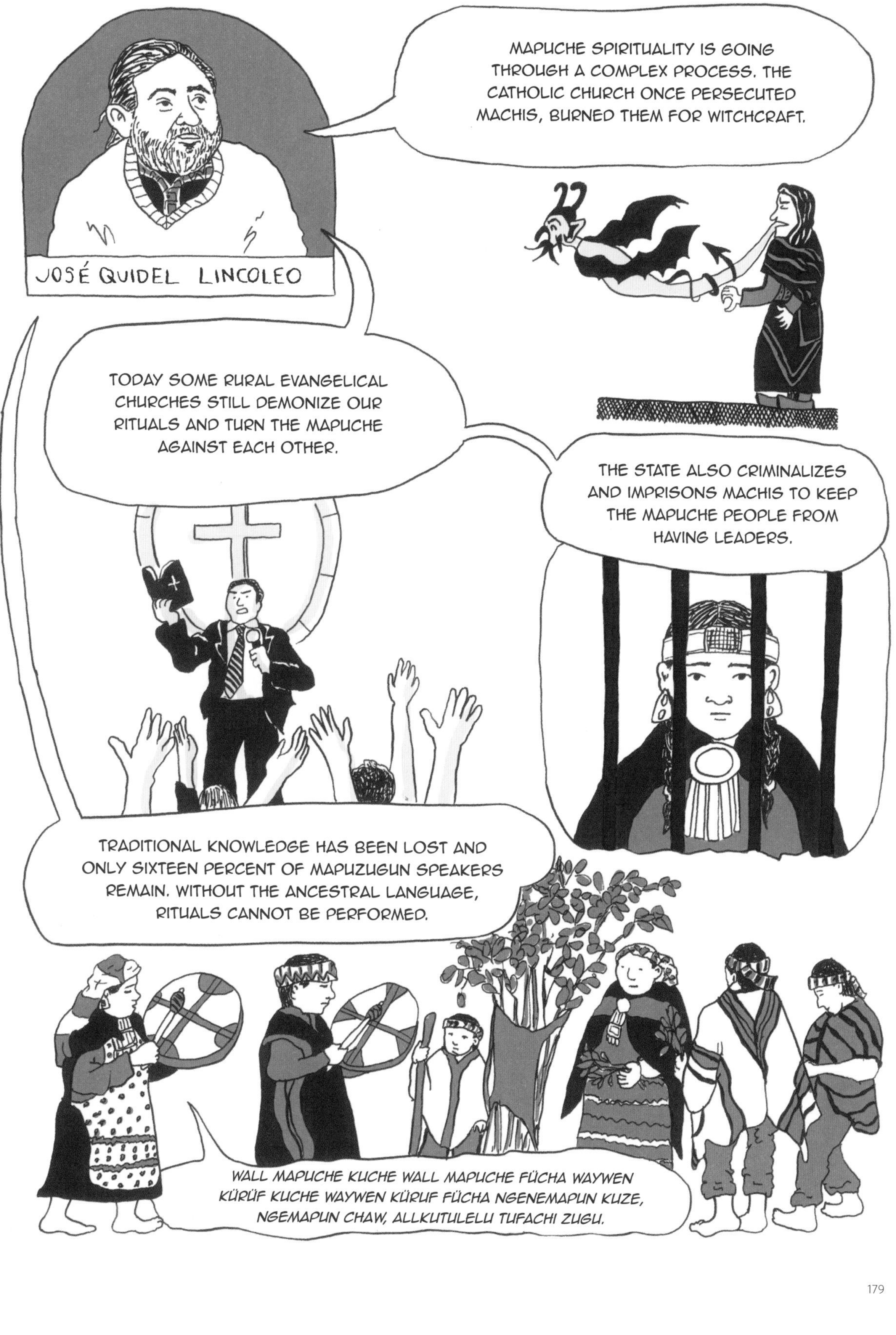
JOSÉ QUIDEL LINCOLEO
MAPUCHE SPIRITUALITY IS GOING THROUGH A COMPLEX PROCESS. THE CATHOLIC CHURCH ONCE PERSECUTED MACHIS, BURNED THEM FOR WITCHCRAFT.
TODAY SOME RURAL EVANGELICAL CHURCHES STILL DEMONIZE OUR RITUALS AND TURN THE MAPUCHE AGAINST EACH OTHER.
THE STATE ALSO CRIMINALIZES AND IMPRISONS MACHIS TO KEEP THE MAPUCHE PEOPLE FROM HAVING LEADERS.
TRADITIONAL KNOWLEDGE HAS BEEN LOST AND ONLY SIXTEEN PERCENT OF MAPUZUGUN SPEAKERS REMAIN. WITHOUT THE ANCESTRAL LANGUAGE, RITUALS CANNOT BE PERFORMED.
WALL MAPUCHE KUCHE WALL MAPUCHE FÜCHA WAYWEN KÜRÜF KUCHE WAYWEN KÜRUF FÜCHA NGENEMAPUN KUZE, NGEMAPUN CHAW, ALLKUTULELU TUFACHI ZUGU.

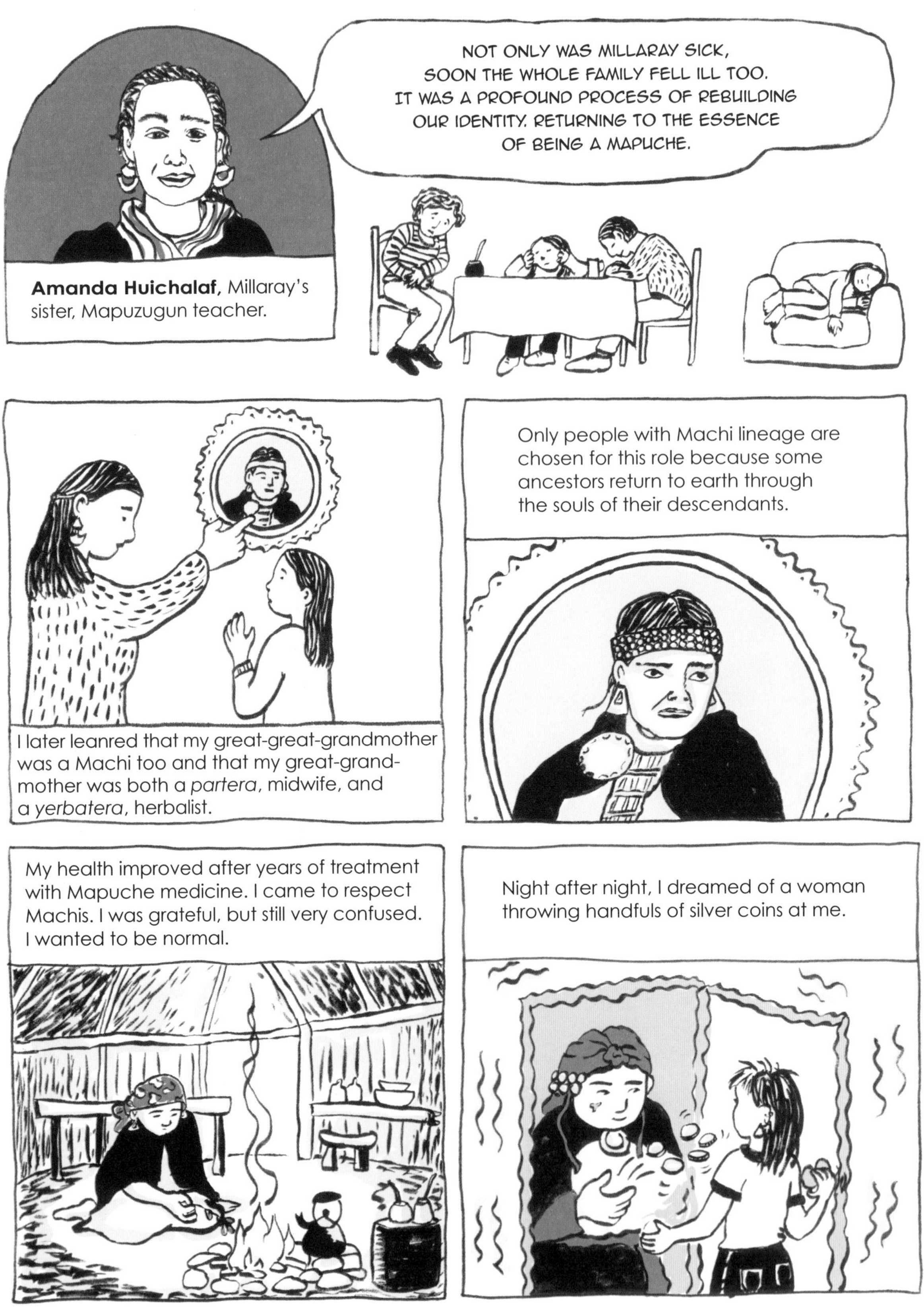
Amanda Huichalaf, Millaray's sister, Mapuzugun teacher.
NOT ONLY WAS MILLARAY SICK, SOON THE WHOLE FAMILY FELL ILL TOO. IT WAS A PROFOUND PROCESS OF REBUILDING OUR IDENTITY. RETURNING TO THE ESSENCE OF BEING A MAPUCHE.
I later leanred that my great-great-grandmother was a Machi too and that my great-grand-mother was both a partera, midwife, and a yerbatera, herbalist.
Only people with Machi lineage are chosen for this role because some ancestors return to earth through the souls of their descendants.
My health improved after years of treatment with Mapuche medicine. I came to respect Machis. I was grateful, but still very confused. I wanted to be normal.
Night after night, I dreamed of a woman throwing handfuls of silver coins at me.

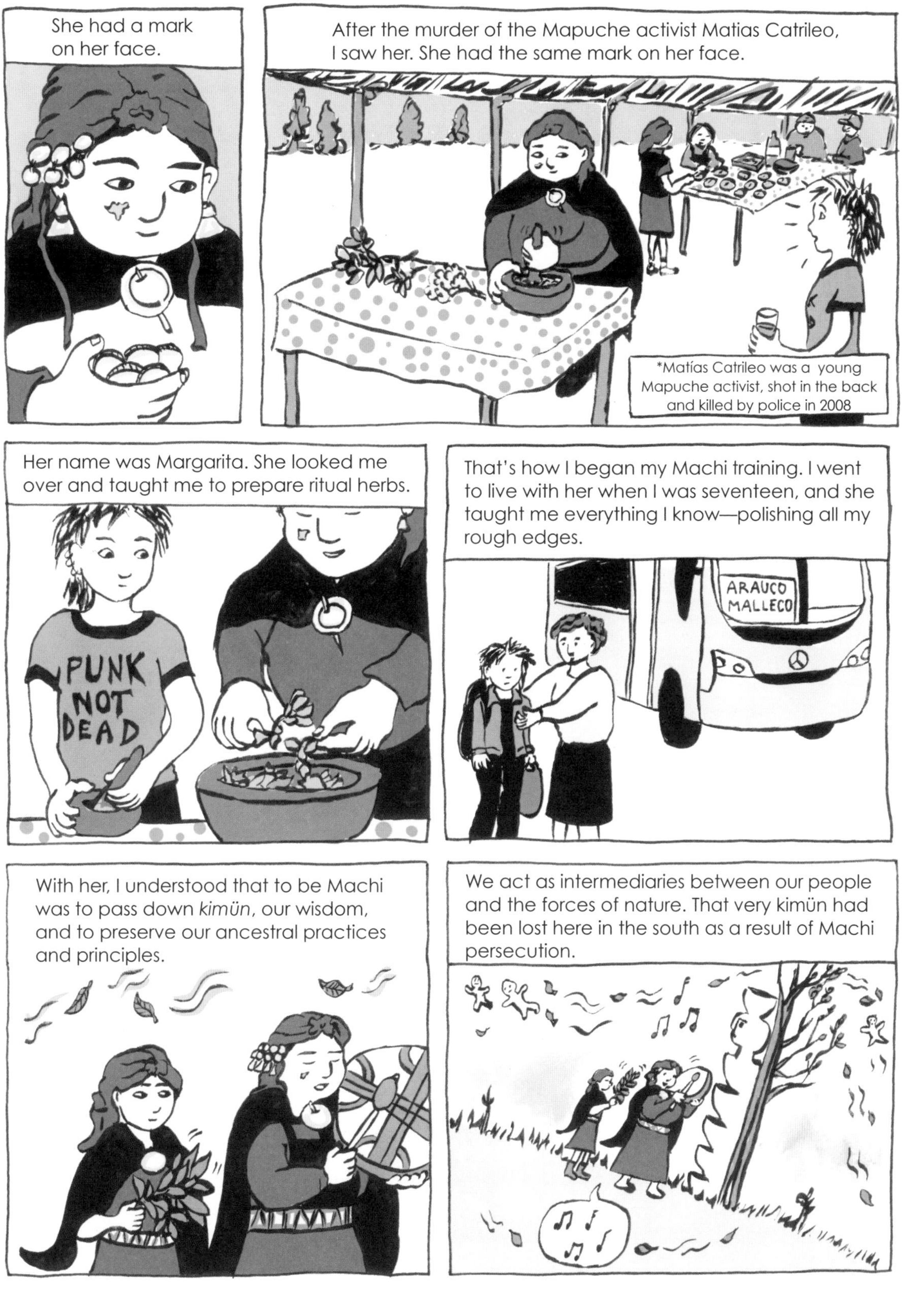
She had a mark on her face.
After the murder of the Mapuche activist Matias Catrileo, I saw her. She had the same mark on her face.
*Matías Catrileo was a young Mapuche activist, shot in the back and killed by police in 2008
Her name was Margarita. She looked me over and taught me to prepare ritual herbs.
PUNK NOT DEAD
That's how I began my Machi training. I went to live with her when I was seventeen, and she taught me everything I know—polishing all my rough edges.
ARAUCO MALLECO
With her, I understood that to be Machi was to pass down *kimün*, our wisdom, and to preserve our ancestral practices and principles.
We act as intermediaries between our people and the forces of nature. That very kimün had been lost here in the south as a result of Machi persecution.

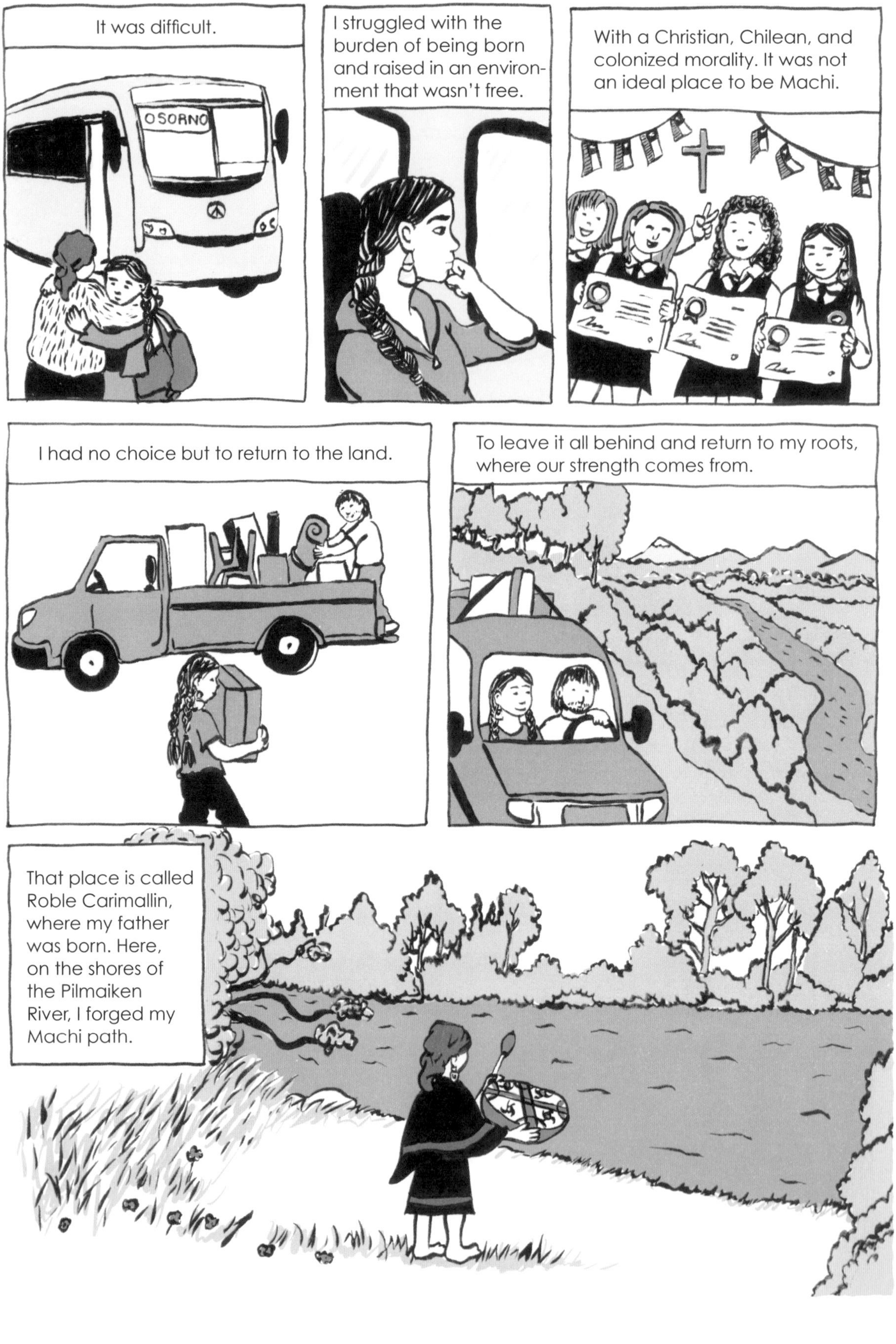
It was difficult.
OSORNO
I struggled with the burden of being born and raised in an environment that wasn't free.
With a Christian, Chilean, and colonized morality. It was not an ideal place to be Machi.
I had no choice but to return to the land.
To leave it all behind and return to my roots, where our strength comes from.
That place is called Roble Carimallin, where my father was born. Here, on the shores of the Pilmaiken River, I forged my Machi path.

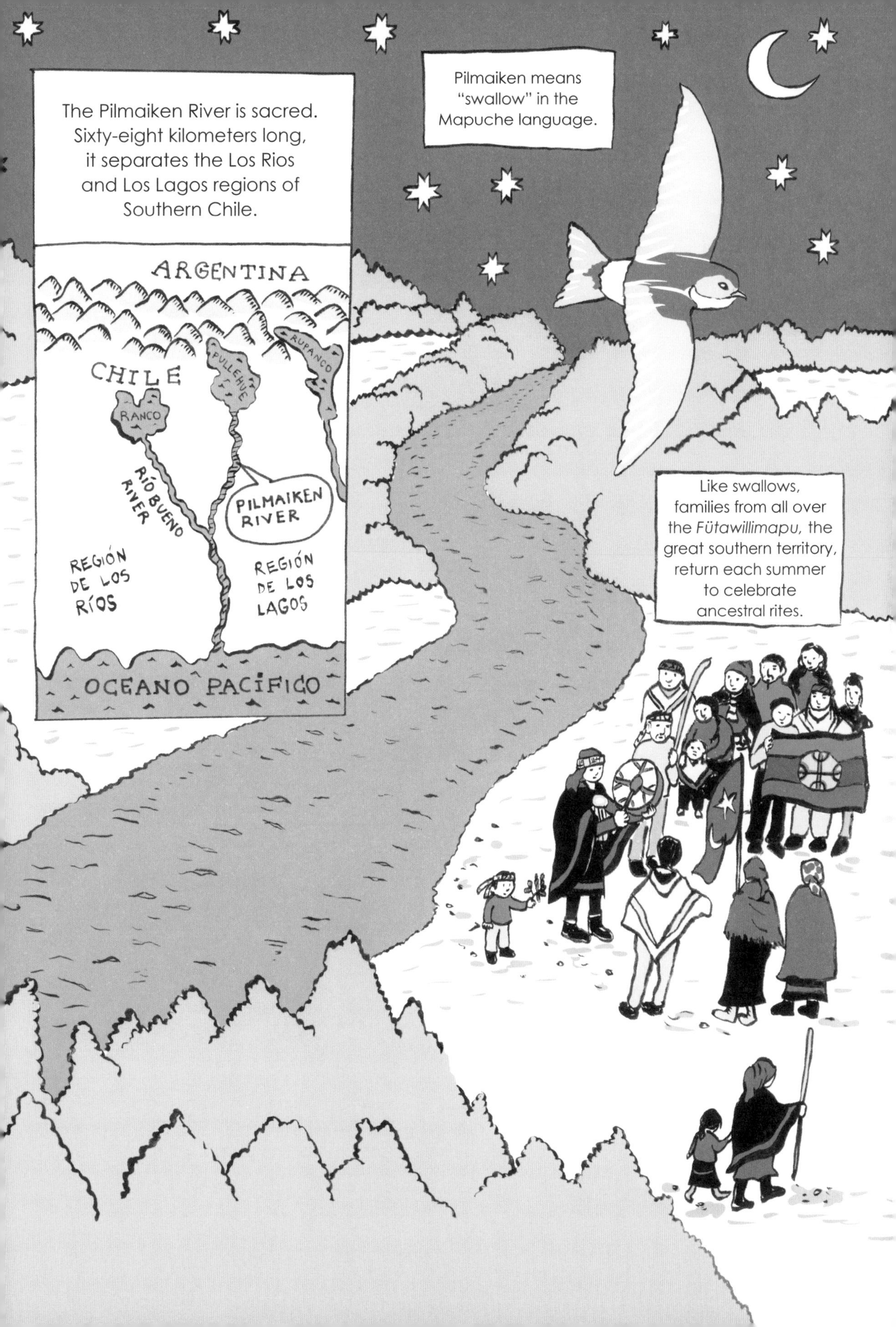
The Pilmaiken River is sacred. Sixty-eight kilometers long, it separates the Los Rios and Los Lagos regions of Southern Chile.
ARGENTINA
CHILE
RANCO
PULLEHUE
RUPANCO
RÍO BUENO RIVER
PILMAIKEN RIVER
REGIÓN DE LOS RÍOS
REGIÓN DE LOS LAGOS
OCEANO PACIFICO
Pilmaiken means "swallow" in the Mapuche language.
Like swallows, families from all over the *Fütawillimapu,* the great southern territory, return each summer to celebrate ancestral rites.

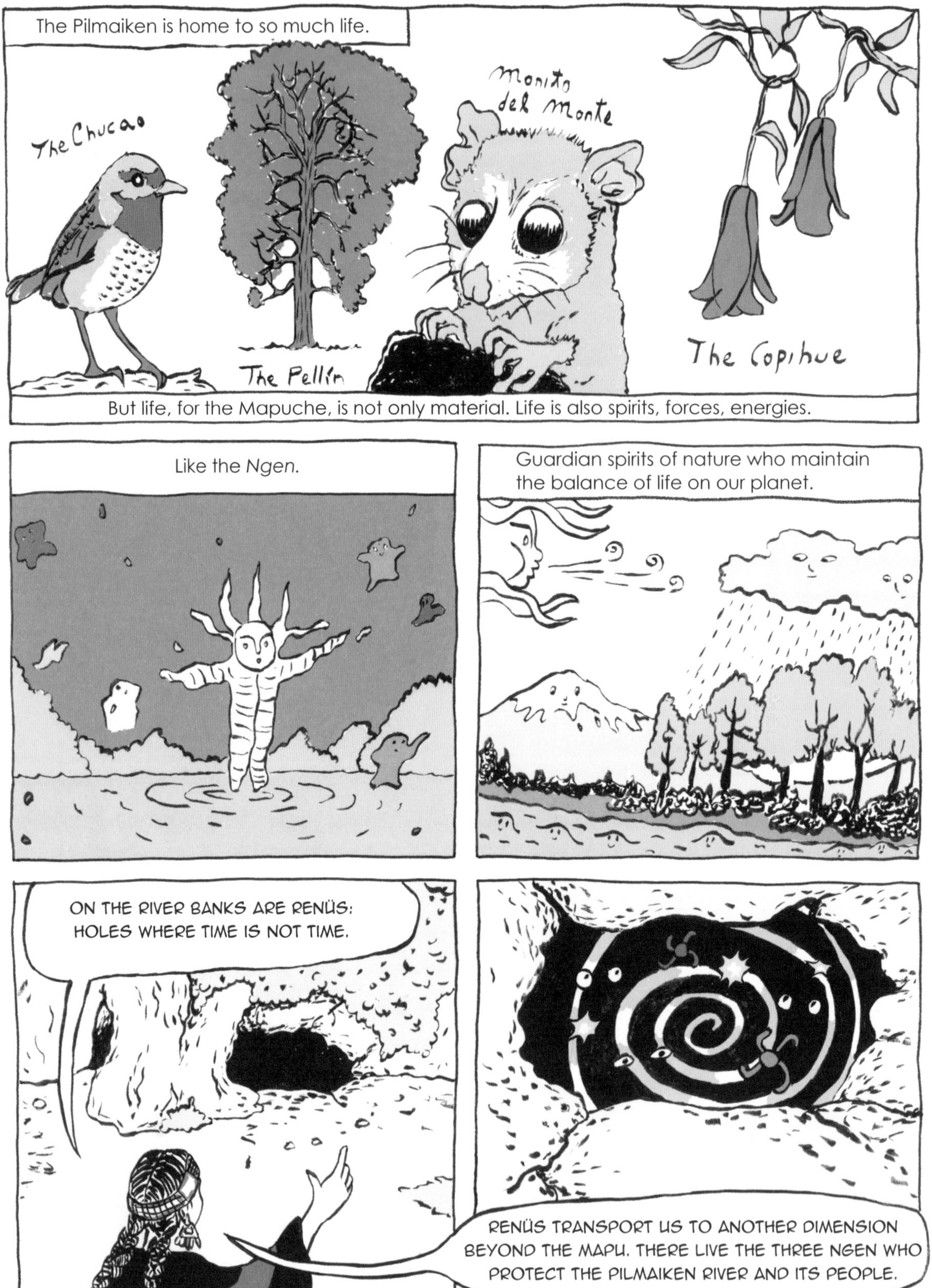
The Pilmaiken is home to so much life.
The Chucao
The Pellín
Monito del Monte
The Copihue
But life, for the Mapuche, is not only material. Life is also spirits, forces, energies.
Like the *Ngen*.
Guardian spirits of nature who maintain the balance of life on our planet.
ON THE RIVER BANKS ARE RENÜS: HOLES WHERE TIME IS NOT TIME.
RENÜS TRANSPORT US TO ANOTHER DIMENSION BEYOND THE MAPU. THERE LIVE THE THREE NGEN WHO PROTECT THE PILMAIKEN RIVER AND ITS PEOPLE.

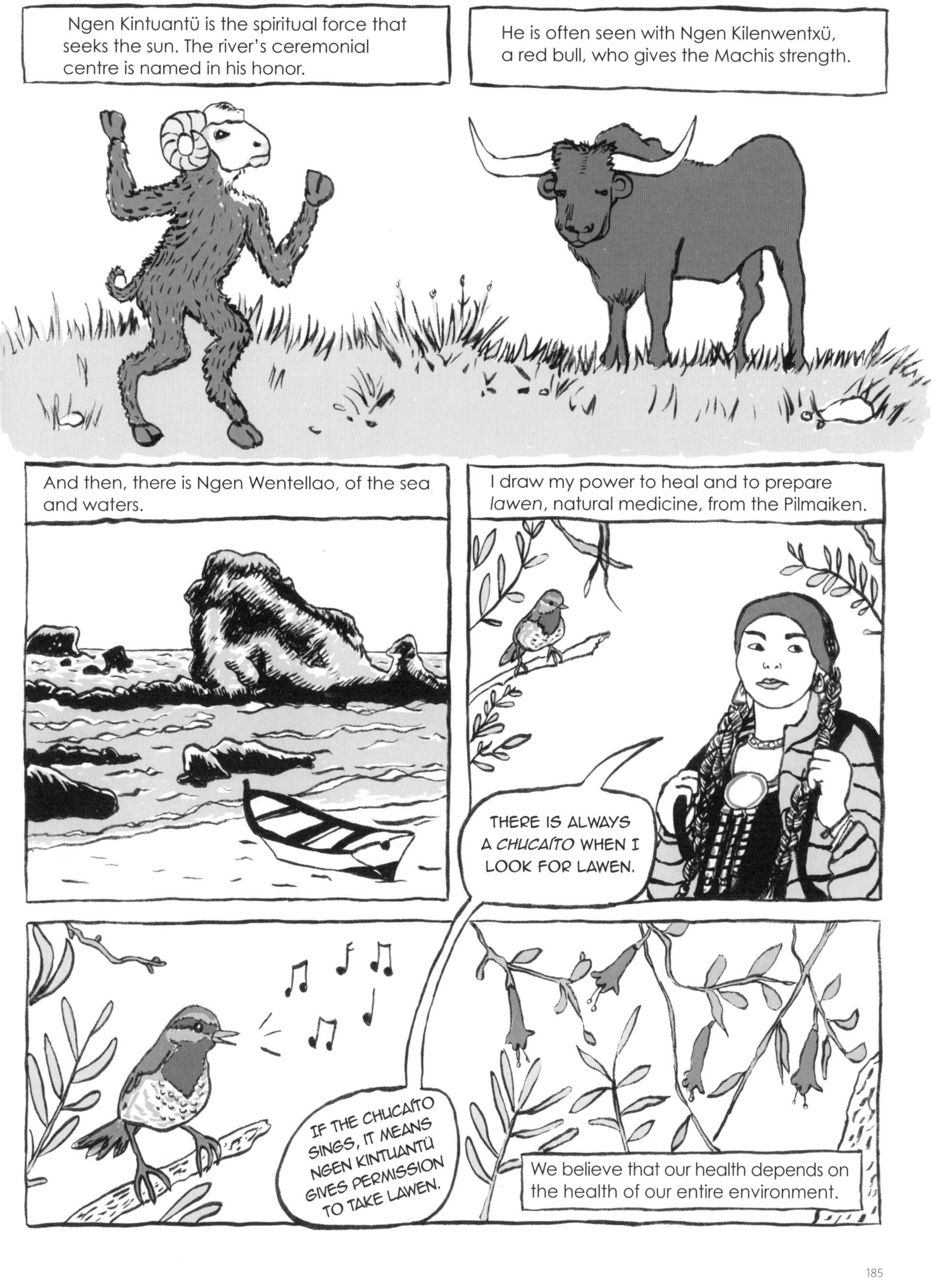
Ngen Kintuantü is the spiritual force that seeks the sun. The river's ceremonial centre is named in his honor.
He is often seen with Ngen Kilenwentxü, a red bull, who gives the Machis strength.
And then, there is Ngen Wentellao, of the sea and waters.
I draw my power to heal and to prepare *lawen*, natural medicine, from the Pilmaiken.
THERE IS ALWAYS A *CHUCAÍTO* WHEN I LOOK FOR LAWEN.
IF THE CHUCAÍTO SINGS, IT MEANS NGEN KINTUANTÜ GIVES PERMISSION TO TAKE LAWEN.
We believe that our health depends on the health of our entire environment.

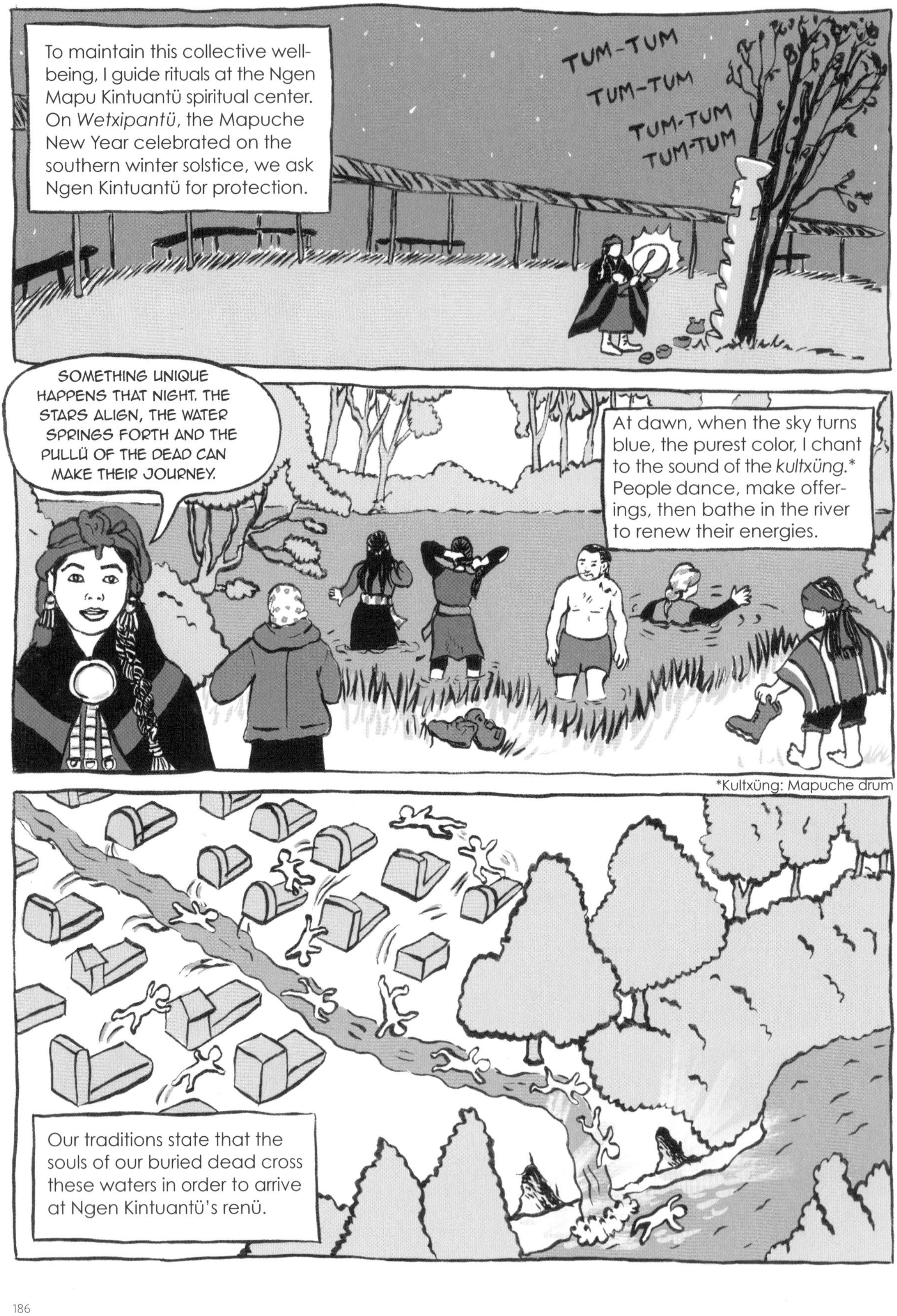
To maintain this collective well-being, I guide rituals at the Ngen Mapu Kintuantü spiritual center. On *Wetxipantü*, the Mapuche New Year celebrated on the southern winter solstice, we ask Ngen Kintuantü for protection.
TUM-TUM
TUM-TUM
TUM-TUM
TUM-TUM
SOMETHING UNIQUE HAPPENS THAT NIGHT. THE STARS ALIGN, THE WATER SPRINGS FORTH AND THE PULLÜ OF THE DEAD CAN MAKE THEIR JOURNEY.
At dawn, when the sky turns blue, the purest color, I chant to the sound of the *kultxüng*.* People dance, make offerings, then bathe in the river to renew their energies.
Our traditions state that the souls of our buried dead cross these waters in order to arrive at Ngen Kintuantü's renü.

*Kultxüng: Mapuche drum

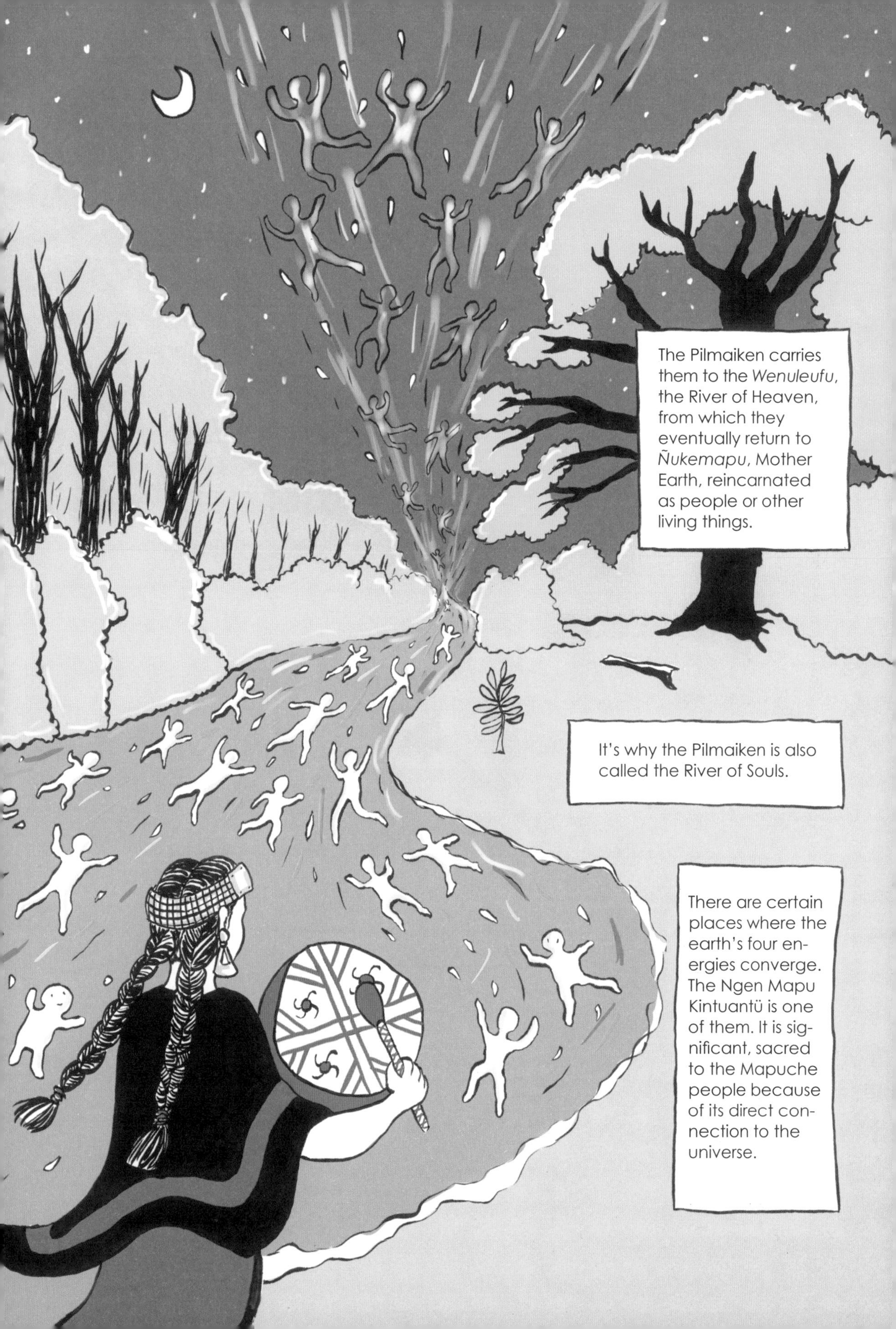
The Pilmaiken carries them to the *Wenuleufu*, the River of Heaven, from which they eventually return to *Ñukemapu*, Mother Earth, reincarnated as people or other living things.
It's why the Pilmaiken is also called the River of Souls.
There are certain places where the earth's four energies converge. The Ngen Mapu Kintuantü is one of them. It is significant, sacred to the Mapuche people because of its direct connection to the universe.

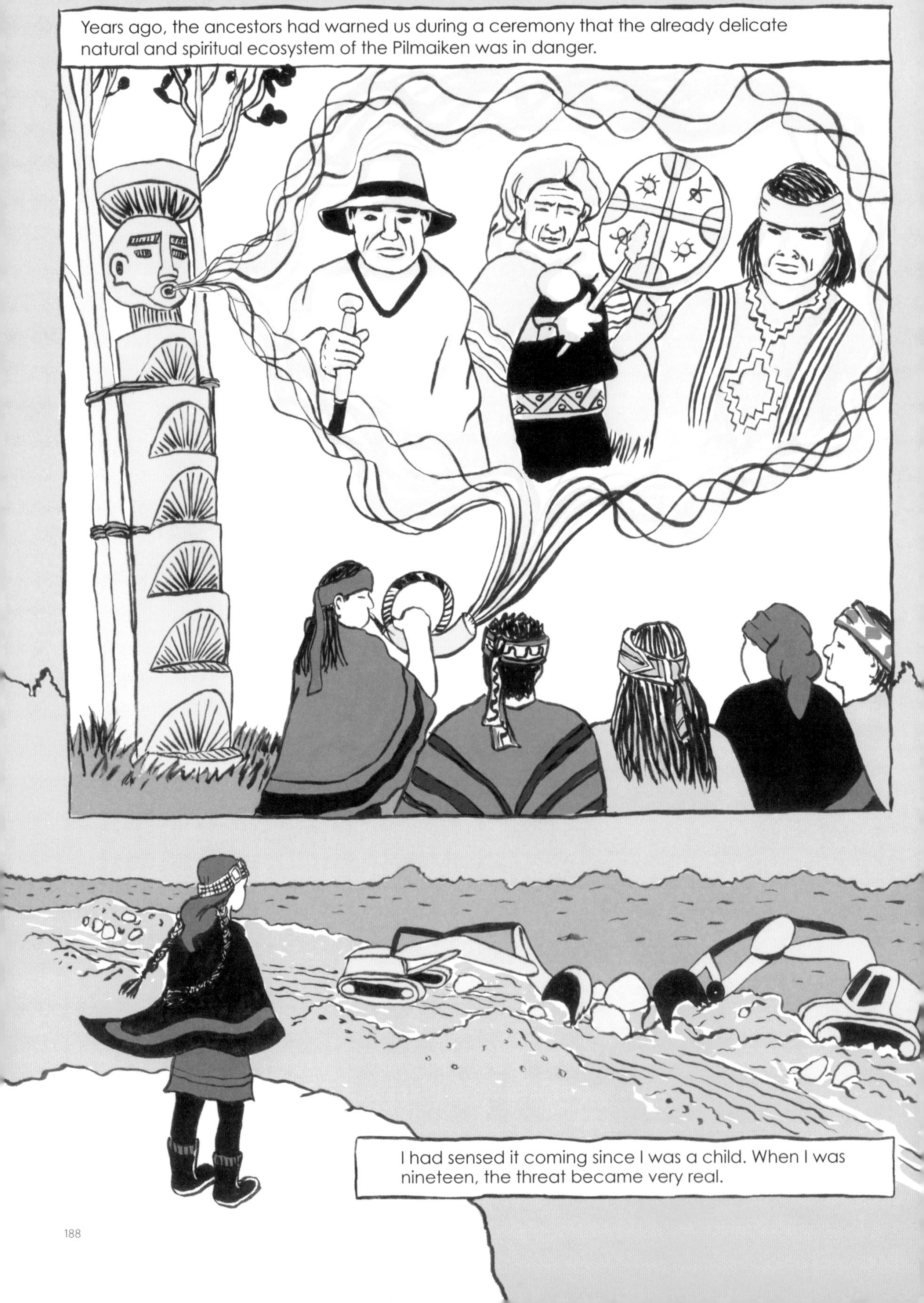
Years ago, the ancestors had warned us during a ceremony that the already delicate natural and spiritual ecosystem of the Pilmaiken was in danger.
I had sensed it coming since I was a child. When I was nineteen, the threat became very real.

THE RESISTANCE OF PILMAIKEN

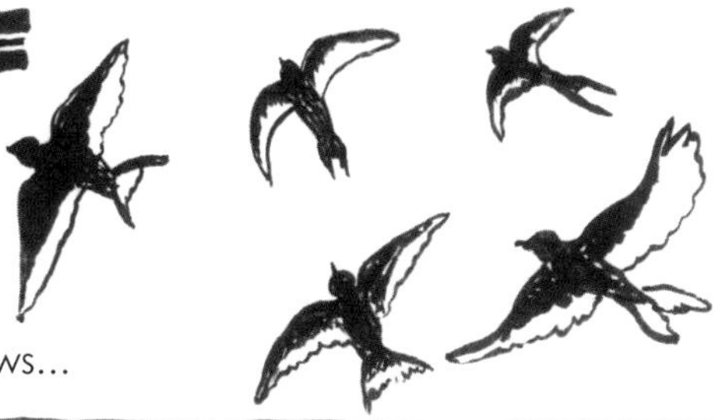

The Ngen Kintuantü is going to be flooded!

The news flew over the Pilmaiken like a flock of swallows…

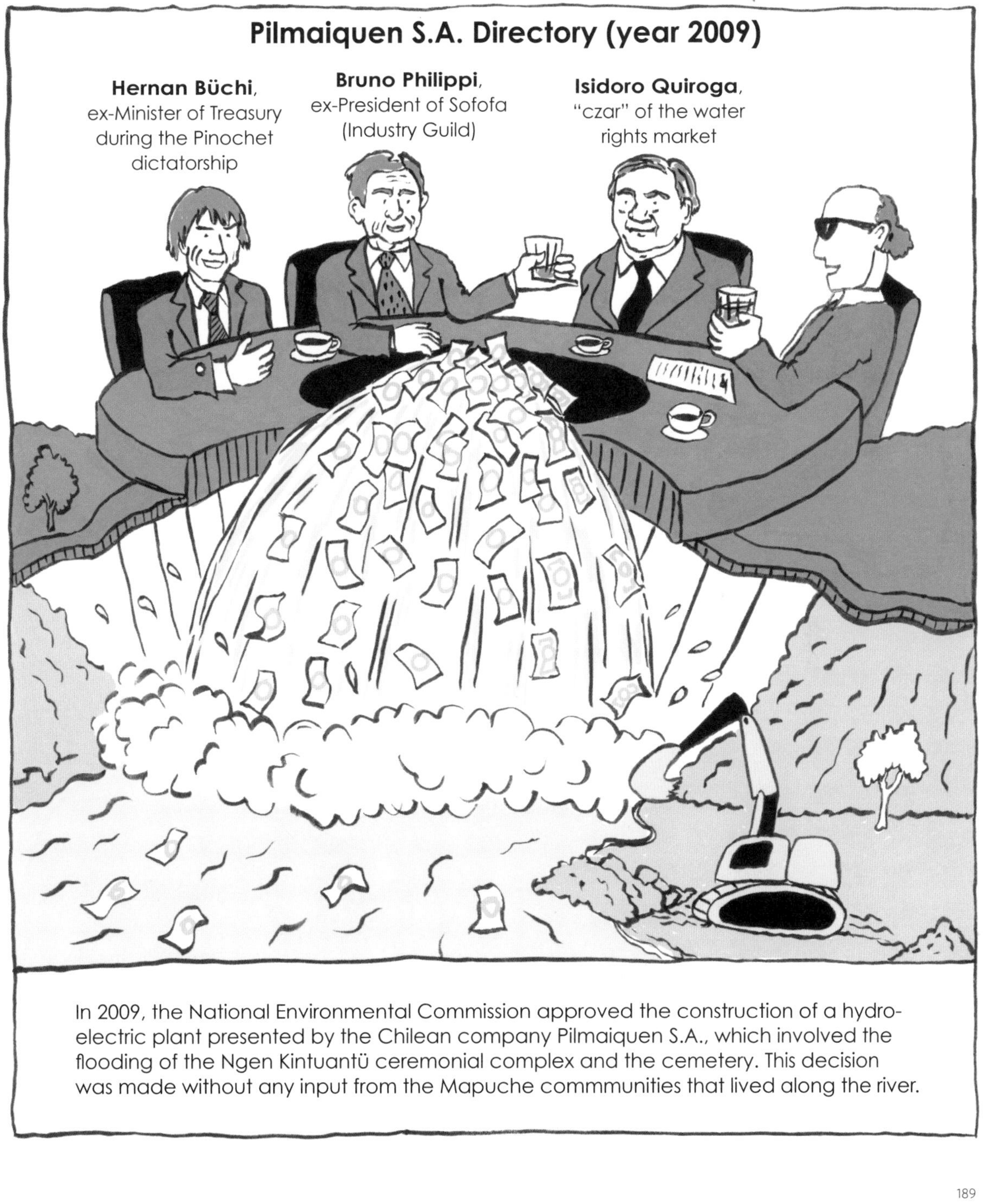
Pilmaiquen S.A. Directory (year 2009)
Hernan Büchi, ex-Minister of Treasury during the Pinochet dictatorship
Bruno Philippi, ex-President of Sofofa (Industry Guild)
Isidoro Quiroga, "czar" of the water rights market

In 2009, the National Environmental Commission approved the construction of a hydro-electric plant presented by the Chilean company Pilmaiquen S.A., which involved the flooding of the Ngen Kintuantü ceremonial complex and the cemetery. This decision was made without any input from the Mapuche commmunities that lived along the river.

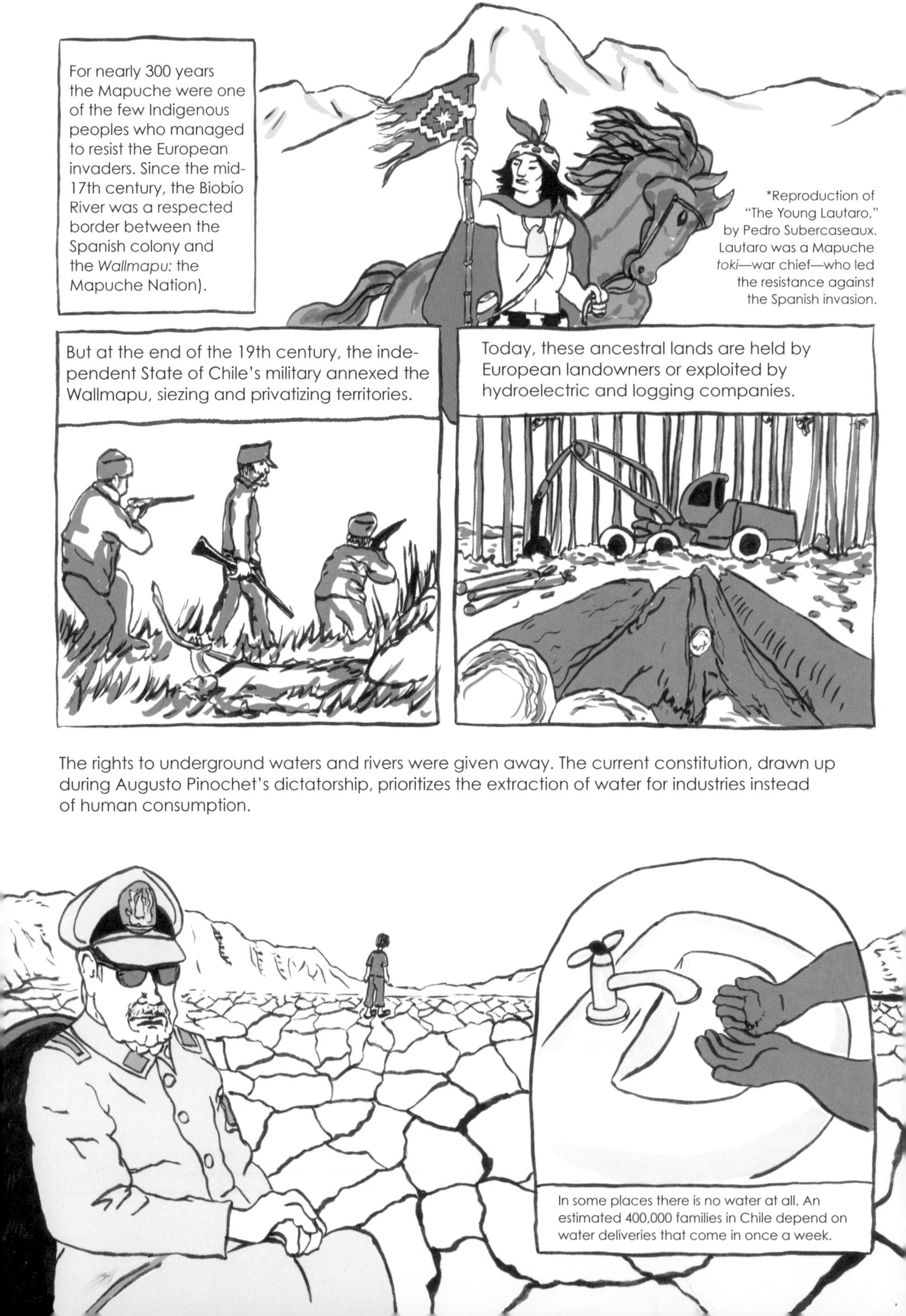
For nearly 300 years the Mapuche were one of the few Indigenous peoples who managed to resist the European invaders. Since the mid-17th century, the Biobío River was a respected border between the Spanish colony and the *Wallmapu:* the Mapuche Nation).
*Reproduction of "The Young Lautaro," by Pedro Subercaseaux. Lautaro was a Mapuche *toki*—war chief—who led the resistance against the Spanish invasion.
But at the end of the 19th century, the independent State of Chile's military annexed the Wallmapu, siezing and privatizing territories.
Today, these ancestral lands are held by European landowners or exploited by hydroelectric and logging companies.
The rights to underground waters and rivers were given away. The current constitution, drawn up during Augusto Pinochet's dictatorship, prioritizes the extraction of water for industries instead of human consumption.
In some places there is no water at all. An estimated 400,000 families in Chile depend on water deliveries that come in once a week.

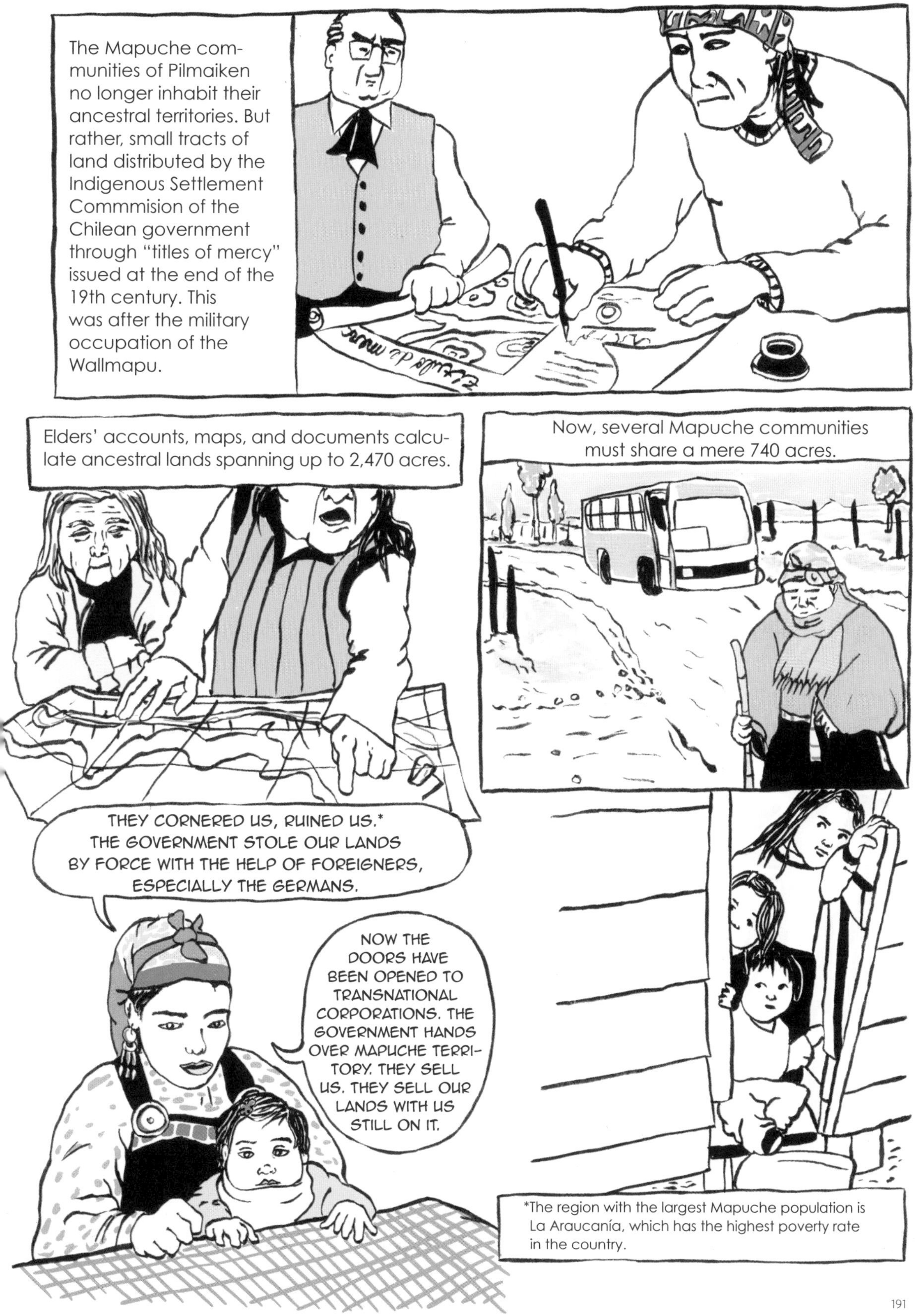
The Mapuche communities of Pilmaiken no longer inhabit their ancestral territories. But rather, small tracts of land distributed by the Indigenous Settlement Commmision of the Chilean government through "titles of mercy" issued at the end of the 19th century. This was after the military occupation of the Wallmapu.
Elders' accounts, maps, and documents calculate ancestral lands spanning up to 2,470 acres.
Now, several Mapuche communities must share a mere 740 acres.
THEY CORNERED US, RUINED US.* THE GOVERNMENT STOLE OUR LANDS BY FORCE WITH THE HELP OF FOREIGNERS, ESPECIALLY THE GERMANS.
NOW THE DOORS HAVE BEEN OPENED TO TRANSNATIONAL CORPORATIONS. THE GOVERNMENT HANDS OVER MAPUCHE TERRITORY. THEY SELL US. THEY SELL OUR LANDS WITH US STILL ON IT.
*The region with the largest Mapuche population is La Araucanía, which has the highest poverty rate in the country.

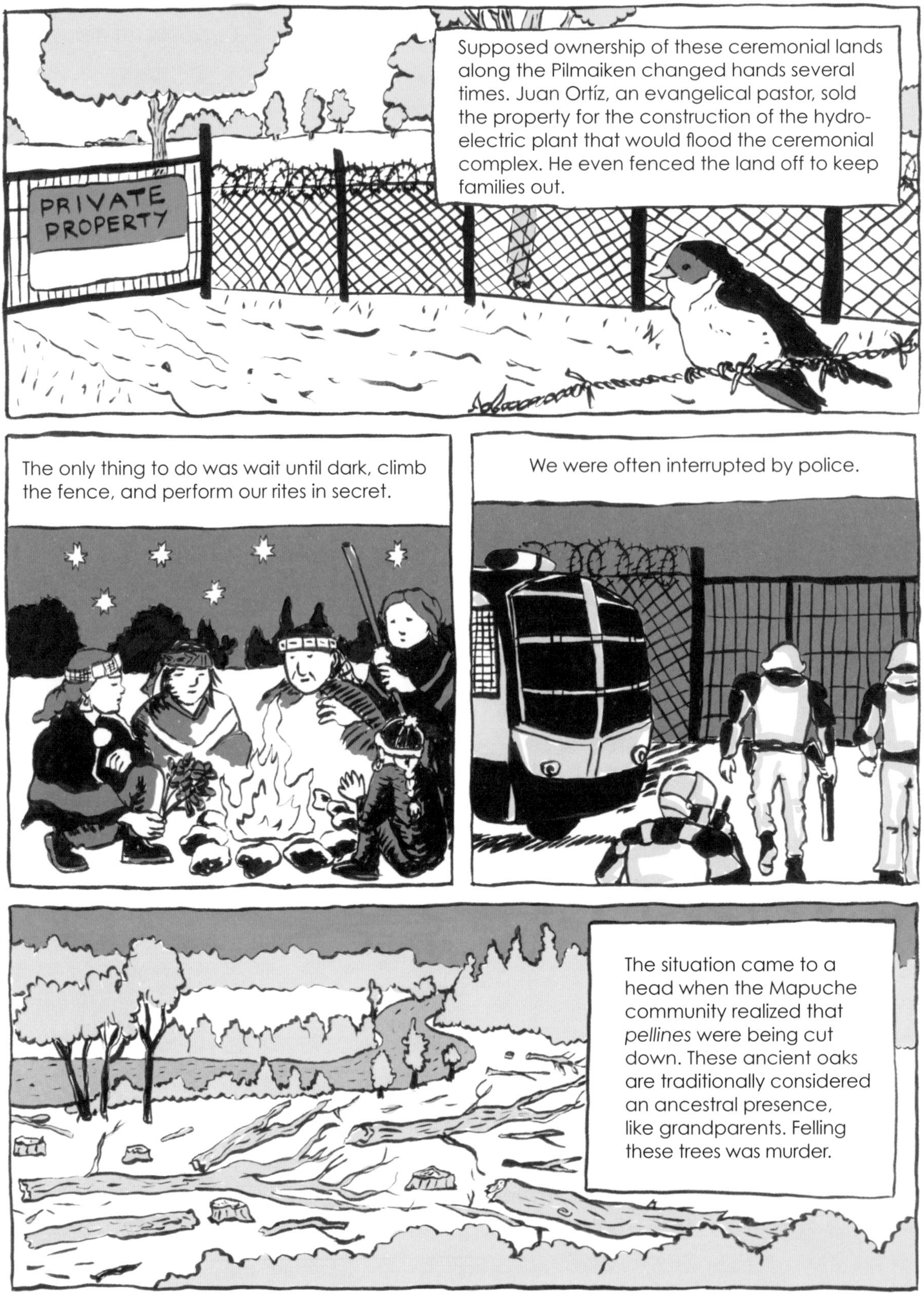
Supposed ownership of these ceremonial lands along the Pilmaiken changed hands several times. Juan Ortíz, an evangelical pastor, sold the property for the construction of the hydro-electric plant that would flood the ceremonial complex. He even fenced the land off to keep families out.
PRIVATE PROPERTY
The only thing to do was wait until dark, climb the fence, and perform our rites in secret.
We were often interrupted by police.
The situation came to a head when the Mapuche community realized that *pellines* were being cut down. These ancient oaks are traditionally considered an ancestral presence, like grandparents. Felling these trees was murder.

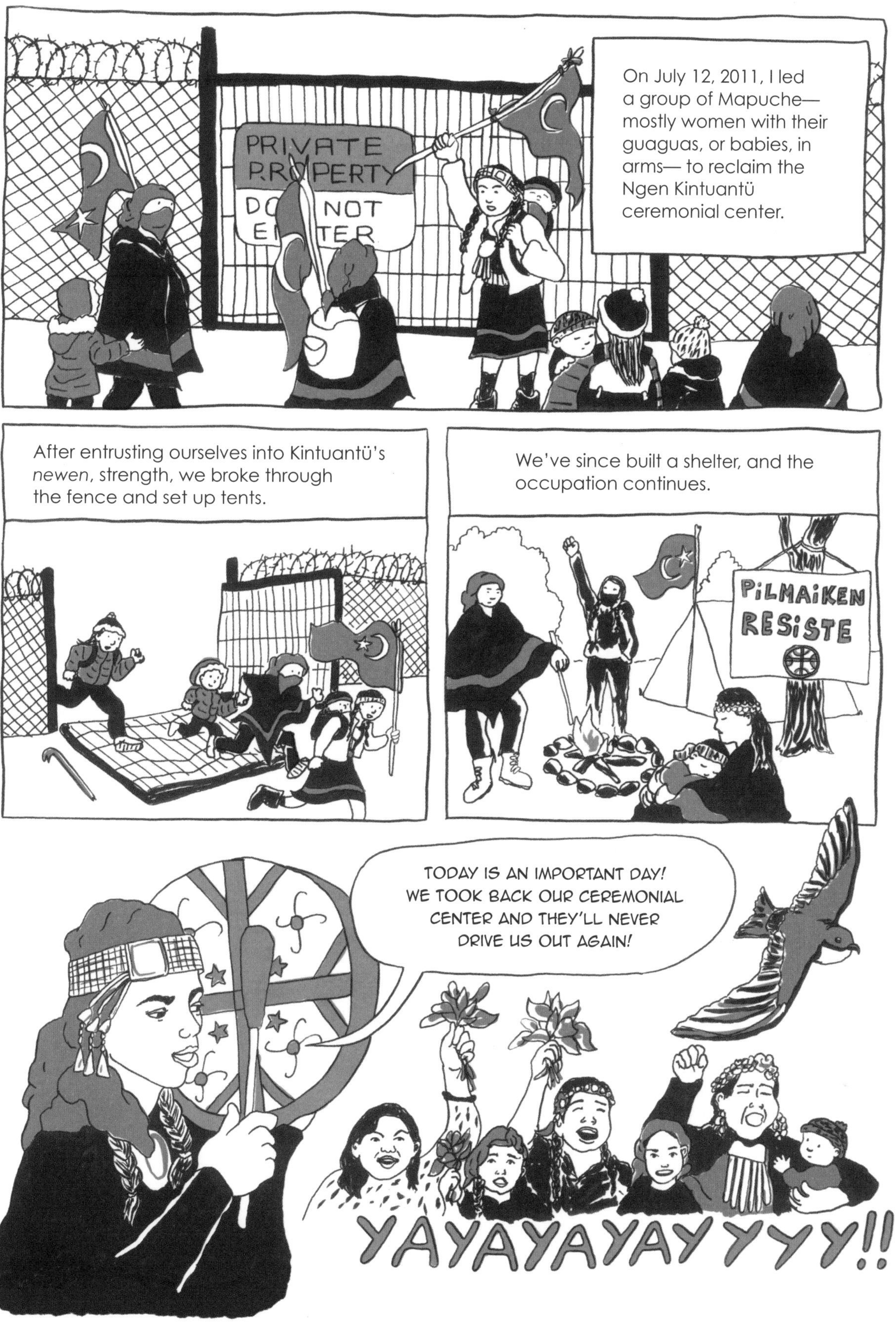

PRIVATE PROPERTY
DO NOT ENTER
On July 12, 2011, I led a group of Mapuche— mostly women with their guaguas, or babies, in arms— to reclaim the Ngen Kintuantü ceremonial center.
After entrusting ourselves into Kintuantü's *newen*, strength, we broke through the fence and set up tents.
We've since built a shelter, and the occupation continues.
PILMAIKEN RESISTE
TODAY IS AN IMPORTANT DAY! WE TOOK BACK OUR CEREMONIAL CENTER AND THEY'LL NEVER DRIVE US OUT AGAIN!
YAYAYAYAYYYY!!

Our re-occupation of the center was followed by legal proceedings. This stopped the flooding for a while. But the threat was much greater than we thought. It wasn't just one plant they were building, but an entire complex with three hydroelectric plants: Rucatayo, Los Lagos, and Osorno.

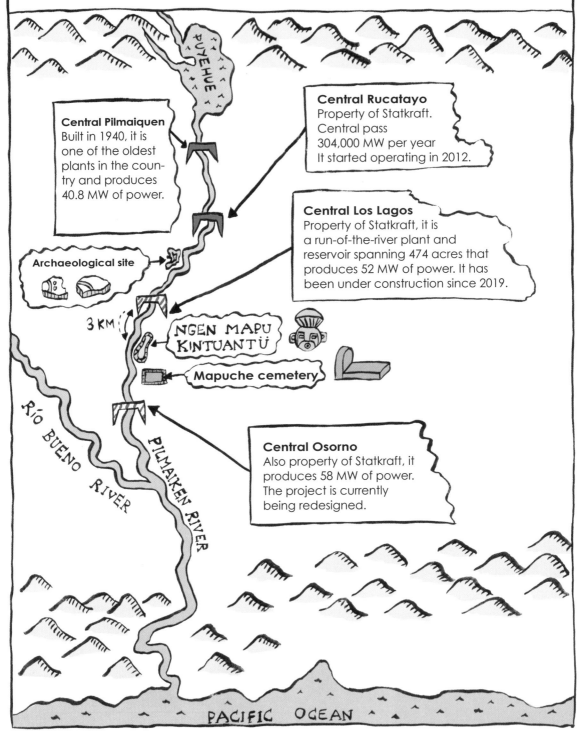

Central Pilmaiquen
Built in 1940, it is one of the oldest plants in the country and produces 40.8 MW of power.

Central Rucatayo
Property of Statkraft.
Central pass
304,000 MW per year
It started operating in 2012.

Central Los Lagos
Property of Statkraft, it is a run-of-the-river plant and reservoir spanning 474 acres that produces 52 MW of power. It has been under construction since 2019.

Archaeological site

3 KM

NGEN MAPU KINTUANTÜ

Mapuche cemetery

Central Osorno
Also property of Statkraft, it produces 58 MW of power. The project is currently being redesigned.

RÍO BUENO RIVER

PILMAIKEN RIVER

PUYEHUE

PACIFIC OCEAN

In 2015, the entire project was acquired by Statkraft, a state-owned Norwegian company with a global presence in the energy sector.

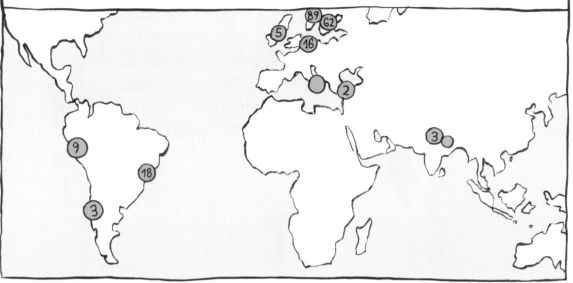

These hydroelectric plants disrupt the river's natural flow. Flooding and logging continue to threaten the Pilmaiken's spiritual and ecological balance.

Commmunities report that hundreds of dead fish have been found in the waters near the Rucatayo power plant.

Sometimes the shore dries up. There aren't as many medicinal herbs as before, and fulffilling my mission, my role as a healer becomes harder.

TERRITORIES ARE ALIVE. IF THEY ARE DESTROYED, THE NGEN LEAVE. AS THE LAND GROWS DISEASED, SO DO PEOPLE. WE HAVE SEEN YOUNG PEOPLE DIE. THE IMBALANCE MAKES THEM SICK.

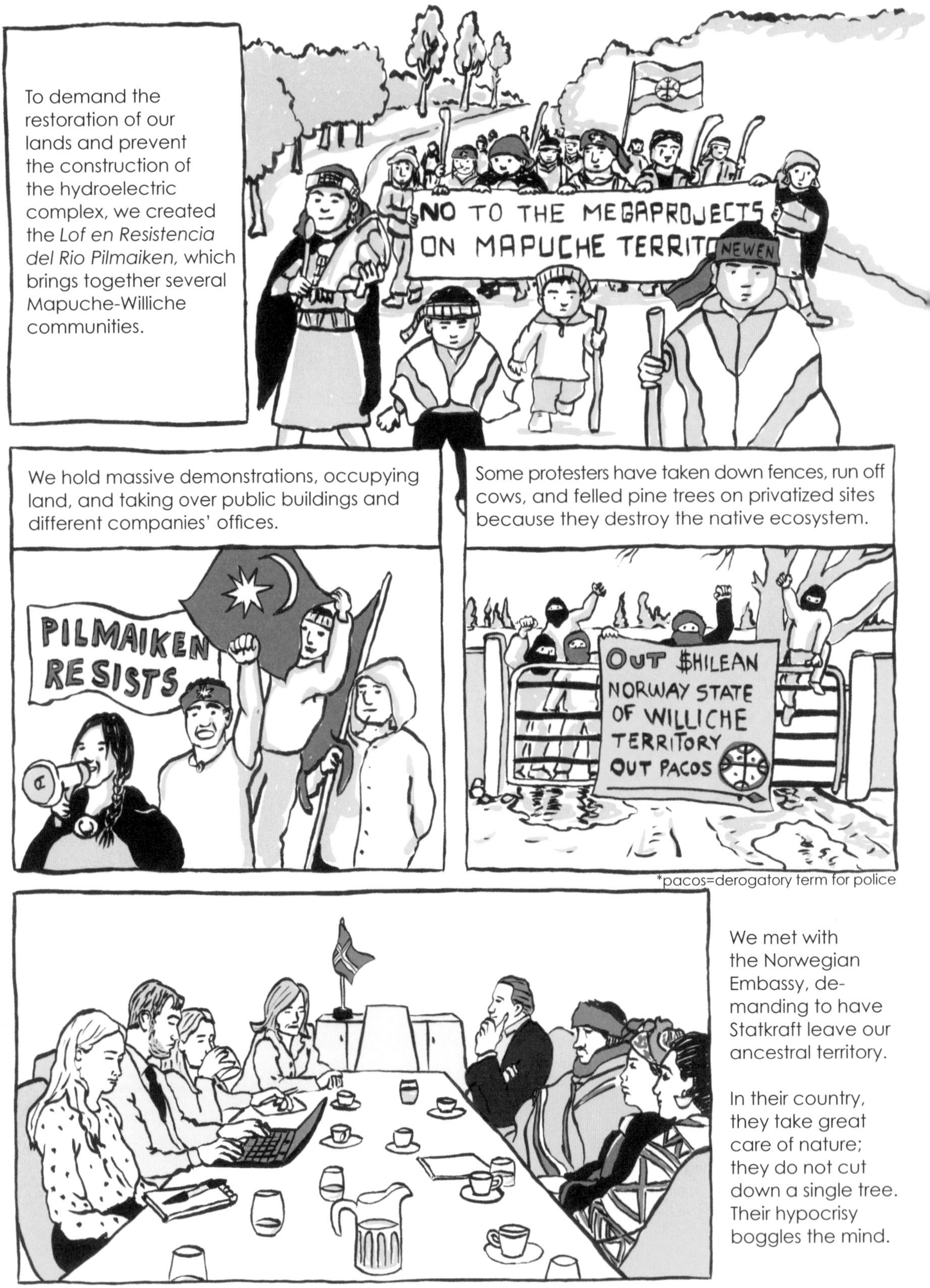
To demand the restoration of our lands and prevent the construction of the hydroelectric complex, we created the *Lof en Resistencia del Rio Pilmaiken*, which brings together several Mapuche-Williche communities.
NO TO THE MEGAPROJECTS ON MAPUCHE TERRIT
NEWEN
We hold massive demonstrations, occupying land, and taking over public buildings and different companies' offices.
PILMAIKEN RESISTS
Some protesters have taken down fences, run off cows, and felled pine trees on privatized sites because they destroy the native ecosystem.
OUT $HILEAN NORWAY STATE OF WILLICHE TERRITORY OUT PACOS
*pacos=derogatory term for police
We met with the Norwegian Embassy, demanding to have Statkraft leave our ancestral territory.
In their country, they take great care of nature; they do not cut down a single tree. Their hypocrisy boggles the mind.

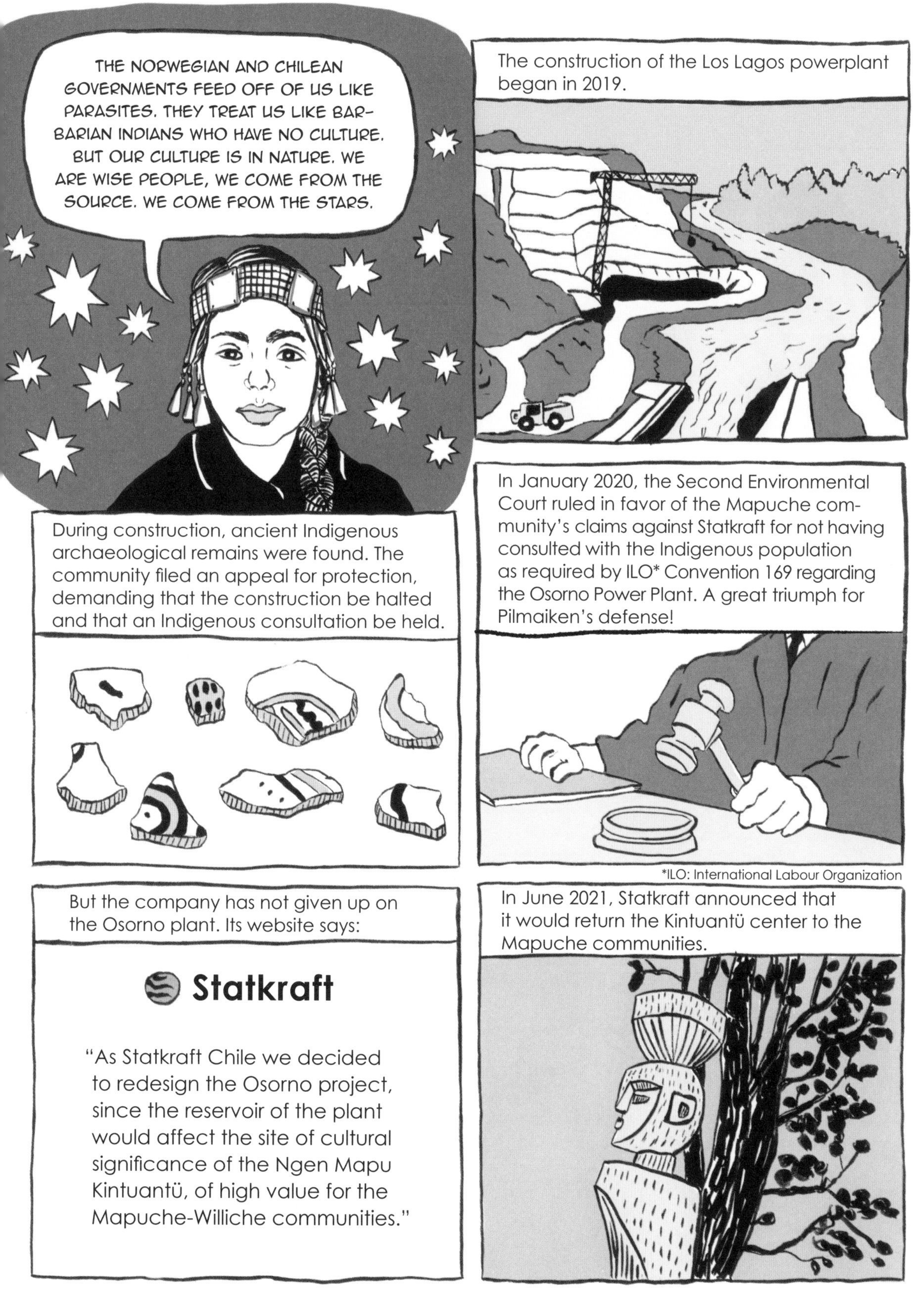
THE NORWEGIAN AND CHILEAN GOVERNMENTS FEED OFF OF US LIKE PARASITES. THEY TREAT US LIKE BARBARIAN INDIANS WHO HAVE NO CULTURE. BUT OUR CULTURE IS IN NATURE. WE ARE WISE PEOPLE, WE COME FROM THE SOURCE. WE COME FROM THE STARS.
The construction of the Los Lagos powerplant began in 2019.
During construction, ancient Indigenous archaeological remains were found. The community filed an appeal for protection, demanding that the construction be halted and that an Indigenous consultation be held.
In January 2020, the Second Environmental Court ruled in favor of the Mapuche community's claims against Statkraft for not having consulted with the Indigenous population as required by ILO* Convention 169 regarding the Osorno Power Plant. A great triumph for Pilmaiken's defense!
*ILO: International Labour Organization
But the company has not given up on the Osorno plant. Its website says:
Statkraft
"As Statkraft Chile we decided to redesign the Osorno project, since the reservoir of the plant would affect the site of cultural significance of the Ngen Mapu Kintuantü, of high value for the Mapuche-Williche communities."
In June 2021, Statkraft announced that it would return the Kintuantü center to the Mapuche communities.

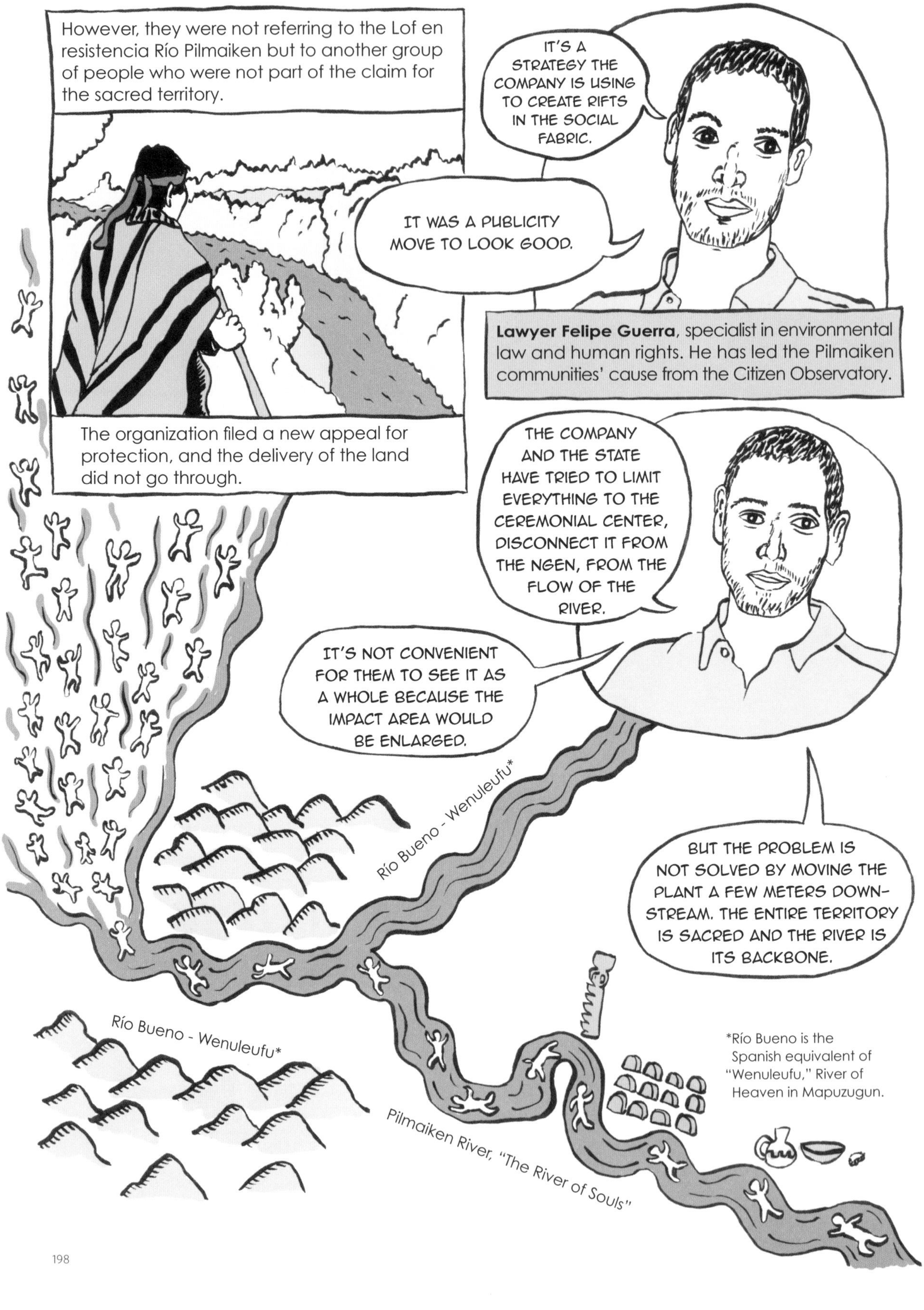
However, they were not referring to the Lof en resistencia Río Pilmaiken but to another group of people who were not part of the claim for the sacred territory.
IT'S A STRATEGY THE COMPANY IS USING TO CREATE RIFTS IN THE SOCIAL FABRIC.
IT WAS A PUBLICITY MOVE TO LOOK GOOD.
Lawyer Felipe Guerra, specialist in environmental law and human rights. He has led the Pilmaiken communities' cause from the Citizen Observatory.
The organization filed a new appeal for protection, and the delivery of the land did not go through.
THE COMPANY AND THE STATE HAVE TRIED TO LIMIT EVERYTHING TO THE CEREMONIAL CENTER, DISCONNECT IT FROM THE NGEN, FROM THE FLOW OF THE RIVER.
IT'S NOT CONVENIENT FOR THEM TO SEE IT AS A WHOLE BECAUSE THE IMPACT AREA WOULD BE ENLARGED.
Río Bueno - Wenuleufu*
BUT THE PROBLEM IS NOT SOLVED BY MOVING THE PLANT A FEW METERS DOWN-STREAM. THE ENTIRE TERRITORY IS SACRED AND THE RIVER IS ITS BACKBONE.
Río Bueno - Wenuleufu*
Pilmaiken River, "The River of Souls"
*Río Bueno is the Spanish equivalent of "Wenuleufu," River of Heaven in Mapuzugun.

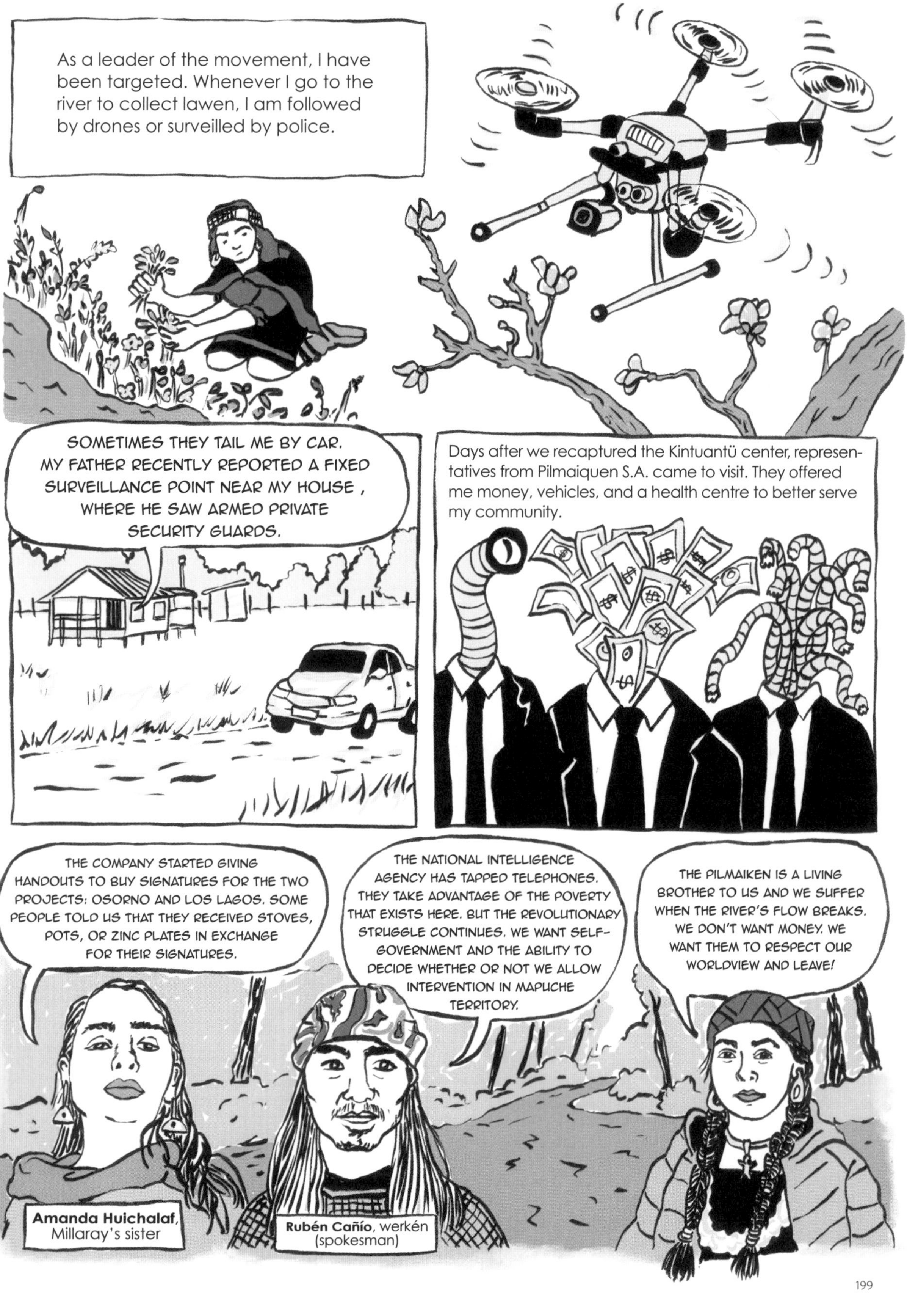
As a leader of the movement, I have been targeted. Whenever I go to the river to collect lawen, I am followed by drones or surveilled by police.
SOMETIMES THEY TAIL ME BY CAR. MY FATHER RECENTLY REPORTED A FIXED SURVEILLANCE POINT NEAR MY HOUSE , WHERE HE SAW ARMED PRIVATE SECURITY GUARDS.
Days after we recaptured the Kintuantü center, representatives from Pilmaiquen S.A. came to visit. They offered me money, vehicles, and a health centre to better serve my community.
THE COMPANY STARTED GIVING HANDOUTS TO BUY SIGNATURES FOR THE TWO PROJECTS: OSORNO AND LOS LAGOS. SOME PEOPLE TOLD US THAT THEY RECEIVED STOVES, POTS, OR ZINC PLATES IN EXCHANGE FOR THEIR SIGNATURES.
THE NATIONAL INTELLIGENCE AGENCY HAS TAPPED TELEPHONES. THEY TAKE ADVANTAGE OF THE POVERTY THAT EXISTS HERE. BUT THE REVOLUTIONARY STRUGGLE CONTINUES. WE WANT SELF-GOVERNMENT AND THE ABILITY TO DECIDE WHETHER OR NOT WE ALLOW INTERVENTION IN MAPUCHE TERRITORY.
THE PILMAIKEN IS A LIVING BROTHER TO US AND WE SUFFER WHEN THE RIVER'S FLOW BREAKS. WE DON'T WANT MONEY. WE WANT THEM TO RESPECT OUR WORLDVIEW AND LEAVE!
Amanda Huichalaf, Millaray's sister
Rubén Caño, werkén (spokesman)

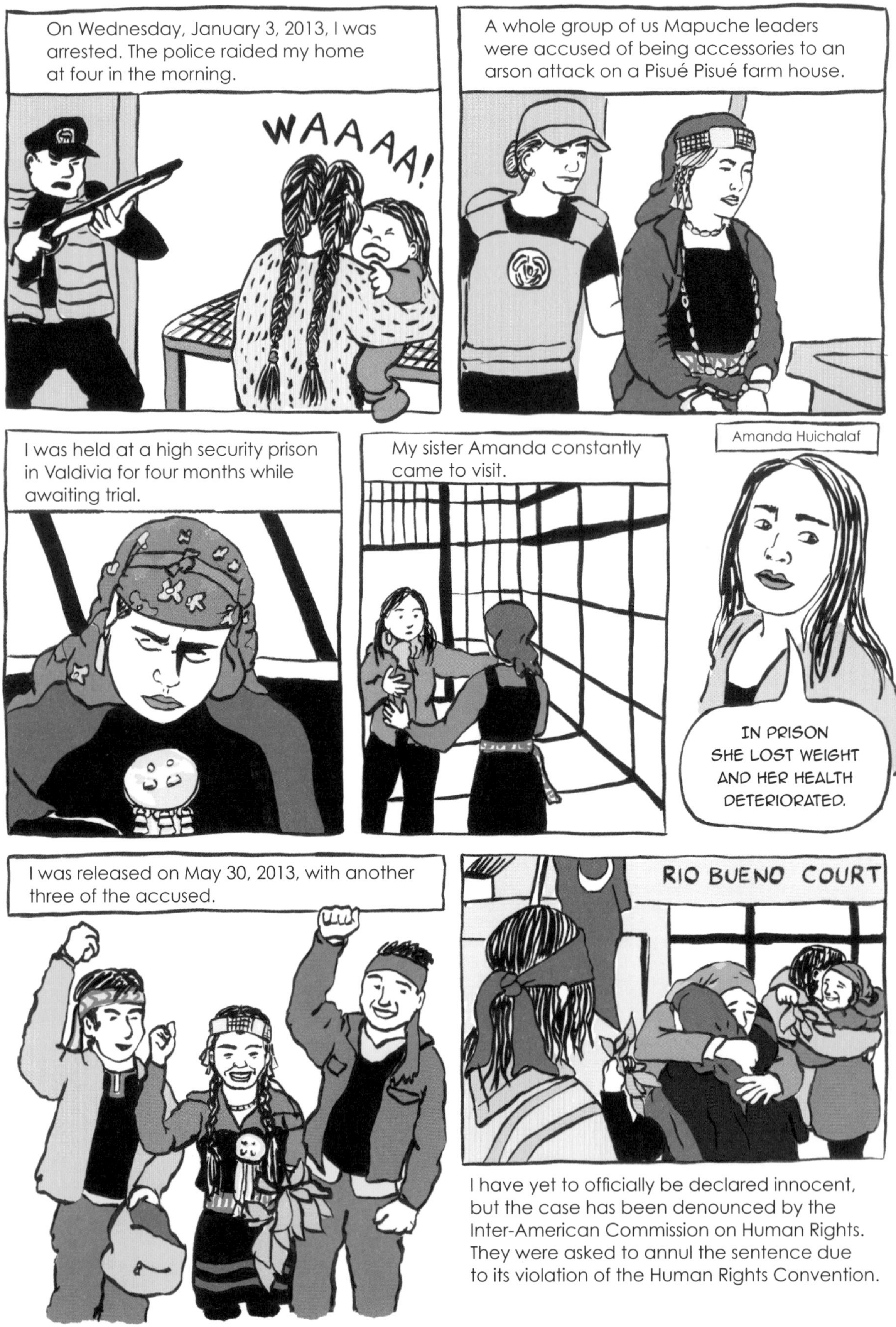
On Wednesday, January 3, 2013, I was arrested. The police raided my home at four in the morning.
WAAAAA!
A whole group of us Mapuche leaders were accused of being accessories to an arson attack on a Pisué Pisué farm house.
I was held at a high security prison in Valdivia for four months while awaiting trial.
My sister Amanda constantly came to visit.
Amanda Huichalaf
IN PRISON SHE LOST WEIGHT AND HER HEALTH DETERIORATED.
I was released on May 30, 2013, with another three of the accused.
RIO BUENO COURT
I have yet to officially be declared innocent, but the case has been denounced by the Inter-American Commission on Human Rights. They were asked to annul the sentence due to its violation of the Human Rights Convention.

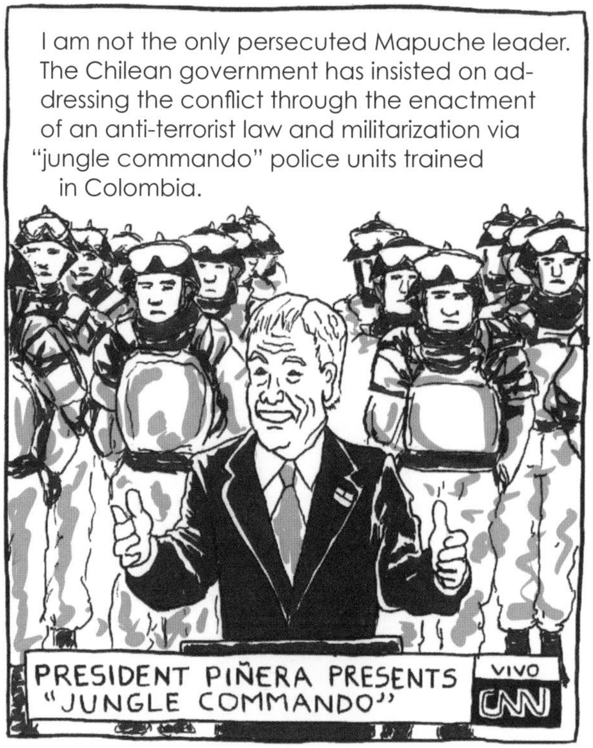
I am not the only persecuted Mapuche leader. The Chilean government has insisted on addressing the conflict through the enactment of an anti-terrorist law and militarization via "jungle commando" police units trained in Colombia.
PRESIDENT PIÑERA PRESENTS "JUNGLE COMMANDO"
VIVO
CNN

All of this despite repeated warnings, as well as national and international reports about murders, human rights violations, unjust imprisonments, and physical and emotional violence against Indigenous youth.

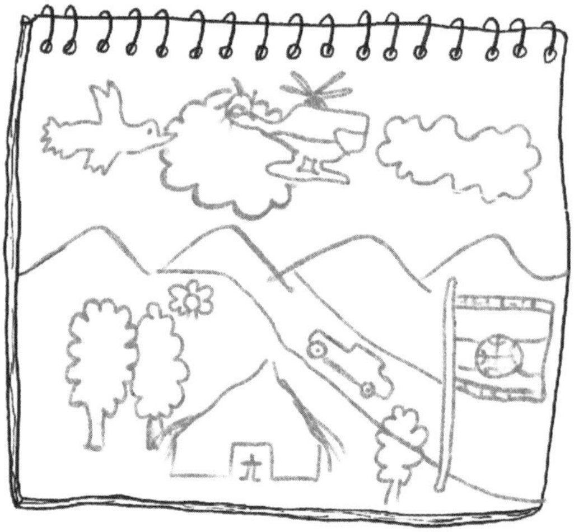

Reproduction of a drawing by a five-year-old Mapuche boy from the Araucanía Region.

MACHI FRANCISCA LINCONAO

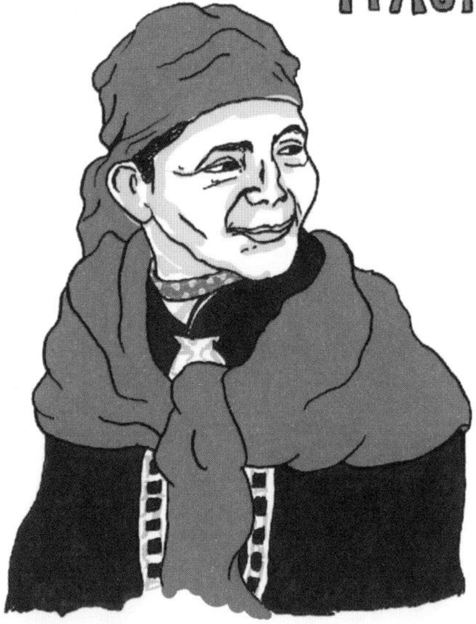

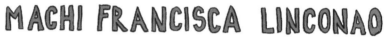

In 2008, sixty-two-year old Machi Francisca sued a forestry company for logging in Rahue, La Araucanía Region. She won under ILO Convention 169. She was arrested in 2016 and accused of arson and participating in the Luchsinger-Mackay murders. The case saw her in and out of jail for years, where she was often on hunger strike. She was finallly acquitted in 2018. In May of 2021, she was elected by her fellow Mapuche as a representative to draft a new Chilean constitution. In a historic decision, the constitutional convention also elected a second Mapuche woman, Elisa Loncón, as its president.

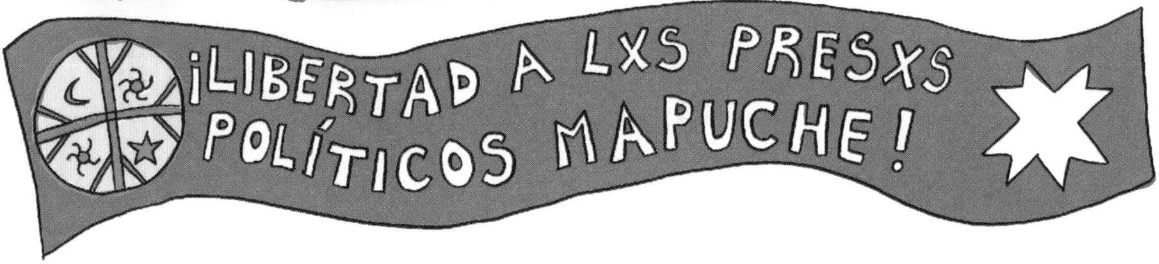
¡LIBERTAD A LXS PRESXS POLÍTICOS MAPUCHE!

ALBERTO CURAMIL

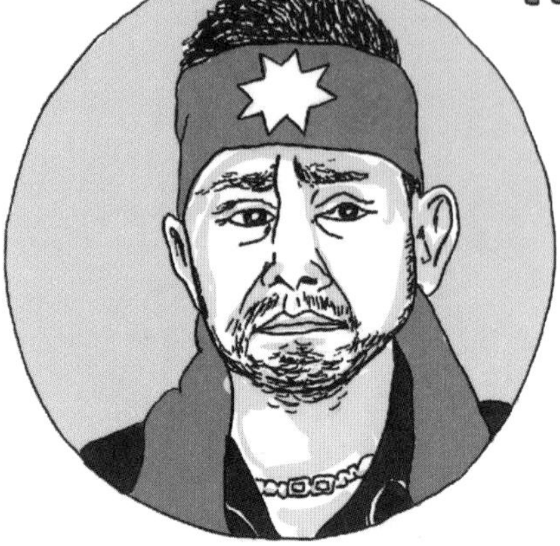

This forty-seven-year-old Longko is a member of the Mapuche Territorial Alliance, an organization that fights for the right to water, food, and land. He was falsely acccused of weapons theft, illegal possesion thereof, and assault after leading a protest that shut down two hydroelectric power plant projects along the Cautín River in La Araucanía. While he was in prison, he won the Goldman Environmental Prize, also known as the Green Nobel.

MACARENA VALDÉS

This thirty-two-year-old Mapuche activist led an environmental campaign opposing a hydro-electric plant along the Tranguil River in Los Ríos. In 2016, her eleven-year old son came home from school to find her hanging from a rope tied to a ceiling beam. It was reported as a suicide. But the autopsy later revealed she was dead before she had been hanged. No one has been held accountable for her murder.

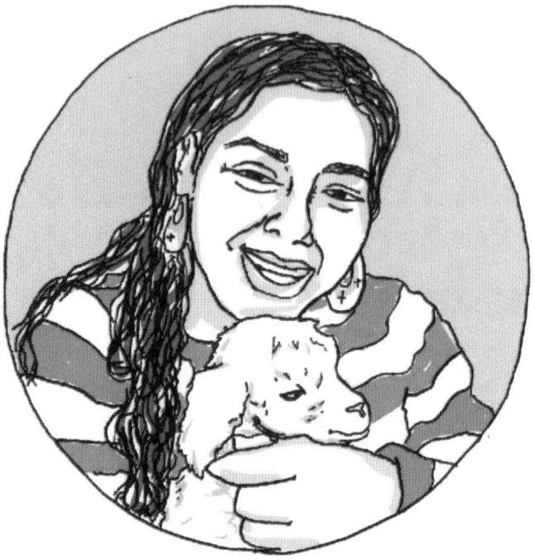

CAMILO CATRILLANCA

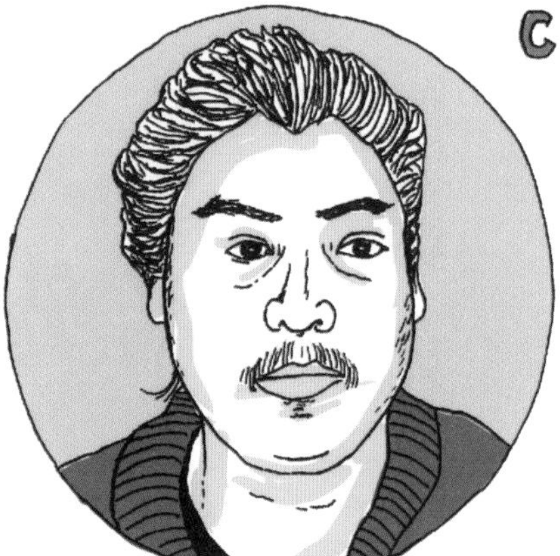

The twenty-three-year-old member of the Mapuche community was shot in the back and killed by "jungle commandos" while driving his tractor in Temucuicui, La Araucanía, in 2018. Authorities claimed that shots were fired during a chase because Catrillanca had stolen a car. This proved to be a setup, and an investigation was opened for obstruction of justice. It triggered social uprising throughout Chile, a prelude to the *revuelta popular* of 2019 and the creation of a new constitutional assembly.

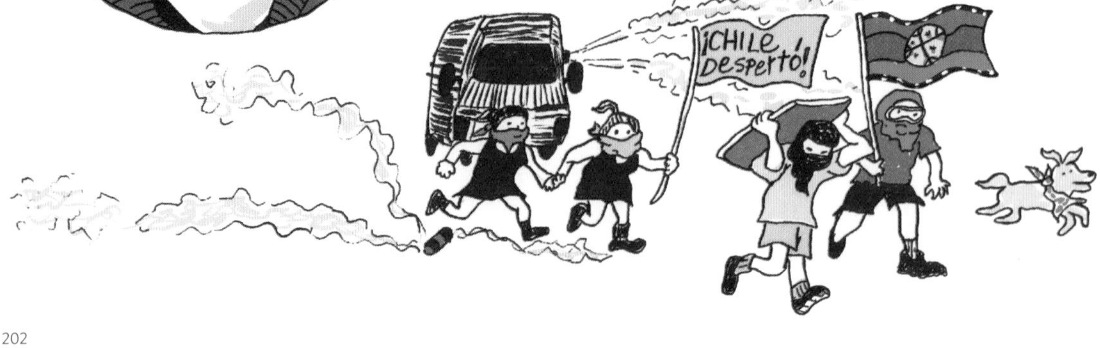
¡CHILE DESPERTÓ!

FACT: Acccording to a global analysis made by the NGO Front Line Defenders in 2019, environmental activism is the most dangerous occupation in Latin America. This region is the most likely to criminalize Indigenous activism, and is also the region in which an Indigenous activist is most likely to be murdered. Their murderers are also the most likely to go unpunished. A report from 2020 indicates that 69% of activists killed that year defended the environment, the rights of Indigenous peoples, and their right to land.

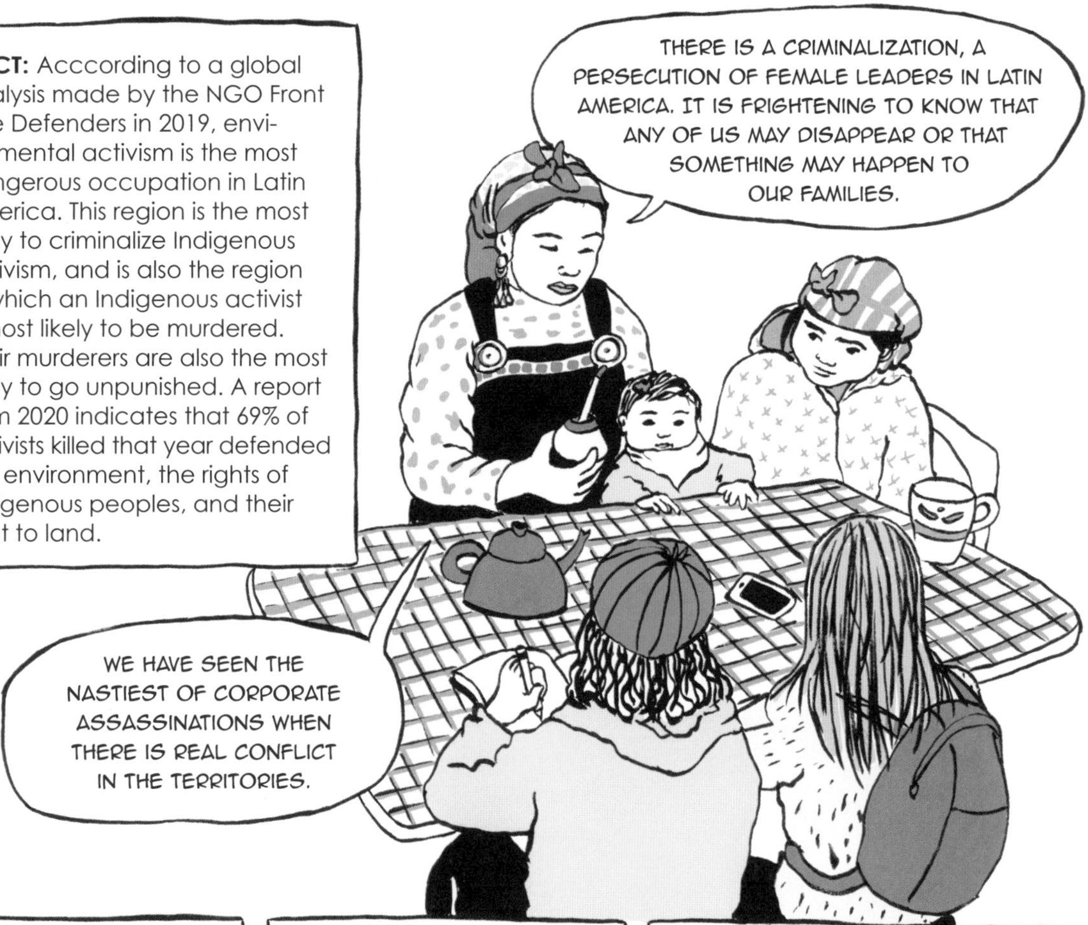
THERE IS A CRIMINALIZATION, A PERSECUTION OF FEMALE LEADERS IN LATIN AMERICA. IT IS FRIGHTENING TO KNOW THAT ANY OF US MAY DISAPPEAR OR THAT SOMETHING MAY HAPPEN TO OUR FAMILIES.
WE HAVE SEEN THE NASTIEST OF CORPORATE ASSASSINATIONS WHEN THERE IS REAL CONFLICT IN THE TERRITORIES.

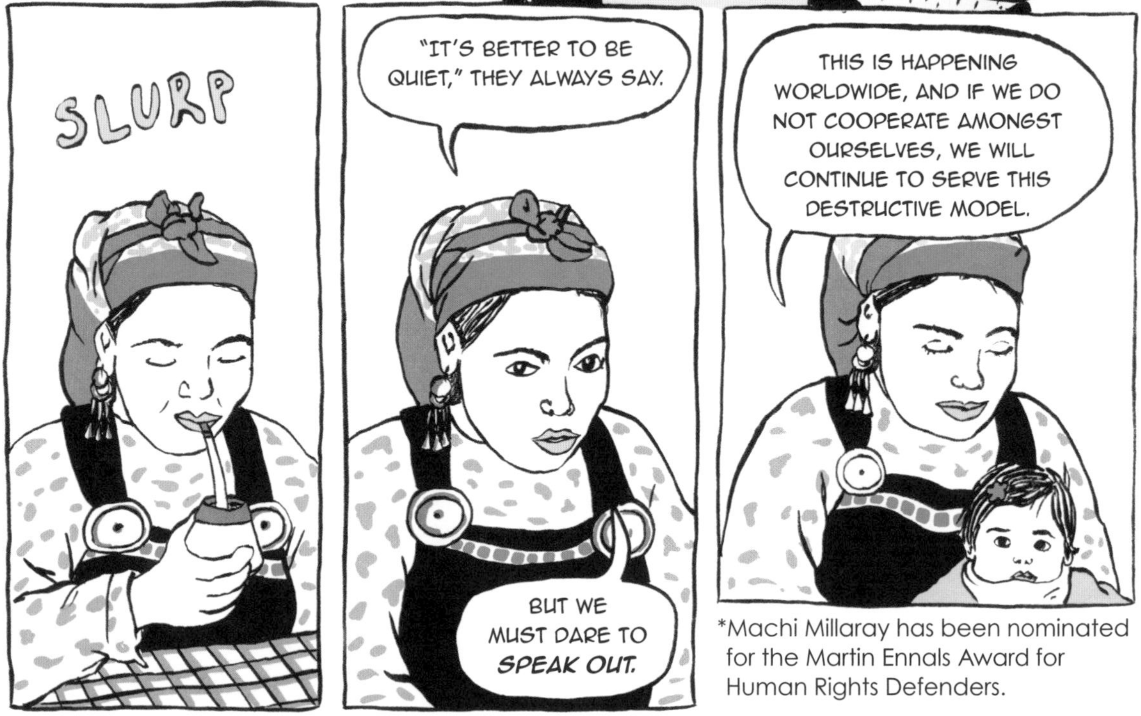
SLURP
"IT'S BETTER TO BE QUIET," THEY ALWAYS SAY.
BUT WE MUST DARE TO *SPEAK OUT.*
THIS IS HAPPENING WORLDWIDE, AND IF WE DO NOT COOPERATE AMONGST OURSELVES, WE WILL CONTINUE TO SERVE THIS DESTRUCTIVE MODEL.

*Machi Millaray has been nominated for the Martin Ennals Award for Human Rights Defenders.

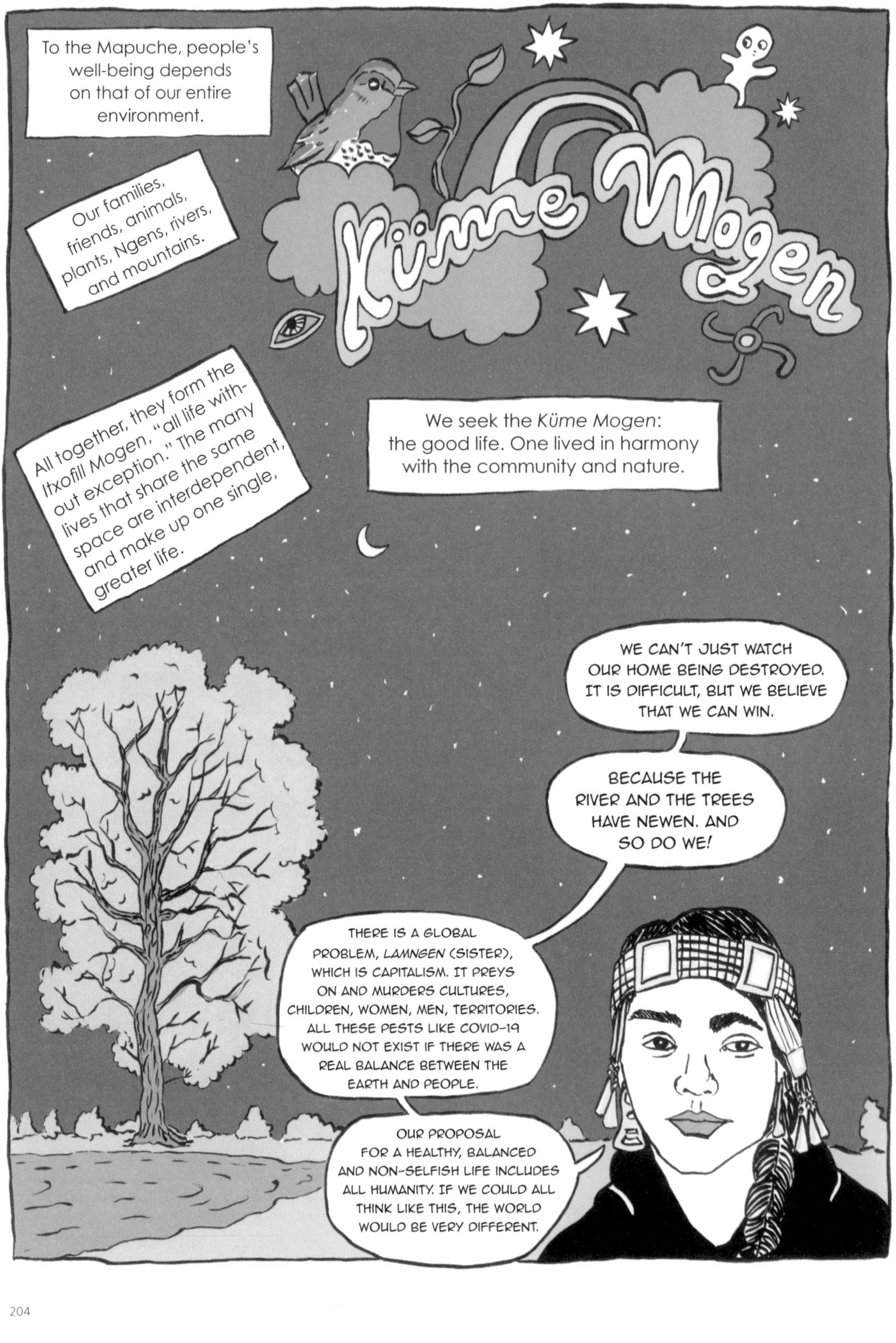
To the Mapuche, people's well-being depends on that of our entire environment.
Our families, friends, animals, plants, Ngens, rivers, and mountains.
Küme Mogen
All together, they form the Itxofill Mogen, "all life without exception." The many lives that share the same space are interdependent, and make up one single, greater life.
We seek the Küme Mogen: the good life. One lived in harmony with the community and nature.
WE CAN'T JUST WATCH OUR HOME BEING DESTROYED. IT IS DIFFICULT, BUT WE BELIEVE THAT WE CAN WIN.
BECAUSE THE RIVER AND THE TREES HAVE NEWEN. AND SO DO WE!
THERE IS A GLOBAL PROBLEM, LAMNGEN (SISTER), WHICH IS CAPITALISM. IT PREYS ON AND MURDERS CULTURES, CHILDREN, WOMEN, MEN, TERRITORIES. ALL THESE PESTS LIKE COVID-19 WOULD NOT EXIST IF THERE WAS A REAL BALANCE BETWEEN THE EARTH AND PEOPLE.
OUR PROPOSAL FOR A HEALTHY, BALANCED AND NON-SELFISH LIFE INCLUDES ALL HUMANITY. IF WE COULD ALL THINK LIKE THIS, THE WORLD WOULD BE VERY DIFFERENT.

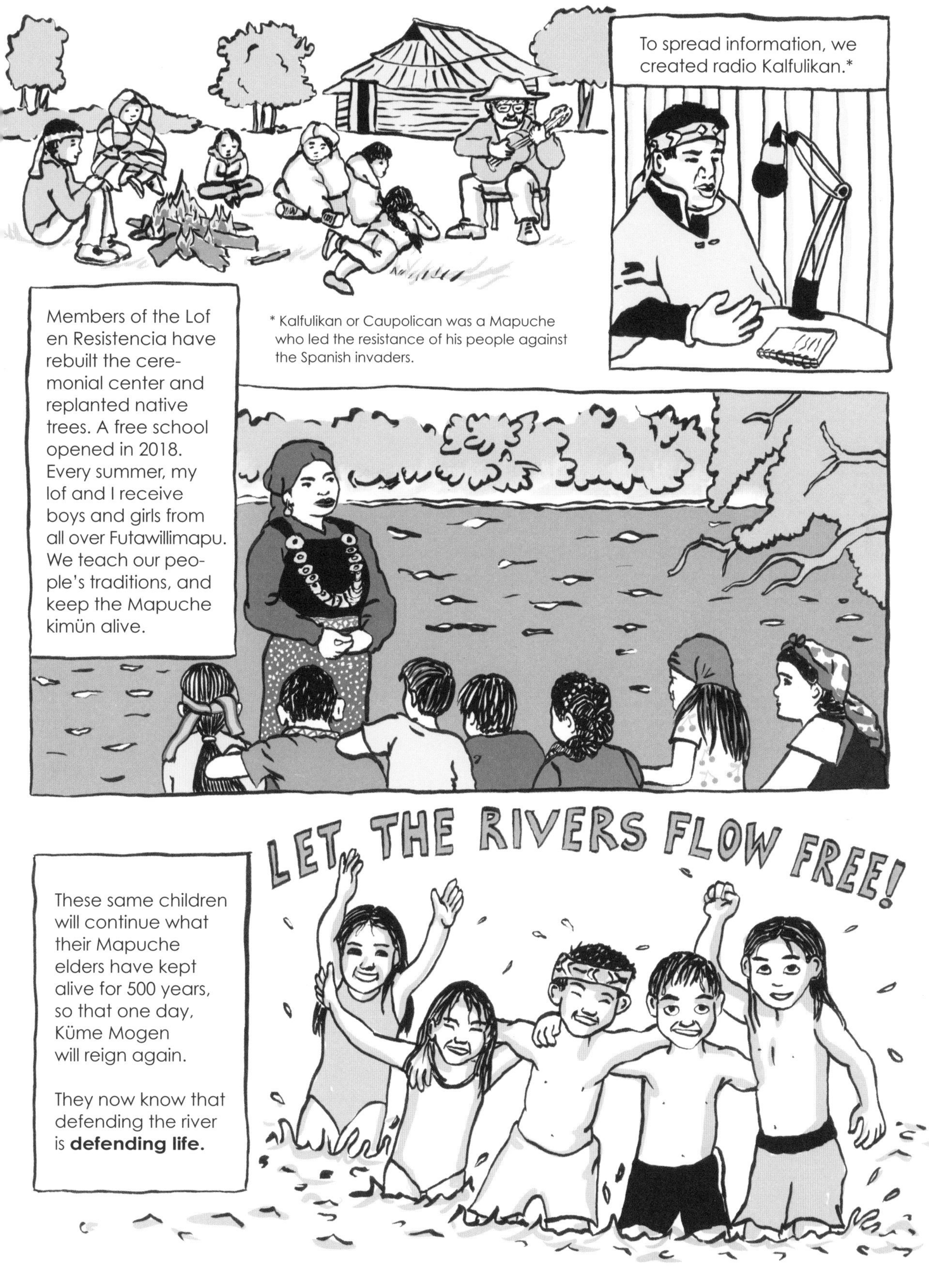

To spread information, we created radio Kalfulikan.*
Members of the Lof en Resistencia have rebuilt the ceremonial center and replanted native trees. A free school opened in 2018. Every summer, my lof and I receive boys and girls from all over Futawillimapu. We teach our people's traditions, and keep the Mapuche kimün alive.
* Kalfulikan or Caupolican was a Mapuche who led the resistance of his people against the Spanish invaders.
LET THE RIVERS FLOW FREE!
These same children will continue what their Mapuche elders have kept alive for 500 years, so that one day, Küme Mogen will reign again.
They now know that defending the river is **defending life.**

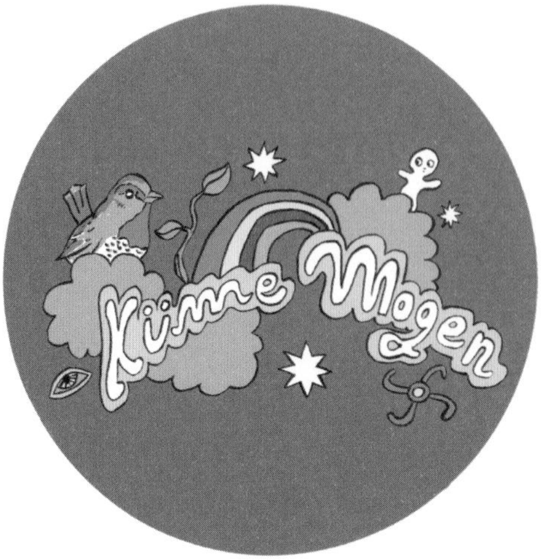
Küme Mogen

Acknowledgments:
Lof en resistencia del río Pilmaiken
Machi Millaray Huichalaf
Amanda Huichalaf
Esteban Vera
Francisco Polla (Corporación Traitraico)
Rubén Cañío
Felipe Guerra
José Quidel
Josefina Buschmann (Mafi)
Nacha Vollenweider
Pablo Sanhueza
Carolina Sepúlveda

HELEN QUIÑONES LOAIZA & TRILCE GARCÍA COSAVALENTE

WARMI MASIY

ANDEAN FEMINISM TAKING SHAPE
IN THE LAND OF THE INCAS

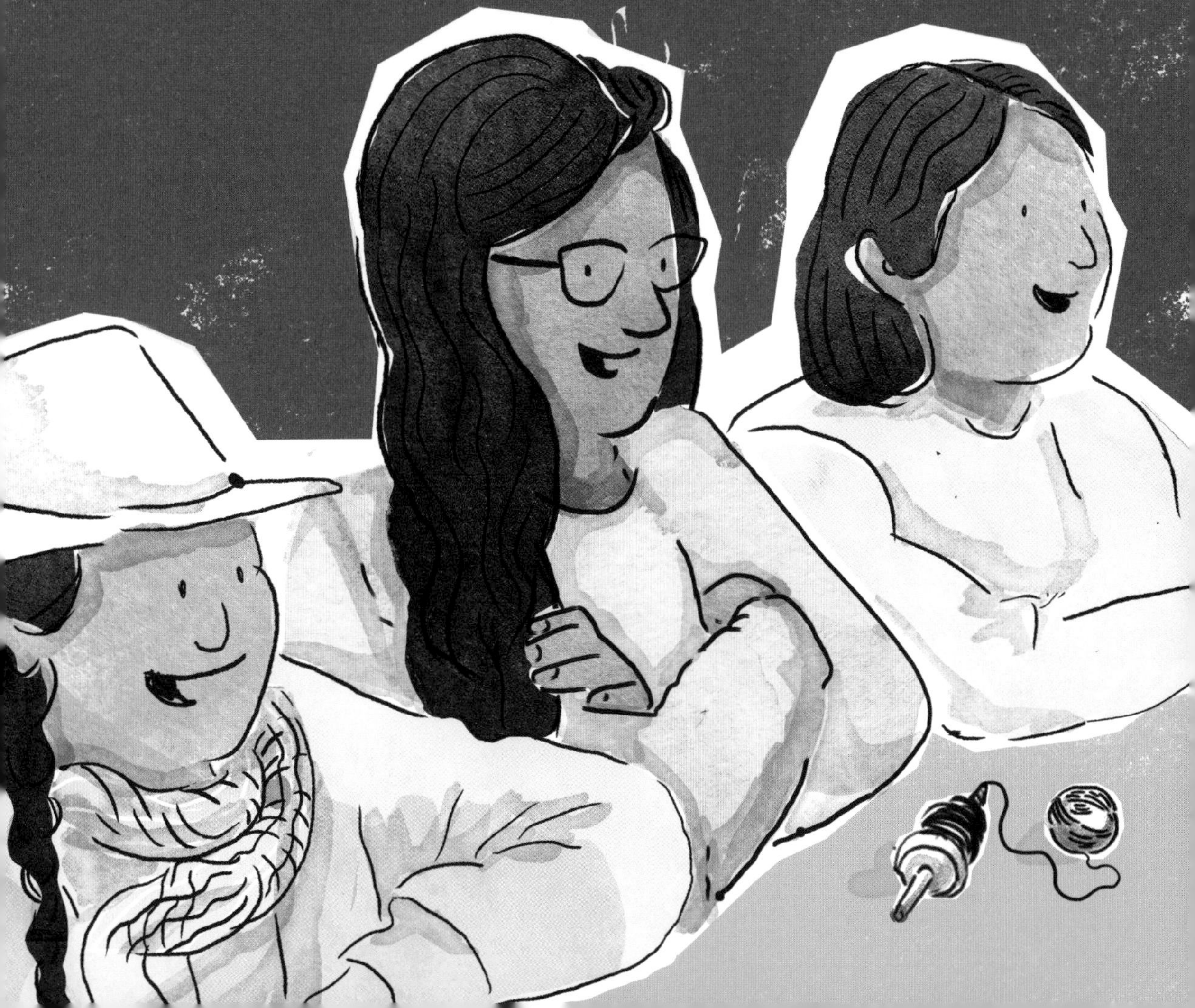

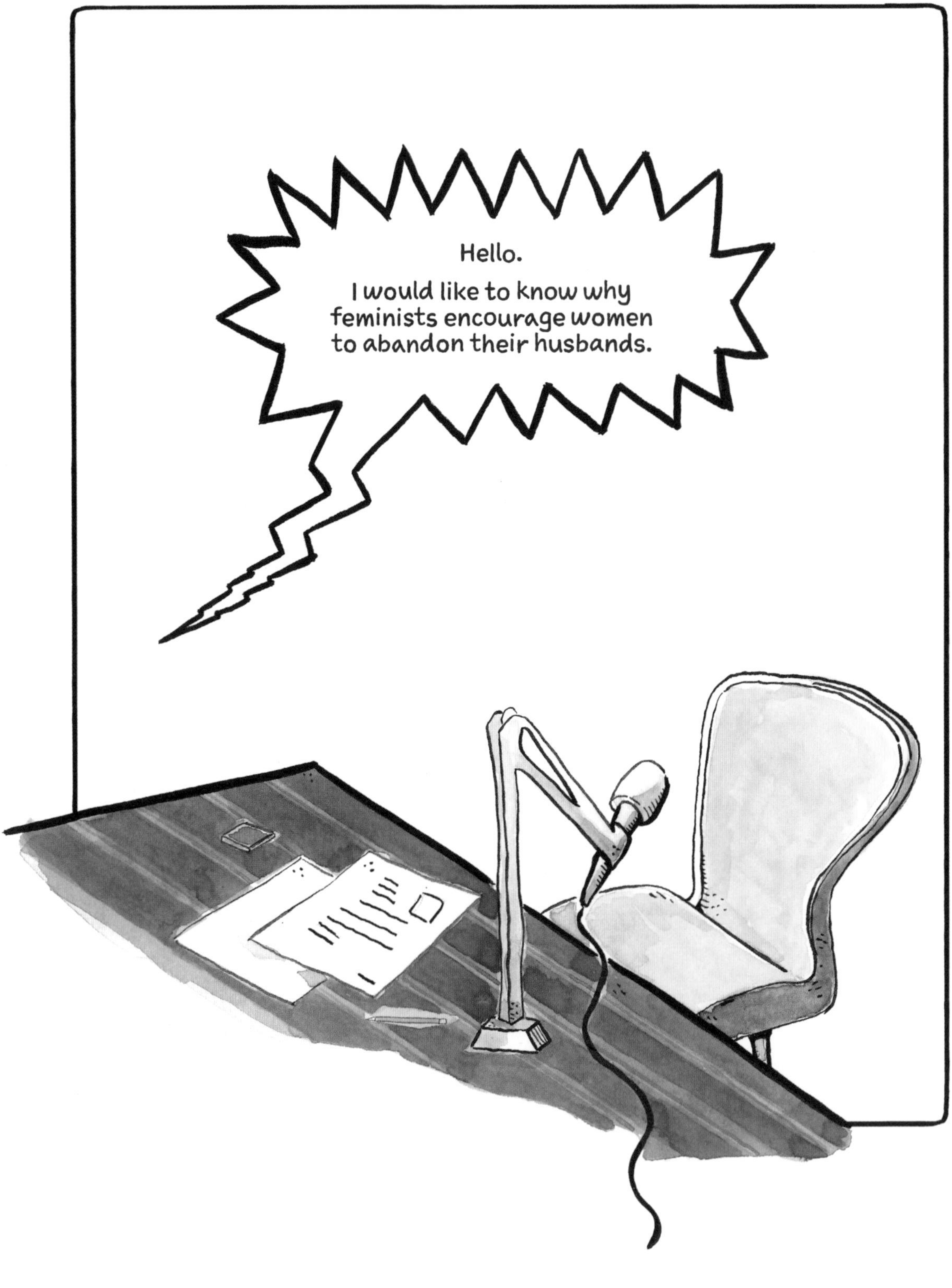
Hello.
I would like to know why feminists encourage women to abandon their husbands.

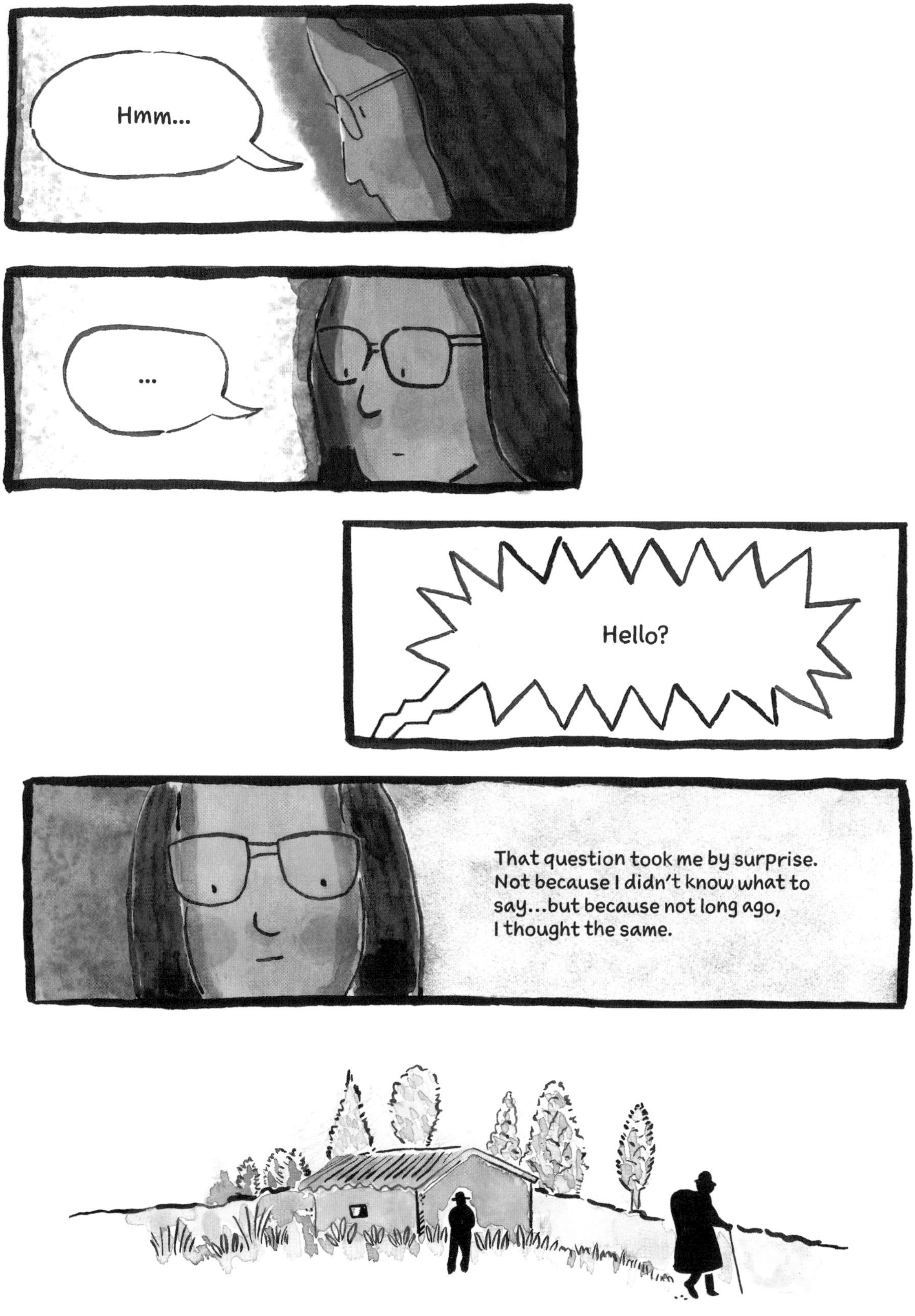
Hmm...
...
Hello?
That question took me by surprise. Not because I didn't know what to say...but because not long ago, I thought the same.

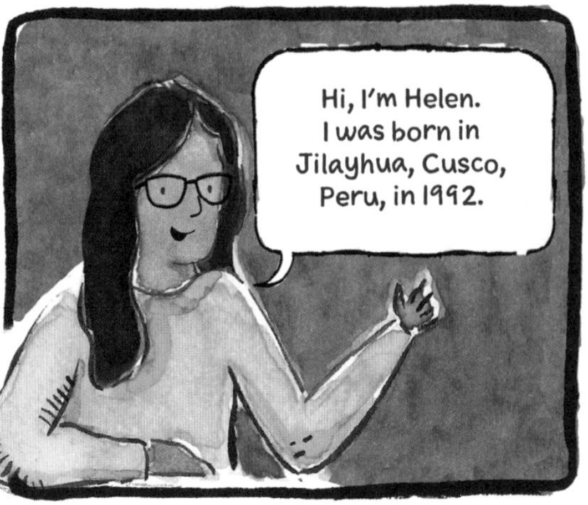
Hi, I'm Helen. I was born in Jilayhua, Cusco, Peru, in 1992.

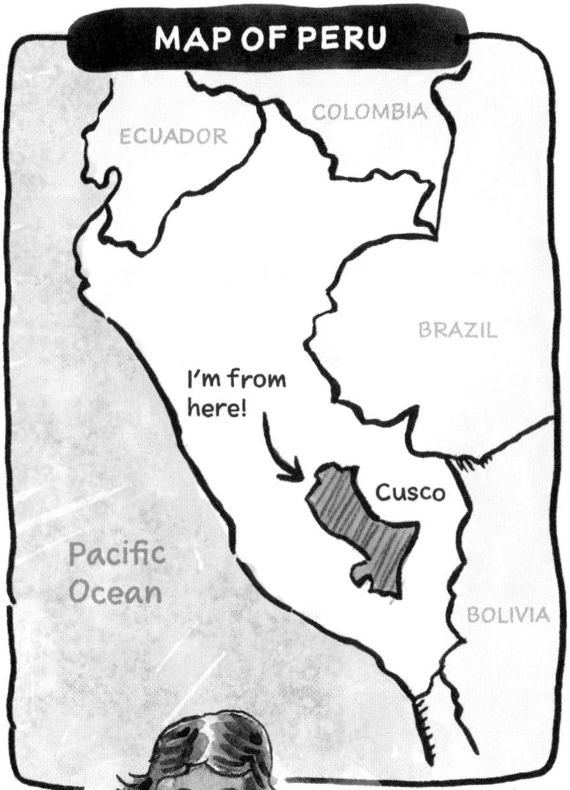
MAP OF PERU
ECUADOR
COLOMBIA
BRAZIL
I'm from here!
Cusco
Pacific Ocean
BOLIVIA

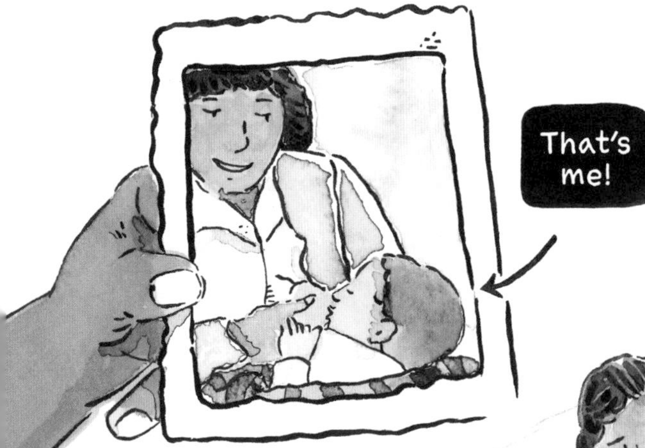
That's me!

I was the fifth daughter. For a rural family, that counts as a great misfortune.

I wasn't very close to my father—he was rather aloof—but I have very good memories of my childhood. Mom always managed to get us through tough times.

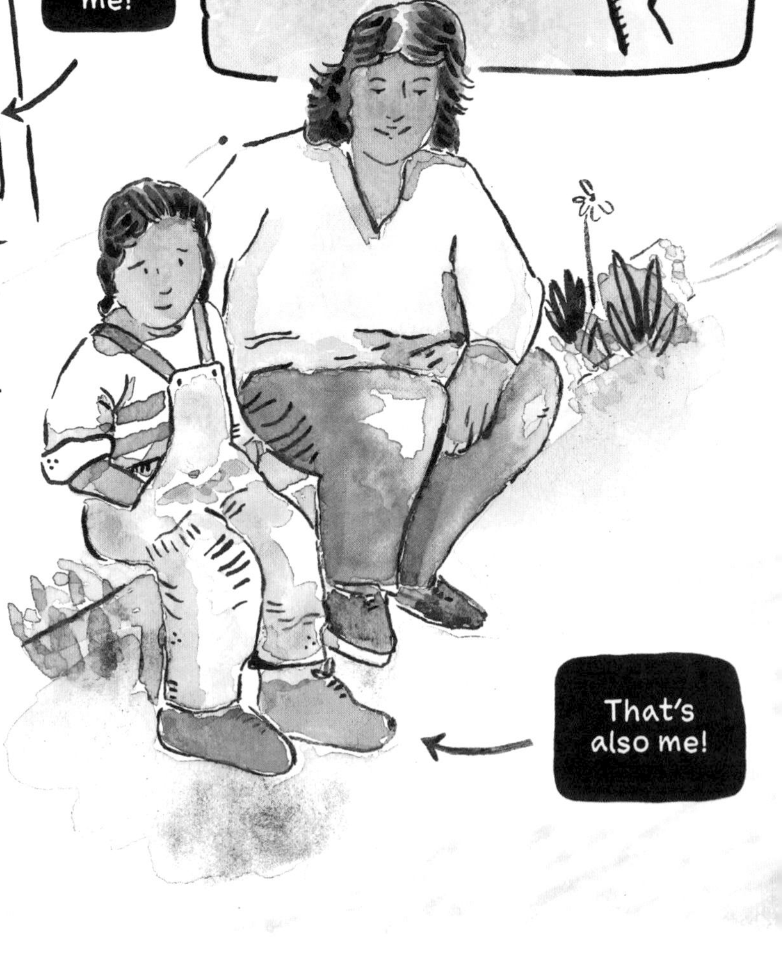
That's also me!

I live in Cusco, where the Incas had their roots. For better or worse, we live in the nostalgia of their powerful empire and in the shadow of the arrival of the Spanish.

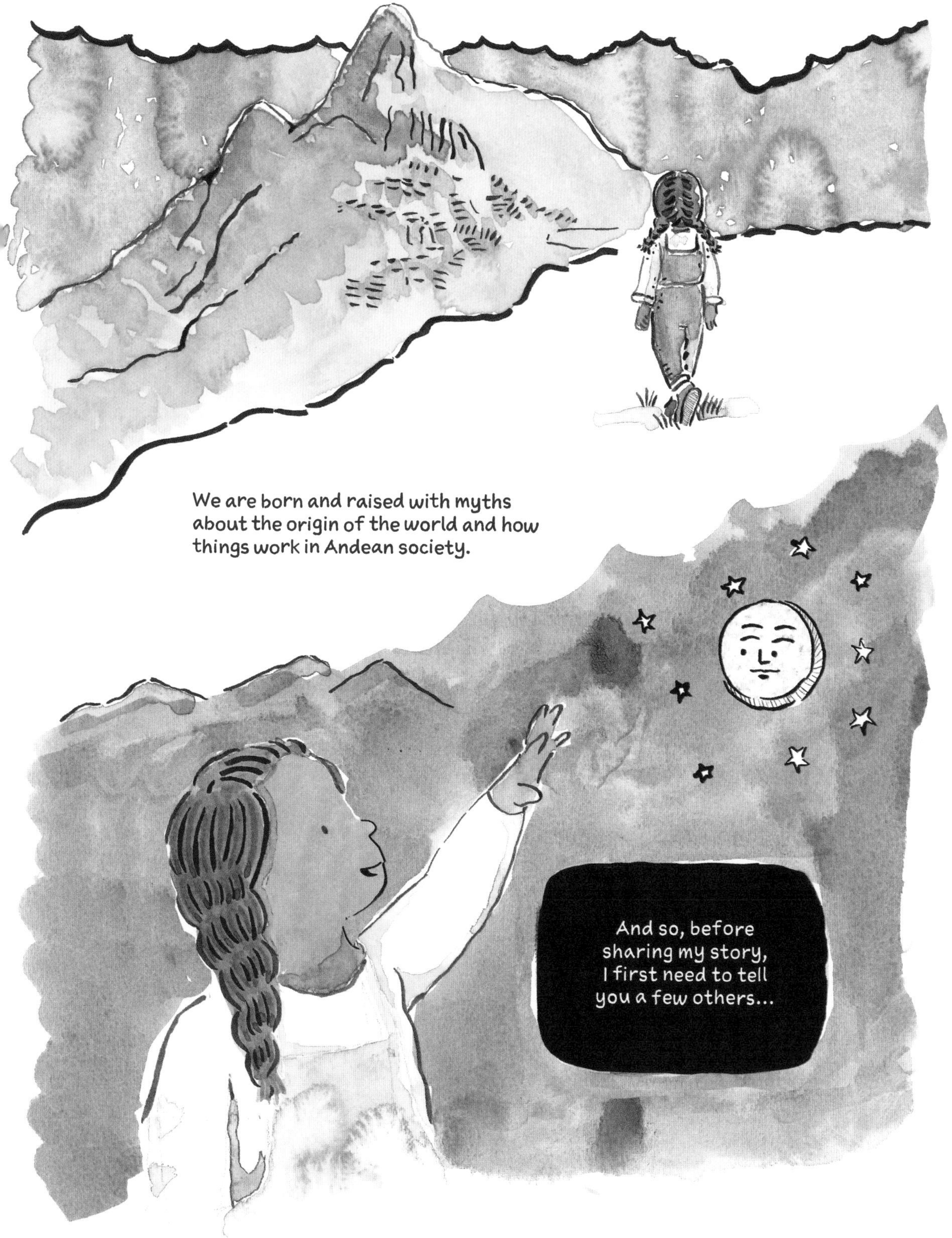
We are born and raised with myths about the origin of the world and how things work in Andean society.
And so, before sharing my story, I first need to tell you a few others...

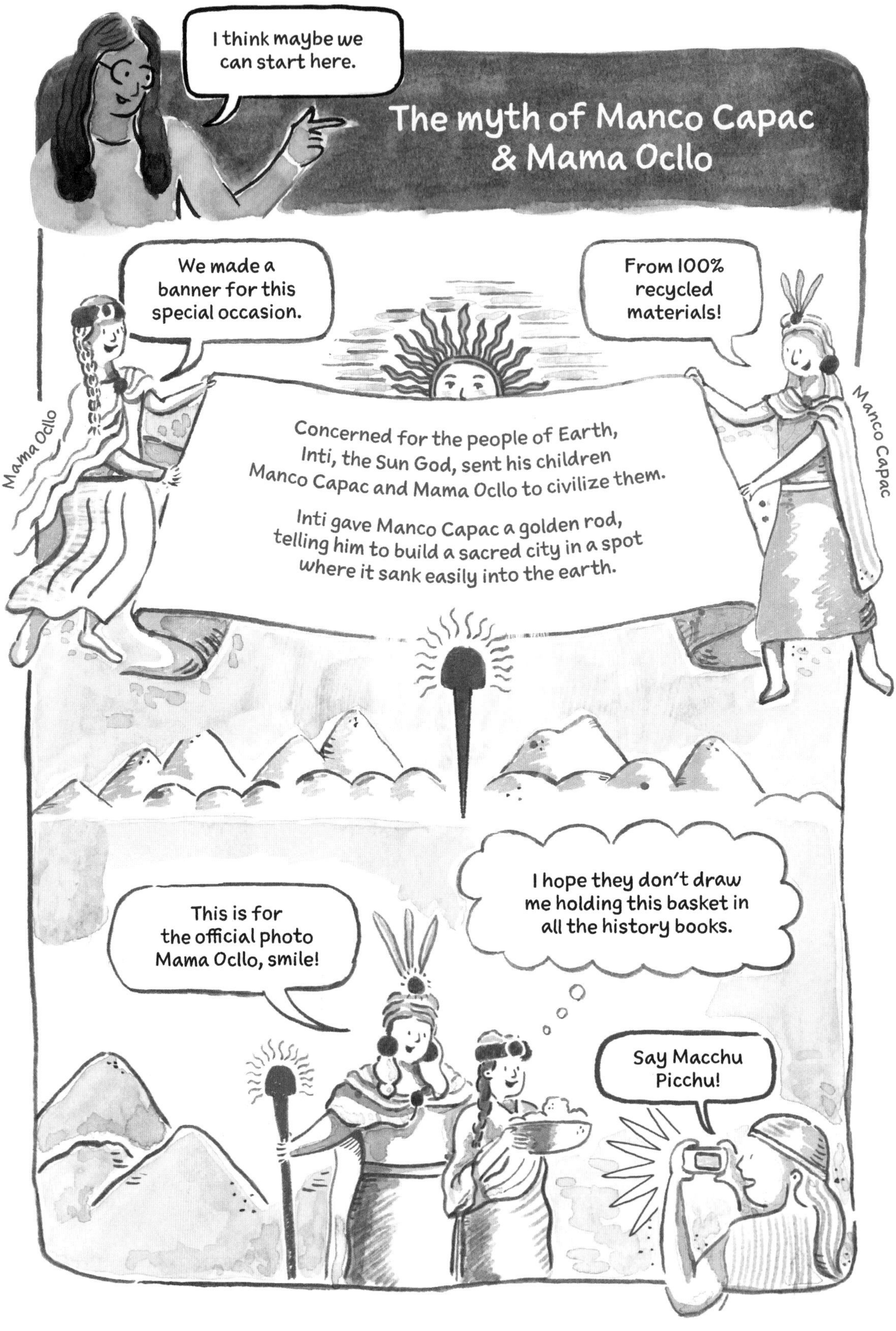
I think maybe we can start here.
The myth of Manco Capac & Mama Ocllo
We made a banner for this special occasion.
From 100% recycled materials!
Mama Ocllo
Manco Capac
Concerned for the people of Earth, Inti, the Sun God, sent his children Manco Capac and Mama Ocllo to civilize them.
Inti gave Manco Capac a golden rod, telling him to build a sacred city in a spot where it sank easily into the earth.
This is for the official photo Mama Ocllo, smile!
I hope they don't draw me holding this basket in all the history books.
Say Macchu Picchu!

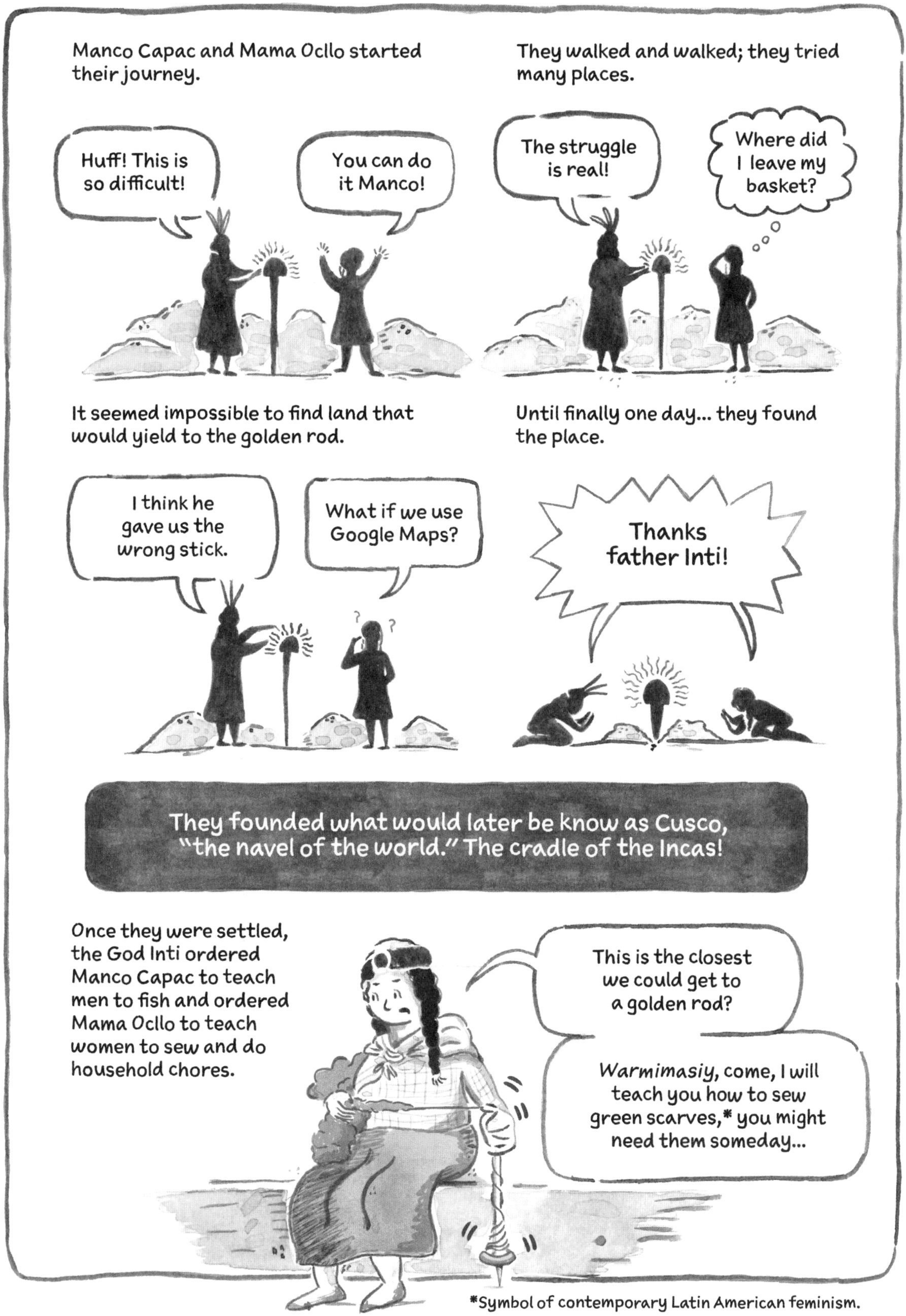

Manco Capac and Mama Ocllo started their journey.
Huff! This is so difficult!
You can do it Manco!
They walked and walked; they tried many places.
The struggle is real!
Where did I leave my basket?
It seemed impossible to find land that would yield to the golden rod.
I think he gave us the wrong stick.
What if we use Google Maps?
Until finally one day... they found the place.
Thanks father Inti!
They founded what would later be know as Cusco, "the navel of the world." The cradle of the Incas!
Once they were settled, the God Inti ordered Manco Capac to teach men to fish and ordered Mama Ocllo to teach women to sew and do household chores.
This is the closest we could get to a golden rod?
Warmimasiy, come, I will teach you how to sew green scarves,* you might need them someday...

*Symbol of contemporary Latin American feminism.

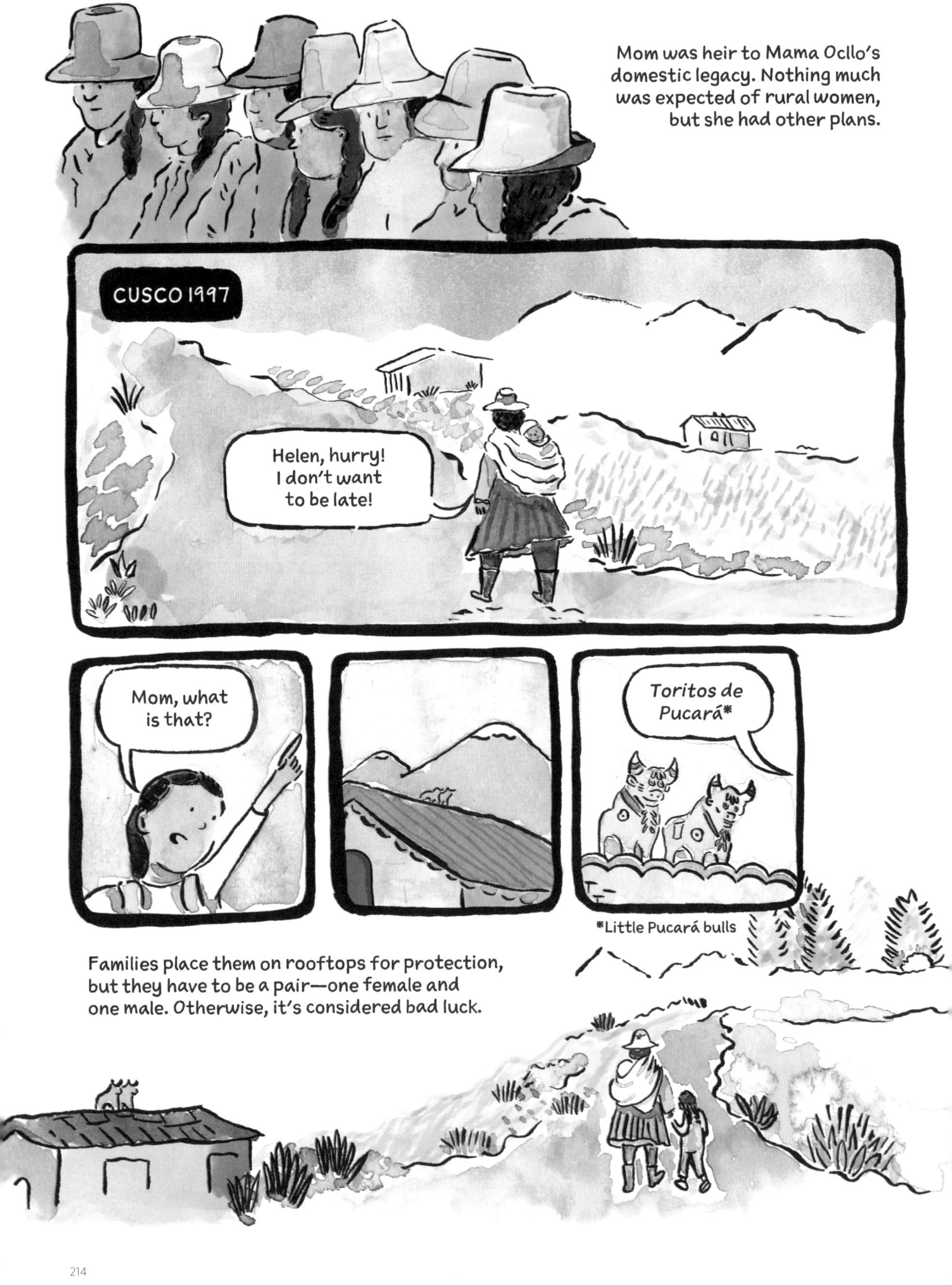
Mom was heir to Mama Ocllo's domestic legacy. Nothing much was expected of rural women, but she had other plans.
CUSCO 1997
Helen, hurry! I don't want to be late!
Mom, what is that?
*Toritos de Pucará**
*Little Pucará bulls
Families place them on rooftops for protection, but they have to be a pair—one female and one male. Otherwise, it's considered bad luck.

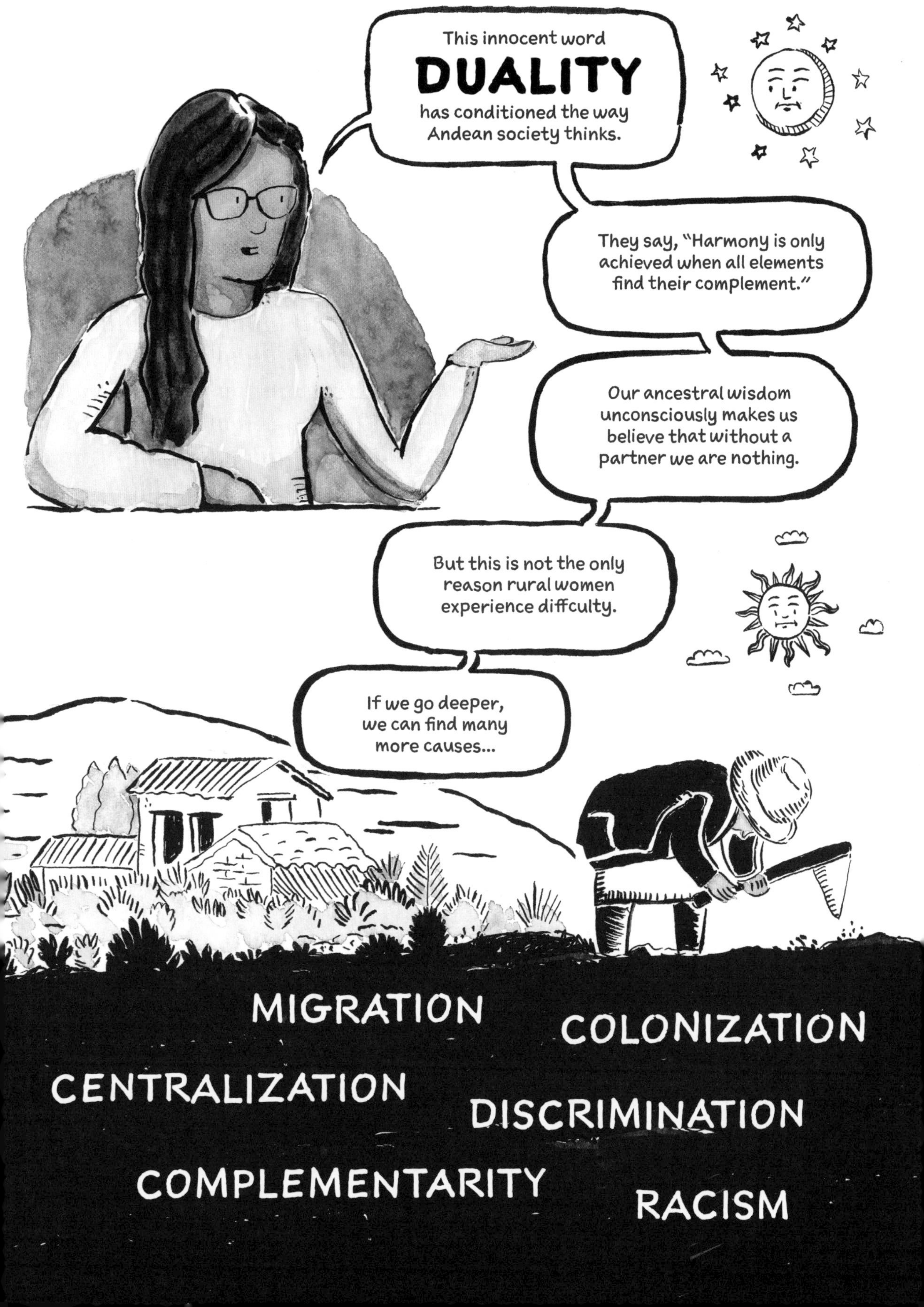
This innocent word DUALITY has conditioned the way Andean society thinks.
They say, "Harmony is only achieved when all elements find their complement."
Our ancestral wisdom unconsciously makes us believe that without a partner we are nothing.
But this is not the only reason rural women experience diffculty.
If we go deeper, we can find many more causes...
MIGRATION
COLONIZATION
CENTRALIZATION
DISCRIMINATION
COMPLEMENTARITY
RACISM

When I was little, mom and I used to go visit families in our village...

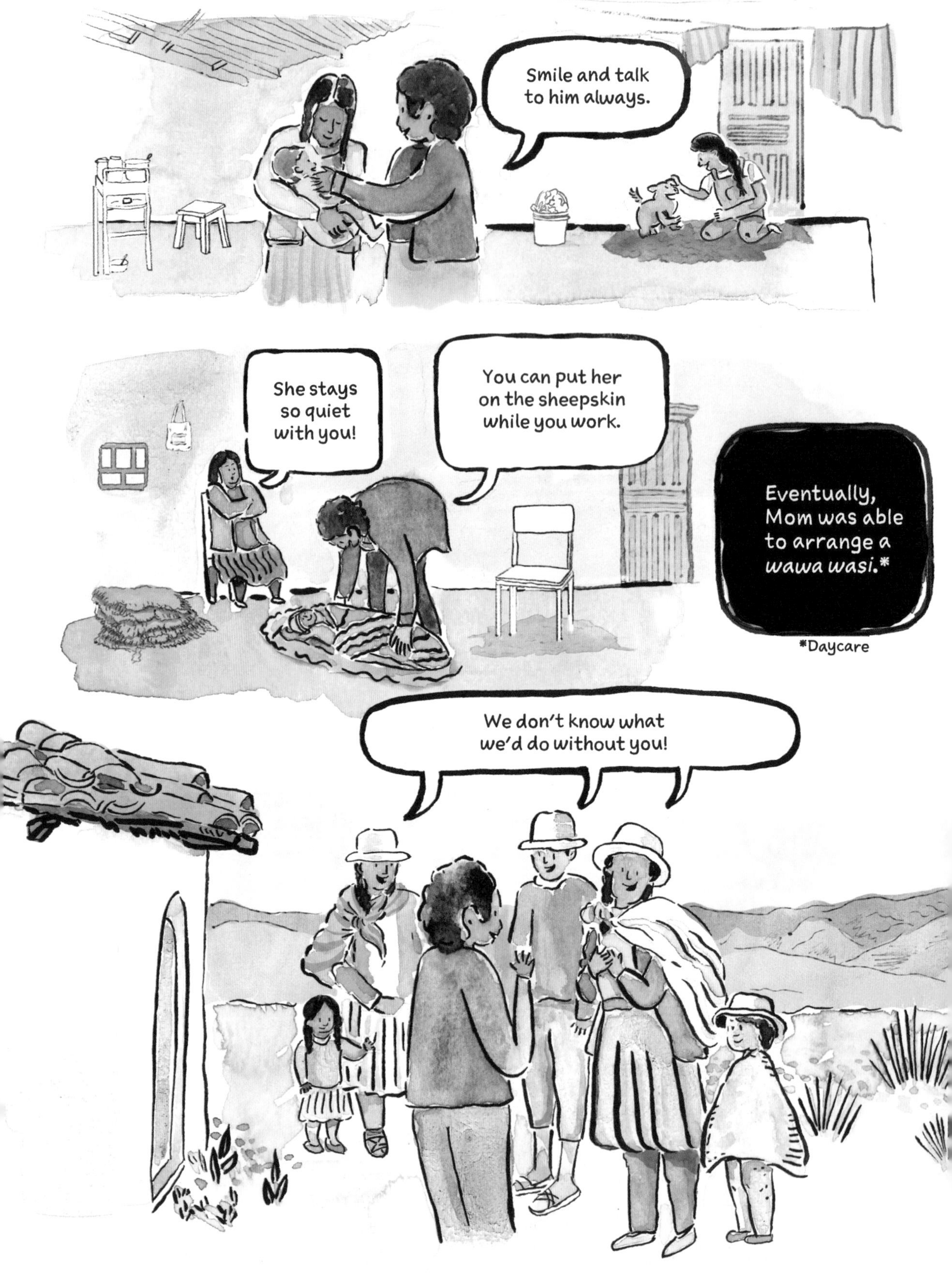
Smile and talk to him always.
She stays so quiet with you!
You can put her on the sheepskin while you work.
Eventually, Mom was able to arrange a *wawa wasi.**
*Daycare
We don't know what we'd do without you!

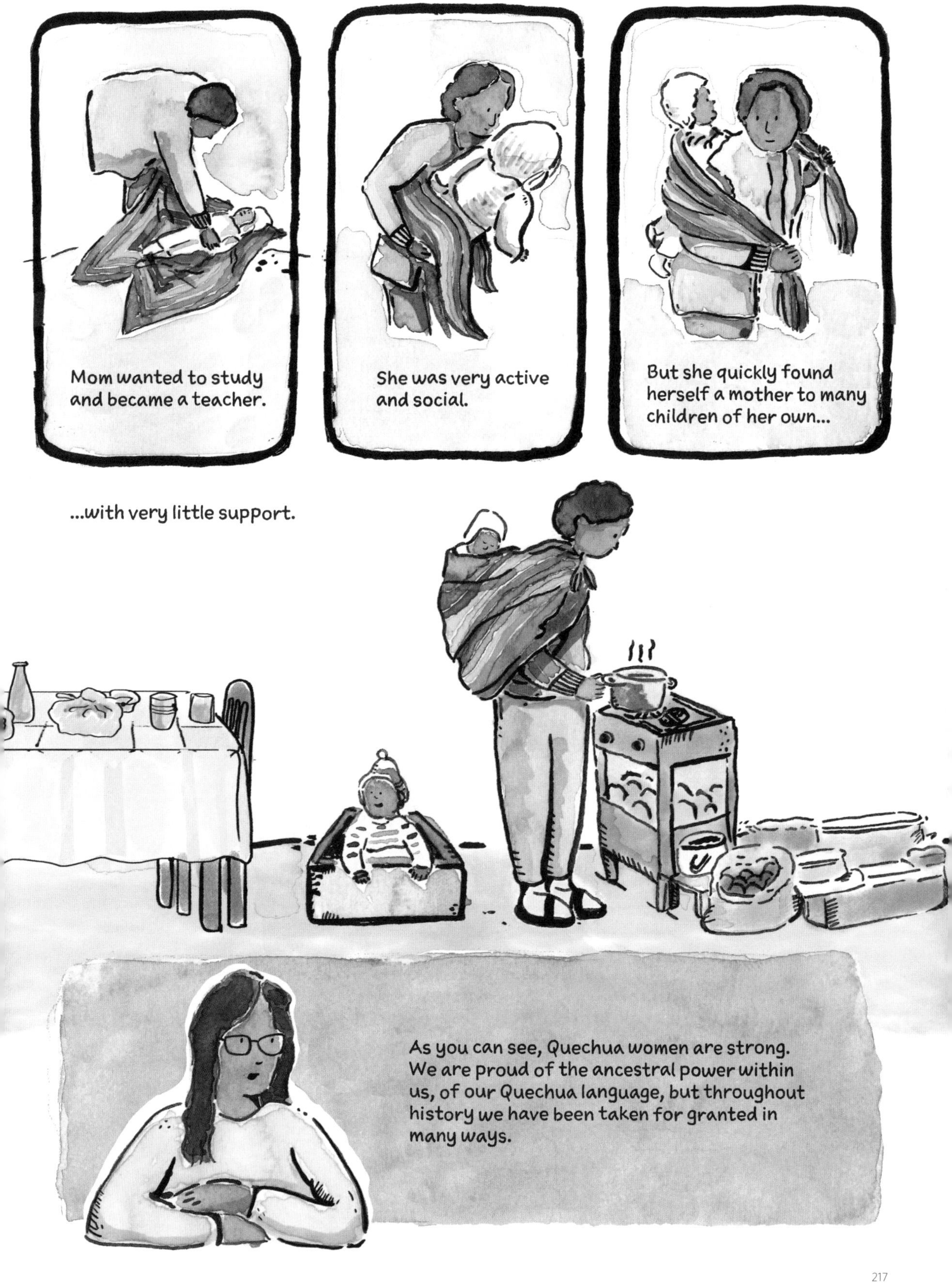
Mom wanted to study and became a teacher.
She was very active and social.
But she quickly found herself a mother to many children of her own...
...with very little support.
As you can see, Quechua women are strong. We are proud of the ancestral power within us, of our Quechua language, but throughout history we have been taken for granted in many ways.

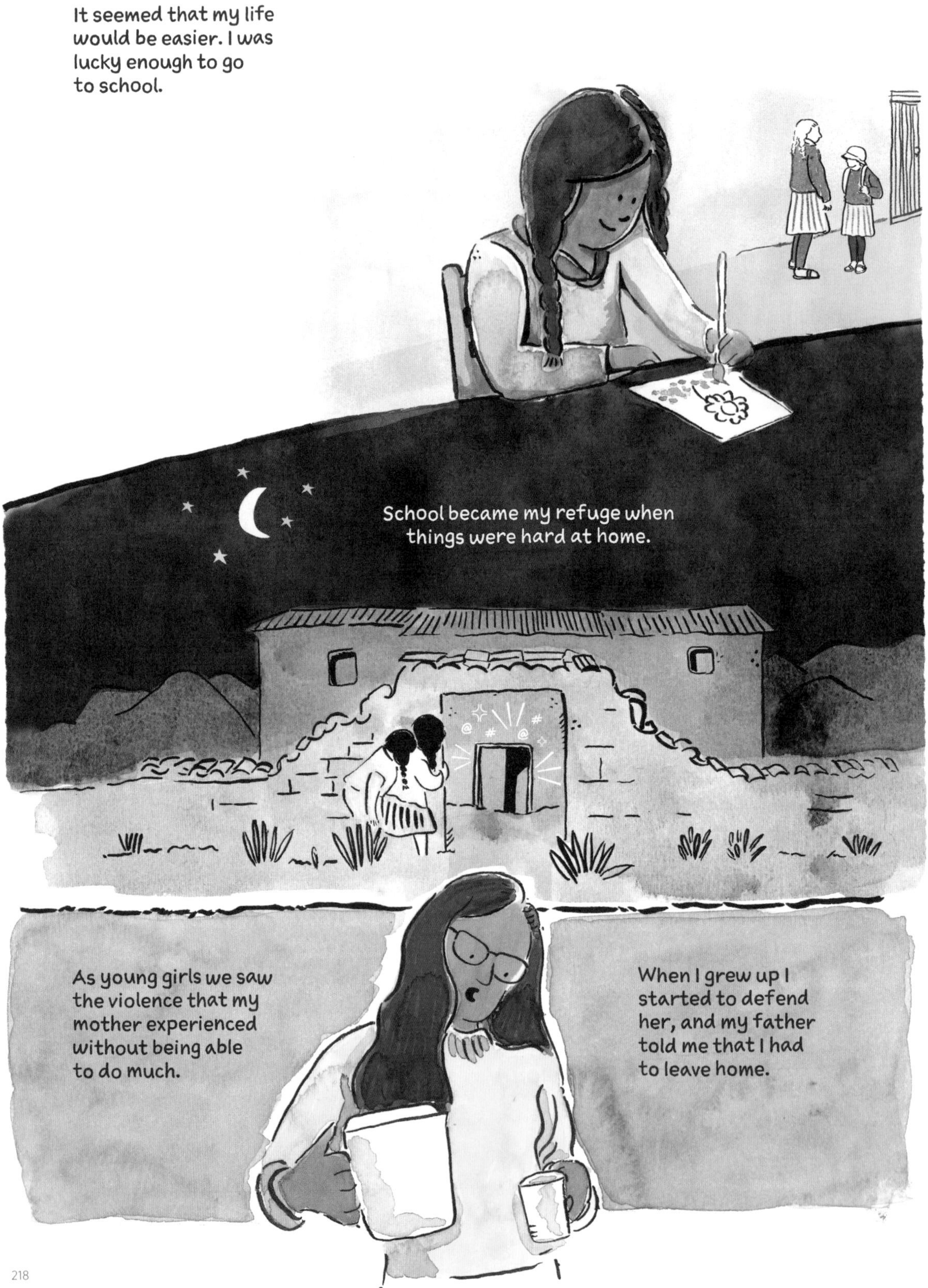
It seemed that my life would be easier. I was lucky enough to go to school.
School became my refuge when things were hard at home.
As young girls we saw the violence that my mother experienced without being able to do much.
When I grew up I started to defend her, and my father told me that I had to leave home.

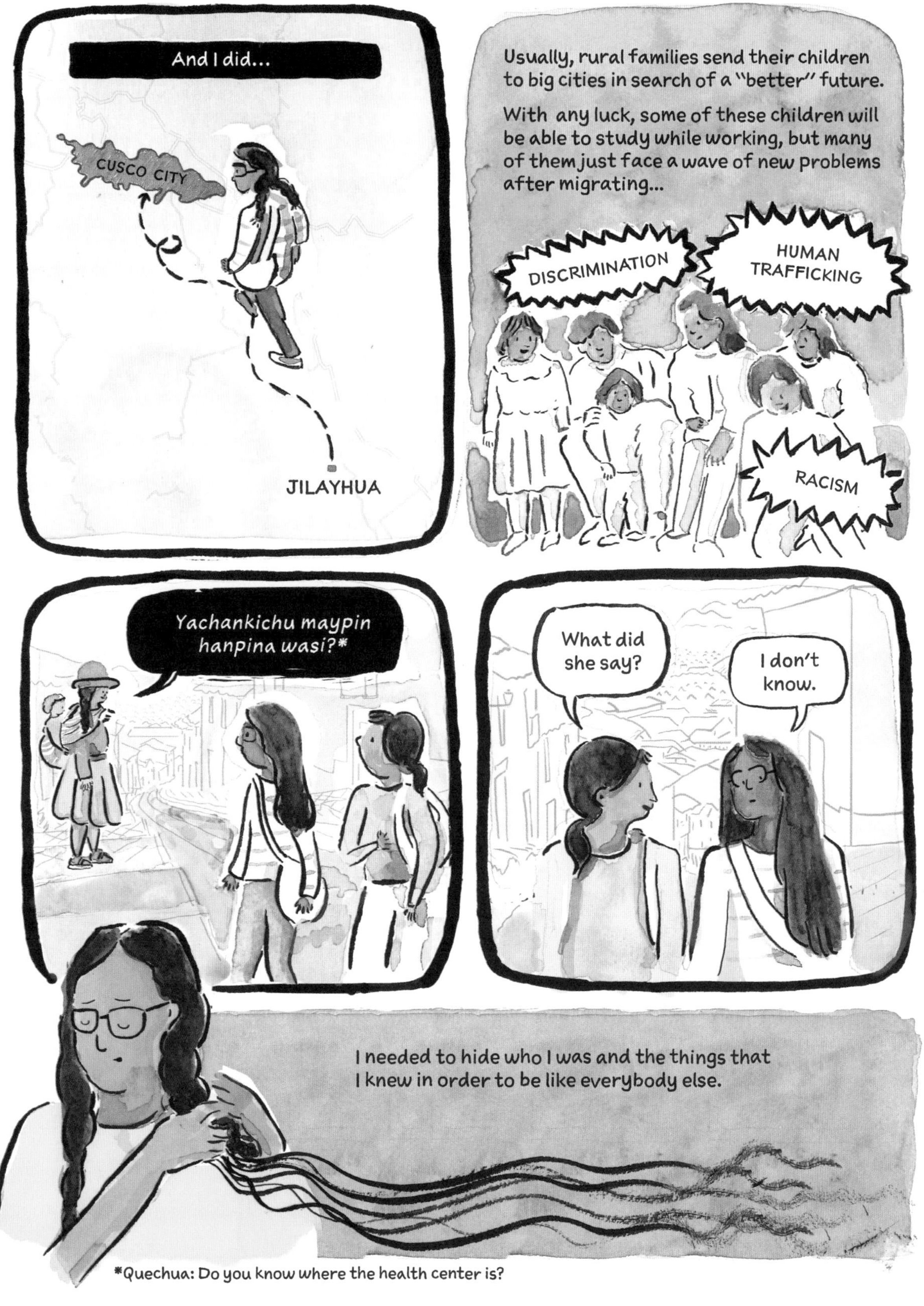

And I did...
CUSCO CITY
JILAYHUA
Usually, rural families send their children to big cities in search of a "better" future.
With any luck, some of these children will be able to study while working, but many of them just face a wave of new problems after migrating...
DISCRIMINATION
HUMAN TRAFFICKING
RACISM
Yachankichu maypin hanpina wasi?*
What did she say?
I don't know.
I needed to hide who I was and the things that I knew in order to be like everybody else.

*Quechua: Do you know where the health center is?

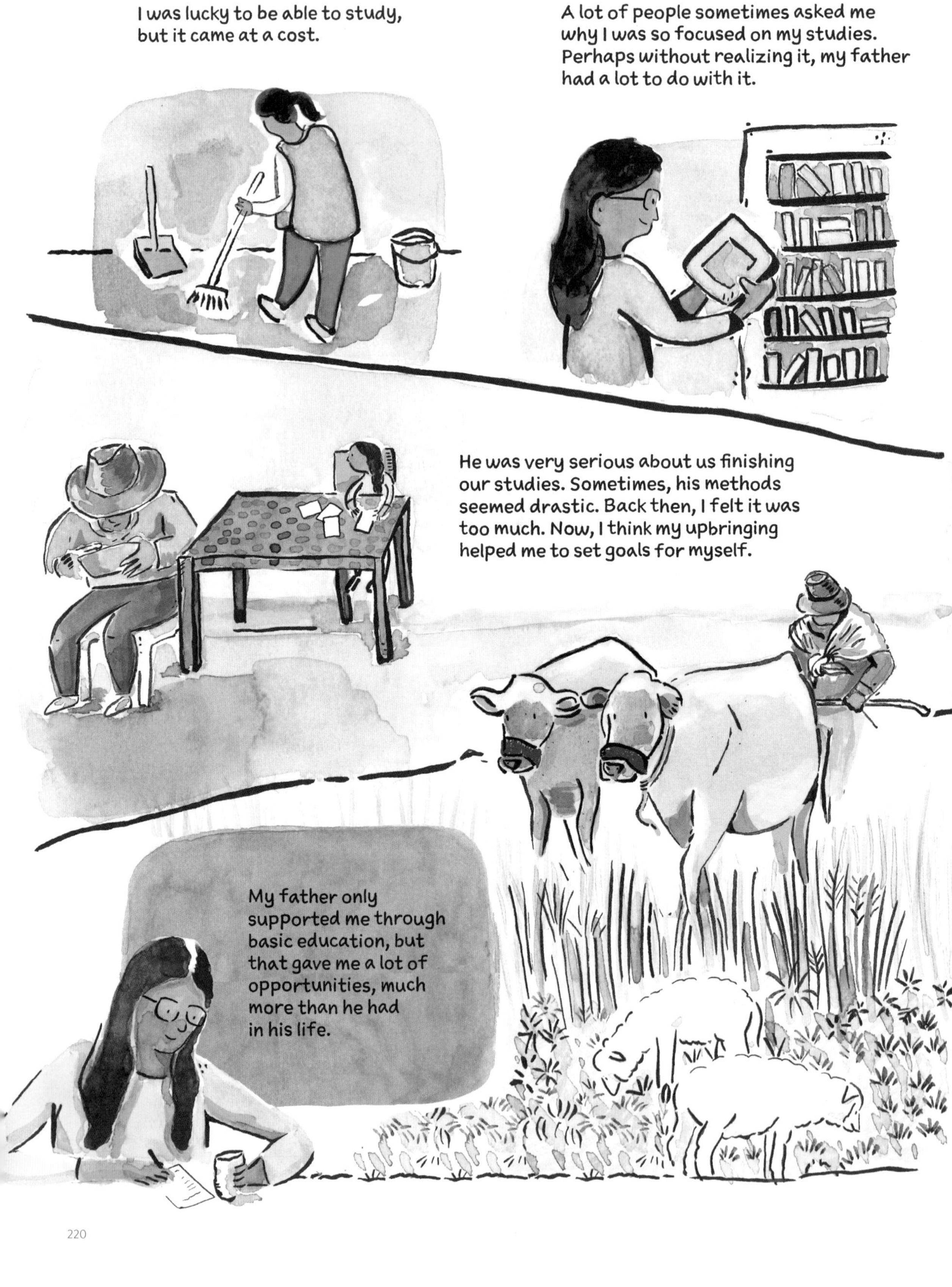
I was lucky to be able to study, but it came at a cost.
A lot of people sometimes asked me why I was so focused on my studies. Perhaps without realizing it, my father had a lot to do with it.
He was very serious about us finishing our studies. Sometimes, his methods seemed drastic. Back then, I felt it was too much. Now, I think my upbringing helped me to set goals for myself.
My father only supported me through basic education, but that gave me a lot of opportunities, much more than he had in his life.

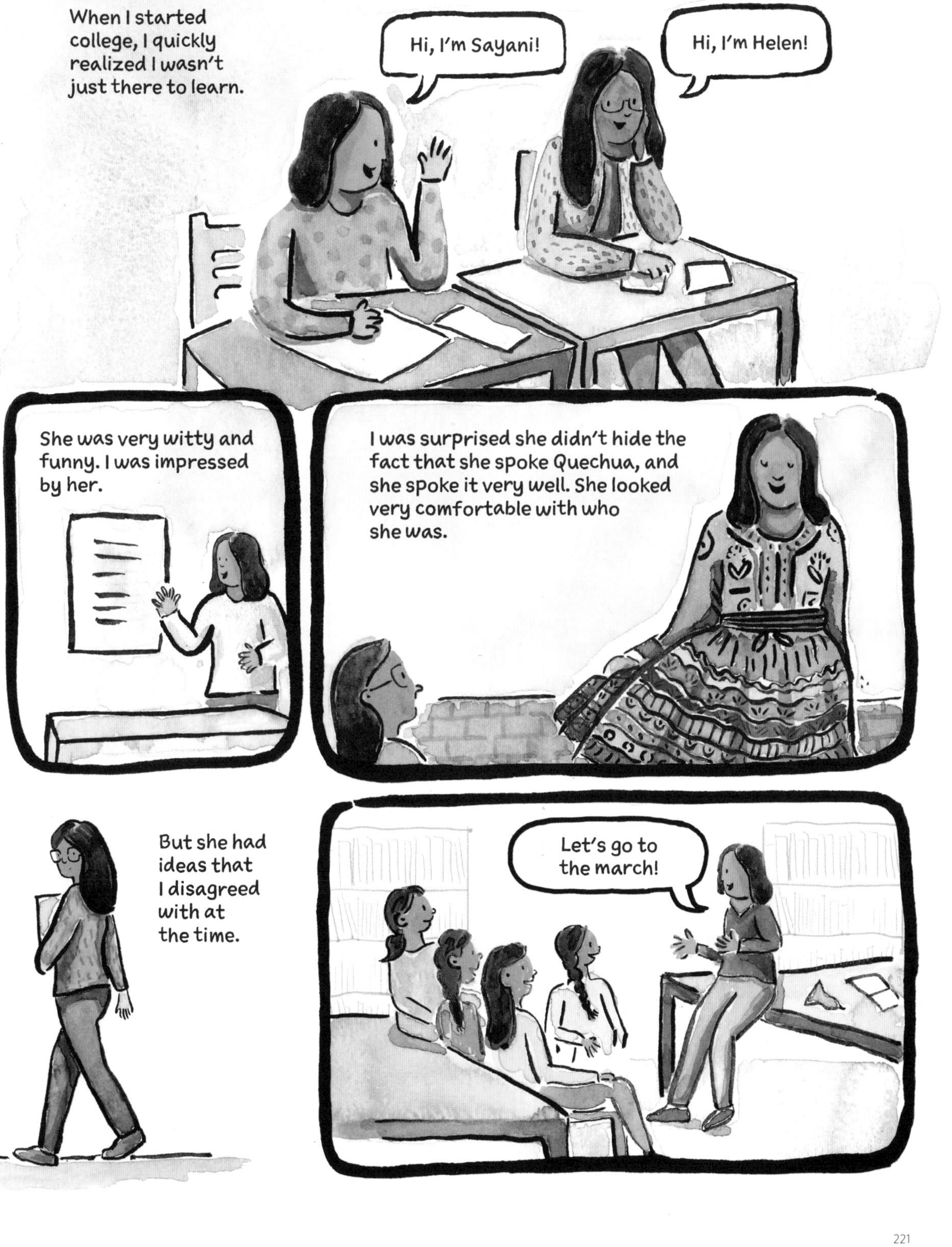
When I started college, I quickly realized I wasn't just there to learn.
Hi, I'm Sayani!
Hi, I'm Helen!
She was very witty and funny. I was impressed by her.
I was surprised she didn't hide the fact that she spoke Quechua, and she spoke it very well. She looked very comfortable with who she was.
But she had ideas that I disagreed with at the time.
Let's go to the march!

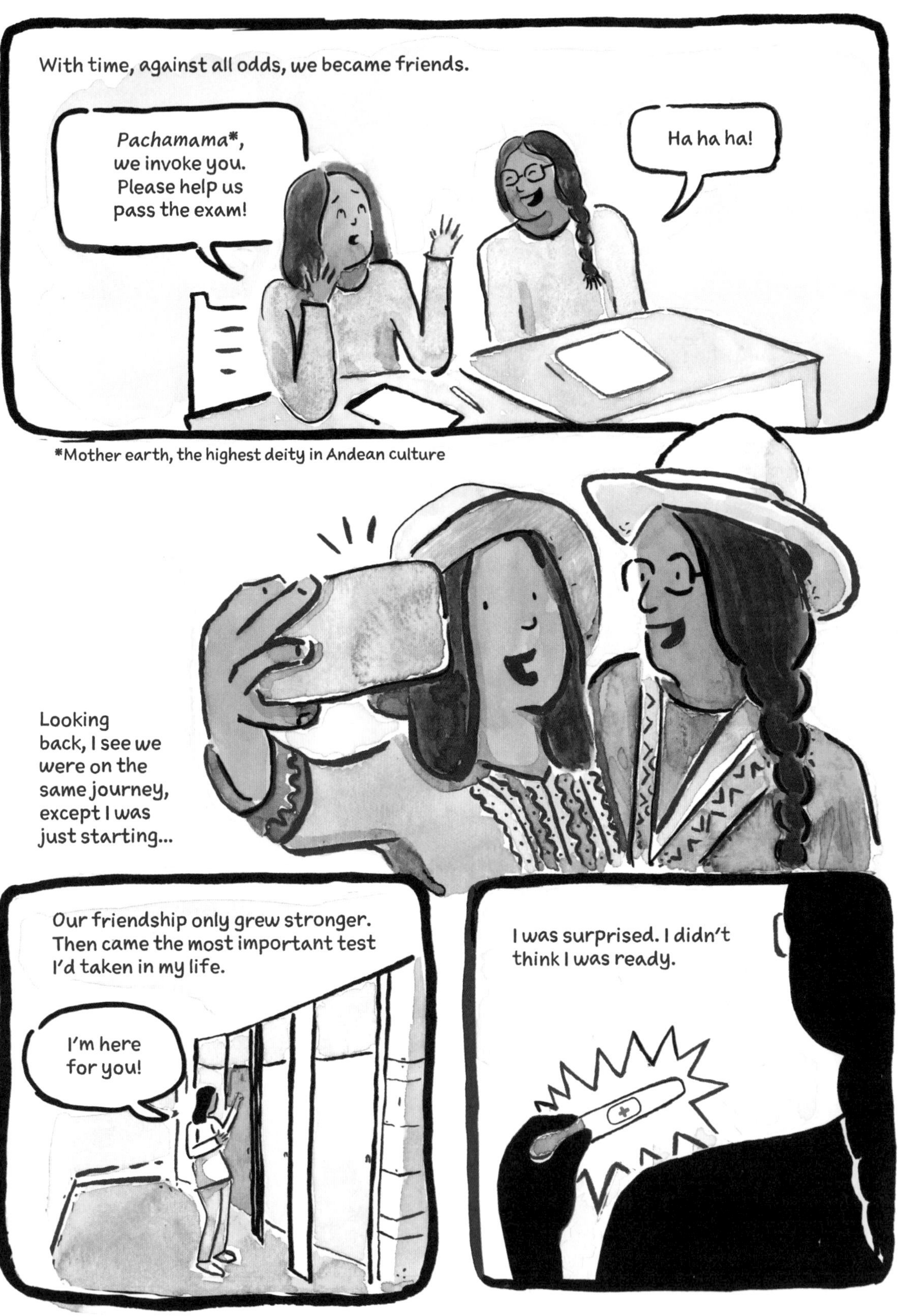
With time, against all odds, we became friends.
*Pachamama**, we invoke you. Please help us pass the exam!
Ha ha ha!
*Mother earth, the highest deity in Andean culture
Looking back, I see we were on the same journey, except I was just starting...
Our friendship only grew stronger. Then came the most important test I'd taken in my life.
I'm here for you!
I was surprised. I didn't think I was ready.

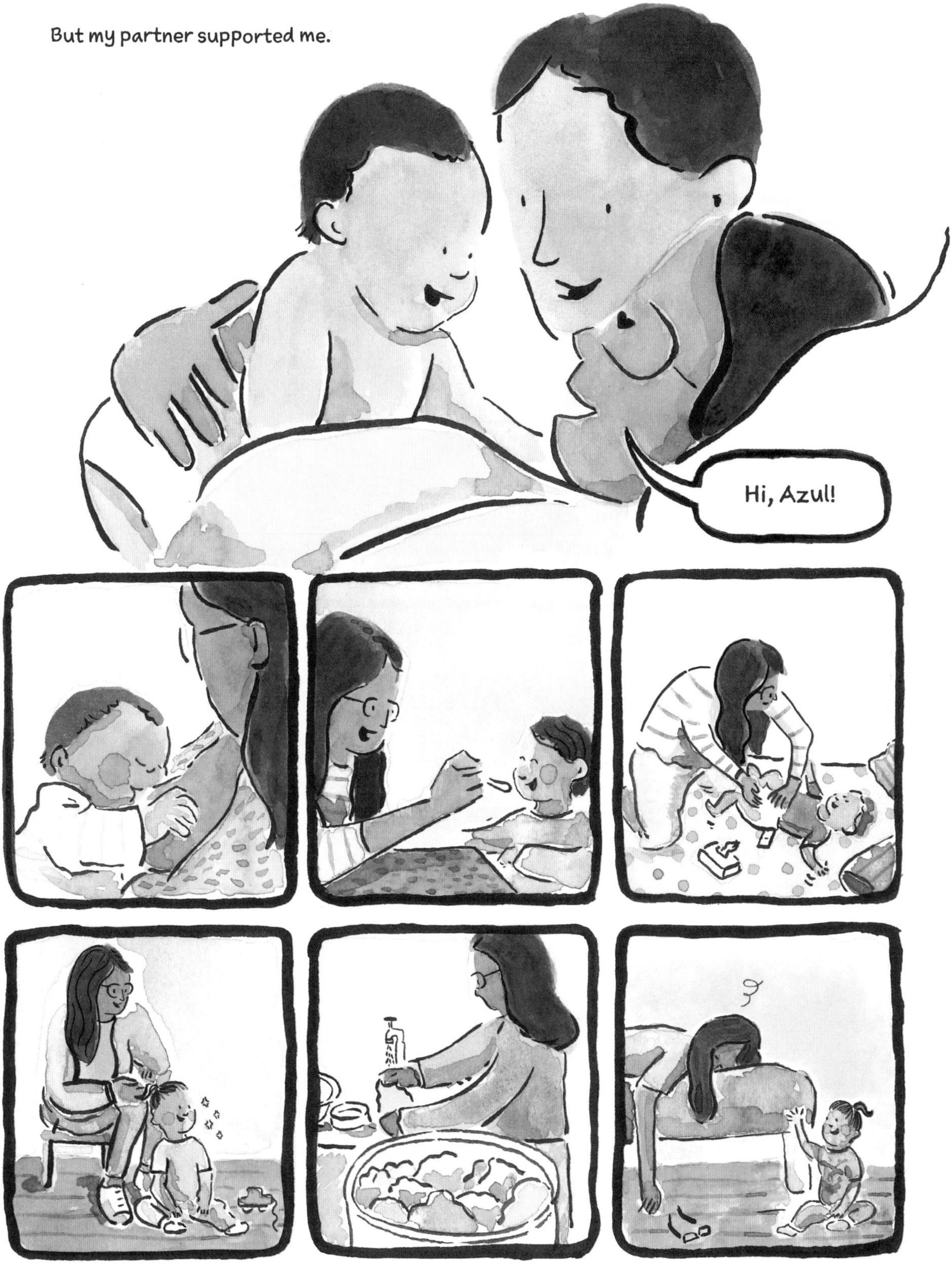
But my partner supported me.
Hi, Azul!

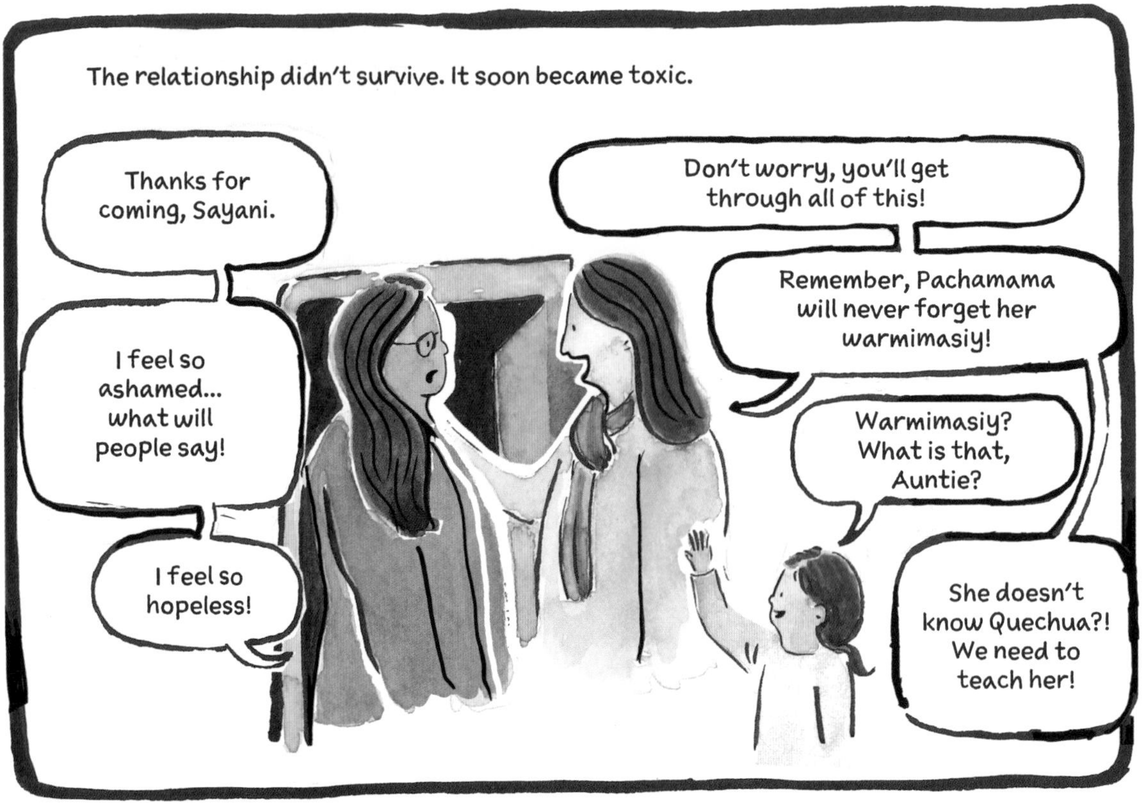
The relationship didn't survive. It soon became toxic.
Thanks for coming, Sayani.
I feel so ashamed... what will people say!
I feel so hopeless!
Don't worry, you'll get through all of this!
Remember, Pachamama will never forget her warmimasiy!
Warmimasiy? What is that, Auntie?
She doesn't know Quechua?! We need to teach her!

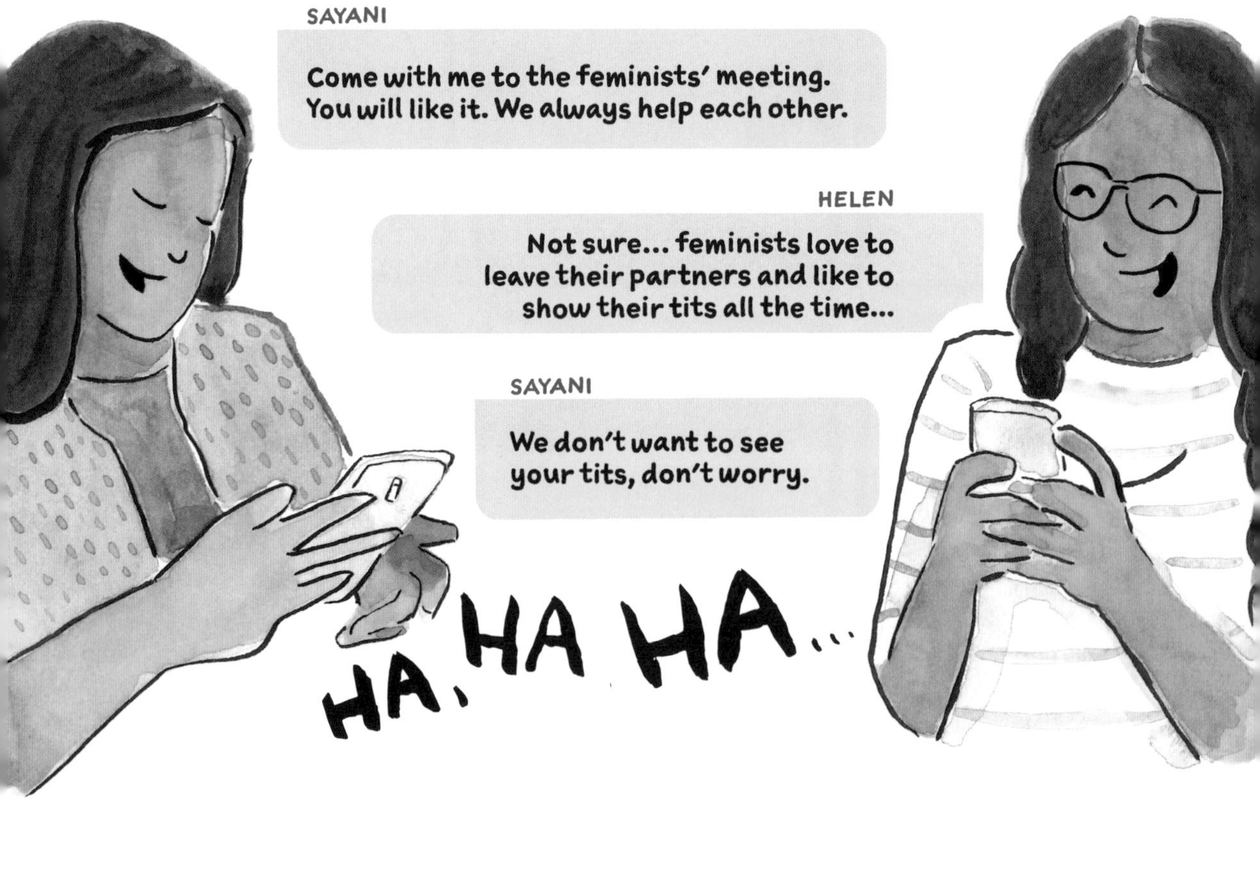
SAYANI
Come with me to the feminists' meeting. You will like it. We always help each other.
HELEN
Not sure... feminists love to leave their partners and like to show their tits all the time...
SAYANI
We don't want to see your tits, don't worry.
HA, HA HA HA...

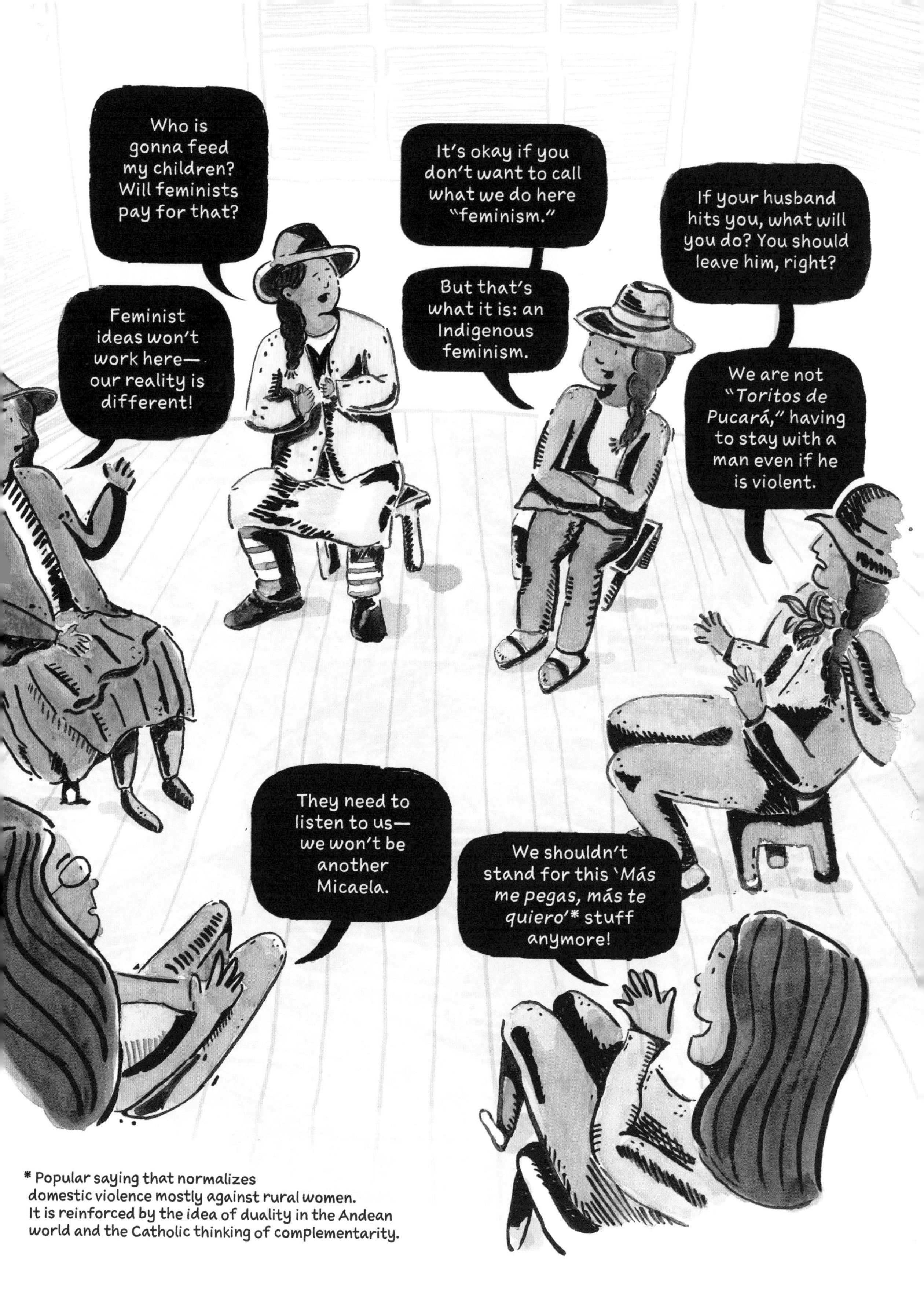
Who is gonna feed my children? Will feminists pay for that?
Feminist ideas won't work here—our reality is different!
It's okay if you don't want to call what we do here "feminism."
But that's what it is: an Indigenous feminism.
If your husband hits you, what will you do? You should leave him, right?
We are not "*Toritos de Pucará*," having to stay with a man even if he is violent.
They need to listen to us—we won't be another Micaela.
We shouldn't stand for this '*Más me pegas, más te quiero*'* stuff anymore!

* Popular saying that normalizes domestic violence mostly against rural women. It is reinforced by the idea of duality in the Andean world and the Catholic thinking of complementarity.

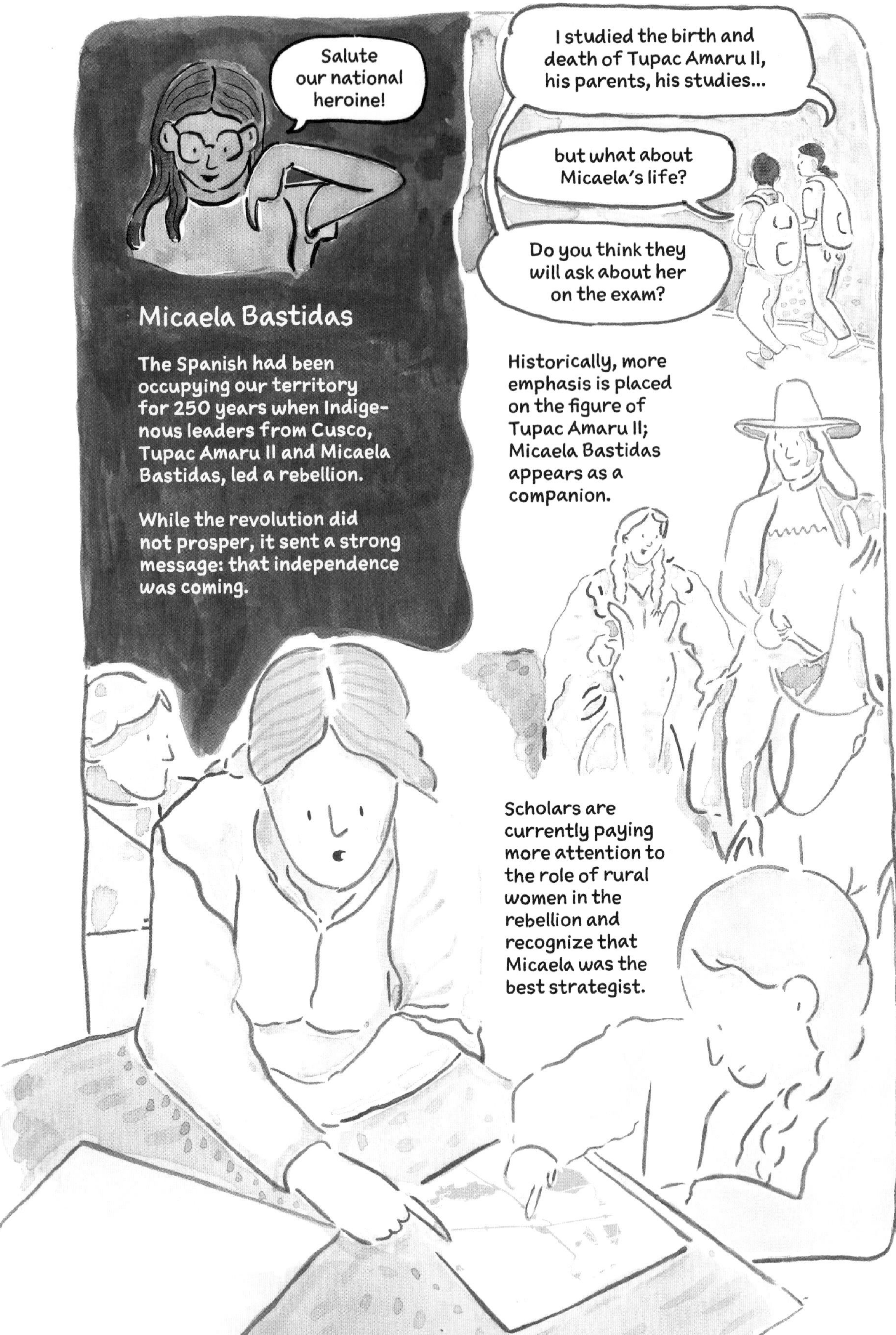
Salute our national heroine!
Micaela Bastidas
The Spanish had been occupying our territory for 250 years when Indigenous leaders from Cusco, Tupac Amaru II and Micaela Bastidas, led a rebellion.
While the revolution did not prosper, it sent a strong message: that independence was coming.
I studied the birth and death of Tupac Amaru II, his parents, his studies...
but what about Micaela's life?
Do you think they will ask about her on the exam?
Historically, more emphasis is placed on the figure of Tupac Amaru II; Micaela Bastidas appears as a companion.
Scholars are currently paying more attention to the role of rural women in the rebellion and recognize that Micaela was the best strategist.

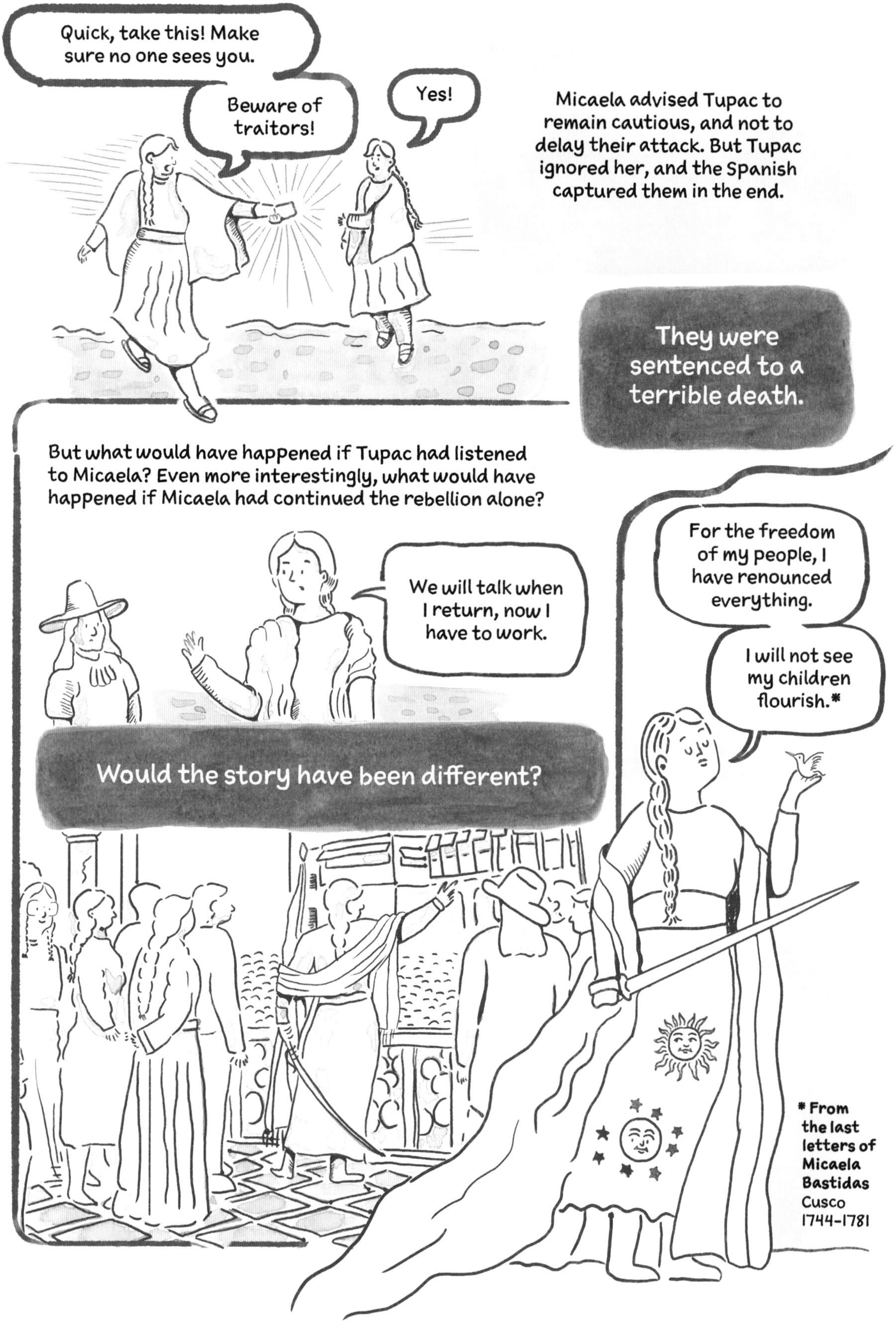
Quick, take this! Make sure no one sees you.
Beware of traitors!
Yes!
Micaela advised Tupac to remain cautious, and not to delay their attack. But Tupac ignored her, and the Spanish captured them in the end.
They were sentenced to a terrible death.
But what would have happened if Tupac had listened to Micaela? Even more interestingly, what would have happened if Micaela had continued the rebellion alone?
We will talk when I return, now I have to work.
Would the story have been different?
For the freedom of my people, I have renounced everything.
I will not see my children flourish.*
* From the last letters of Micaela Bastidas Cusco 1744-1781

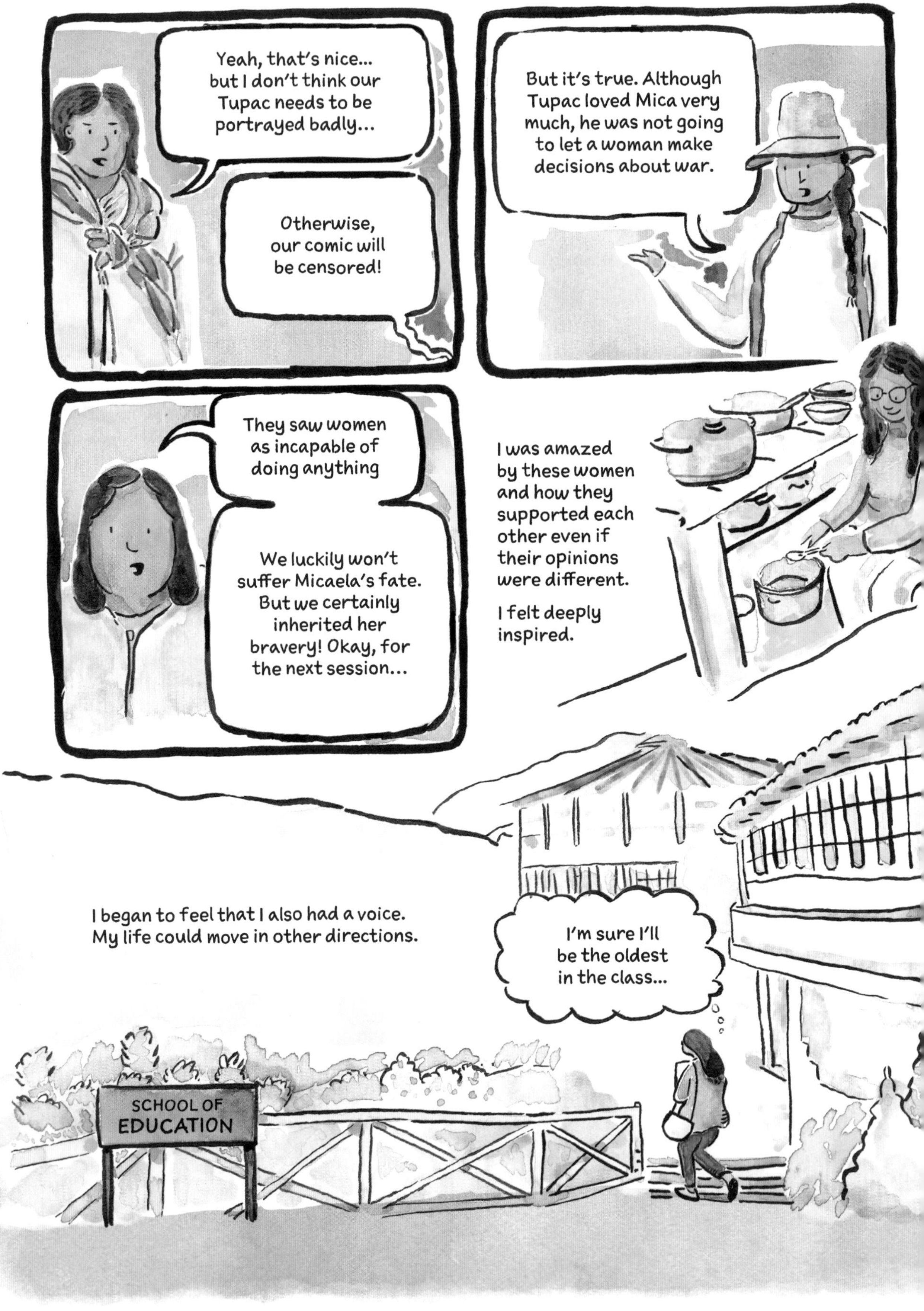
Yeah, that's nice... but I don't think our Tupac needs to be portrayed badly...
Otherwise, our comic will be censored!
But it's true. Although Tupac loved Mica very much, he was not going to let a woman make decisions about war.
They saw women as incapable of doing anything
We luckily won't suffer Micaela's fate. But we certainly inherited her bravery! Okay, for the next session...
I was amazed by these women and how they supported each other even if their opinions were different.
I felt deeply inspired.
I began to feel that I also had a voice. My life could move in other directions.
I'm sure I'll be the oldest in the class...
SCHOOL OF EDUCATION

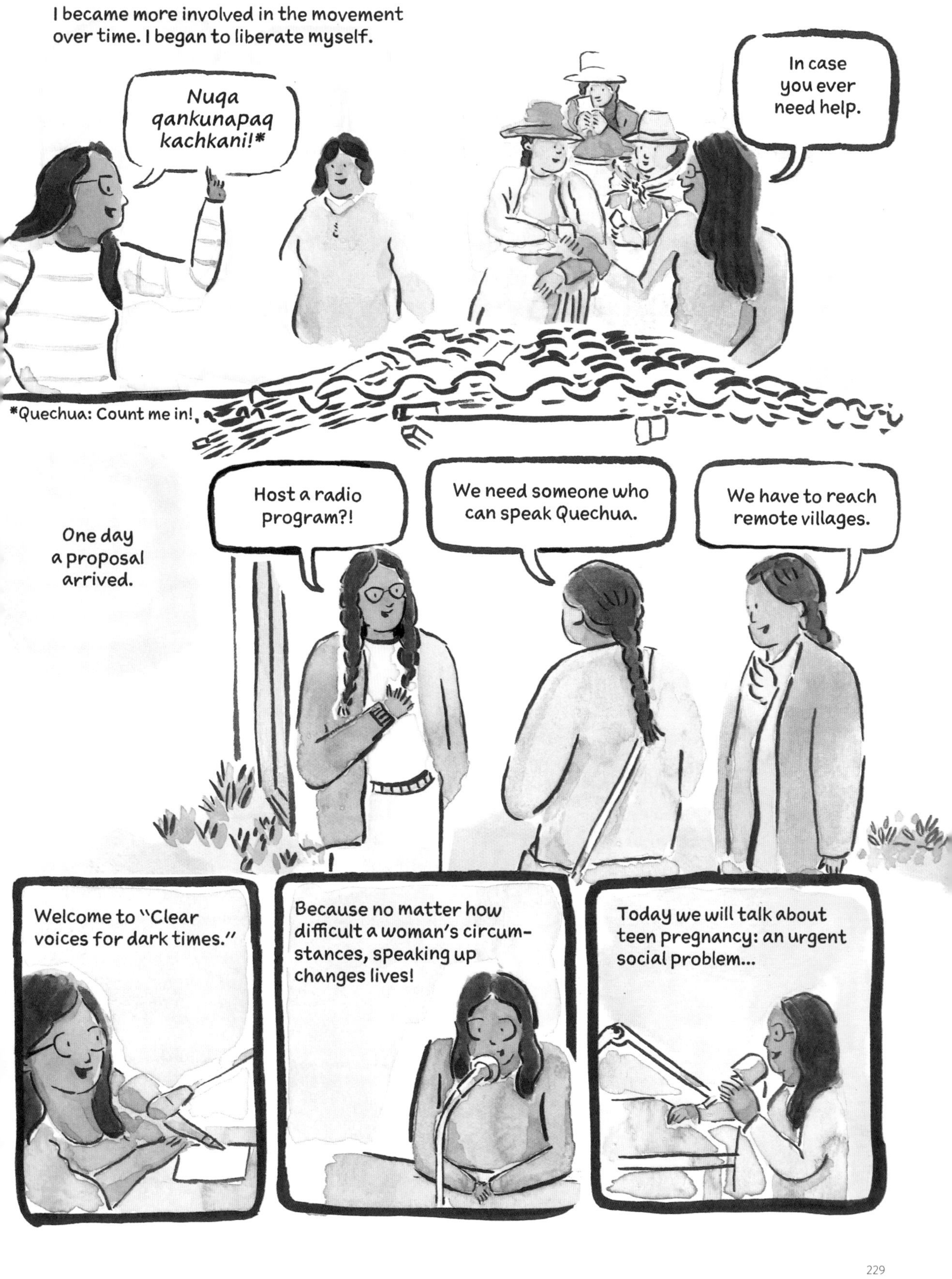
I became more involved in the movement over time. I began to liberate myself.
Nuqa qankunapaq kachkani!*
In case you ever need help.
*Quechua: Count me in!
One day a proposal arrived.
Host a radio program?!
We need someone who can speak Quechua.
We have to reach remote villages.
Welcome to "Clear voices for dark times."
Because no matter how difficult a woman's circumstances, speaking up changes lives!
Today we will talk about teen pregnancy: an urgent social problem...

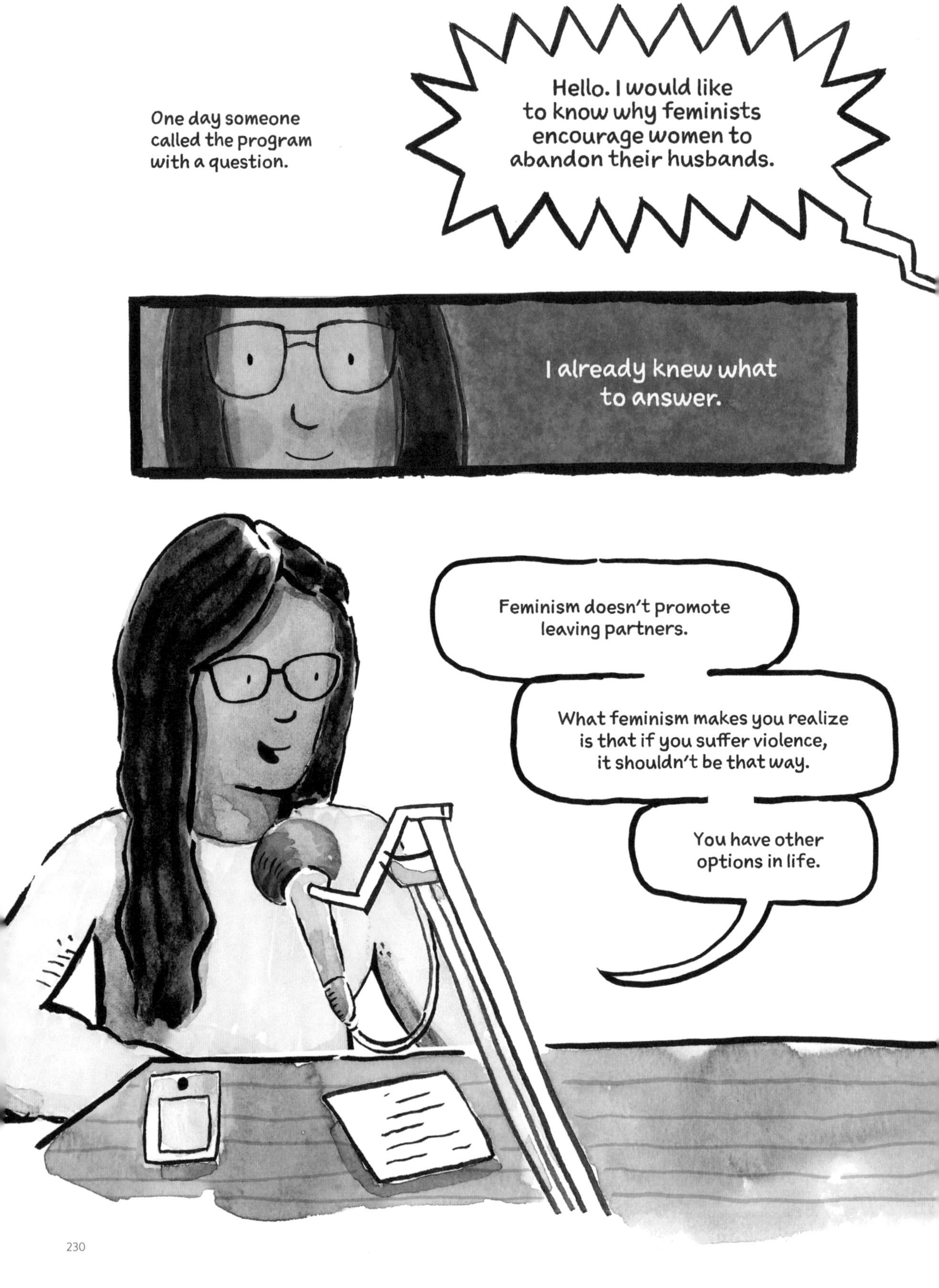
One day someone called the program with a question.
Hello. I would like to know why feminists encourage women to abandon their husbands.
I already knew what to answer.
Feminism doesn't promote leaving partners.
What feminism makes you realize is that if you suffer violence, it shouldn't be that way.
You have other options in life.

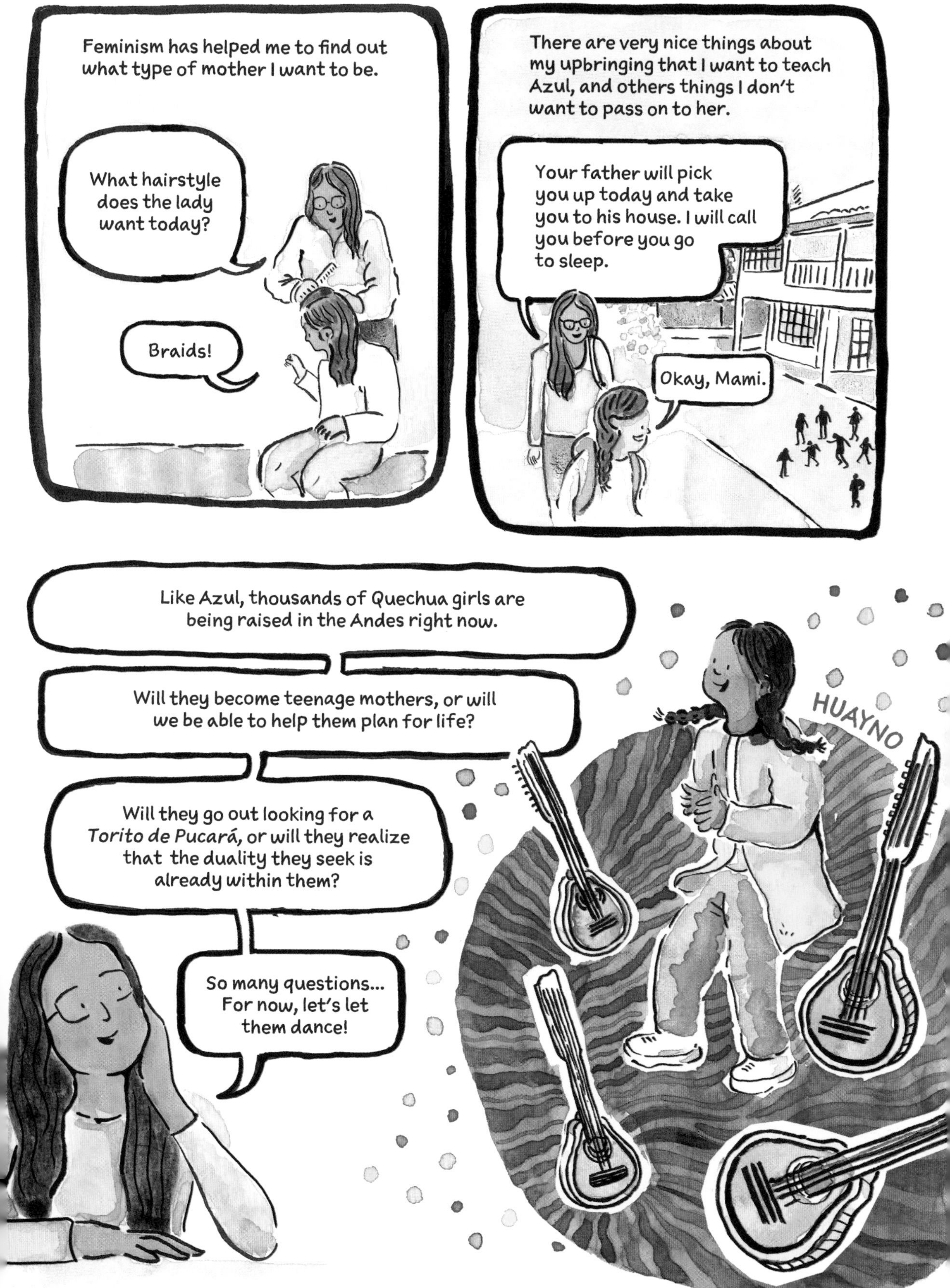
Feminism has helped me to find out what type of mother I want to be.
What hairstyle does the lady want today?
Braids!
There are very nice things about my upbringing that I want to teach Azul, and others things I don't want to pass on to her.
Your father will pick you up today and take you to his house. I will call you before you go to sleep.
Okay, Mami.
Like Azul, thousands of Quechua girls are being raised in the Andes right now.
Will they become teenage mothers, or will we be able to help them plan for life?
Will they go out looking for a *Torito de Pucará*, or will they realize that the duality they seek is already within them?
So many questions... For now, let's let them dance!
HUAYNO

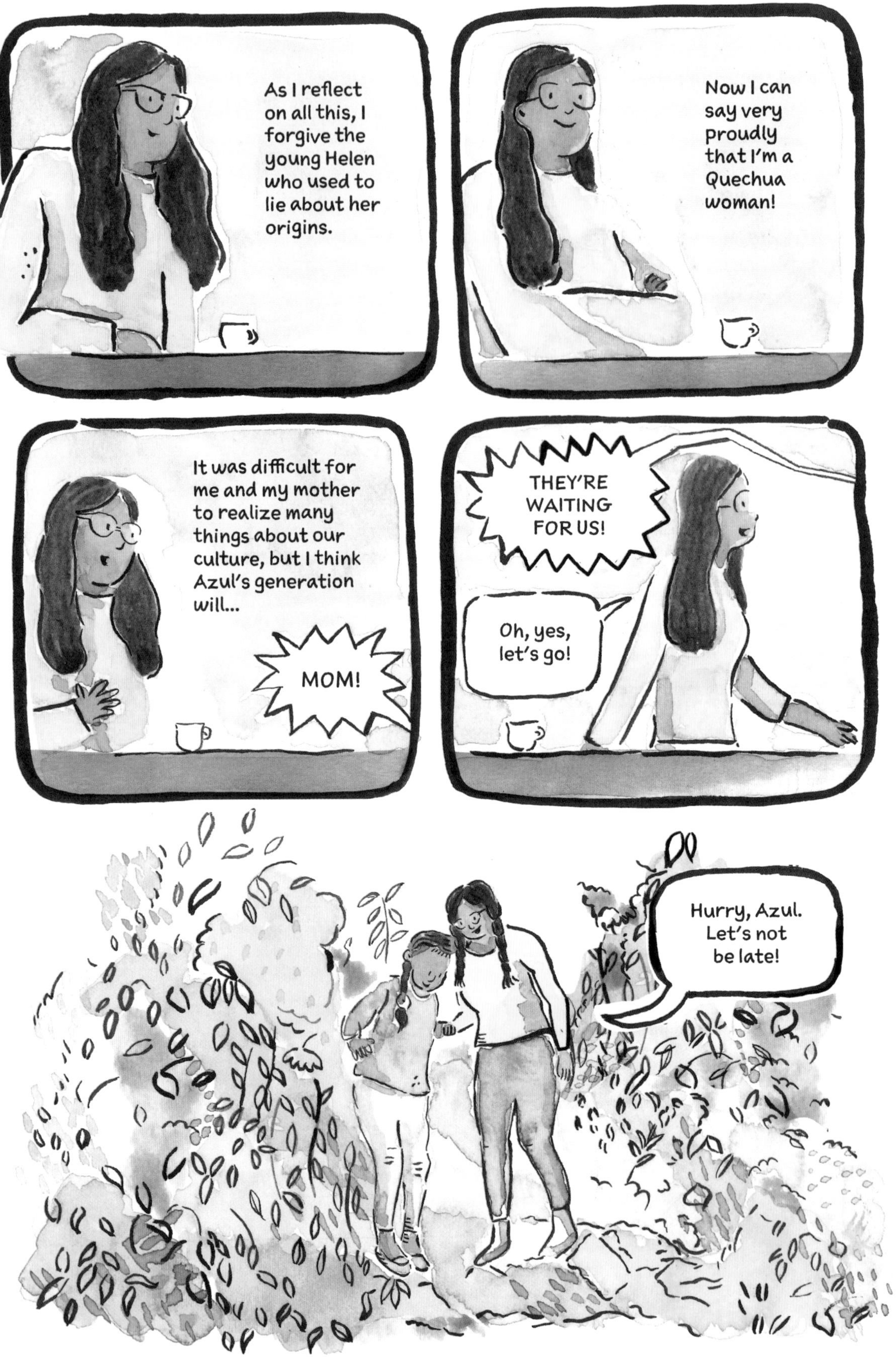
As I reflect on all this, I forgive the young Helen who used to lie about her origins.
Now I can say very proudly that I'm a Quechua woman!
It was difficult for me and my mother to realize many things about our culture, but I think Azul's generation will...
MOM!
THEY'RE WAITING FOR US!
Oh, yes, let's go!
Hurry, Azul. Let's not be late!

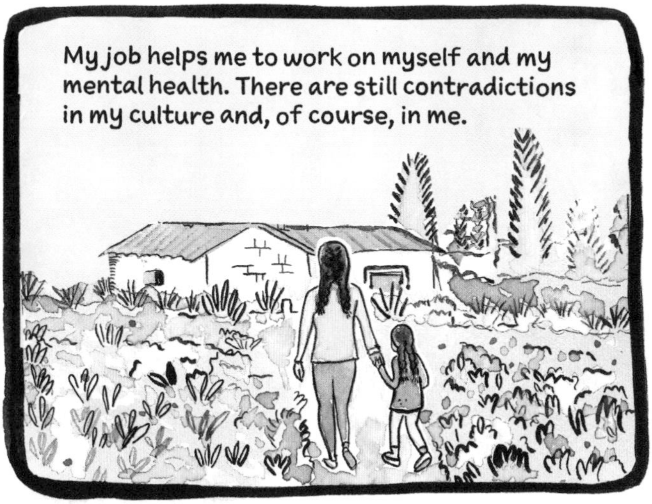
My job helps me to work on myself and my mental health. There are still contradictions in my culture and, of course, in me.

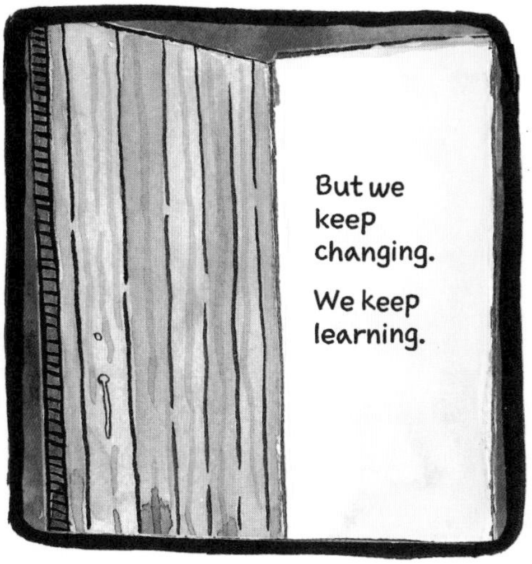
But we keep changing.
We keep learning.

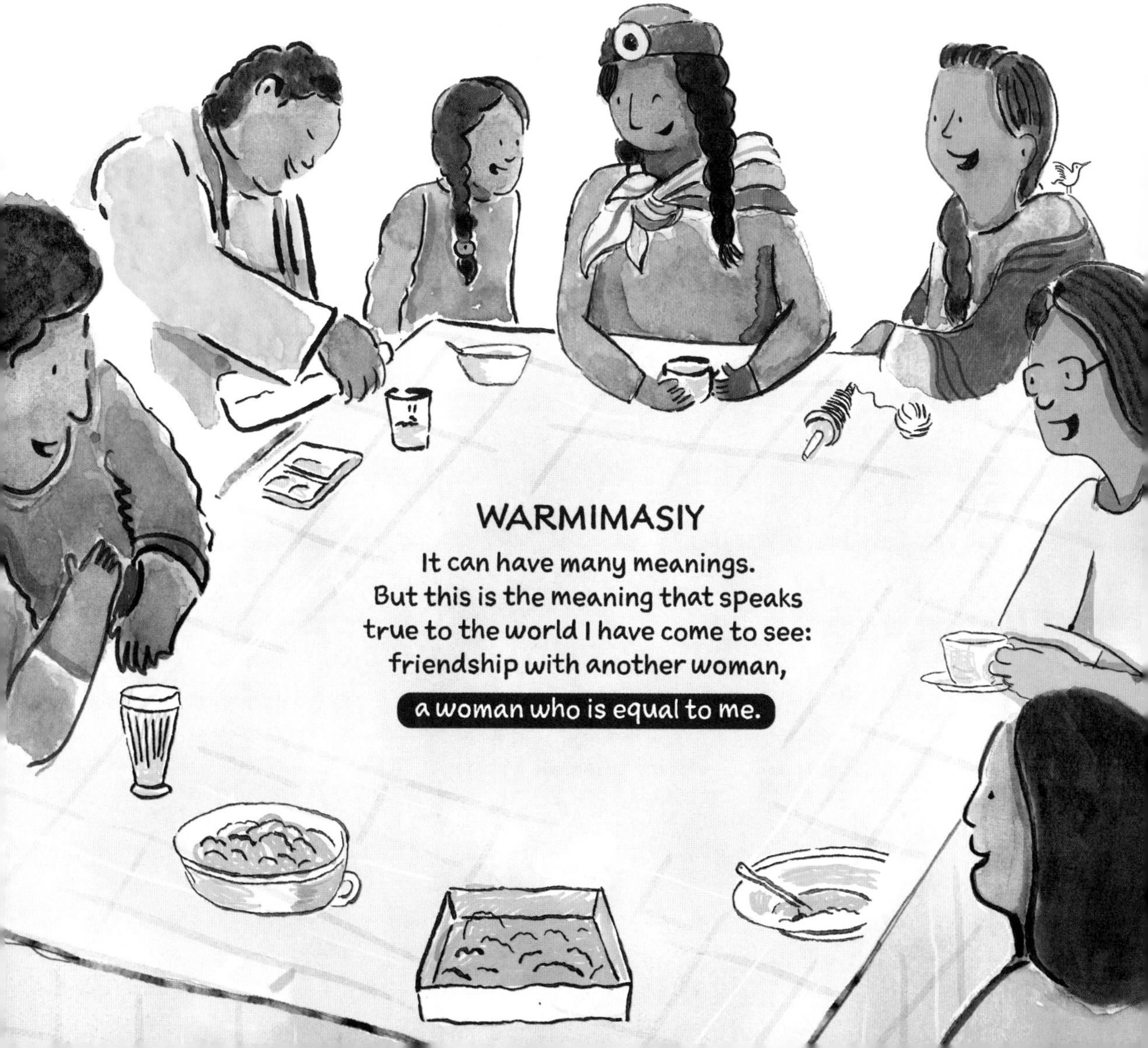
WARMIMASIY
It can have many meanings. But this is the meaning that speaks true to the world I have come to see: friendship with another woman,
a woman who is equal to me.

*Hinaqa
ñañaykunaturaykuna,
huk sunqulla,
huk kallpalla puririnanchis,
maqanakuyta, awqanakuyta
tatichispa,
chinkachispa;
allin kawsay
rayku.* ❋

This is how it is, sisters
and brothers. We must
continue with one heart, one
strength to find the best way
to reach a better life, free
from all kinds of violence.

Helen Quiñones Loaiza

Thanks to Movimiento de Promoción por los Derechos
Humanos de las Mujeres – Amhauta, particularly to
Charito Salazar Segovia for all the support and
access to information she provided in Cusco.

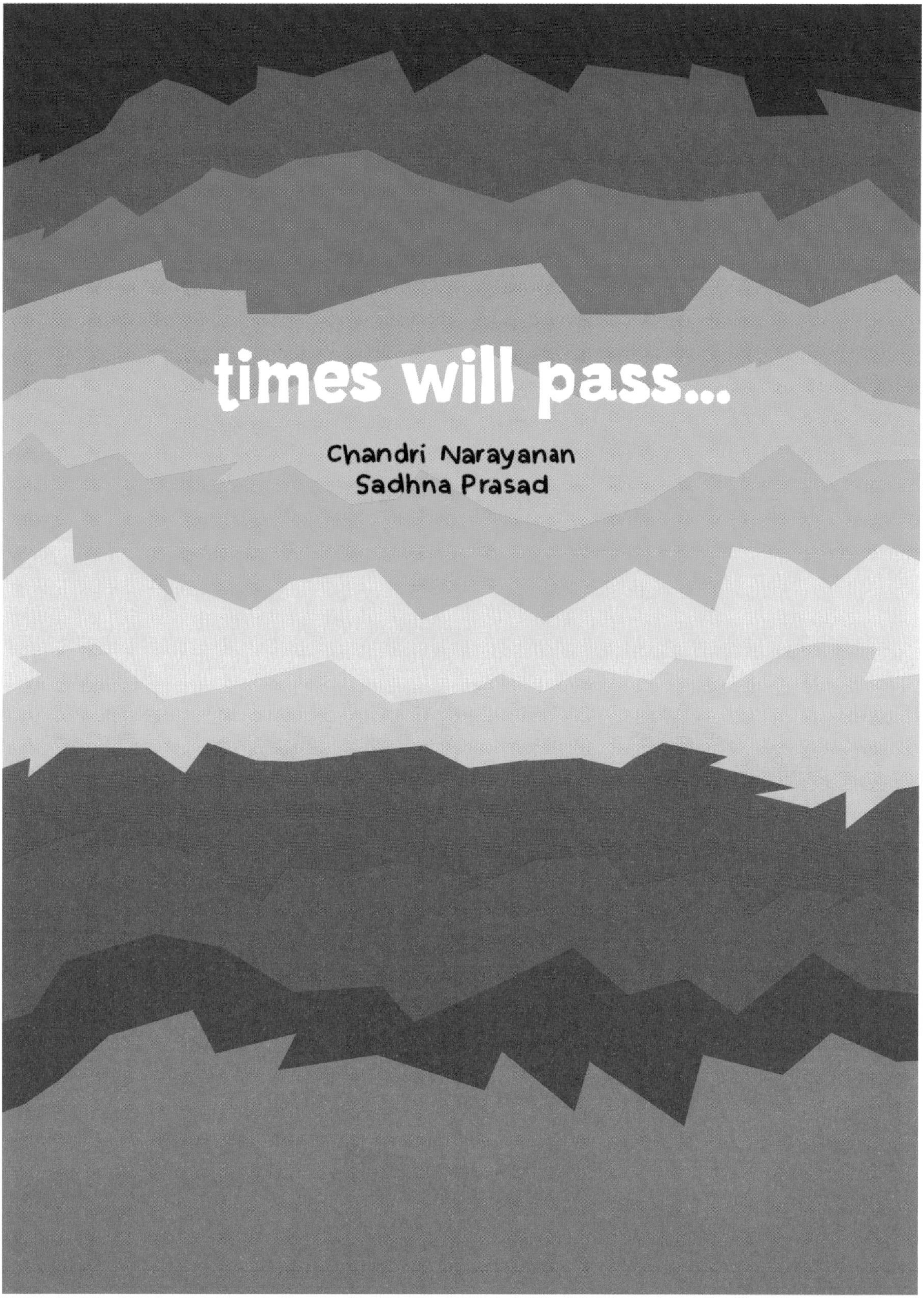

times will pass...

Chandri Narayanan
Sadhna Prasad

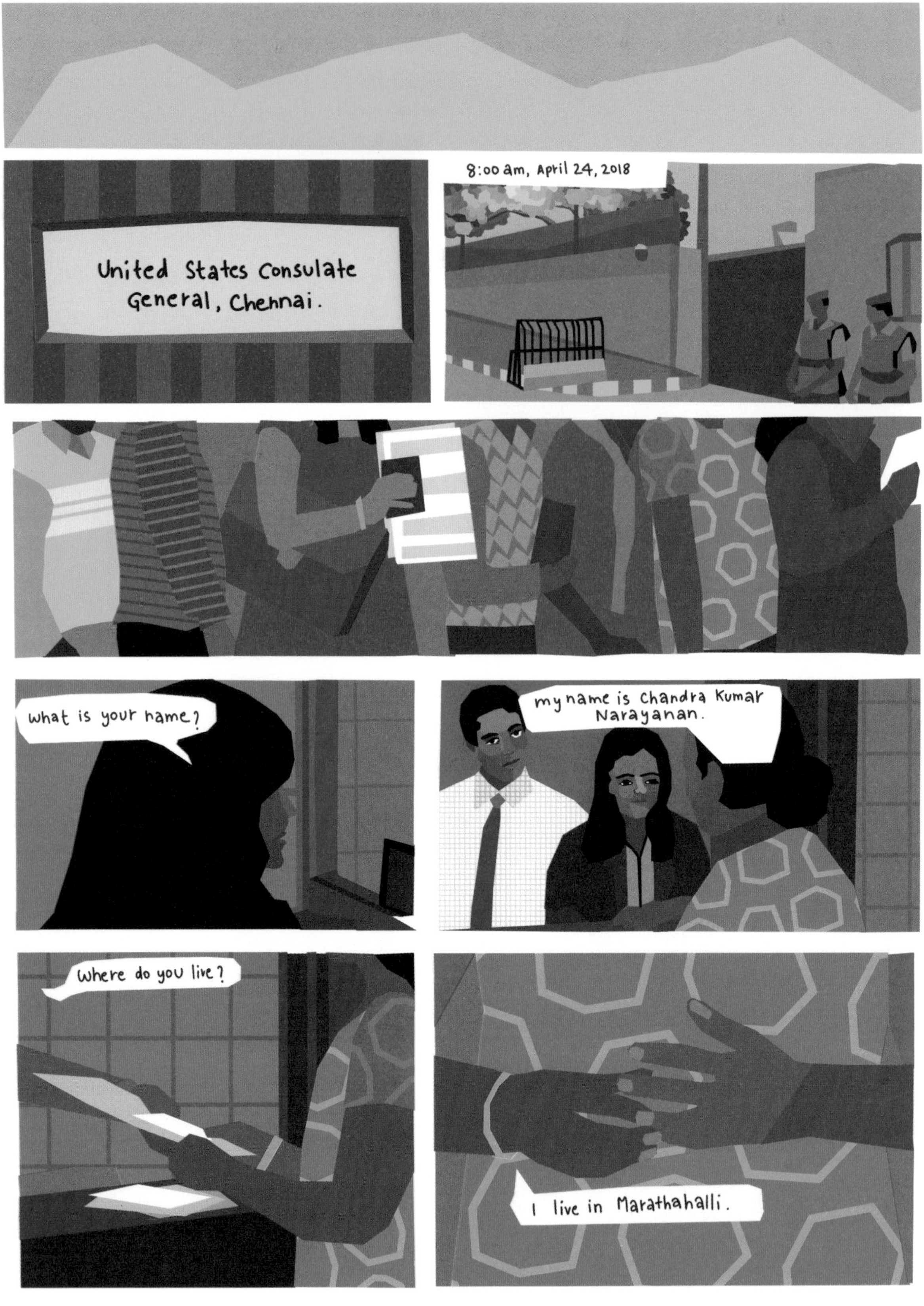
United States Consulate General, Chennai.
8:00 am, April 24, 2018
what is your name?
my name is Chandra Kumar Narayanan.
where do you live?
I live in Marathahalli.

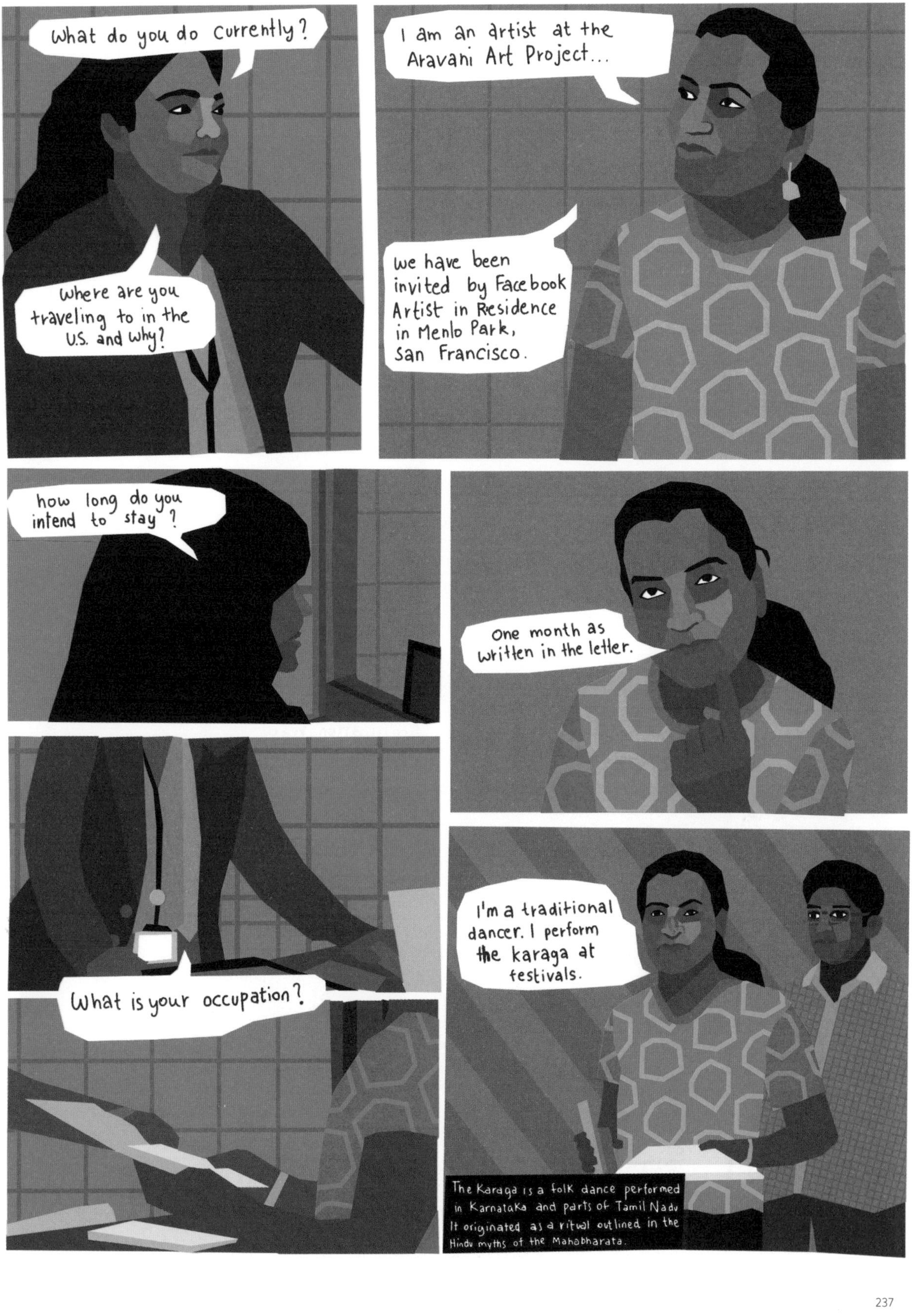
What do you do currently?
Where are you traveling to in the U.S. and why?
I am an artist at the Aravani Art Project...
We have been invited by Facebook Artist in Residence in Menlo Park, San Francisco.
how long do you intend to stay?
One month as written in the letter.
What is your occupation?
I'm a traditional dancer. I perform the karaga at festivals.
The Karaga is a folk dance performed in Karnataka and parts of Tamil Nadu It originated as a ritual outlined in the Hindu myths of the Mahabharata.

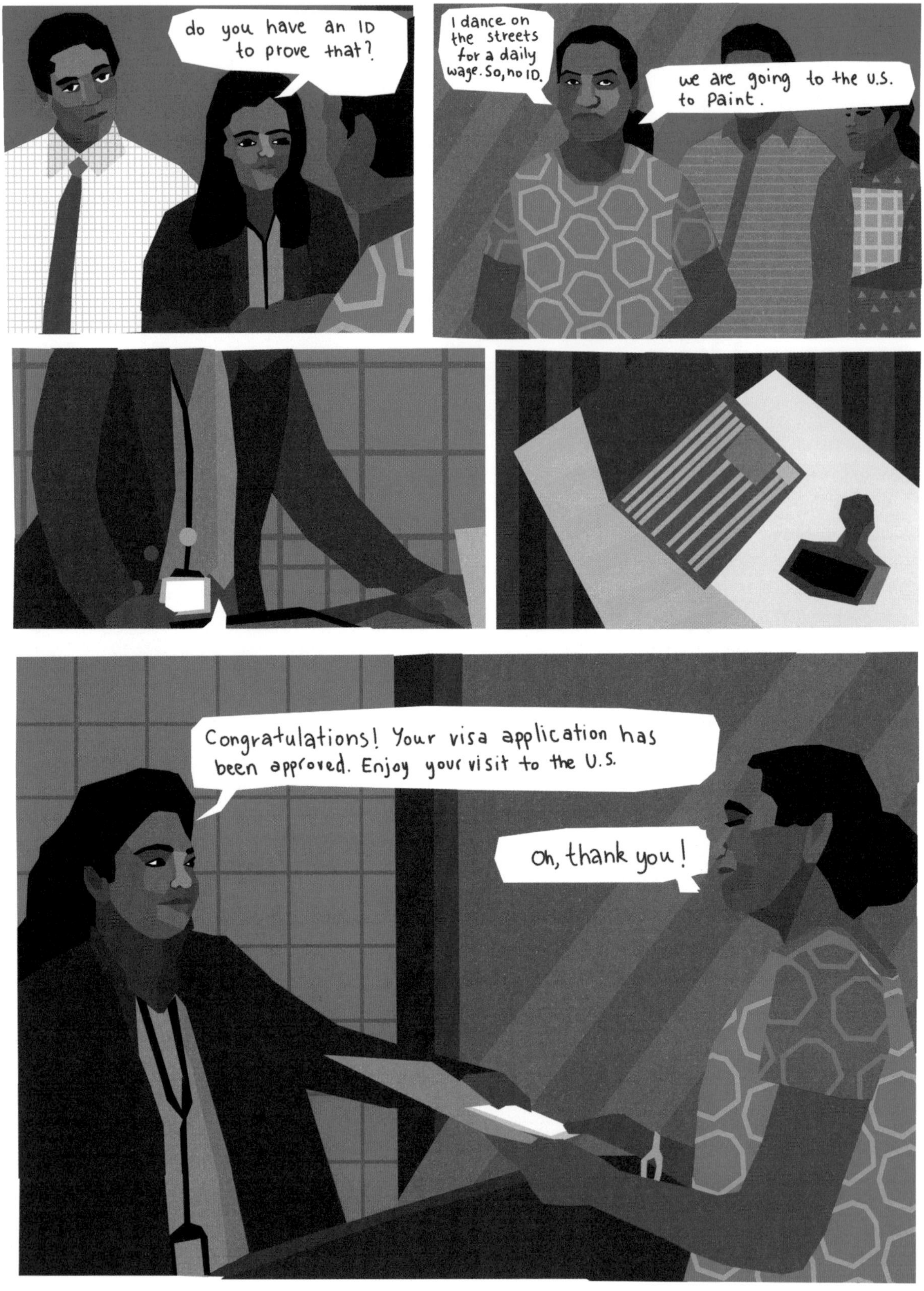
do you have an ID to prove that?
I dance on the streets for a daily wage. So, no ID.
we are going to the U.S. to Paint.
Congratulations! Your visa application has been approved. Enjoy your visit to the U.S.
Oh, thank you!

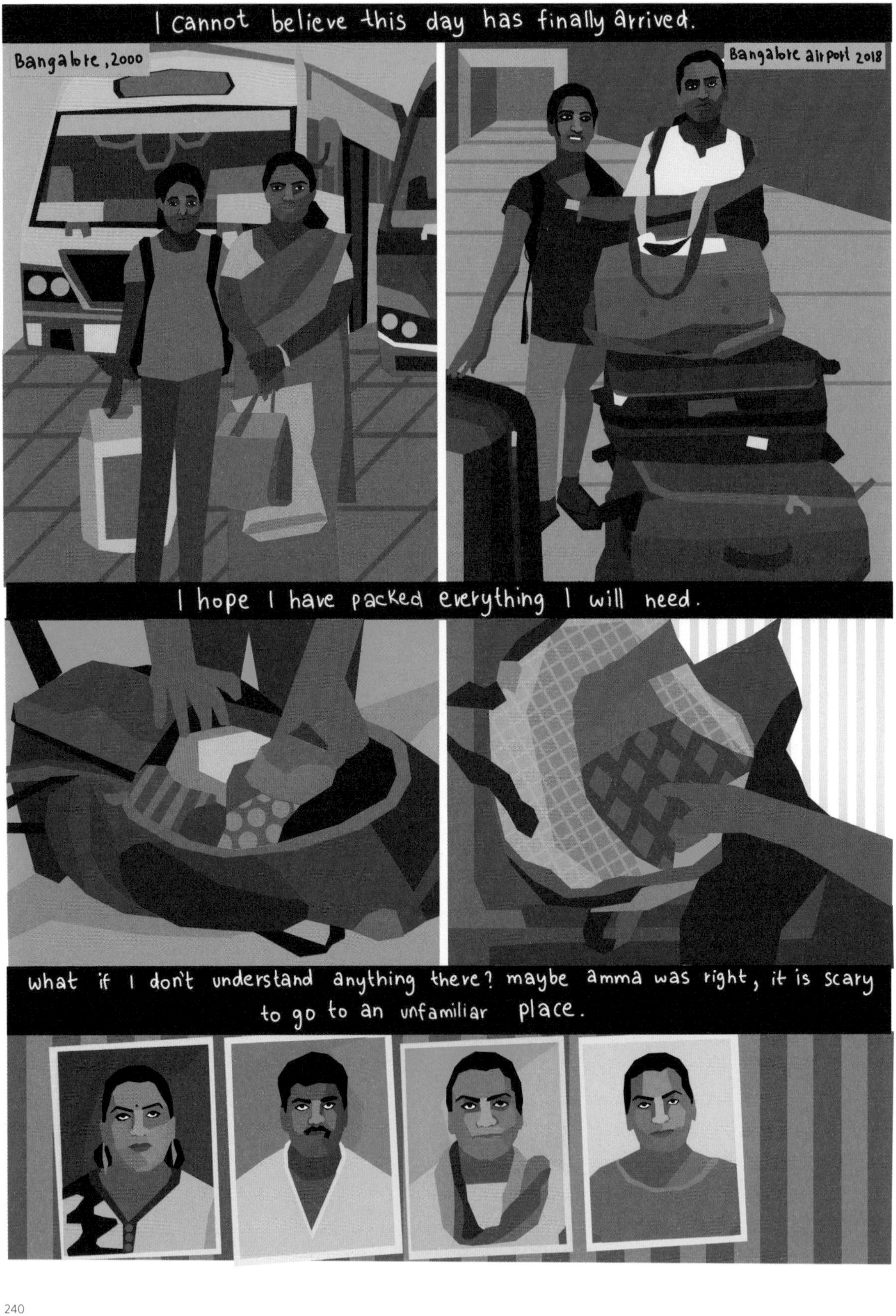
I cannot believe this day has finally arrived.
Bangalore, 2000
Bangalore airport 2018
I hope I have packed everything I will need.
what if I don't understand anything there? maybe amma was right, it is scary to go to an unfamiliar place.

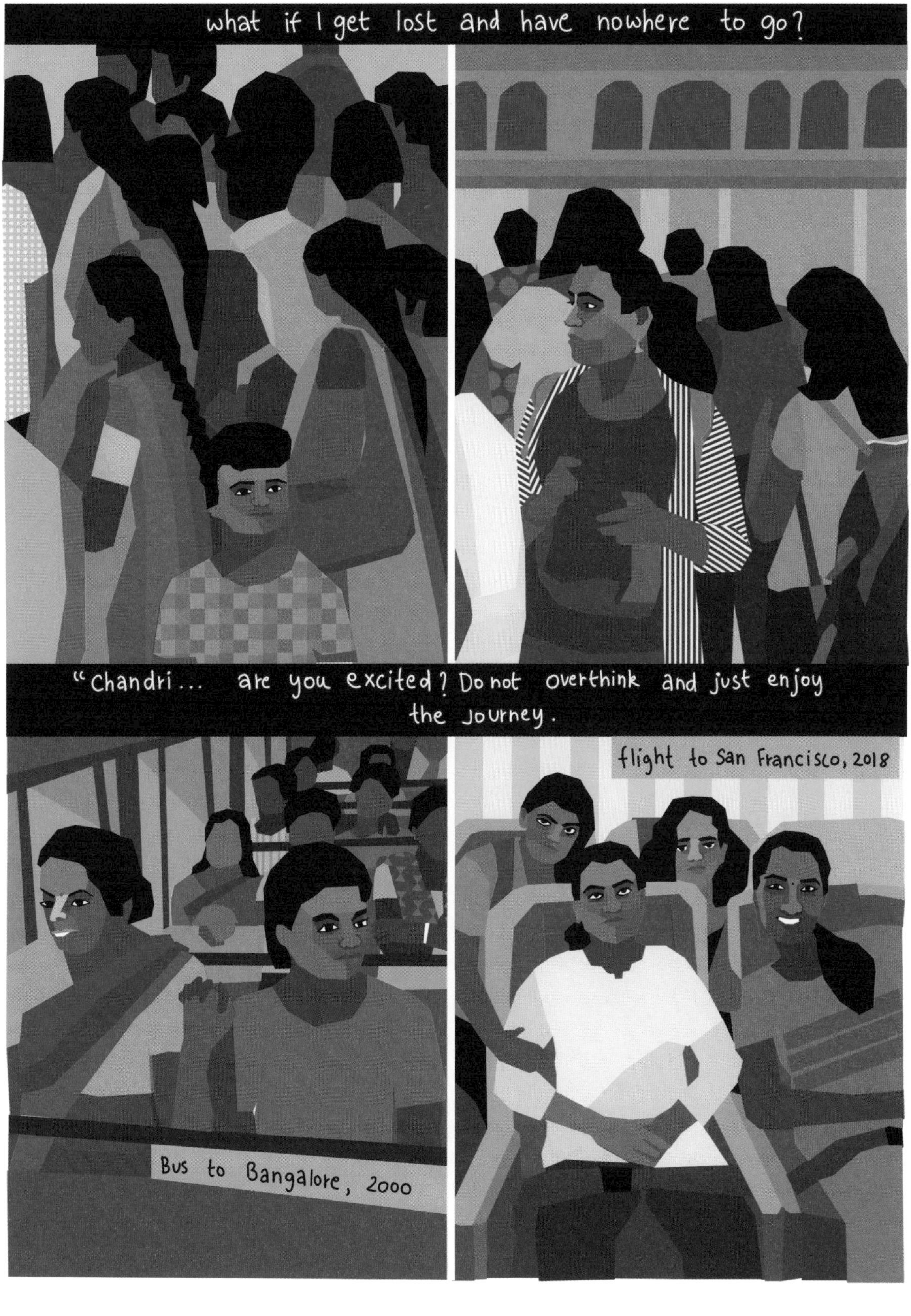
what if I get lost and have nowhere to go?
"Chandri... are you excited? Do not overthink and just enjoy the journey.
Bus to Bangalore, 2000
flight to San Francisco, 2018

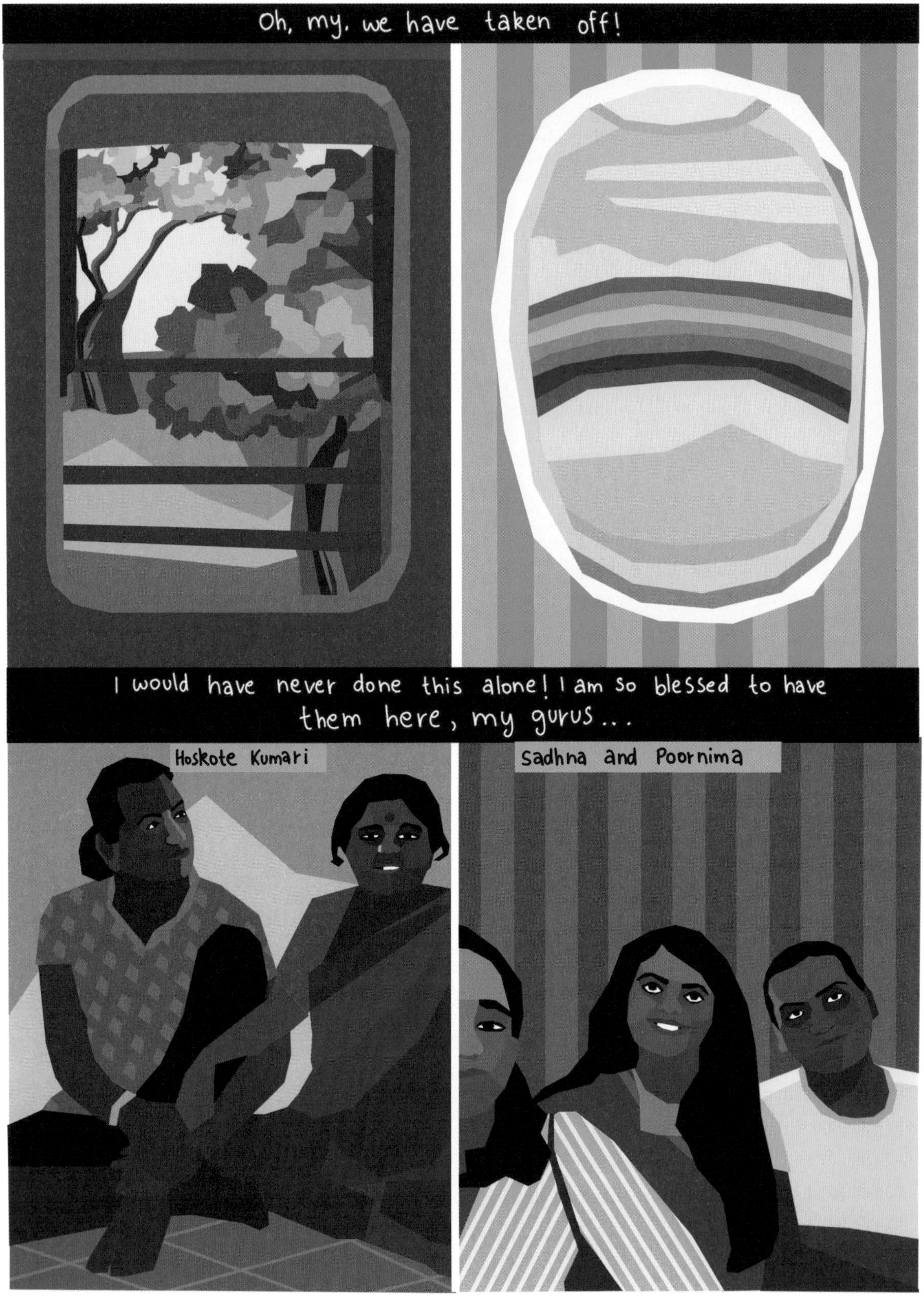

Oh, my. we have taken off!
I would have never done this alone! I am so blessed to have them here, my gurus...
Hoskote Kumari
Sadhna and Poornima

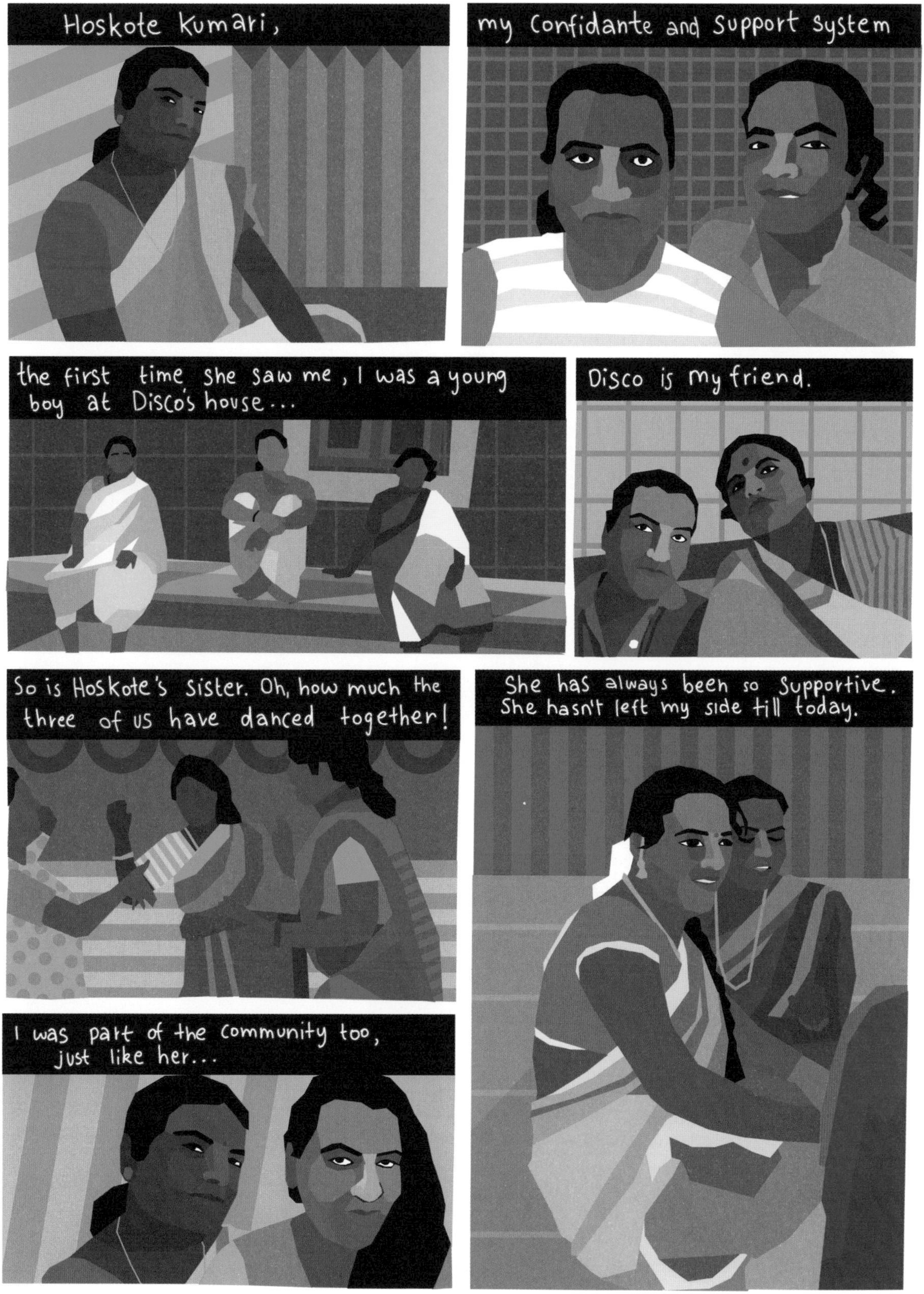
Hoskote Kumari,
my Confidante and Support system
the first time she saw me, I was a young boy at Disco's house...
Disco is my friend.
So is Hoskote's sister. Oh, how much the three of us have danced together!
I was part of the community too, just like her...
She has always been so supportive. She hasn't left my side till today.

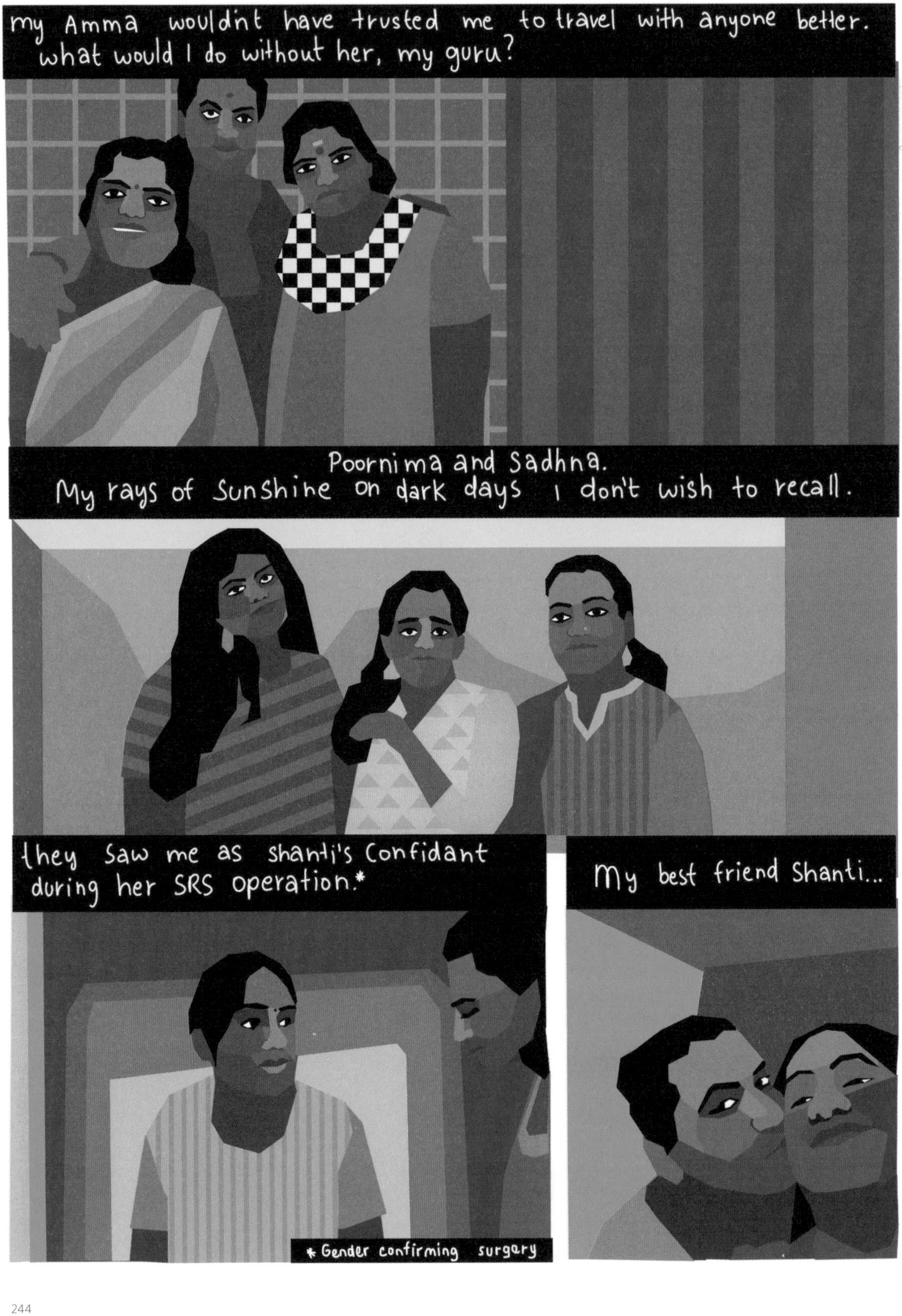
my Amma wouldn't have trusted me to travel with anyone better. what would I do without her, my guru?
Poornima and Sadhna.
My rays of Sunshine on dark days I don't wish to recall.
they saw me as shanti's confidant during her SRS operation.*
My best friend Shanti...
* Gender confirming surgery

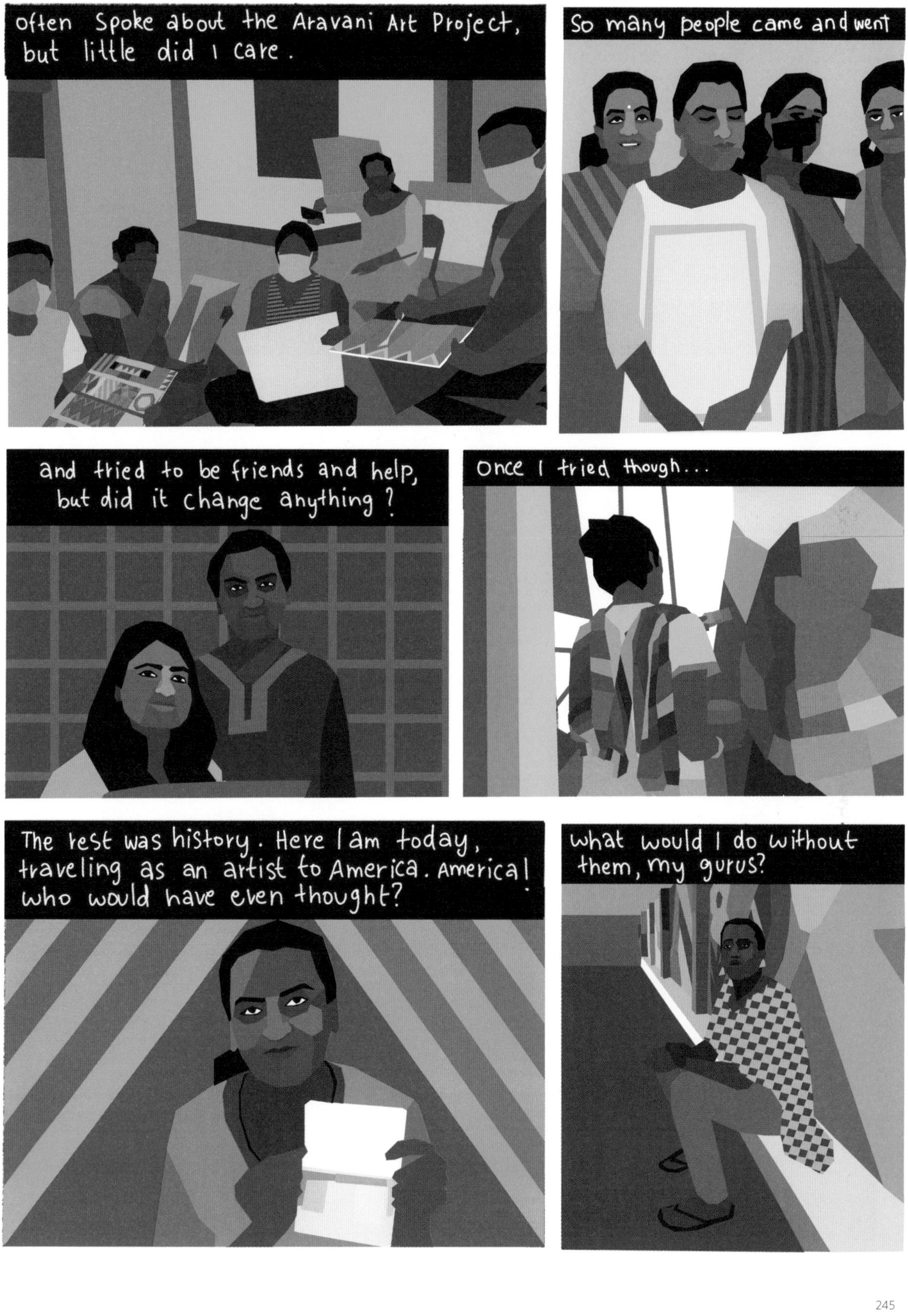

often Spoke about the Aravani Art Project, but little did I care.
So many people came and went
and tried to be friends and help, but did it change anything ?
Once I tried though...
The rest was history. Here I am today, traveling as an artist to America. America! who would have even thought?
what would I do without them, my gurus?

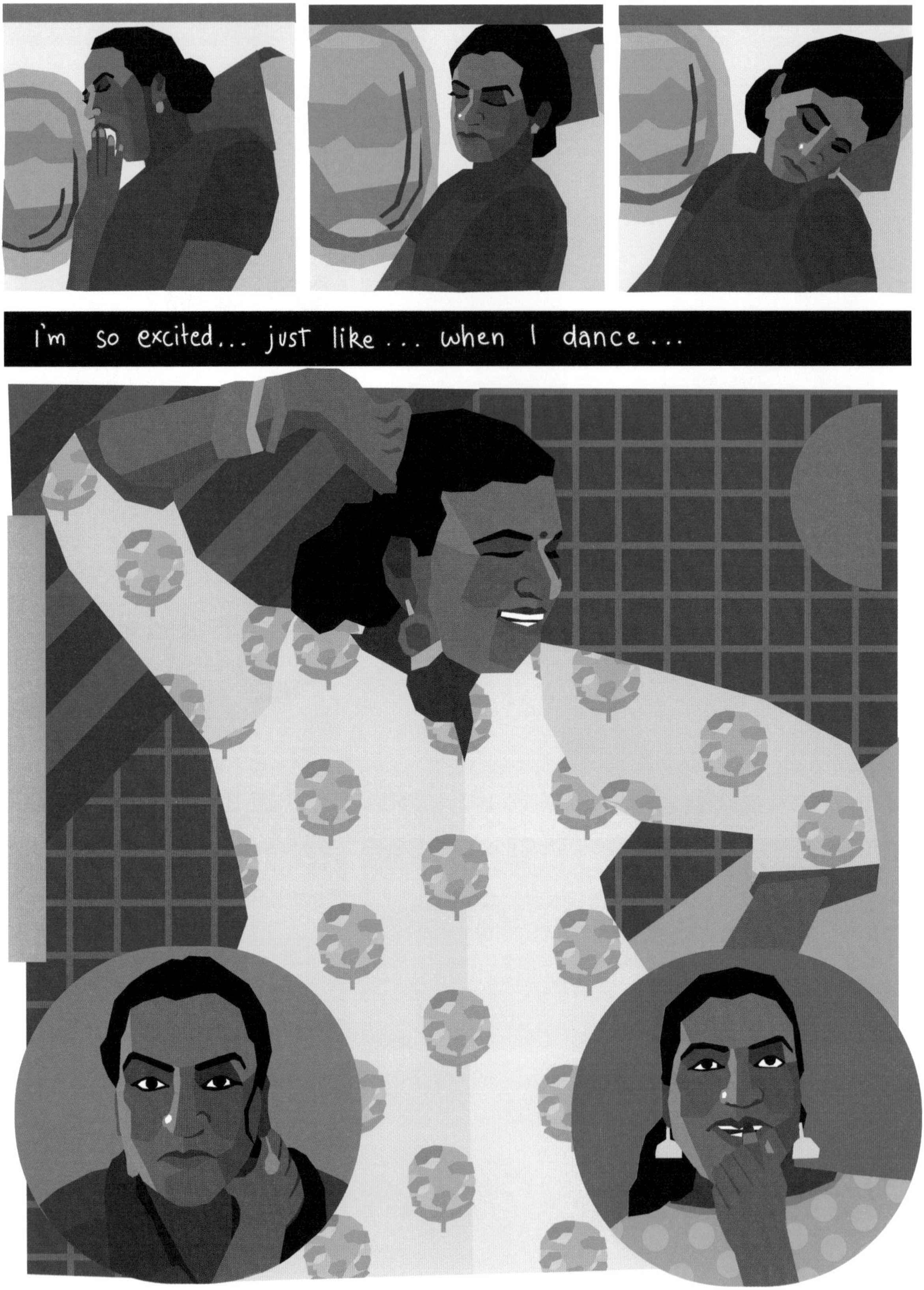
I'm so excited... just like... when I dance...

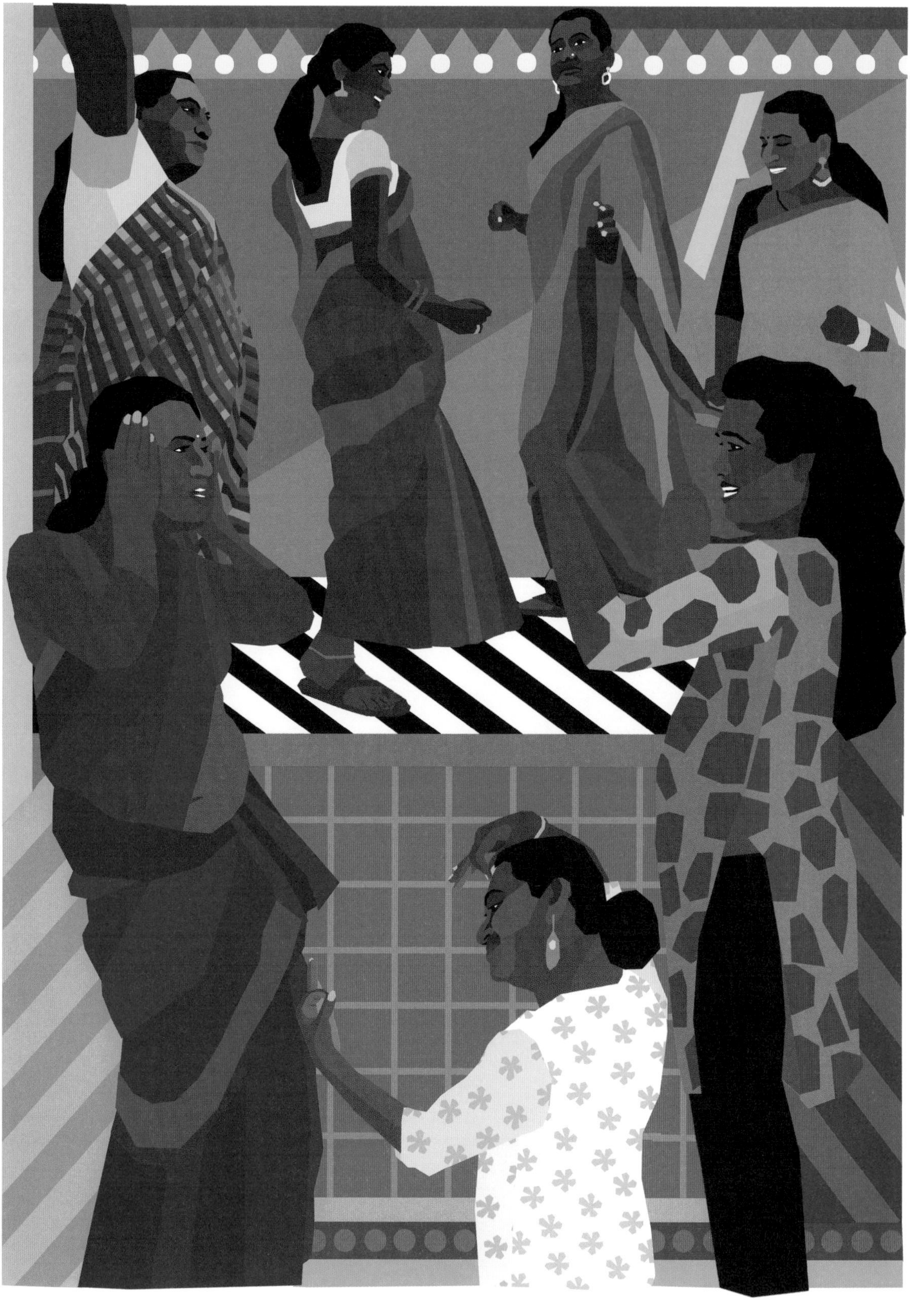

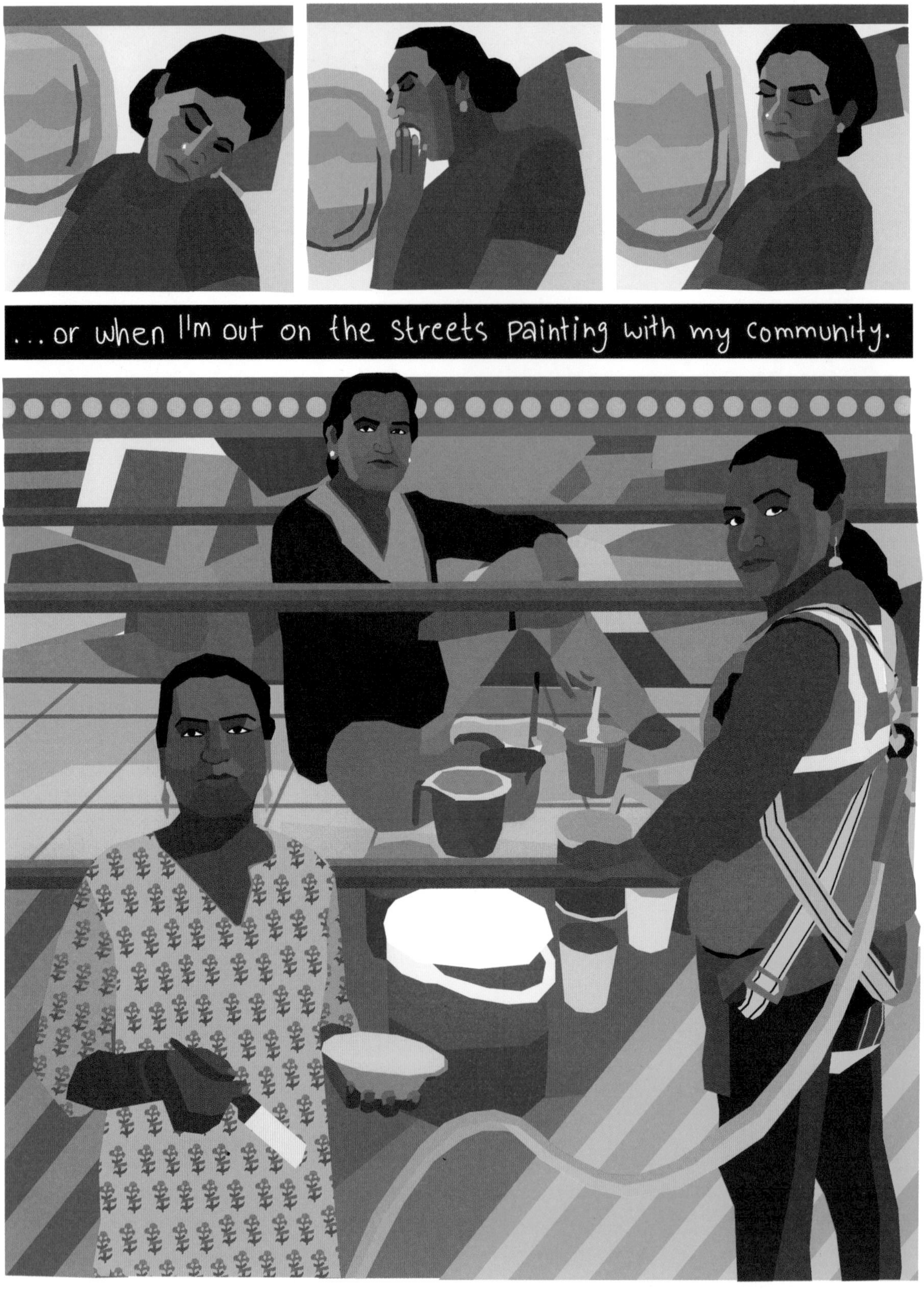
...or when I'm out on the streets painting with my community.

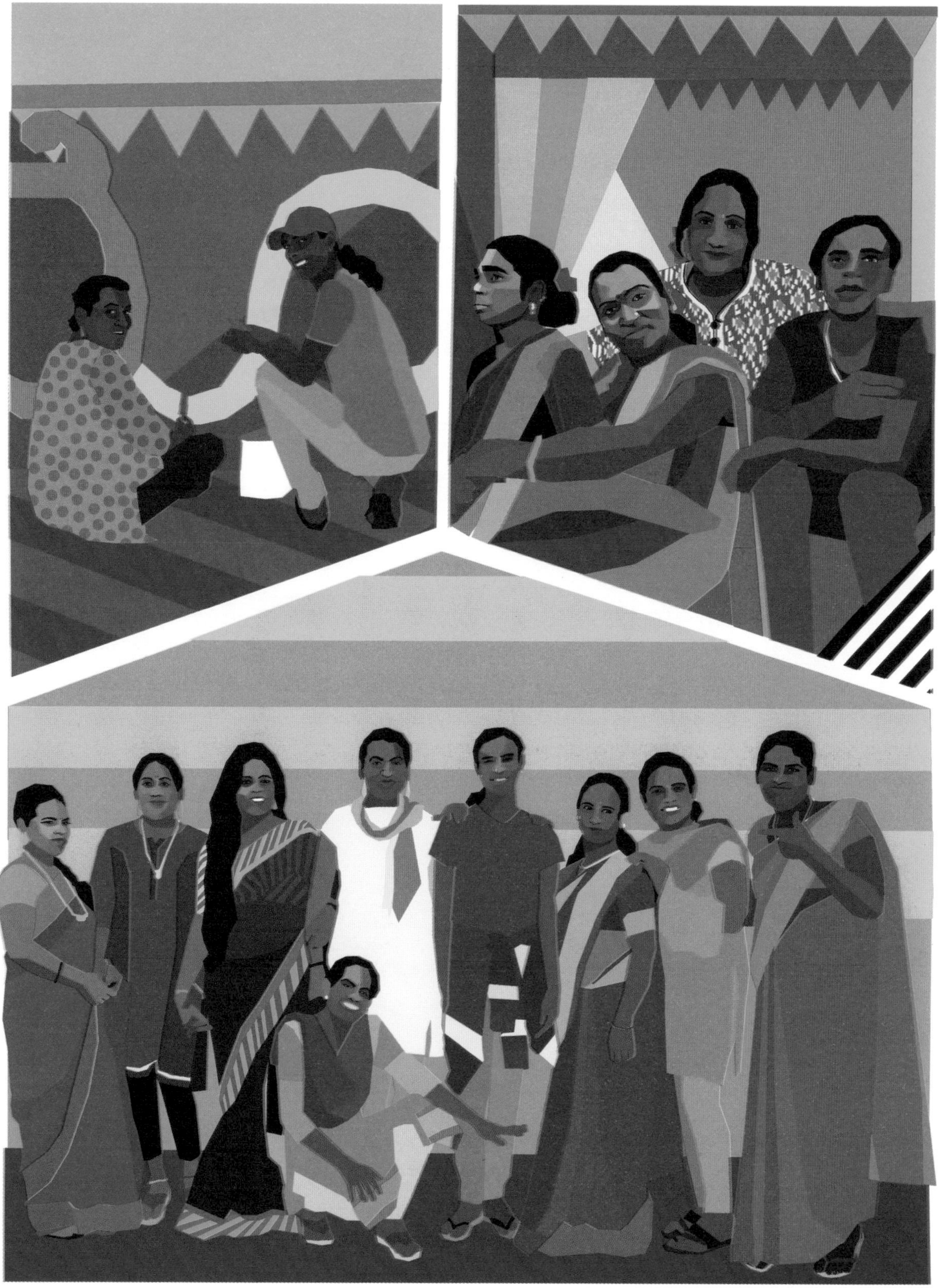

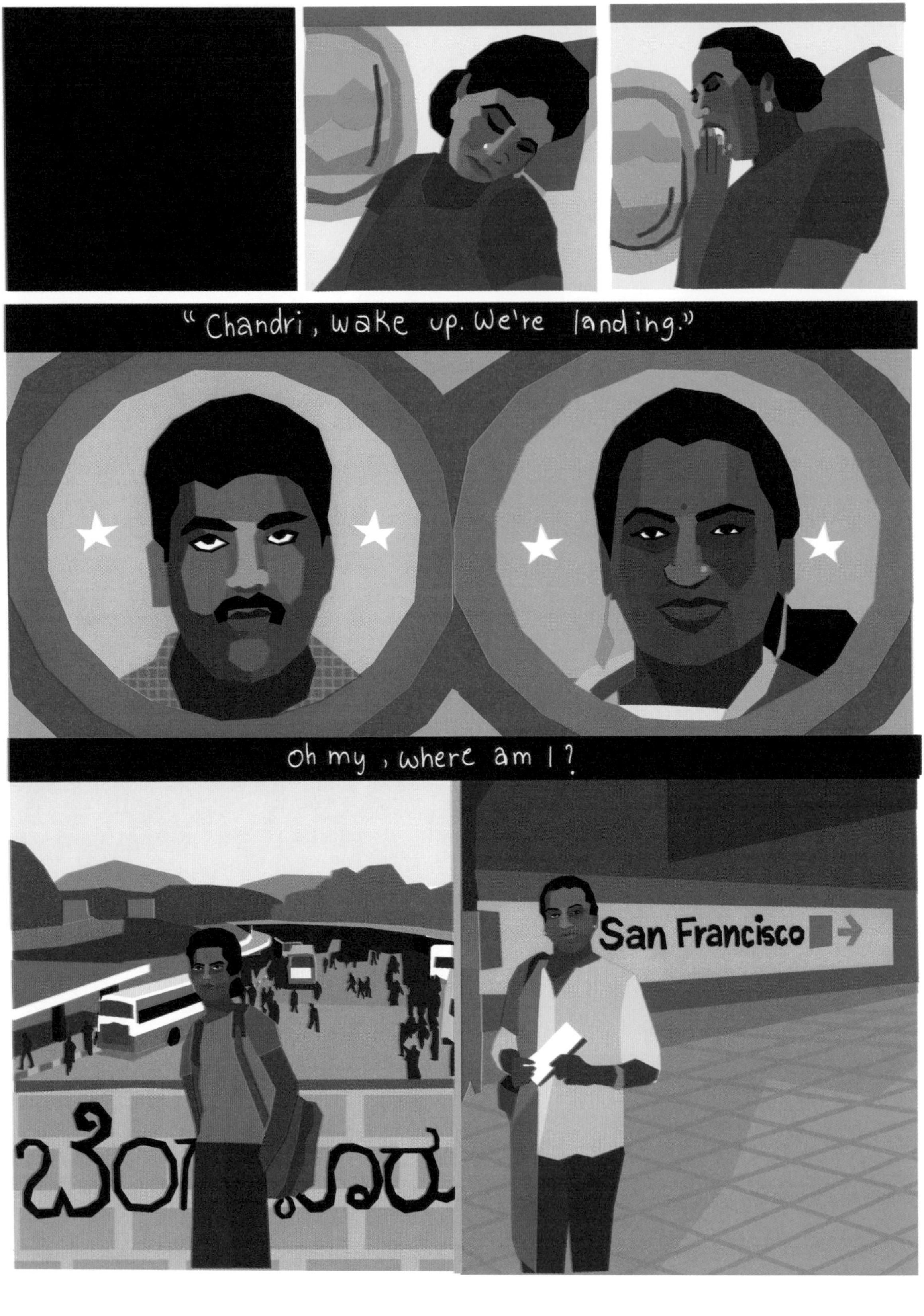
"Chandri, wake up. We're landing."
Oh my, where am I?
San Francisco

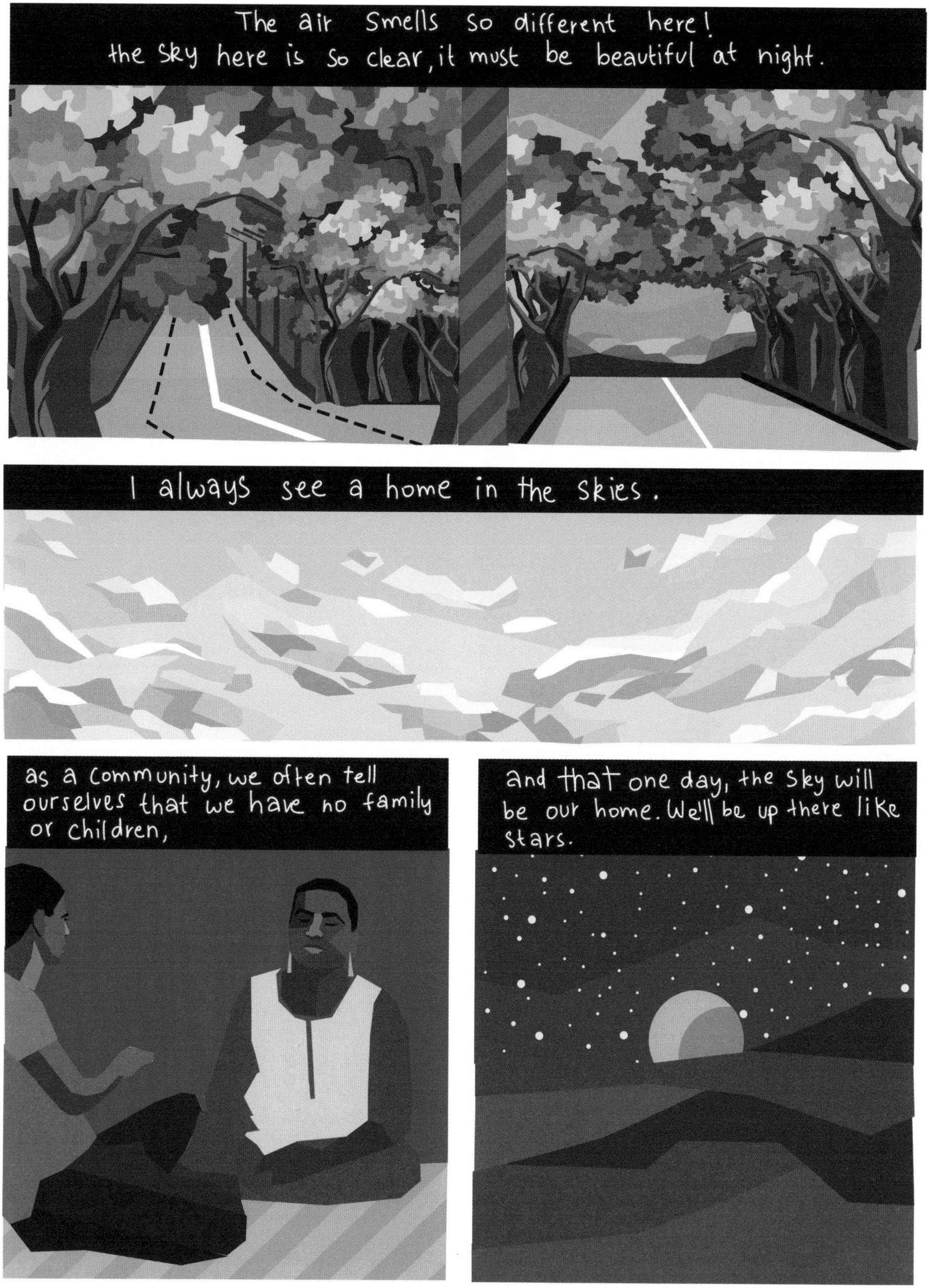
The air smells so different here!
the sky here is so clear, it must be beautiful at night.
I always see a home in the skies.
as a community, we often tell ourselves that we have no family or children,
and that one day, the sky will be our home. We'll be up there like stars.

The whole Sky feels like home.

The stars remind me of my maternal grandmother's house

and Sleeping out in the open as a Child when I was growing up in that village house in Tamil Nadu.

Very few families lived in my village, it was a tight-knit Community.

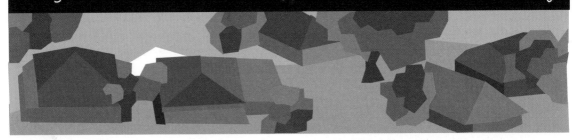

as a Child, I loved playing with my mother and listening to her stories.

as I got older, I still enjoyed playing. But My mother watched me enjoy dancing and wearing my Sister's clothes.

my mother could tell that this feminine behavior was not well received.

When I was ten, she told me that if I went on this way I would get chicken pox. It scared me.

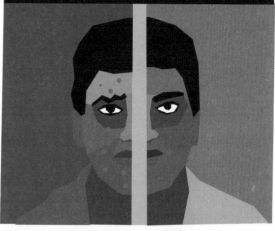

what memories!

This air now smells familiar to me.

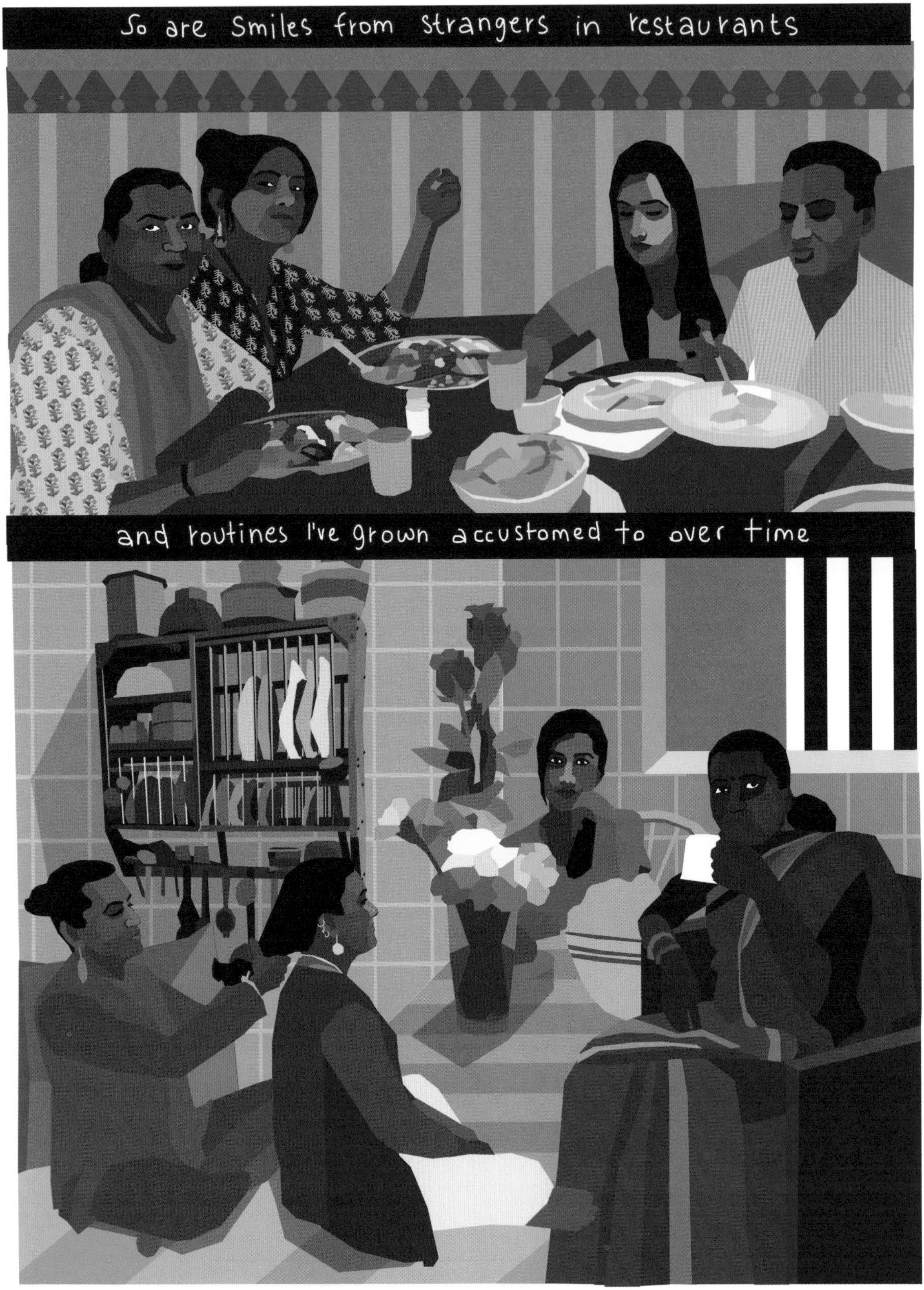
So are Smiles from strangers in restaurants
and routines I've grown accustomed to over time

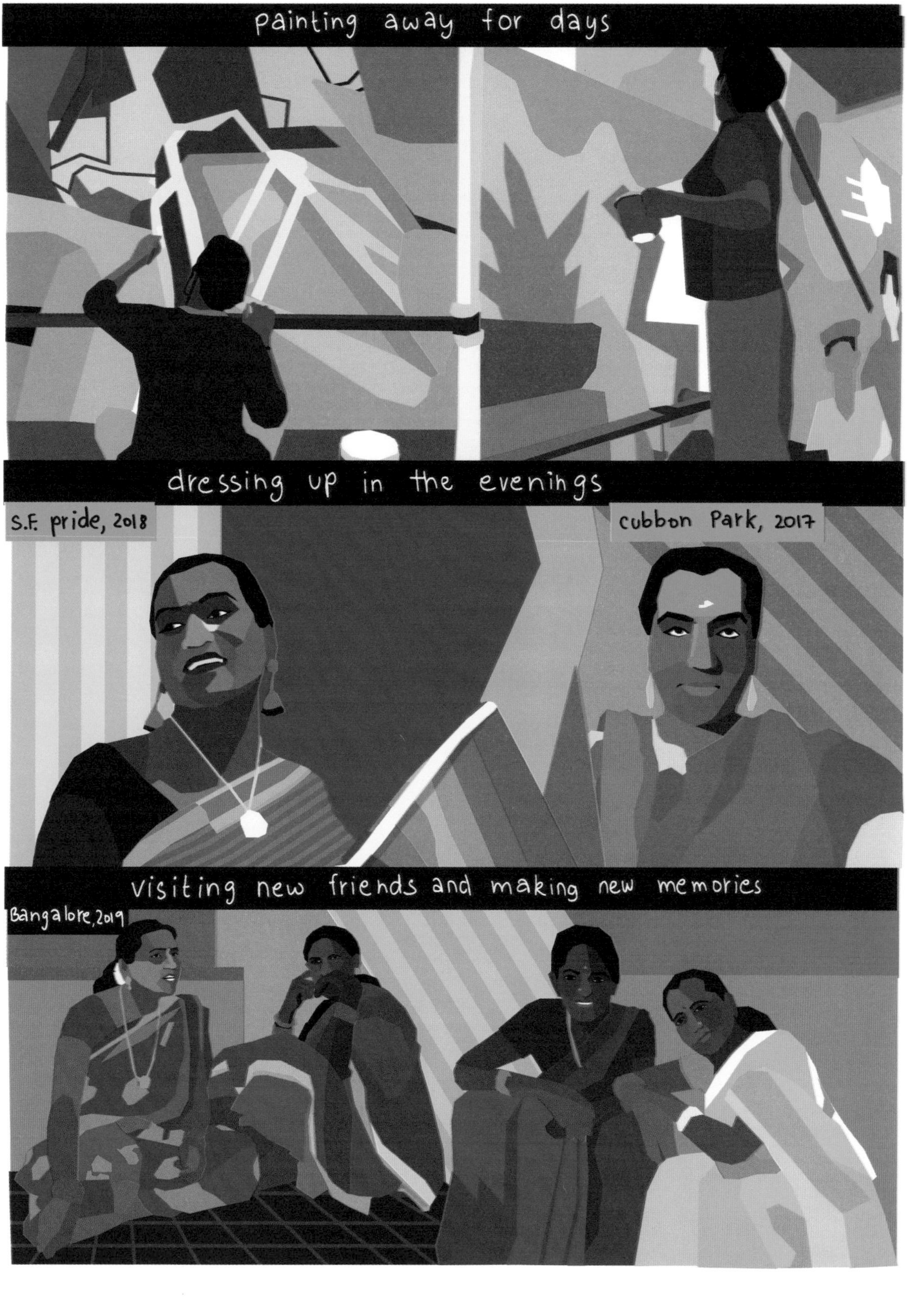
painting away for days
dressing up in the evenings
S.F. pride, 2018
cubbon Park, 2017
visiting new friends and making new memories
Bangalore, 2019

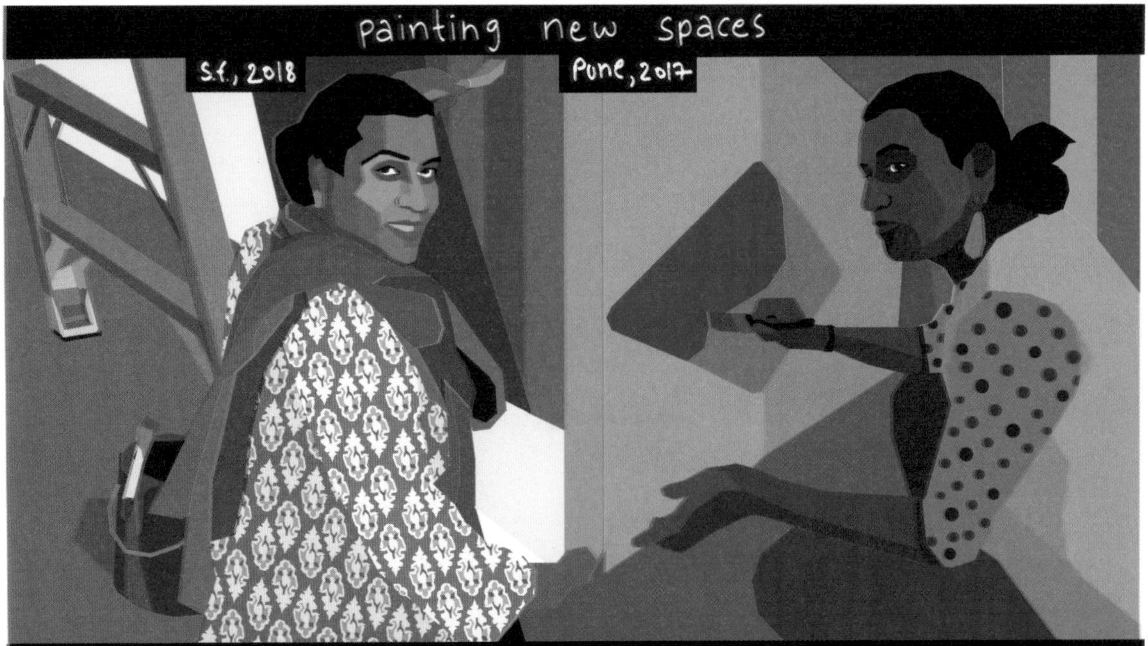
painting new spaces
S.F., 2018
Pune, 2017

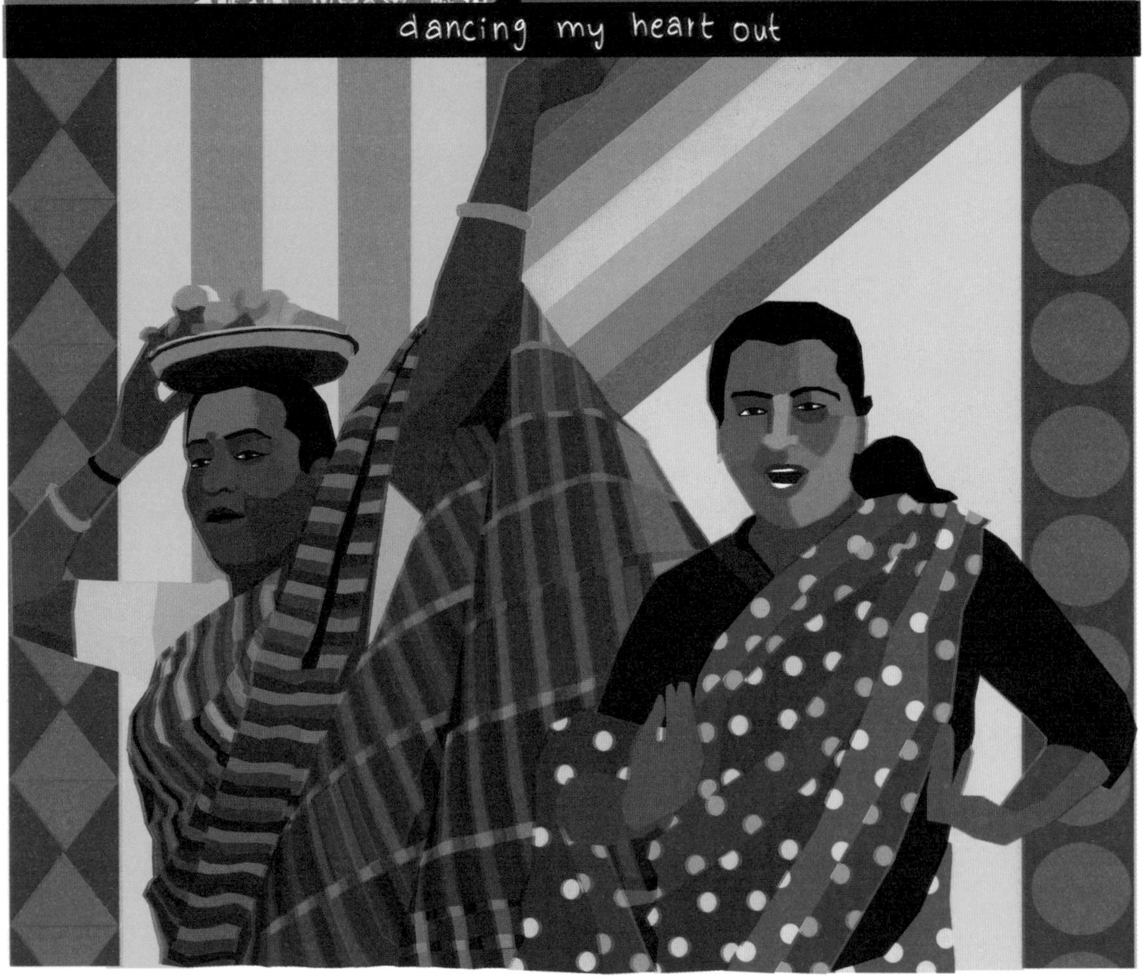
dancing my heart out

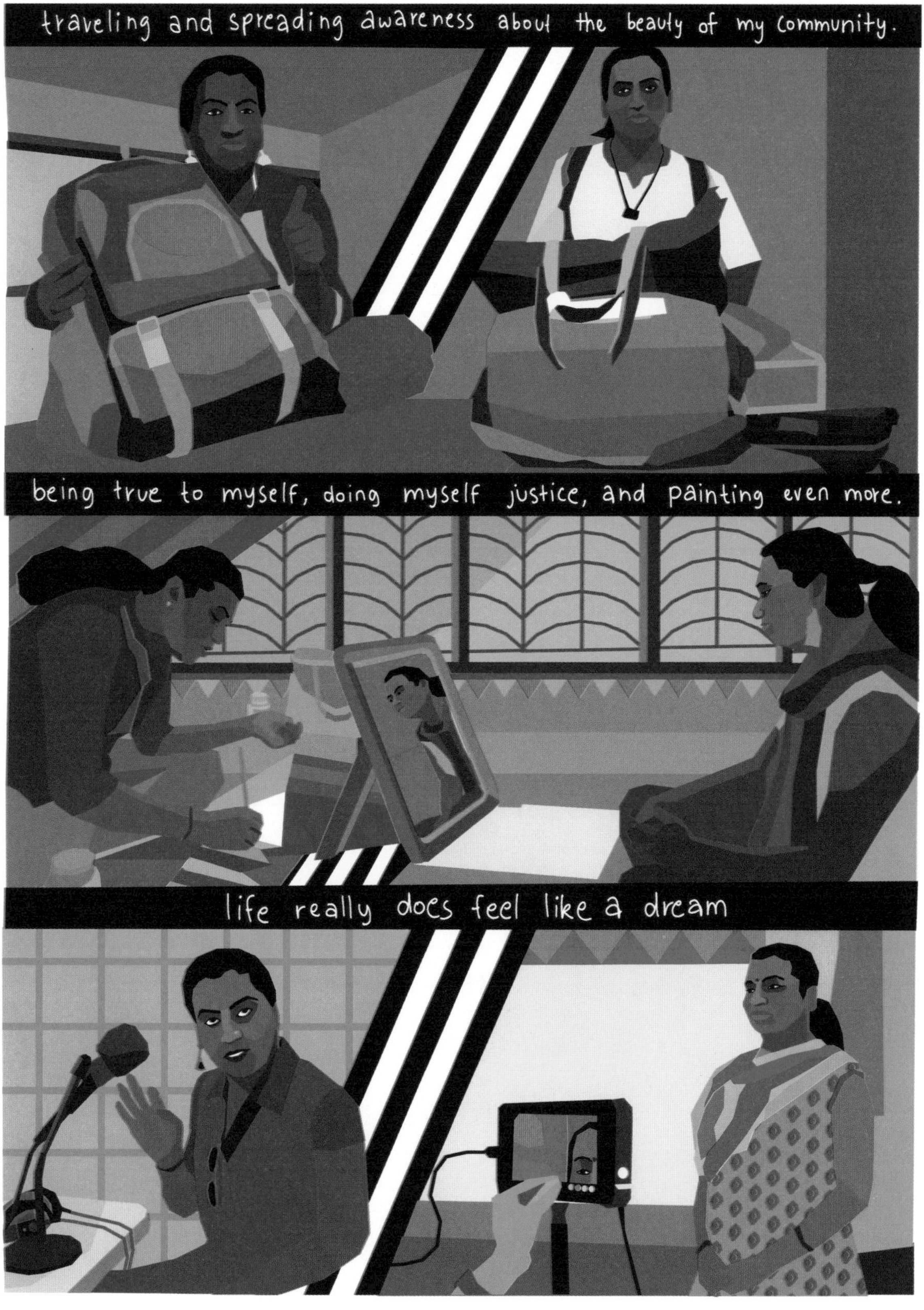
traveling and spreading awareness about the beauty of my community.
being true to myself, doing myself justice, and painting even more.
life really does feel like a dream

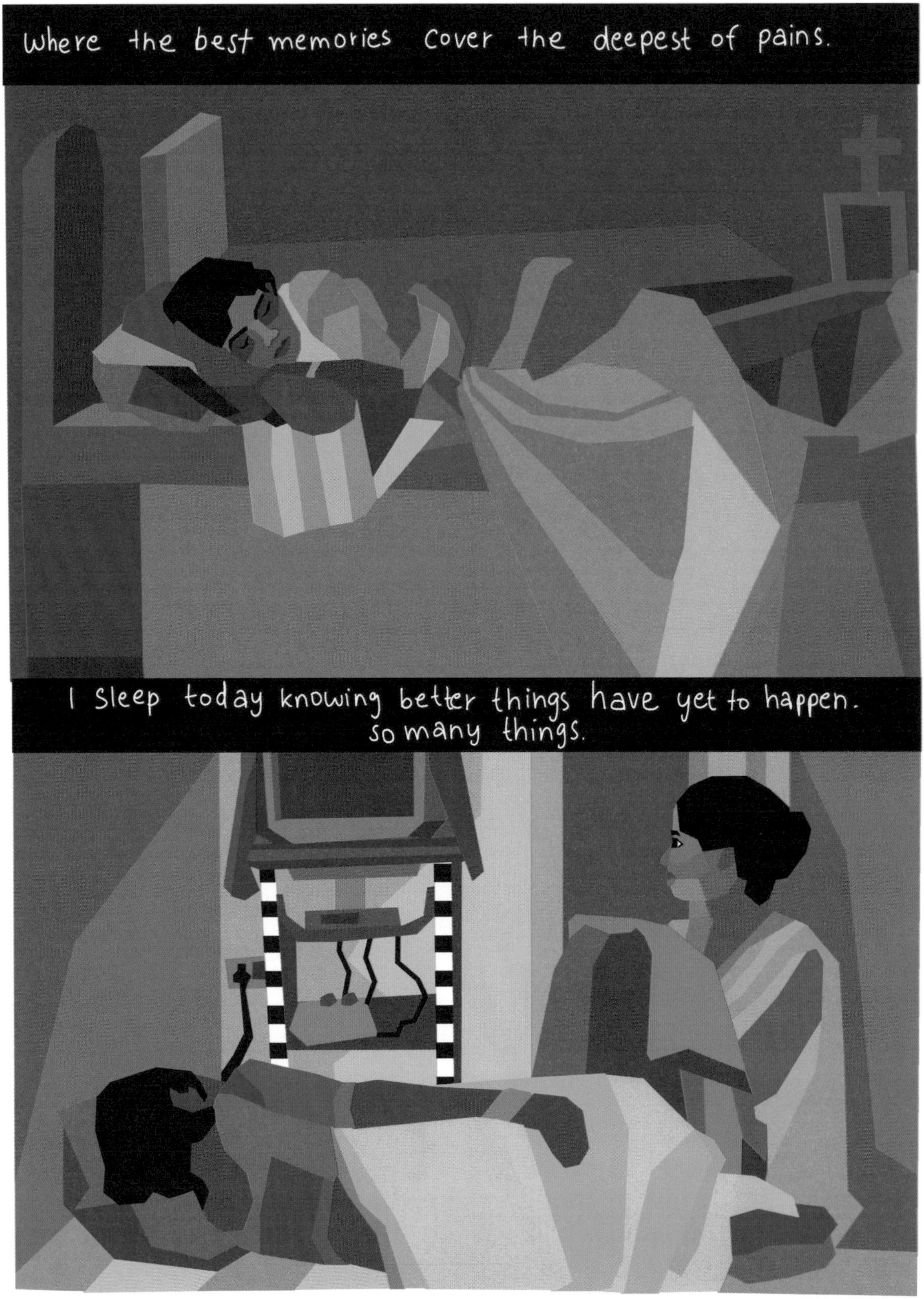
Where the best memories cover the deepest of pains.
I sleep today knowing better things have yet to happen. So many things.

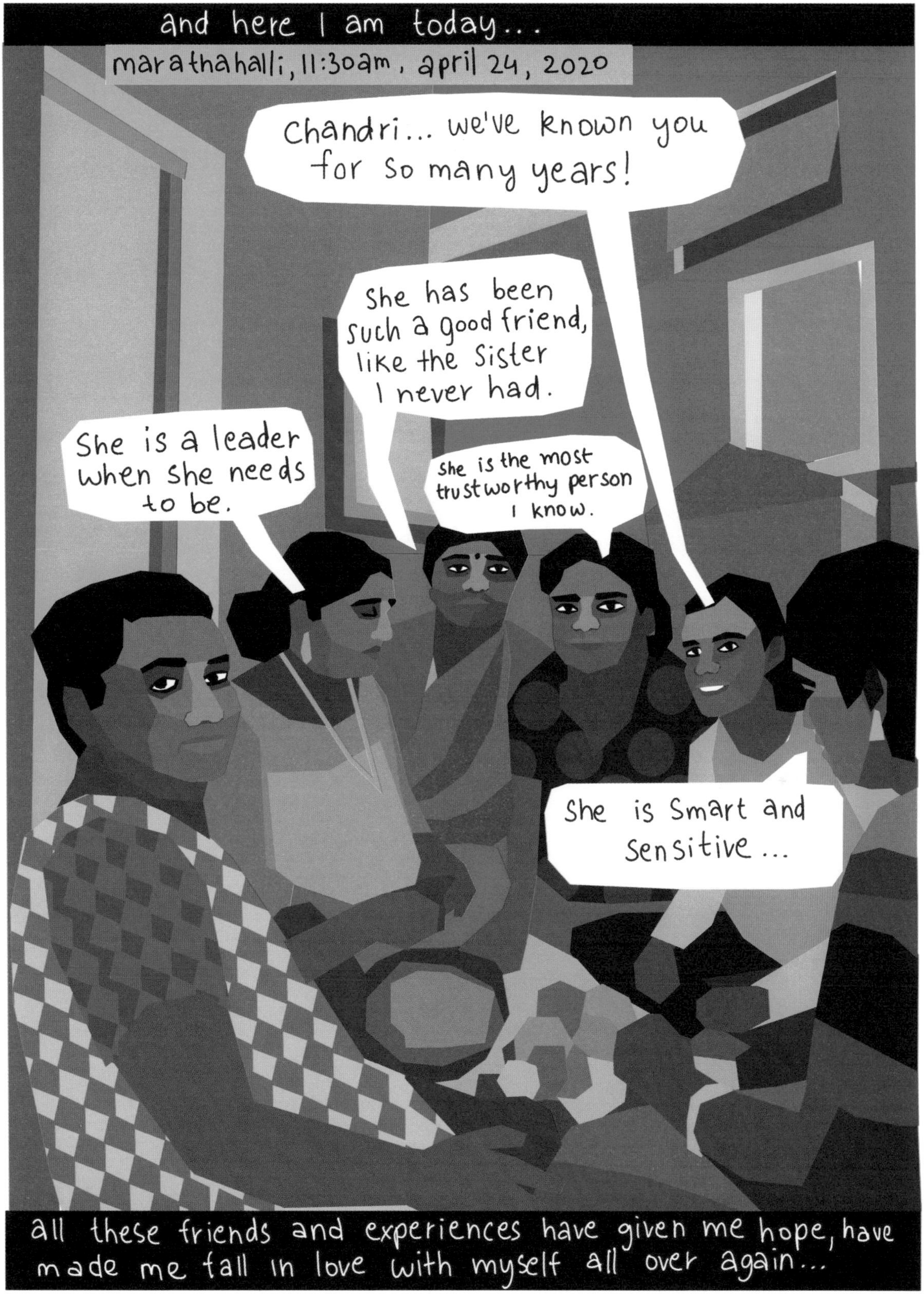
and here I am today...
marathahalli, 11:30am, april 24, 2020
Chandri... we've known you for so many years!
She has been such a good friend, like the sister I never had.
She is a leader when she needs to be.
she is the most trustworthy person I know.
She is Smart and sensitive...
all these friends and experiences have given me hope, have made me fall in love with myself all over again...

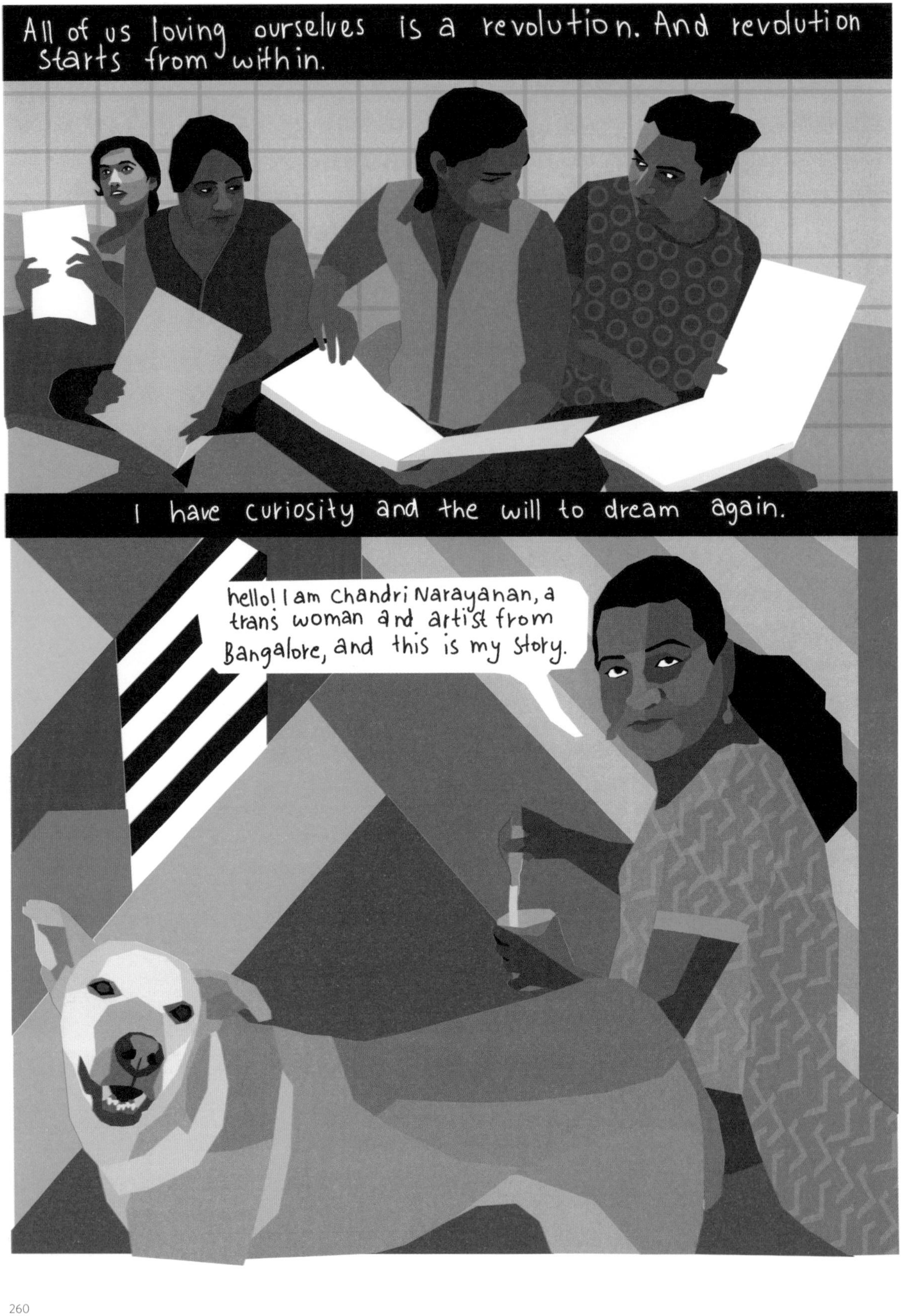
All of us loving ourselves is a revolution. And revolution starts from within.
I have curiosity and the will to dream again.
hello! I am Chandri Narayanan, a trans woman and artist from Bangalore, and this is my story.

Story and Narration : Chandri Narayanan
Storyboarding and Visual Design : Sadhna Prasad
Lifestory Mapping EXA Workshop; Aliyeh Rizvi,Native Place
English Type design : Chirag Swamy

meet the artists

LET THE RIVER FLOW FREE

NINA MARTINEZ is an illustrator from Manila. She graduated in 2016 from the University of the Philippines with a BFA in Visual Communication. When she's not illustrating for a diverse range of media, she writes and draws original comics about ghosts, God, and growing up. To learn more about her work, please visit ninamartinezart.com.

Founded in 2015, GANTALA PRESS is an independent, non-profit, volunteer-run Filipina feminist press and literary collective that centers women's stories and issues in their publications, discussions, and workshops. They believe in the potential of feminist publishing and that working in solidarity with women artists and collectives is a vital political action. They were responsible for the English translation of this story. To learn more about their work, please visit gantalapress.org.

GANTALA
PRESS

MAMA DULU

CITLALLI ANDRANGO is from Turuku, a Kichwa Otavalo community in the northern Ecuadorian Andes. She works as a film producer and actress. Her work usually revolves around identity. To learn more about her work, please visit her instagram acccount: @citlalli.a.c.

CECILIA LARREA is an Ecuadorian artist. She has been involved in the film industry for many years and has illustrated a couple of movie posters. Her illustrations, using her character Casimira, talk about everyday issues, and address political and social problems. To learn more about her work, please visit celarrea.com.

SHANTI: BEYOND THE VEIL

BANDANA TULACHAN is an illustrator and designer from Kathmandu, Nepal. She's been publishing children's books, comics, and illustrations since 2012. She uses her work to explore issues of self and identity. Her book, *Sanu and the Big Storm*, was published by FinePrint Books. She is a cofounder of Virangana Comics, a platform for comics artists in Nepal. To learn more about her work, please visit bandanatulachan.com.np.

THE ANARCHIST CHOLAS: A SHORT STORY...

VANESSA PEÑUELA and CÉSAR VARGAS are two visual artists from Bogotá, Colombia, interested in political, social, and historical issues related to Latin American and Caribbean realities. They have more recently explored the intersection of class, race, and gender issues as they affect Latin American women. Learn more about Vanessa's work on instagram at @guagua_de_pan, and more about César's work at behance.net/cesarvargas1.

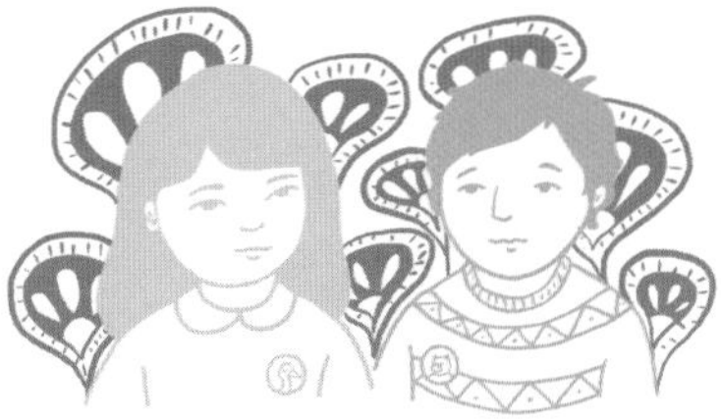

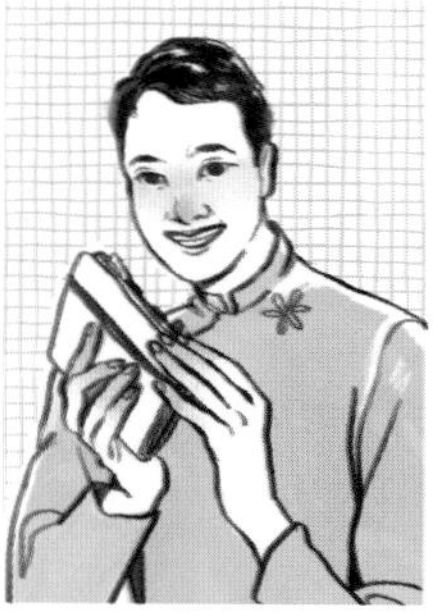

TRACING BETWEEN COLORS OF THE HIGHLANDS

DƯƠNG MẠNH HÙNG (b. 1991) is a writer and translator who has collaborated with a diverse range of publishers and art spaces in Southeast Asia. He is a cofounder of Bar De Force Press, an independent publisher that seeks to connect Vietnam to the global literary scene through multilingual translated works. To learn more about his work, follow the press' facebook and instagram accounts: @bardeforcepress.

PHẠM THU TRÀ was born in Hanoi and is a young illustrator who recently graduated with a BA in Graphic Design in Italy. Trà is now working full-time as an art director and freelance illustrator in her hometown. Her work focuses on the Anthropocene and the flaws that make humans intrinsically fascinating. To learn more about her work visit cameliapham.com.

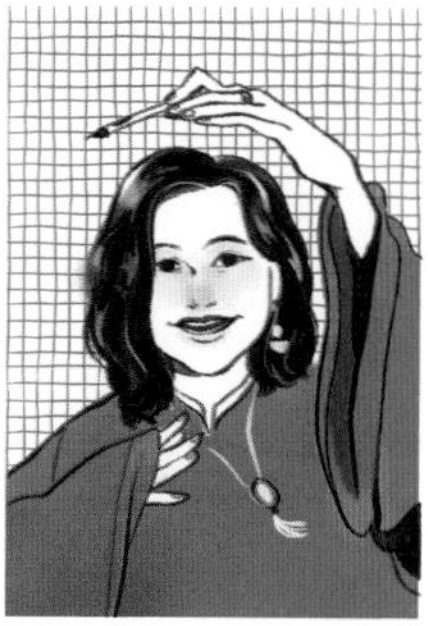

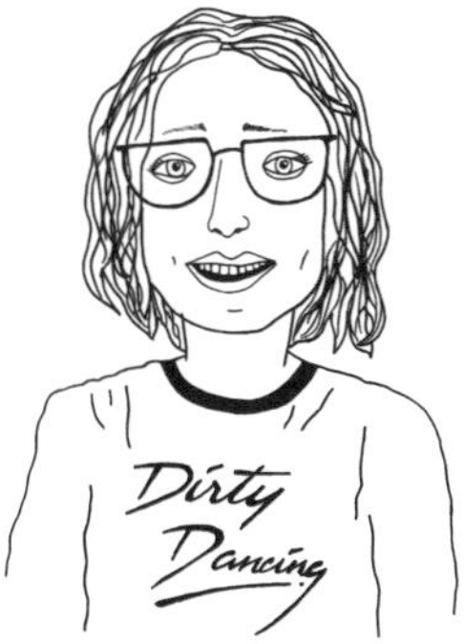
Dirty
Dancing

MILLARAY HUICHALAF: THE PROTECTRESS OF THE SACRED RIVER

CONSUELO TERRA is a journalist, illustrator, and comics creator. Her first graphic novel *Mamá, yo te recuerdo,* with Emiliano Valenzuela, was published in 2021 by Reservoir Books. She drew the comic "Water Stations Save Lives" for the anthology book *Border-X, a Crisis in Graphic Detail* in 2020. Her comics about pop culture, feminism, and human rights have been published by *NerdNews.cl* and *La Voz Latina Newspaper*. She created the artwork and contributed to the script and reseach for *Millaray*. To learn more about her work, visit her instagram account: @consuterra.

As a journalist, GRETA DI GIROLAMO has worked for *The Clinic, El Desconcierto, Revista Paula, Vice* and on independent projects related to childhood, ecology, feminism, and human rights. Greta is one of the creators of *Respirantes*, a children's series about life in areas that have sustained permanent environmental damage. She had the original idea for *Millaray and* was responsible for the research, interviews, production, and script of the story. Visit her instagram account to learn more about her work: @lagretalmar.

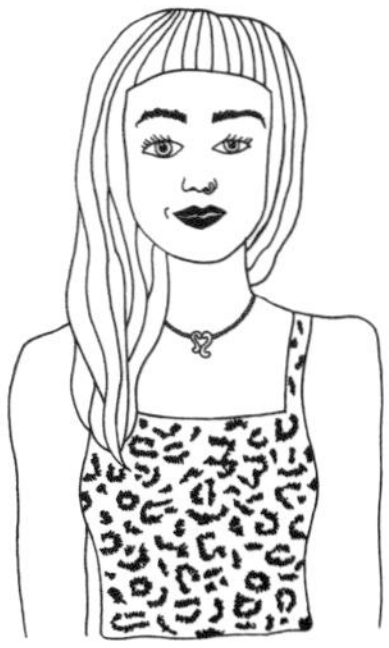

WARMIMASIY: ANDEAN FEMINISM...

TRILCE GARCÍA COSAVALENTE is a graphic designer and illustrator who fell in love with graphic narratives. She believes that a visual communicator can be an agent of social change. She was responsible for the script, illustrations, and English translation of *Warmimasiy*. To learn more about her work, visit trilcegarcia.com.

HELEN QUIÑONES LOAIZA is a social communicator, educator, translator, and interpreter of native languages (Quechua) with a special interest in the fight for gender equality. Through her work in radio she has reached the hearts of many people around the country, especially in the rural Quechua areas. She was reponsible for the story and Quechua translations in *Warmimasiy*. To learn more about her work, visit her facebook page: @Warmimasiy.

TIMES WILL PASS...

CHANDRI NARAYANAN is an passionate artist and trans woman who is committed to all areas of her practice. She is a skilled muralist, storyteller, orator, and teacher. Apart from painting, she has a keen interest in music, dance, and she is quite the foodie. Learn more about her work at aravaniartproject.com.

SADHNA PRASAD is an independent illustrator, artist, and muralist based in India. She is also the cofounder and graphic director of the Aravani Art Project in Bangalore, India. All her work involves exploring stories and narratives by examining stereotypes about women, and showcasing everyday life and the use of colour across Indian art forms. To learn more about her work, please visit her instagram account: @sadh.press.

ABOUT THE EDITORS

This project was originally edited by Sonja Eismann, and coordinated by Ingo Schöningh and Maya.

SONJA EISMANN is an author, journalist, professor, indie comics fan, and one of the founders and editors of *Missy Magazine*, a feminist periodical on politics, pop culture, and style based in Berlin, Germany.

Since 2020, DR. INGO SCHÖNINGH is the Goethe-Institut's regional head of cultural programs in Southeast Asia, based in Jakarta. He's been on assignment in Hanoi, Seoul, and Tokyo, and he really likes this world.

MAYA identifies herself as a 'facilitator.' Since 2009, she has been actively organizing and realizing several Indonesian and international art and cultural initiatives. She currently works as a program manager for visual art and discourse at the Goethe-Institut Indonesia.